SHONEN JUMP

NARUTO

THE MOVIE

LEGEND of the STONE of GELEL

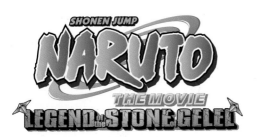

Original Concept by Masashi Kishimoto
Edited by Jump Comics

English Adaptation/Annie Blacklock
Touch-up Art & Lettering/Rina Mapa
Design/Sean Lee
Editor/Carol Fox

Editor in Chief, Books/Alvin Lu
Editor in Chief, Magazines/Marc Weidenbaum
VP, Publishing Licensing/Rika Inouye
VP, Sales and Product Marketing/Gonzalo Ferreyra
VP, Creative/Linda Espinosa
Publisher/Hyoe Narita

NARUTO GEKIJOBAN ANIME COMICS – DAIGEKITOTSU!
MABOROSHI NO CHITEIISEKI DATTEBAYO © 2002 MASASHI
KISHIMOTO © NMP 2005 All rights reserved. First published in Japan in
2006 by SHUEISHA Inc., Tokyo. English translation rights arranged by
SHUEISHA Inc.

The stories, characters and incidents mentioned in this publication are
entirely fictional.

No portion of this book may be reproduced or transmitted in any form
or by any means without written permission from the copyright holders.

Printed in Singapore

Published by VIZ Media, LLC
P.O. Box 77010
San Francisco, CA 94107

10 9 8 7 6 5 4 3 2 1
First printing, November 2008

www.viz.com

PARENTAL ADVISORY
NARUTO THE MOVIE ANI-MANGA is rated T for
Teen and is recommended for ages 13 and up. This
volume contains violence.
ratings.viz.com

THE WORLD'S
MOST POPULAR MANGA

SHONEN JUMP
ANI-MANGA
www.shonenjump.com

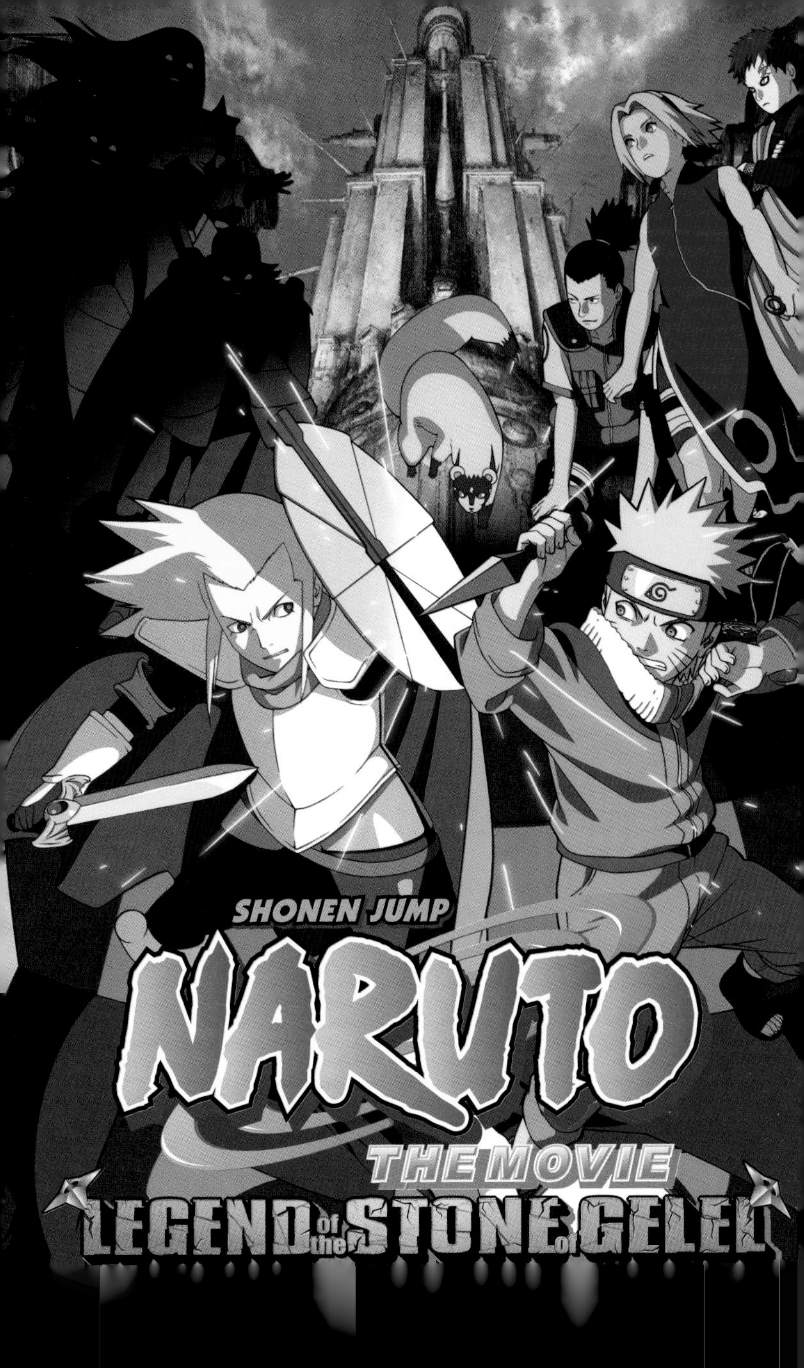
SHONEN JUMP
NARUTO
THE MOVIE
LEGEND of the STONE of GELEL

Main characters

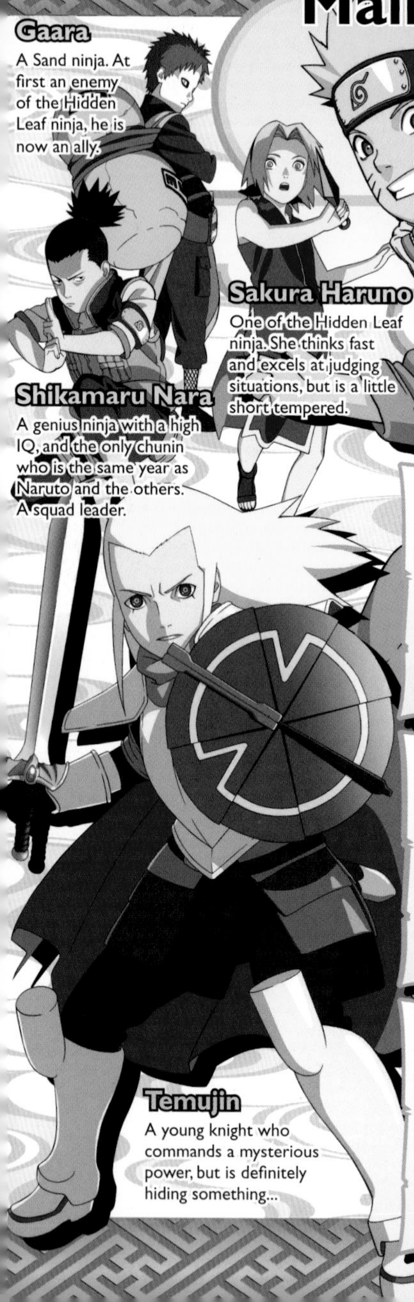

Gaara
A Sand ninja. At first an enemy of the Hidden Leaf ninja, he is now an ally.

Sakura Haruno
One of the Hidden Leaf ninja. She thinks fast and excels at judging situations, but is a little short tempered.

Naruto Uzumaki
A young ninja who is determined to become Hokage, the most powerful ninja in the Hidden Leaf Village. The fox spirit he carries inside of him gives him chakra far beyond the ordinary!

Shikamaru Nara
A genius ninja with a high IQ, and the only chunin who is the same year as Naruto and the others. A squad leader.

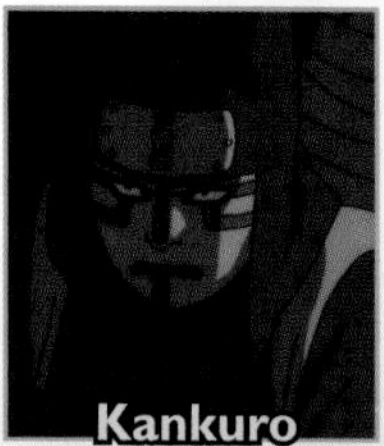

Kankuro

Gaara's older brother, another Sand ninja, is a puppeteer who controls mechanical things with chakra.

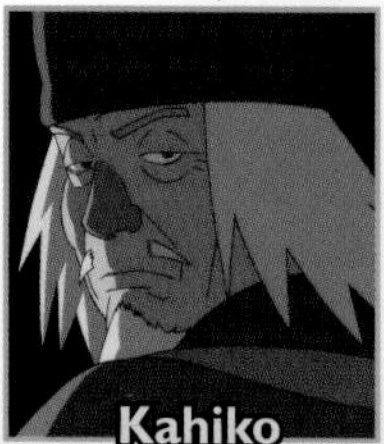

Kahiko

Chief of a wandering caravan. He asked the Hidden Leaf ninja to search for Nerugui the ferret. Very well versed in the legends of his people.

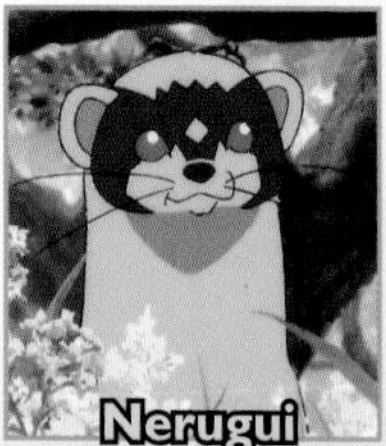

Nerugui

A ferret kept by Kahiko's caravan. The pet of a once-flourishing empire's royal family, he has been alive since time immemorial.

Temujin
A young knight who commands a mysterious power, but is definitely hiding something...

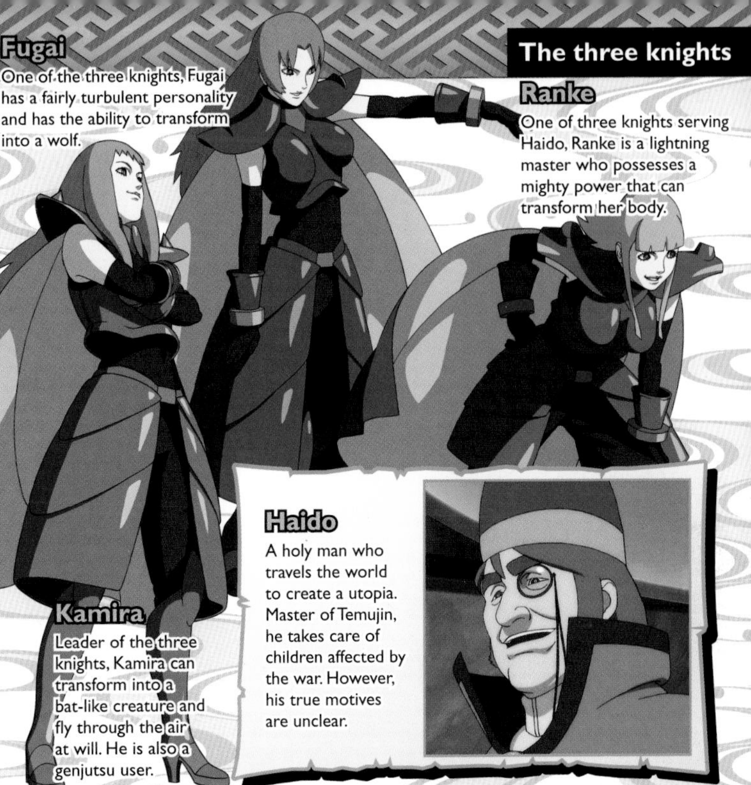

The three knights

Fugai
One of the three knights, Fugai has a fairly turbulent personality and has the ability to transform into a wolf.

Ranke
One of three knights serving Haido, Ranke is a lightning master who possesses a mighty power that can transform her body.

Kamira
Leader of the three knights, Kamira can transform into a bat-like creature and fly through the air at will. He is also a genjutsu user.

Haido
A holy man who travels the world to create a utopia. Master of Temujin, he takes care of children affected by the war. However, his true motives are unclear.

The Story of Naruto

Determined to become the next Hokage, the Hidden Leaf Village's most powerful ninja, former "problem child" Naruto Uzumaki trains day and night!

Naruto's treasured friend Sasuke has slipped out of the Hidden Leaf Village and sided with its enemy, Orochimaru, to gain tremendous power. As they go about their missions, Naruto and the others are gathering information about Orochimaru in hopes of finding Sasuke. During this time, Naruto sets out on a seemingly simple new mission to look for a lost pet. His three-ninja team sets off, with Shikamaru filling in for Sasuke. But things are about to move in a way that no one expected!

SHONEN JUMP

NARUTO THE MOVIE

LEGEND of the STONE of GELEL

ANI-MANGA

Contents

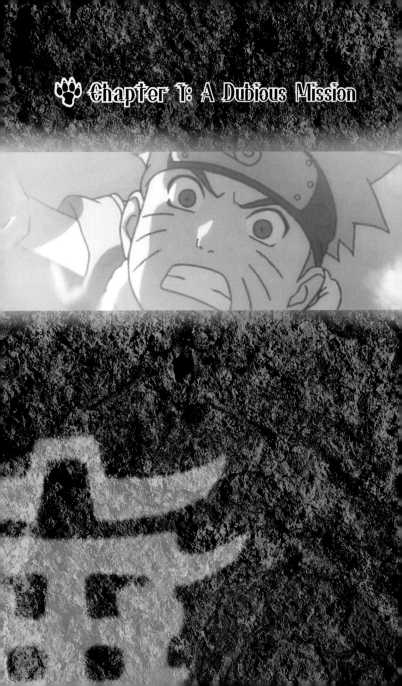

Chapter 1: A Dubious Mission

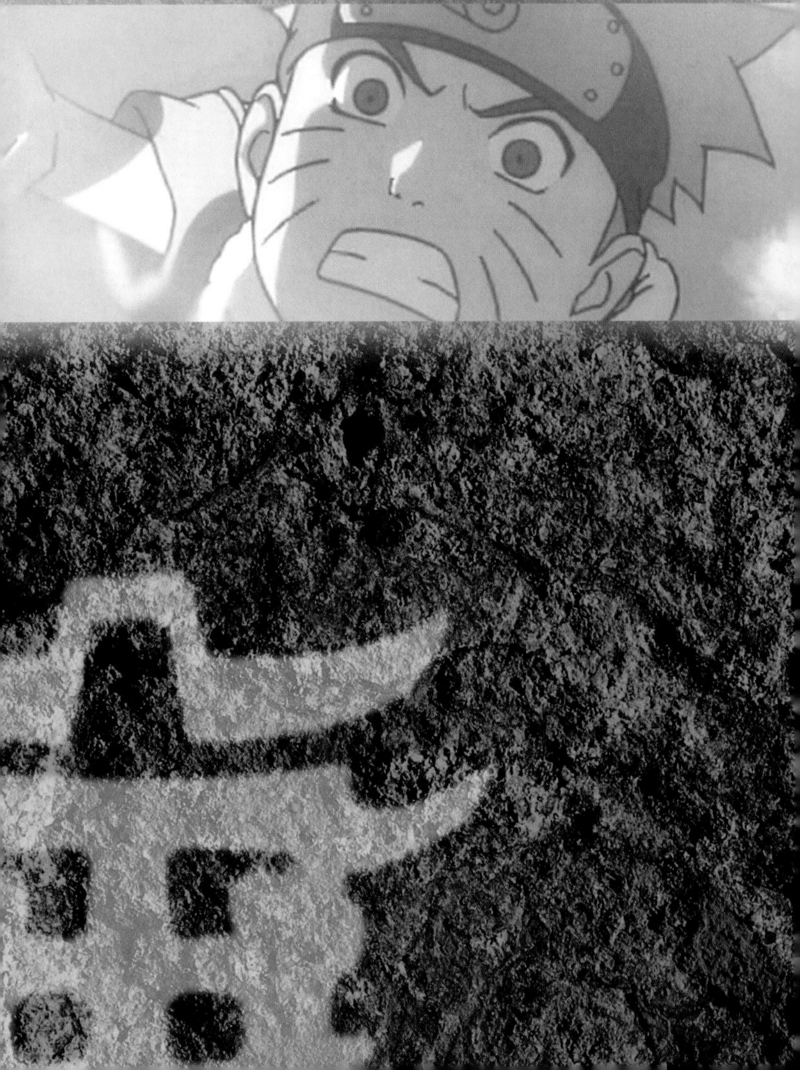

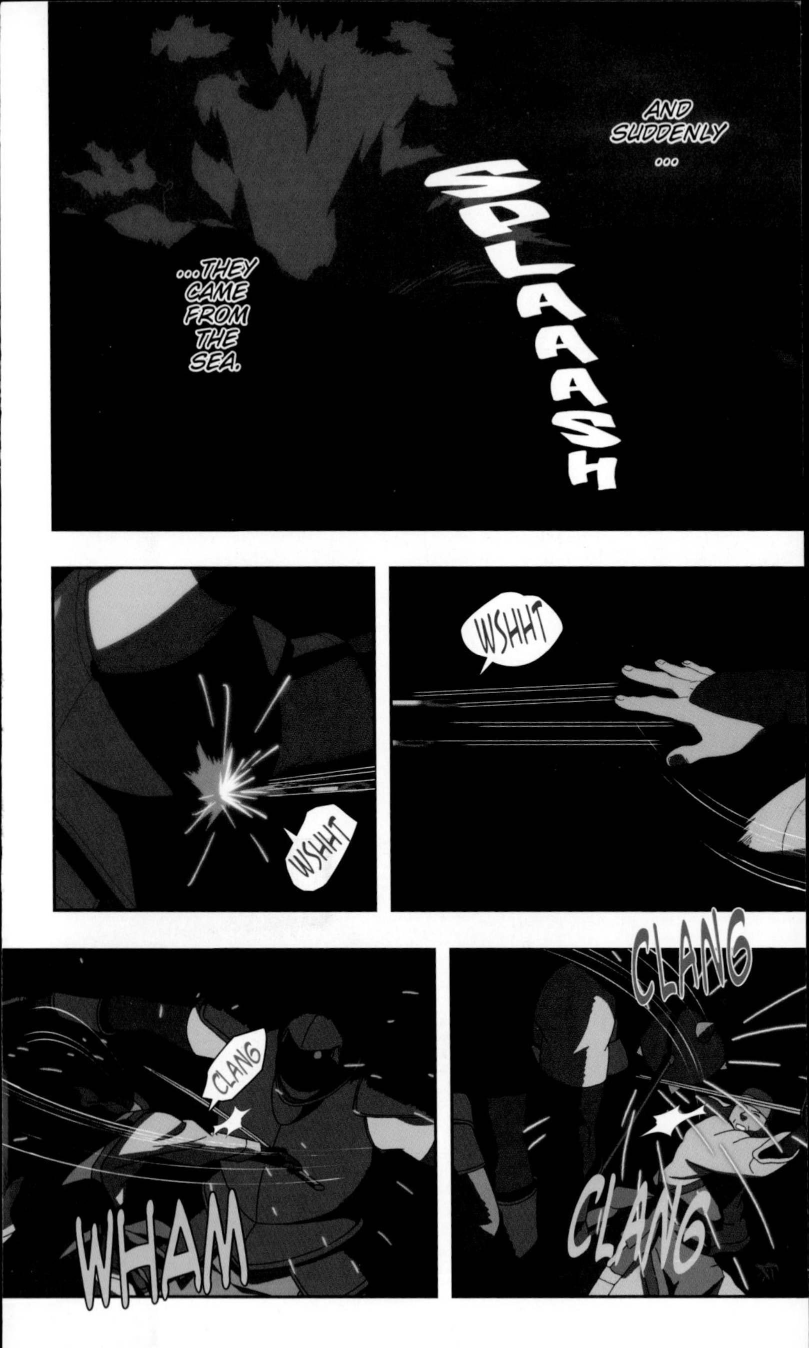
AND SUDDENLY ...
SPLAAASH
...THEY CAME FROM THE SEA.
WSHHT
WSHHT
CLANG
CLANG
CLANG
WHAM

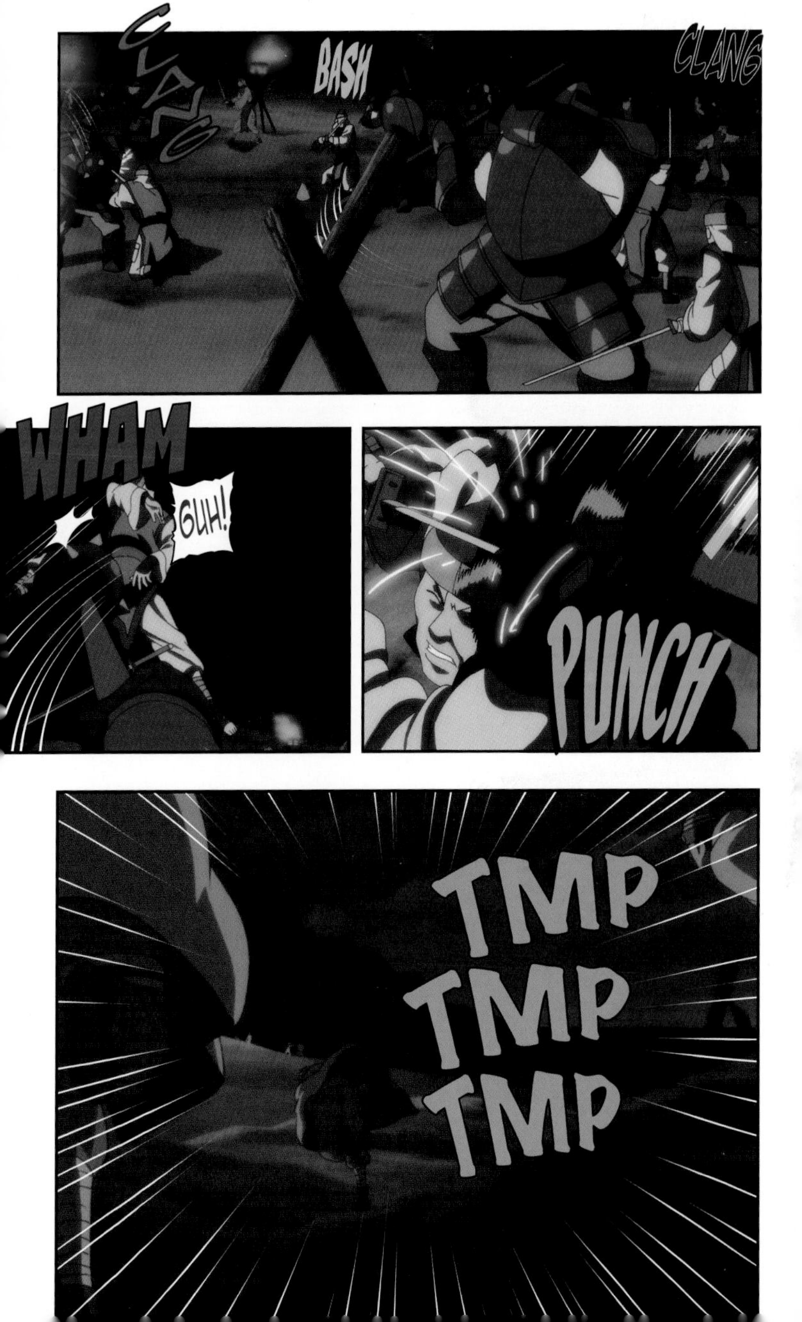
CLANG
BASH
CLANG
PUNCH
WHAM
GUH!
TMP
TMP
TMP

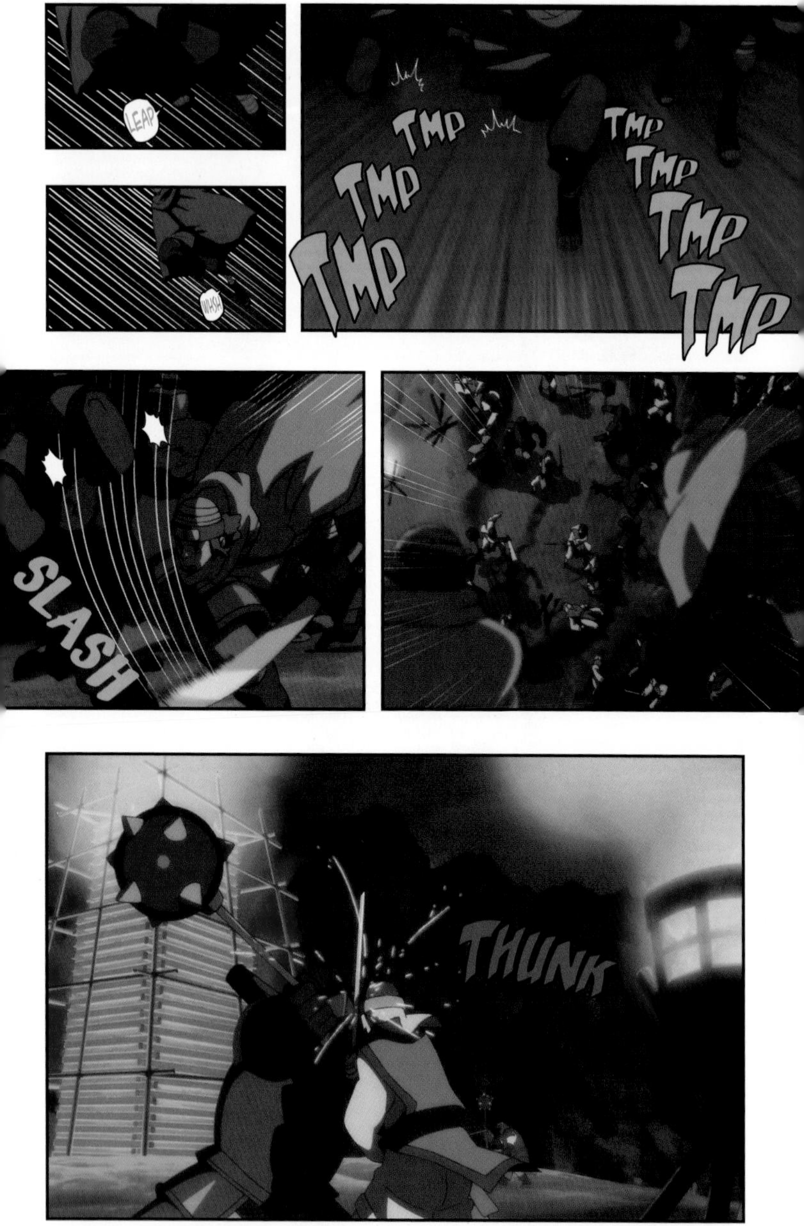
TMP
TMP
TMP
TMP
TMP
TMP
TMP
TMP
LEAP
WHSH
SLASH
THUNK

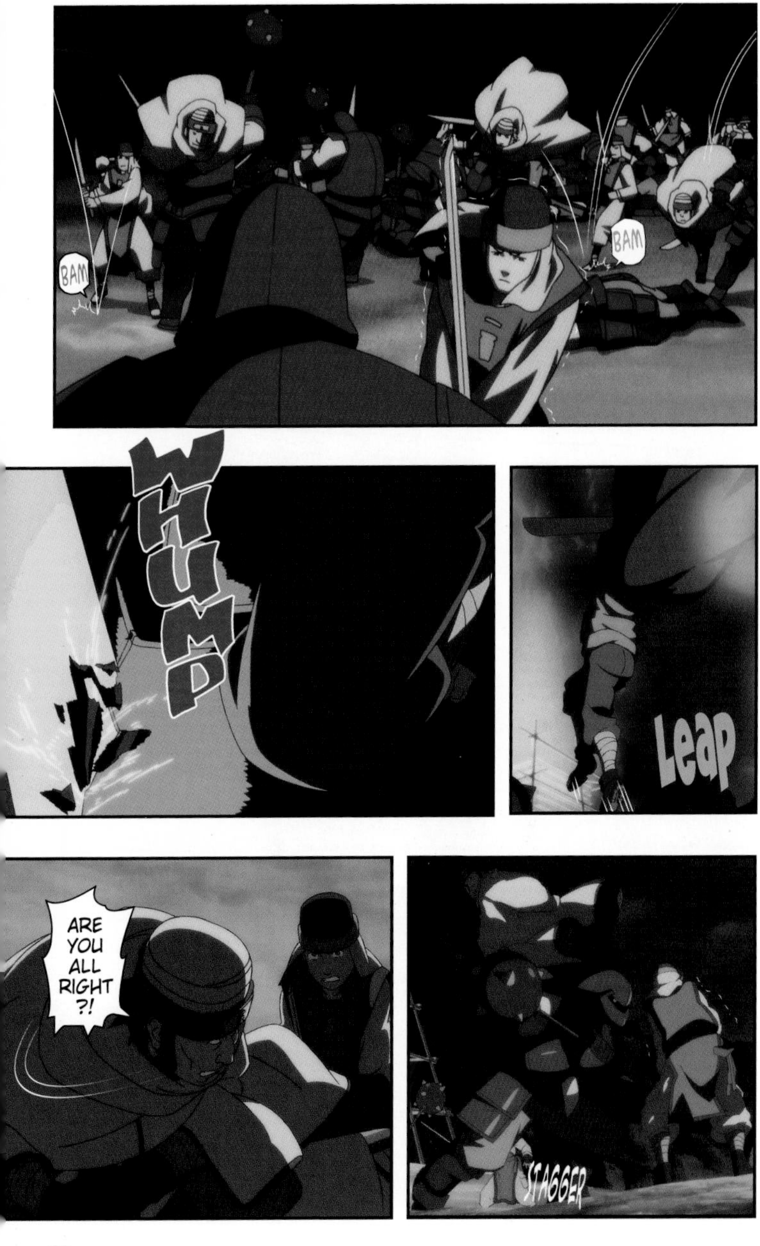
BAM
BAM
Leap
WHUMP
STAGGER
ARE YOU ALL RIGHT ?!

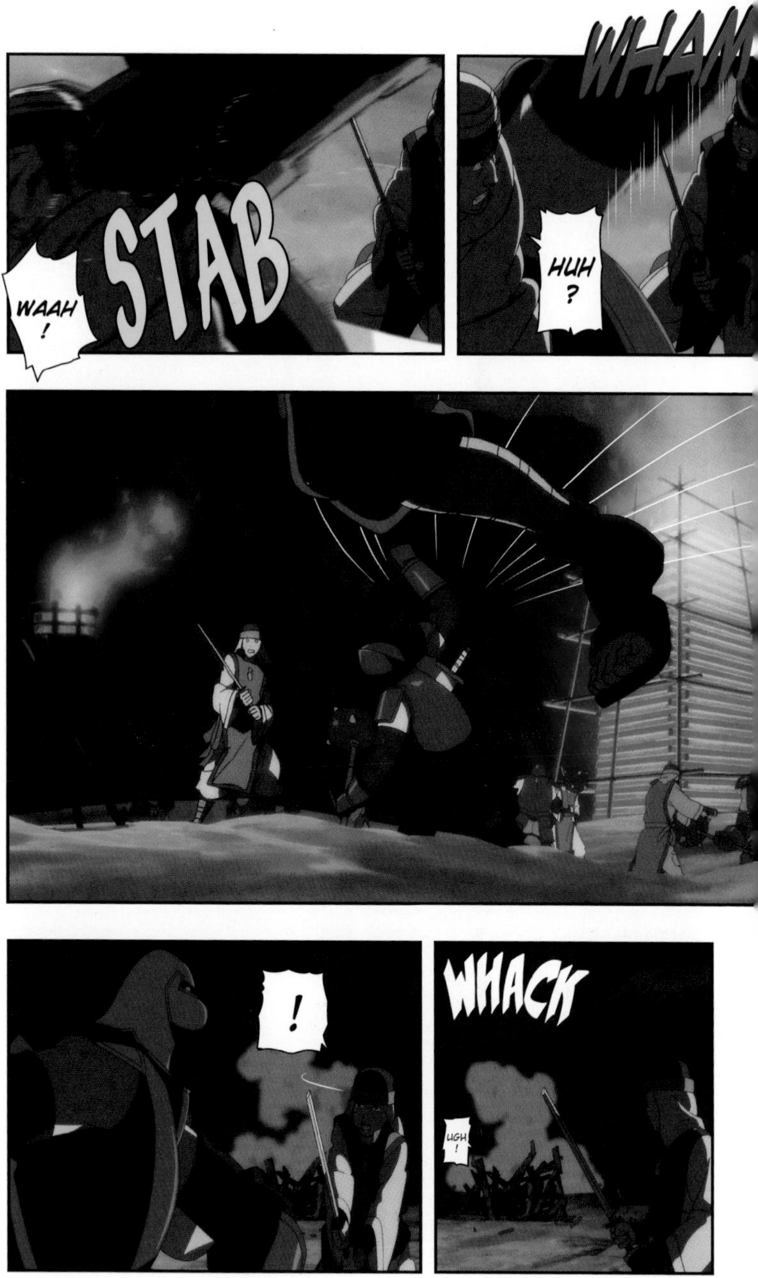
WHAM
HUH?
STAB
WAAH!
WHACK
UGH!
!

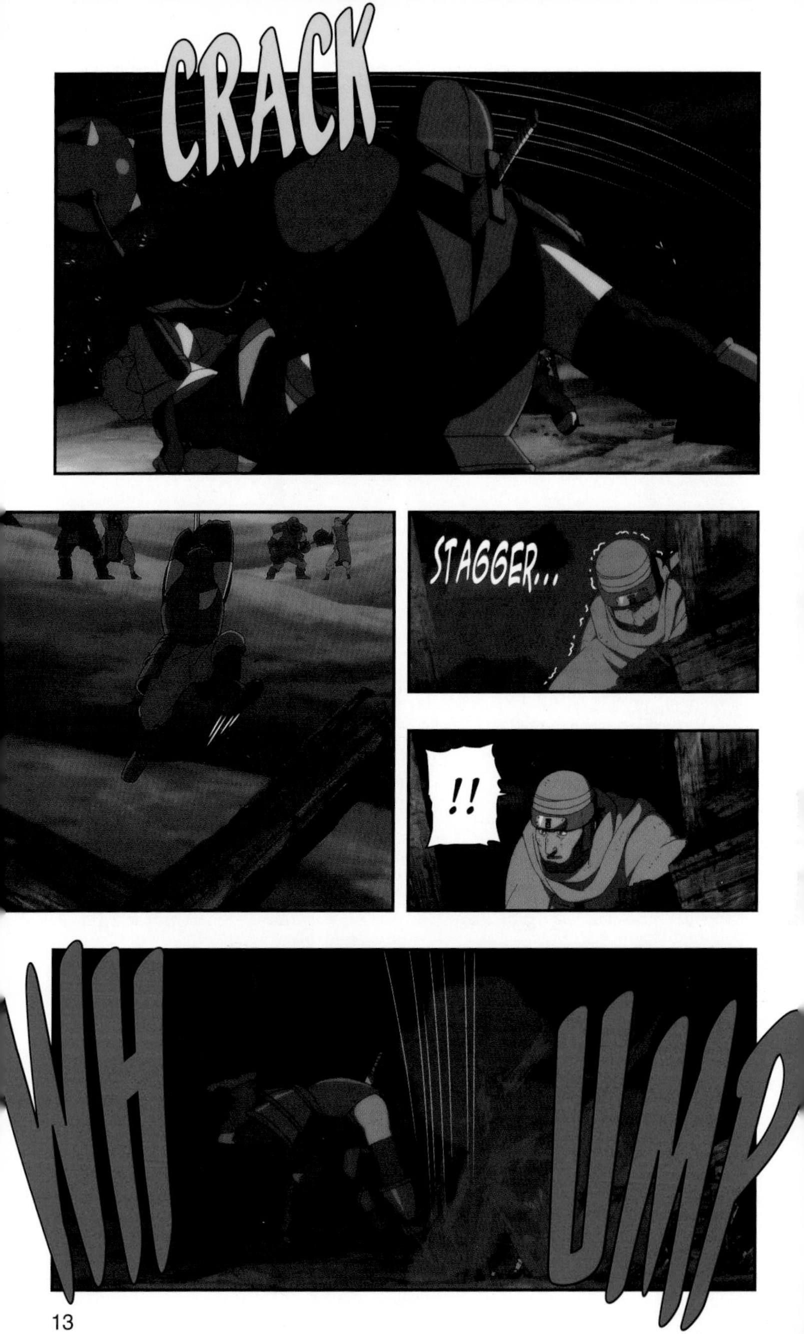
CRACK
STAGGER...
!!
WHUMP

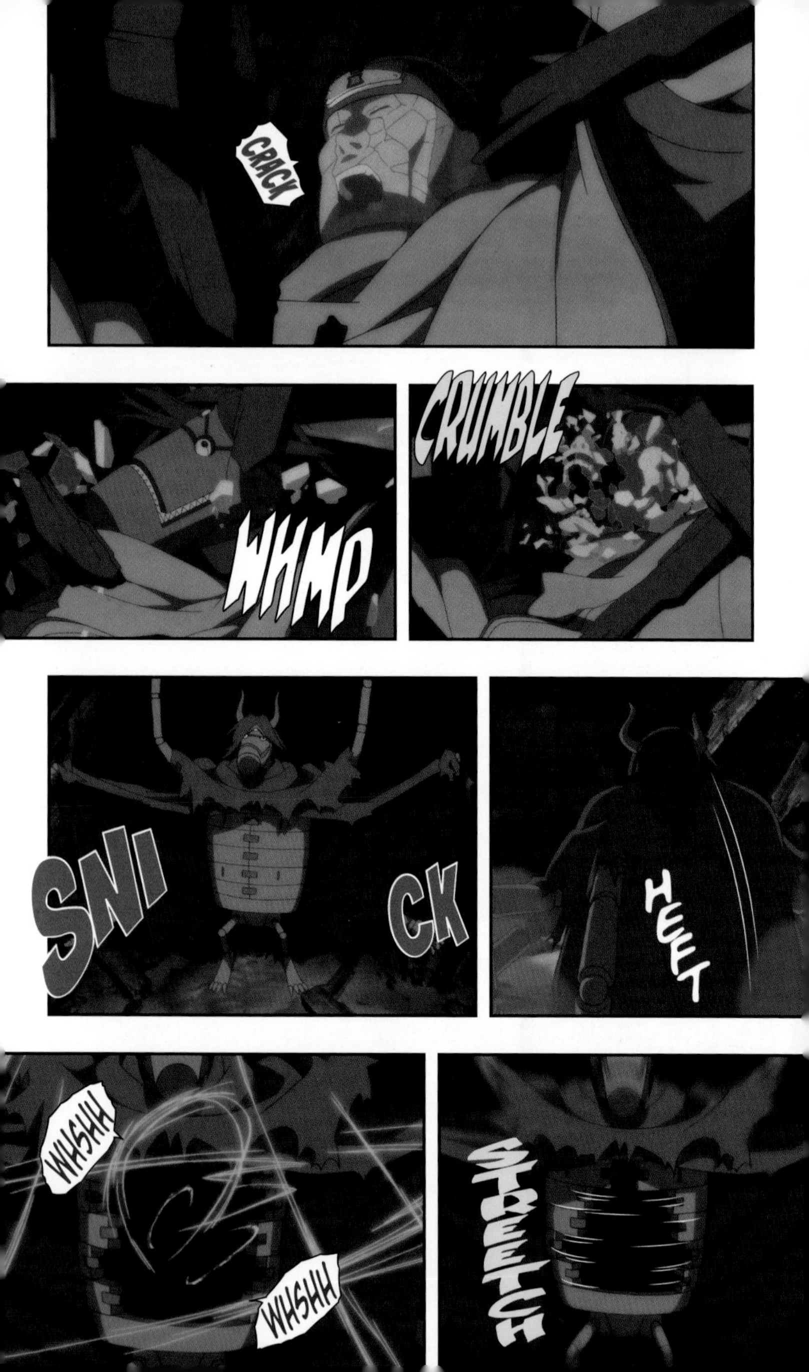
CRACK
CRUMBLE
WHMP
HEFT
SNI
CK
STREETCH
WHSHH
WHSHH

WHIPPA WHIPPA WHIPPA
TUG
NAB
SLAM
WHIRR
WHIRR

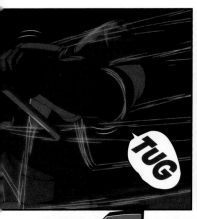

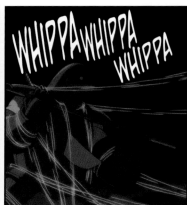

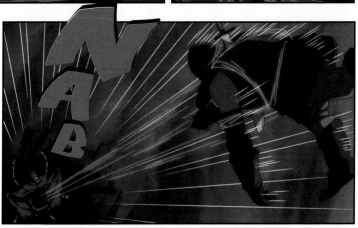

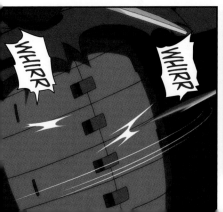

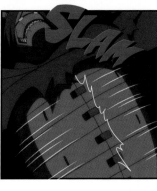

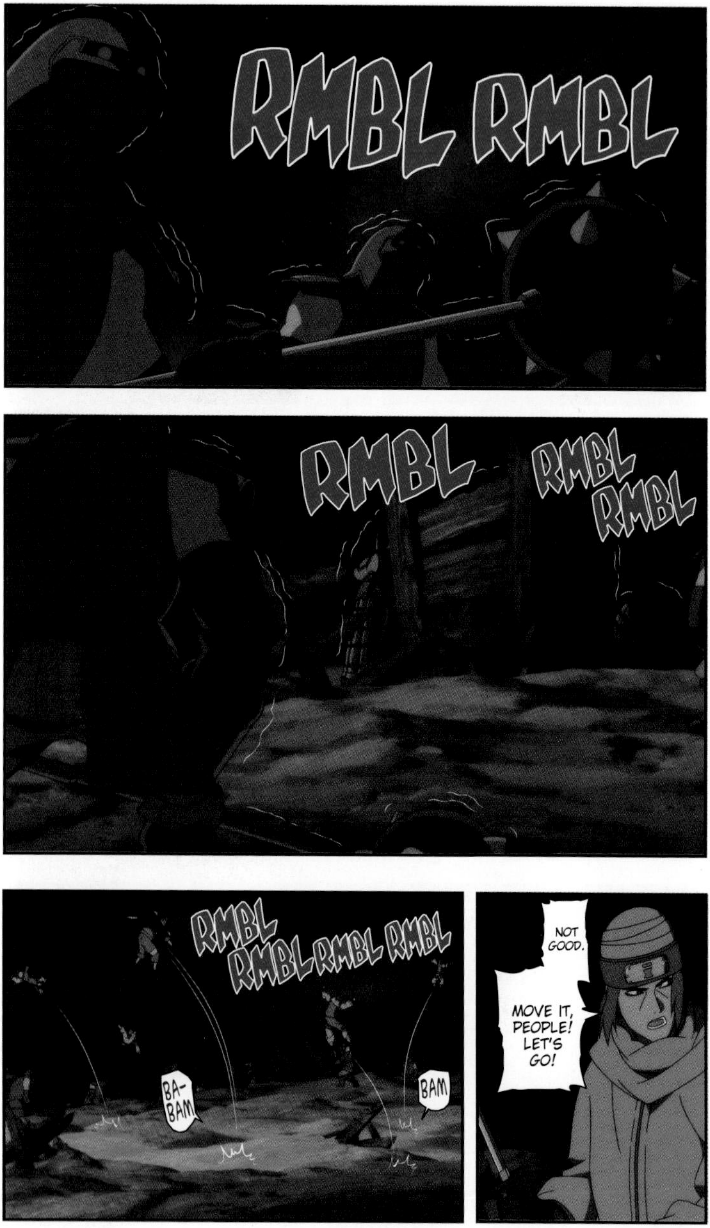
RMBL RMBL
RMBL
RMBL RMBL
NOT GOOD.
MOVE IT, PEOPLE! LET'S GO!
RMBL RMBL RMBL RMBL
BA-BAM
BAM

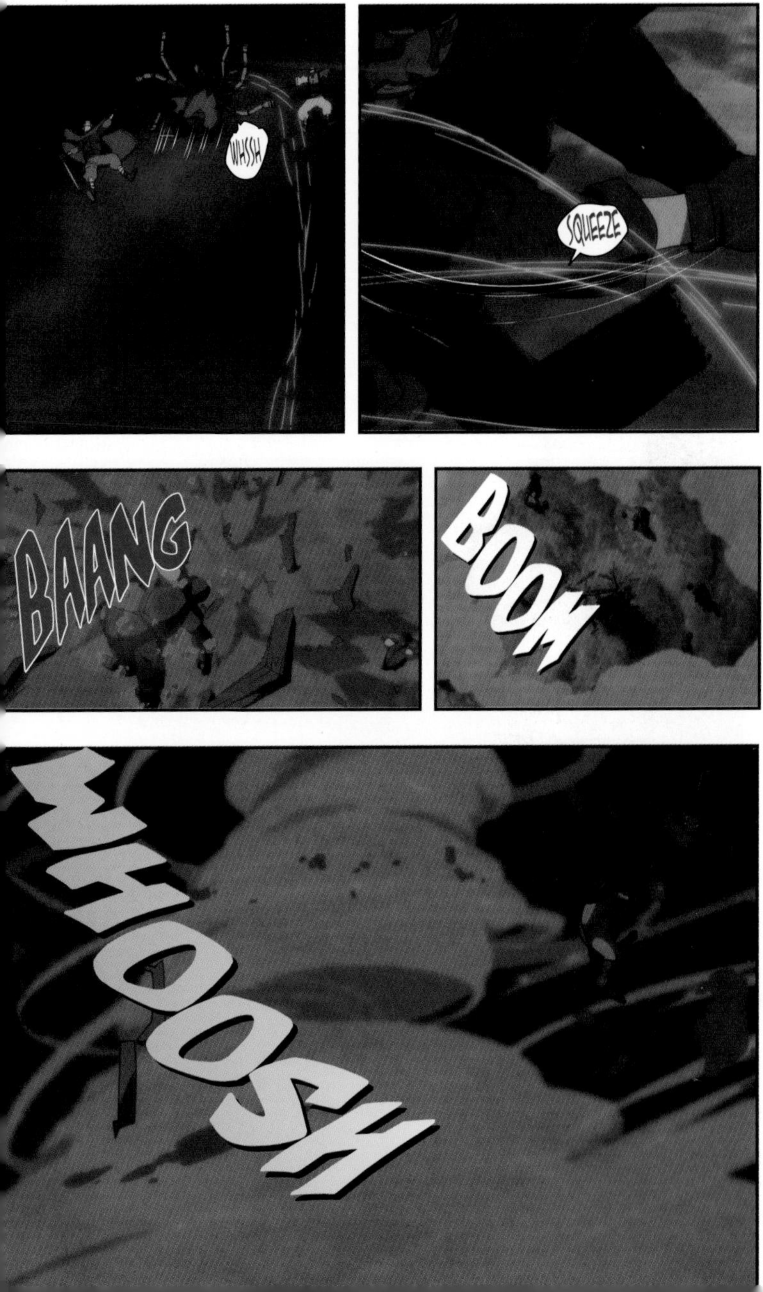
SQUEEZE
WHSSH
BOOM
BAANG
WHOOSH

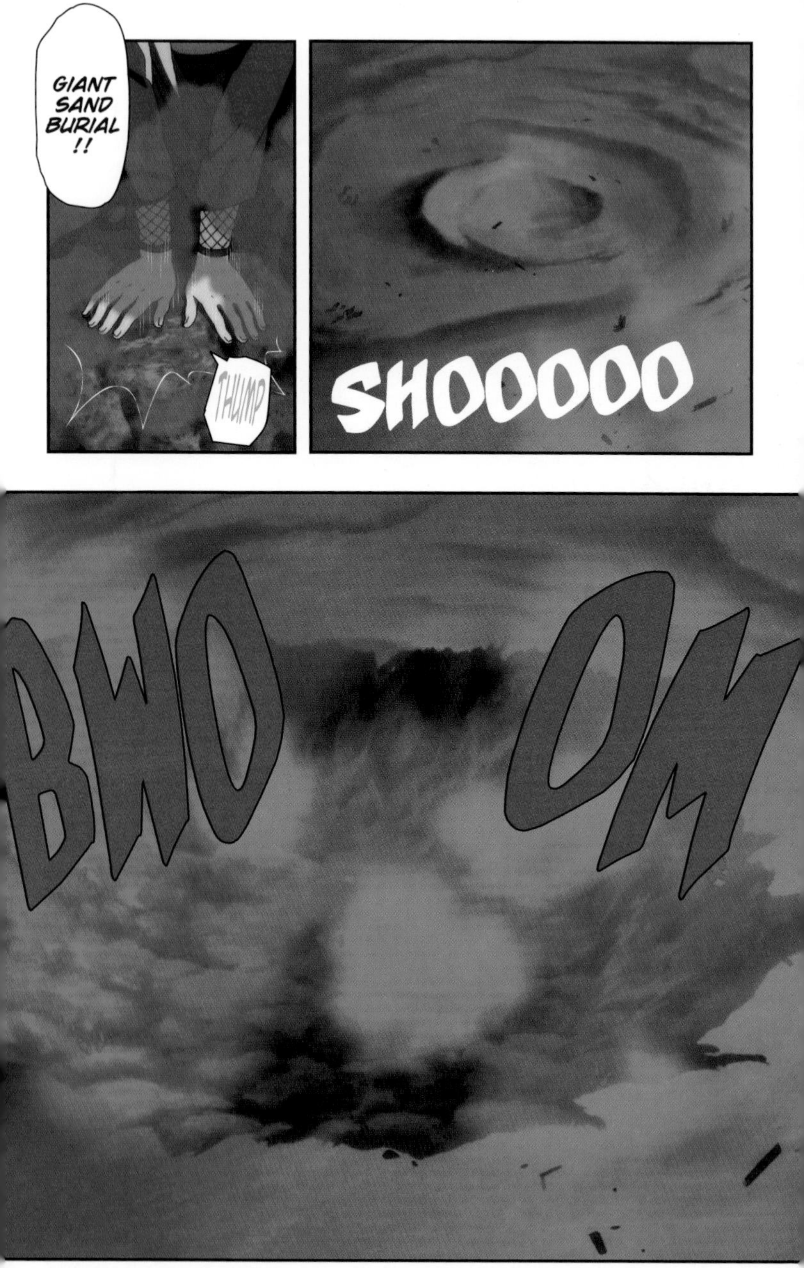
SHOOOOO
GIANT SAND BURIAL!!
THUMP
BWOOM

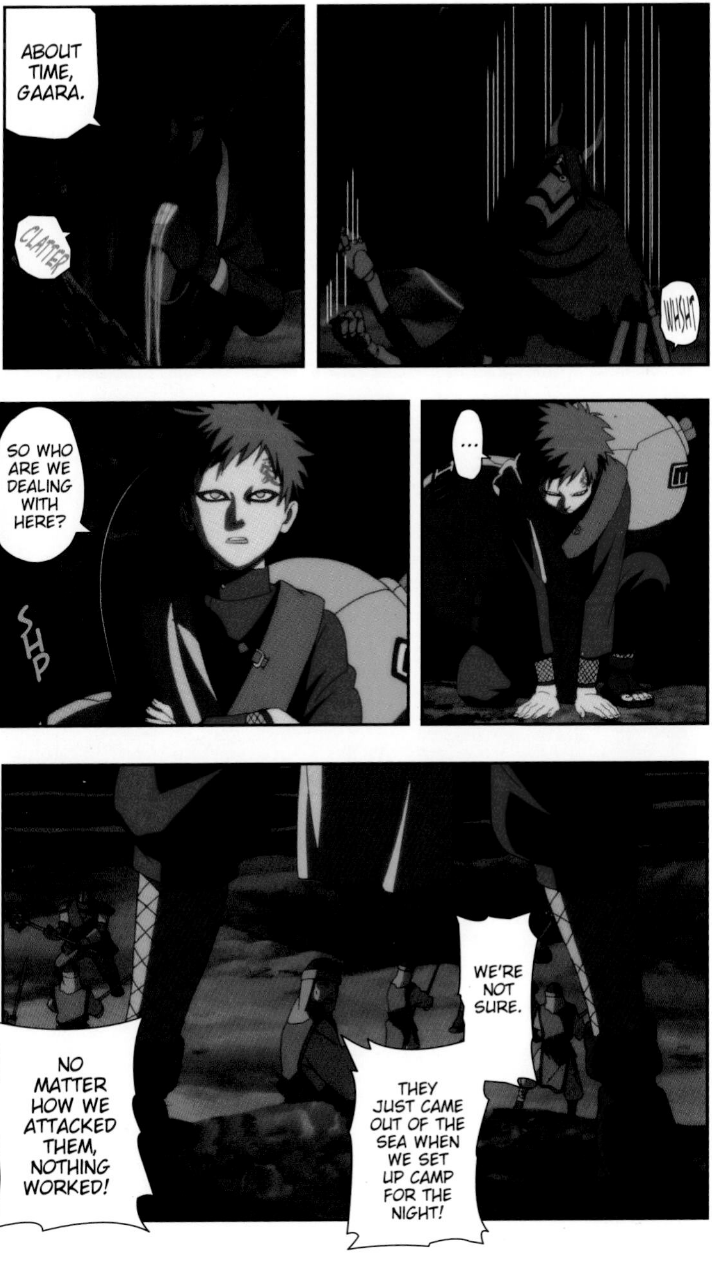
WHSHT
ABOUT TIME, GAARA.
CLATTER
...
SO WHO ARE WE DEALING WITH HERE?
SHP
WE'RE NOT SURE.
THEY JUST CAME OUT OF THE SEA WHEN WE SET UP CAMP FOR THE NIGHT!
NO MATTER HOW WE ATTACKED THEM, NOTHING WORKED!

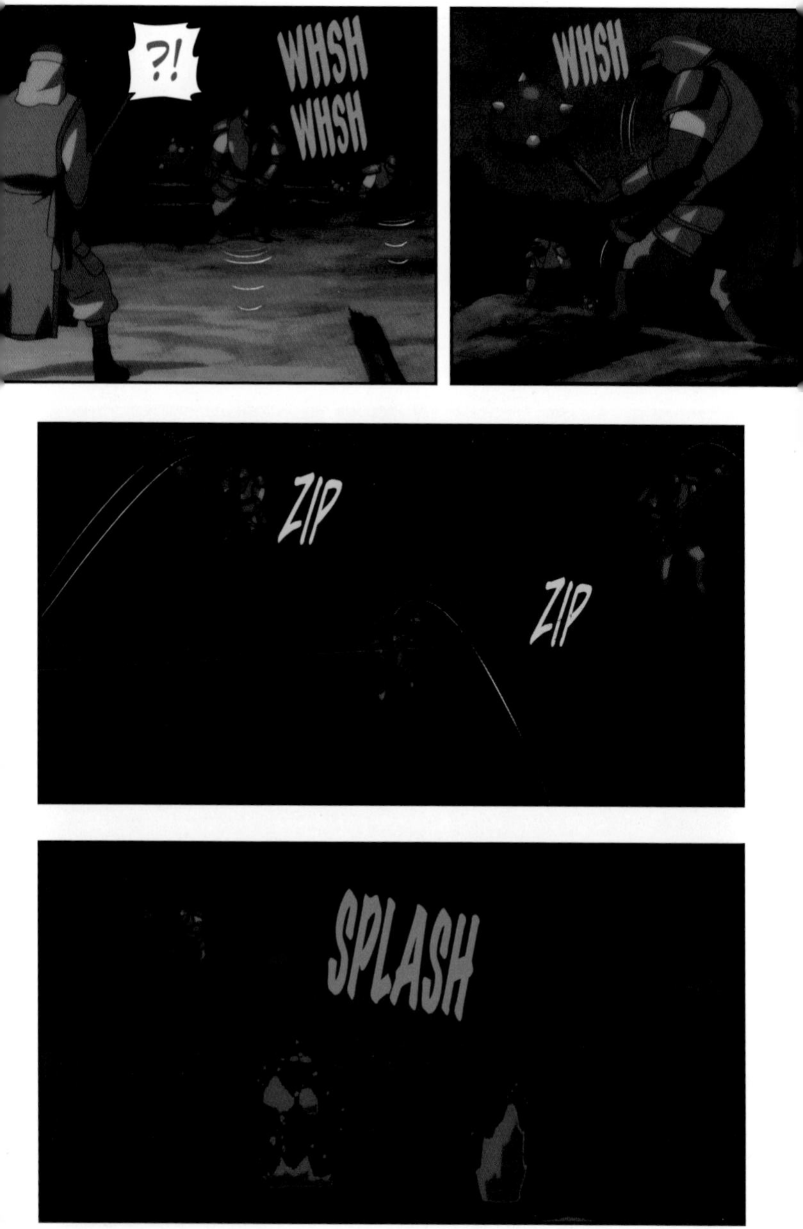
WHSH
?!
WHSH
WHSH
ZIP
ZIP
SPLASH

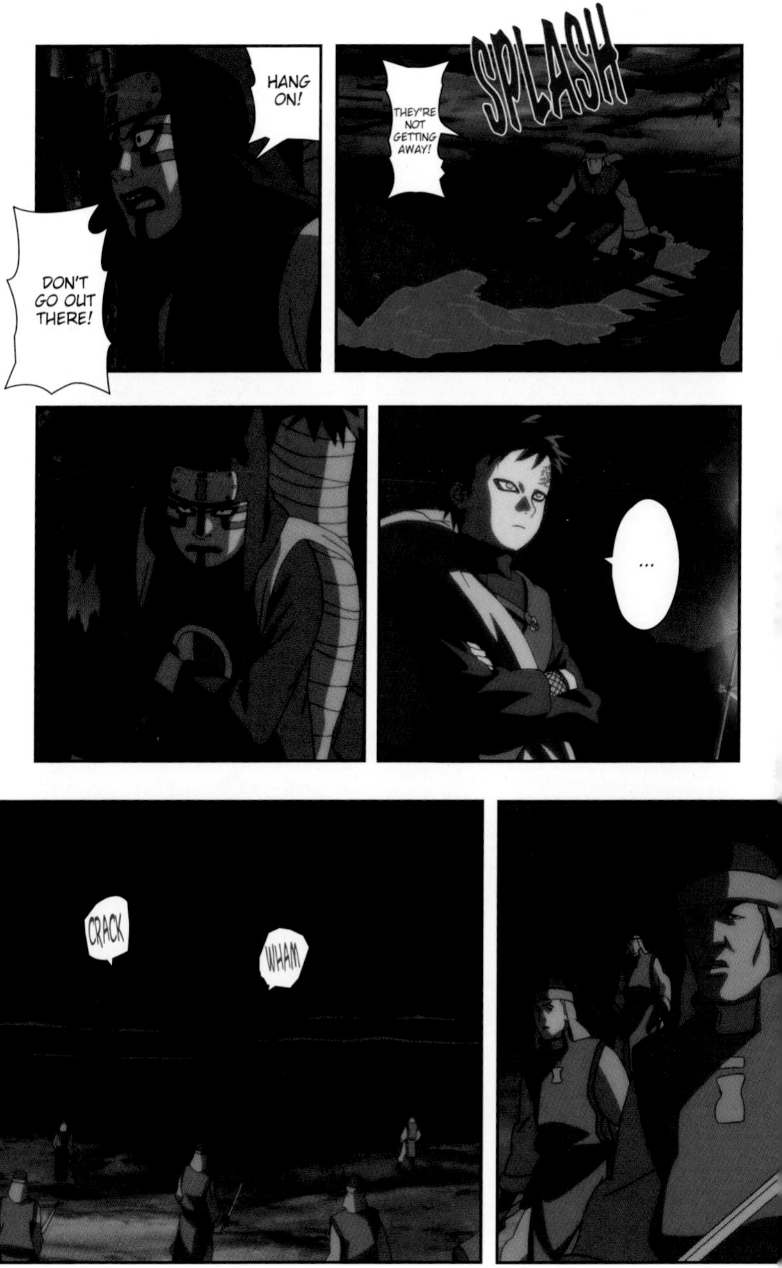
THEY'RE NOT GETTING AWAY!
SPLASH
HANG ON!
DON'T GO OUT THERE!
...
CRACK
WHAM

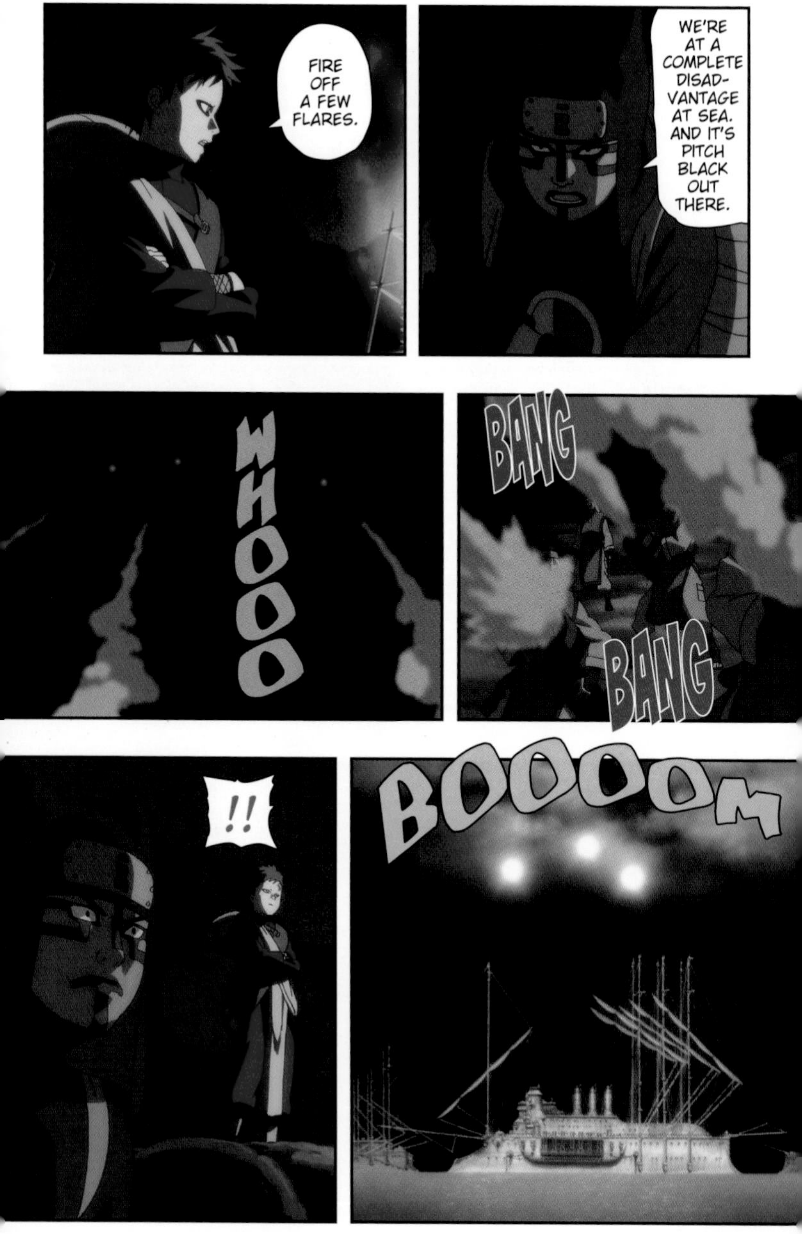
WE'RE AT A COMPLETE DISAD-VANTAGE AT SEA. AND IT'S PITCH BLACK OUT THERE.
FIRE OFF A FEW FLARES.
BANG
BANG
WHOOO
BOOOOM
!!

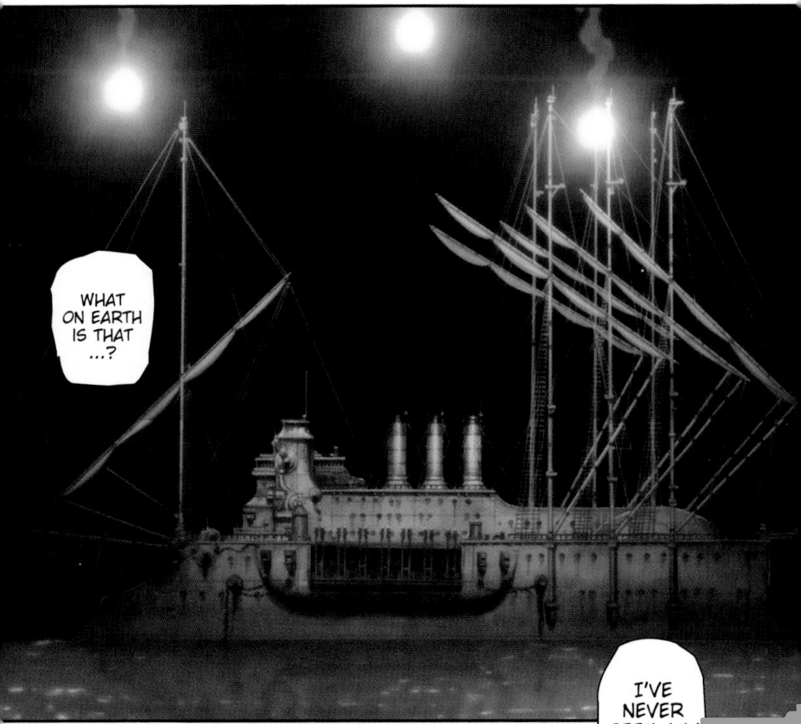
WHAT ON EARTH IS THAT ...?

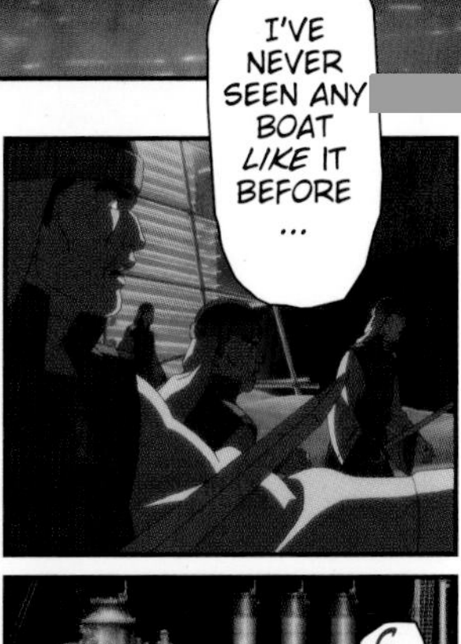
I'VE NEVER SEEN ANY BOAT *LIKE* IT BEFORE ...

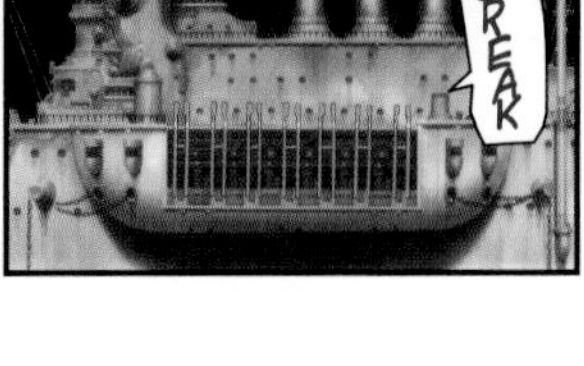
CREAK

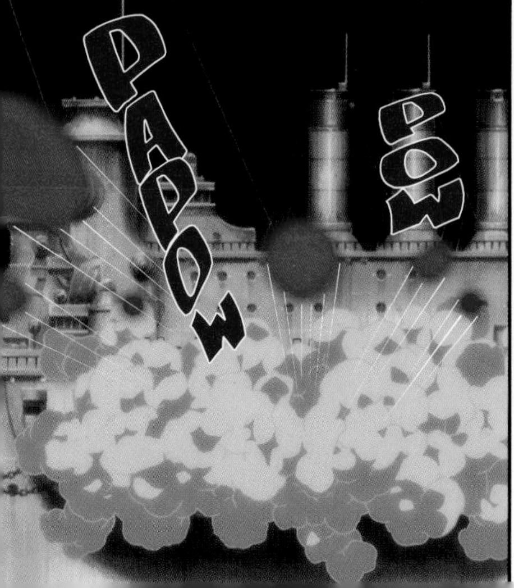
PAPOW
POW

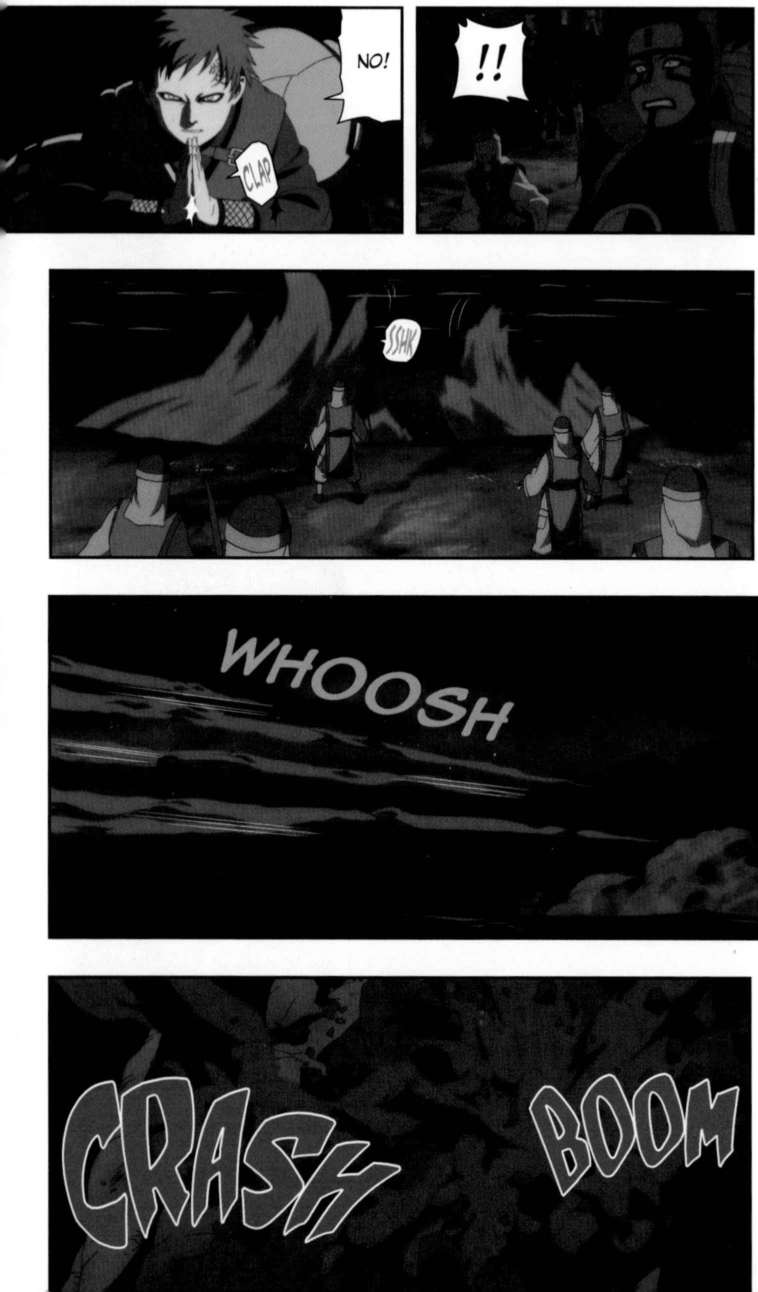
!!
NO!
CLAP
SSHK
WHOOSH
BOOM
CRASH

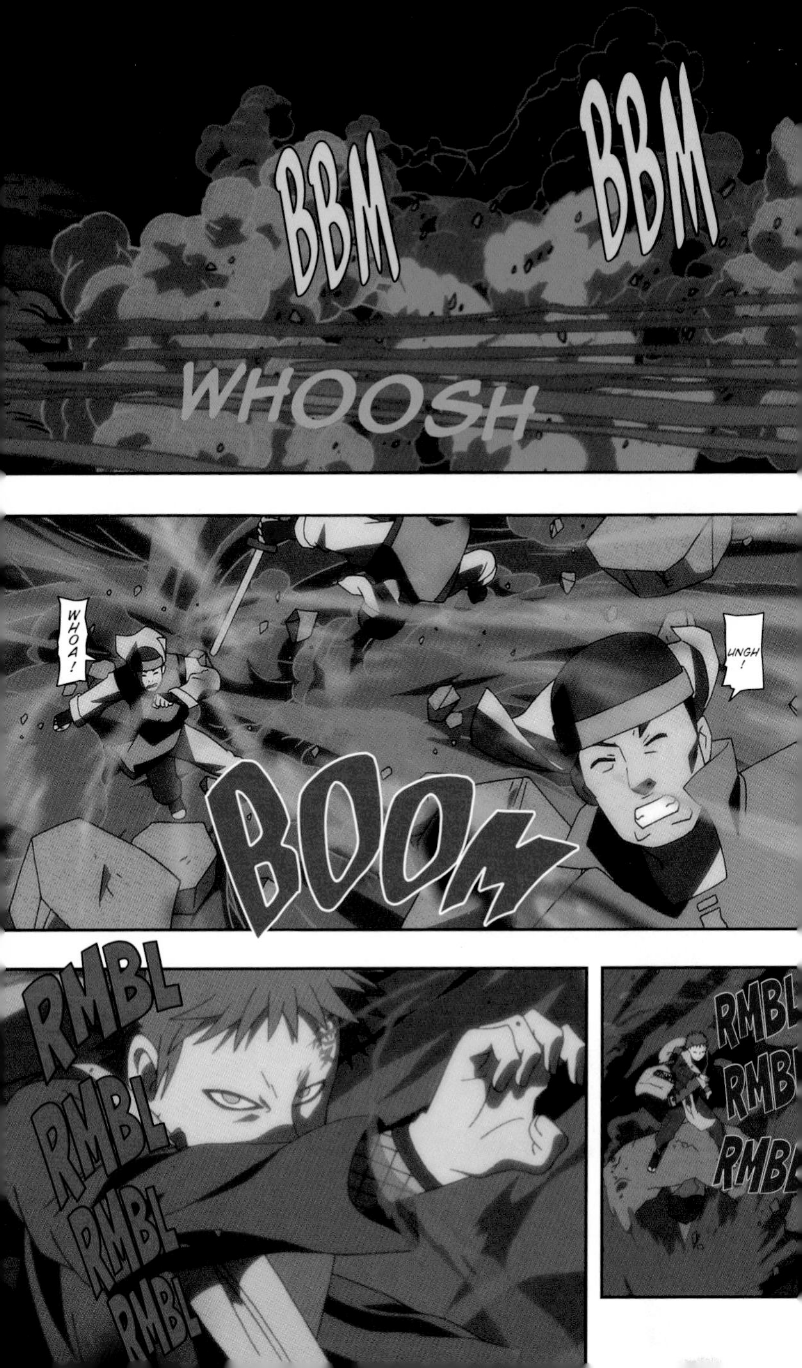
BBM
BBM
WHOOSH
UNGH!
BOOM
WHOA!
RMBL
RMBL
RMBL
RMBL
RMBL
RMBL
RMBL

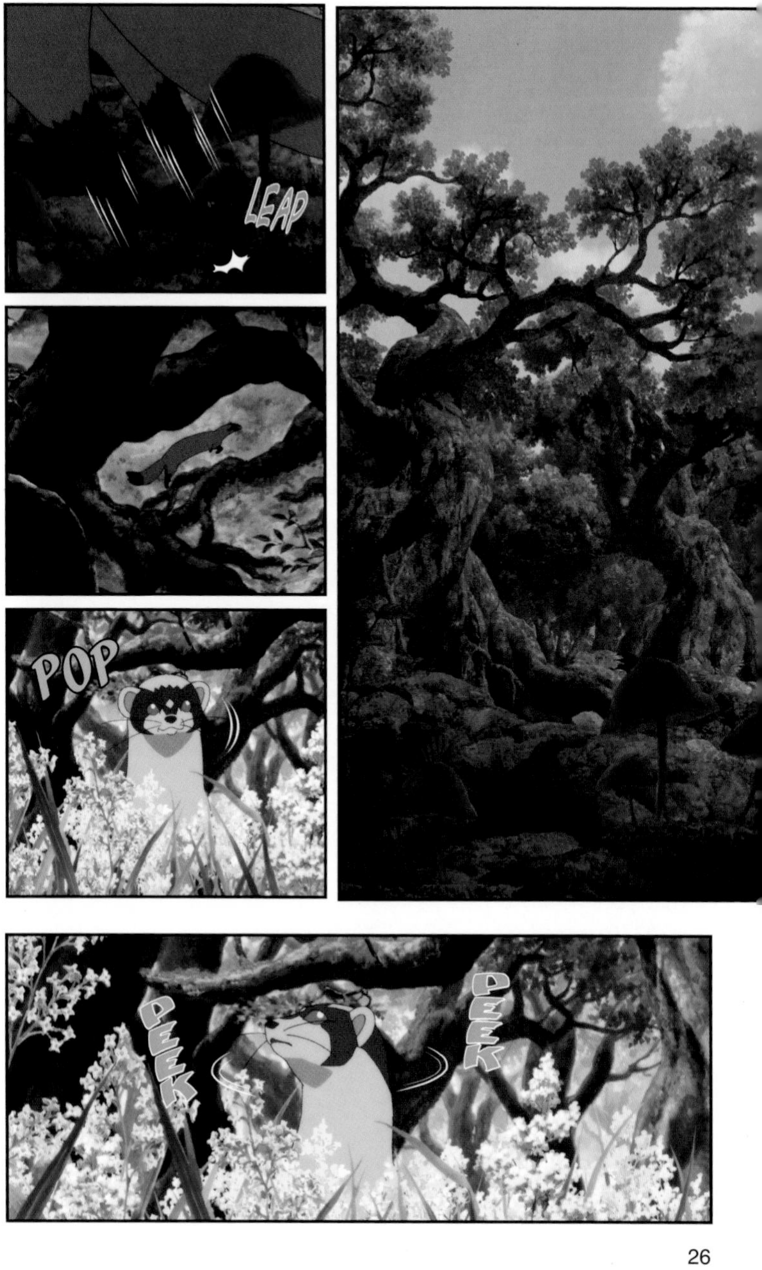
LEAP
POP
PEEK
PEEK

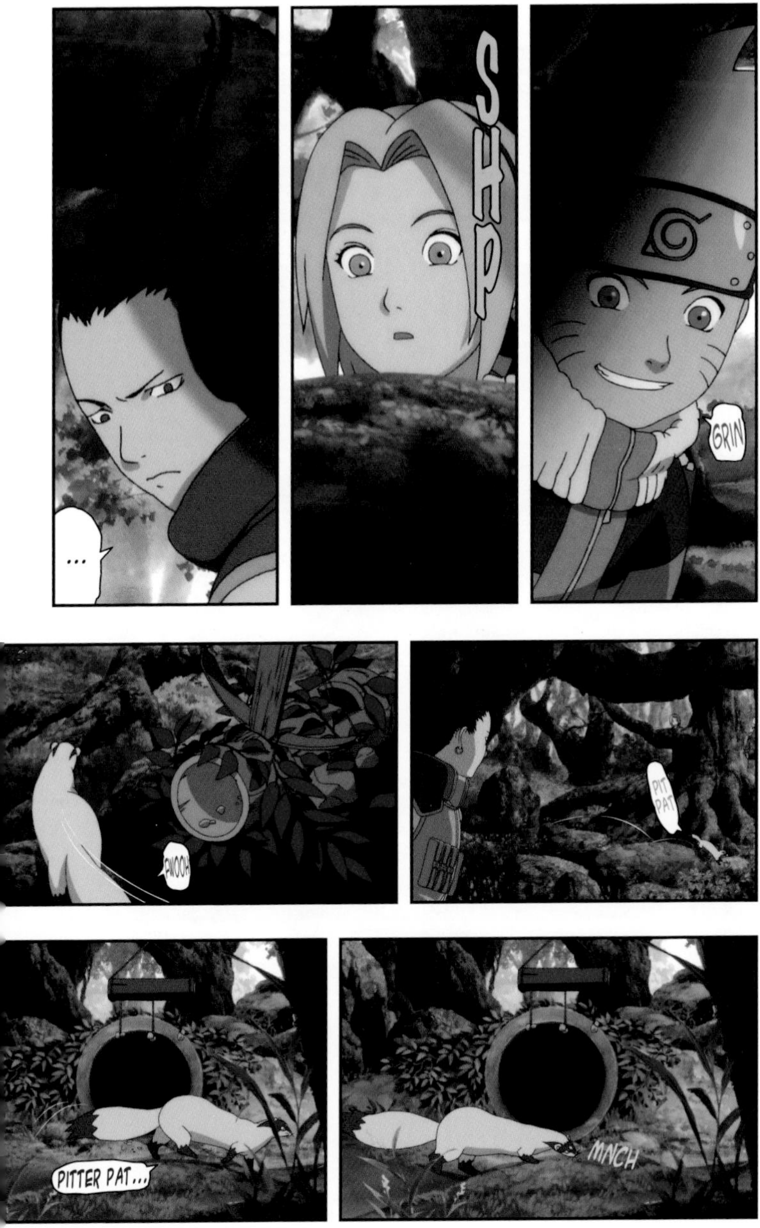
GRIN
SHP
...
PIT PAT
FWOOH
MNCH
PITTER PAT...

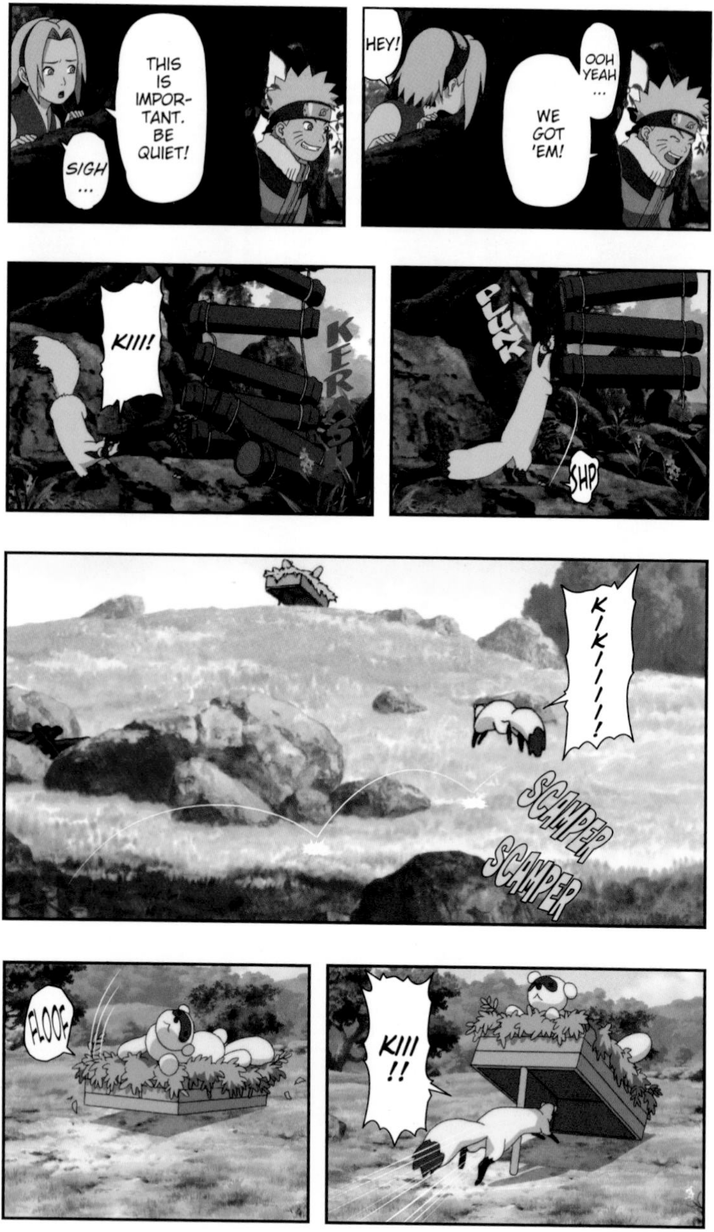
OOH YEAH...
HEY!
WE GOT 'EM!
THIS IS IMPORTANT. BE QUIET!
SIGH...
PLUNK
SHP
KERASH
KIII!
KIKIIII!
SCAMPER SCAMPER
KIII!!
FLOOF

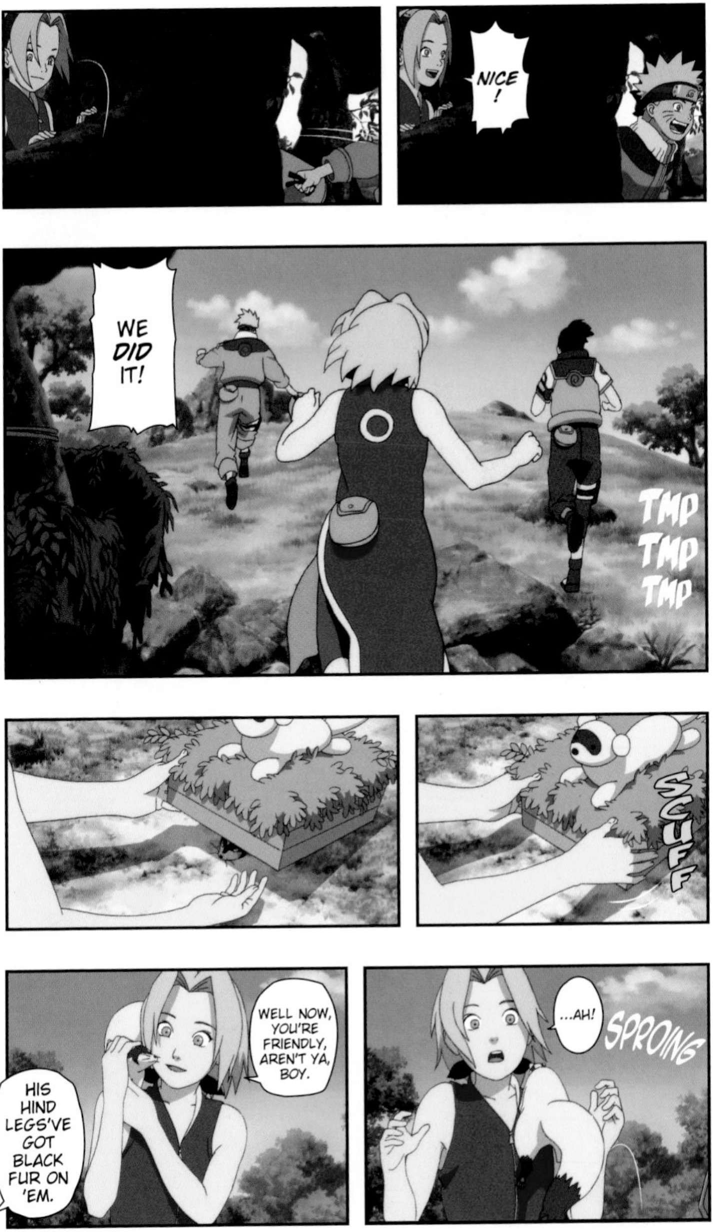
NICE!
WE DID IT!
TMP TMP TMP
SCUFF
...AH!
SPROING
WELL NOW, YOU'RE FRIENDLY, AREN'T YA, BOY.
HIS HIND LEGS'VE GOT BLACK FUR ON 'EM.

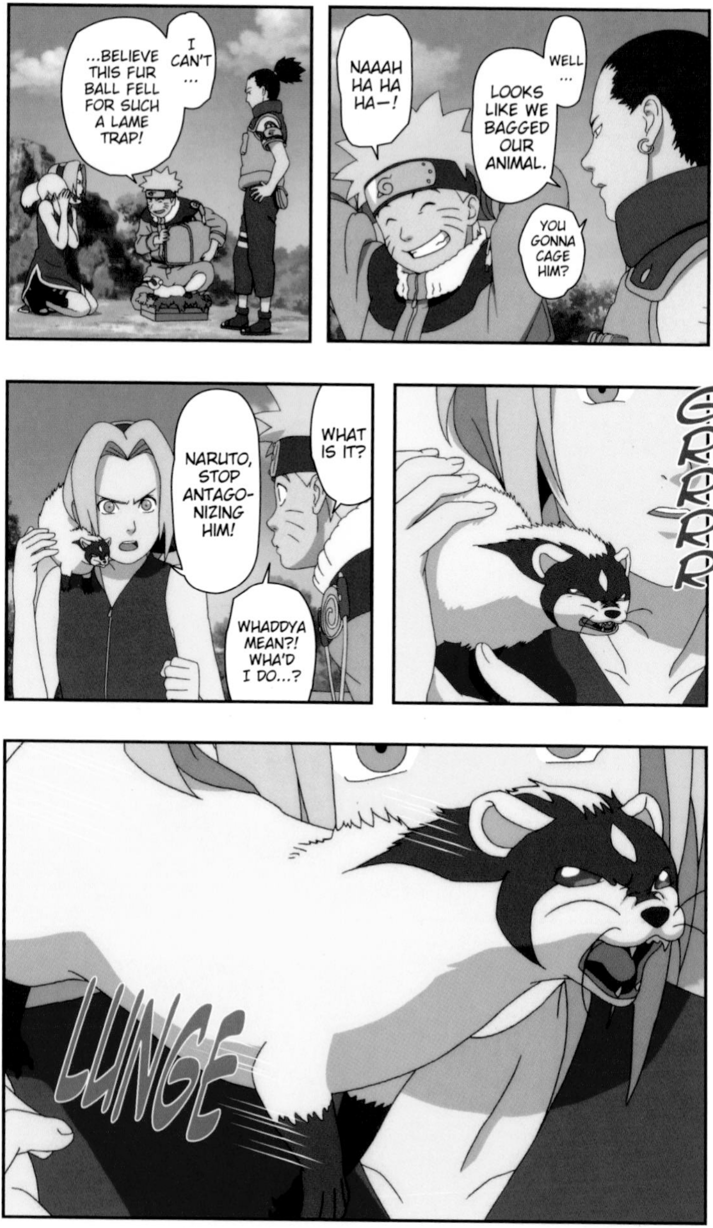
WELL...
LOOKS LIKE WE BAGGED OUR ANIMAL.
NAAAH HA HA HA—!
YOU GONNA CAGE HIM?
I CAN'T...
...BELIEVE THIS FUR BALL FELL FOR SUCH A LAME TRAP!
GRRRRR
WHAT IS IT?
NARUTO, STOP ANTAGONIZING HIM!
WHADDYA MEAN?! WHA'D I DO...?
LUNGE

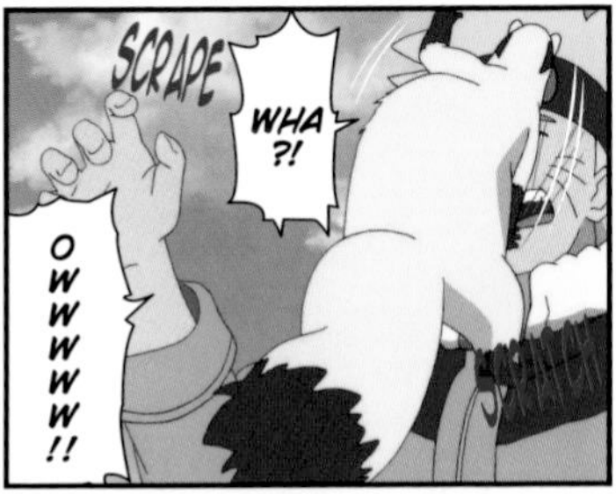
SCRAPE
WHA ?!
OWWWWWW!!
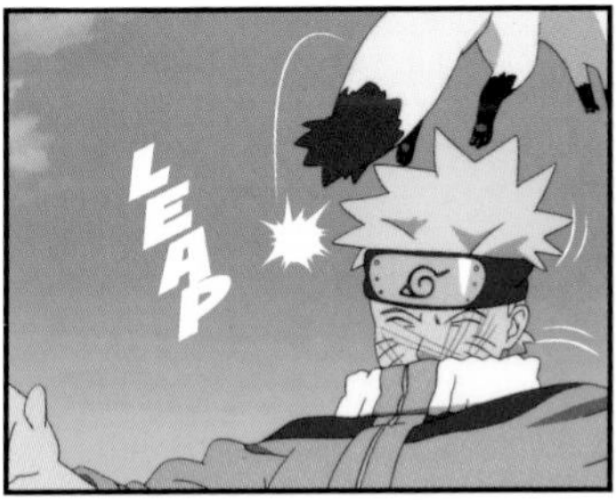
LEAP
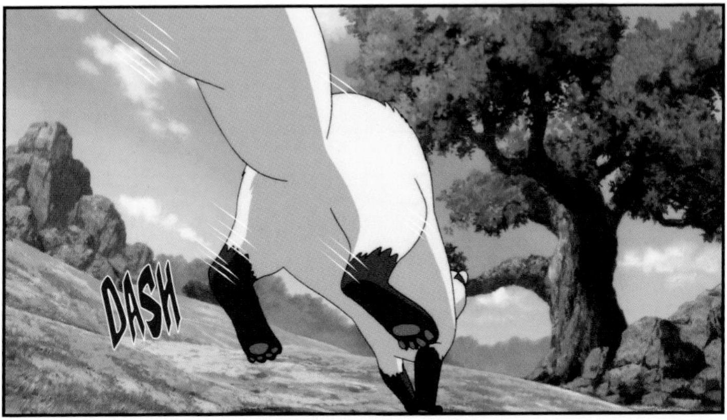
DASH
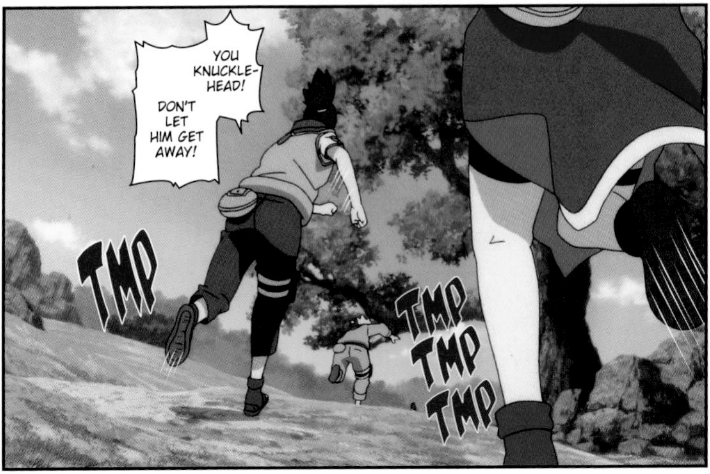
YOU KNUCKLE-HEAD!
DON'T LET HIM GET AWAY!
TMP
TMP TMP TMP

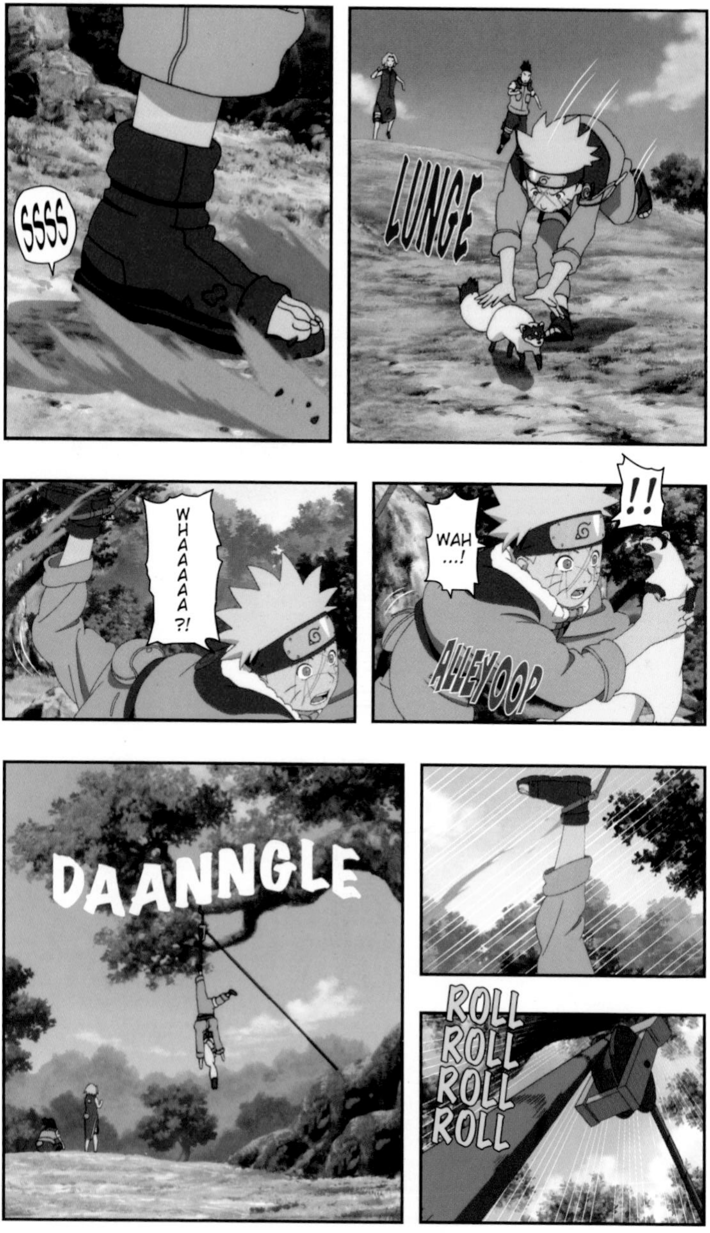
LUNGE
SSSS
WAH ...!
!!
ALLEY OOP
WHAAAAAA?!
ROLL ROLL ROLL ROLL
DAANNGLE

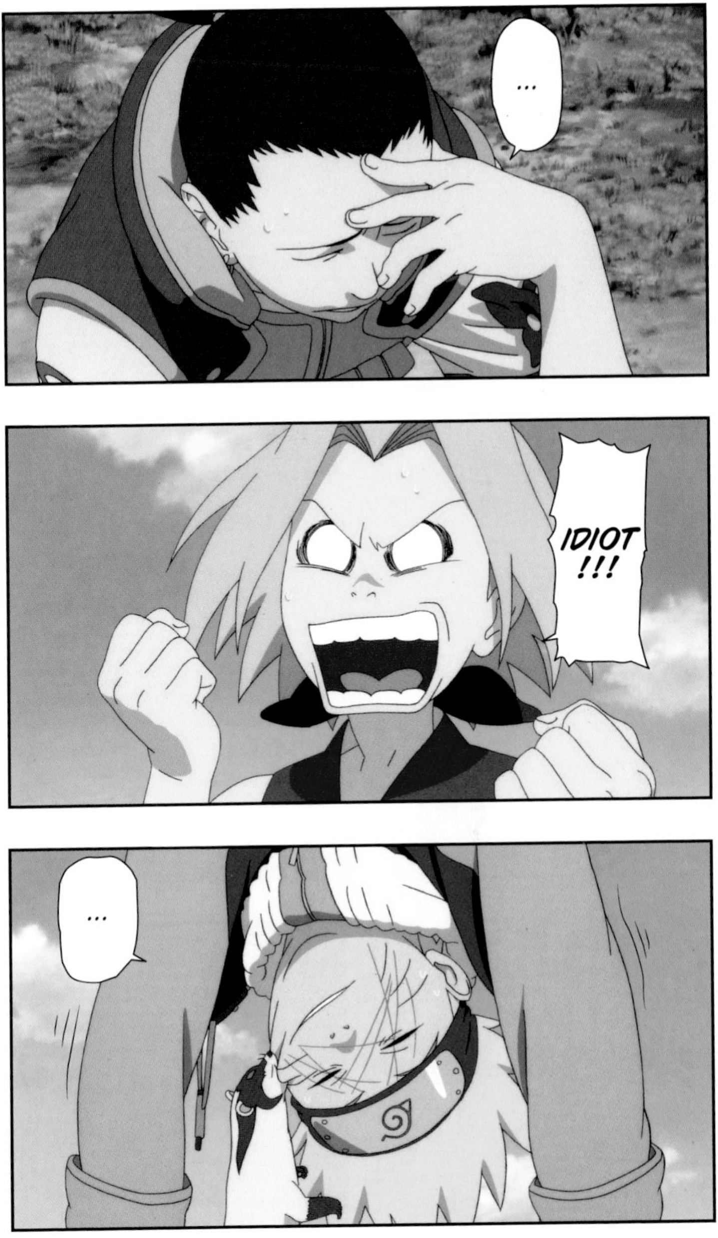
...
IDIOT!!!
...

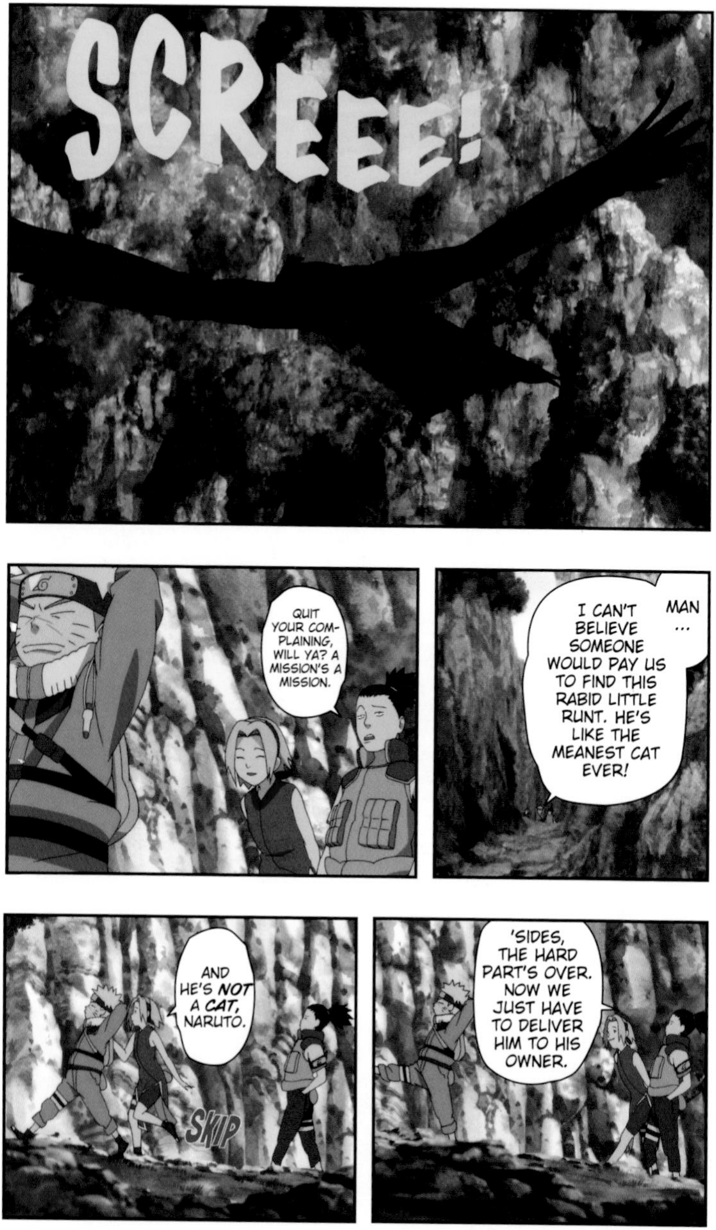
SCREEE!
MAN ...
I CAN'T BELIEVE SOMEONE WOULD PAY US TO FIND THIS RABID LITTLE RUNT. HE'S LIKE THE MEANEST CAT EVER!
QUIT YOUR COM- PLAINING, WILL YA? A MISSION'S A MISSION.
'SIDES, THE HARD PART'S OVER. NOW WE JUST HAVE TO DELIVER HIM TO HIS OWNER.
AND HE'S ***NOT*** A ***CAT***, NARUTO.
SKIP

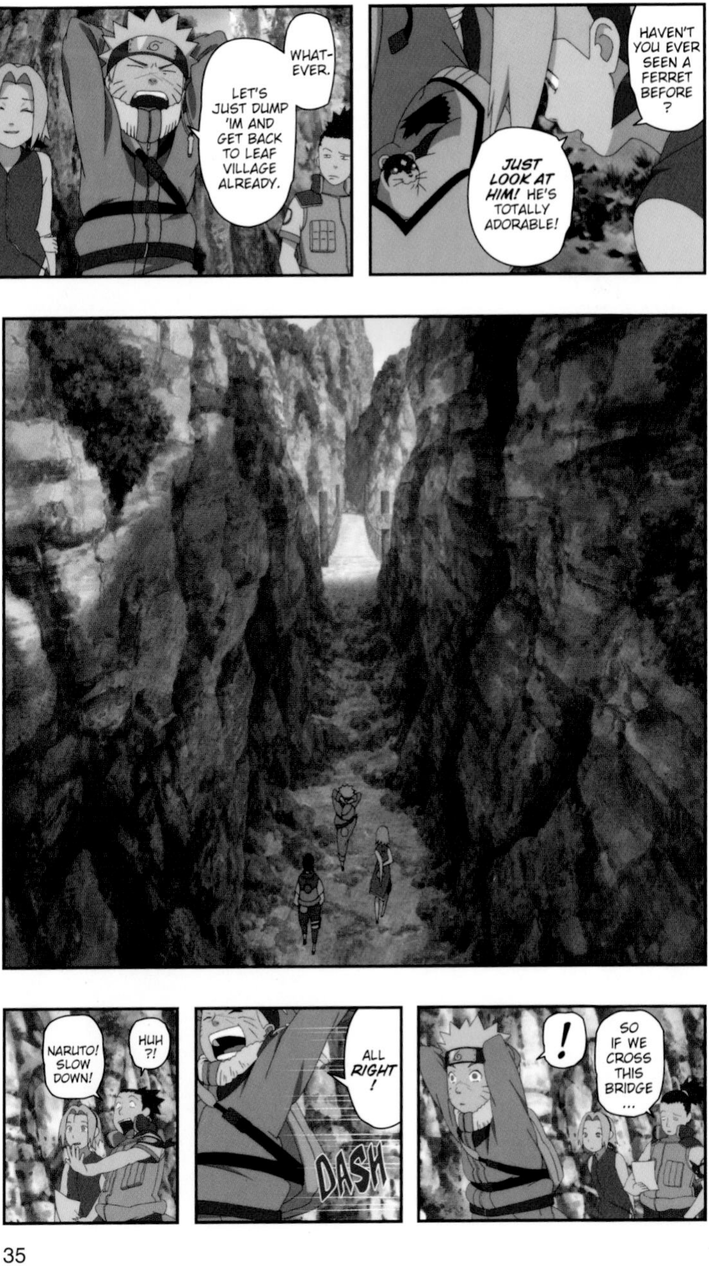
HAVEN'T YOU EVER SEEN A FERRET BEFORE?
JUST LOOK AT HIM! HE'S TOTALLY ADORABLE!
WHAT-EVER.
LET'S JUST DUMP 'IM AND GET BACK TO LEAF VILLAGE ALREADY.
SO IF WE CROSS THIS BRIDGE...
!
ALL *RIGHT*!
DASH
HUH?!
NARUTO! SLOW DOWN!

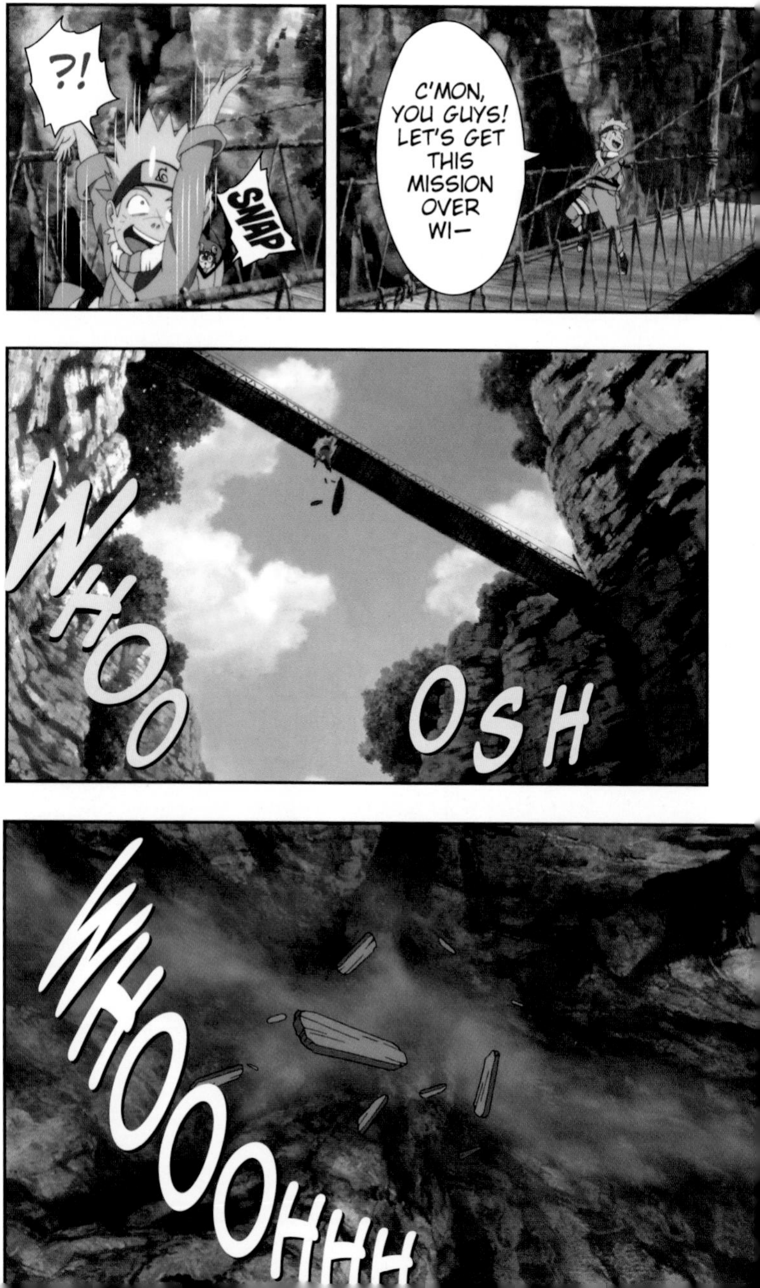
C'MON, YOU GUYS! LET'S GET THIS MISSION OVER WI—
?!
SNAP
WHOO OSH
WHOOOOHHH

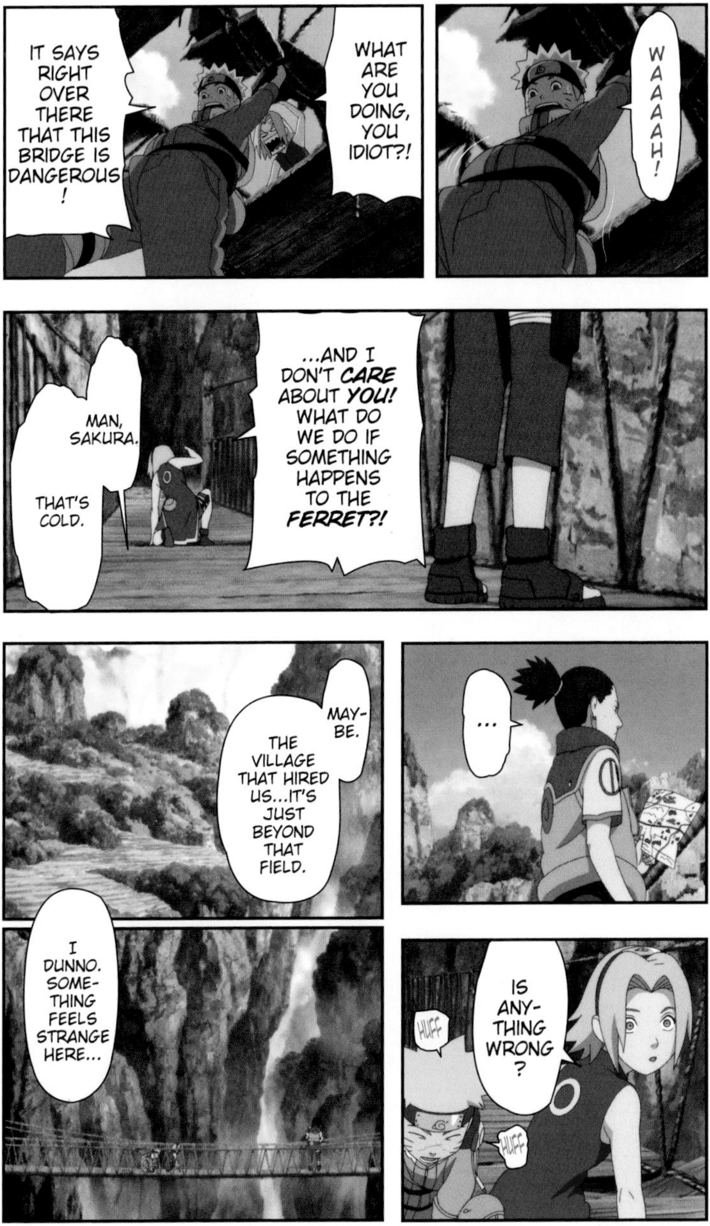
WAAAAAH!
WHAT ARE YOU DOING, YOU IDIOT?!
IT SAYS RIGHT OVER THERE THAT THIS BRIDGE IS DANGEROUS!
...AND I DON'T **CARE** ABOUT **YOU!** WHAT DO WE DO IF SOMETHING HAPPENS TO THE **FERRET?!**
MAN, SAKURA.
THAT'S COLD.
...
MAY-BE.
THE VILLAGE THAT HIRED US...IT'S JUST BEYOND THAT FIELD.
IS ANY-THING WRONG?
HUFF
HUFF
I DUNNO. SOME-THING FEELS STRANGE HERE...

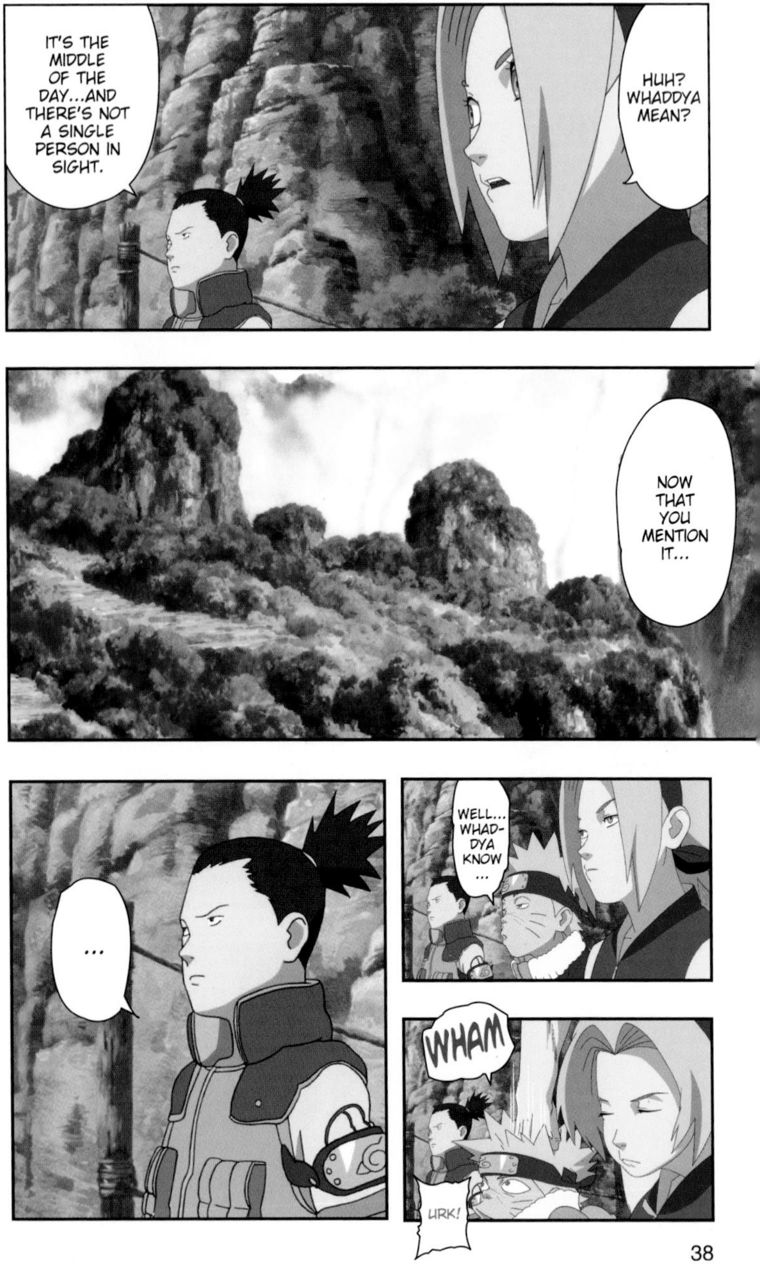
HUH? WHADDYA MEAN?
IT'S THE MIDDLE OF THE DAY...AND THERE'S NOT A SINGLE PERSON IN SIGHT.
NOW THAT YOU MENTION IT...
WELL... WHAD-DYA KNOW ...
WHAM
URK!
...

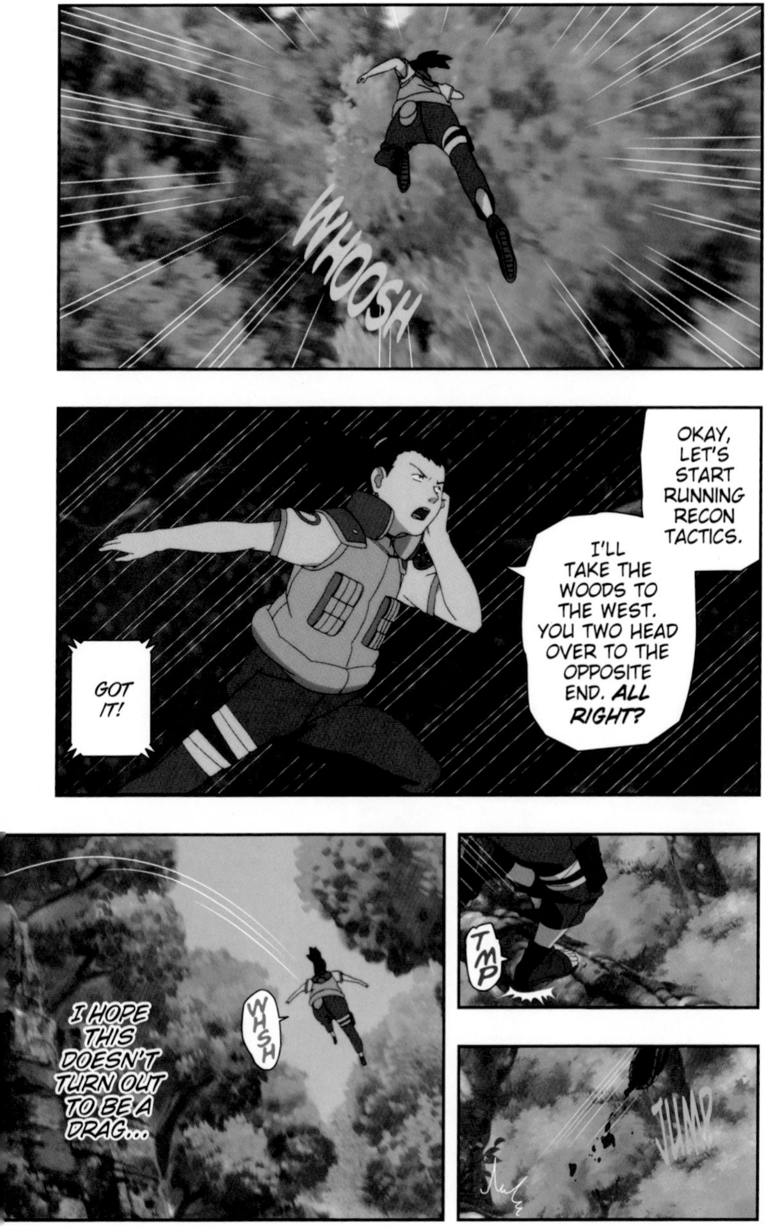
WHOOSH
OKAY, LET'S START RUNNING RECON TACTICS.
I'LL TAKE THE WOODS TO THE WEST. YOU TWO HEAD OVER TO THE OPPOSITE END. ALL RIGHT?
GOT IT!
TMP
JUMP
WHSH
I HOPE THIS DOESN'T TURN OUT TO BE A DRAG...

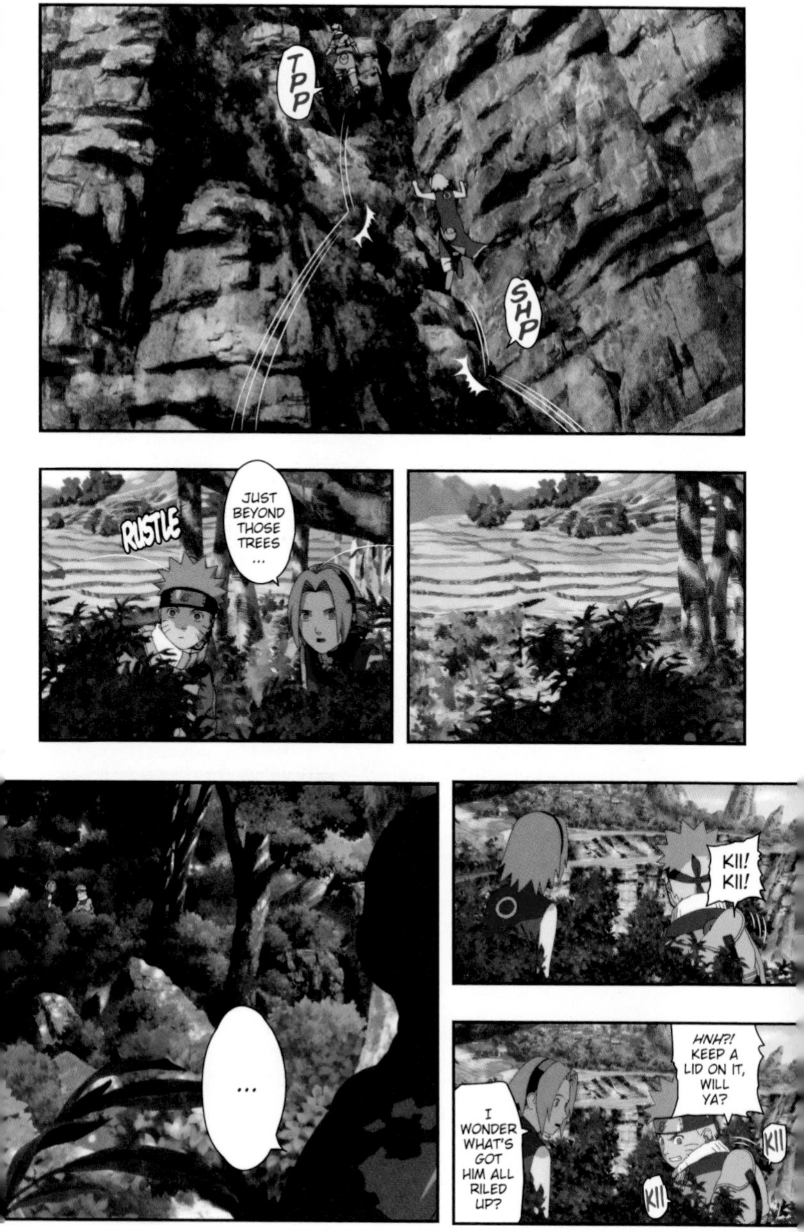
TPP
SHP
RUSTLE
JUST BEYOND THOSE TREES ...
KII! KII!
HNH?! KEEP A LID ON IT, WILL YA?
KII
I WONDER WHAT'S GOT HIM ALL RILED UP?
KII
...

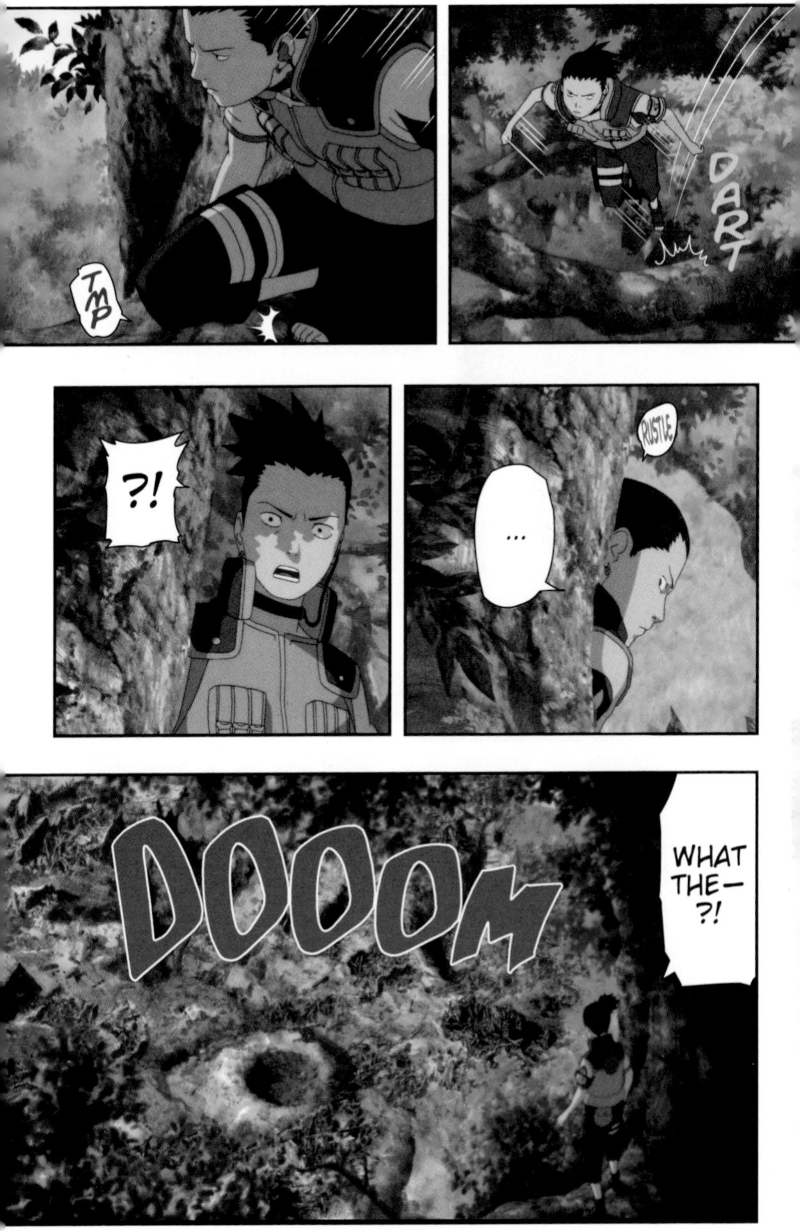
DART
TMP
RUSTLE
...
?!
WHAT THE— ?!
DOOOM

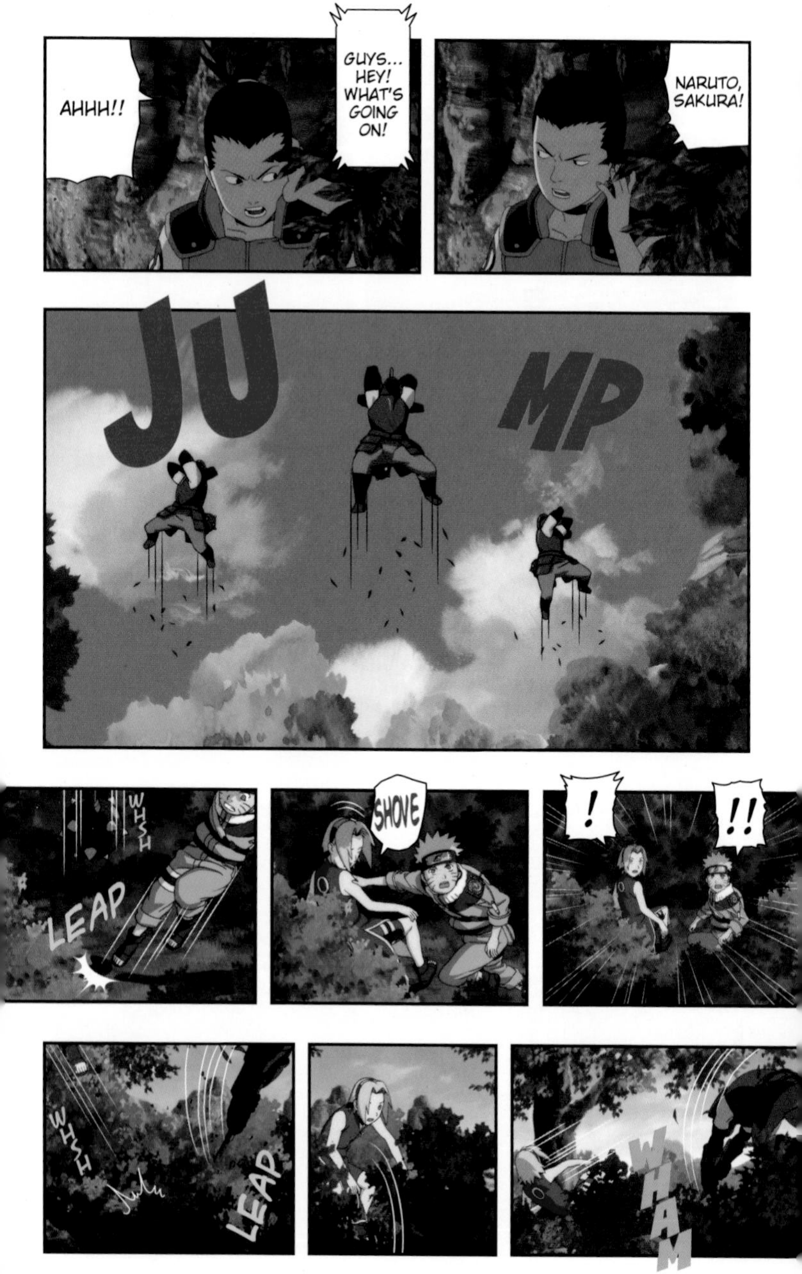
NARUTO, SAKURA!
GUYS... HEY! WHAT'S GOING ON!
AHHH!!
JUMP
!
!!
SHOVE
WHSH
LEAP
WHAM
WHSH
LEAP

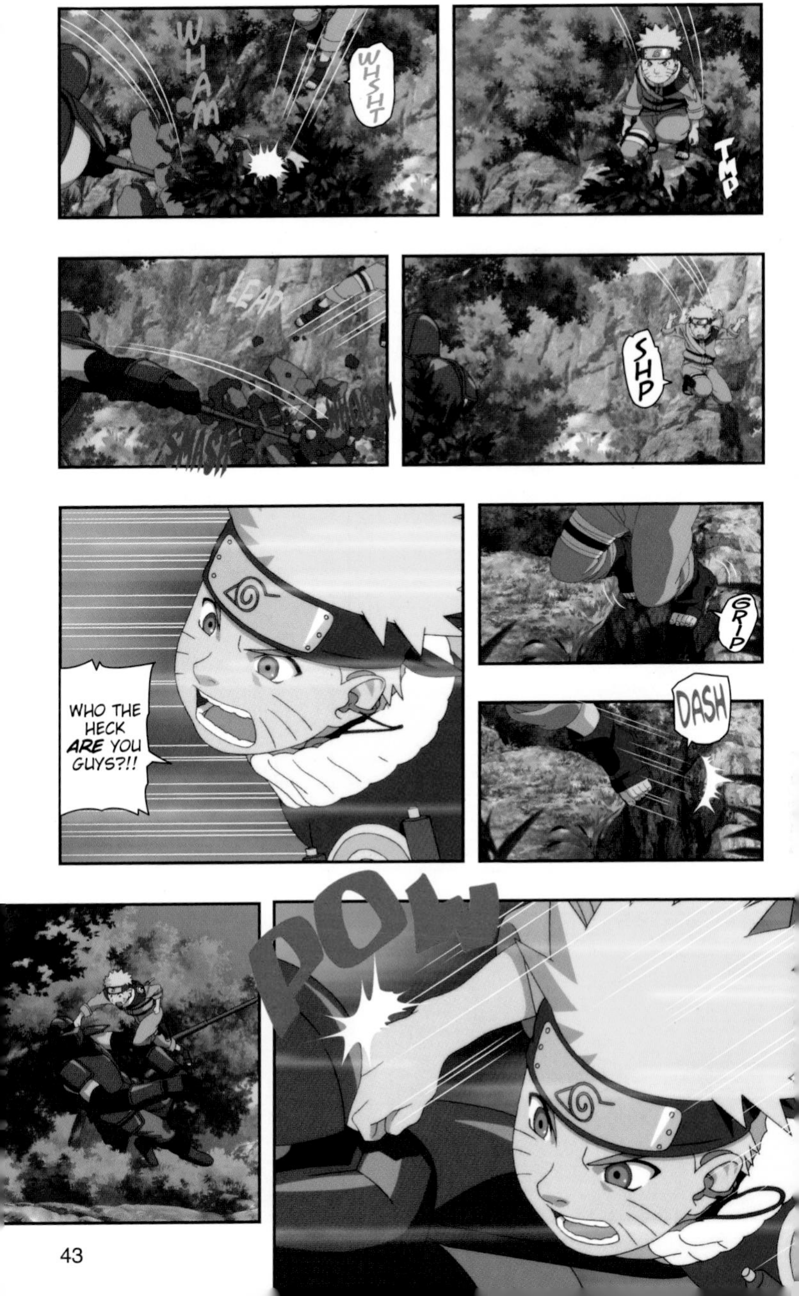
TMP
WHAM
WHSHT
SHP
LEAP
WHOOSH
SMASH
GRIP
DASH
WHO THE HECK **ARE** YOU GUYS?!!
POW

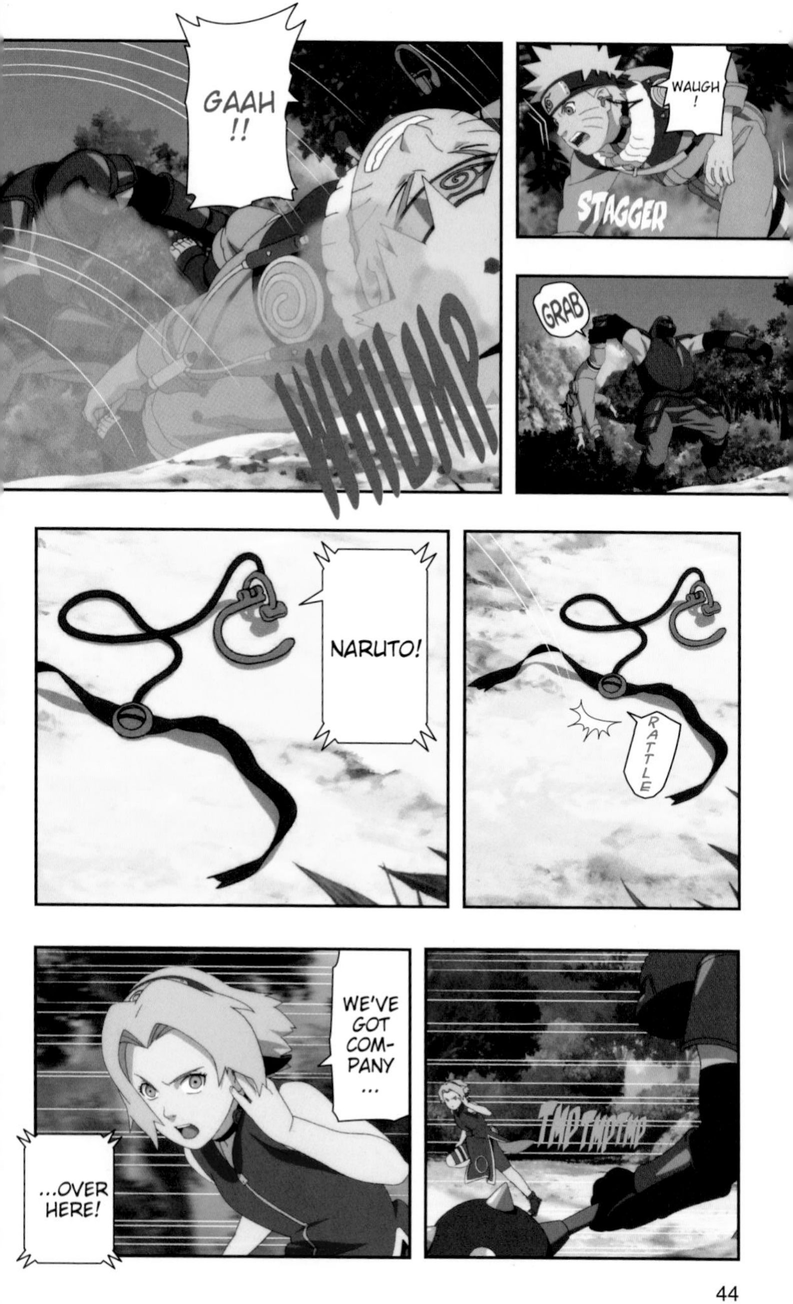
WAUGH!
STAGGER
GRAB
GAAH!!
WHUMP
RATTLE
NARUTO!
TMPTMPTMP
WE'VE GOT COMPANY...
...OVER HERE!

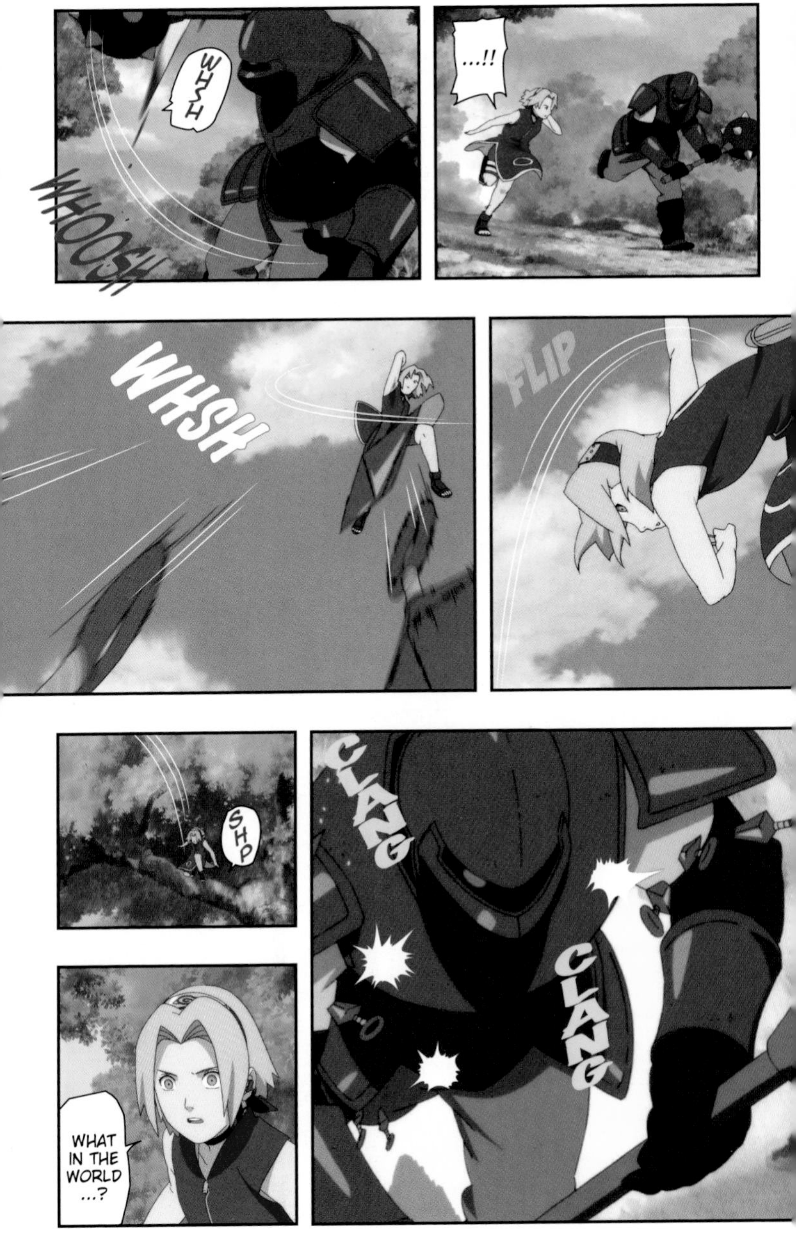
...!!
WHSH
WHOOSH
FLIP
WHSH
CLANG
CLANG
CLANG
SHP
WHAT IN THE WORLD ...?

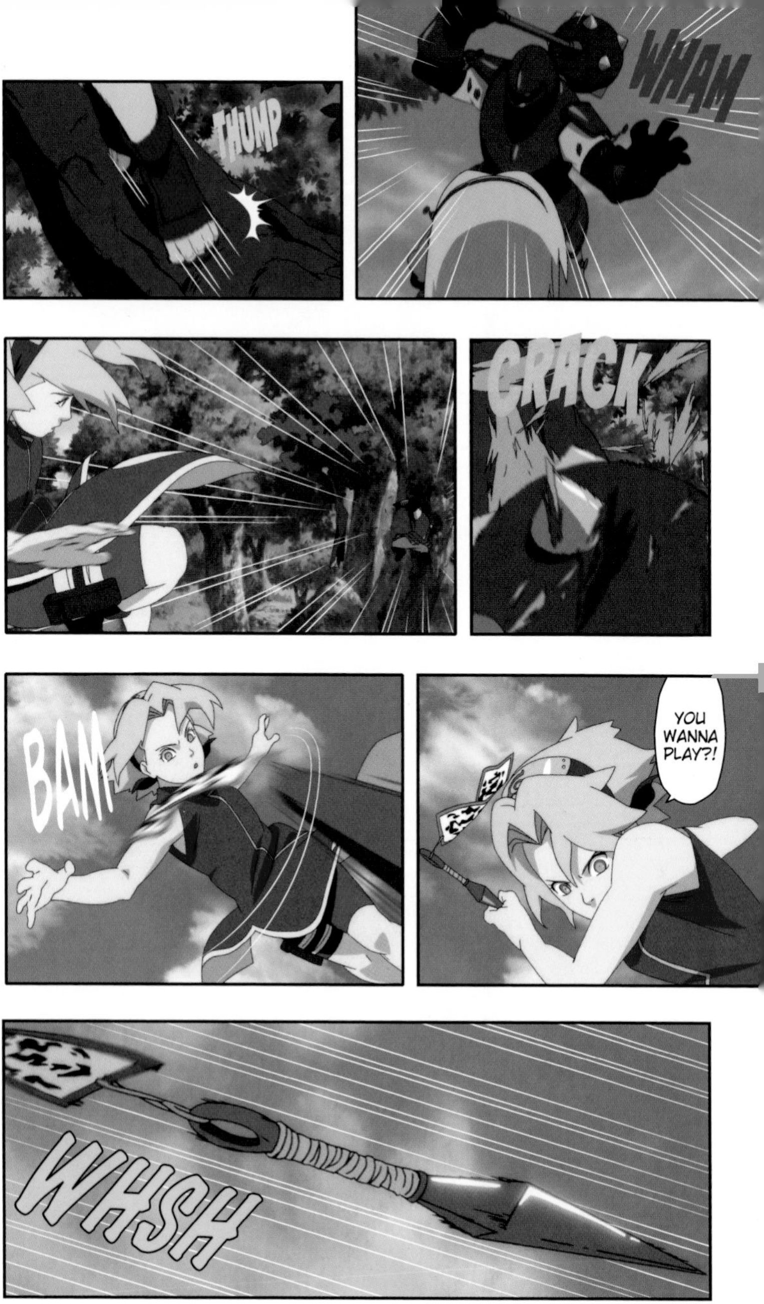
WHAM
THUMP
CRACK
YOU WANNA PLAY?!
BAM
WHSH

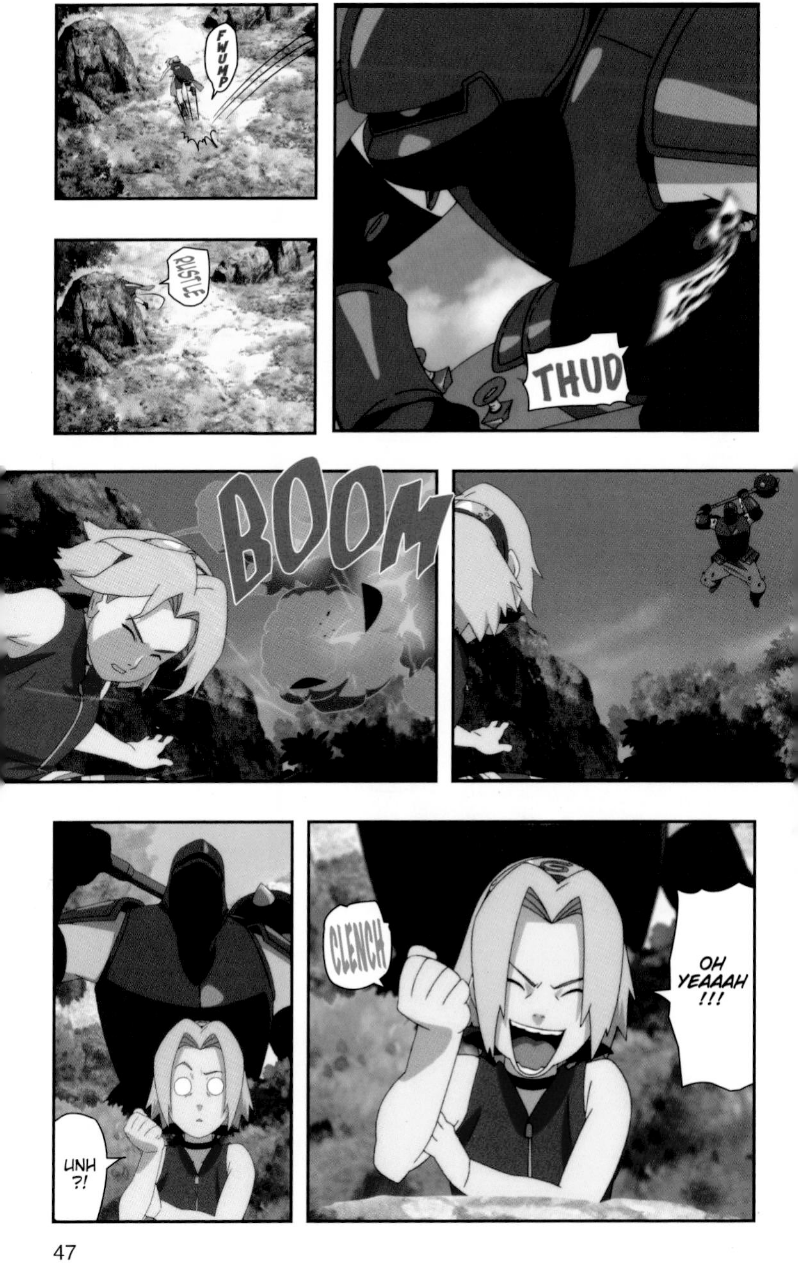
THUD
FWUMP
RUSTLE
BOOM
OH YEAAAH !!!
CLENCH
UNH ?!

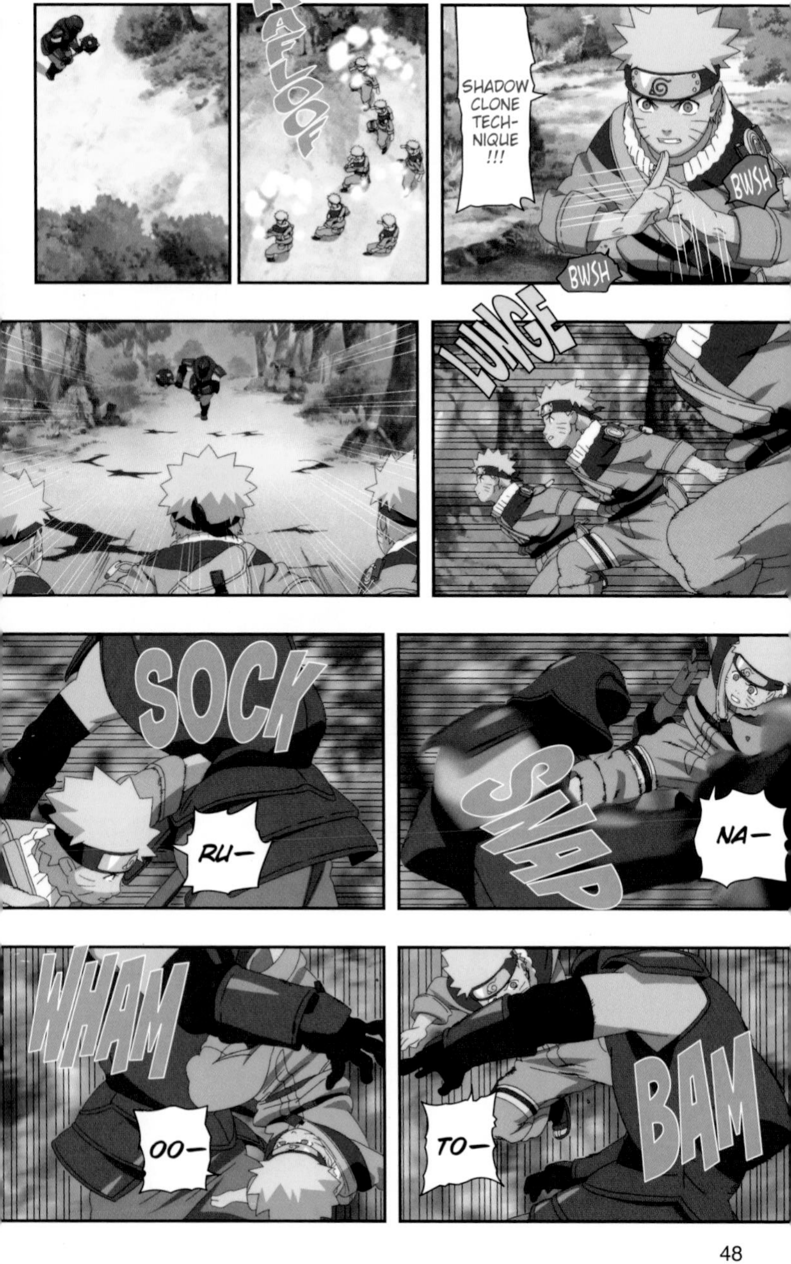
SHADOW CLONE TECH-NIQUE !!!
BWSH
BWSH
KAFLOOF
LUNGE
SNAP
NA—
SOCK
RU—
BAM
TO—
WHAM
OO—

POW

POW

UZU-MAKI! BAR-RAGE!

WHOOSH

POW

POW

TMP

TMP

BOOF

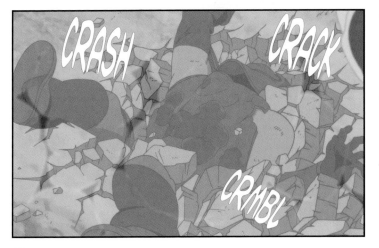

CRASH

CRACK

CRMBL

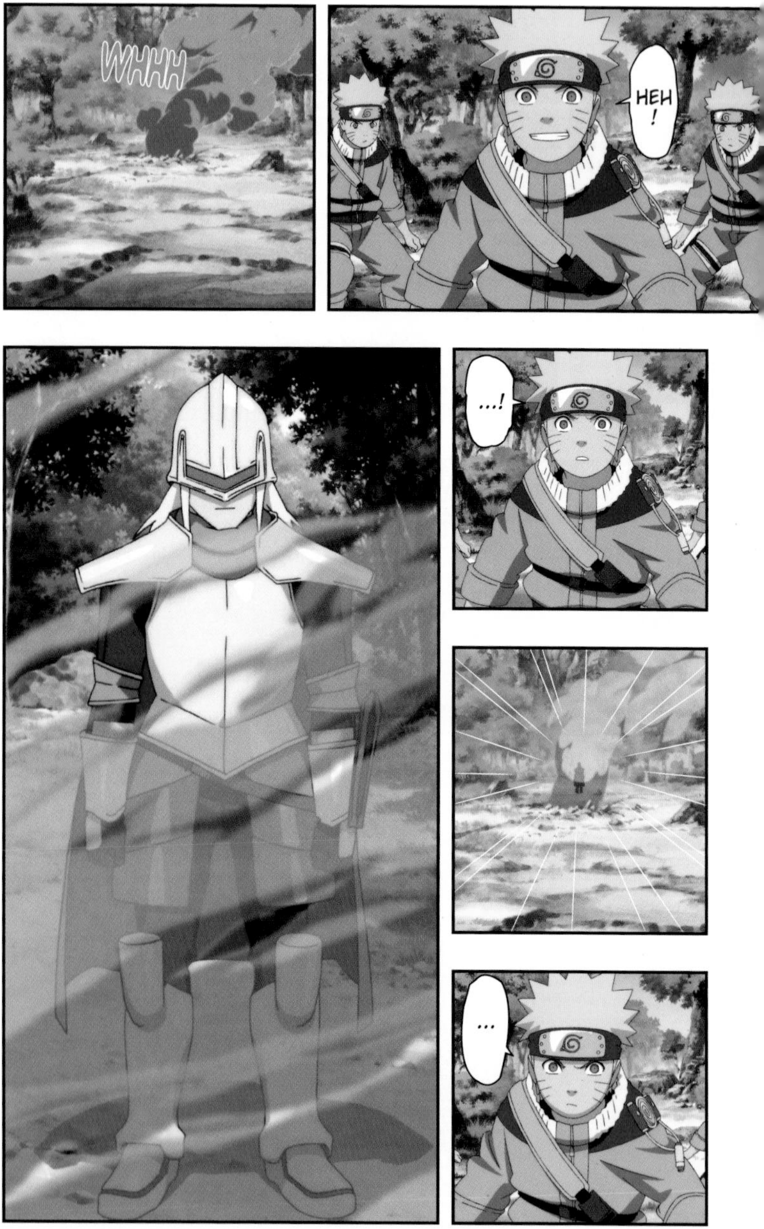
HEH!
WHHH
...!
...

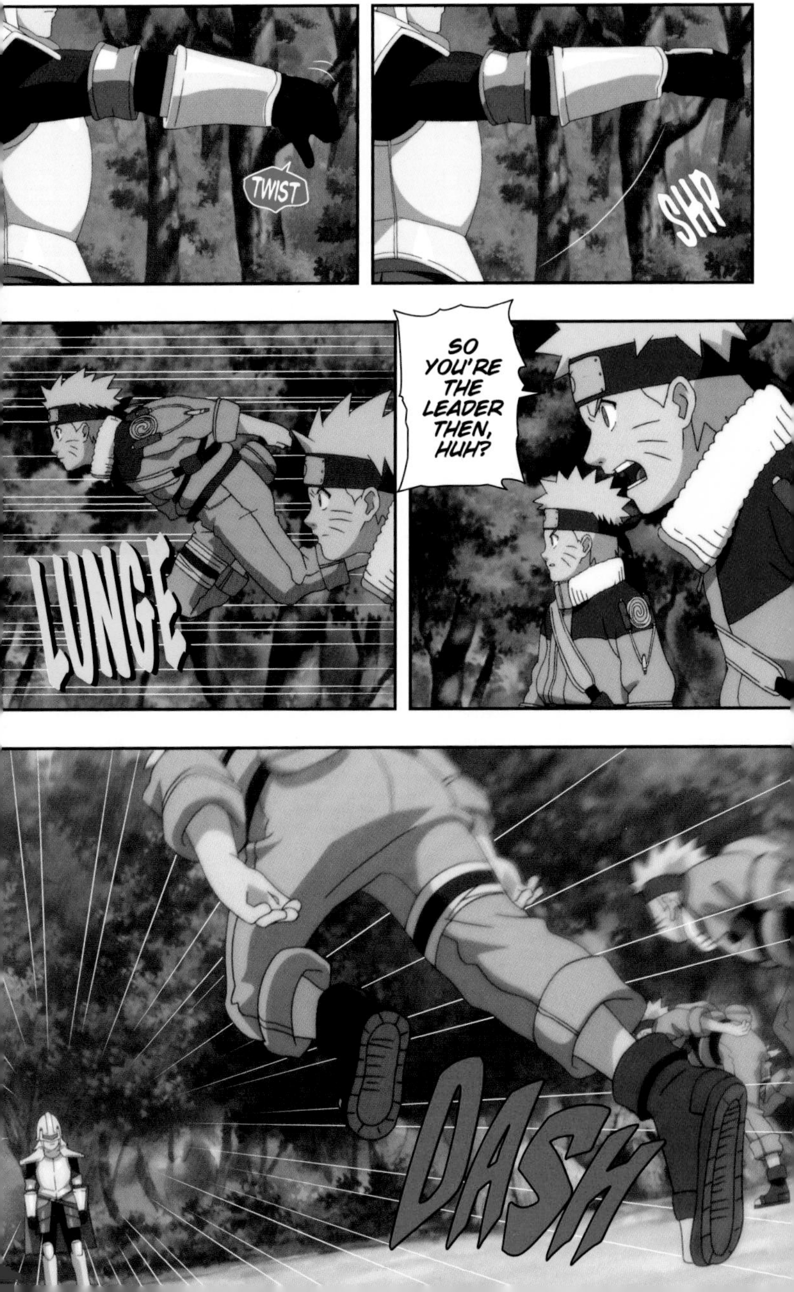
SHP
TWIST
SO YOU'RE THE LEADER THEN, HUH?
LUNGE
DASH

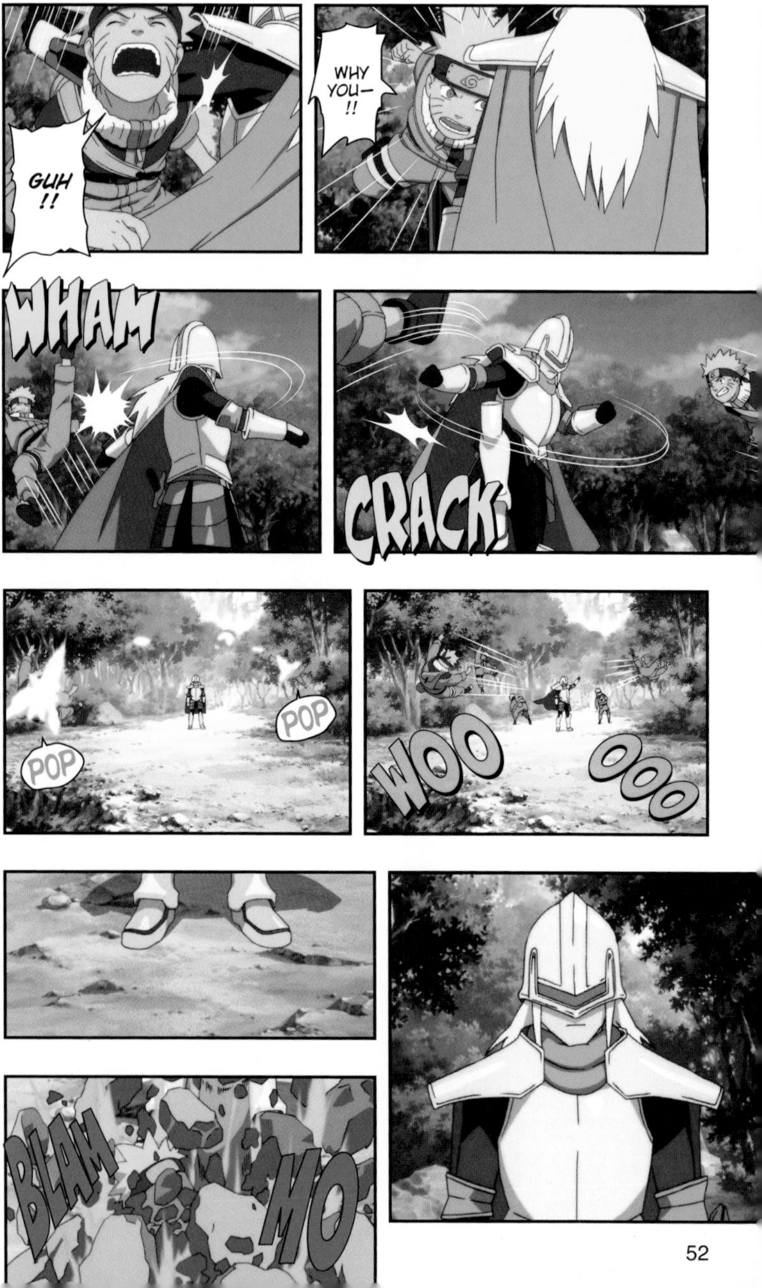
WHY YOU— !!
GUH !!
CRACK
WHAM
WOO OOO
POP
POP
BLAM
MO

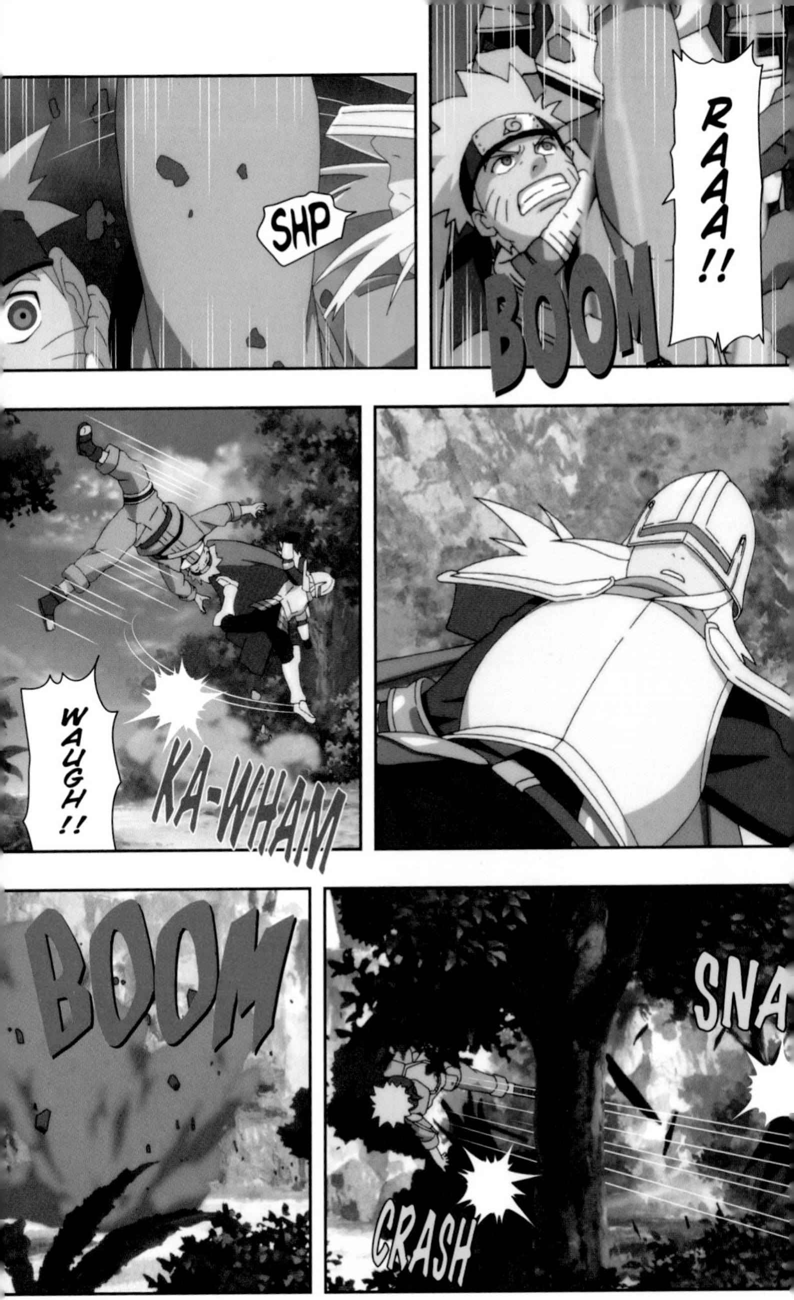
RAAAA!!
BOOM
SHP
WAUGH!!
KA-WHAM
SNA
CRASH
BOOM

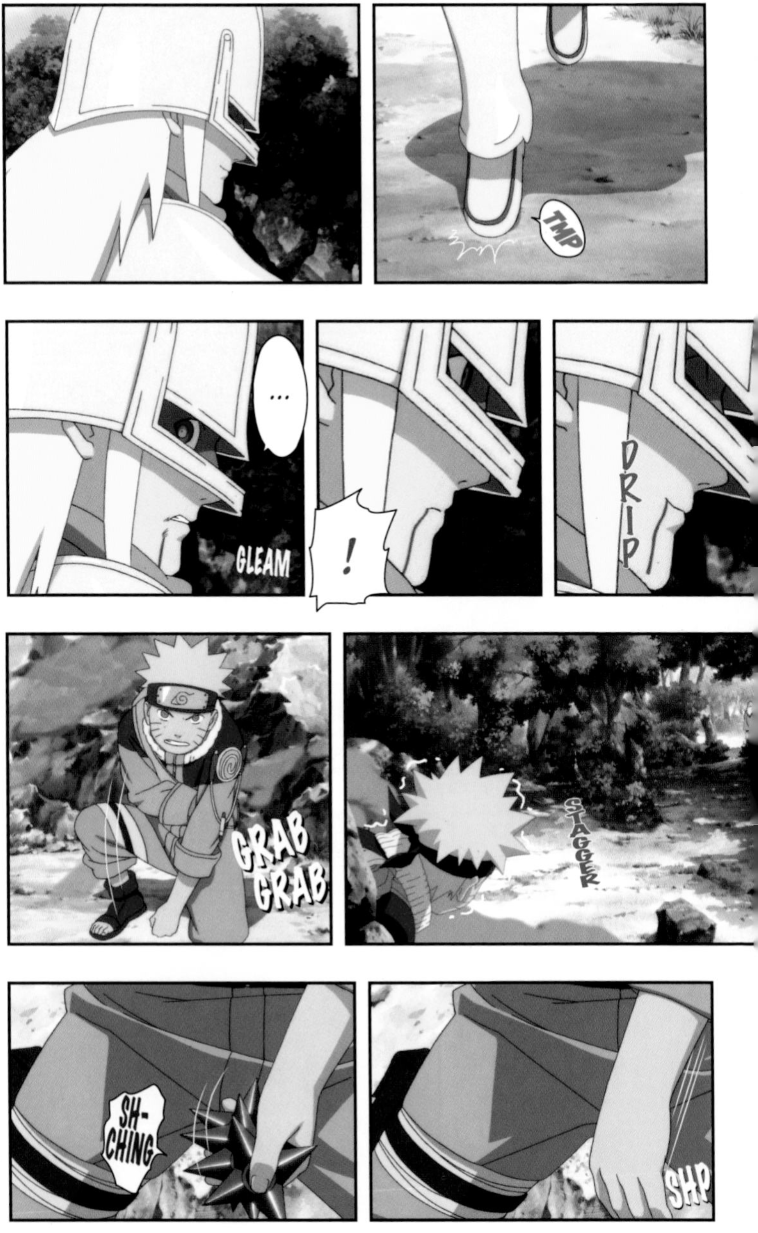
TMP
DRIP
!
...
GLEAM
STAGGER
GRAB GRAB
SHP
SH-CHING

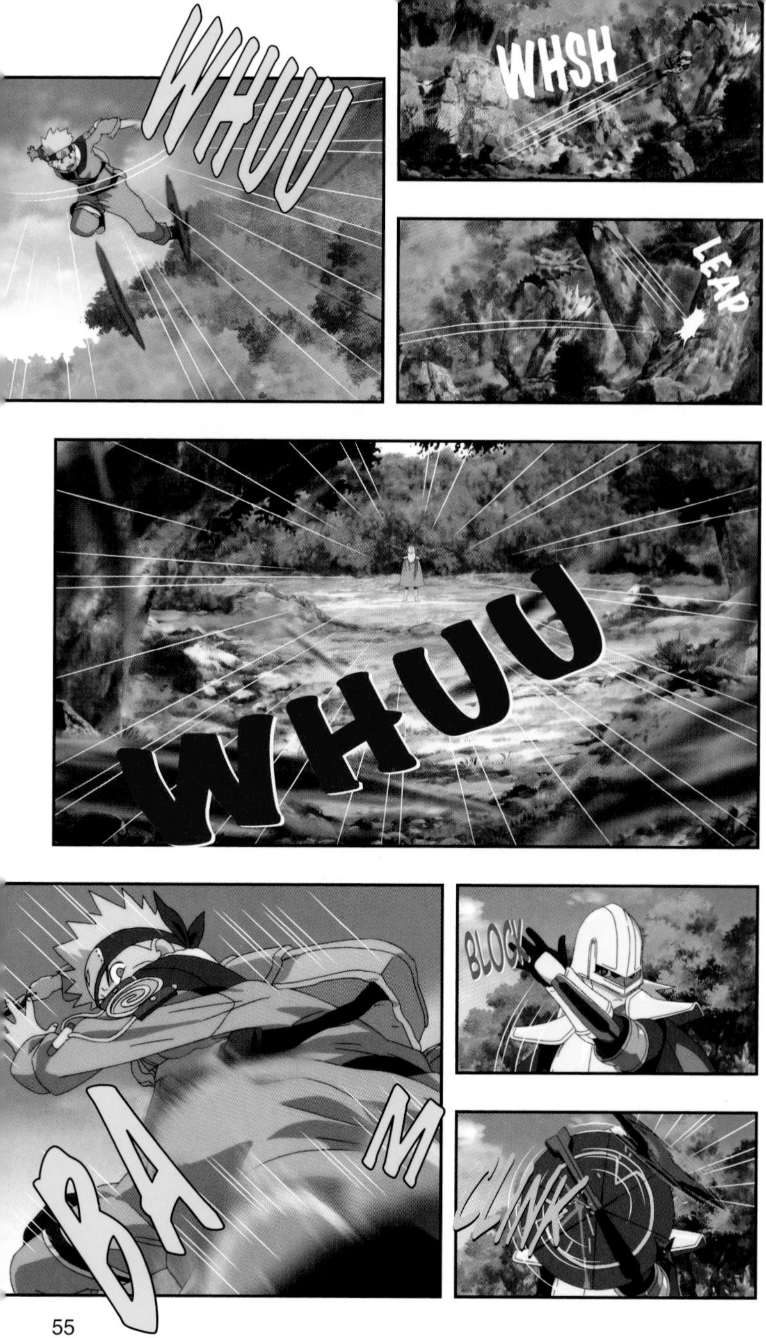
WHSH
LEAP
WHUU
WHUU
BLOCK
CLINK
BAM

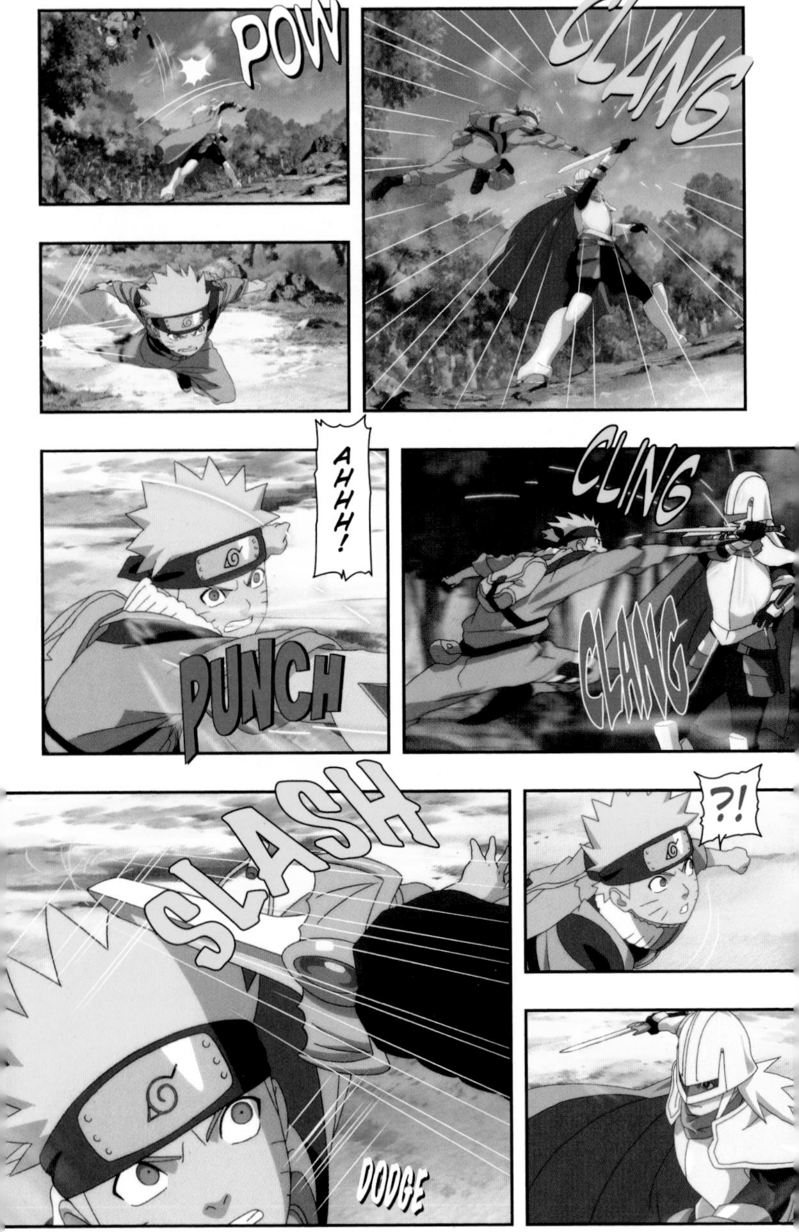
CLANG
POW
CLING
CLANG
AHHHH!
PUNCH
?!
SLASH
DODGE

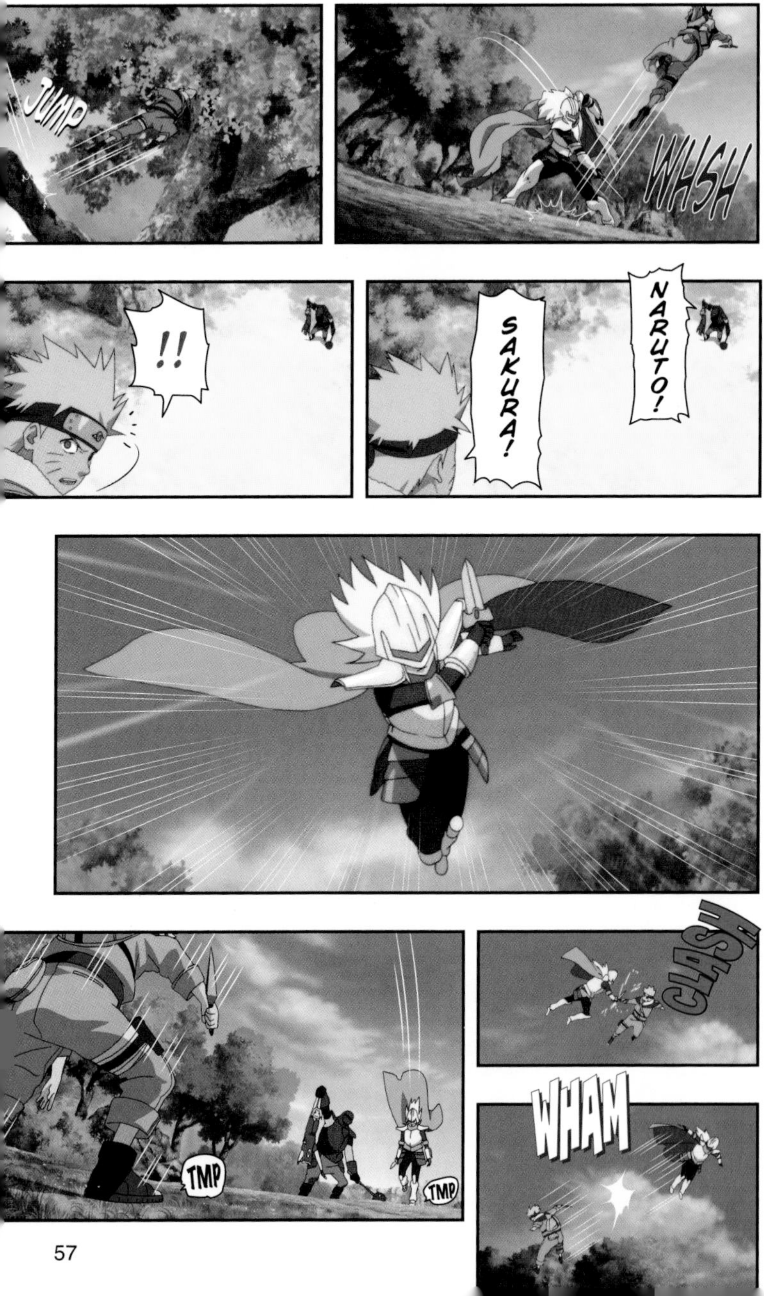
WHSH
JUMP
NARUTO!
SAKURA!
!!
CLASH
WHAM
TMP
TMP

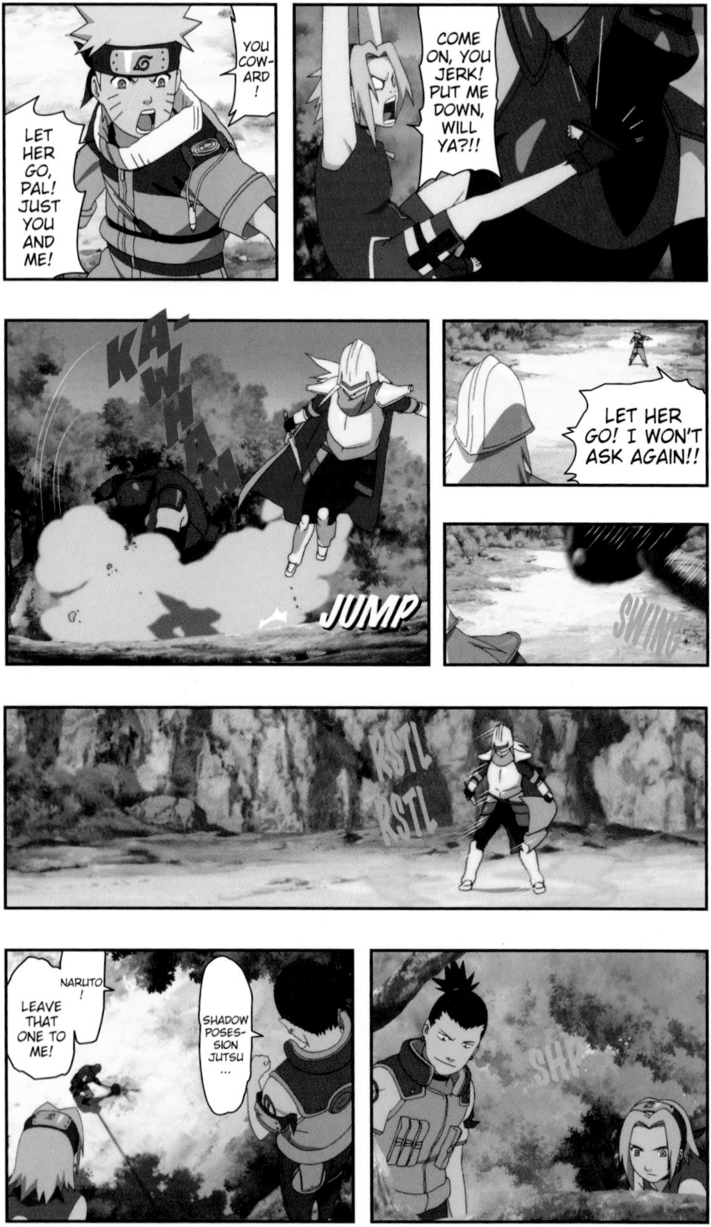
COME ON, YOU JERK! PUT ME DOWN, WILL YA?!!
YOU COW-ARD!
LET HER GO, PAL! JUST YOU AND ME!
LET HER GO! I WON'T ASK AGAIN!!
SWING
KA-WHAM
JUMP
RSTL RSTL
SHP
SHADOW POSES-SION JUTSU ...
NARUTO!
LEAVE THAT ONE TO ME!

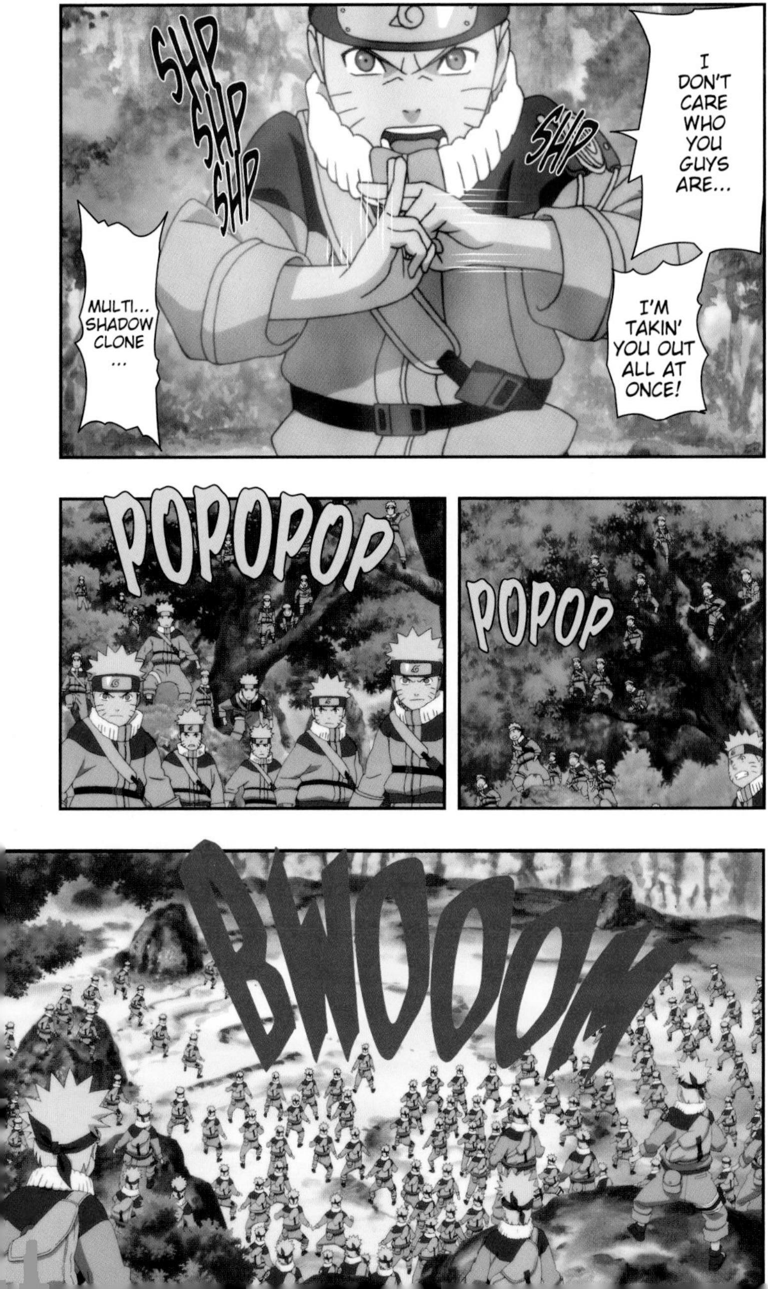
SHP
I DON'T CARE WHO YOU GUYS ARE...
I'M TAKIN' YOU OUT ALL AT ONCE!
SHP SHP SHP SHP
MULTI... SHADOW CLONE ...
POPOP
POPOPOP
BWOOOM

GLOW

SHFF

GLOW

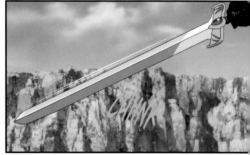

LET'S GO!

DASH

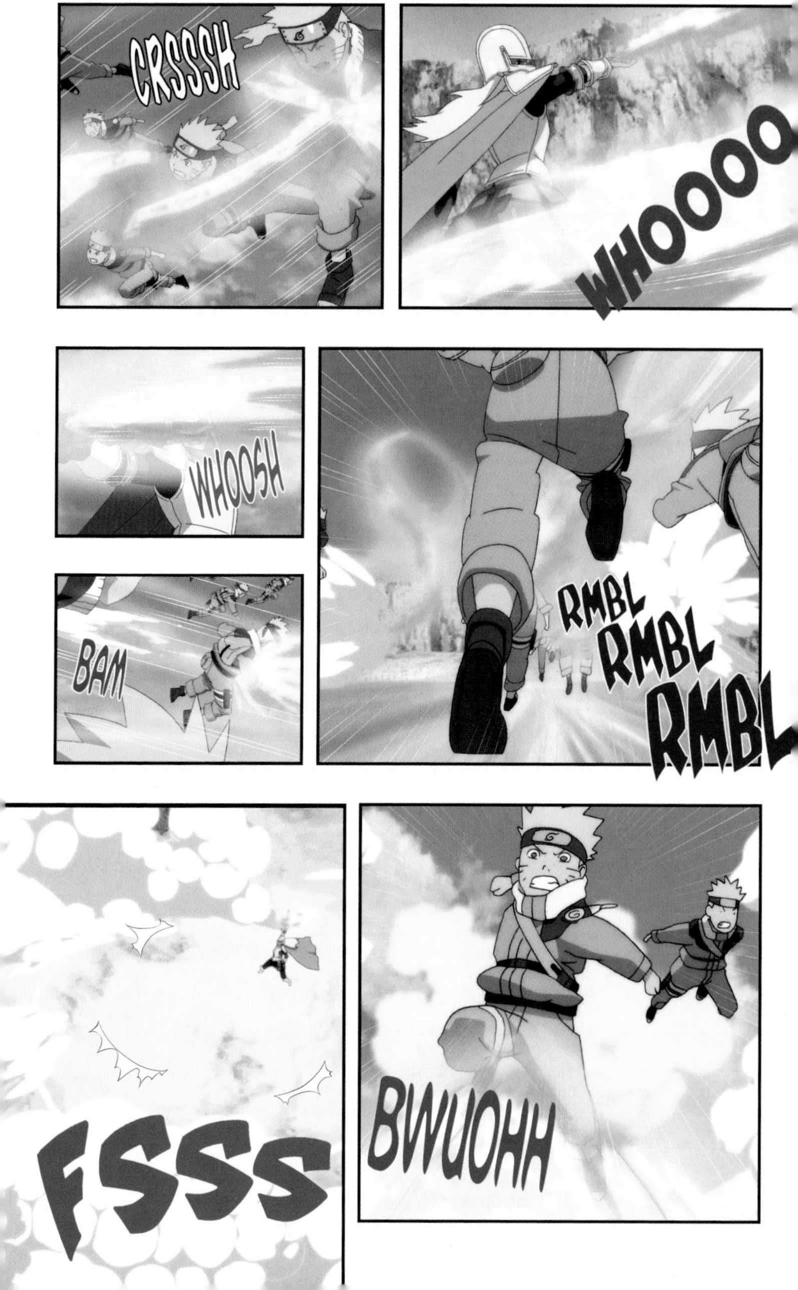
WHOOOO
CRSSSH
RMBL
RMBL
RMBL
WHOOSH
BAM
BWUOHH
FSSS

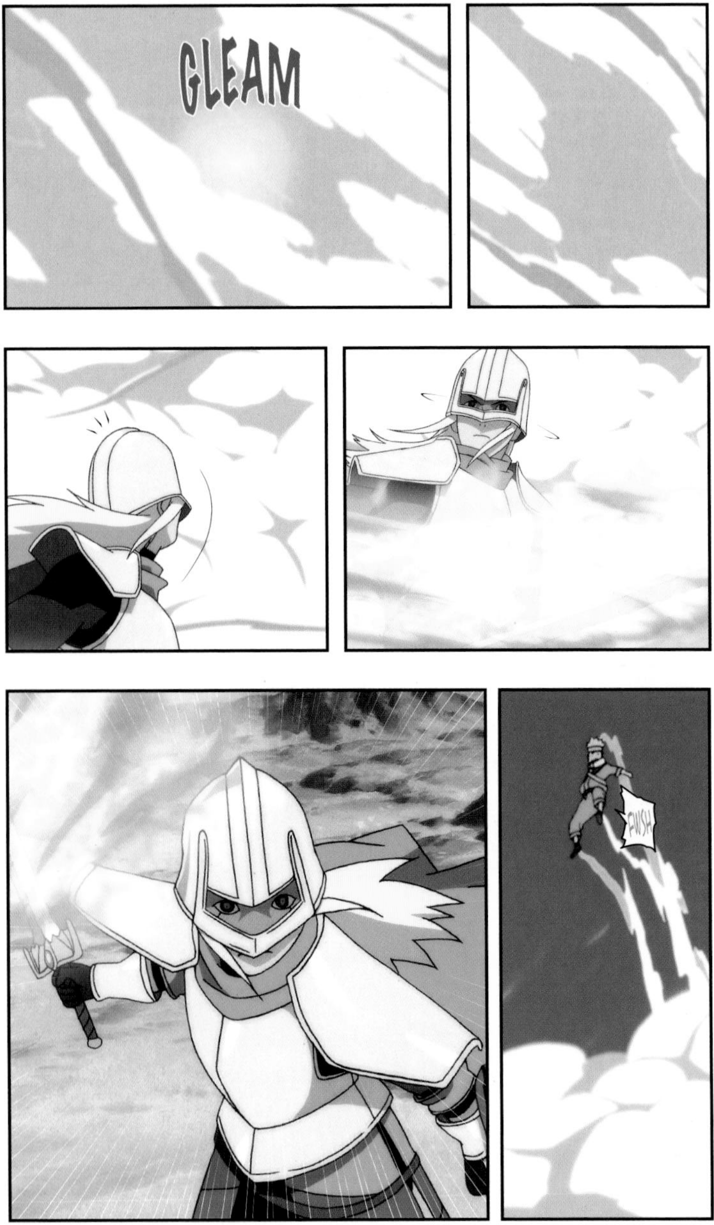
GLEAM
FWISH

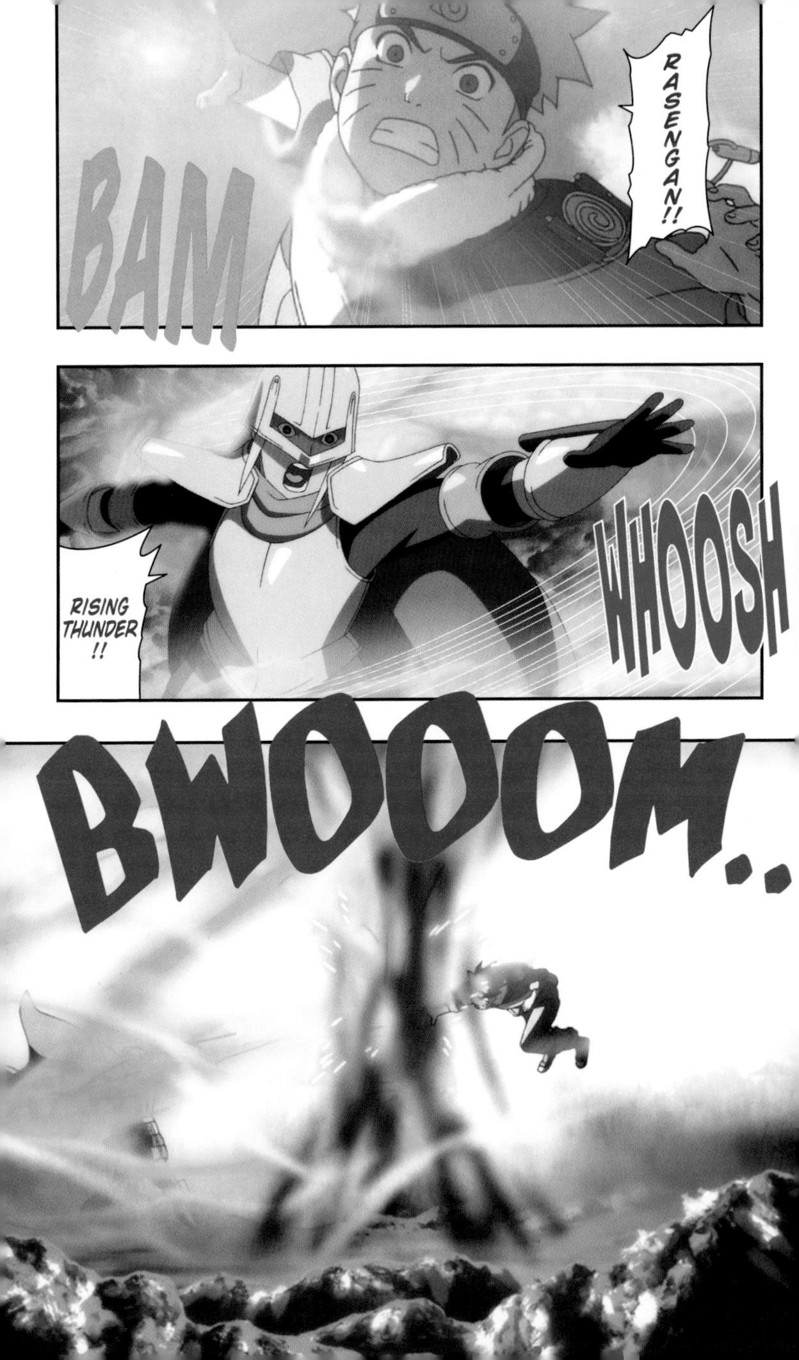
RASENGAN!!
BAM
WHOOSH
RISING THUNDER !!
BWOOOM..

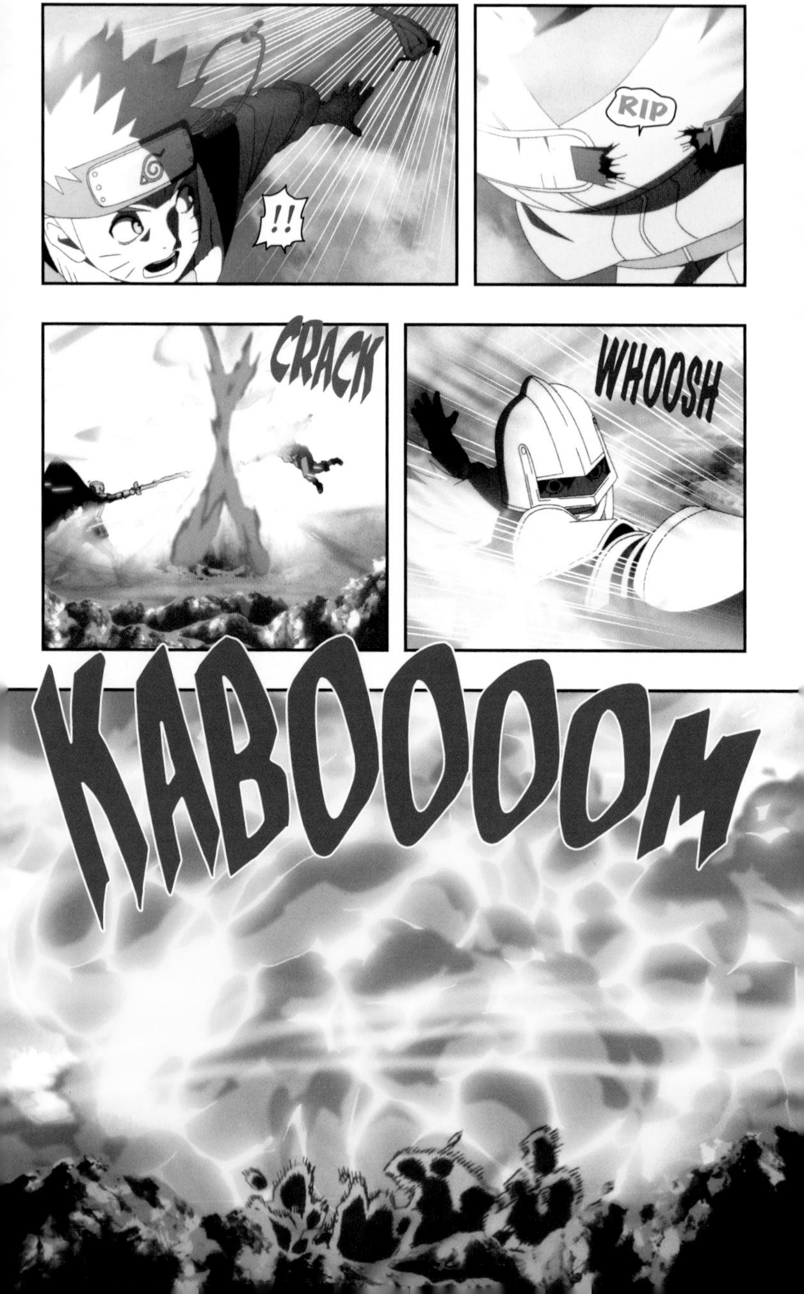
RIP
!!
WHOOSH
CRACK
KABOOOOM

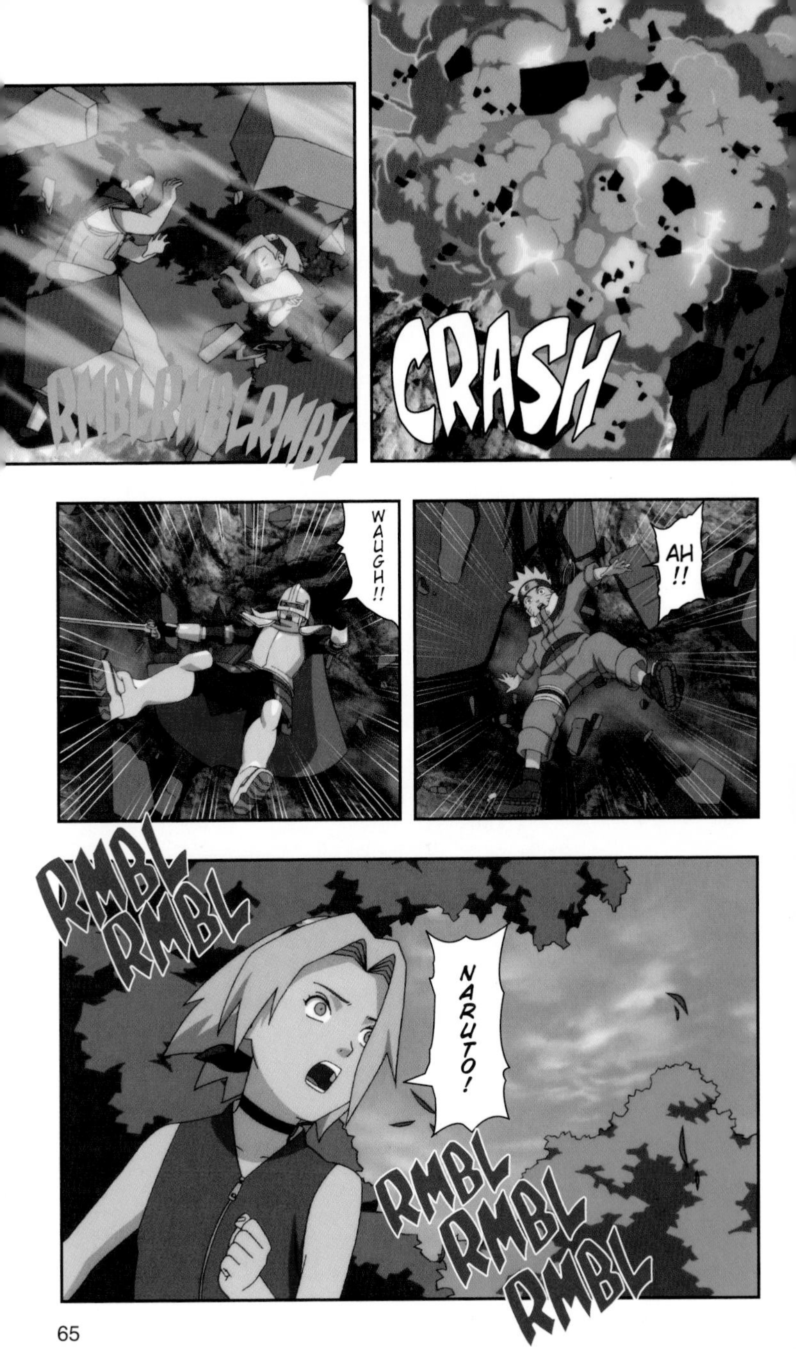
CRASH
RMBLRMBLRMBL
AH!!
WAUGH!!
RMBL RMBL
NARUTO!
RMBL RMBL RMBL

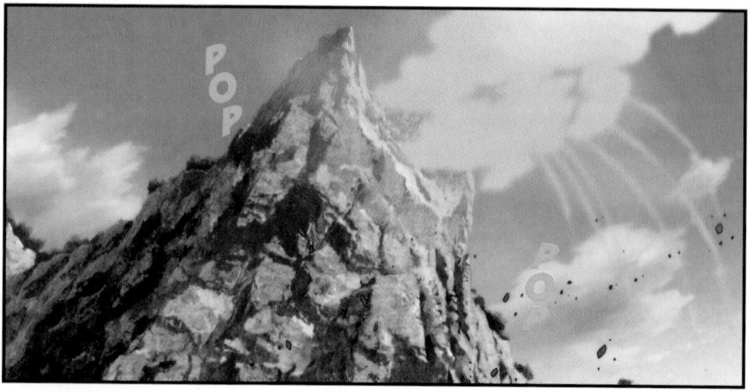
POP
POP
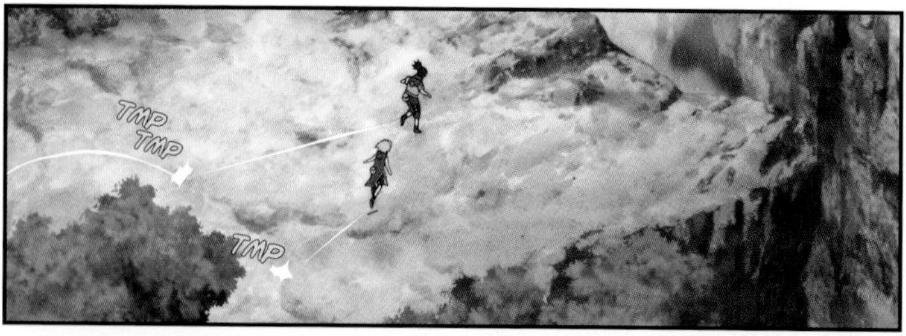
TMP TMP
TMP
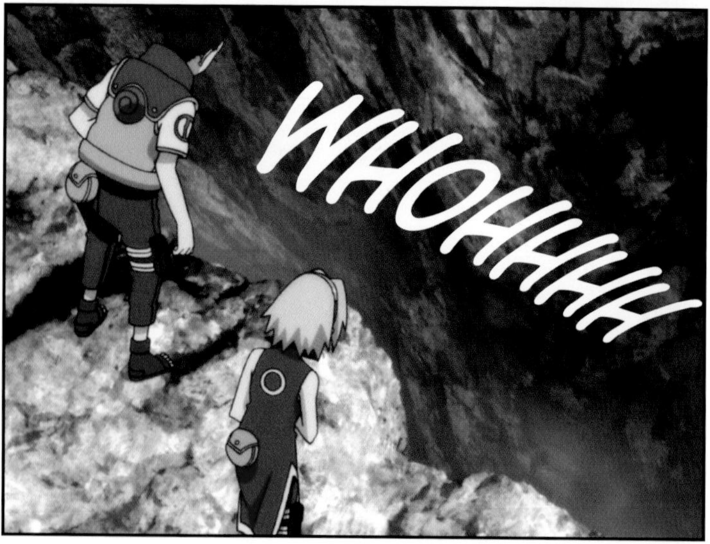
WHOHHHH

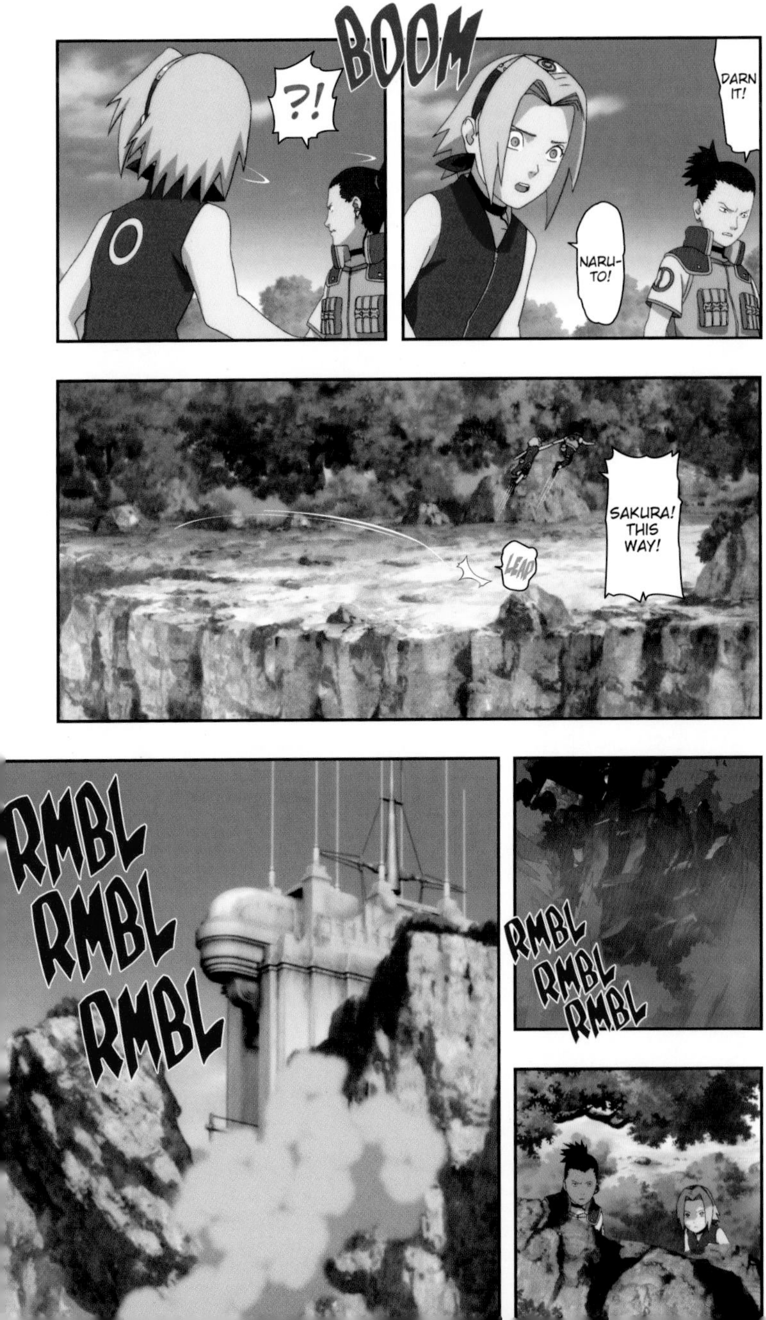
BOOM
DARN IT!
NARU-TO!
?!
SAKURA! THIS WAY!
LEAP
RMBL RMBL RMBL
RMBL RMBL RMBL

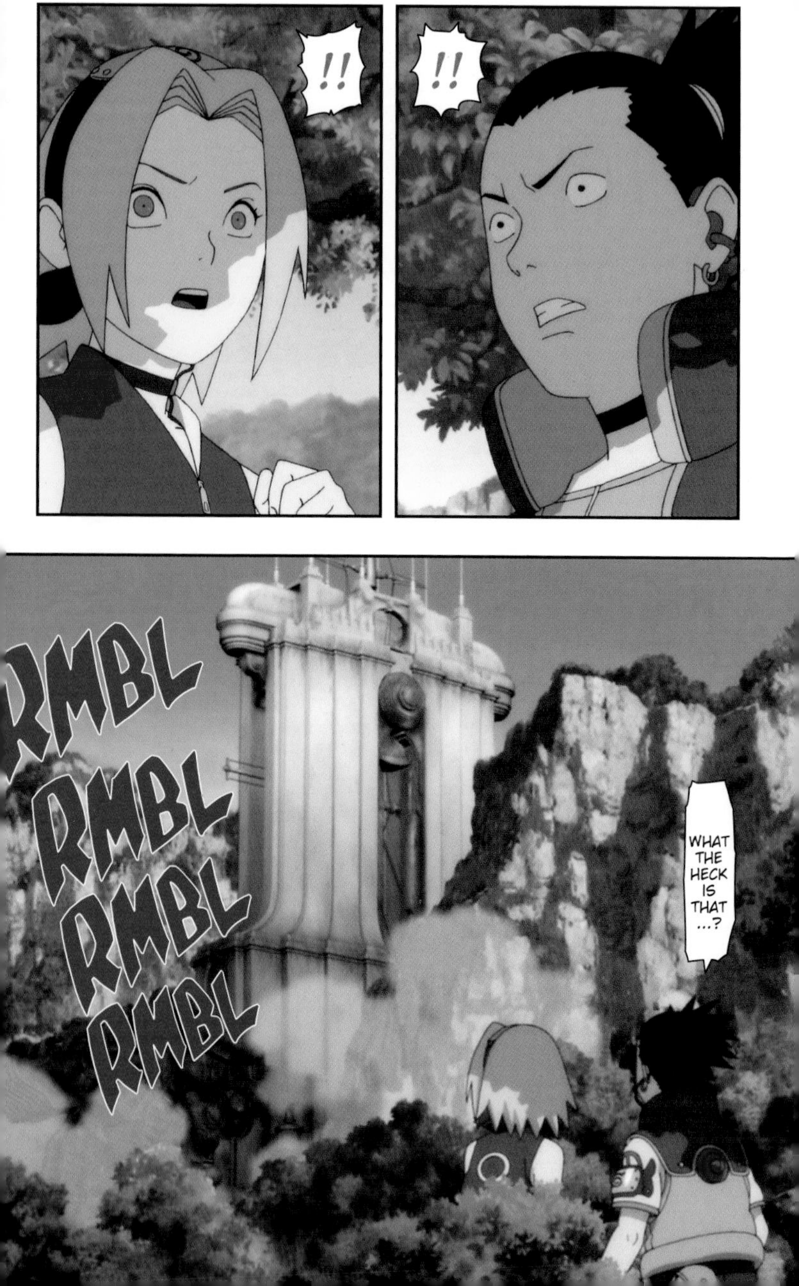
!!
!!
WHAT THE HECK IS THAT ...?
RMBL RMBL RMBL RMBL

Chapter 2: Temujin the Knight

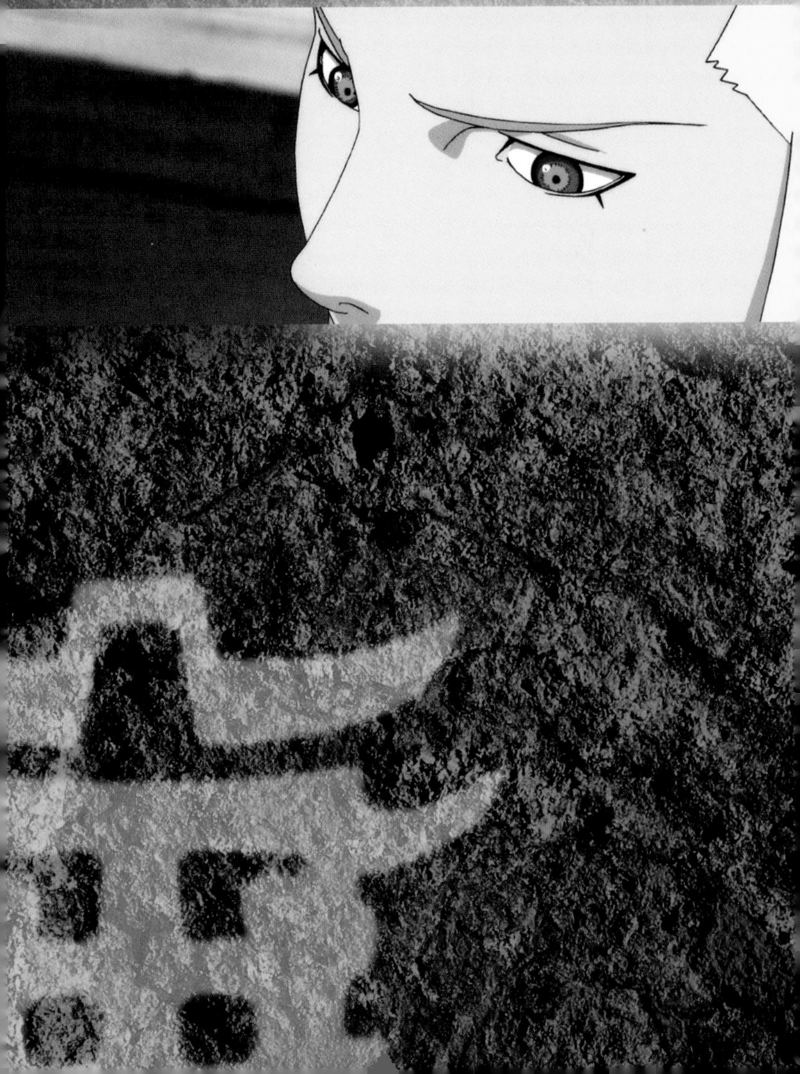

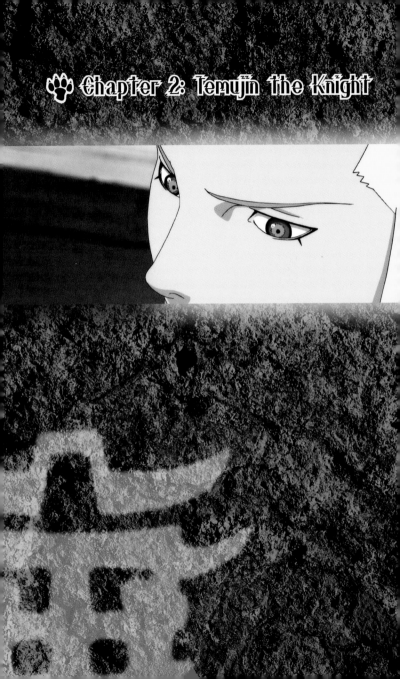

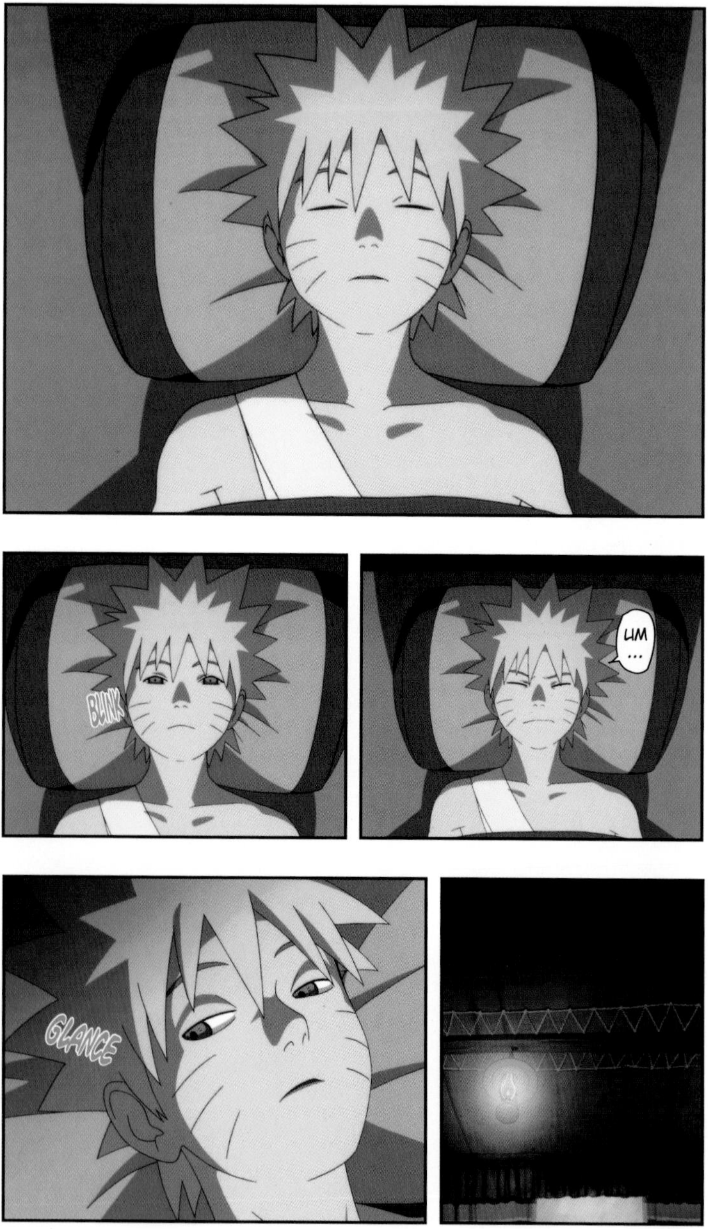
UM ...
BLINK
GLANCE

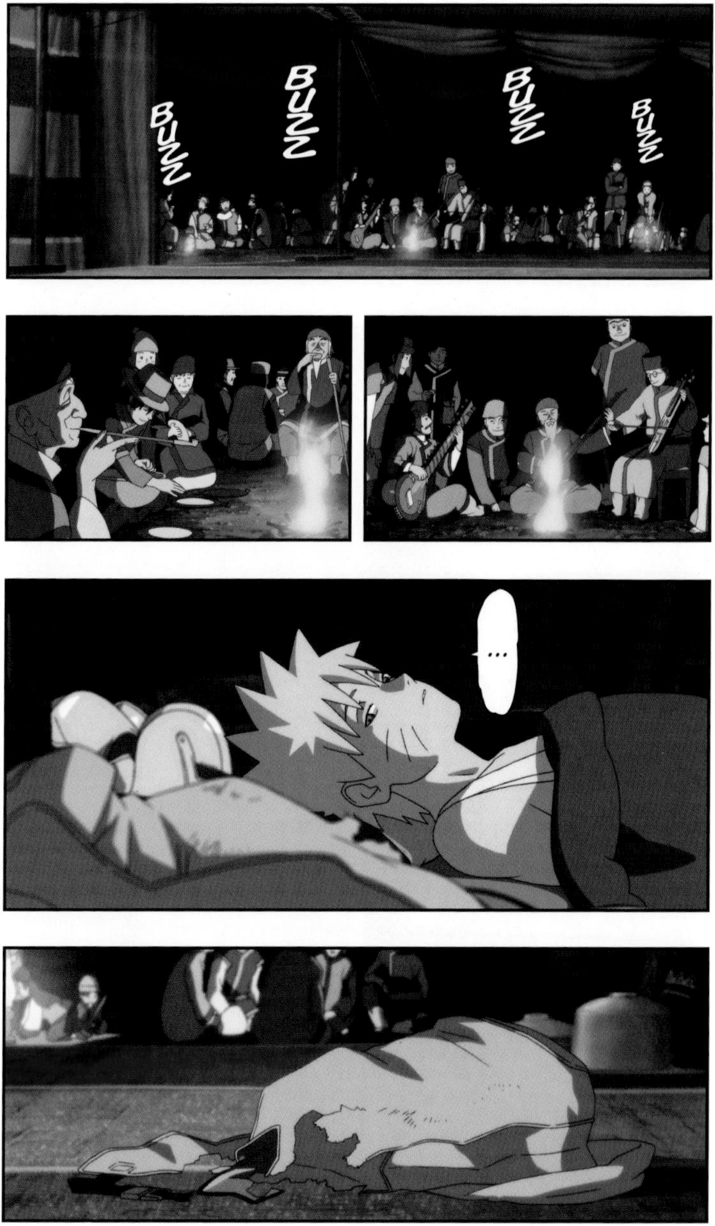
BUZZ
BUZZ
BUZZ
BUZZ
...

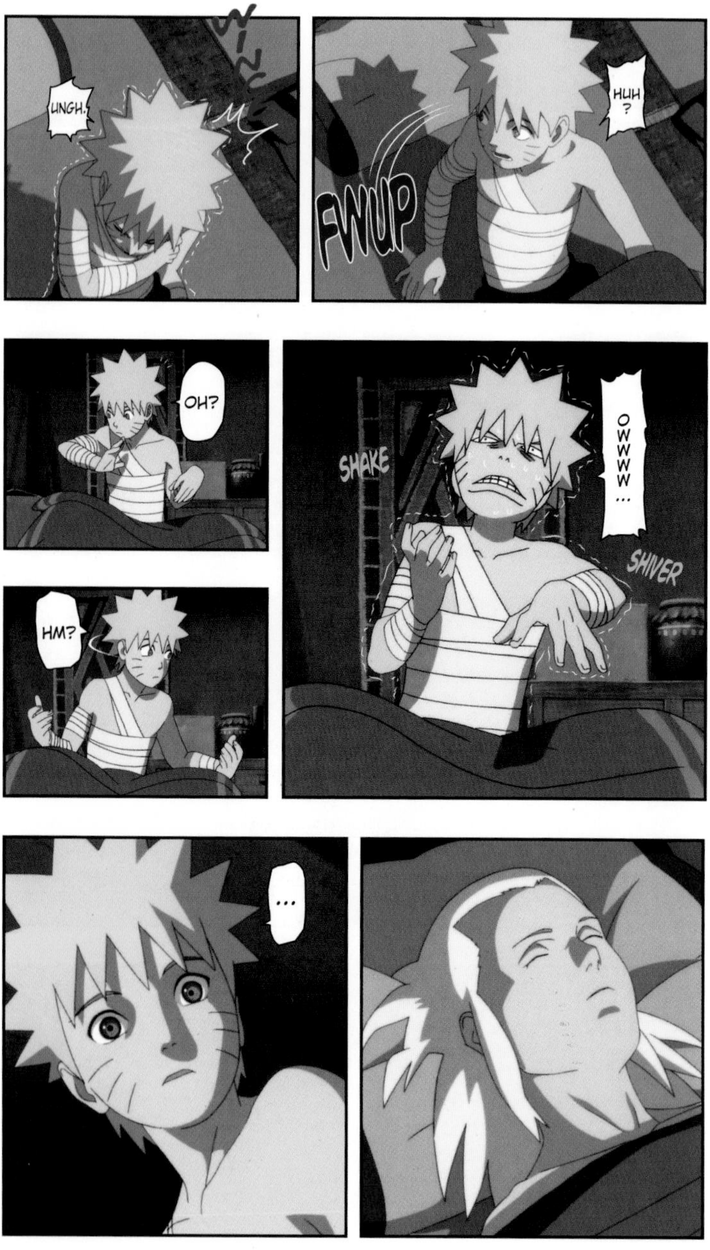
HUH ?
FWUP
UNGH.
WINCE
OWWWW...
SHAKE
SHIVER
OH?
HM?
...

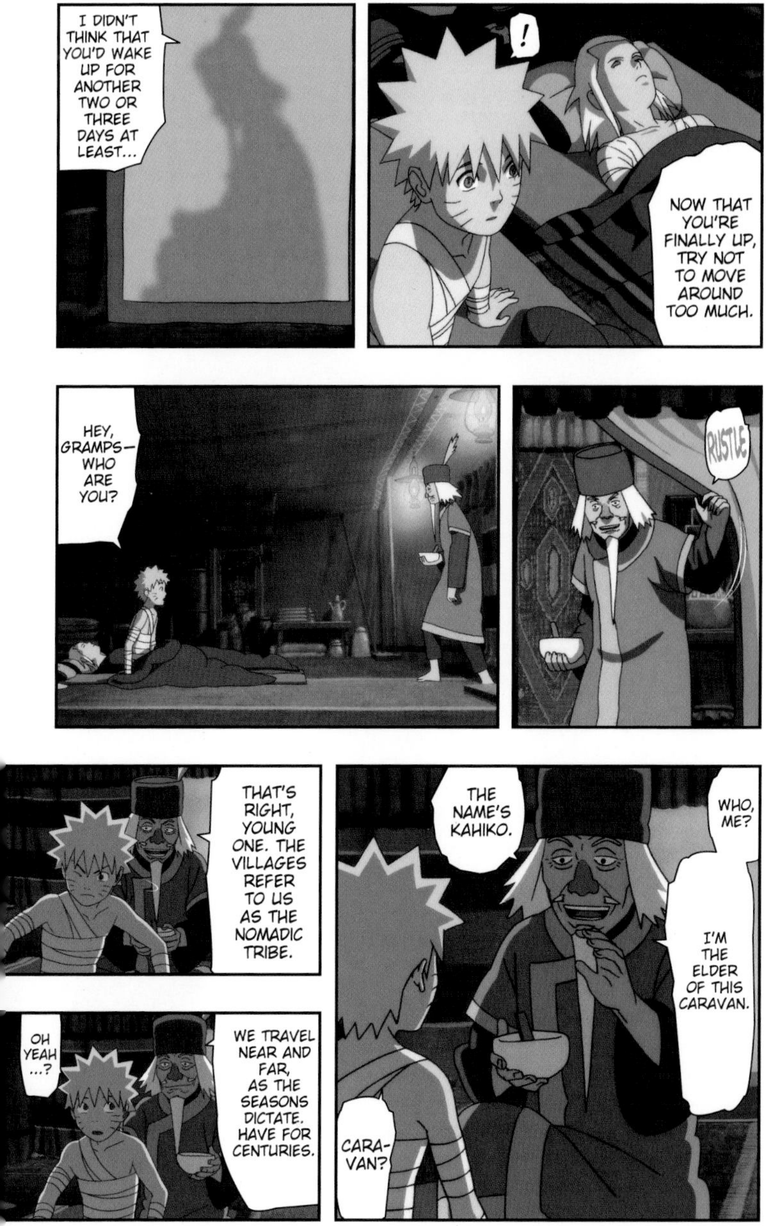
!
NOW THAT YOU'RE FINALLY UP, TRY NOT TO MOVE AROUND TOO MUCH.
I DIDN'T THINK THAT YOU'D WAKE UP FOR ANOTHER TWO OR THREE DAYS AT LEAST...
RUSTLE
HEY, GRAMPS— WHO ARE YOU?
WHO, ME?
THE NAME'S KAHIKO.
I'M THE ELDER OF THIS CARAVAN.
CARA-VAN?
THAT'S RIGHT, YOUNG ONE. THE VILLAGES REFER TO US AS THE NOMADIC TRIBE.
WE TRAVEL NEAR AND FAR, AS THE SEASONS DICTATE. HAVE FOR CENTURIES.
OH YEAH ...?

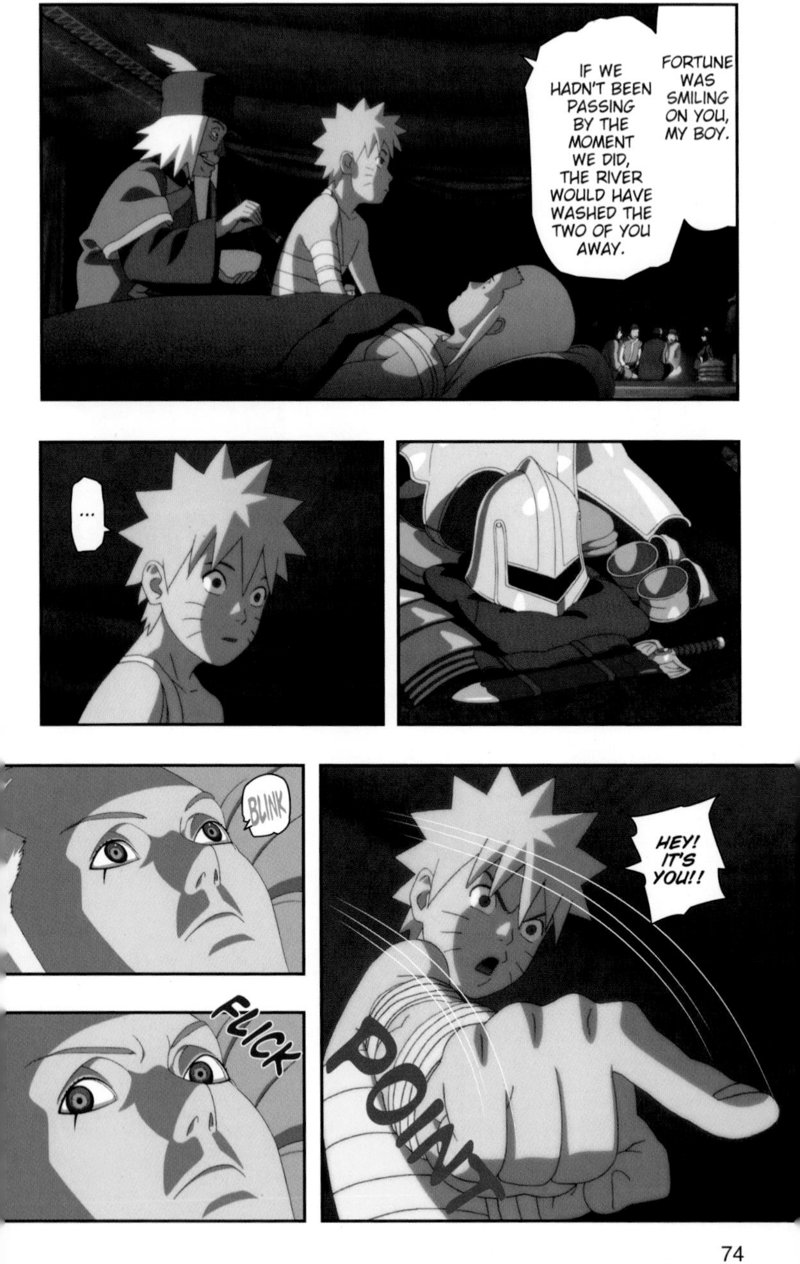
FORTUNE WAS SMILING ON YOU, MY BOY.
IF WE HADN'T BEEN PASSING BY THE MOMENT WE DID, THE RIVER WOULD HAVE WASHED THE TWO OF YOU AWAY.
...
HEY! IT'S YOU!!
POINT
BLINK
FLICK

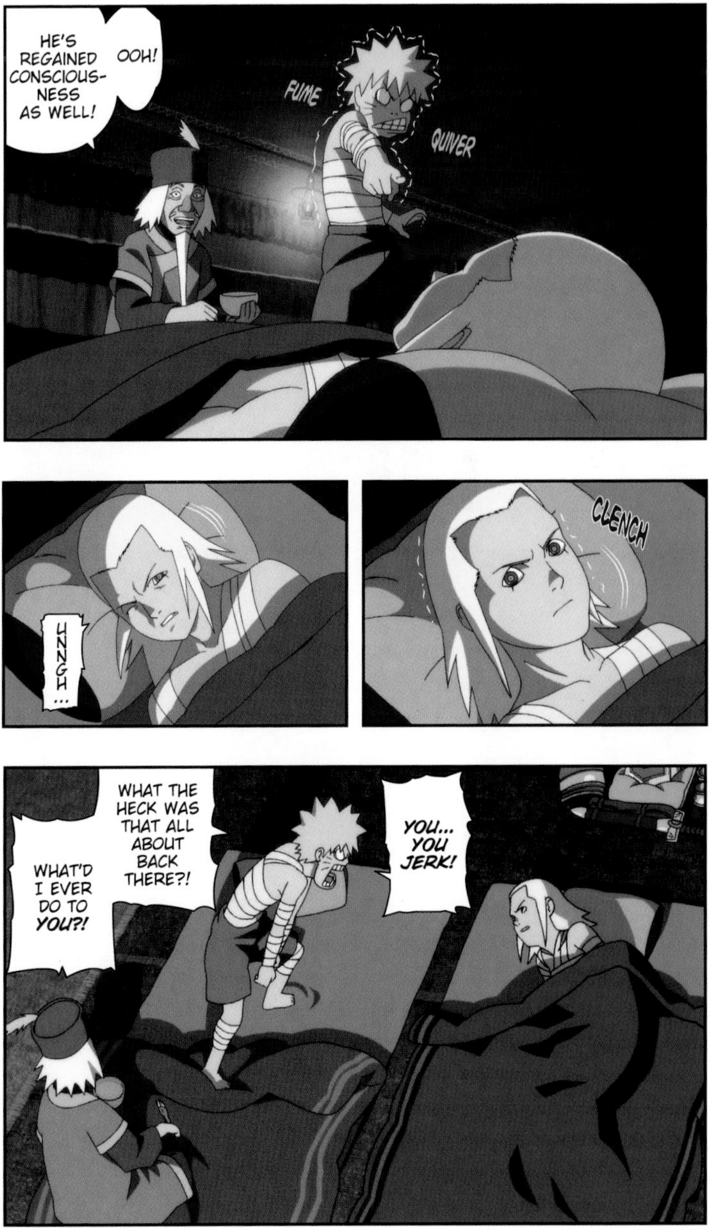
FUME
QUIVER
OOH!
HE'S REGAINED CONSCIOUSNESS AS WELL!
CLENCH
UNNGH...
YOU... YOU JERK!
WHAT THE HECK WAS THAT ALL ABOUT BACK THERE?!
WHAT'D I EVER DO TO *YOU?!*

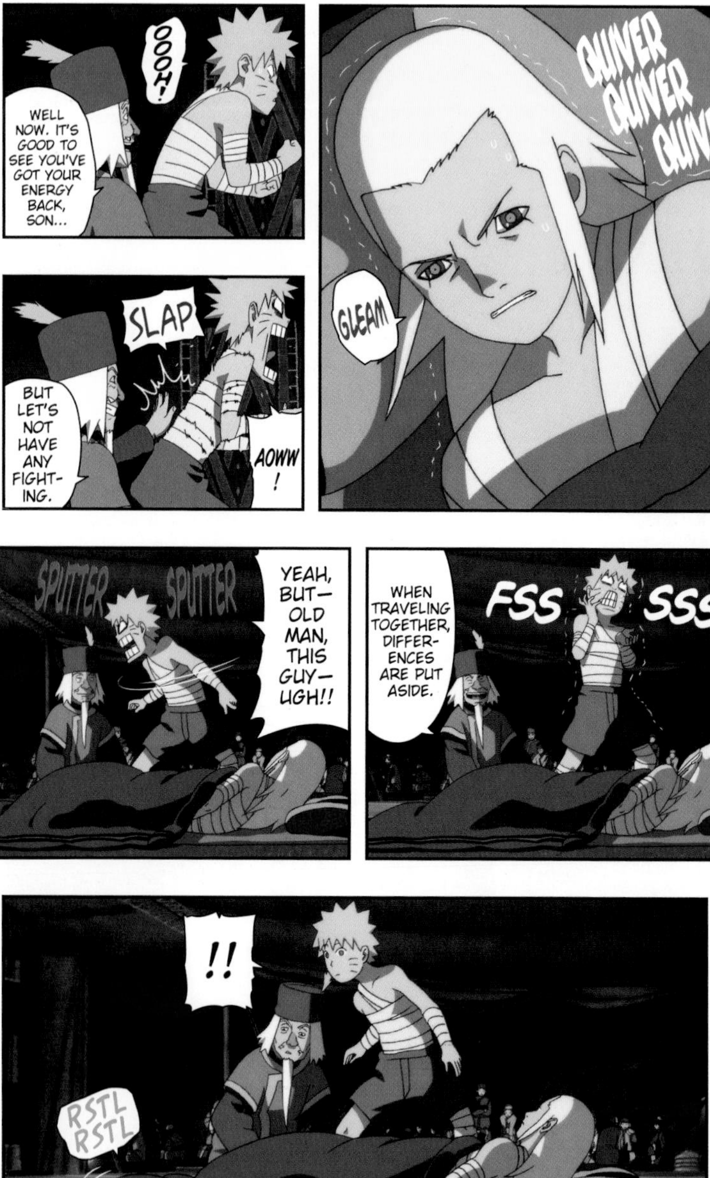
QUIVER QUIVER QUIVER
GLEAM
OOOH!
WELL NOW. IT'S GOOD TO SEE YOU'VE GOT YOUR ENERGY BACK, SON...
SLAP
BUT LET'S NOT HAVE ANY FIGHT-ING.
AOWW!
FSS SSS
WHEN TRAVELING TOGETHER, DIFFER-ENCES ARE PUT ASIDE.
SPUTTER SPUTTER
YEAH, BUT— OLD MAN, THIS GUY— UGH!!
!!
RSTL RSTL

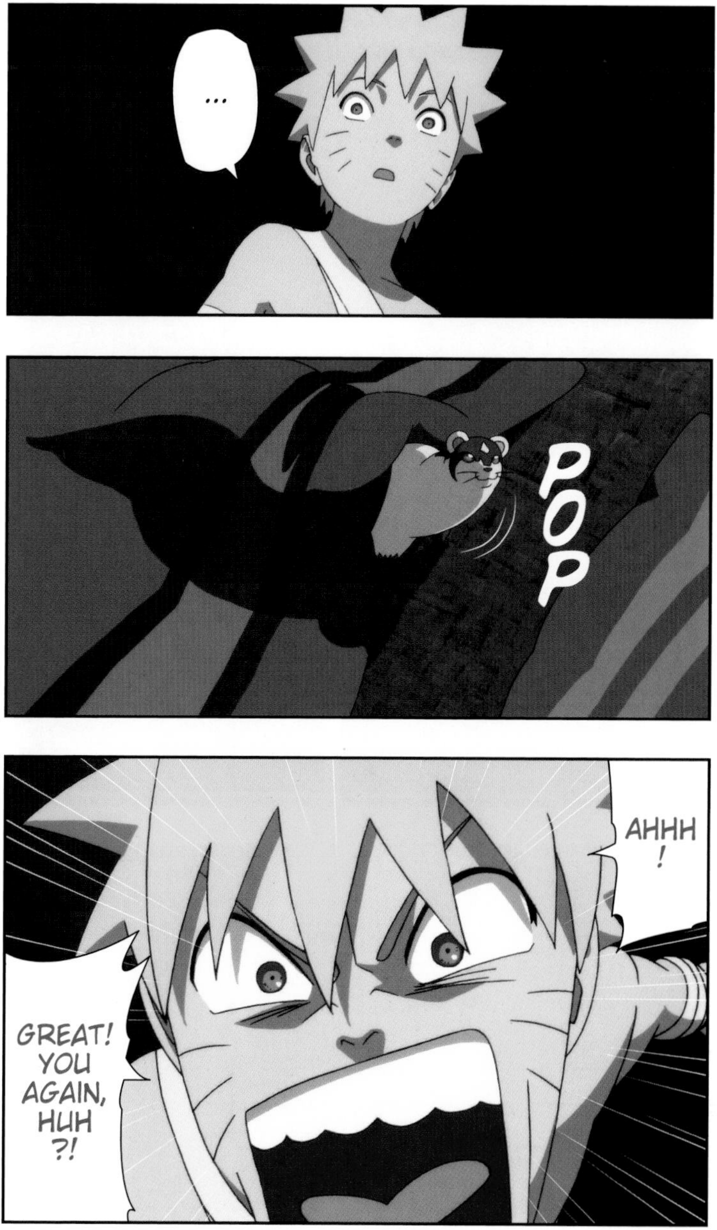
...
POP POP
AHHH !
GREAT! YOU AGAIN, HUH ?!

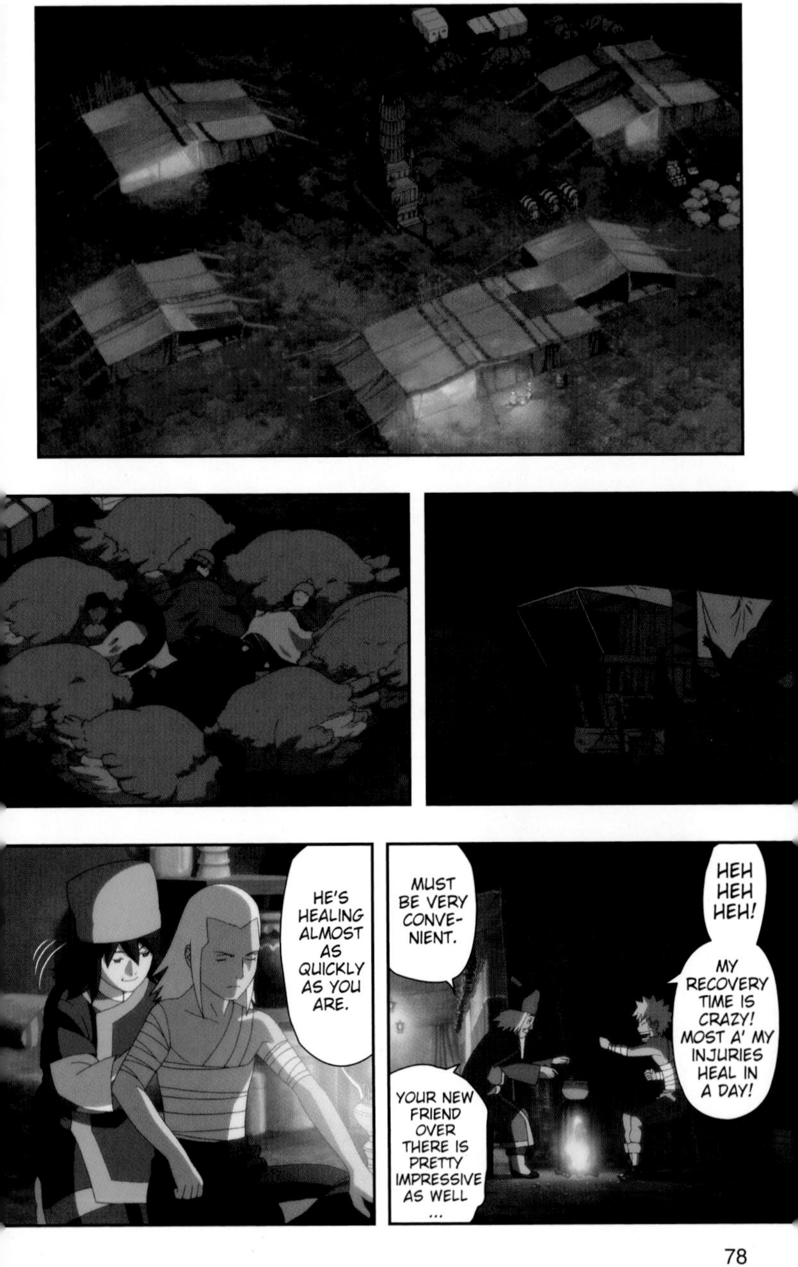
HEH HEH HEH!
MY RECOVERY TIME IS CRAZY! MOST A' MY INJURIES HEAL IN A DAY!
MUST BE VERY CONVE-NIENT.
YOUR NEW FRIEND OVER THERE IS PRETTY IMPRESSIVE AS WELL ...
HE'S HEALING ALMOST AS QUICKLY AS YOU ARE.

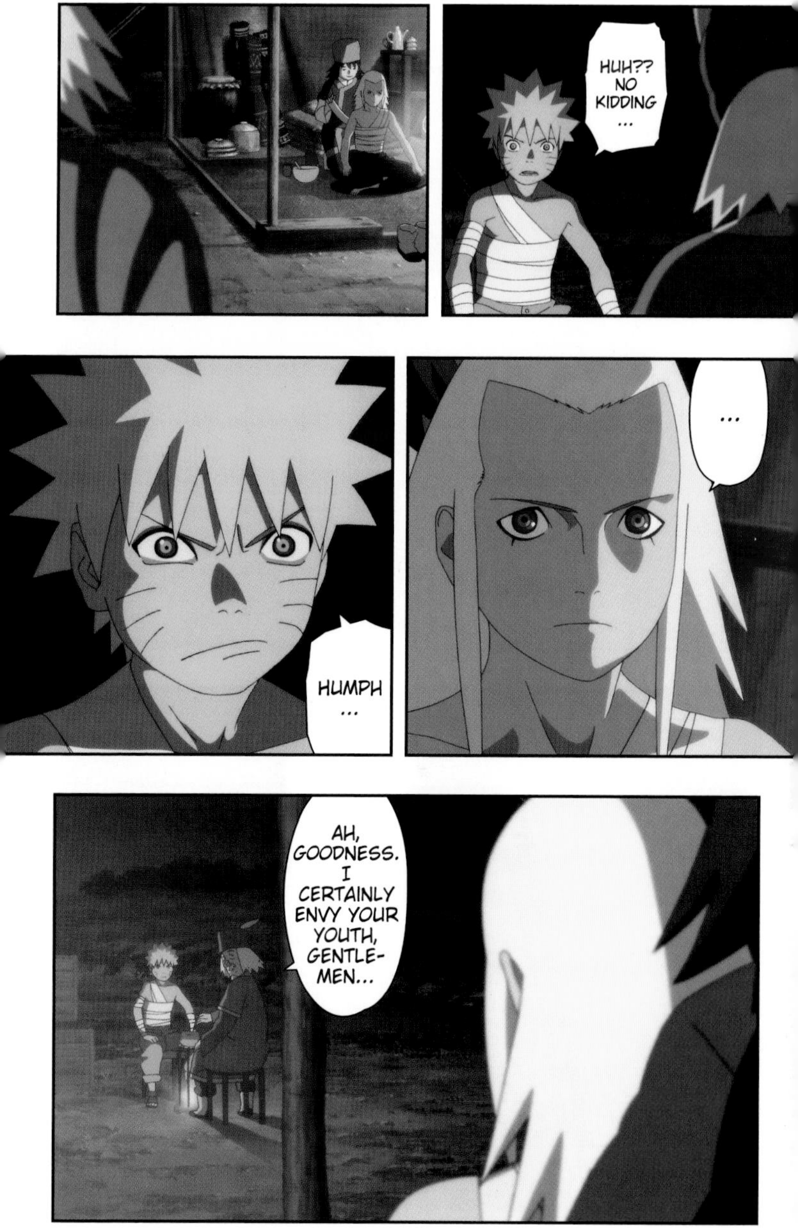
HUH?? NO KIDDING ...
...
HUMPH ...
AH, GOODNESS. I CERTAINLY ENVY YOUR YOUTH, GENTLEMEN...

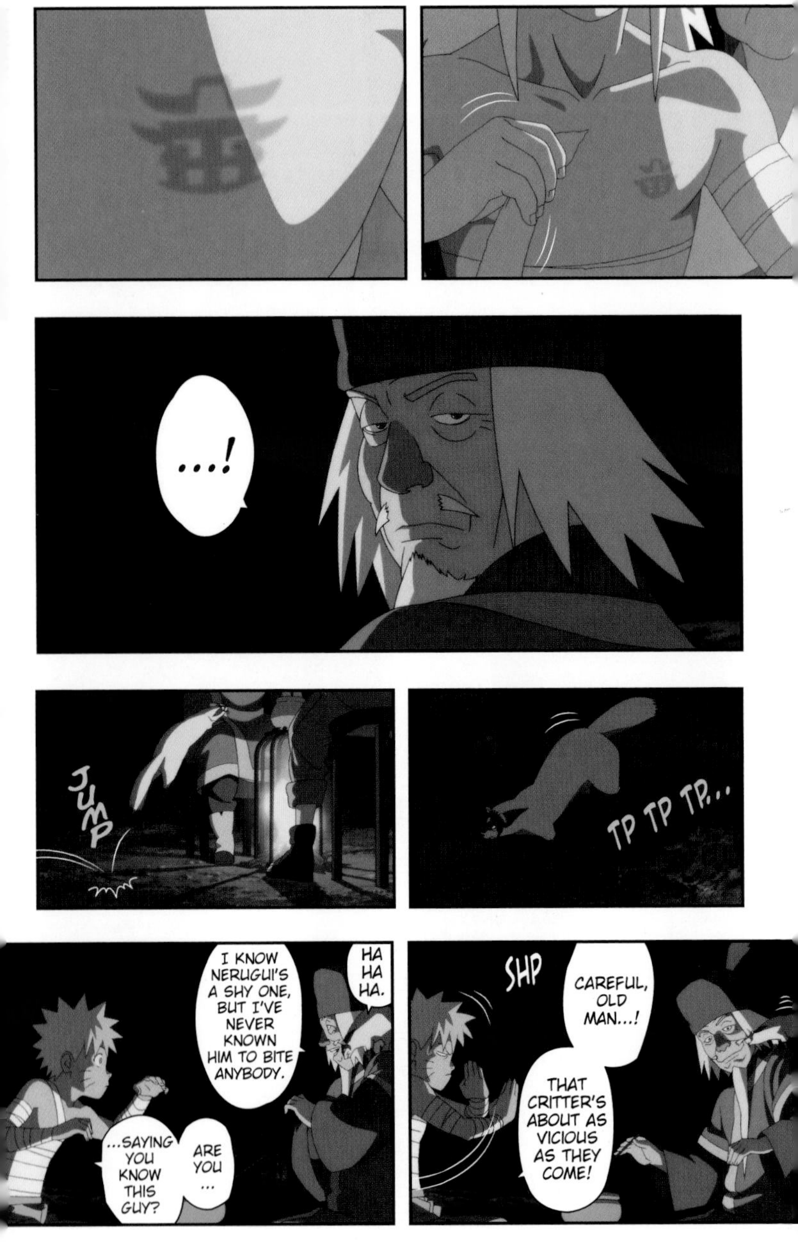
...!
TP TP TP...
JUMP
SHP
CAREFUL, OLD MAN...!
THAT CRITTER'S ABOUT AS VICIOUS AS THEY COME!
HA HA HA.
I KNOW NERUGUI'S A SHY ONE, BUT I'VE NEVER KNOWN HIM TO BITE ANYBODY.
ARE YOU ...
...SAYING YOU KNOW THIS GUY?

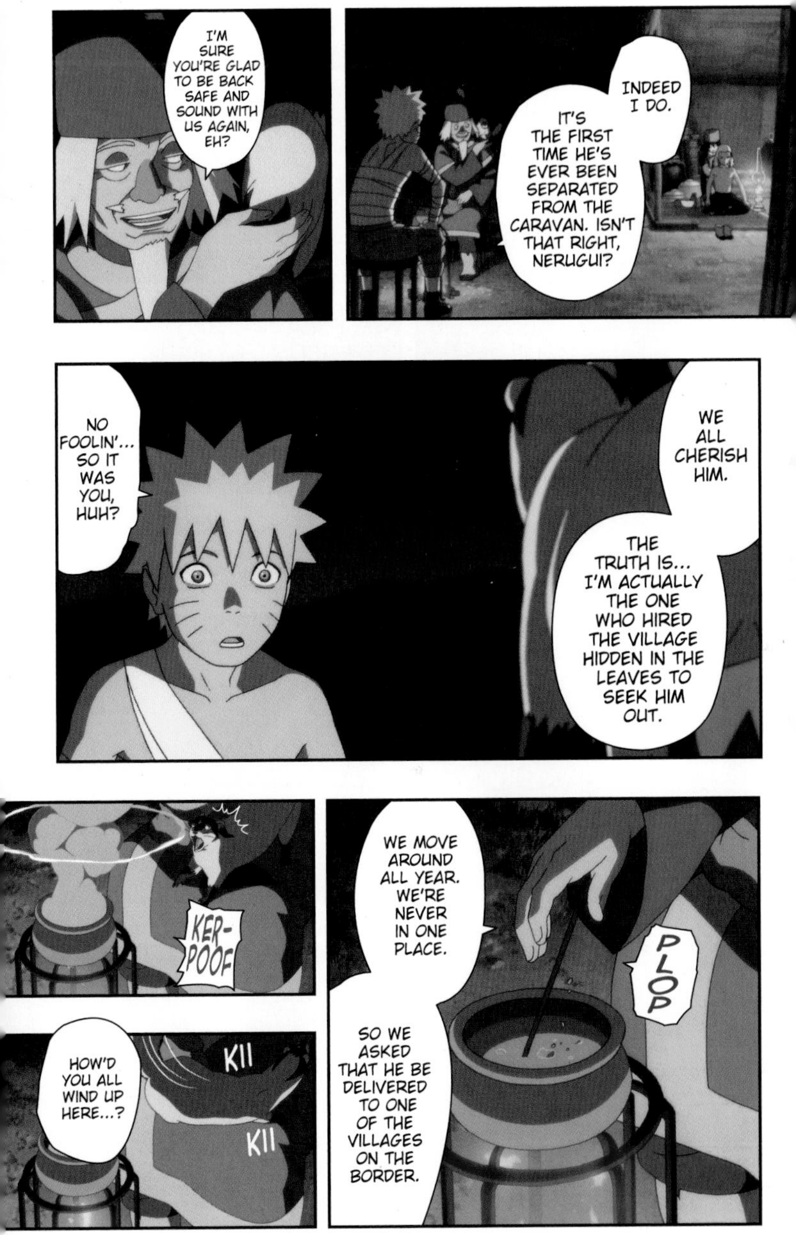
INDEED I DO.
IT'S THE FIRST TIME HE'S EVER BEEN SEPARATED FROM THE CARAVAN. ISN'T THAT RIGHT, NERUGUI?
I'M SURE YOU'RE GLAD TO BE BACK SAFE AND SOUND WITH US AGAIN, EH?
WE ALL CHERISH HIM.
THE TRUTH IS... I'M ACTUALLY THE ONE WHO HIRED THE VILLAGE HIDDEN IN THE LEAVES TO SEEK HIM OUT.
NO FOOLIN'... SO IT WAS YOU, HUH?
WE MOVE AROUND ALL YEAR. WE'RE NEVER IN ONE PLACE.
PLOP
SO WE ASKED THAT HE BE DELIVERED TO ONE OF THE VILLAGES ON THE BORDER.
KER-POOF
KII
HOW'D YOU ALL WIND UP HERE...?
KII

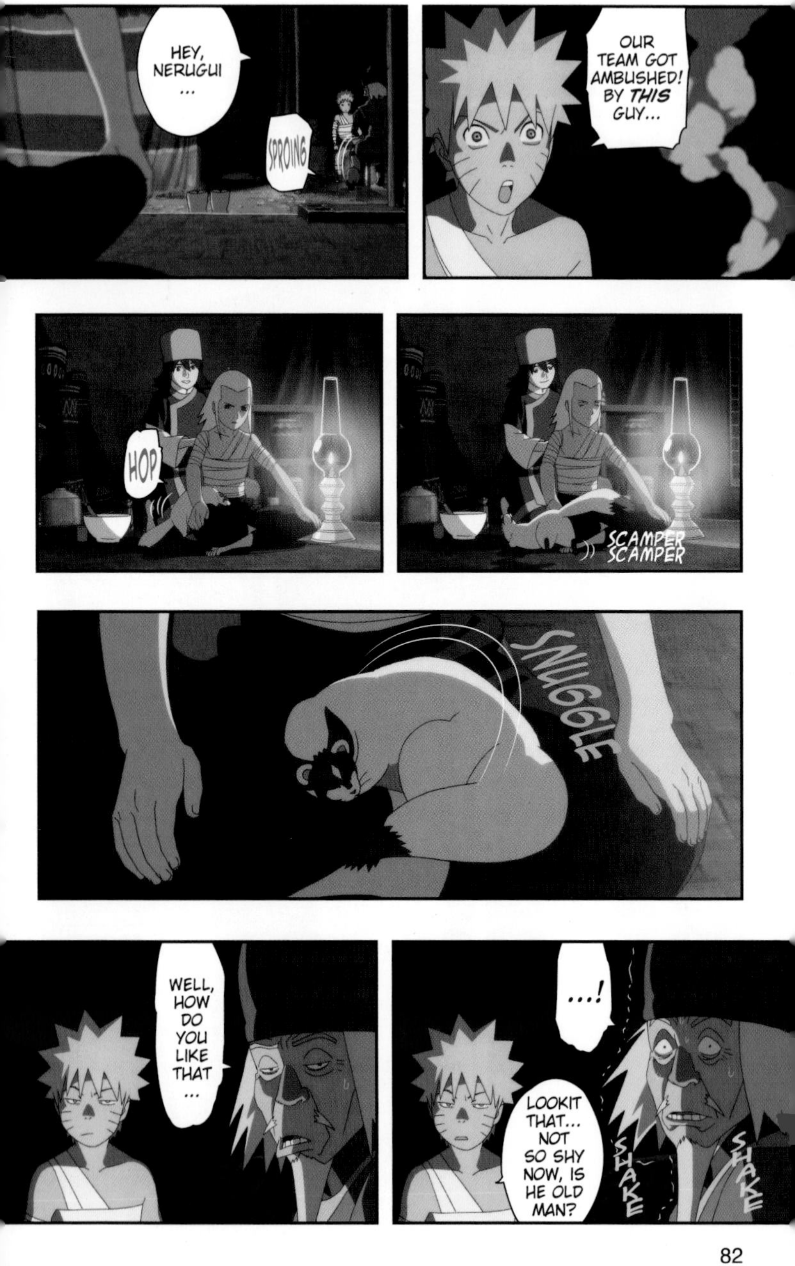
OUR TEAM GOT AMBUSHED! BY THIS GUY...
HEY, NERUGUI ...
SPROING
SCAMPER SCAMPER
HOP
SNUGGLE
...!
LOOKIT THAT... NOT SO SHY NOW, IS HE OLD MAN?
SHAKE
SHAKE
WELL, HOW DO YOU LIKE THAT ...

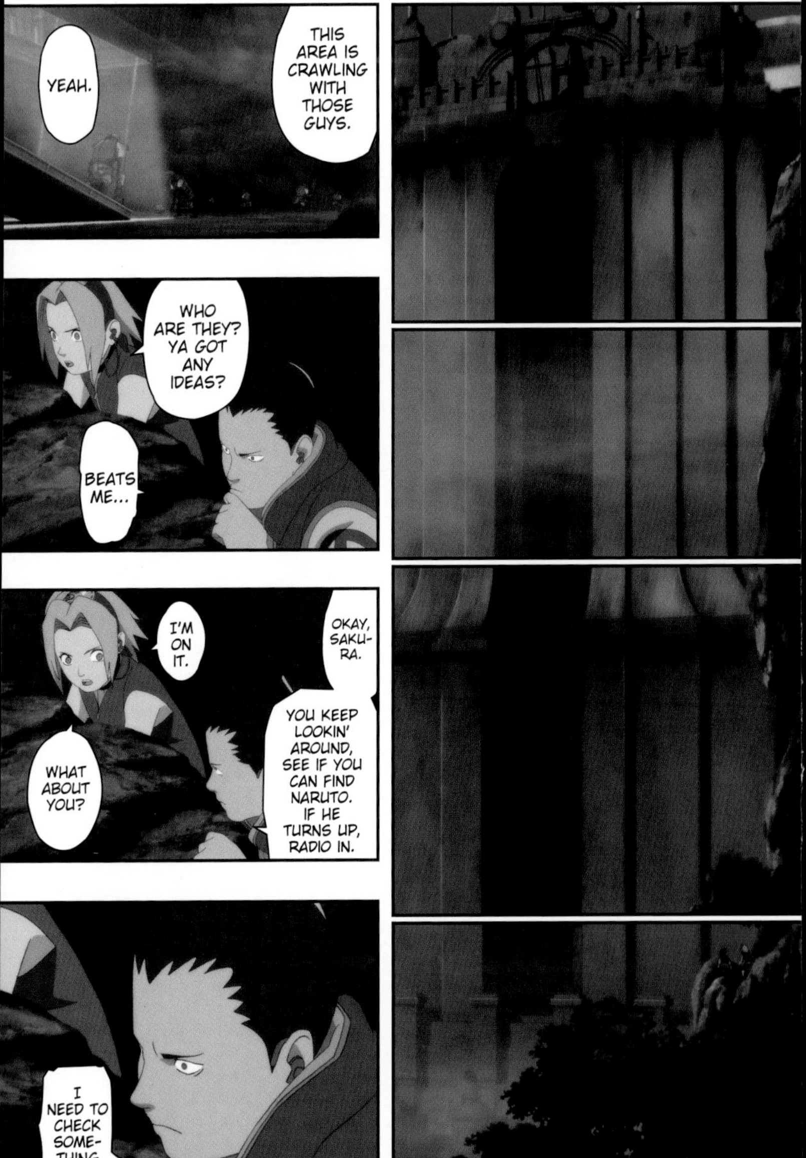
THIS AREA IS CRAWLING WITH THOSE GUYS.
YEAH.
WHO ARE THEY? YA GOT ANY IDEAS?
BEATS ME...
OKAY, SAKURA.
YOU KEEP LOOKIN' AROUND, SEE IF YOU CAN FIND NARUTO. IF HE TURNS UP, RADIO IN.
I'M ON IT.
WHAT ABOUT YOU?
I NEED TO CHECK SOMETHING OUT...

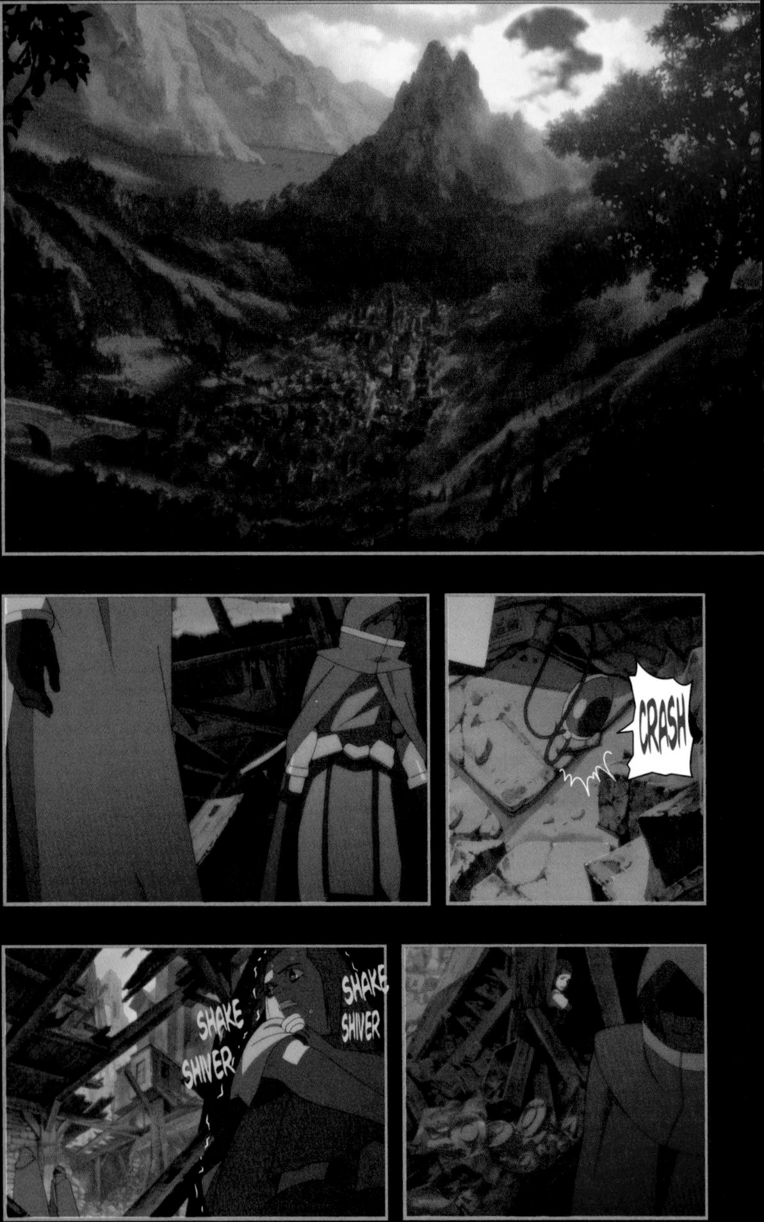
CRASH
SHAKE
SHIVER
SHAKE
SHIVER

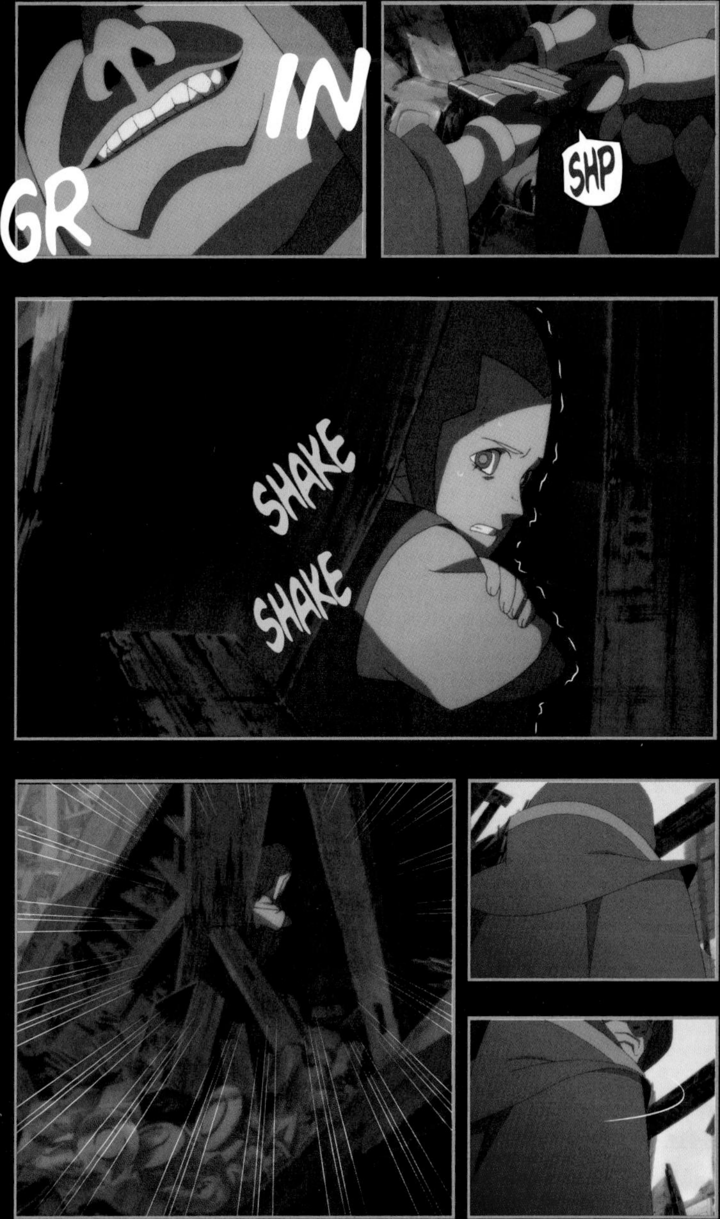
SHP
GRIN
SHAKE
SHAKE

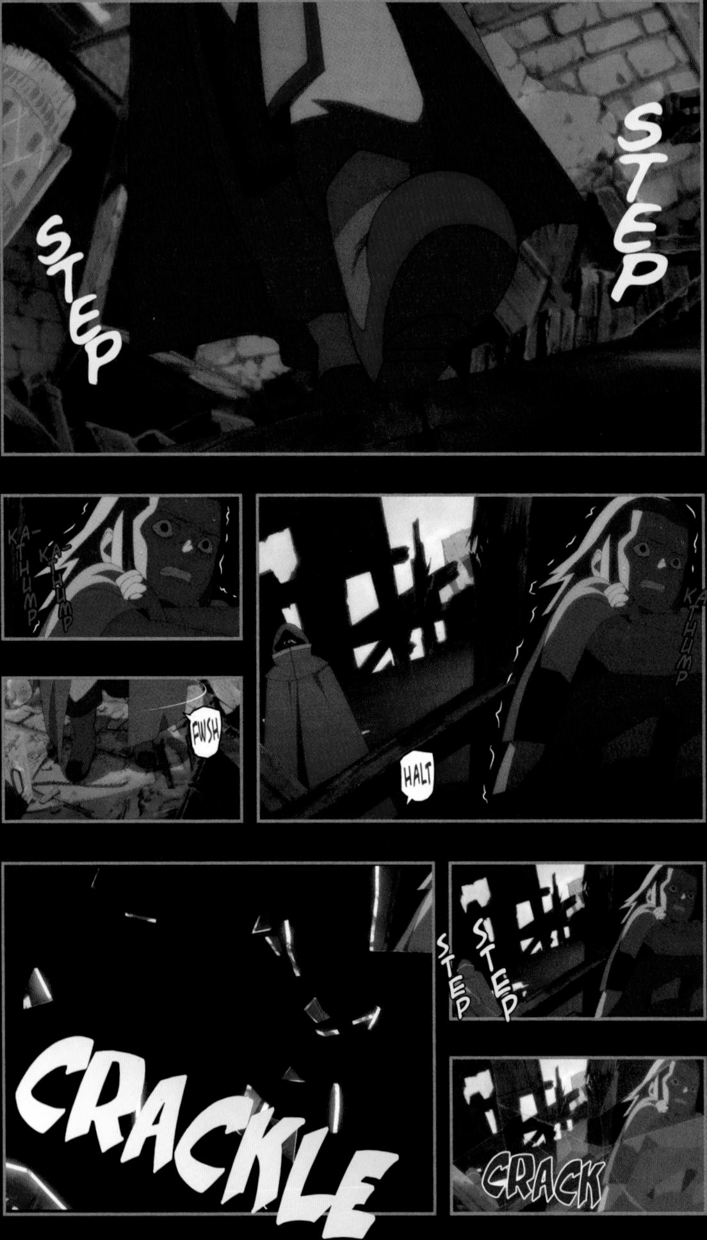
STEP
STEP
HALT
KA-THUMP
KA-THUMP
KA-THUMP
FWSH
STEP
STEP
CRACK
CRACKLE

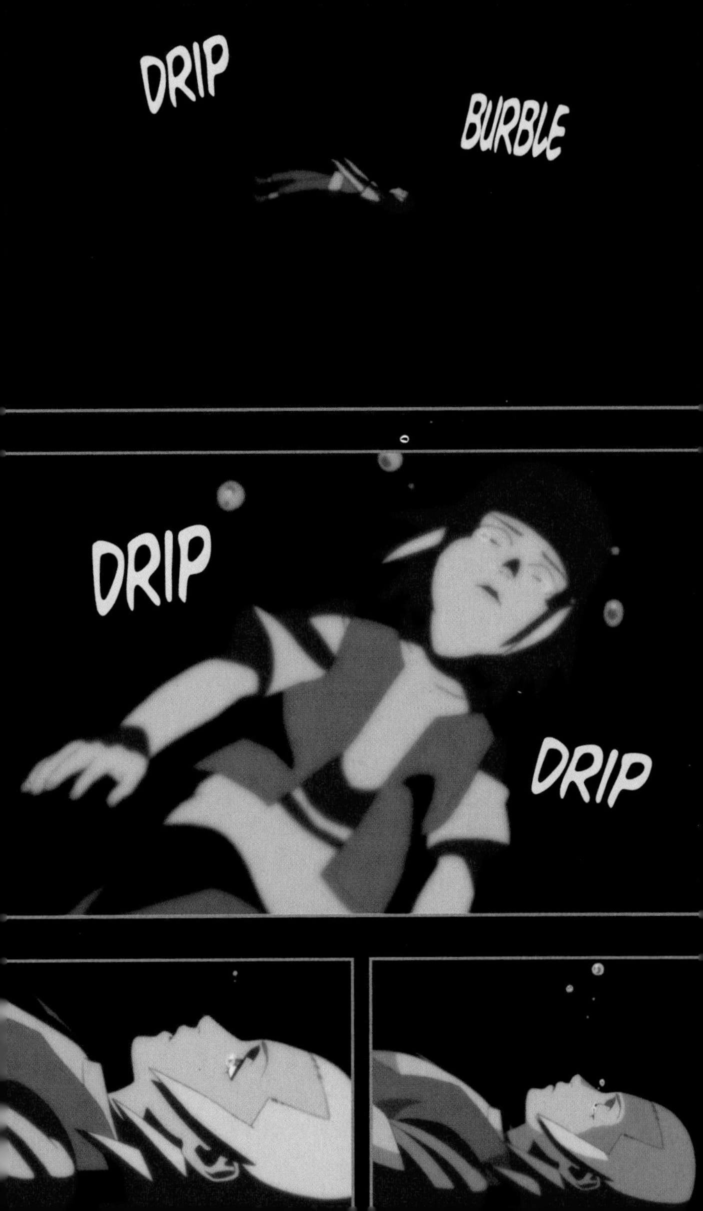
BURBLE
DRIP
DRIP
DRIP

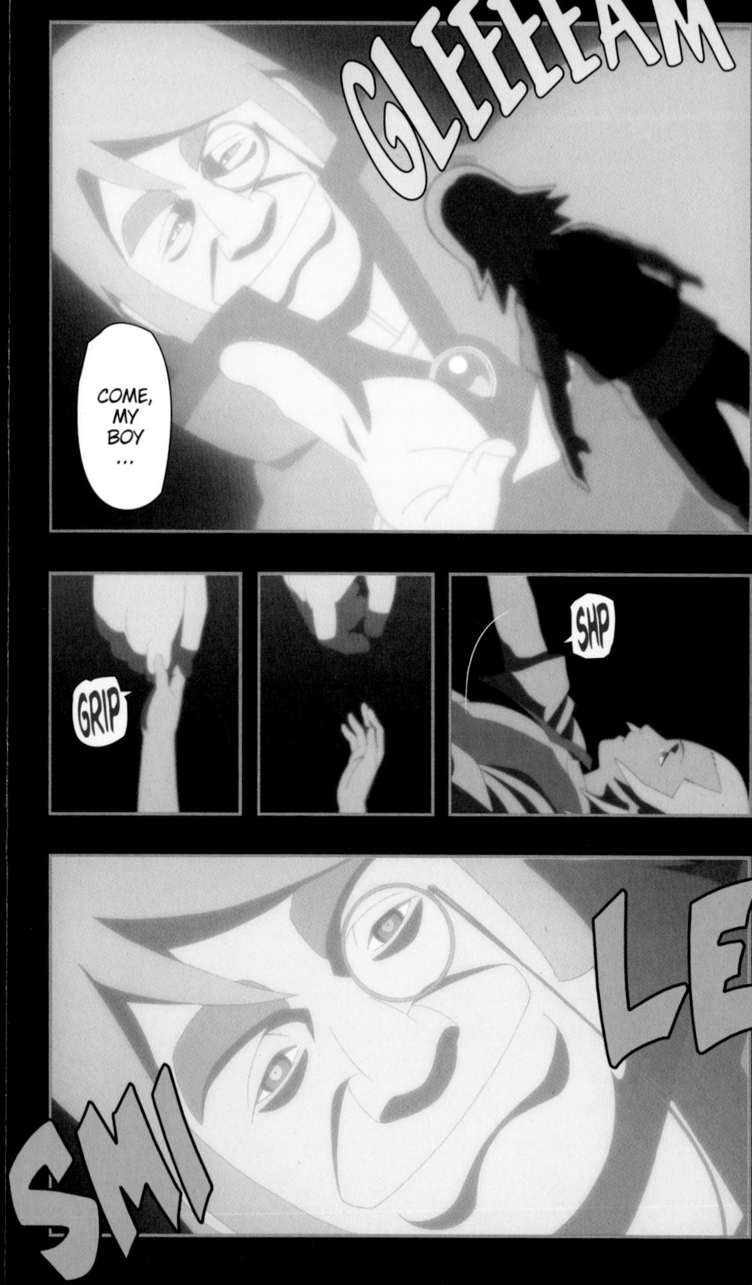
GLEEEEAM
COME, MY BOY ...
SHP
GRIP
LE
SMI

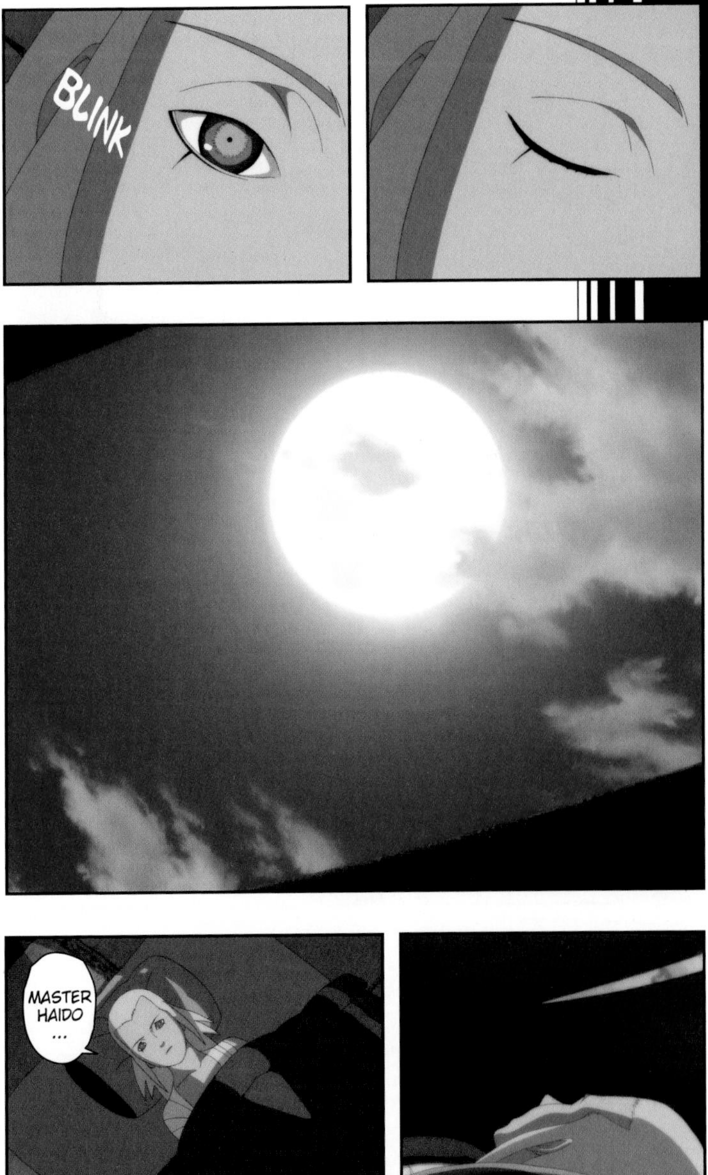
BLINK
MASTER HAIDO ...

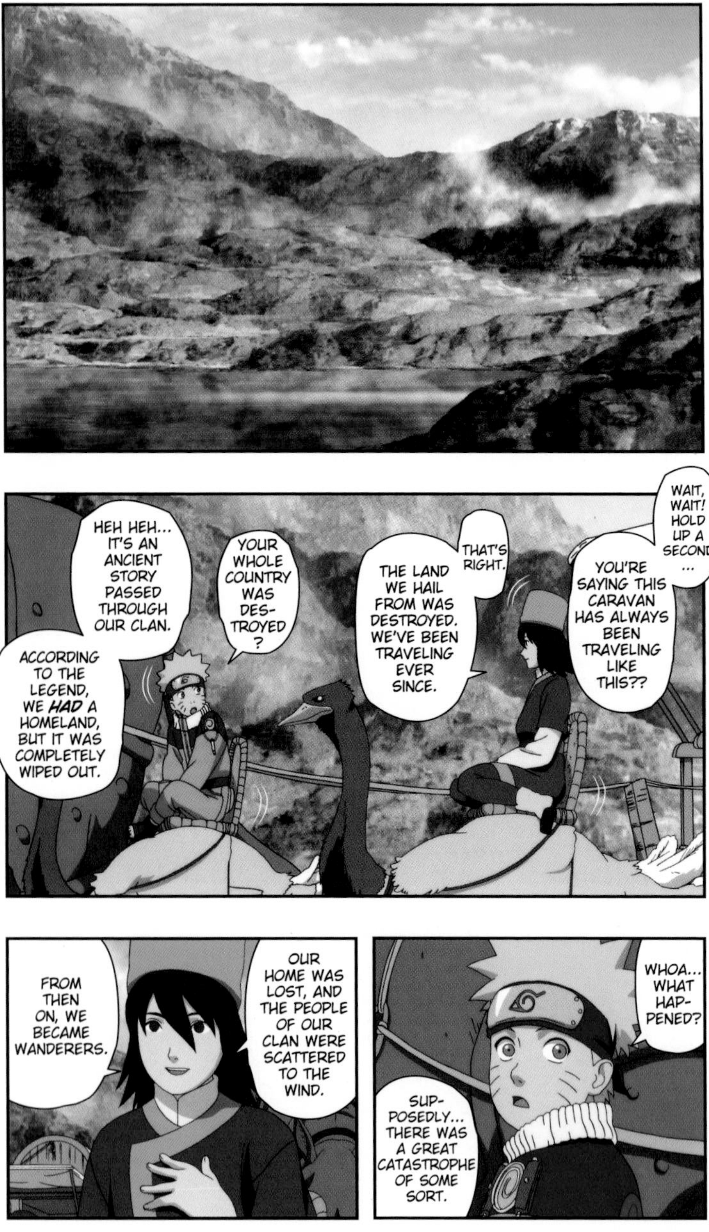
WAIT, WAIT! HOLD UP A SECOND...
YOU'RE SAYING THIS CARAVAN HAS ALWAYS BEEN TRAVELING LIKE THIS??
THAT'S RIGHT.
THE LAND WE HAIL FROM WAS DESTROYED. WE'VE BEEN TRAVELING EVER SINCE.
YOUR WHOLE COUNTRY WAS DES-TROYED?
HEH HEH... IT'S AN ANCIENT STORY PASSED THROUGH OUR CLAN.
ACCORDING TO THE LEGEND, WE *HAD* A HOMELAND, BUT IT WAS COMPLETELY WIPED OUT.
WHOA... WHAT HAP-PENED?
SUP-POSEDLY... THERE WAS A GREAT CATASTROPHE OF SOME SORT.
OUR HOME WAS LOST, AND THE PEOPLE OF OUR CLAN WERE SCATTERED TO THE WIND.
FROM THEN ON, WE BECAME WANDERERS.

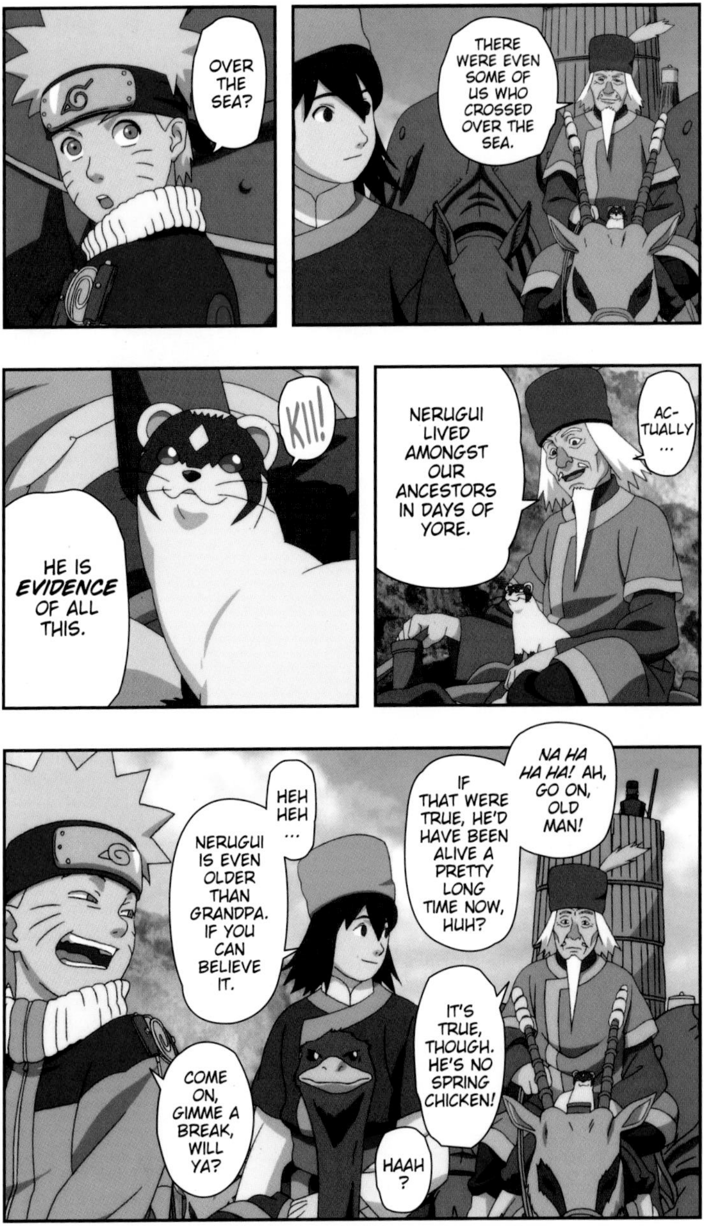
THERE WERE EVEN SOME OF US WHO CROSSED OVER THE SEA.
OVER THE SEA?
ACTUALLY...
NERUGUI LIVED AMONGST OUR ANCESTORS IN DAYS OF YORE.
KII!
HE IS *EVIDENCE* OF ALL THIS.
NA HA HA HA! AH, GO ON, OLD MAN!
IF THAT WERE TRUE, HE'D HAVE BEEN ALIVE A PRETTY LONG TIME NOW, HUH?
HEH HEH...
NERUGUI IS EVEN OLDER THAN GRANDPA. IF YOU CAN BELIEVE IT.
IT'S TRUE, THOUGH. HE'S NO SPRING CHICKEN!
COME ON, GIMME A BREAK, WILL YA?
HAAH?

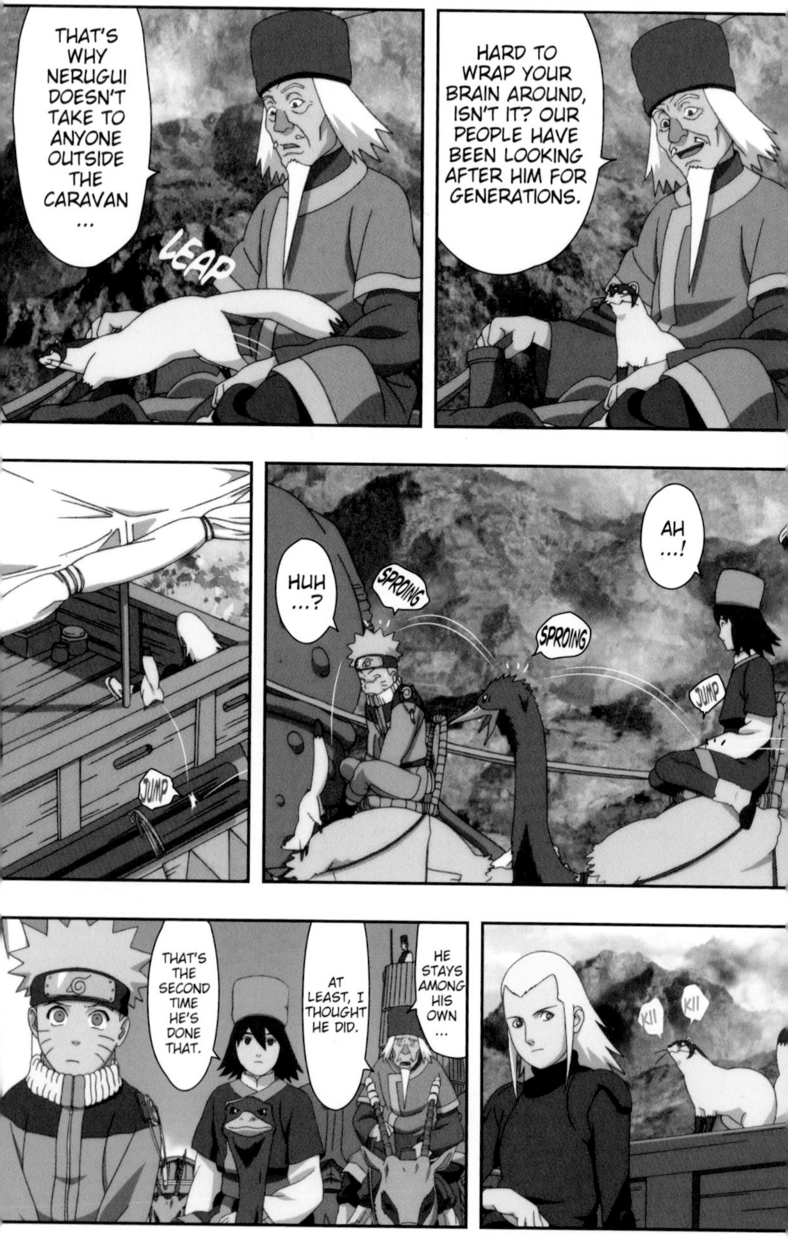
HARD TO WRAP YOUR BRAIN AROUND, ISN'T IT? OUR PEOPLE HAVE BEEN LOOKING AFTER HIM FOR GENERATIONS.
THAT'S WHY NERUGUI DOESN'T TAKE TO ANYONE OUTSIDE THE CARAVAN ...
LEAP
AH ...!
JUMP
SPROING
SPROING
HUH ...?
JUMP
KII
KII
HE STAYS AMONG HIS OWN ...
AT LEAST, I THOUGHT HE DID.
THAT'S THE SECOND TIME HE'S DONE THAT.

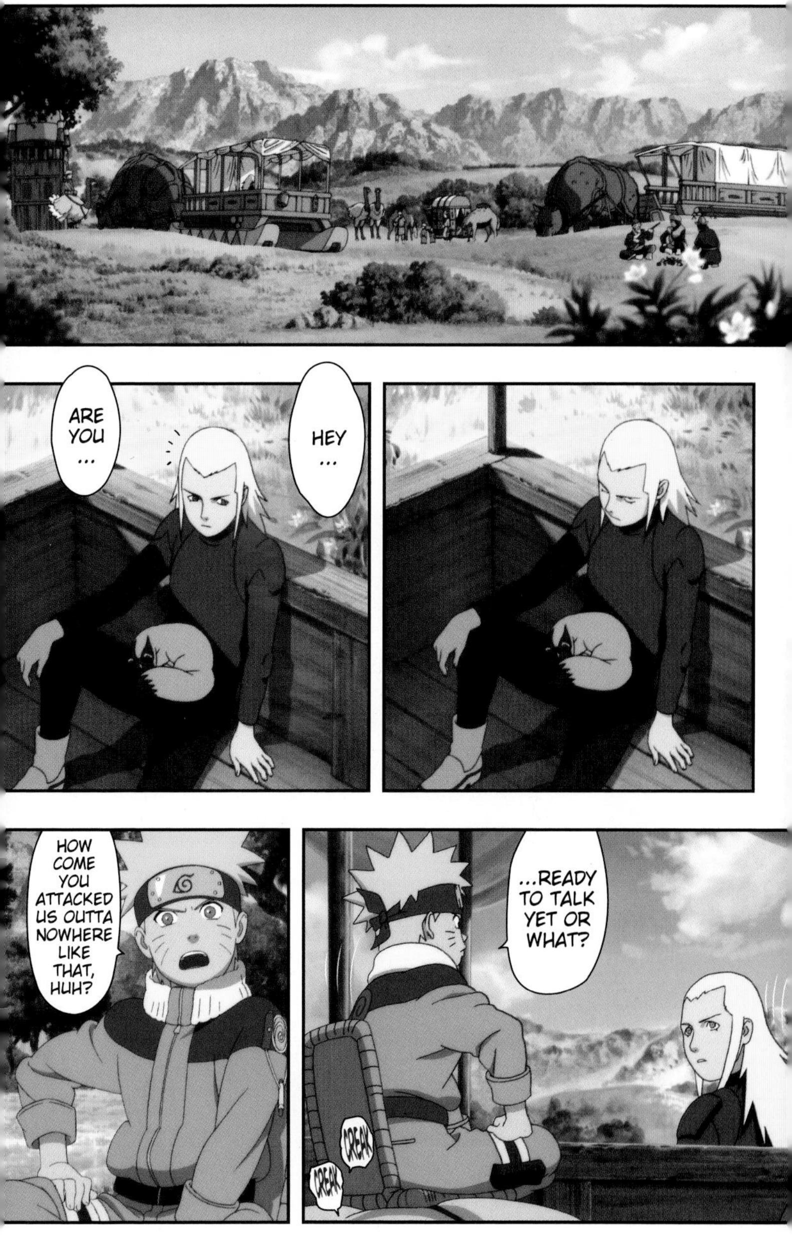
HEY...
ARE YOU...
...READY TO TALK YET OR WHAT?
CREAK
CREAK
HOW COME YOU ATTACKED US OUTTA NOWHERE LIKE THAT, HUH?

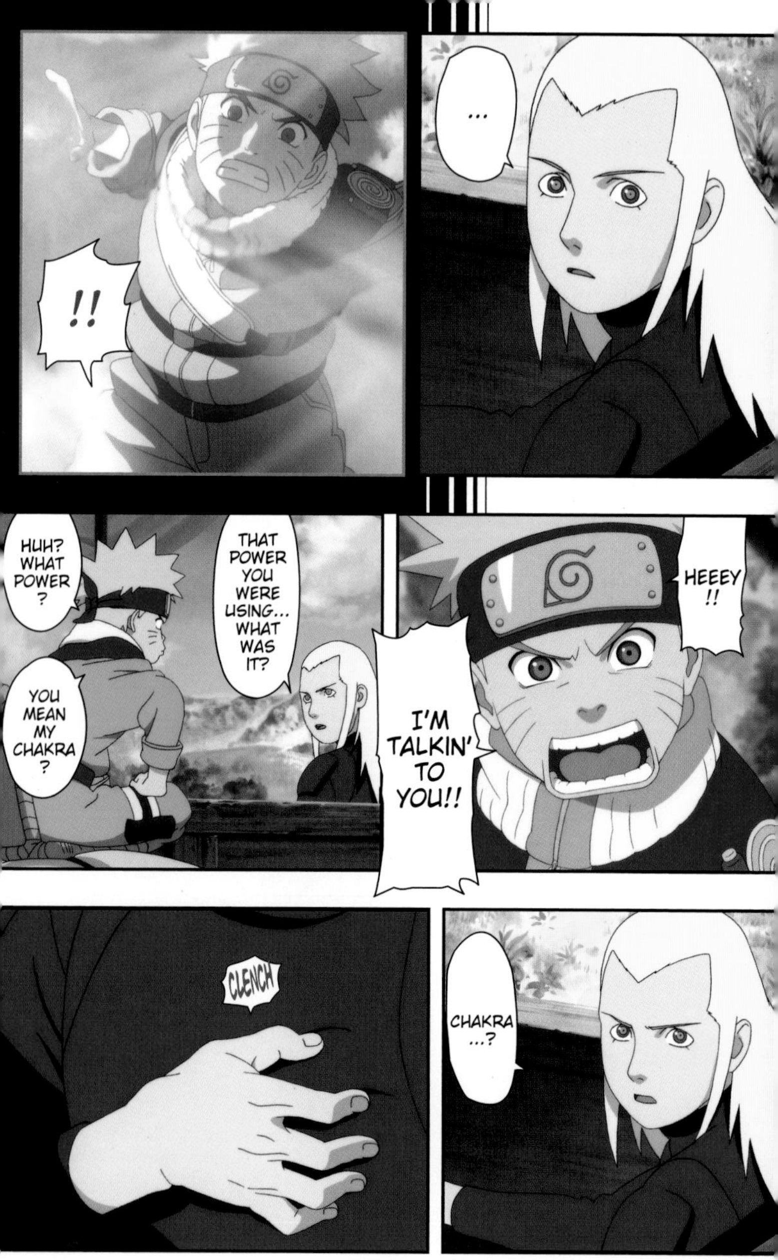
...
!!
HEEEY!!
I'M TALKIN' TO YOU!!
THAT POWER YOU WERE USING... WHAT WAS IT?
HUH? WHAT POWER?
YOU MEAN MY CHAKRA?
CHAKRA...?
CLENCH

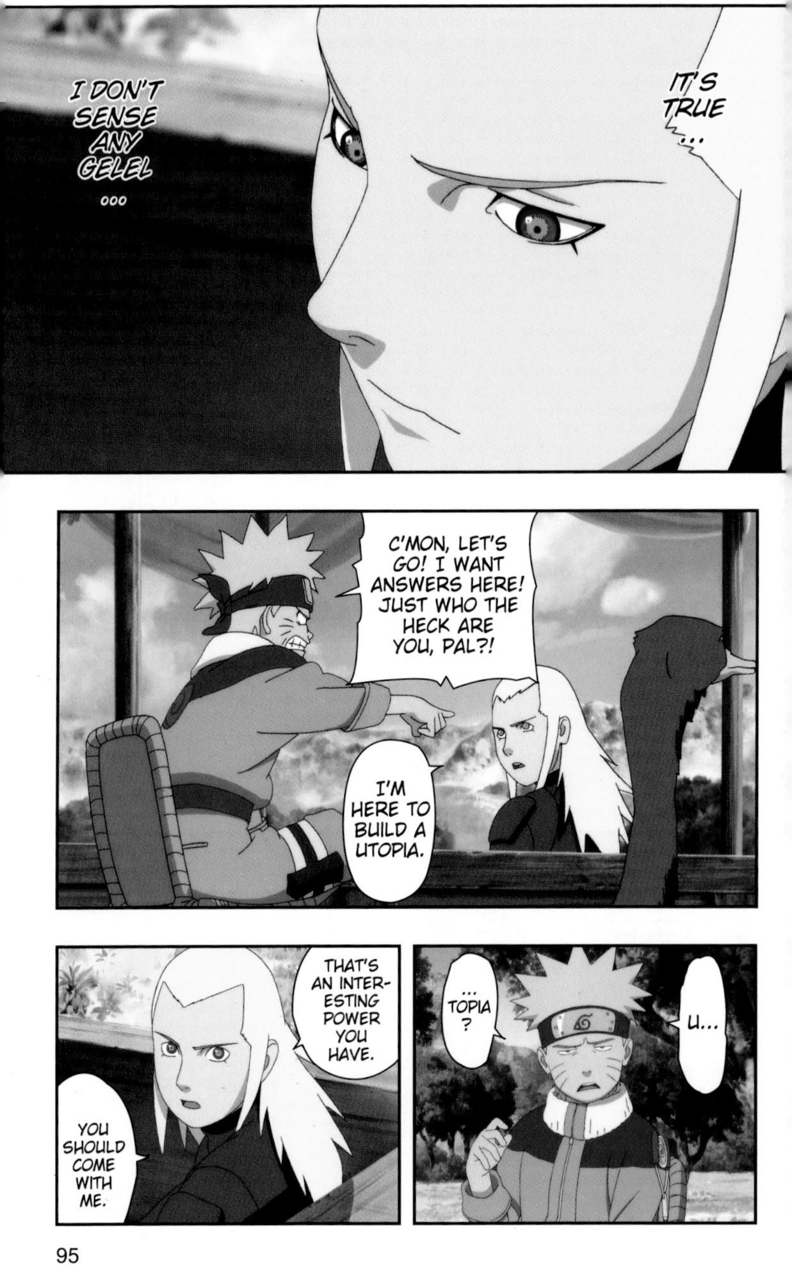
IT'S TRUE...
I DON'T SENSE ANY GELEL...
C'MON, LET'S GO! I WANT ANSWERS HERE! JUST WHO THE HECK ARE YOU, PAL?!
I'M HERE TO BUILD A UTOPIA.
U...
...TOPIA?
THAT'S AN INTER-ESTING POWER YOU HAVE.
YOU SHOULD COME WITH ME.

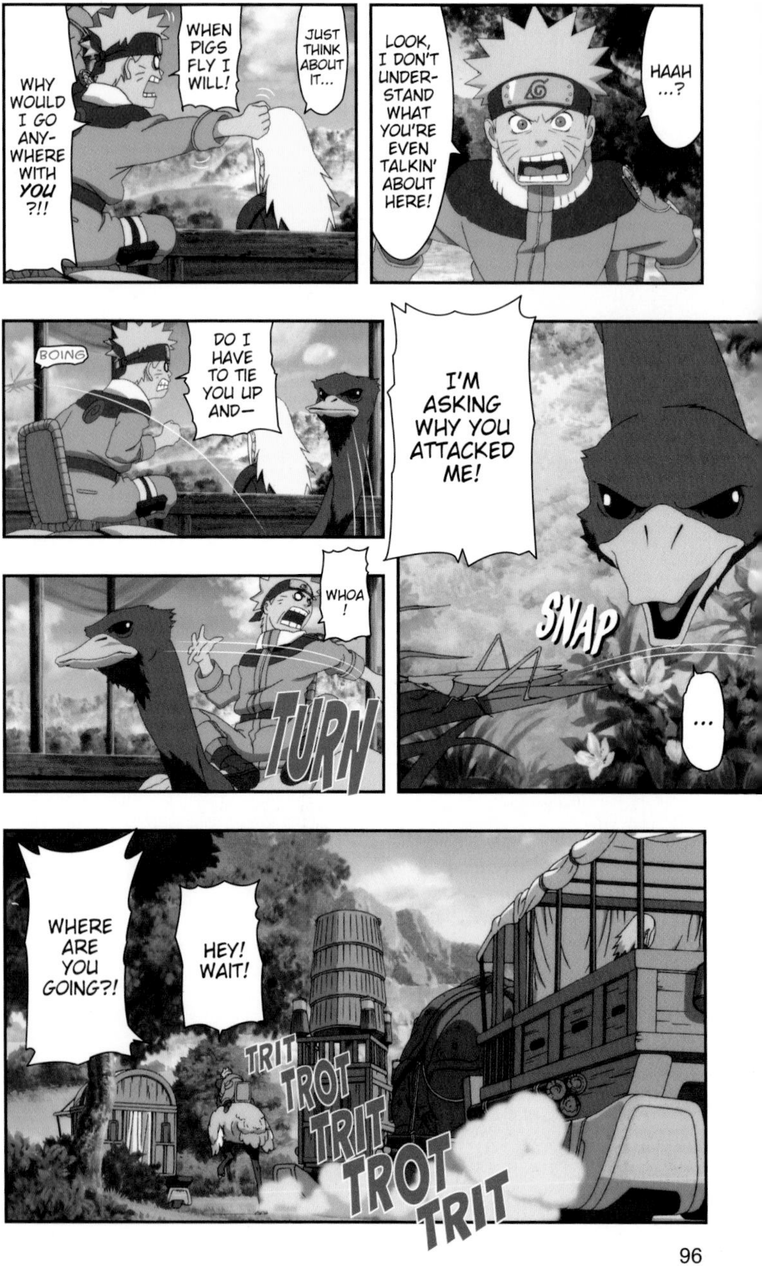
HAAH ...?
LOOK, I DON'T UNDER-STAND WHAT YOU'RE EVEN TALKIN' ABOUT HERE!
JUST THINK ABOUT IT...
WHEN PIGS FLY I WILL!
WHY WOULD I GO ANY-WHERE WITH YOU ?!!
I'M ASKING WHY YOU ATTACKED ME!
SNAP
...
DO I HAVE TO TIE YOU UP AND—
BOING
WHOA !
TURN
HEY! WAIT!
WHERE ARE YOU GOING?!
TRIT TROT TRIT TROT TRIT

FLEX

...

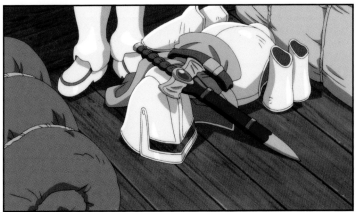

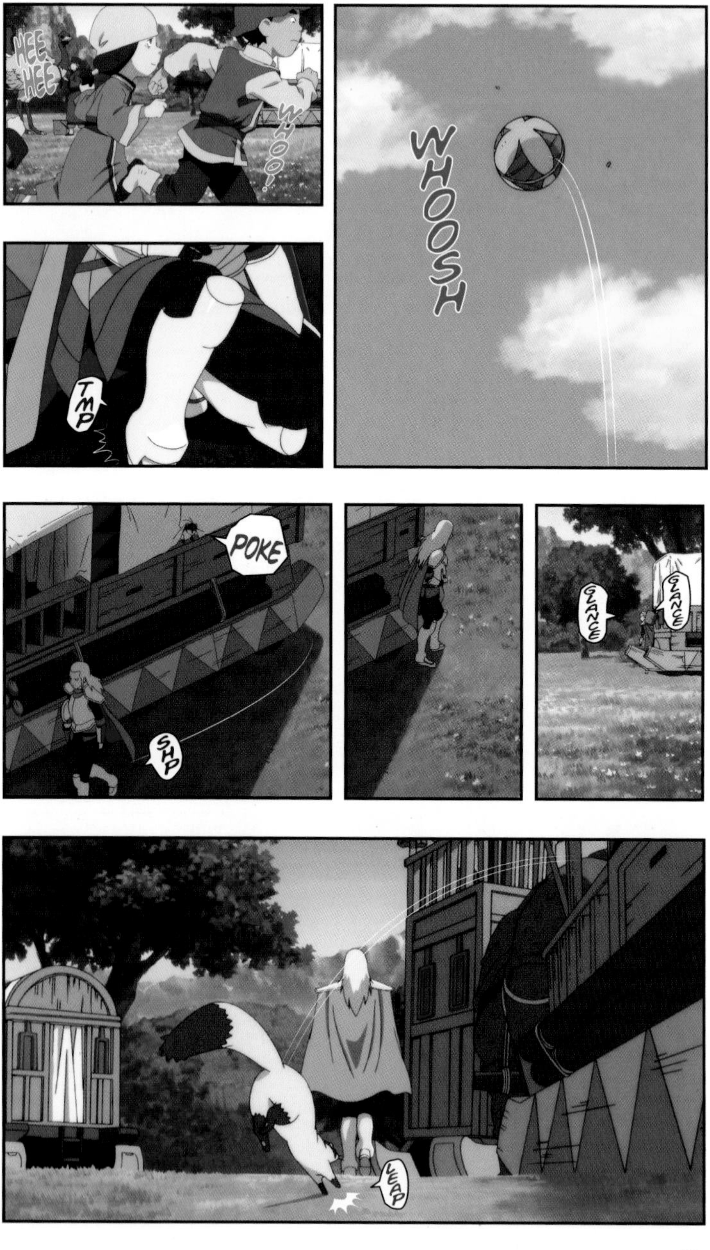
WHOOSH
WHOOO!
HEE HEE
TMP
GLANCE
GLANCE
POKE
SHP
LEAP

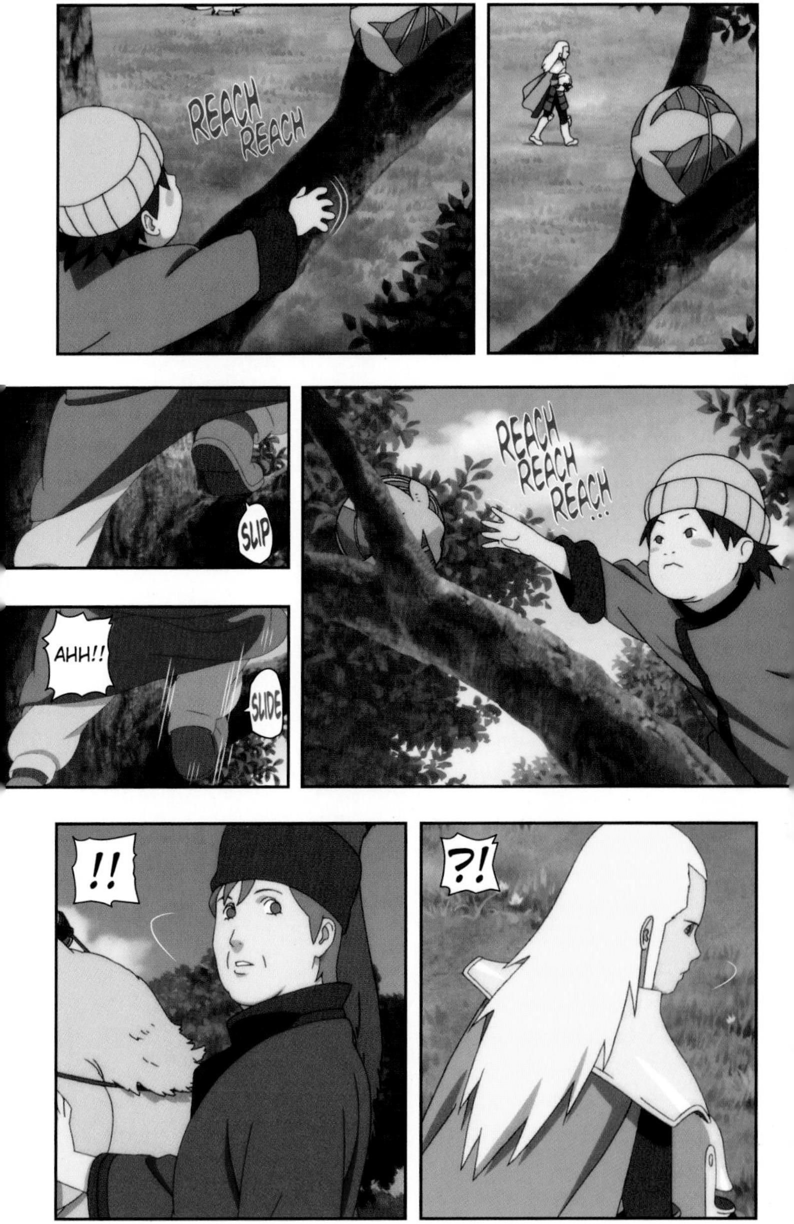
REACH REACH
REACH REACH REACH...
SLIP
AHH!!
SLIDE
?!
!!

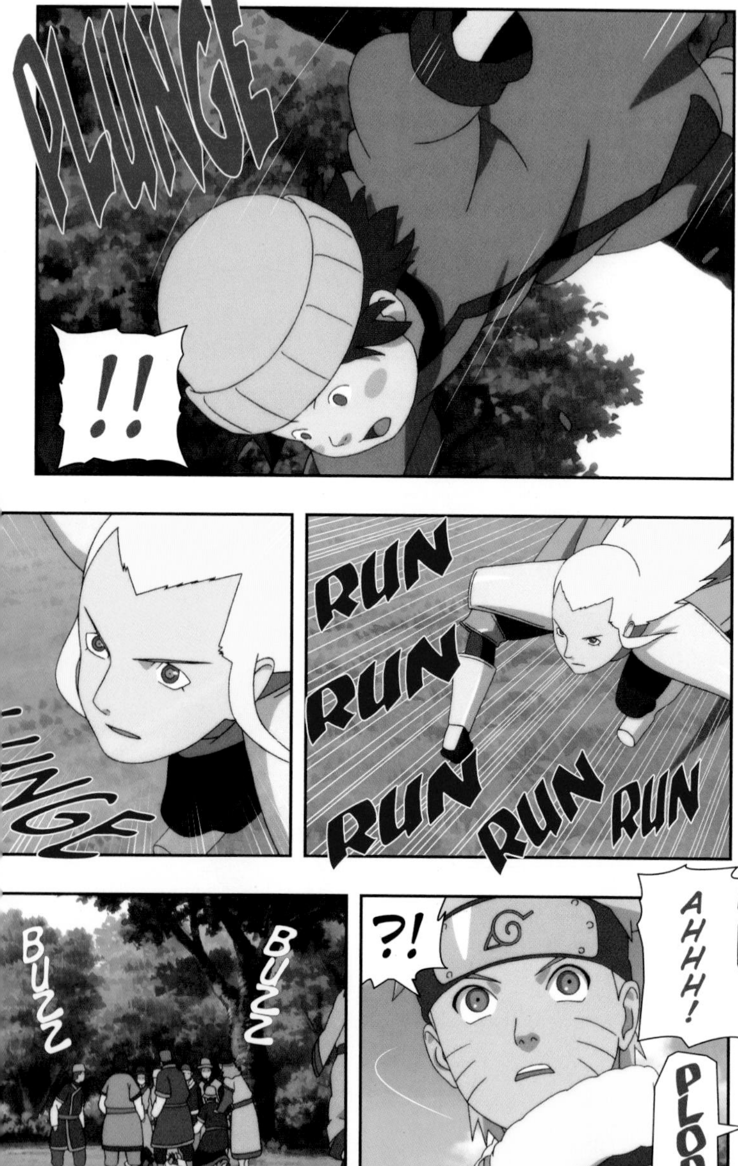
PLUNGE
!!
RUN
RUN
RUN
RUN
RUN
?!
AHHHH!
PLOP
BUZZ
BUZZ

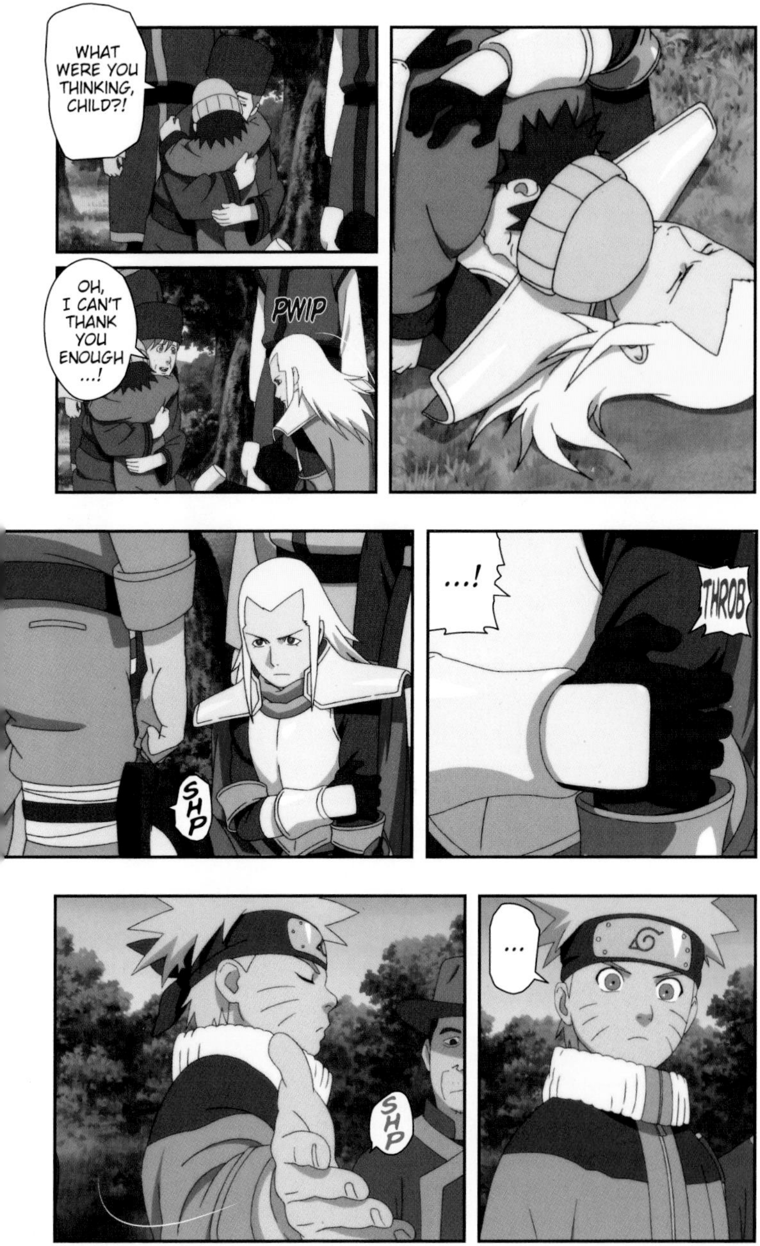
WHAT WERE YOU THINKING, CHILD?!
OH, I CAN'T THANK YOU ENOUGH ...!
PWIP
...!
THROB
SHP
...
SHP

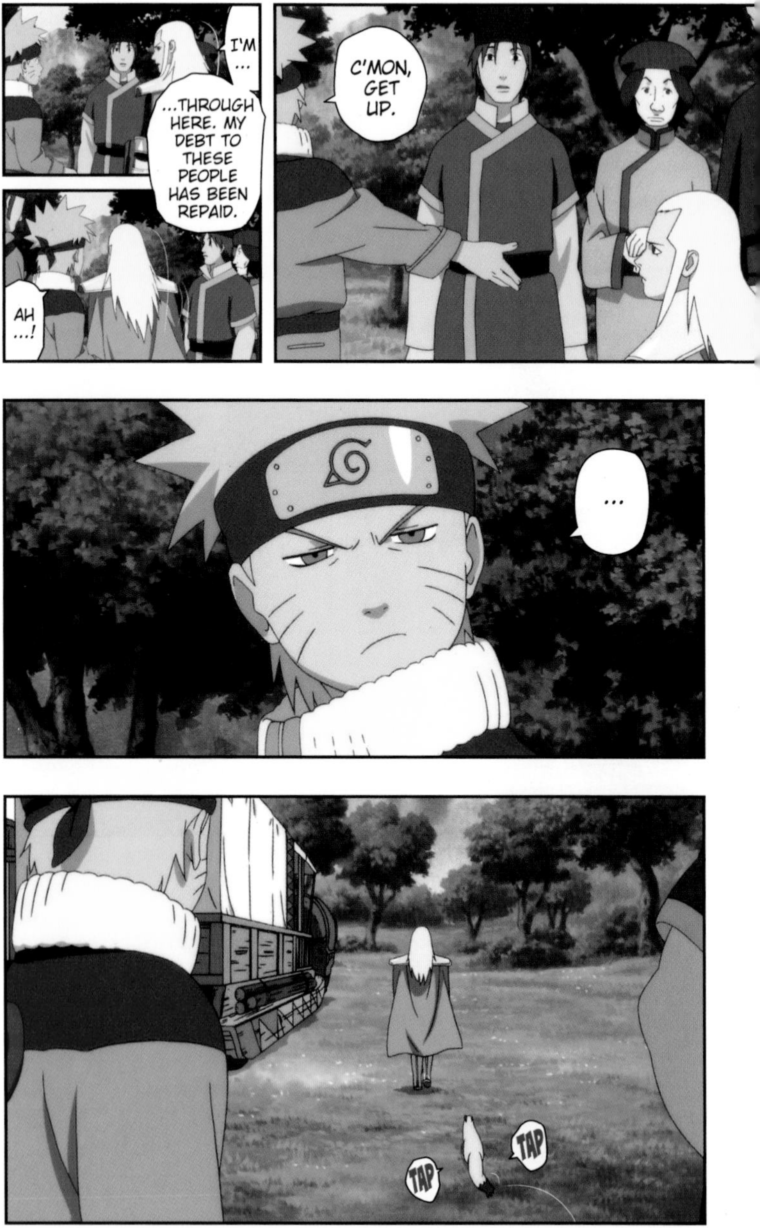
C'MON, GET UP.
I'M ...
...THROUGH HERE. MY DEBT TO THESE PEOPLE HAS BEEN REPAID.
AH ...!
...
TAP
TAP

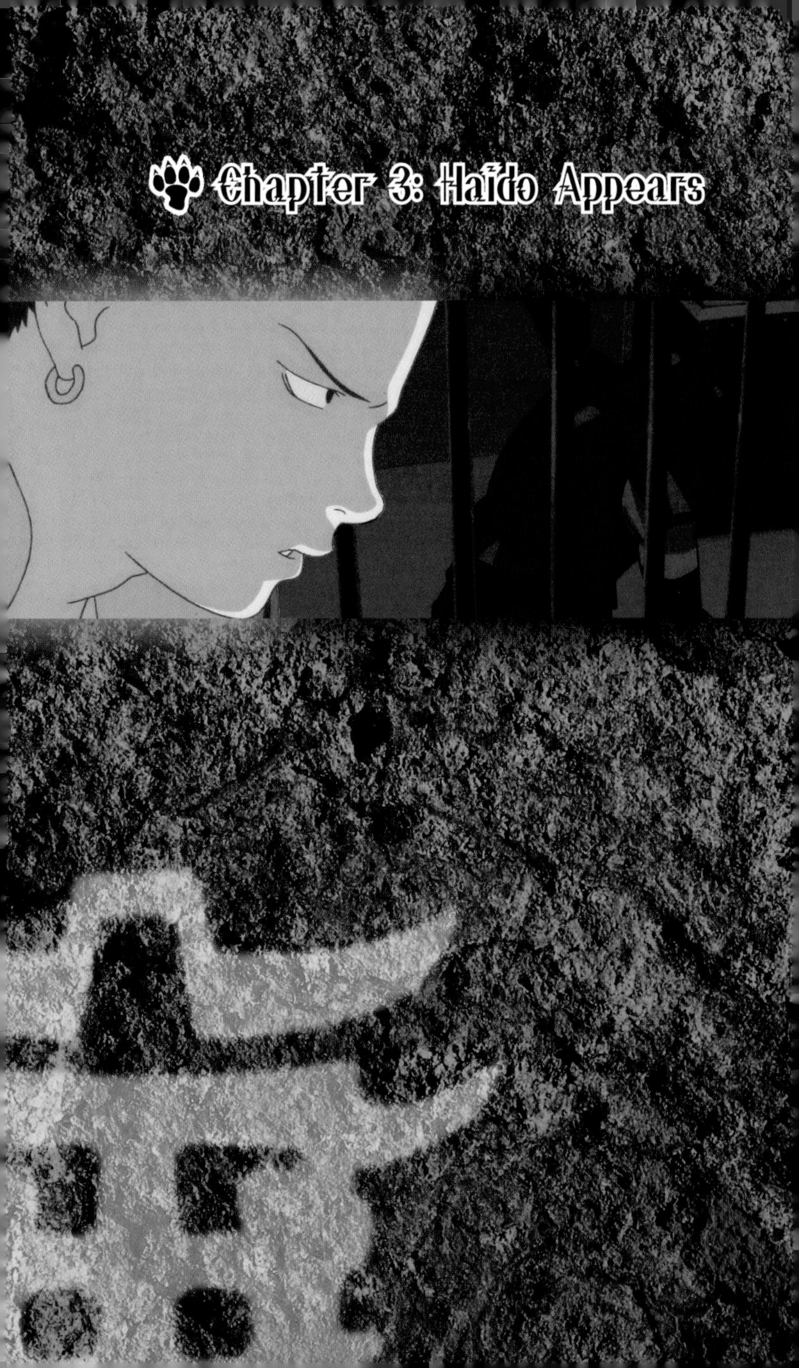
Chapter 3: Haido Appears

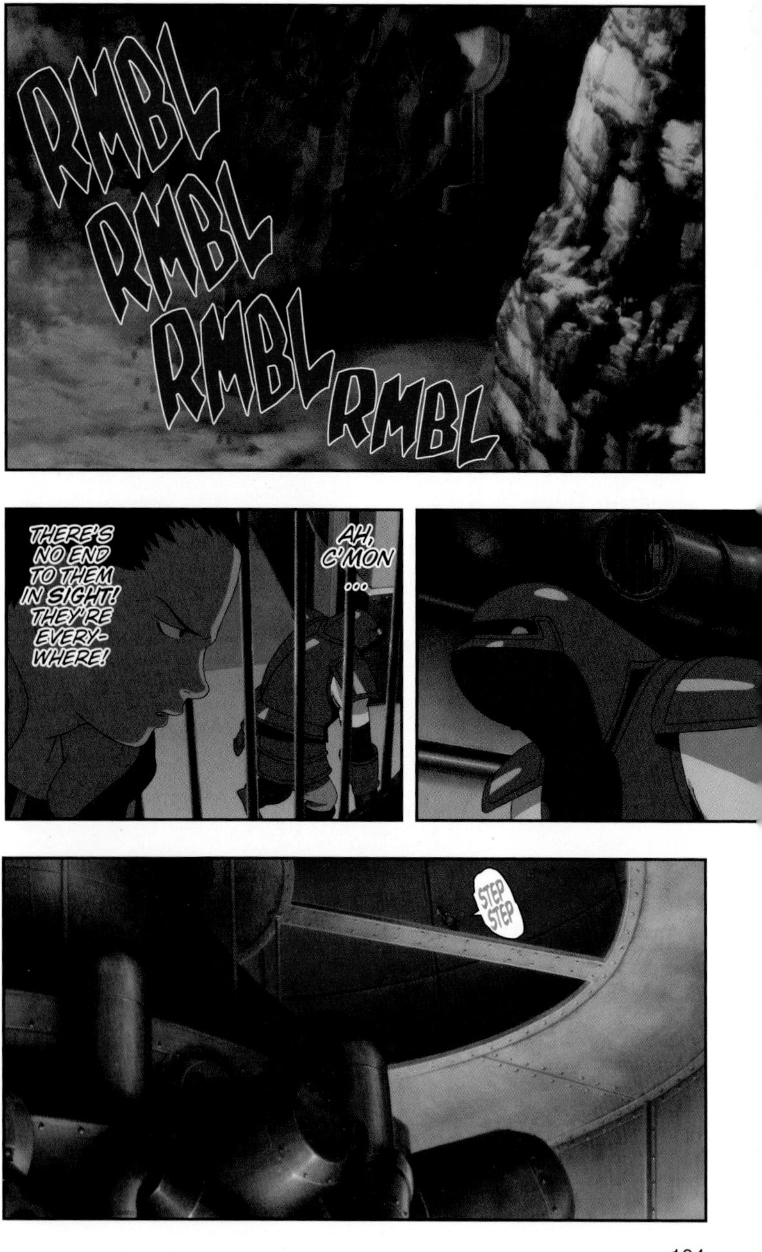
RMBL RMBL RMBL RMBL
AH, C'MON...
THERE'S NO END TO THEM IN SIGHT! THEY'RE EVERY-WHERE!
STEP STEP

TMP
TMP
TMP

?!

PAUSE

BWO

OM

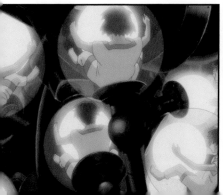

DOESN'T LOOK LIKE THEY'RE CONSCIOUS.

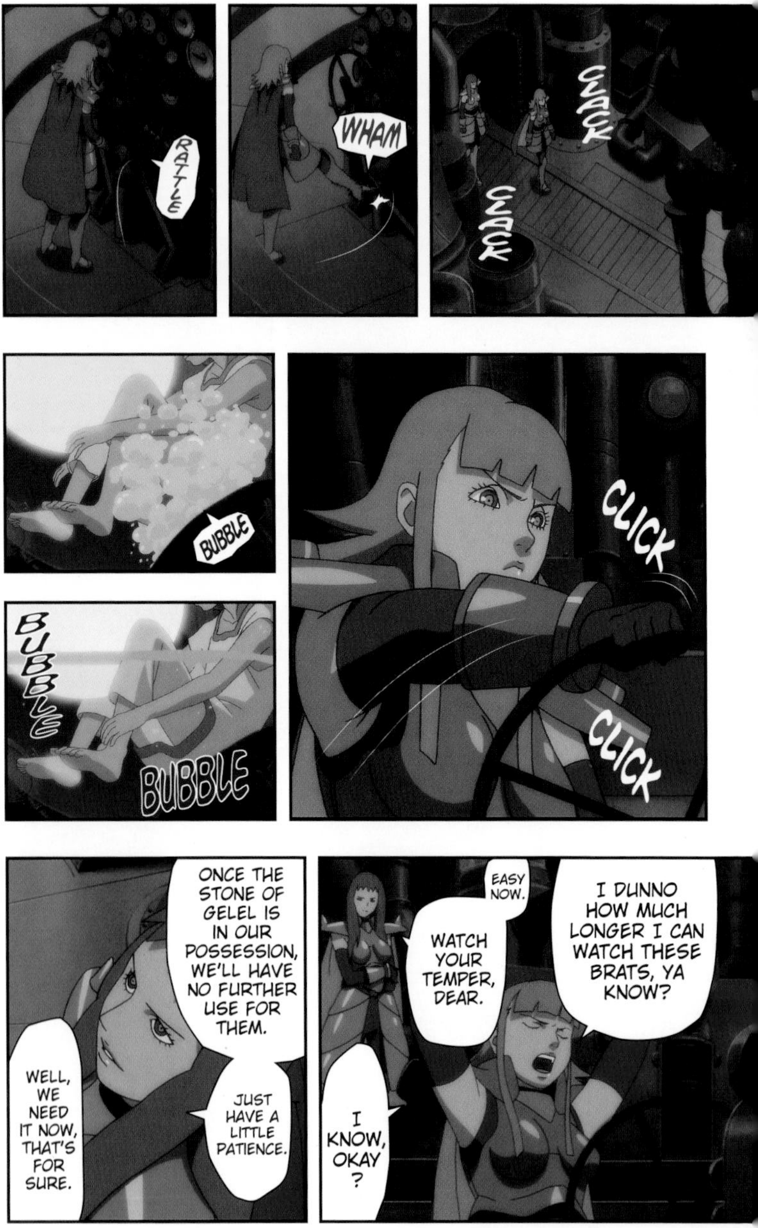
CLACK
CLACK
WHAM
RATTLE
CLICK
CLICK
BUBBLE
BUBBLE
BUBBLE
I DUNNO HOW MUCH LONGER I CAN WATCH THESE BRATS, YA KNOW?
EASY NOW.
WATCH YOUR TEMPER, DEAR.
I KNOW, OKAY?
ONCE THE STONE OF GELEL IS IN OUR POSSESSION, WE'LL HAVE NO FURTHER USE FOR THEM.
JUST HAVE A LITTLE PATIENCE.
WELL, WE NEED IT NOW, THAT'S FOR SURE.

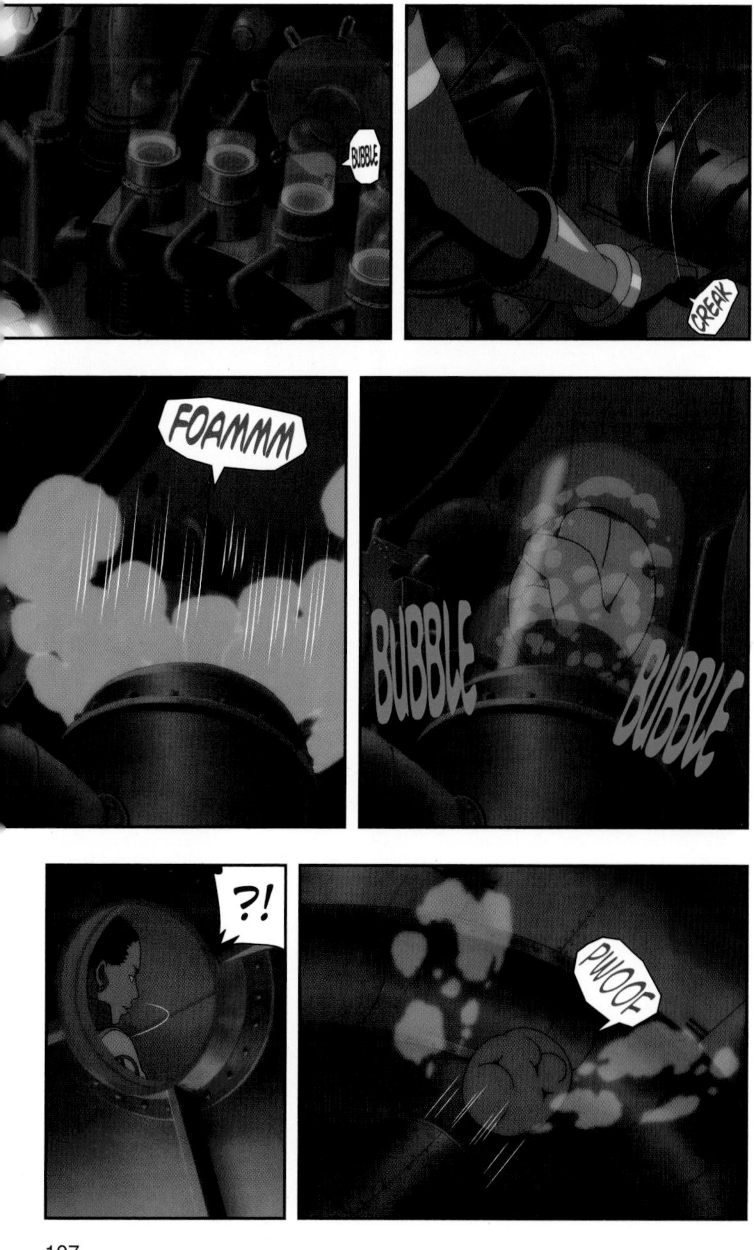
CREAK
BUBBLE
BUBBLE
BUBBLE
FOAMMM
PWOOF
?!

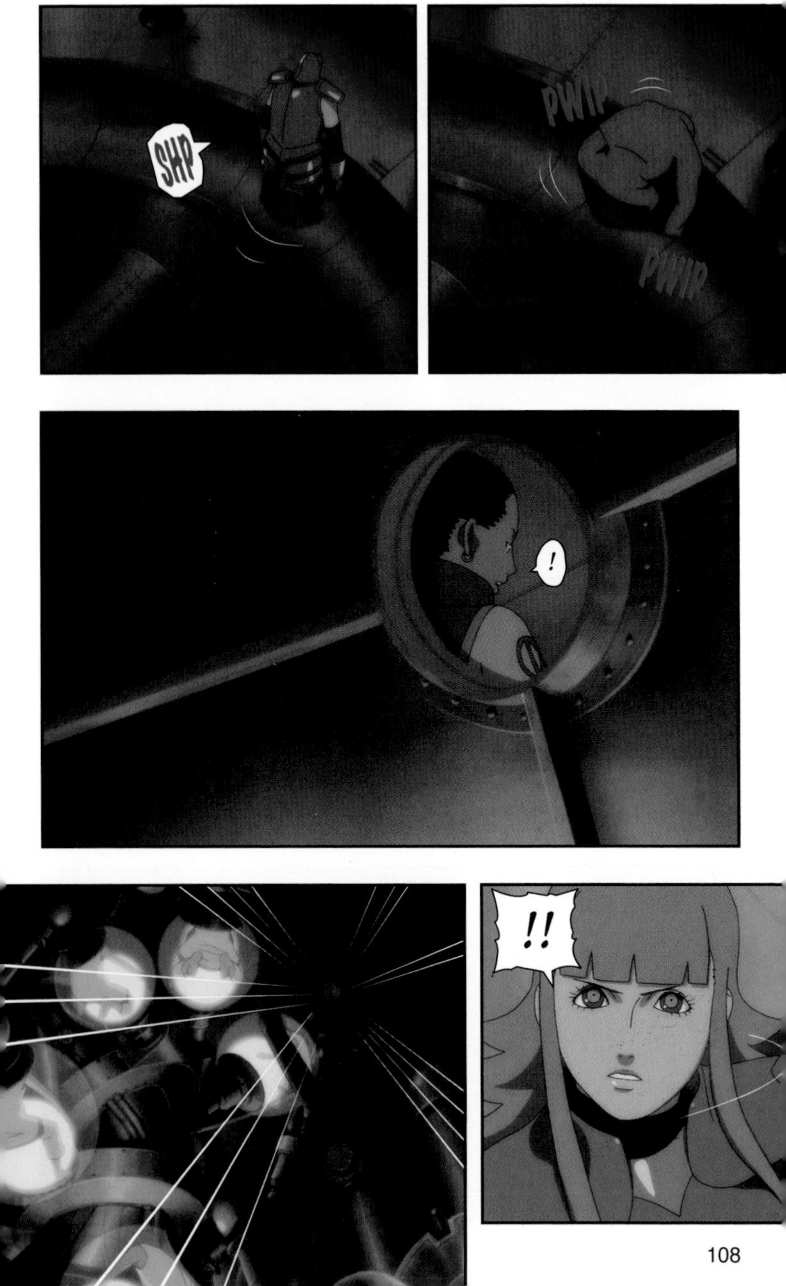
PWIP
PWIP
SHP
!
!!

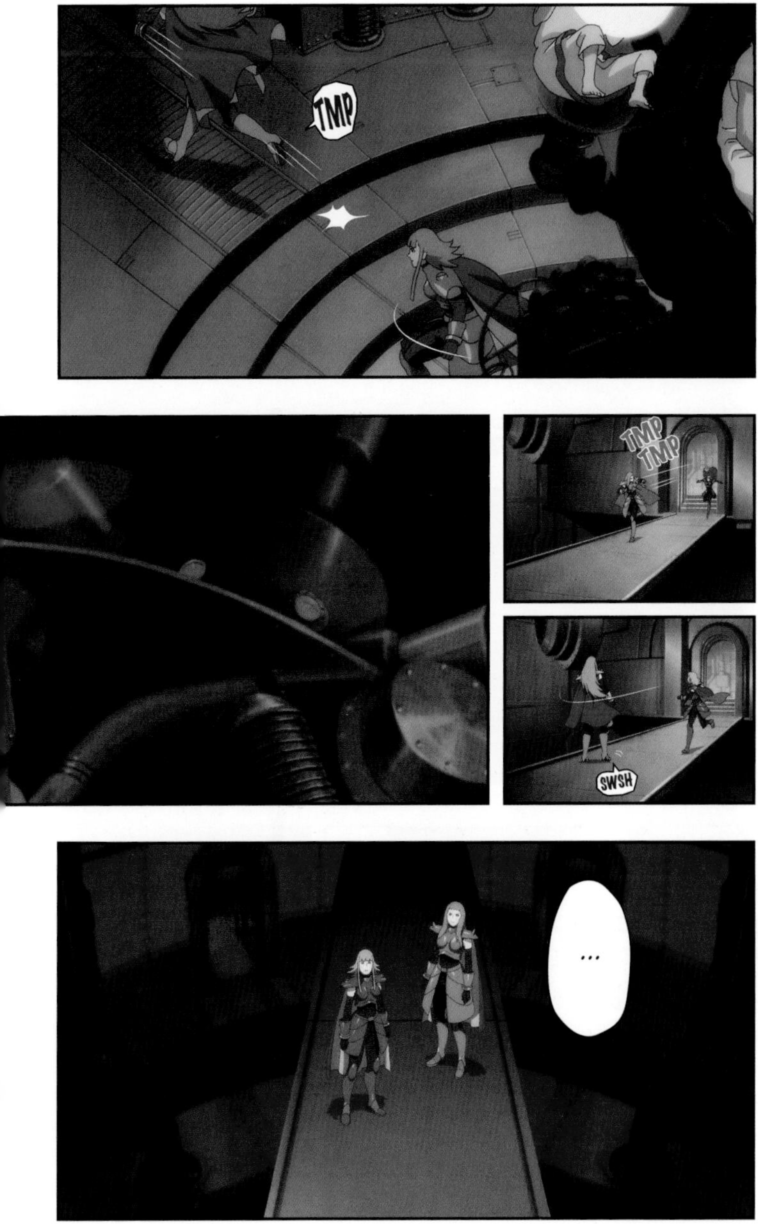
TMP
TMP TMP
SWSH
...

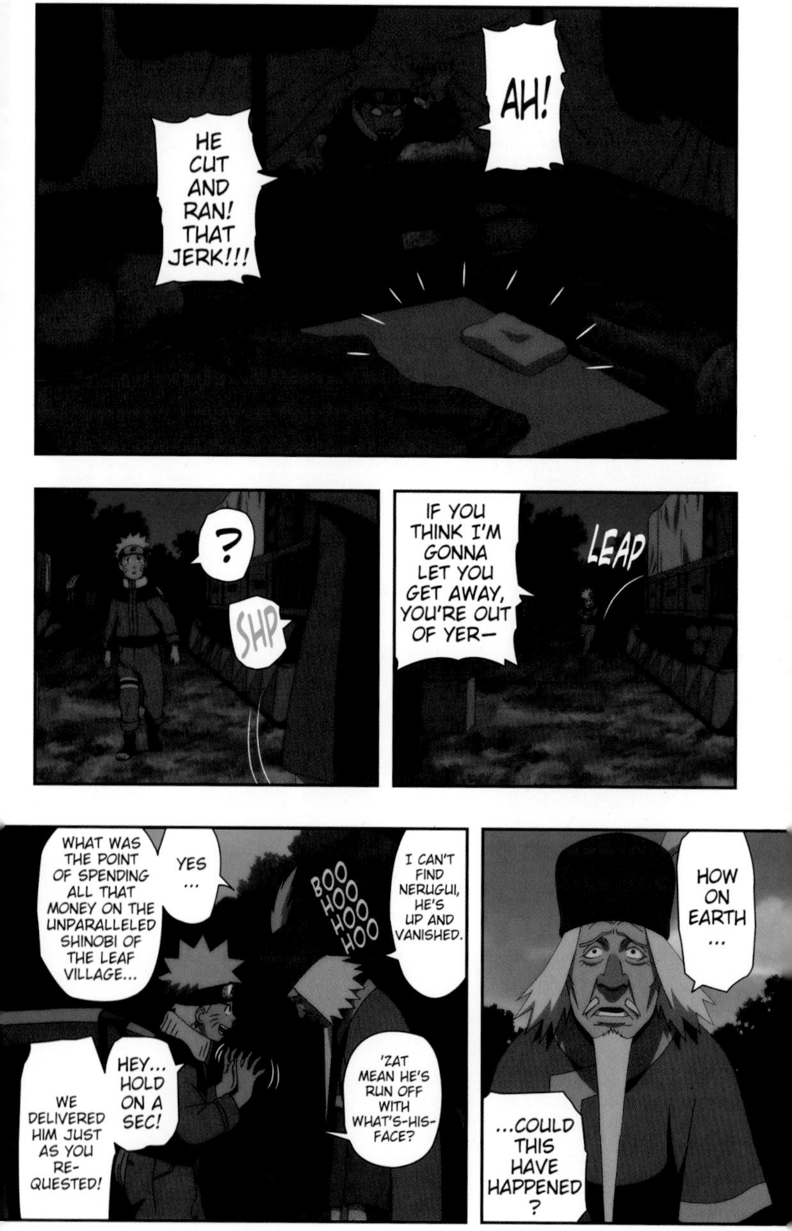
AH!
HE CUT AND RAN! THAT JERK!!!
IF YOU THINK I'M GONNA LET YOU GET AWAY, YOU'RE OUT OF YER—
LEAP
?
SHP
HOW ON EARTH...
...COULD THIS HAVE HAPPENED?
BOOOOO HOOOO HOOO HOO
I CAN'T FIND NERUGUI, HE'S UP AND VANISHED.
YES...
WHAT WAS THE POINT OF SPENDING ALL THAT MONEY ON THE UNPARALLELED SHINOBI OF THE LEAF VILLAGE...
'ZAT MEAN HE'S RUN OFF WITH WHAT'S-HIS-FACE?
HEY... HOLD ON A SEC!
WE DELIVERED HIM JUST AS YOU RE-QUESTED!

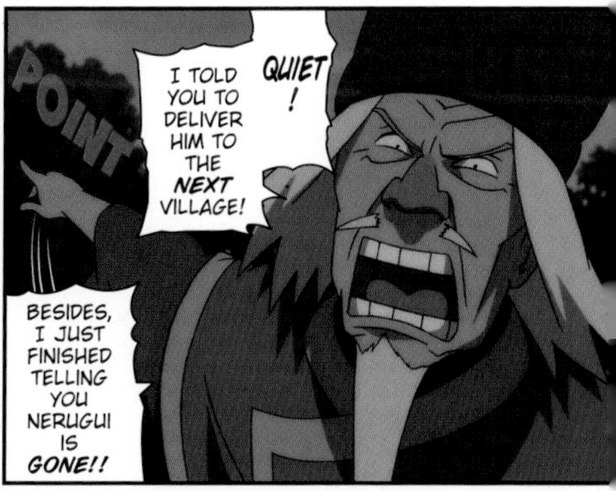
QUIET!
I TOLD YOU TO DELIVER HIM TO THE NEXT VILLAGE!
POINT
BESIDES, I JUST FINISHED TELLING YOU NERUGUI IS GONE!!

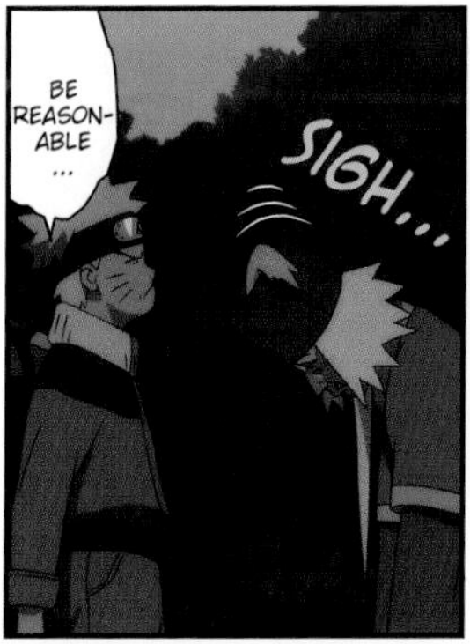
SIGH...
BE REASONABLE...

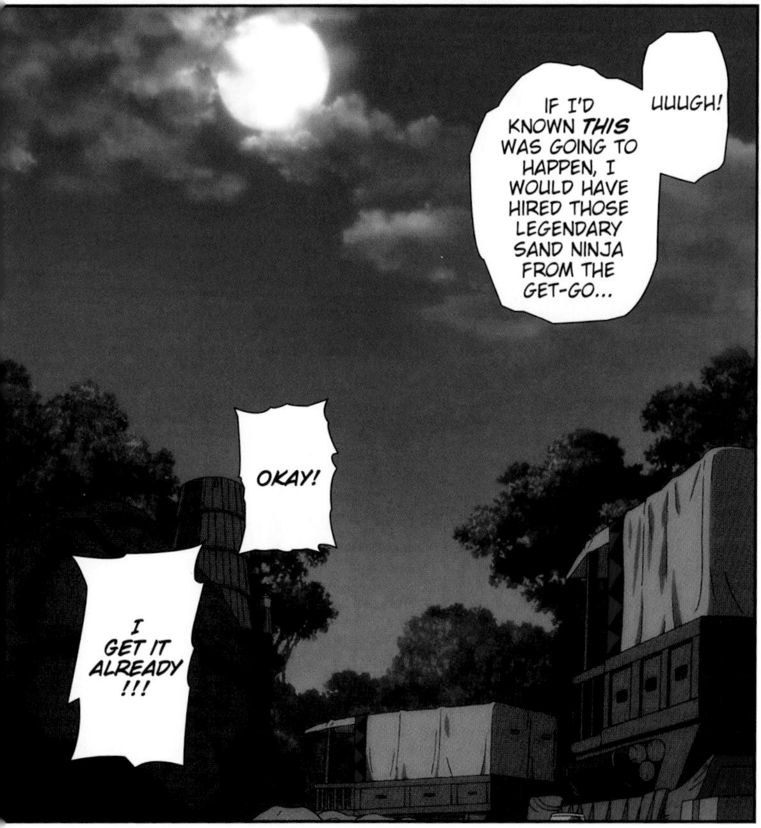
UUUGH!
IF I'D KNOWN THIS WAS GOING TO HAPPEN, I WOULD HAVE HIRED THOSE LEGENDARY SAND NINJA FROM THE GET-GO...
OKAY!
I GET IT ALREADY!!!

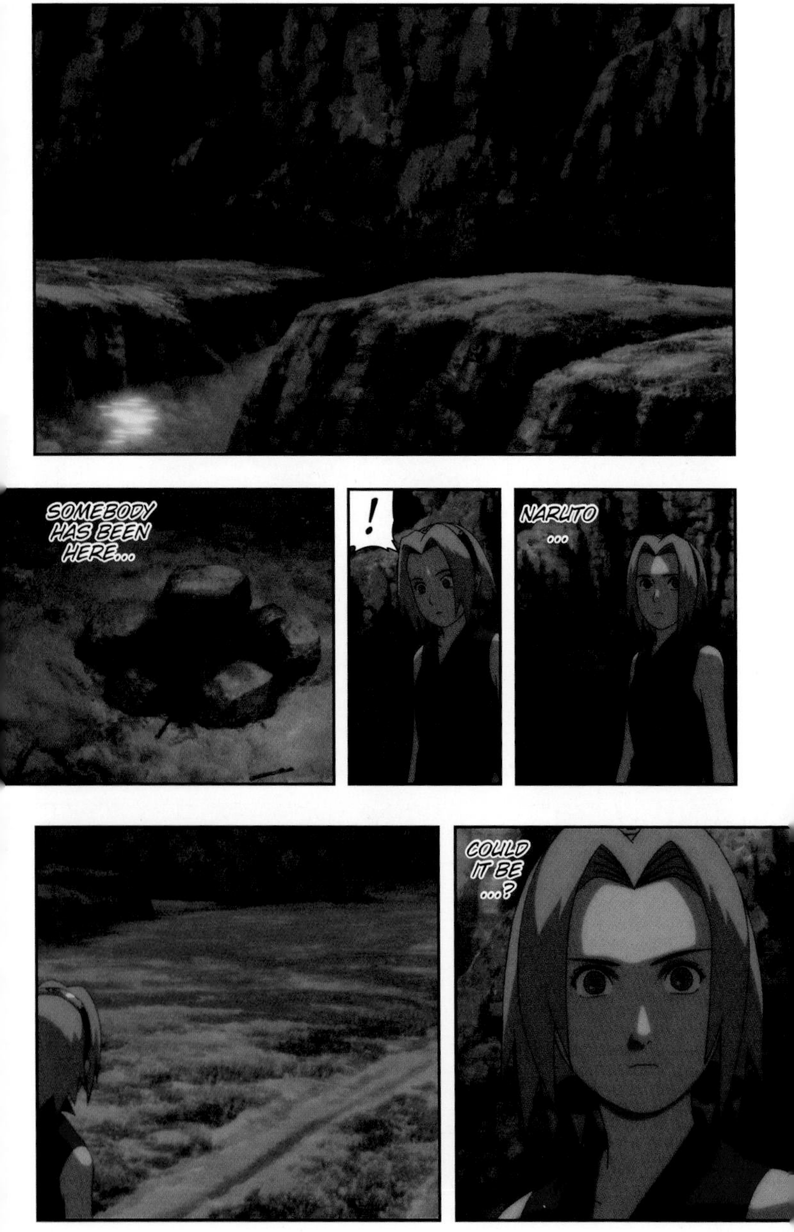
NARUTO ...
!
SOMEBODY HAS BEEN HERE...
COULD IT BE ...?

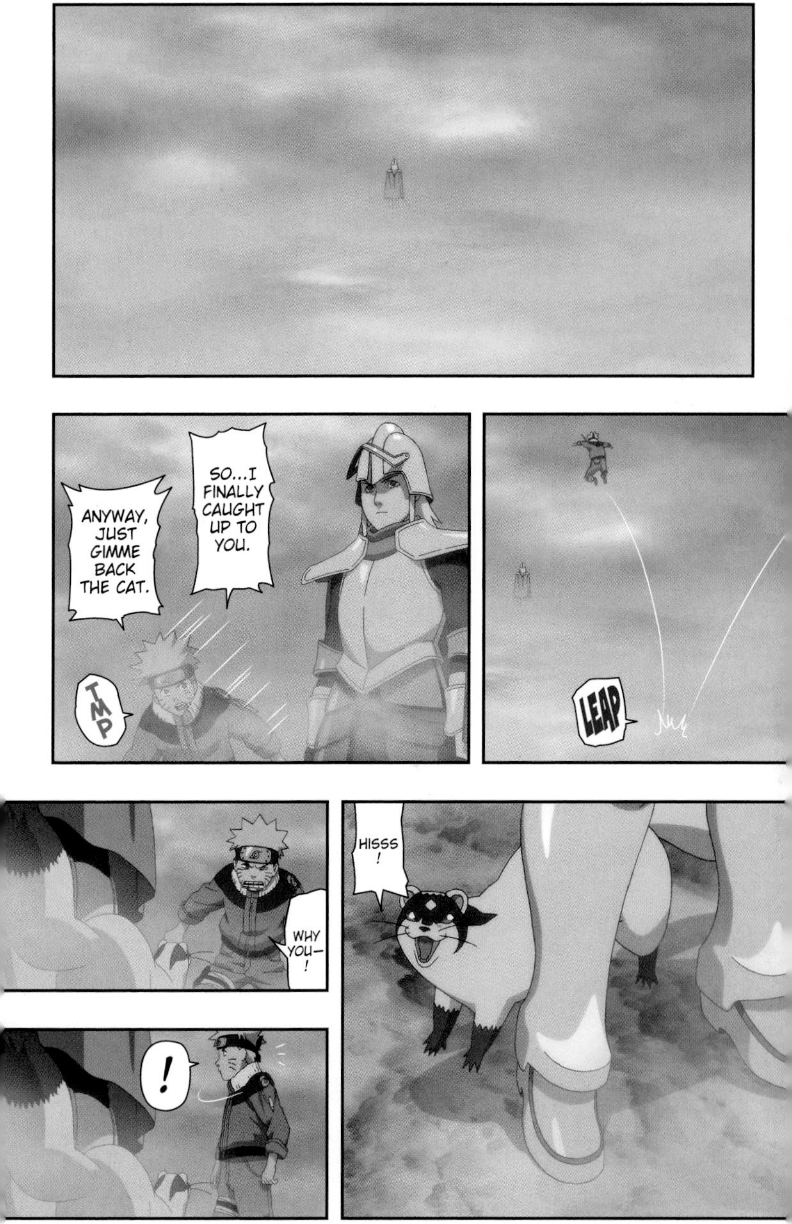
LEAP
SO...I FINALLY CAUGHT UP TO YOU.
ANYWAY, JUST GIMME BACK THE CAT.
TMP
HISSS!
WHY YOU—!
!

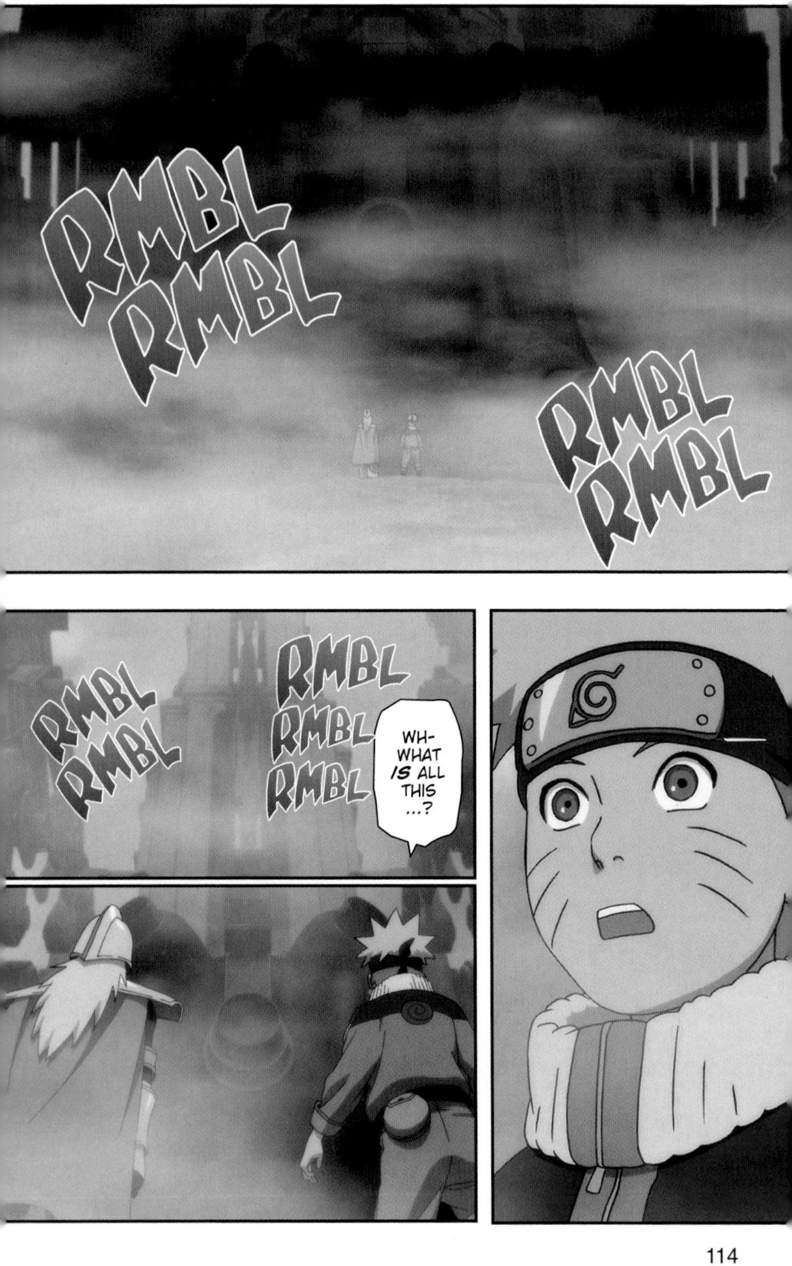
RMBL RMBL
RMBL RMBL
WH- WHAT *IS* ALL THIS ...?
RMBL RMBL RMBL
RMBL RMBL

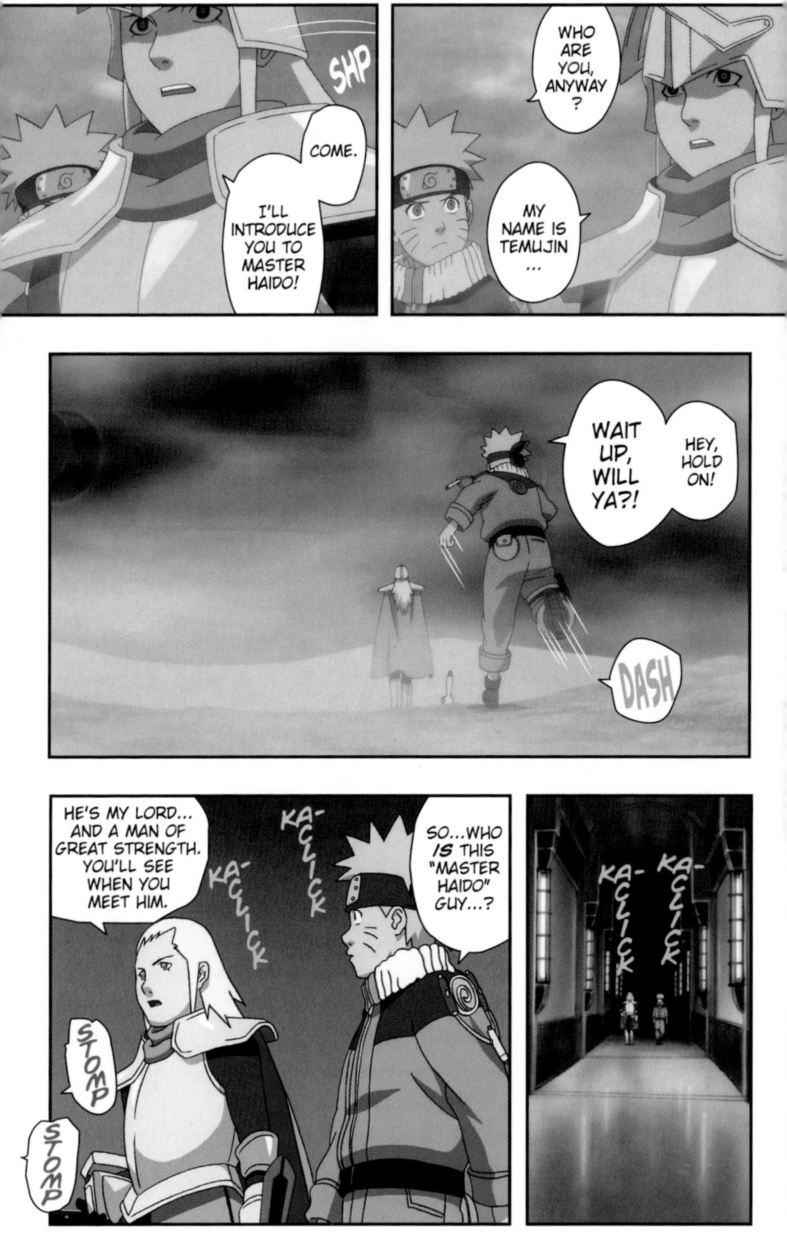
WHO ARE YOU, ANYWAY?
MY NAME IS TEMUJIN...
SHP
COME.
I'LL INTRODUCE YOU TO MASTER HAIDO!
HEY, HOLD ON!
WAIT UP, WILL YA?!
DASH
KA-CLICK
KA-CLICK
SO...WHO *IS* THIS "MASTER HAIDO" GUY...?
KA-CLICK
KA-CLICK
HE'S MY LORD... AND A MAN OF GREAT STRENGTH. YOU'LL SEE WHEN YOU MEET HIM.
STOMP
STOMP

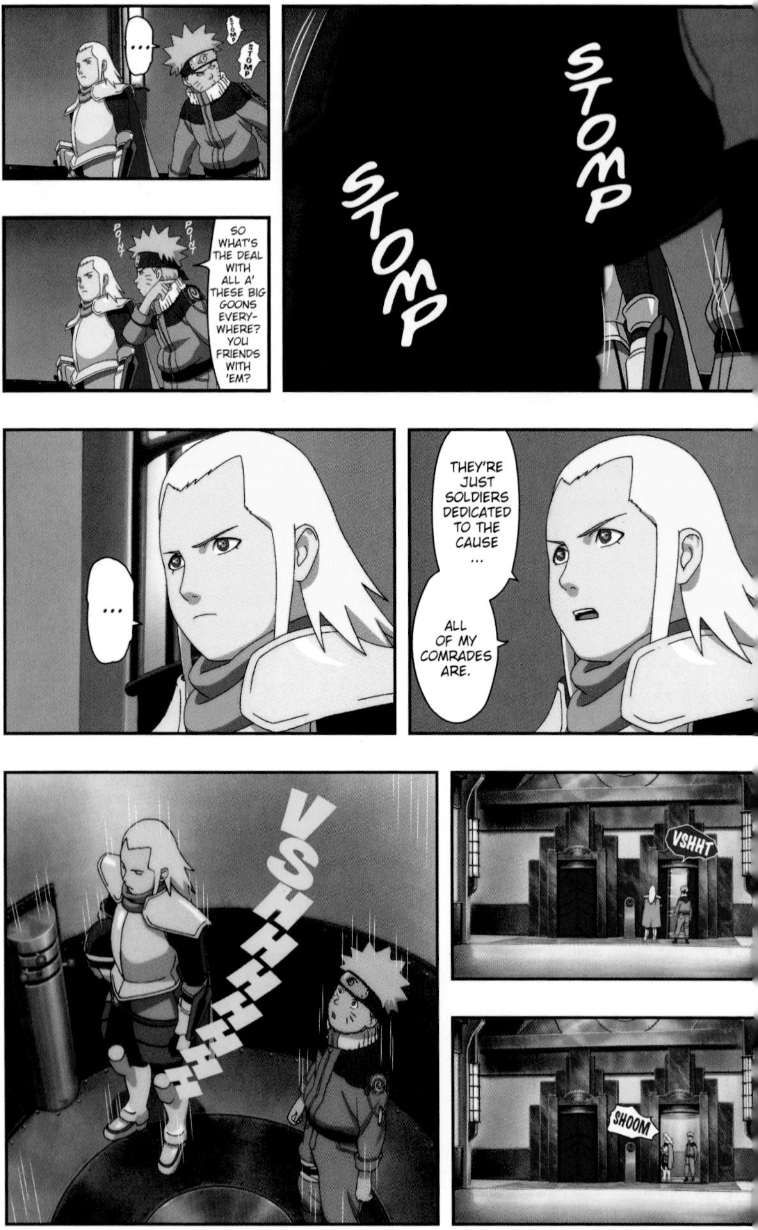
STOMP
STOMP
...
STOMP
STOMP
POINT
POINT
SO WHAT'S THE DEAL WITH ALL A' THESE BIG GOONS EVERY-WHERE? YOU FRIENDS WITH 'EM?
THEY'RE JUST SOLDIERS DEDICATED TO THE CAUSE...
ALL OF MY COMRADES ARE.
...
VSHHT
SHOOM
VSHHHHHHH

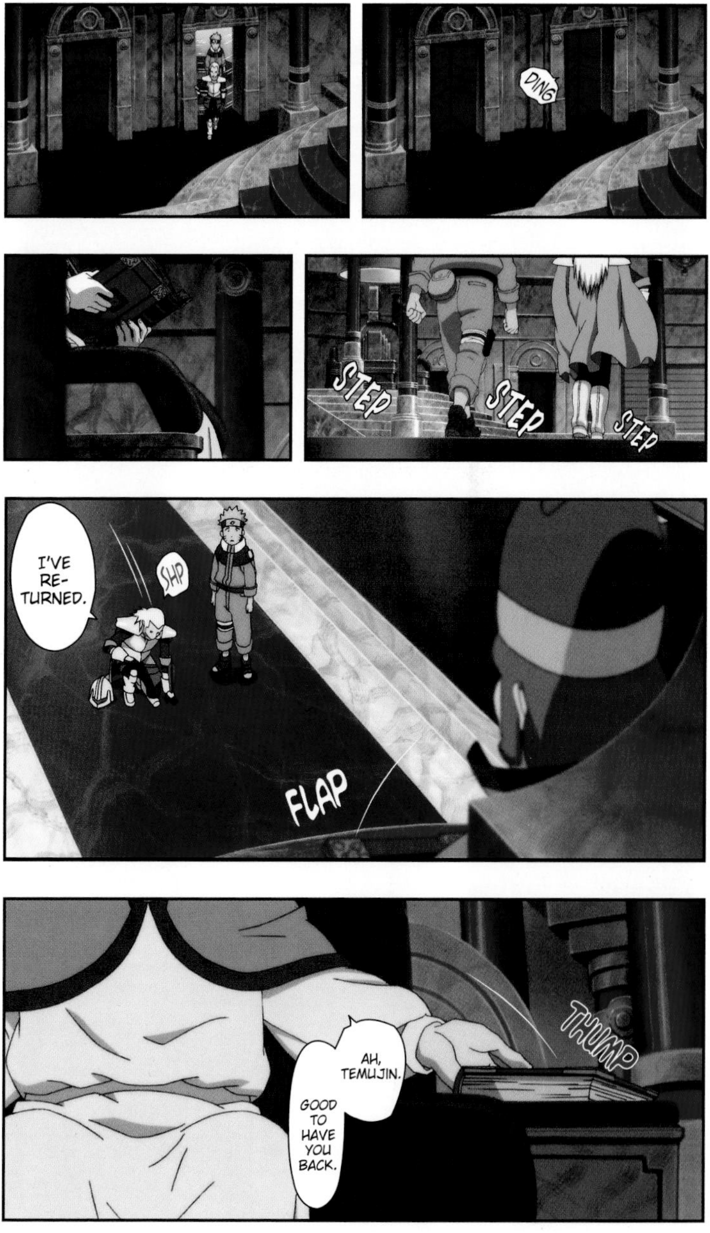
DING
STEP
STEP
STEP
I'VE RE-TURNED.
SHP
FLAP
THUMP
AH, TEMUJIN.
GOOD TO HAVE YOU BACK.

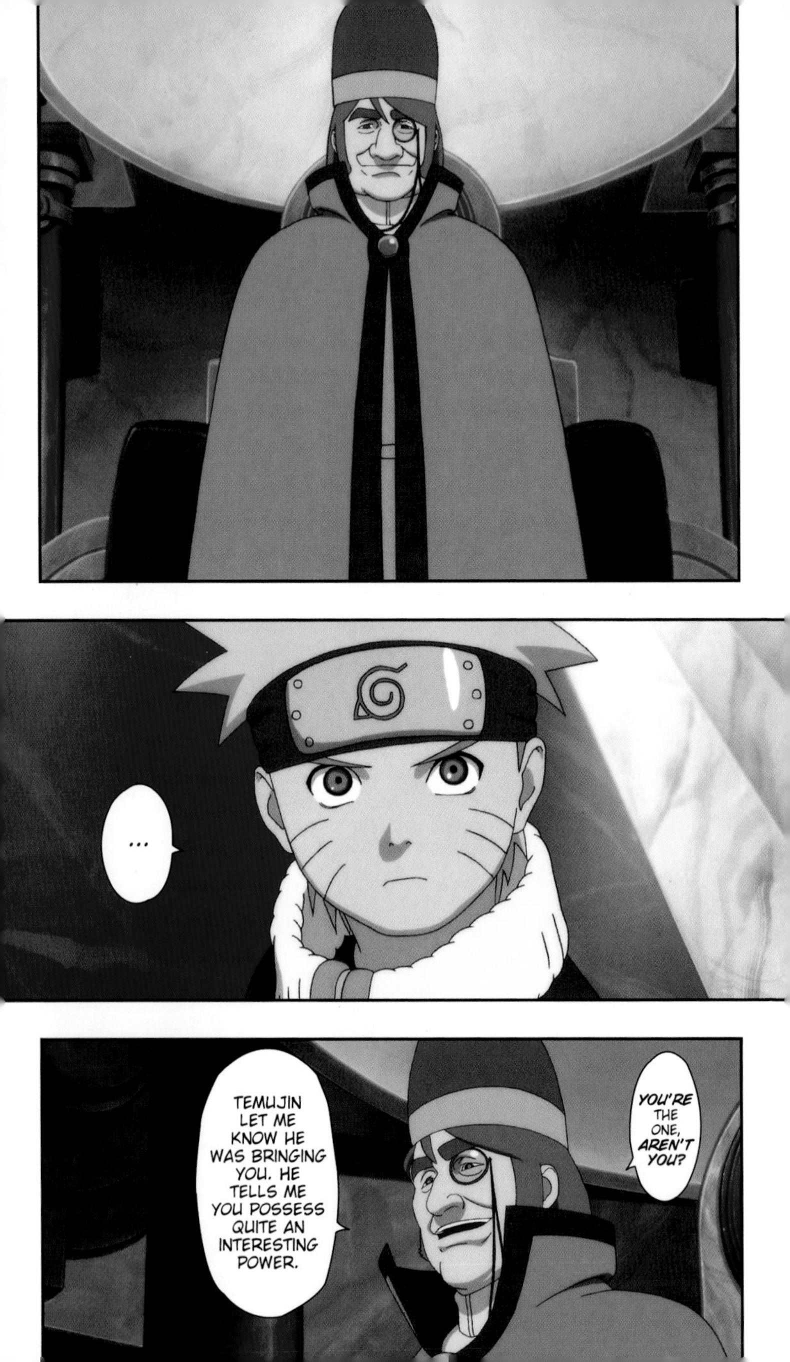
...
YOU'RE THE ONE, *AREN'T YOU?*
TEMUJIN LET ME KNOW HE WAS BRINGING YOU. HE TELLS ME YOU POSSESS QUITE AN INTERESTING POWER.

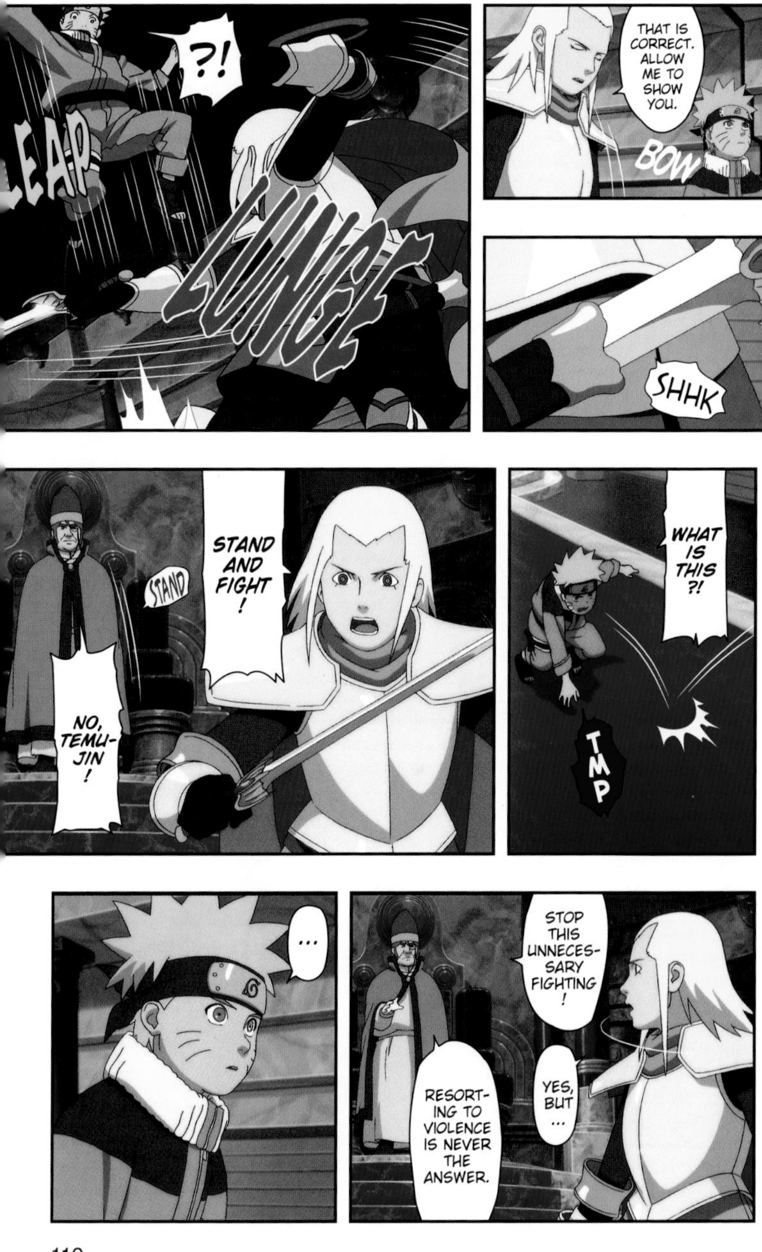
THAT IS CORRECT. ALLOW ME TO SHOW YOU.
BOW
SHHK
LUNGE
?!
LEAP
WHAT IS THIS ?!
TMP
STAND AND FIGHT !
STAND
NO, TEMUJIN !
STOP THIS UNNECES-SARY FIGHTING !
YES, BUT ...
RESORT-ING TO VIOLENCE IS NEVER THE ANSWER.
...

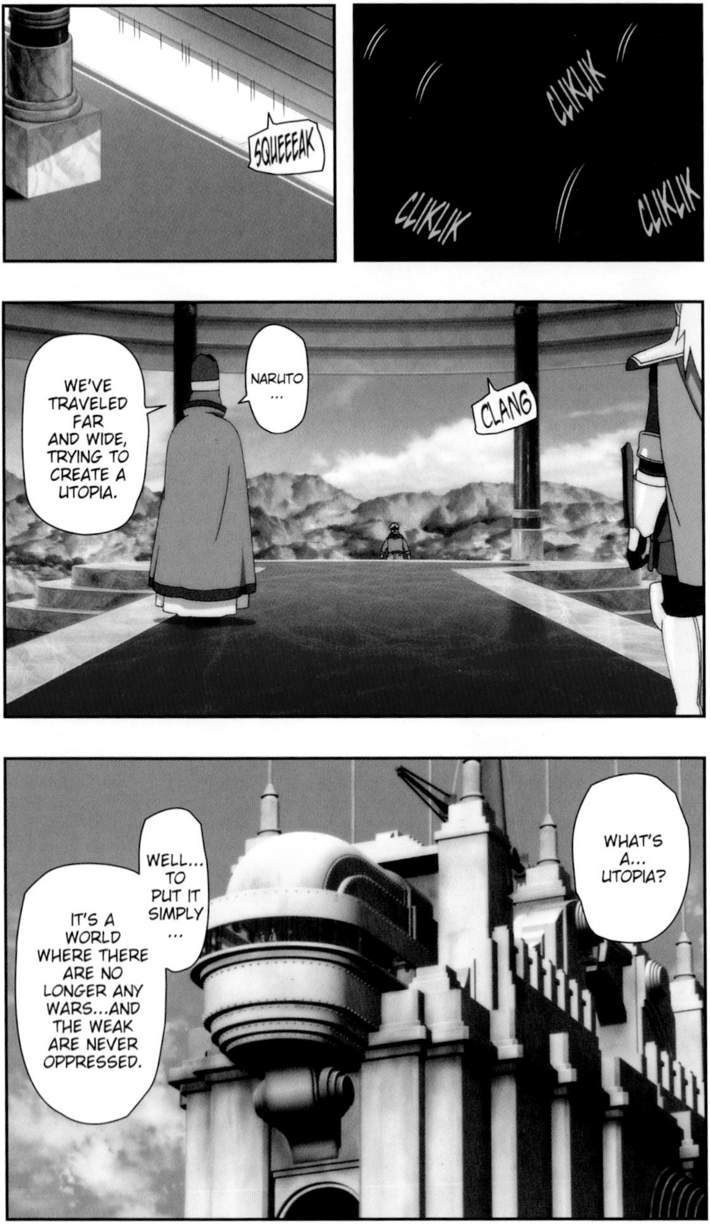
CLIKLIK
CLIKLIK
CLIKLIK
SQUEEEAK
CLANG
NARUTO …
WE'VE TRAVELED FAR AND WIDE, TRYING TO CREATE A UTOPIA.
WHAT'S A… UTOPIA?
WELL… TO PUT IT SIMPLY …
IT'S A WORLD WHERE THERE ARE NO LONGER ANY WARS…AND THE WEAK ARE NEVER OPPRESSED.

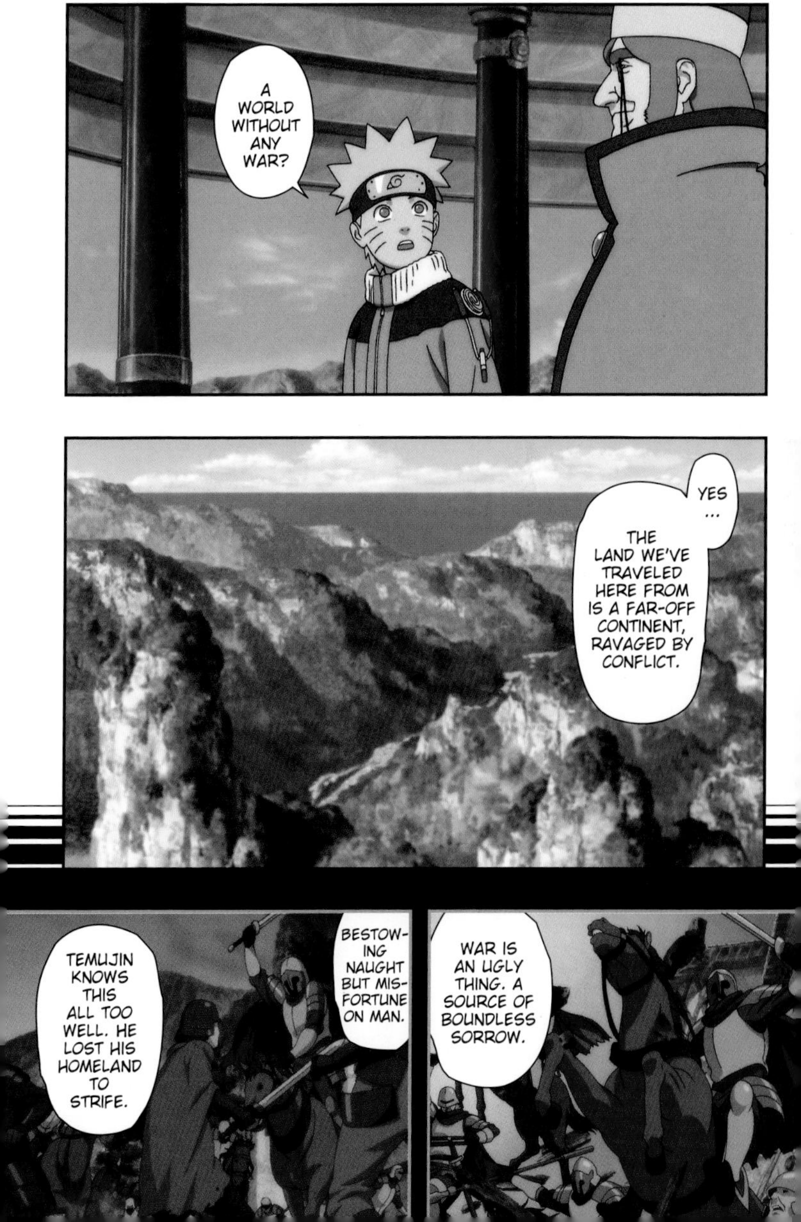
A WORLD WITHOUT ANY WAR?
YES ...
THE LAND WE'VE TRAVELED HERE FROM IS A FAR-OFF CONTINENT, RAVAGED BY CONFLICT.
WAR IS AN UGLY THING. A SOURCE OF BOUNDLESS SORROW.
BESTOW-ING NAUGHT BUT MIS-FORTUNE ON MAN.
TEMUJIN KNOWS THIS ALL TOO WELL. HE LOST HIS HOMELAND TO STRIFE.

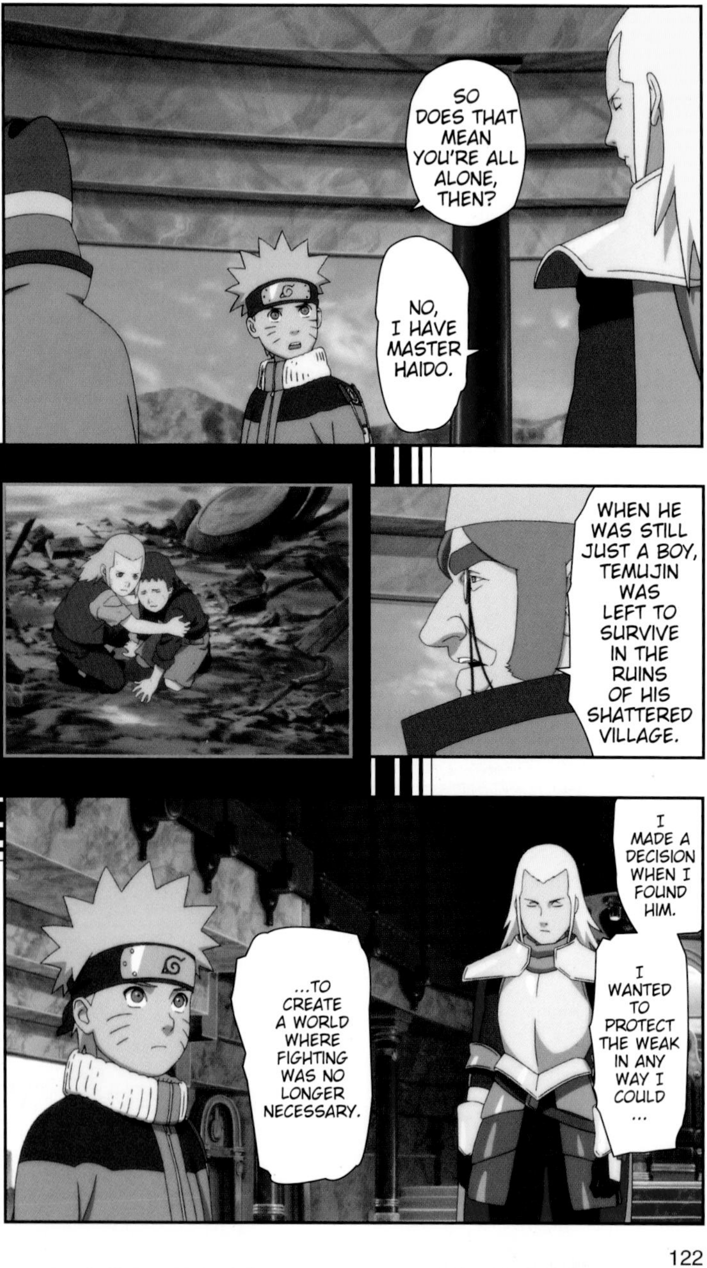
SO DOES THAT MEAN YOU'RE ALL ALONE, THEN?
NO, I HAVE MASTER HAIDO.
WHEN HE WAS STILL JUST A BOY, TEMUJIN WAS LEFT TO SURVIVE IN THE RUINS OF HIS SHATTERED VILLAGE.
I MADE A DECISION WHEN I FOUND HIM.
I WANTED TO PROTECT THE WEAK IN ANY WAY I COULD...
...TO CREATE A WORLD WHERE FIGHTING WAS NO LONGER NECESSARY.

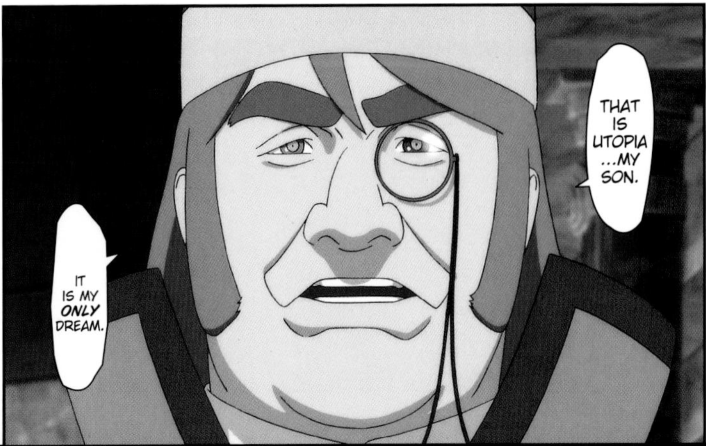
THAT IS UTOPIA ...MY SON.
IT IS MY *ONLY* DREAM.
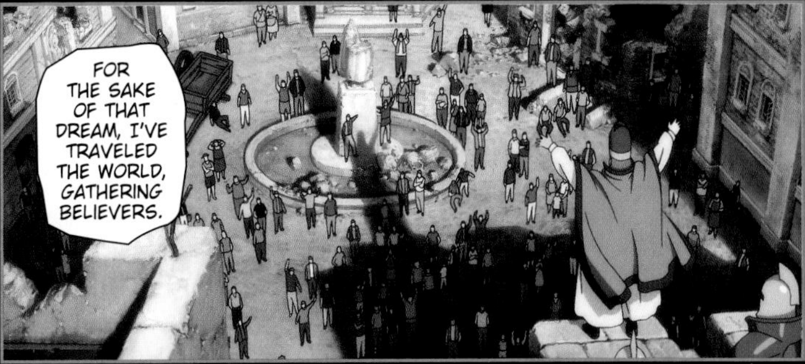
FOR THE SAKE OF THAT DREAM, I'VE TRAVELED THE WORLD, GATHERING BELIEVERS.
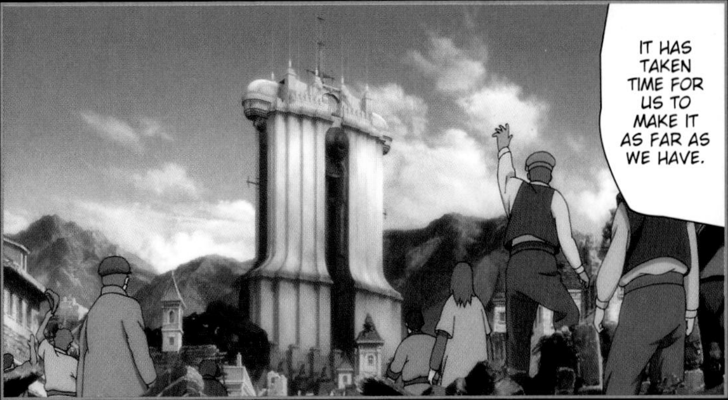
IT HAS TAKEN TIME FOR US TO MAKE IT AS FAR AS WE HAVE.

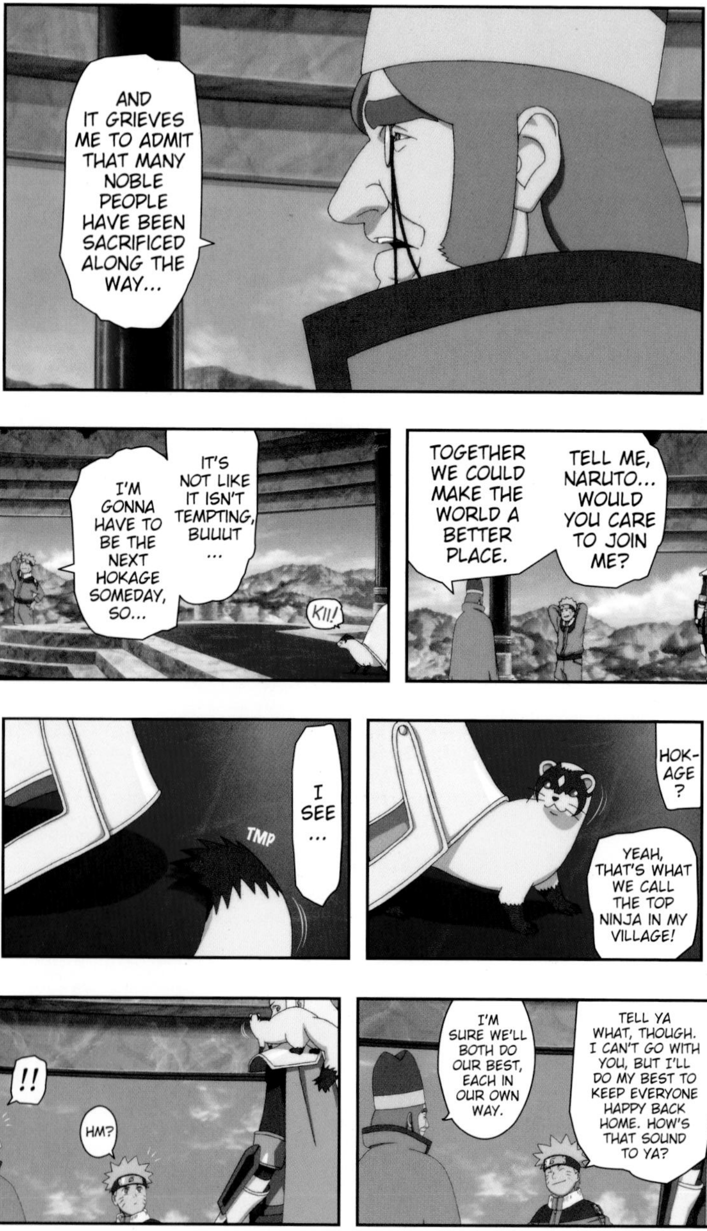
AND IT GRIEVES ME TO ADMIT THAT MANY NOBLE PEOPLE HAVE BEEN SACRIFICED ALONG THE WAY...
TELL ME, NARUTO... WOULD YOU CARE TO JOIN ME?
TOGETHER WE COULD MAKE THE WORLD A BETTER PLACE.
IT'S NOT LIKE IT ISN'T TEMPTING, BUUUT...
I'M GONNA HAVE TO BE THE NEXT HOKAGE SOMEDAY, SO...
KII!
HOK-AGE?
YEAH, THAT'S WHAT WE CALL THE TOP NINJA IN MY VILLAGE!
I SEE...
TMP
TELL YA WHAT, THOUGH. I CAN'T GO WITH YOU, BUT I'LL DO MY BEST TO KEEP EVERYONE HAPPY BACK HOME. HOW'S THAT SOUND TO YA?
I'M SURE WE'LL BOTH DO OUR BEST, EACH IN OUR OWN WAY.
RSTL
!!
HM?

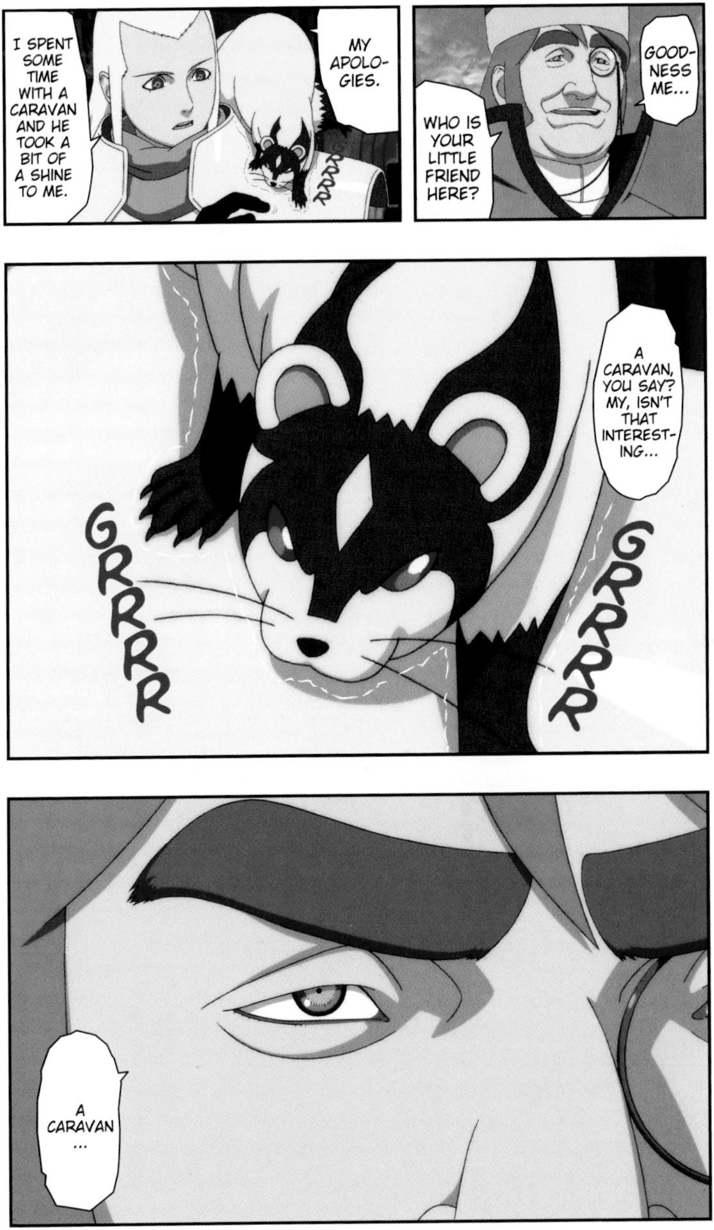
GOODNESS ME...
WHO IS YOUR LITTLE FRIEND HERE?
MY APOLOGIES.
I SPENT SOME TIME WITH A CARAVAN AND HE TOOK A BIT OF A SHINE TO ME.
GRRRR
A CARAVAN, YOU SAY? MY, ISN'T THAT INTERESTING...
GRRRR
GRRRR
A CARAVAN...

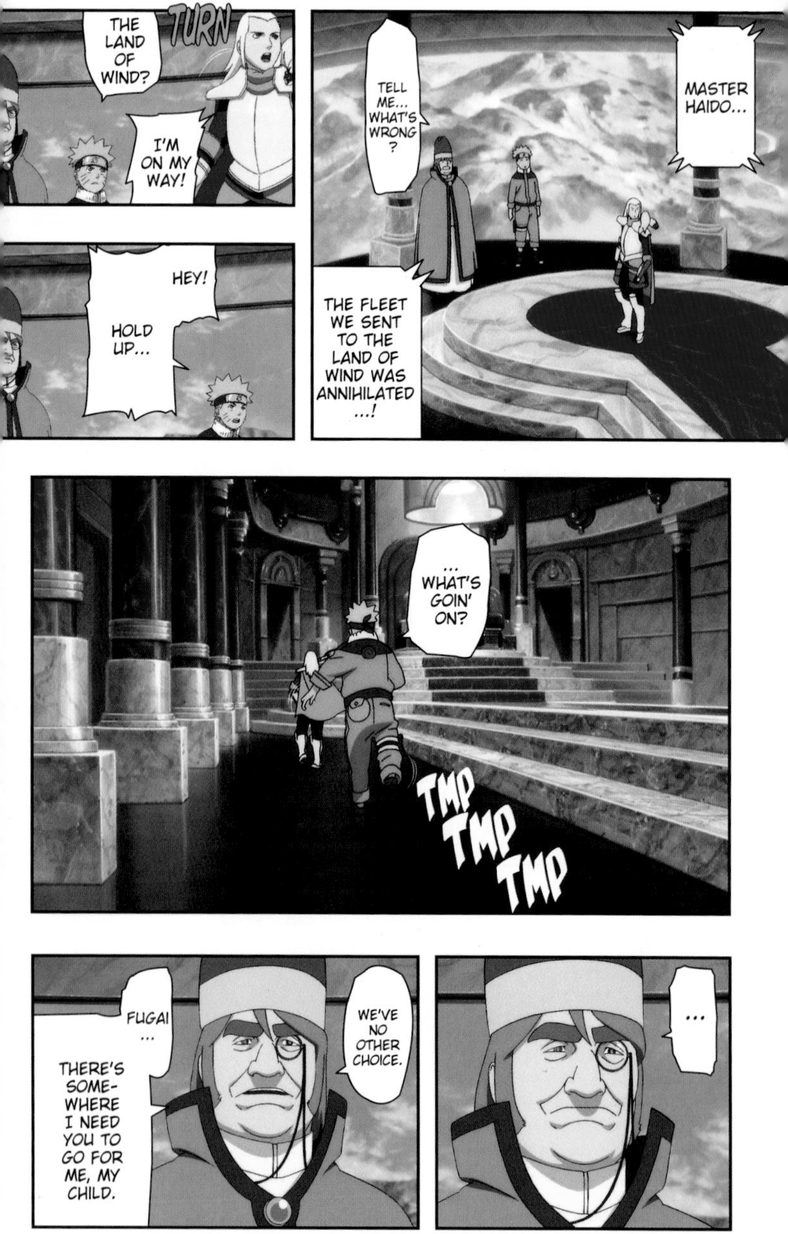
MASTER HAIDO...
TELL ME... WHAT'S WRONG?
THE FLEET WE SENT TO THE LAND OF WIND WAS ANNIHILATED...!
TURN
THE LAND OF WIND?
I'M ON MY WAY!
HEY!
HOLD UP...
...WHAT'S GOIN' ON?
TMP TMP TMP
...
WE'VE NO OTHER CHOICE.
FUGAI...
THERE'S SOMEWHERE I NEED YOU TO GO FOR ME, MY CHILD.

Chapter 4: Gaara and the Attack

愛

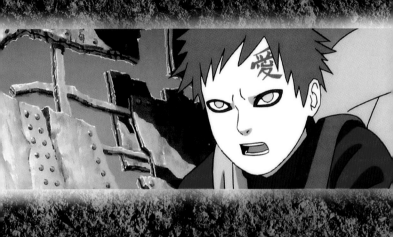

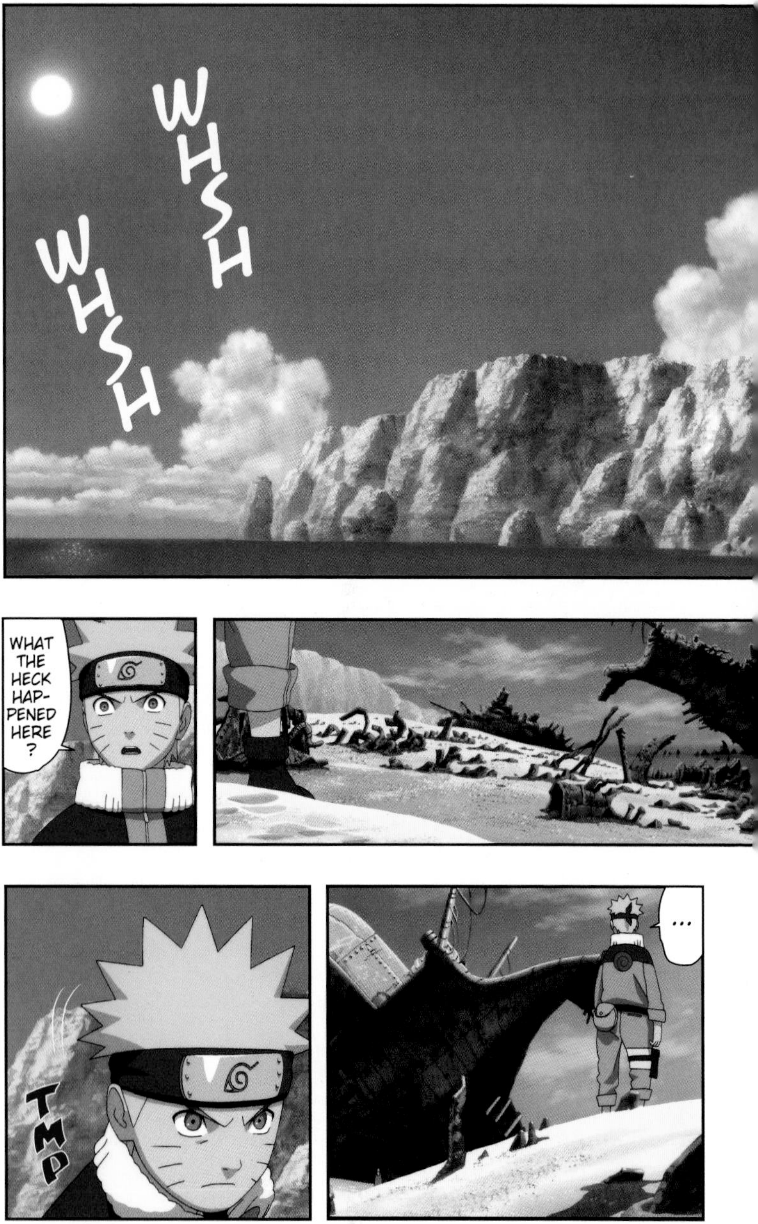
WHSH
WHSH
WHAT THE HECK HAP-PENED HERE?
...
TMP

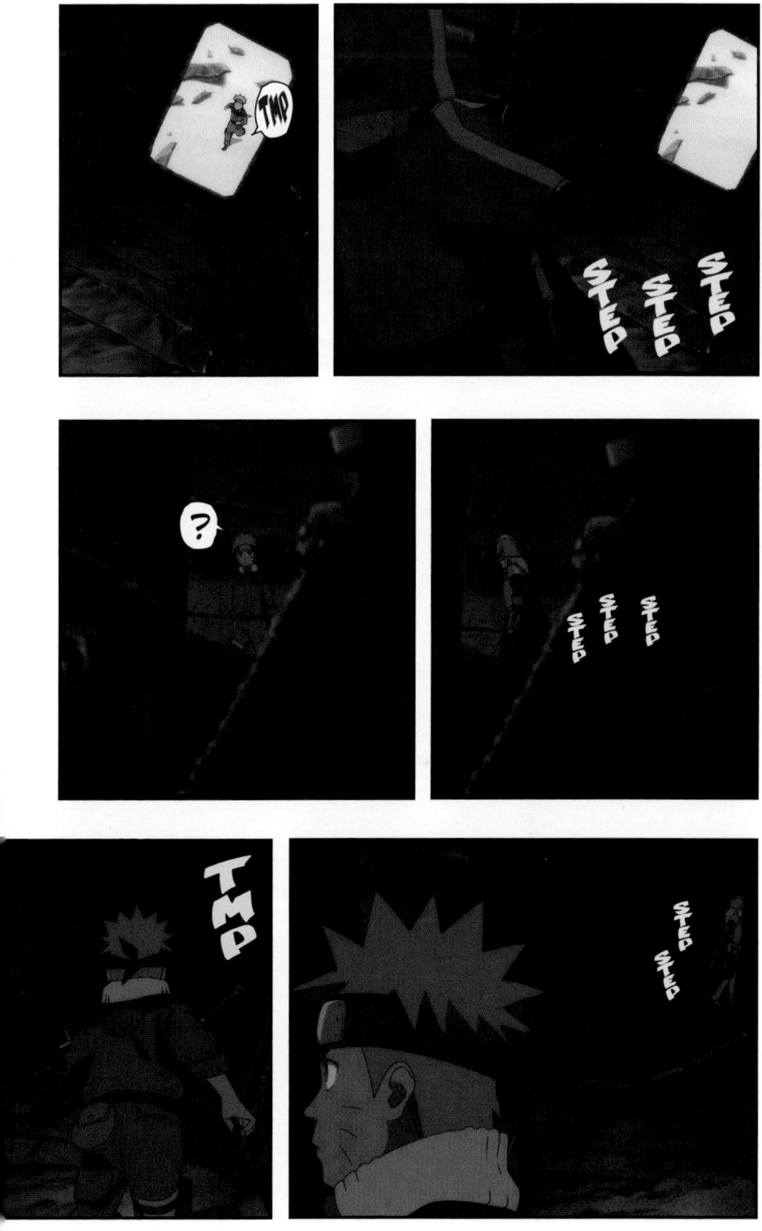
STEP STEP STEP
TMP
STEP STEP STEP
?
STEP STEP
TMP

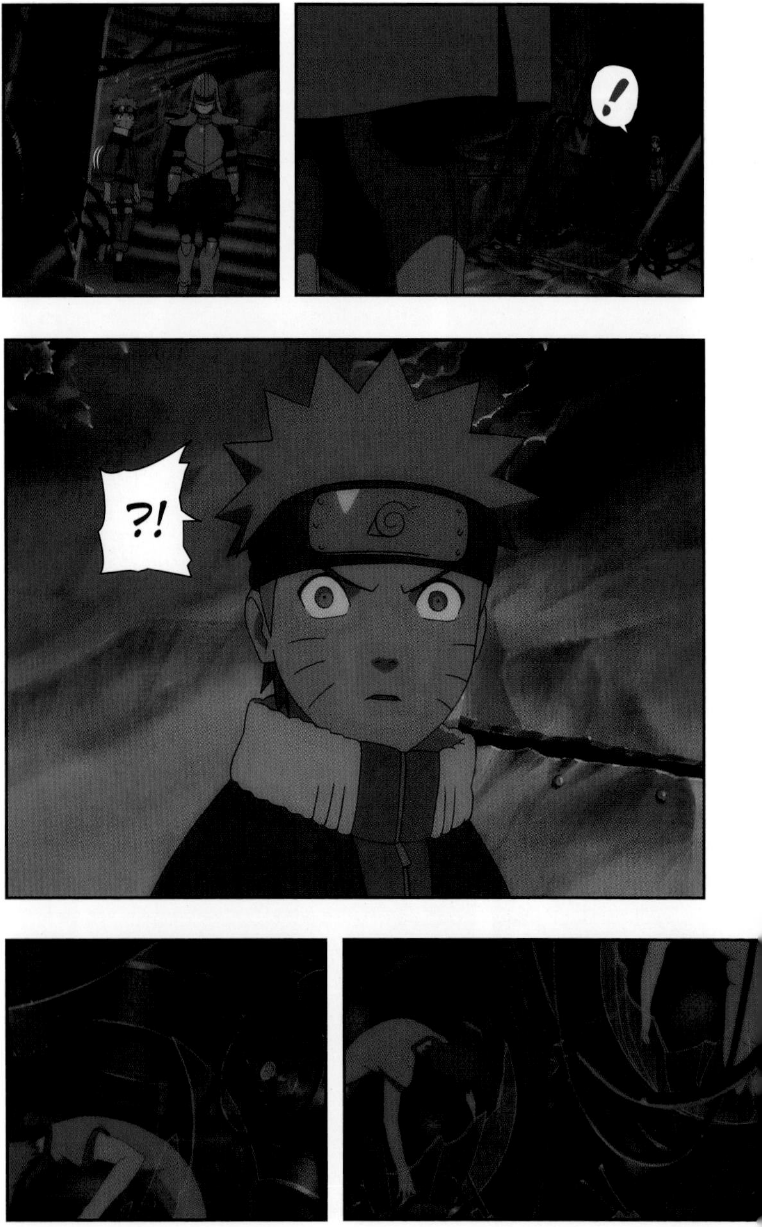
!
?!

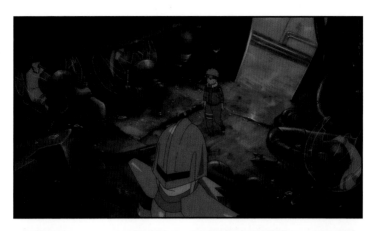

HOLD UP! WHAT'S ALL THIS ABOUT ?!

...

WELL ?!

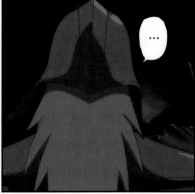

...

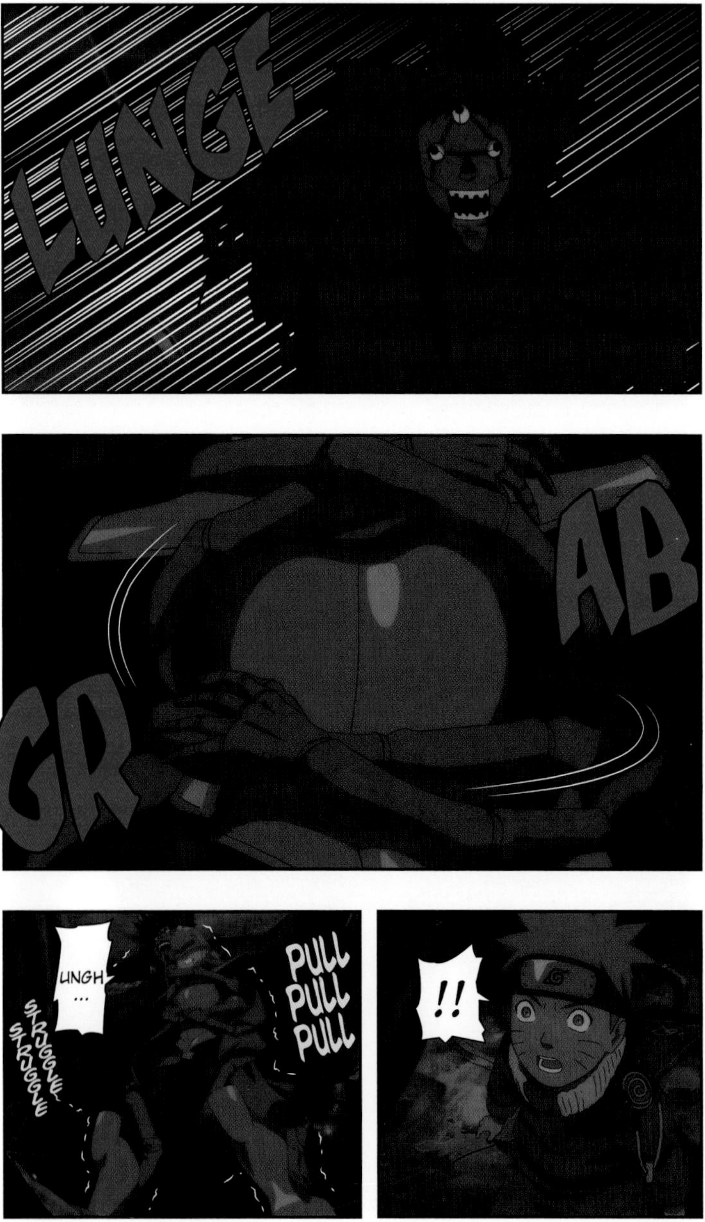
LUNGE
GRAB
!!
PULL PULL PULL
UNGH...
STRUGGLE STRUGGLE

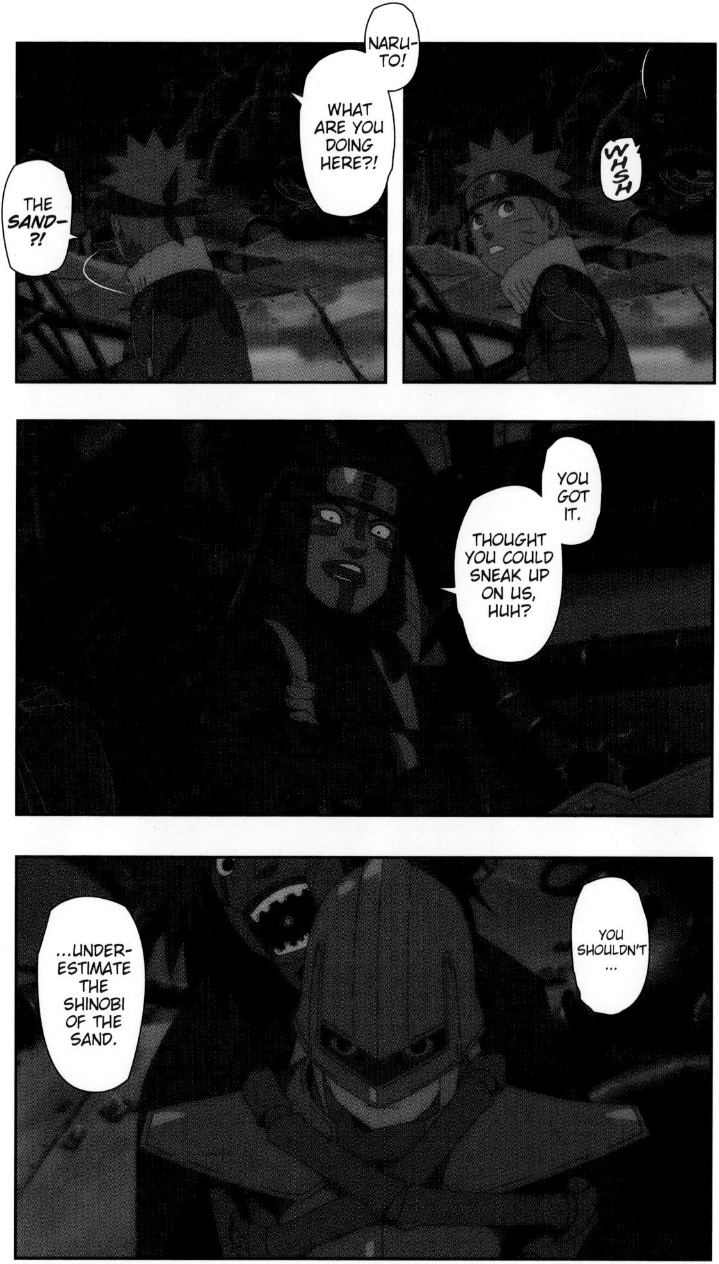
WHSH
NARU-TO!
WHAT ARE YOU DOING HERE?!
THE SAND-?!
YOU GOT IT.
THOUGHT YOU COULD SNEAK UP ON US, HUH?
YOU SHOULDN'T...
...UNDER-ESTIMATE THE SHINOBI OF THE SAND.

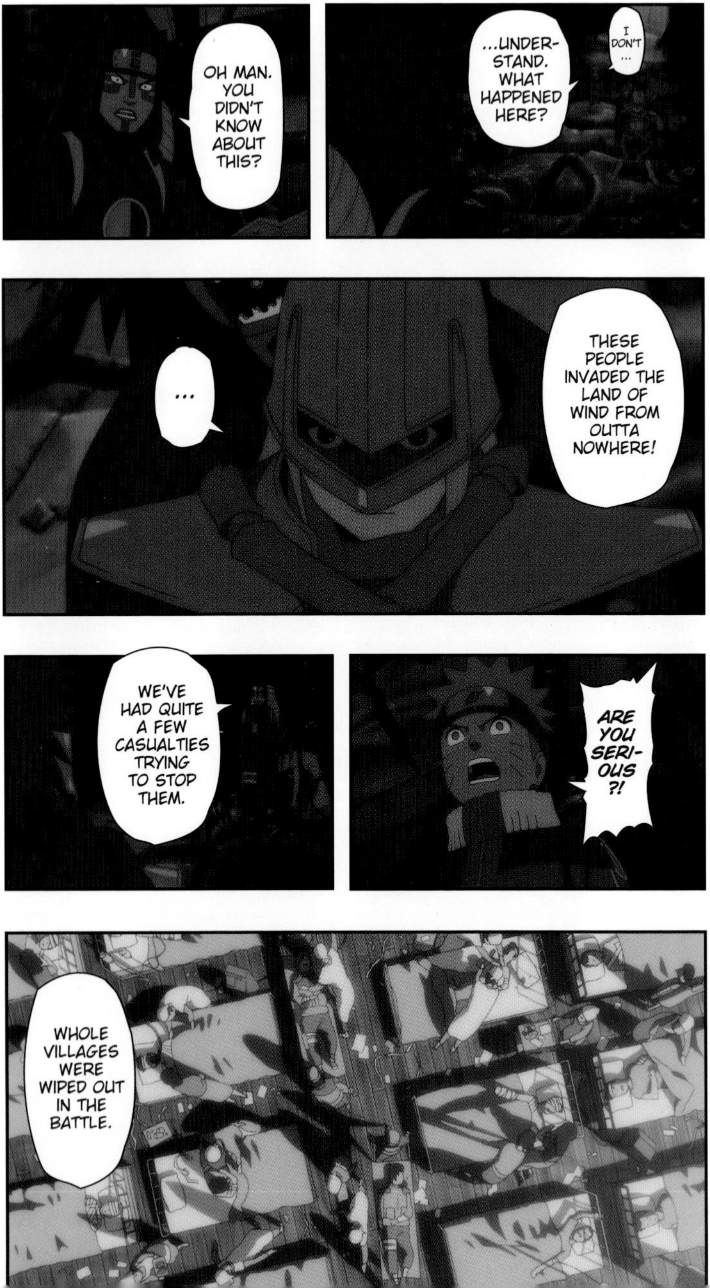
I DON'T...
...UNDERSTAND. WHAT HAPPENED HERE?
OH MAN. YOU DIDN'T KNOW ABOUT THIS?
THESE PEOPLE INVADED THE LAND OF WIND FROM OUTTA NOWHERE!
...
ARE YOU SERIOUS?!
WE'VE HAD QUITE A FEW CASUALTIES TRYING TO STOP THEM.
WHOLE VILLAGES WERE WIPED OUT IN THE BATTLE.

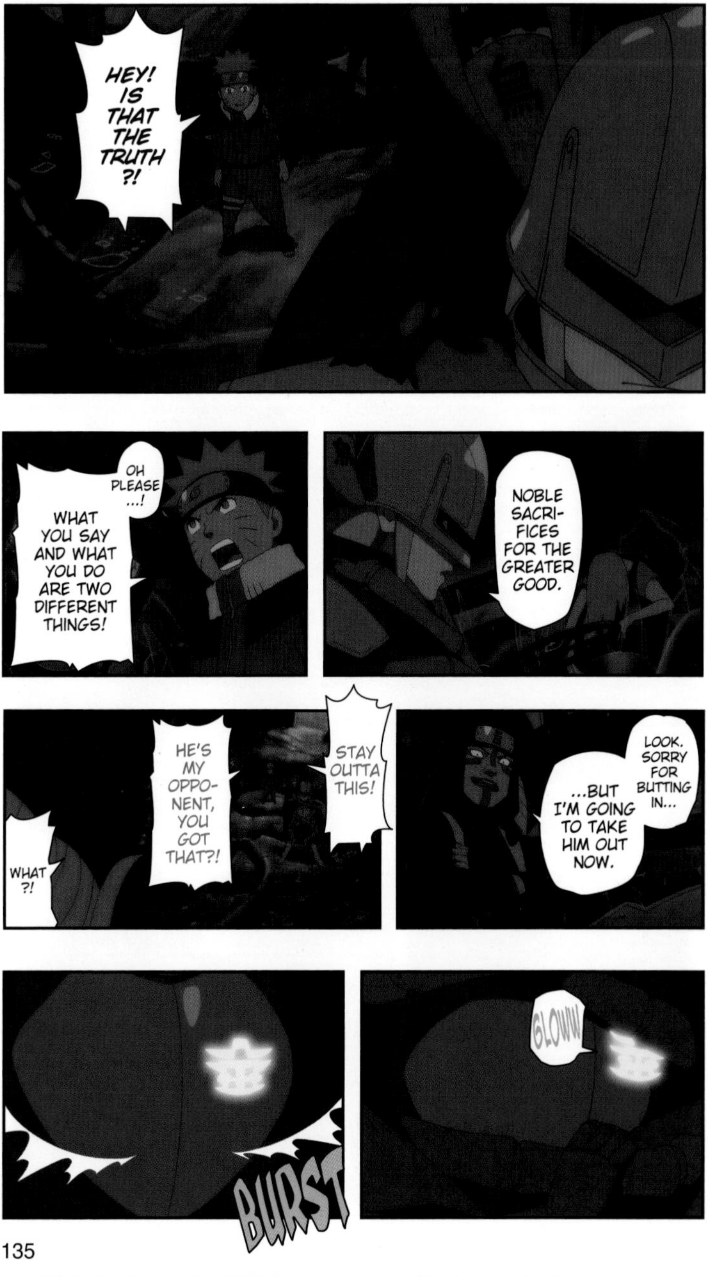
HEY! IS THAT THE TRUTH?!
NOBLE SACRI-FICES FOR THE GREATER GOOD.
OH PLEASE...!
WHAT YOU SAY AND WHAT YOU DO ARE TWO DIFFERENT THINGS!
LOOK. SORRY FOR BUTTING IN...
...BUT I'M GOING TO TAKE HIM OUT NOW.
STAY OUTTA THIS!
HE'S MY OPPO-NENT, YOU GOT THAT?!
WHAT?!
GLOWW
BURST

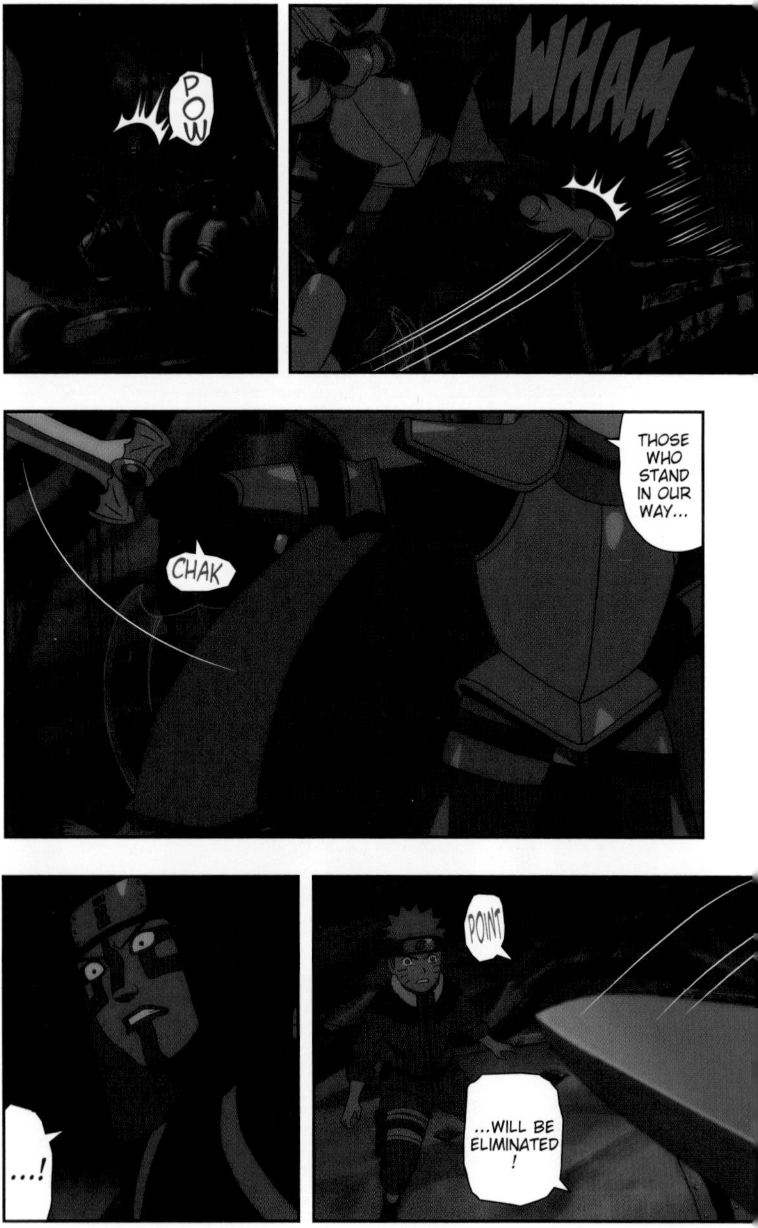
WHAM
POW
THOSE WHO STAND IN OUR WAY...
CHAK
POINT
...WILL BE ELIMINATED!
...!

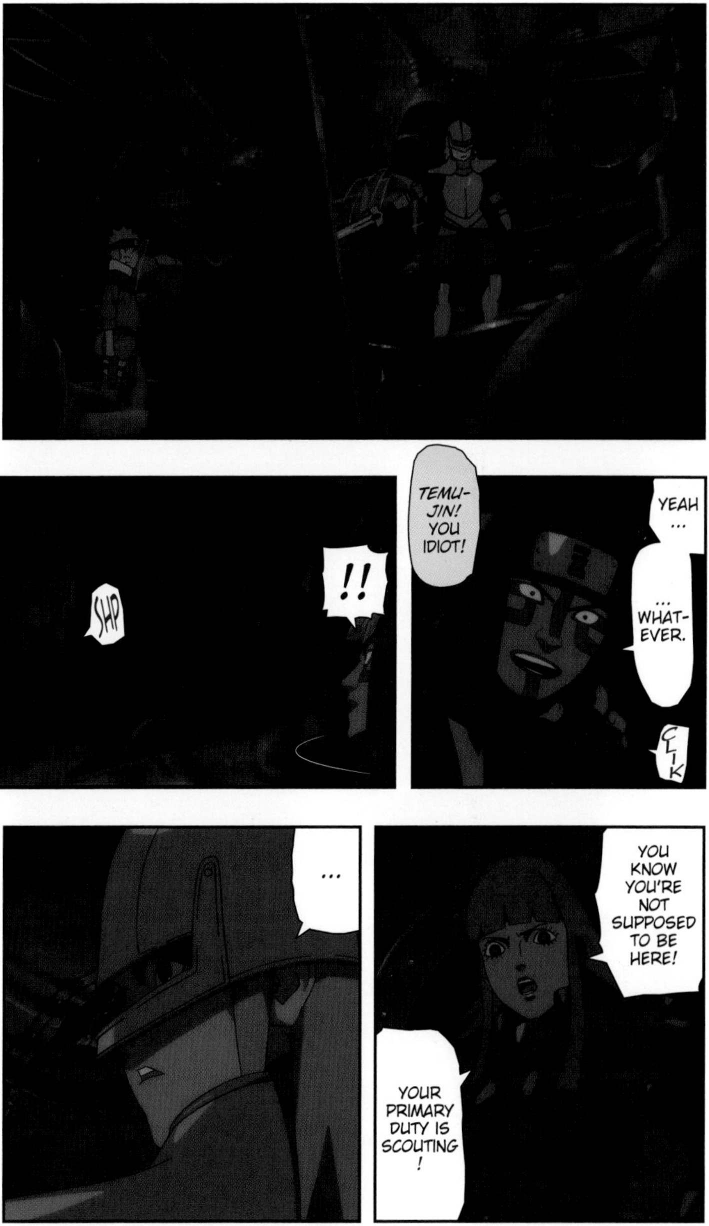
TEMUJIN! YOU IDIOT!
YEAH...
...WHATEVER.
CLIK
!!
SHP
YOU KNOW YOU'RE NOT SUPPOSED TO BE HERE!
YOUR PRIMARY DUTY IS SCOUTING!
...

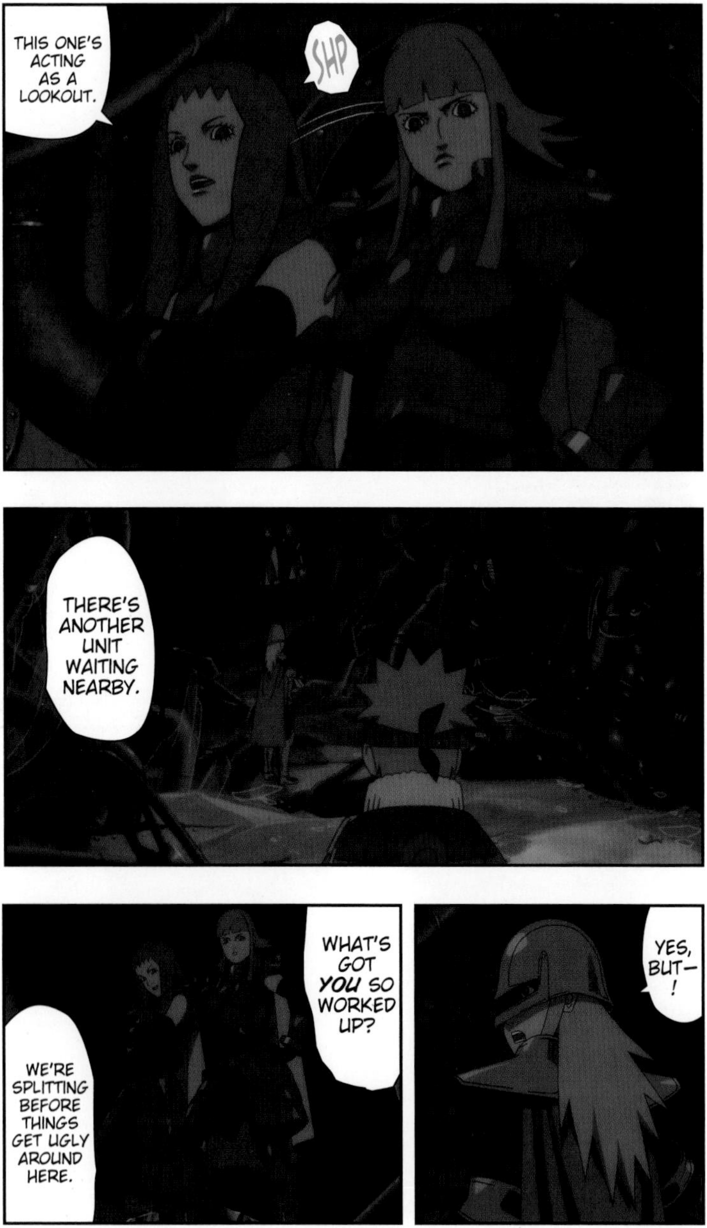
SHP
THIS ONE'S ACTING AS A LOOKOUT.
THERE'S ANOTHER UNIT WAITING NEARBY.
YES, BUT—!
WHAT'S GOT *YOU* SO WORKED UP?
WE'RE SPLITTING BEFORE THINGS GET UGLY AROUND HERE.

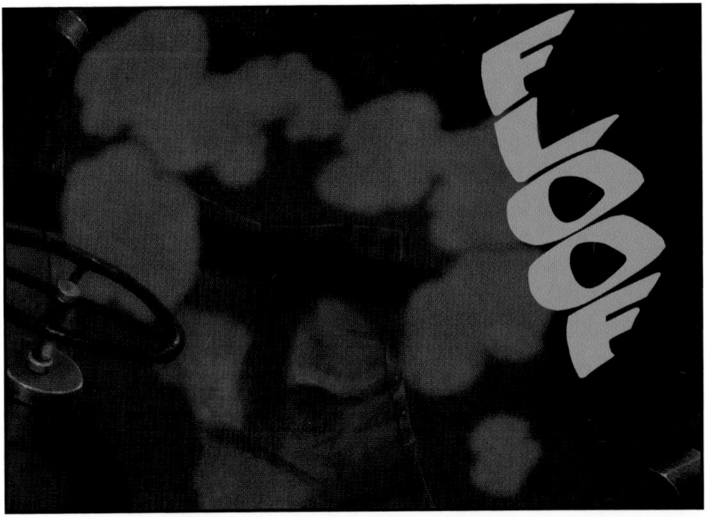
FLOOF
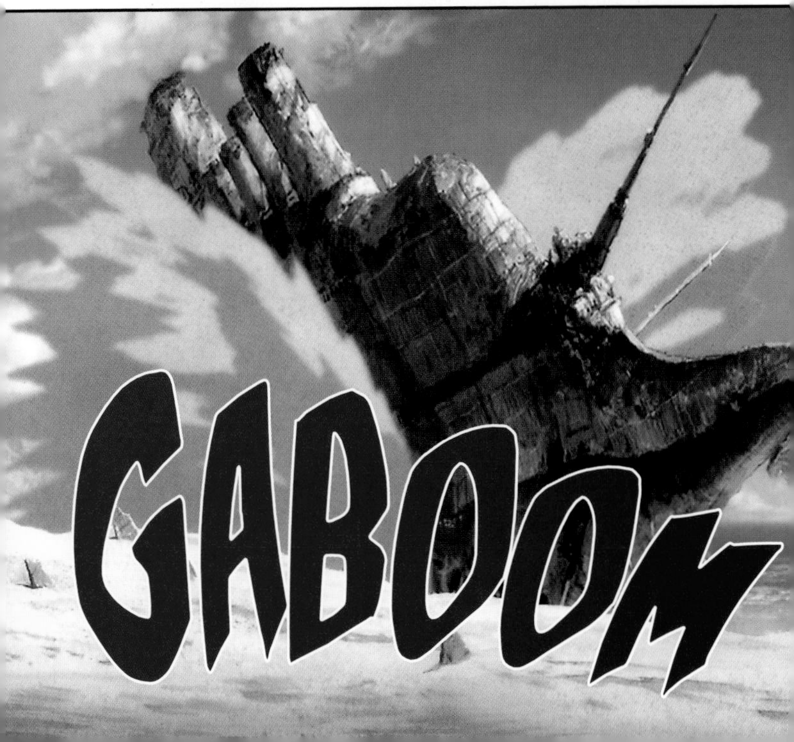
GABOOM

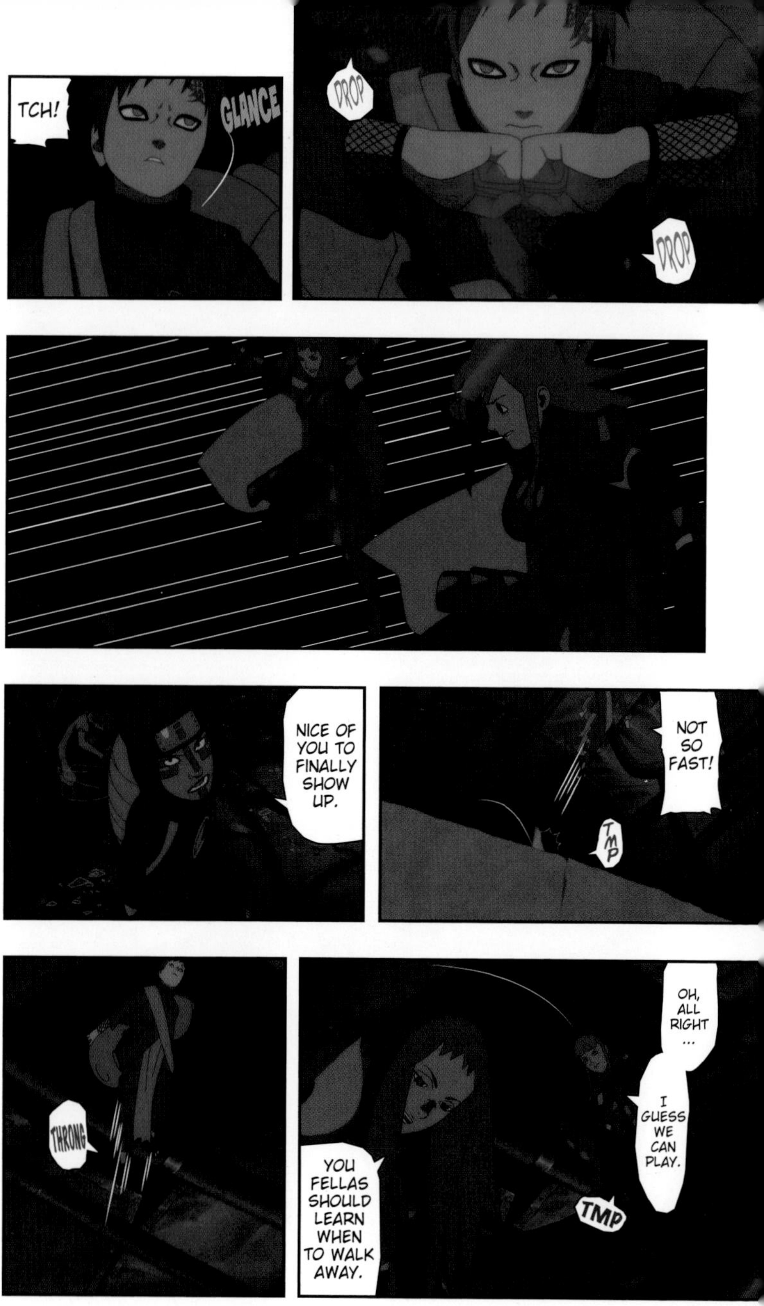
DROP
DROP
TCH!
GLANCE
NOT SO FAST!
TMP
NICE OF YOU TO FINALLY SHOW UP.
OH, ALL RIGHT...
I GUESS WE CAN PLAY.
TMP
YOU FELLAS SHOULD LEARN WHEN TO WALK AWAY.
THRONG

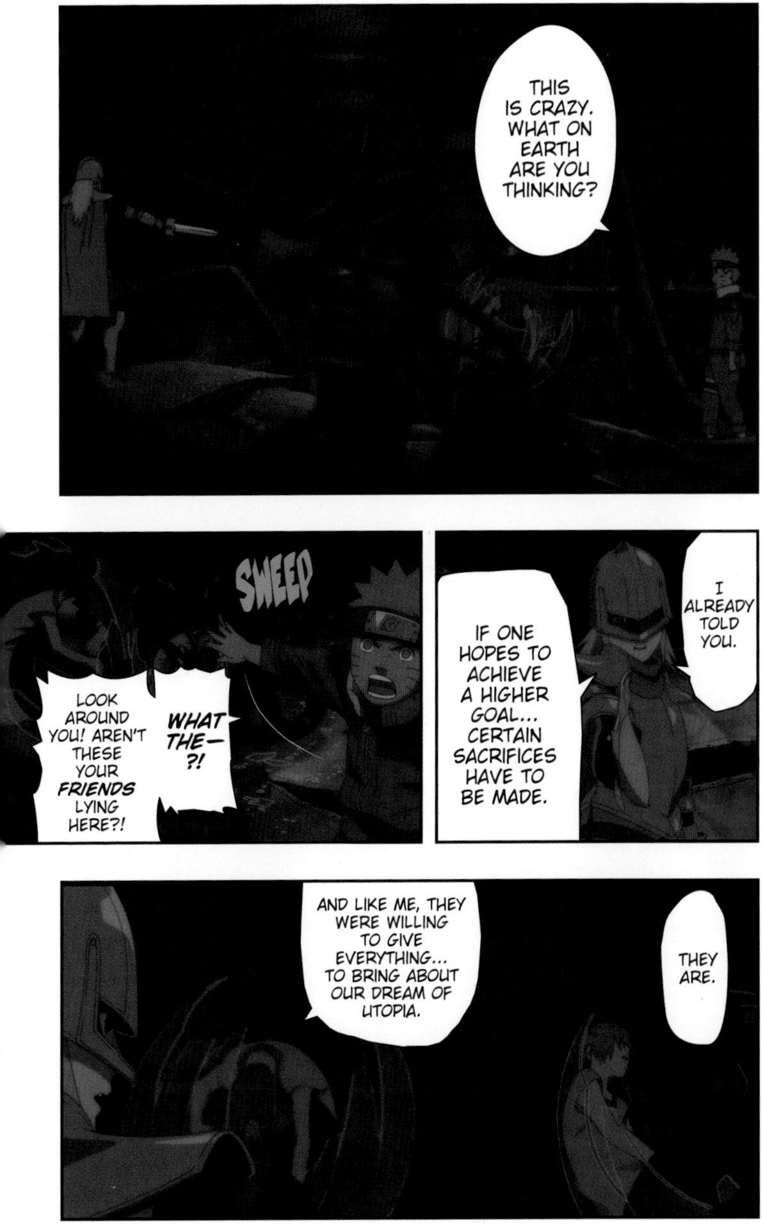
THIS IS CRAZY. WHAT ON EARTH ARE YOU THINKING?
I ALREADY TOLD YOU.
IF ONE HOPES TO ACHIEVE A HIGHER GOAL... CERTAIN SACRIFICES HAVE TO BE MADE.
SWEEP
WHAT THE—?!
LOOK AROUND YOU! AREN'T THESE YOUR FRIENDS LYING HERE?!
THEY ARE.
AND LIKE ME, THEY WERE WILLING TO GIVE EVERYTHING... TO BRING ABOUT OUR DREAM OF UTOPIA.

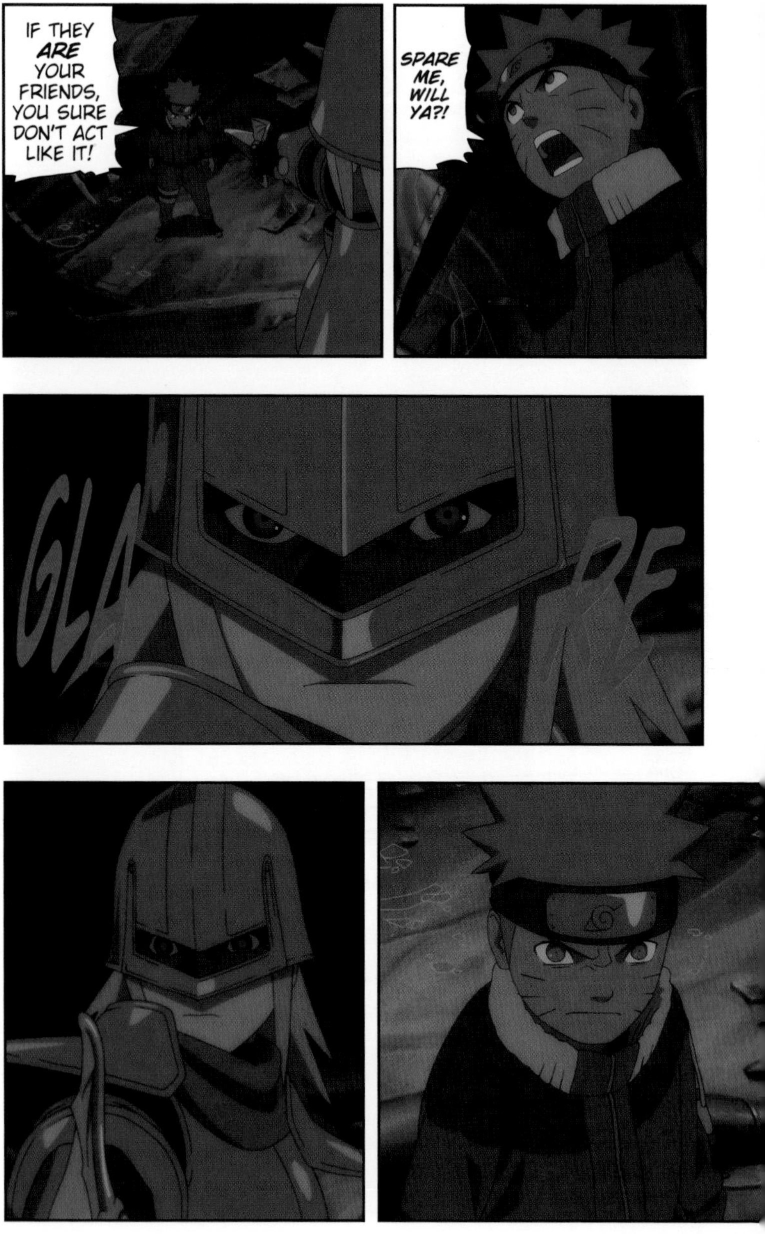
SPARE ME, WILL YA?!
IF THEY ARE YOUR FRIENDS, YOU SURE DON'T ACT LIKE IT!
GLARE

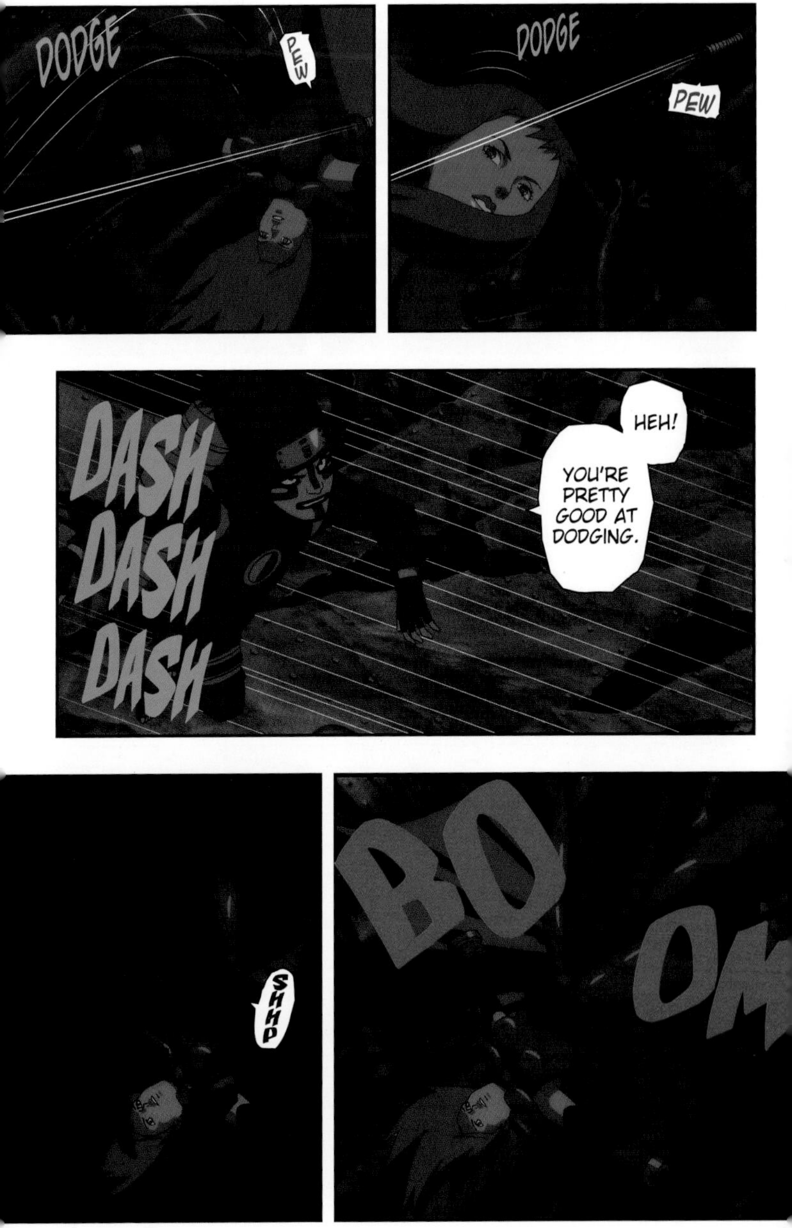

DODGE
PEW
DODGE
PEW
HEH!
YOU'RE PRETTY GOOD AT DODGING.
DASH DASH DASH
BOOM
SHHP

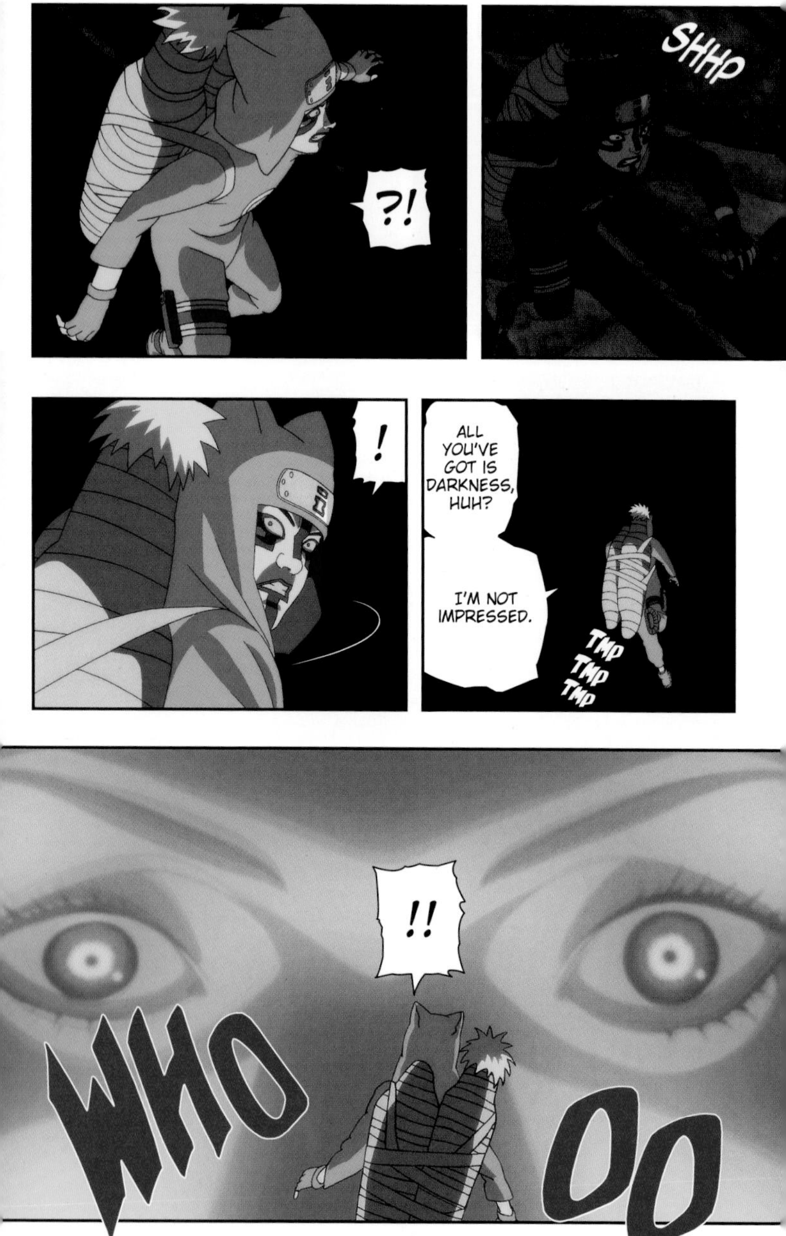
SHHP
?!
ALL YOU'VE GOT IS DARKNESS, HUH?
I'M NOT IMPRESSED.
TMP TMP TMP
!
!!
WHOOO

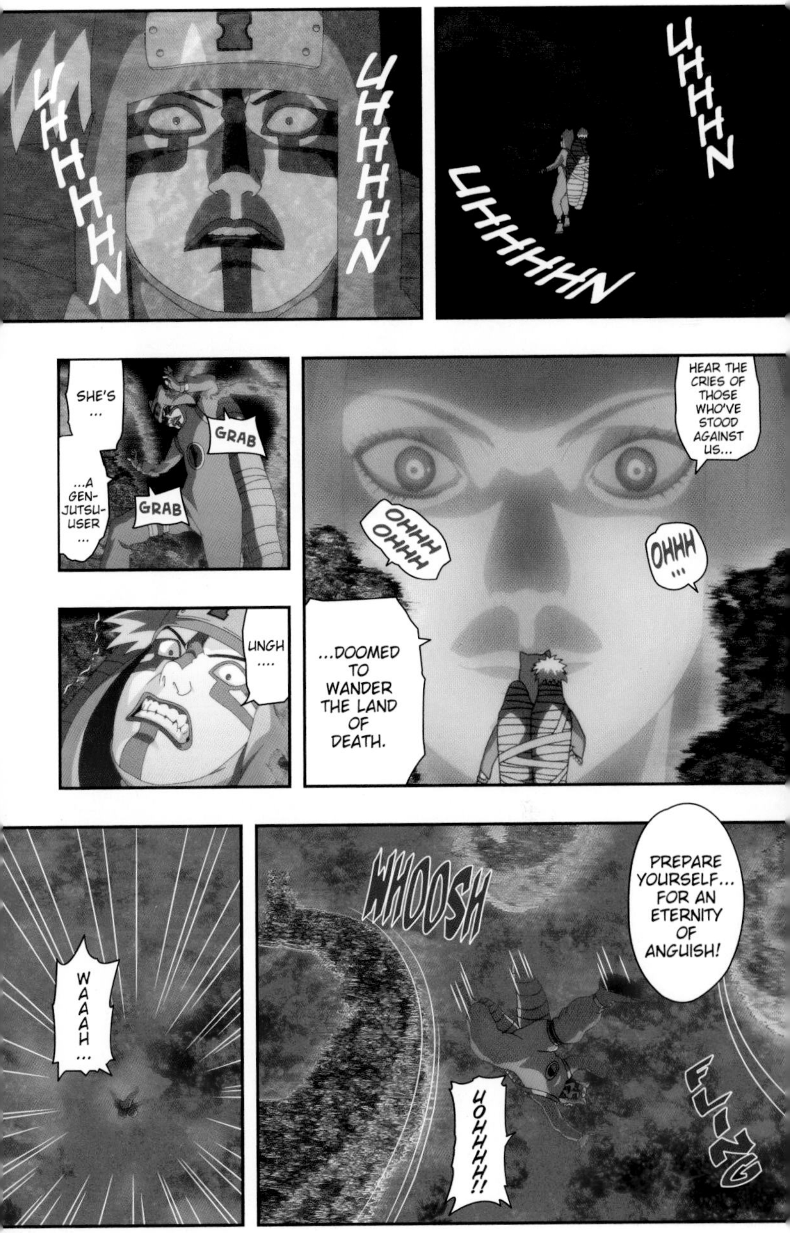
UHHHN
UHHHHHN
UHHHHHN
UHHHHHN
HEAR THE CRIES OF THOSE WHO'VE STOOD AGAINST US...
OHHH...
OHHH OHHH
...DOOMED TO WANDER THE LAND OF DEATH.
SHE'S...
GRAB
GRAB
...A GEN-JUTSU-USER...
UNGH....
PREPARE YOURSELF... FOR AN ETERNITY OF ANGUISH!
WHOOSH
FLING
UOHHHH!!
WAAAH...

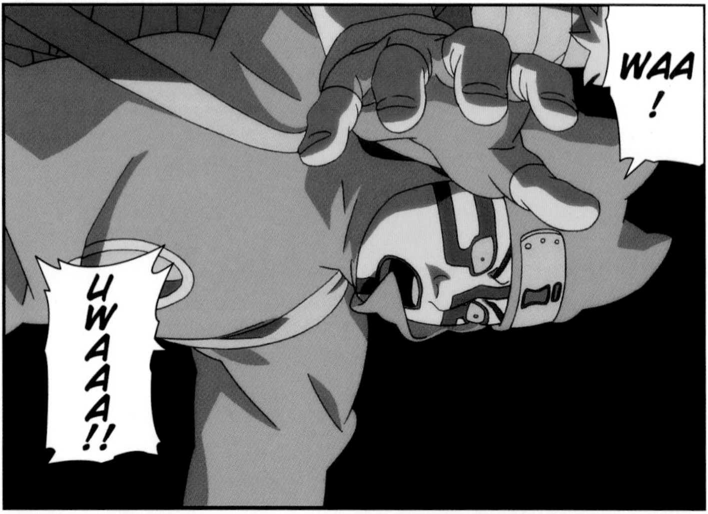
WAA!
UWAAAA!!

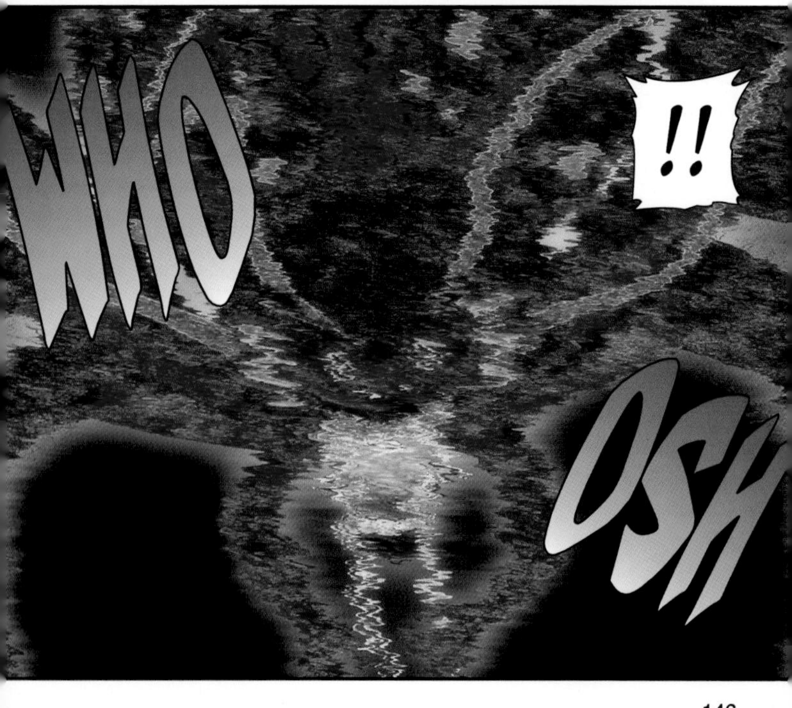
!!
WHO
OSH

RMBL RMBL RMBL RMBL
SPROUT
?!
SPROUT
WRAP
SHWIRL
POOF
CHOMP
CHOMP
CHOMP
URGH
CHOMP
CHOMP

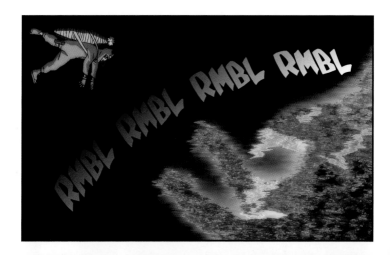

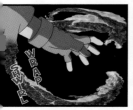

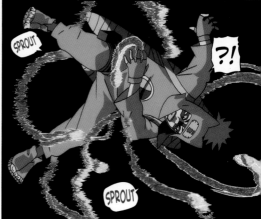

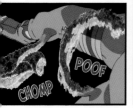

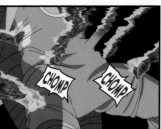

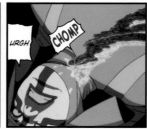

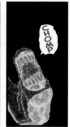

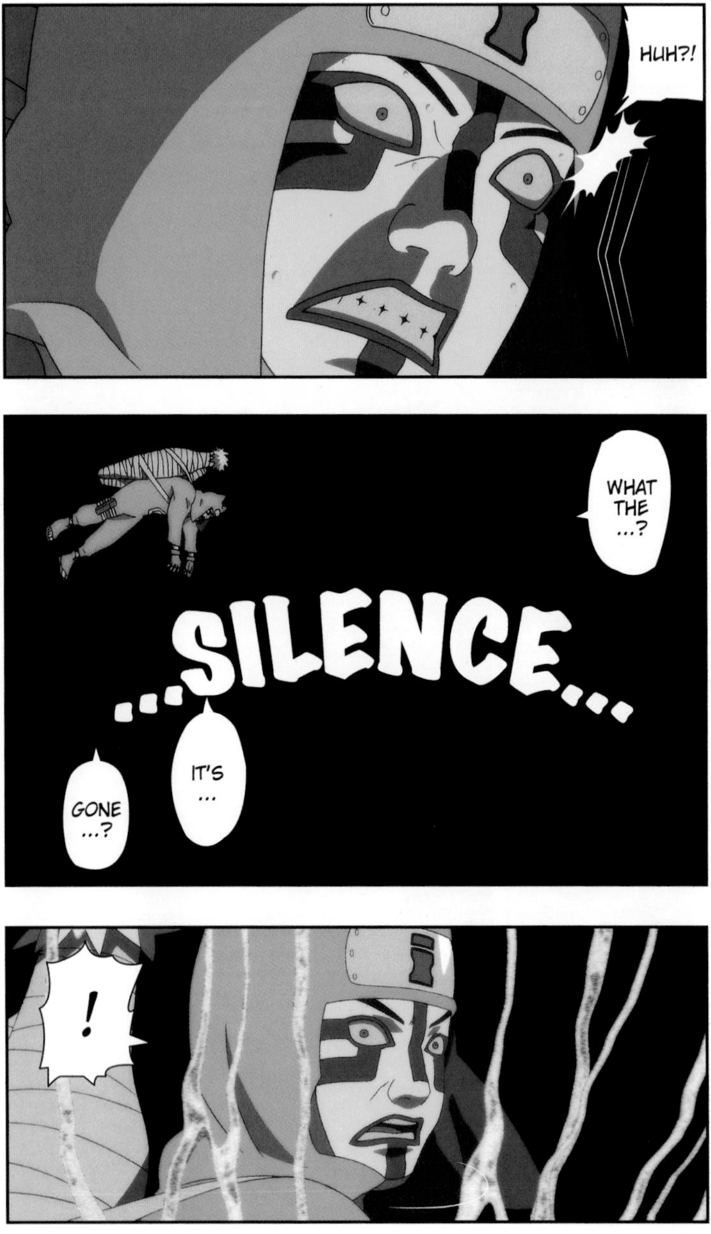
HUH?!
WHAT THE ...?
...SILENCE...
IT'S ...
GONE ...?
!

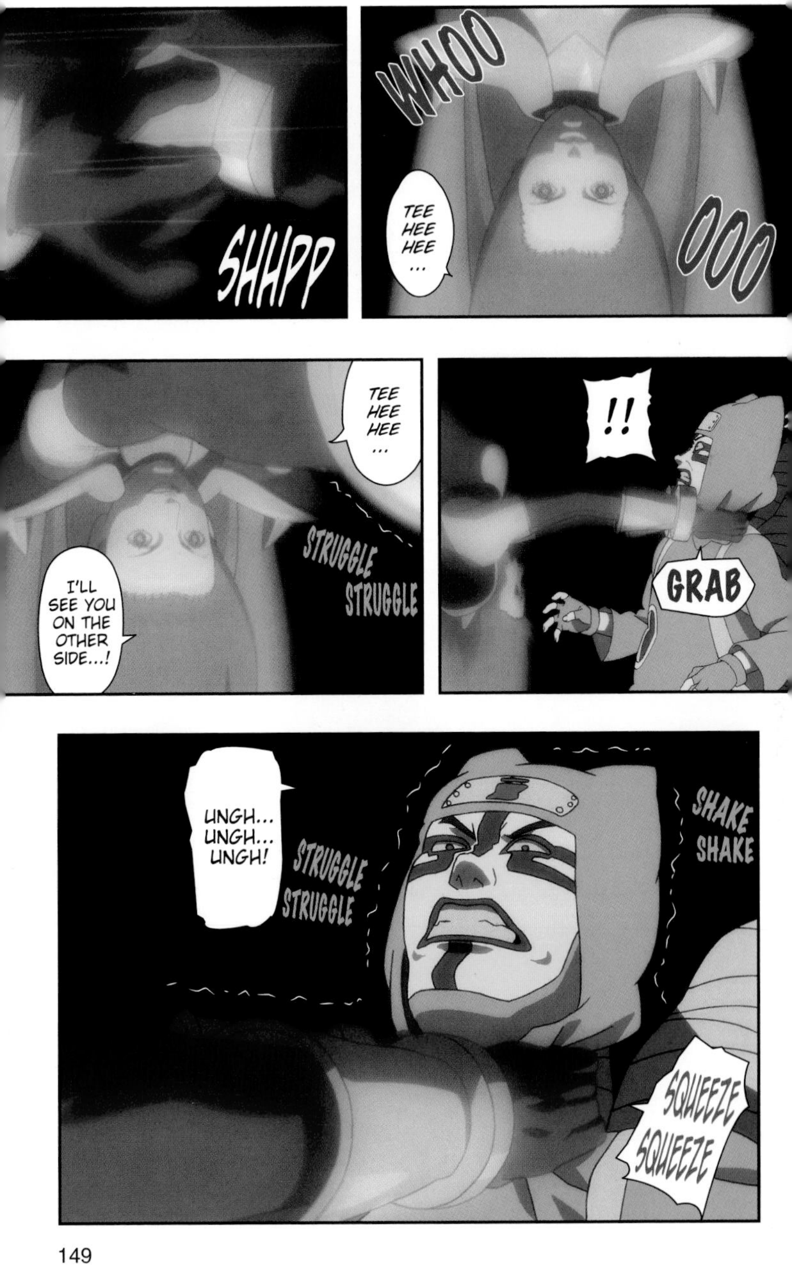
WHOO
TEE HEE HEE...
OOO
SHHPP
!!
GRAB
TEE HEE HEE...
STRUGGLE STRUGGLE
I'LL SEE YOU ON THE OTHER SIDE...!
SHAKE SHAKE
UNGH... UNGH... UNGH!
STRUGGLE STRUGGLE
SQUEEZE SQUEEZE

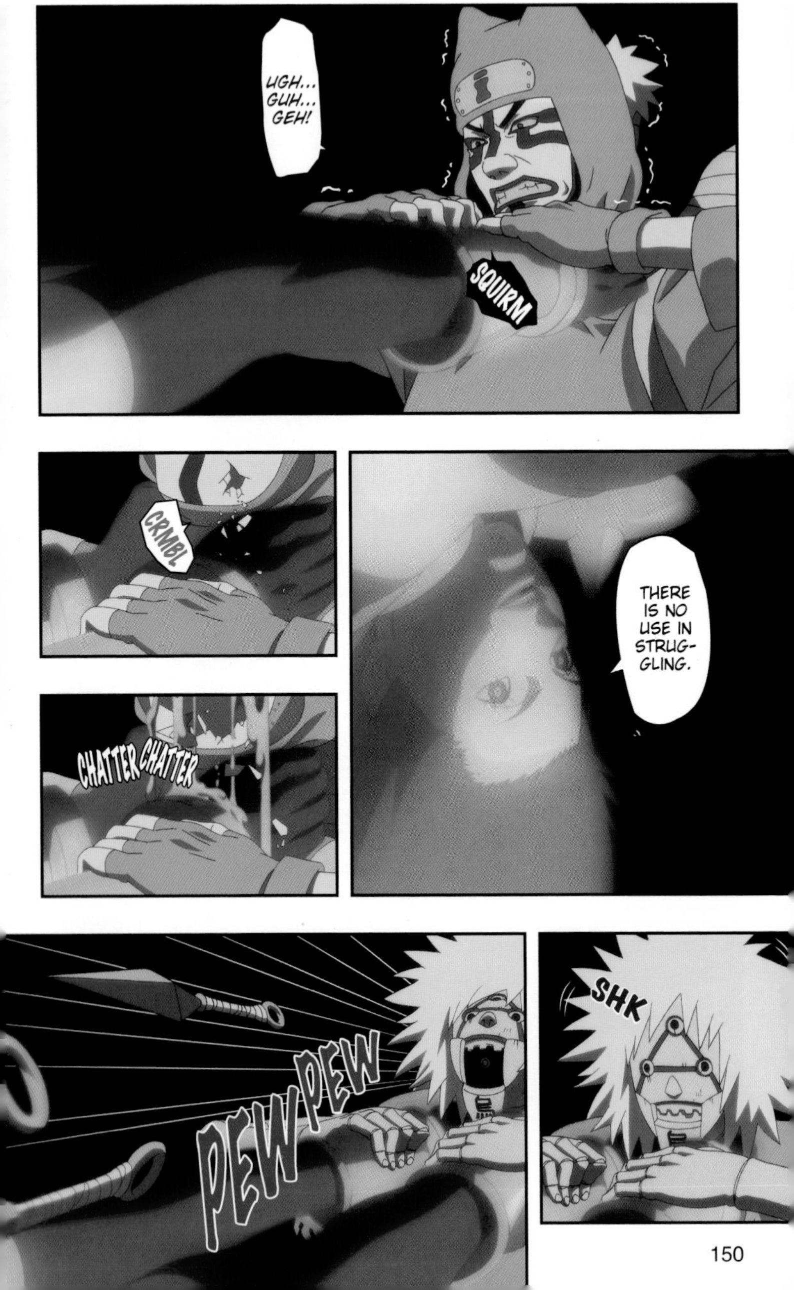
UGH... GUH... GEH!
SQUIRM
THERE IS NO USE IN STRUG- GLING.
CRMBL
CHATTER CHATTER
SHK
PEW PEW

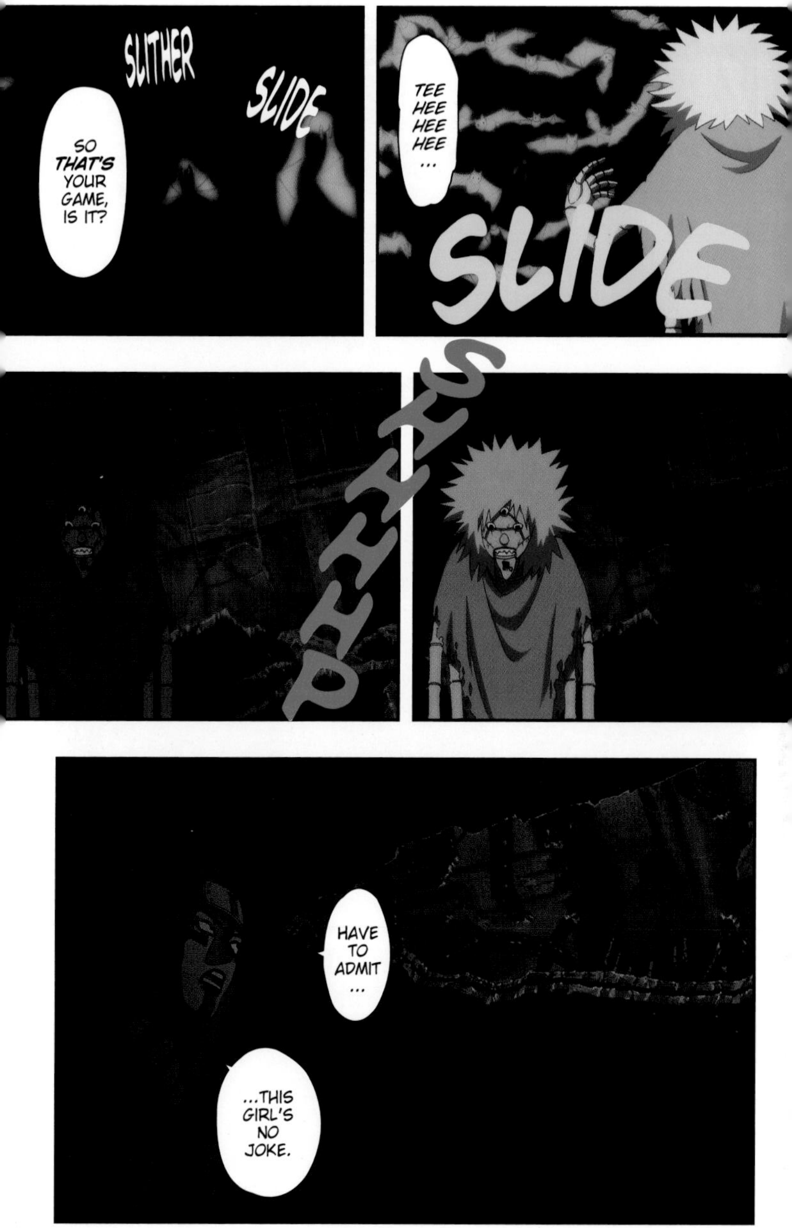
TEE HEE HEE HEE...
SLIDE
SLITHER
SLIDE
SO THAT'S YOUR GAME, IS IT?
SHHHP
HAVE TO ADMIT...
...THIS GIRL'S NO JOKE.

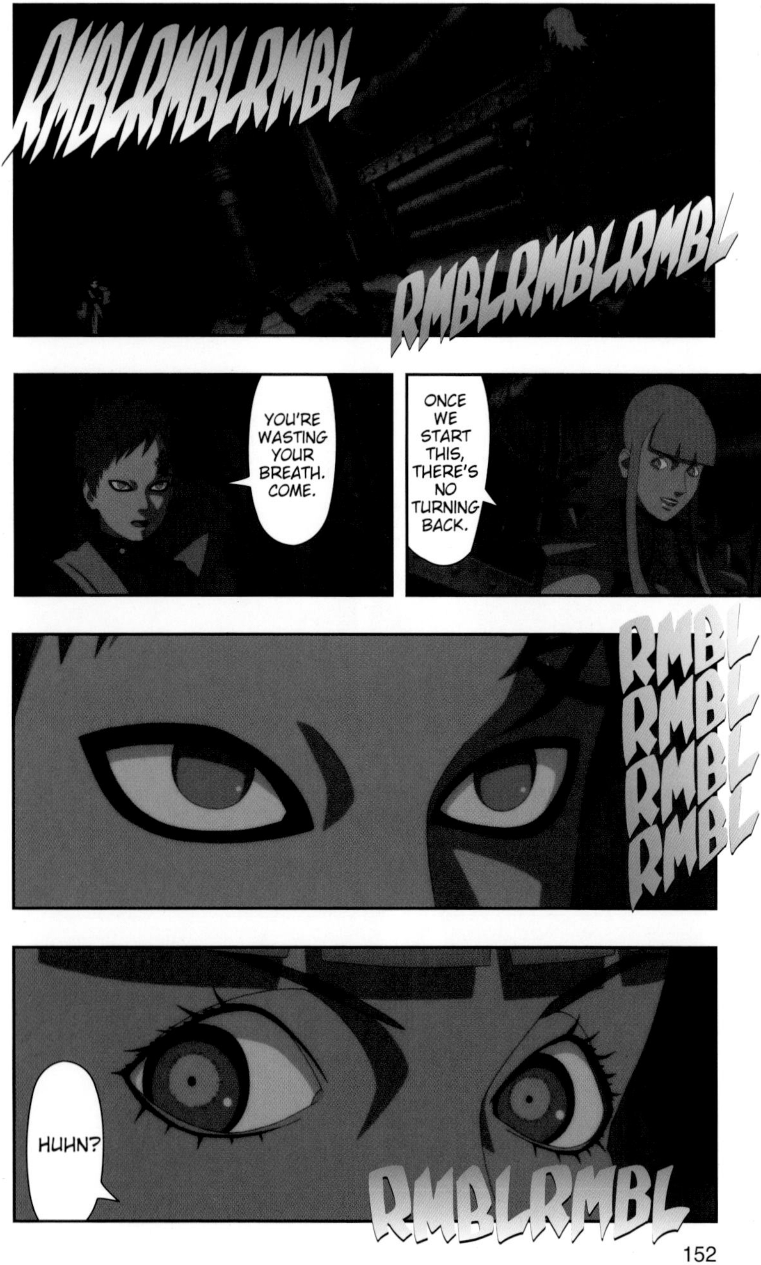
RMBLRMBLRMBL
RMBLRMBLRMBL
ONCE WE START THIS, THERE'S NO TURNING BACK.
YOU'RE WASTING YOUR BREATH. COME.
RMBL RMBL RMBL RMBL
HUHN?
RMBLRMBL

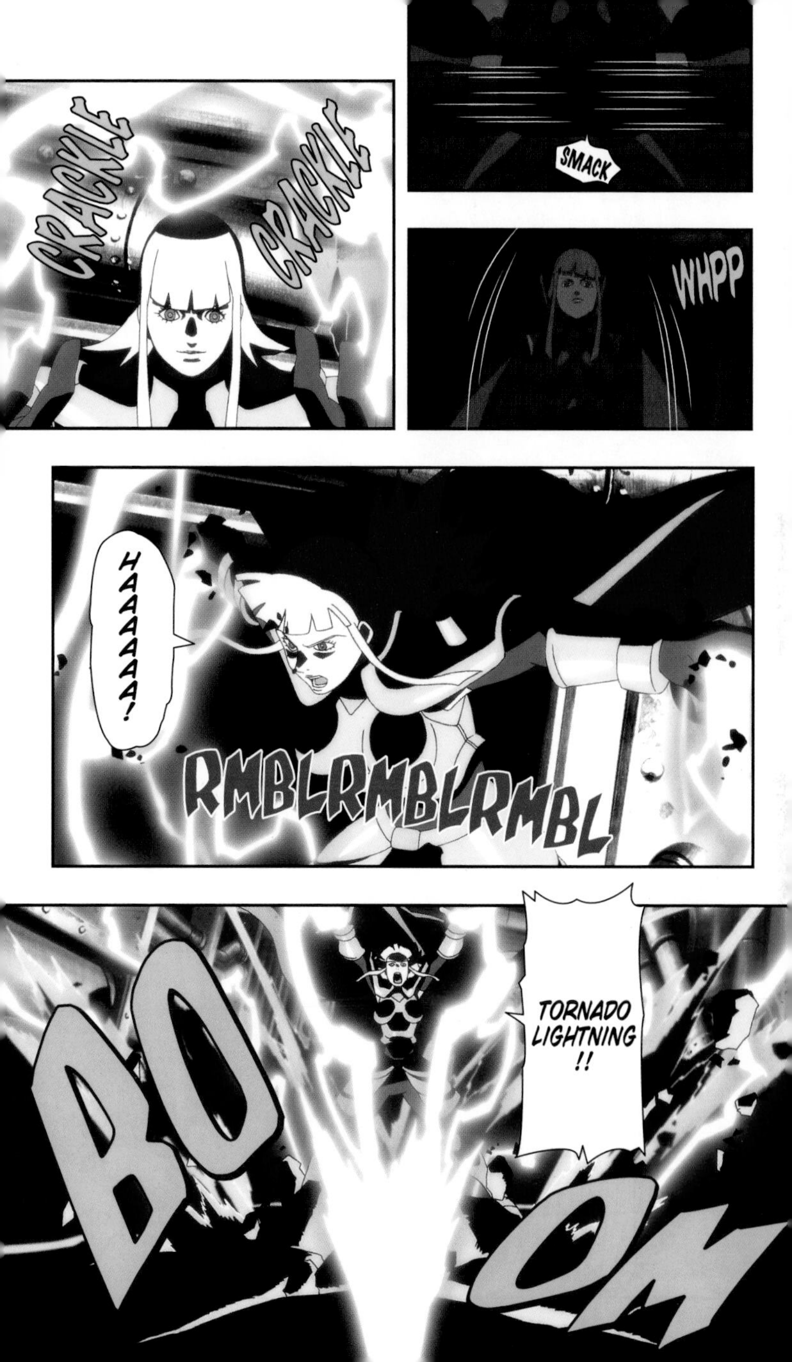
SMACK
WHPP
CRACKLE
CRACKLE
HAAAAAAA!
RMBLRMBLRMBL
TORNADO LIGHTNING !!
BOOM

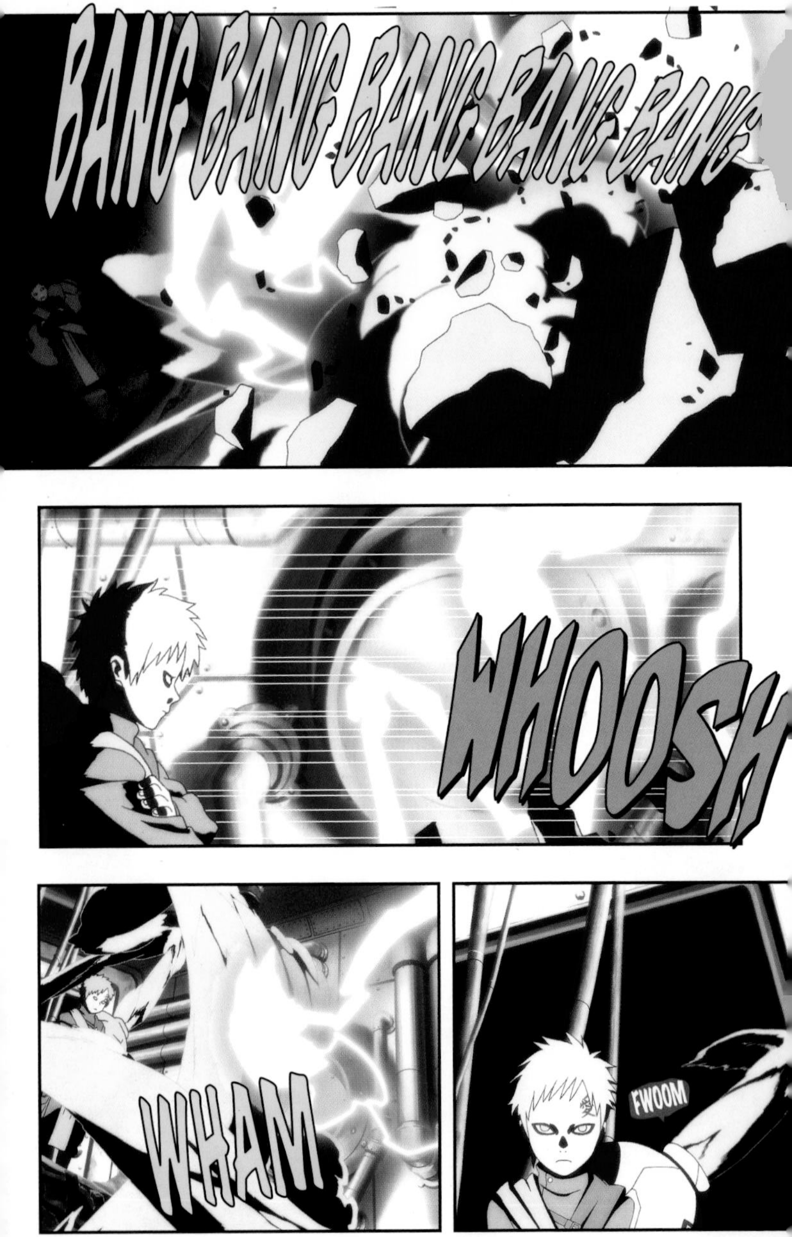
BANG BANG BANG BANG BANG
WHOOSH
FWOOM
WHAM

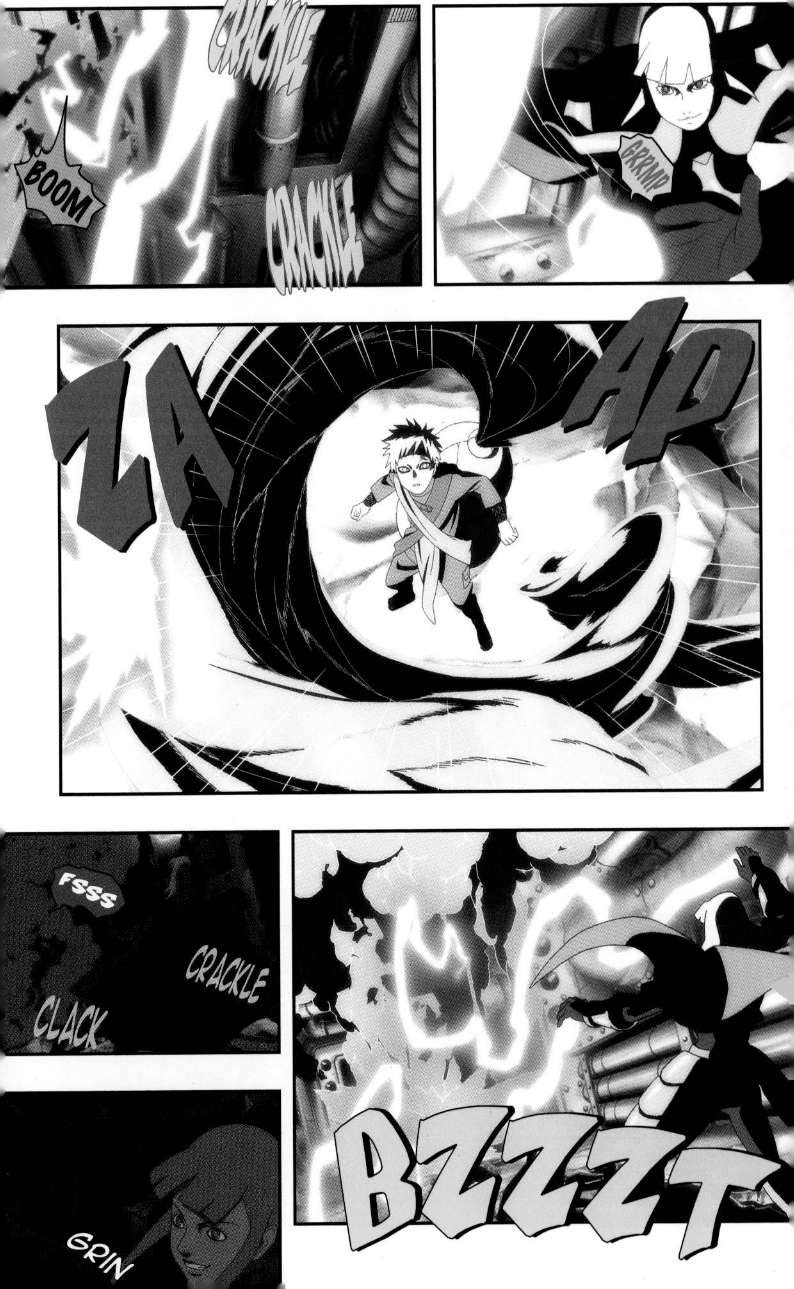
GRRMP
CRACKLE
BOOM
CRACKLE
ZA
AP
BZZZT
FSSS
CRACKLE
CLACK
GRIN

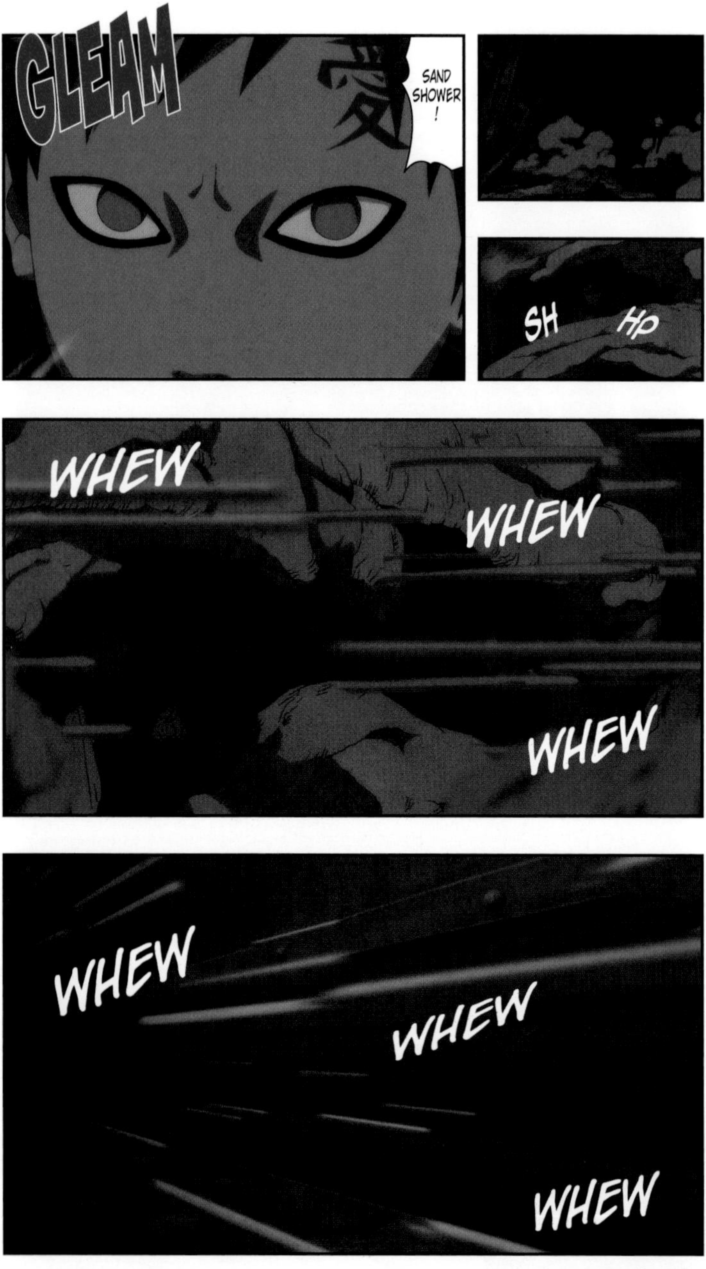
SH
HP
GLEAM
SAND SHOWER!
WHEW
WHEW
WHEW
WHEW
WHEW
WHEW

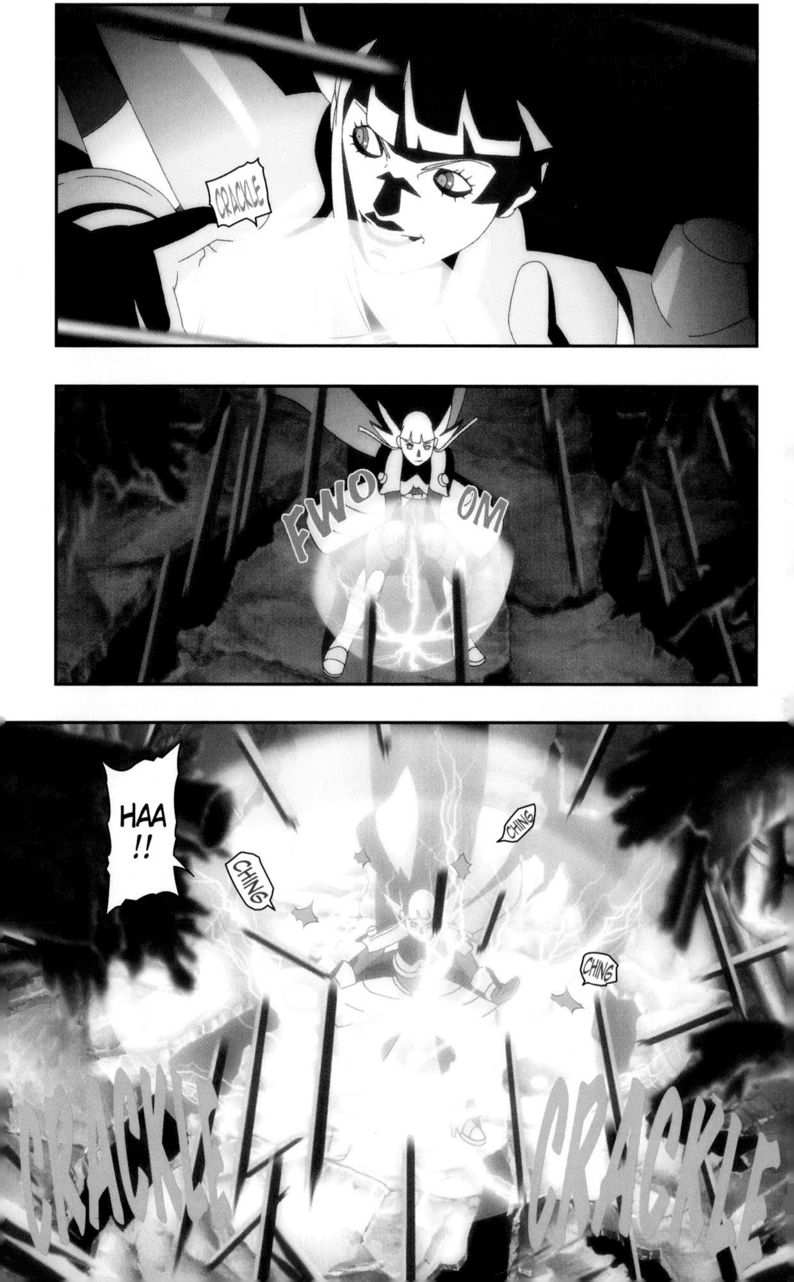
CRACKLE
FWOOM
HAA!!
CHING
CHING
CHING
CRACKLE
CRACKLE

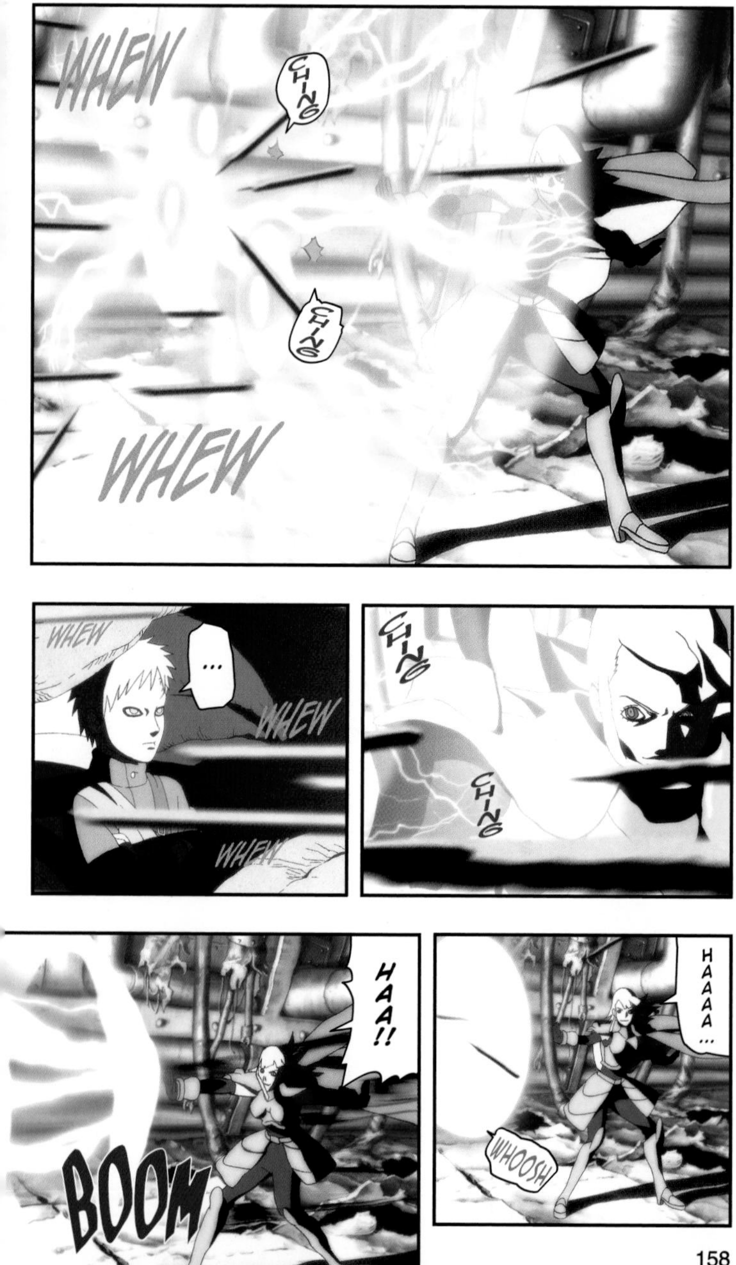
WHEW
CHING
CHING
WHEW
CHING
CHING
WHEW
...
WHEW
WHEW
HAAAA...
WHOOSH
HAAA!!
BOOM

HALT
SSS
SSS
SSS
SSS
SSS
SHWP
TEE HEE HEE... WHAT'S THE MATTER?
DON'T YOU WANNA PLAY?!!
BOOM

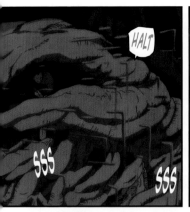

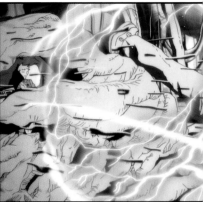

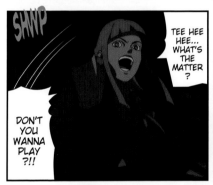

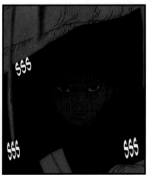

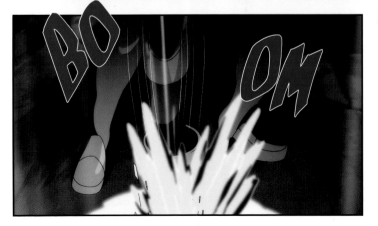

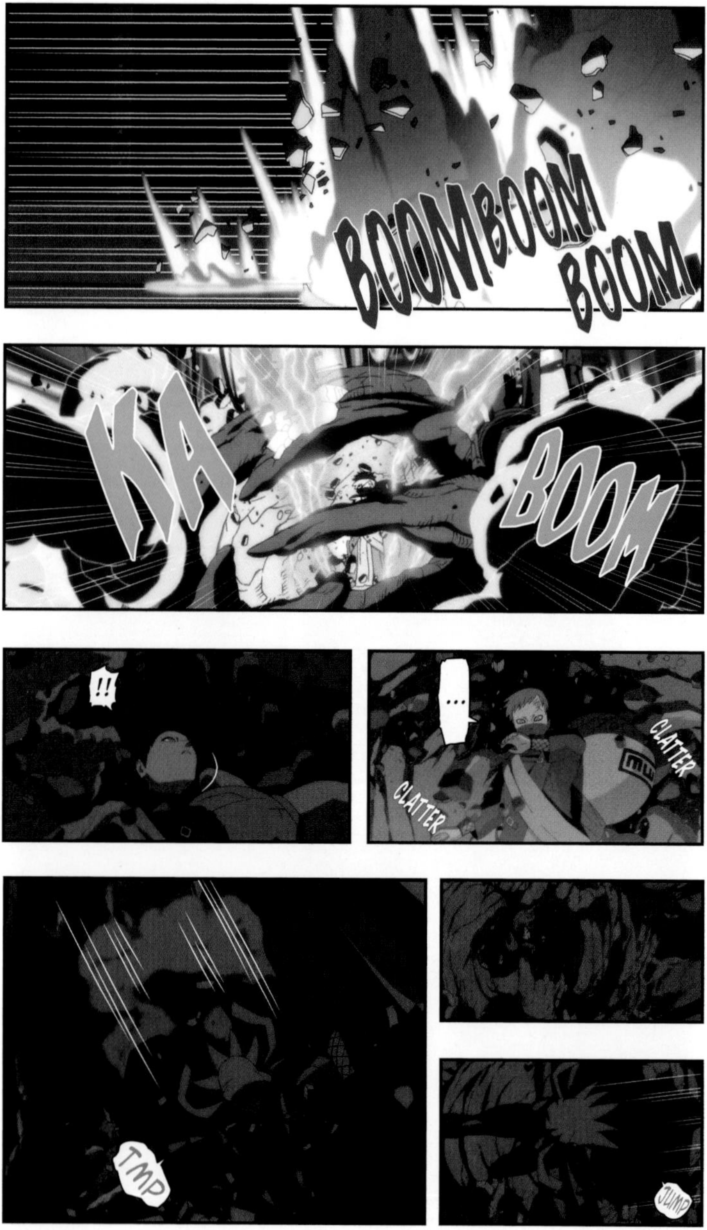
BOOM BOOM
BOOM
KA BOOM
....
CLATTER
CLATTER
!!
JUMP
TMP

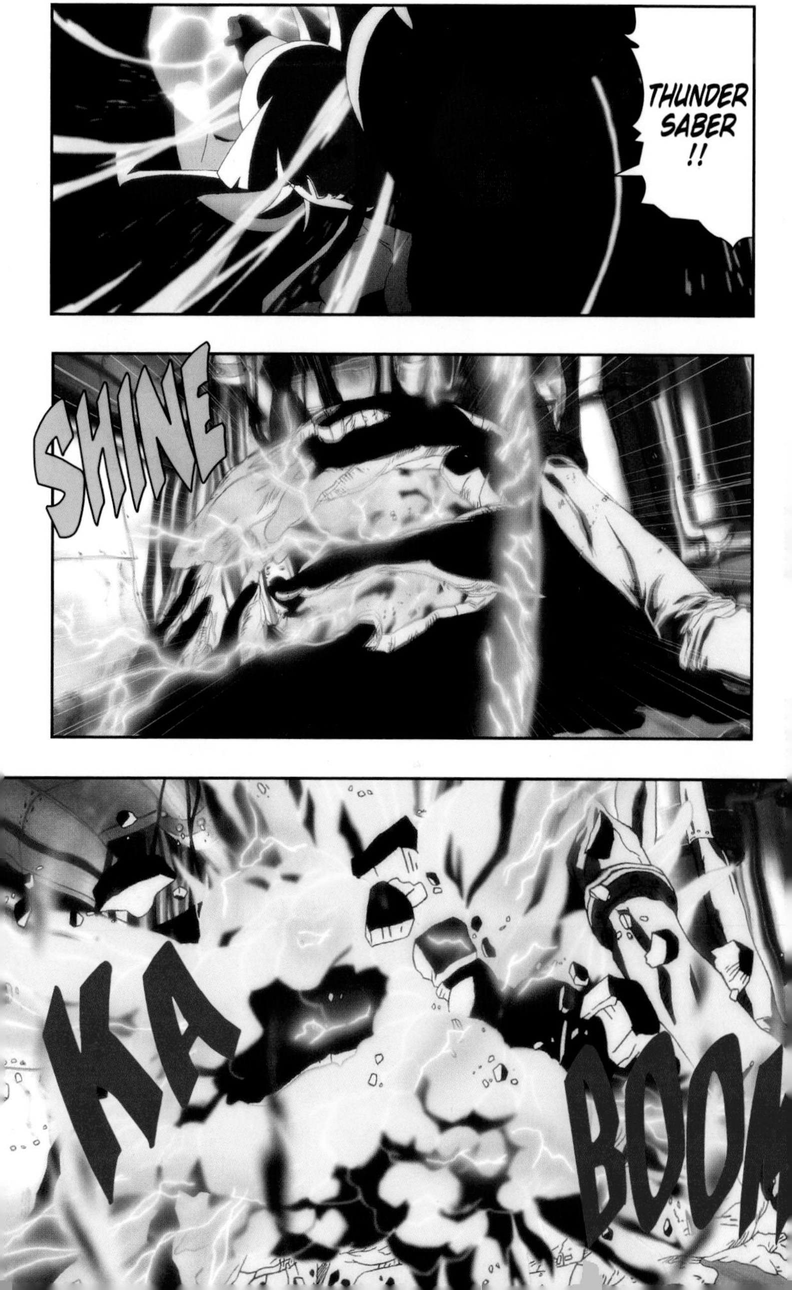
THUNDER SABER !!
SHINE
KA
BOOM

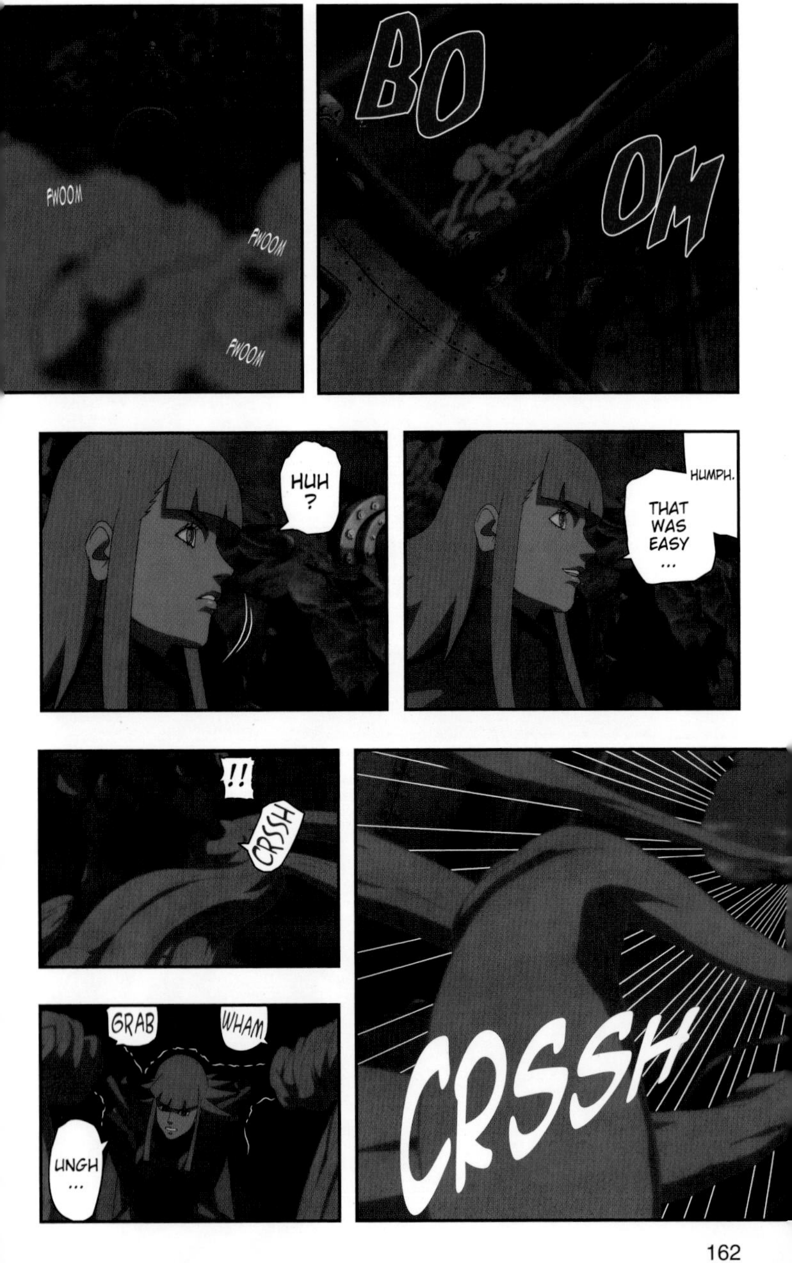
BOOM
FWOOM
FWOOM
FWOOM
HUMPH.
THAT WAS EASY ...
HUH?
CRSSH
!!
CRSSH
WHAM
GRAB
UNGH ...

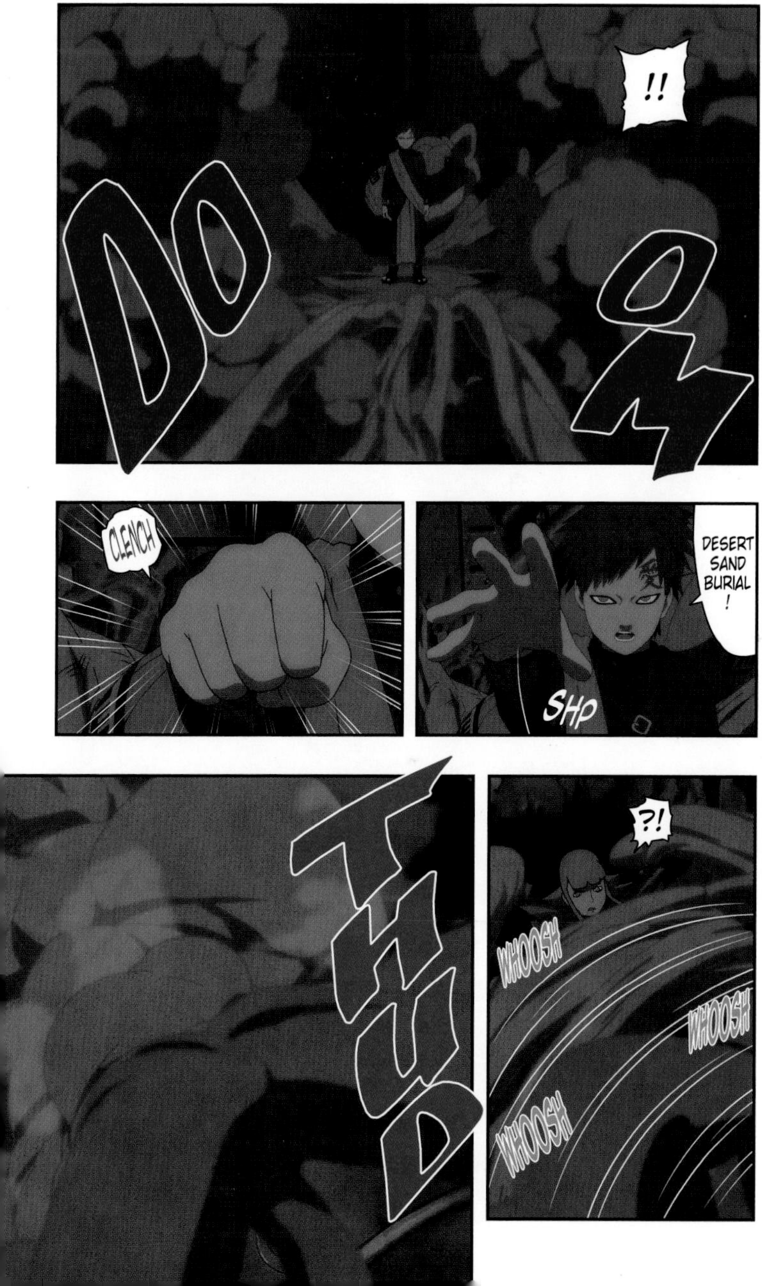
!!
DOOM
DESERT SAND BURIAL!
SHP
CLENCH
?!
WHOOSH
WHOOSH
WHOOSH
THUD

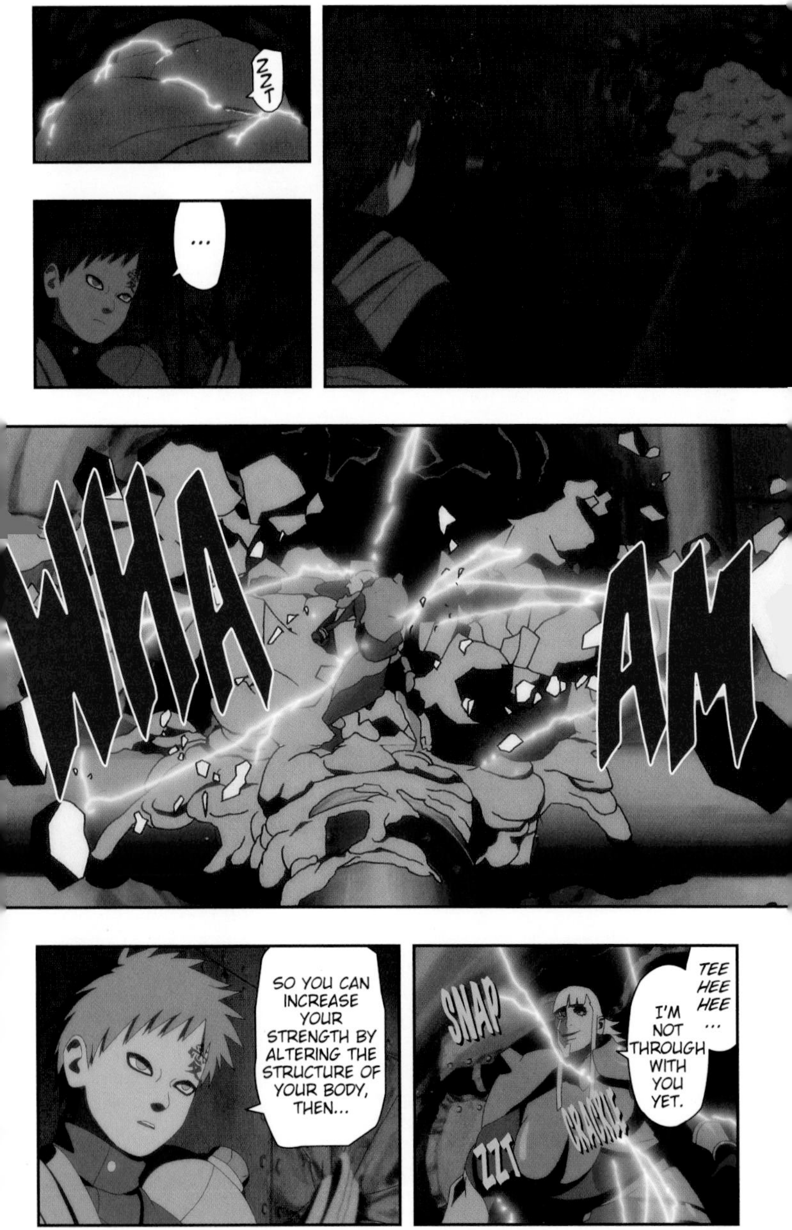
ZZT
...
WHAAM
SNAP
TEE HEE HEE...
I'M NOT THROUGH WITH YOU YET.
CRACKLE
ZZT
SO YOU CAN INCREASE YOUR STRENGTH BY ALTERING THE STRUCTURE OF YOUR BODY, THEN...

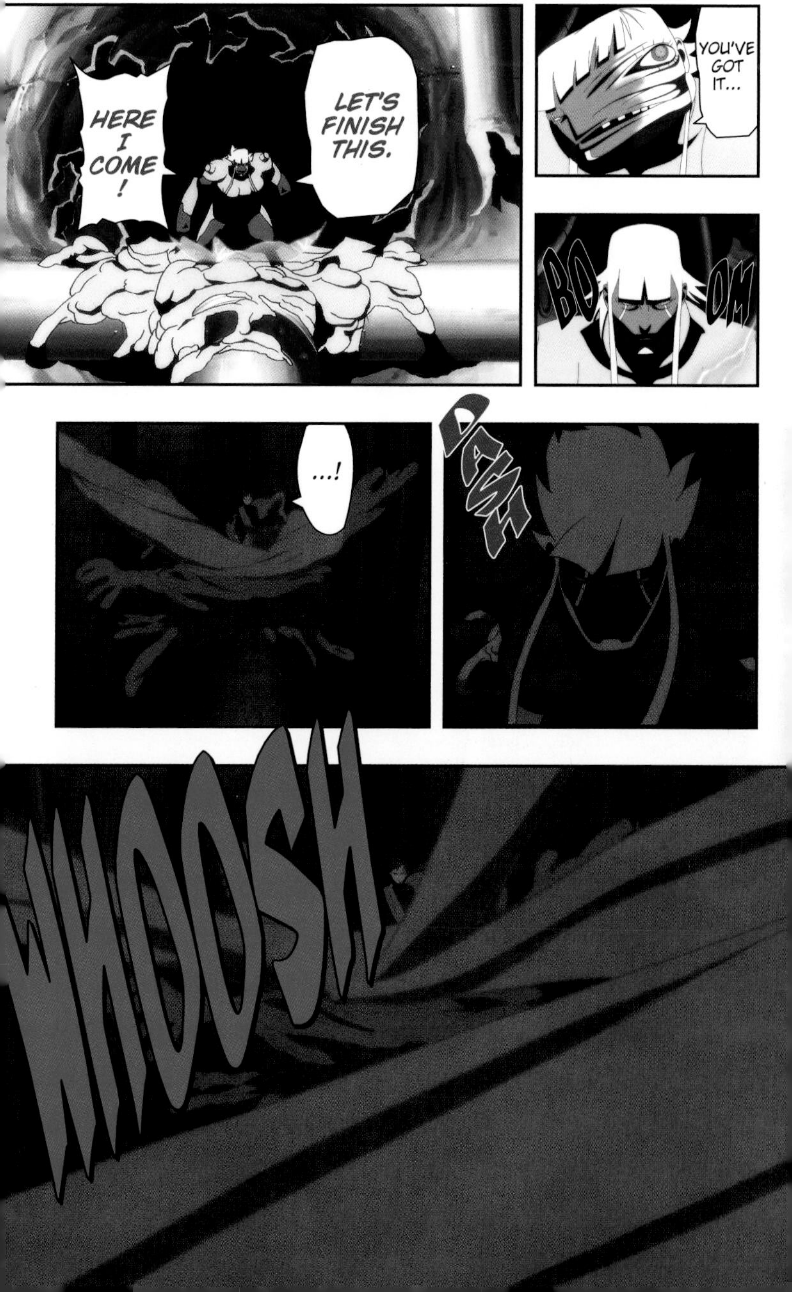
YOU'VE GOT IT...
BOOM
LET'S FINISH THIS.
HERE I COME!
DASH
...!
WHOOSH

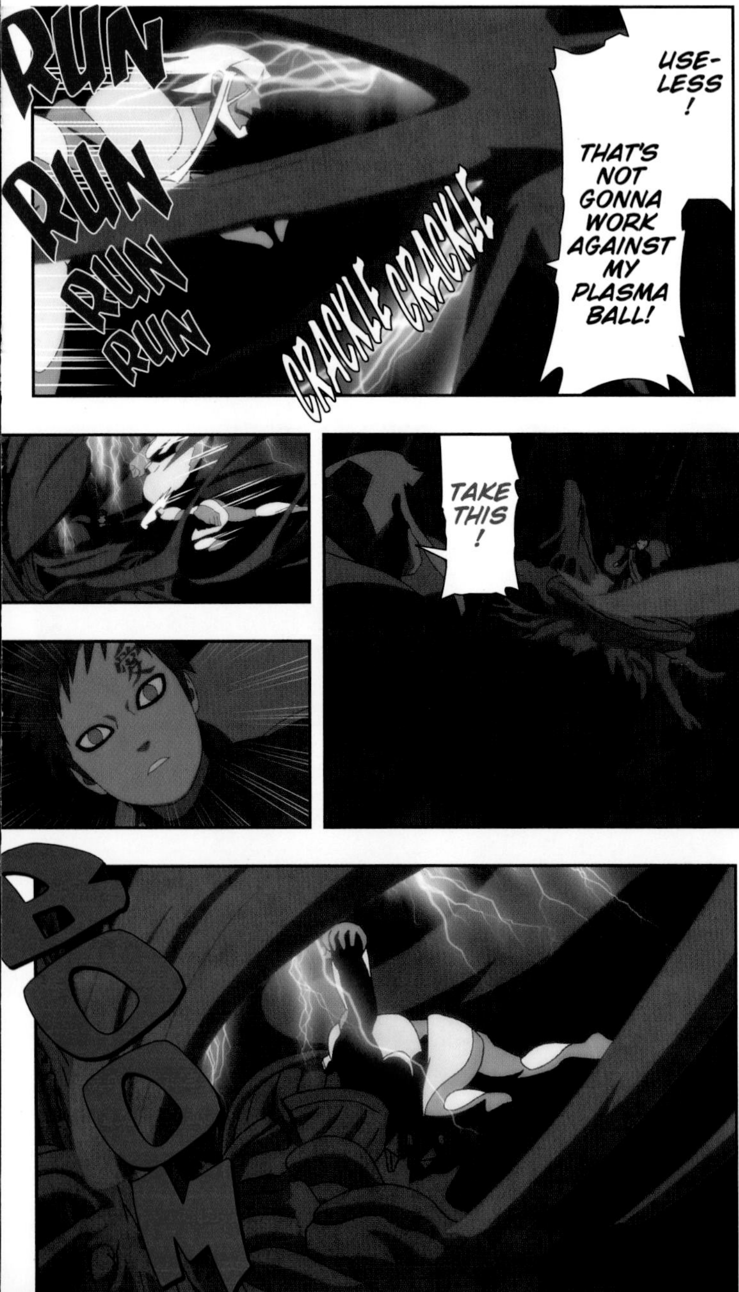
USE-LESS!
THAT'S NOT GONNA WORK AGAINST MY PLASMA BALL!
CRACKLE CRACKLE
RUN RUN RUN RUN
TAKE THIS!
BOOM

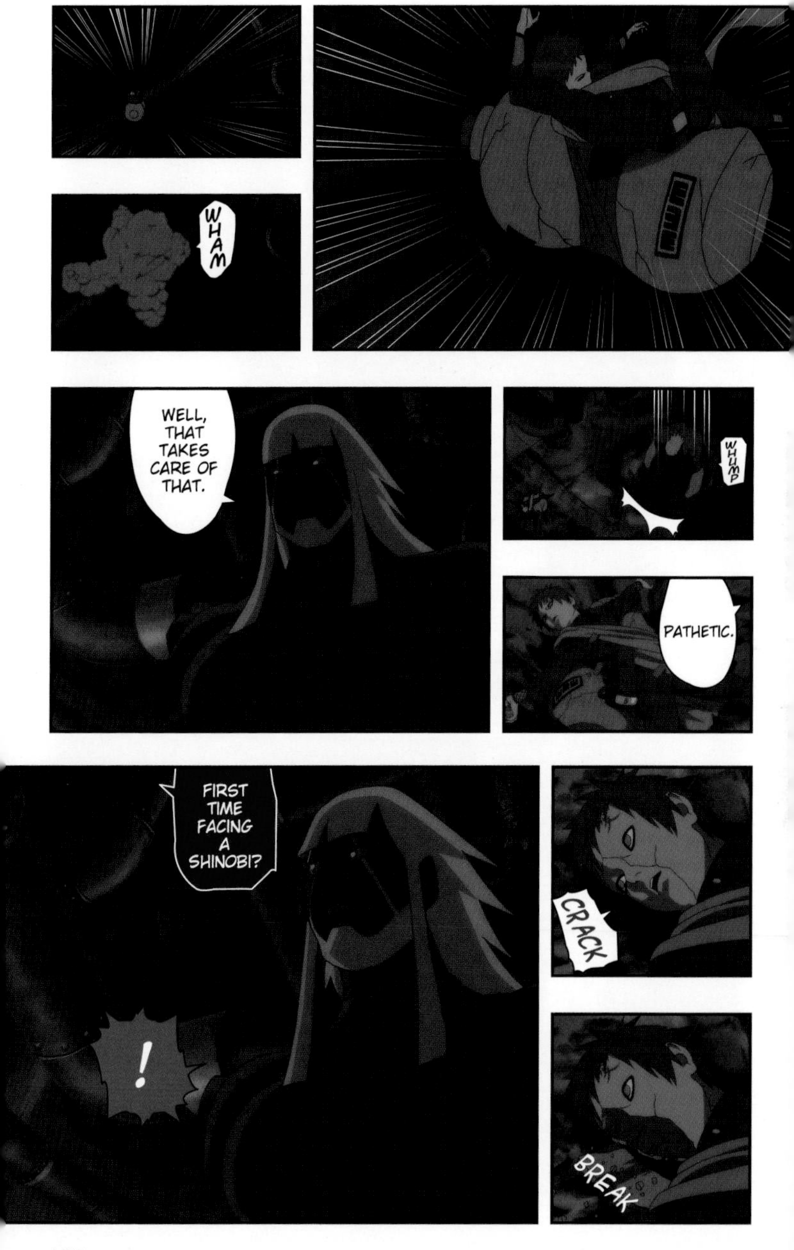
WHAM
WHUMP
PATHETIC.
WELL, THAT TAKES CARE OF THAT.
CRACK
BREAK
FIRST TIME FACING A SHINOBI?
!

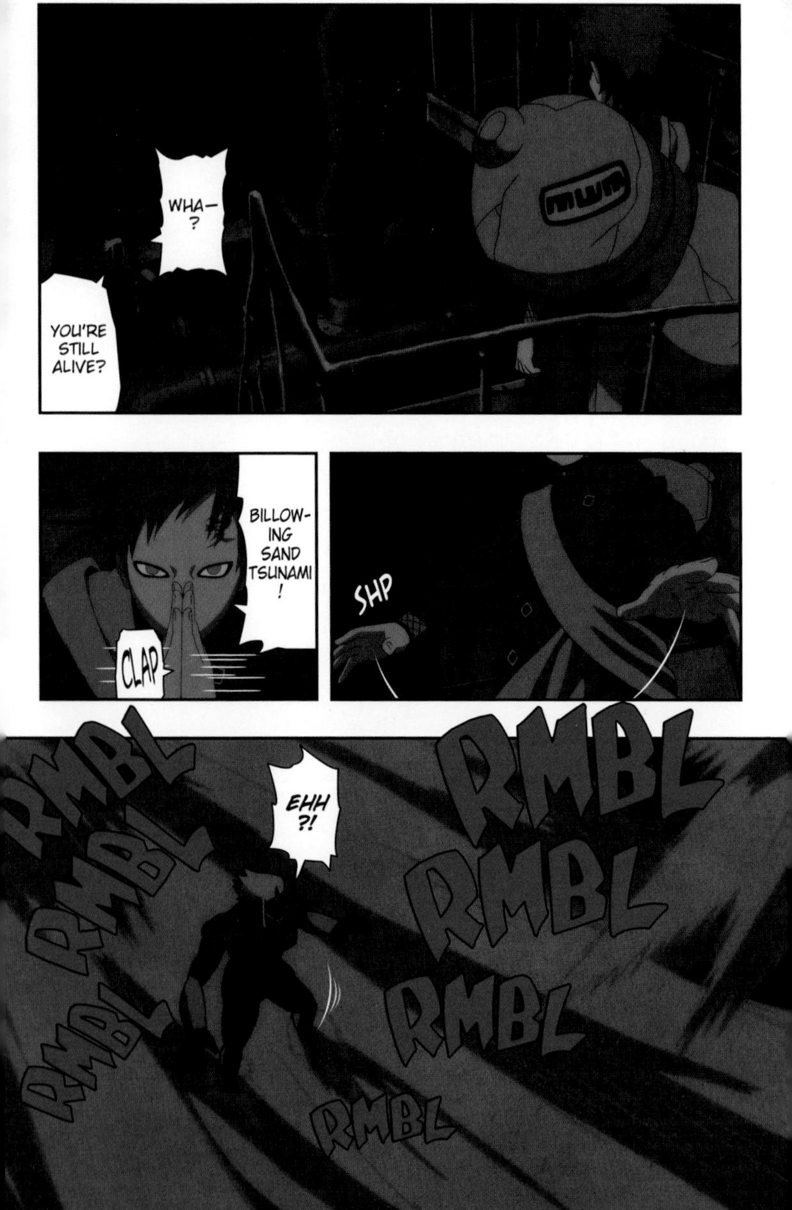
WHA— ?
YOU'RE STILL ALIVE?
SHP
BILLOW-ING SAND TSUNAMI!
CLAP
RMBL RMBL
EHH ?!
RMBL
RMBL
RMBL
RMBL
RMBL
RMBL

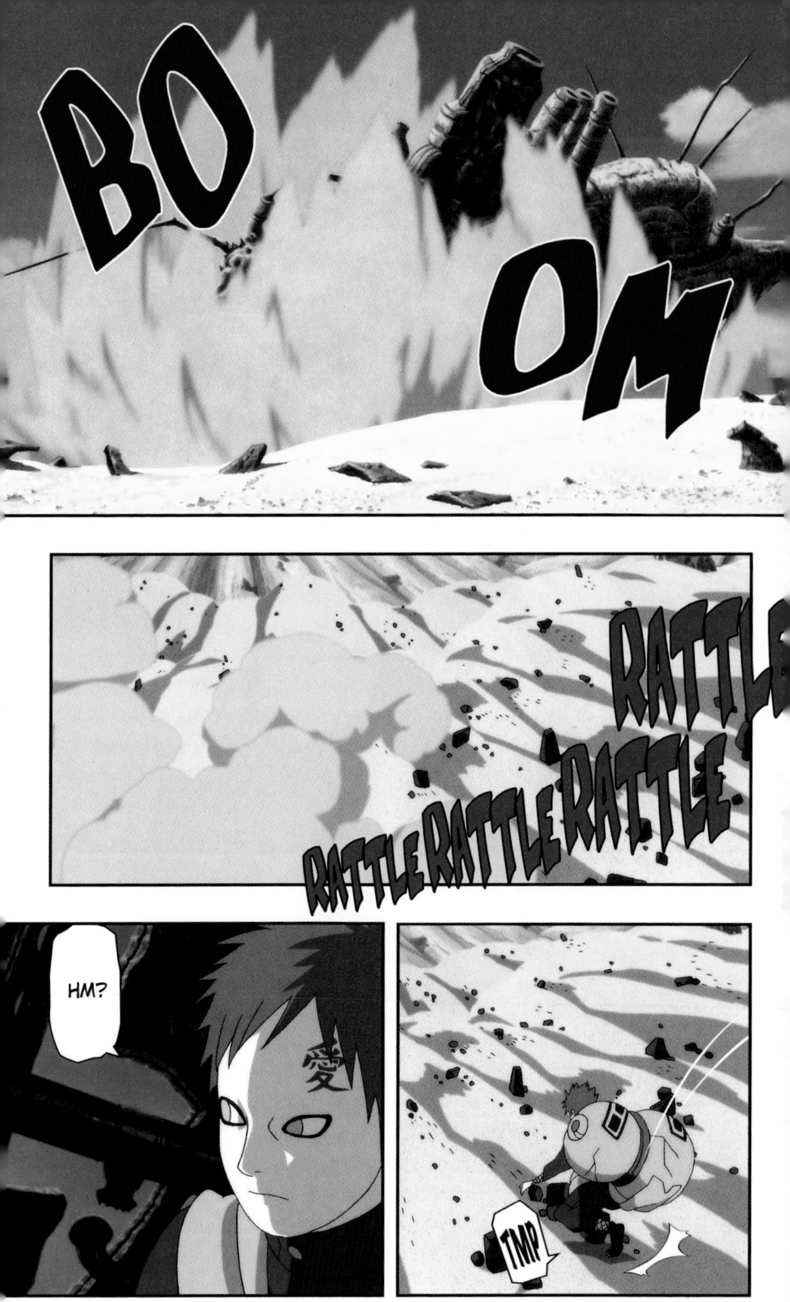
BOOM
RATTLE
RATTLE RATTLE RATTLE
TMP
HM?

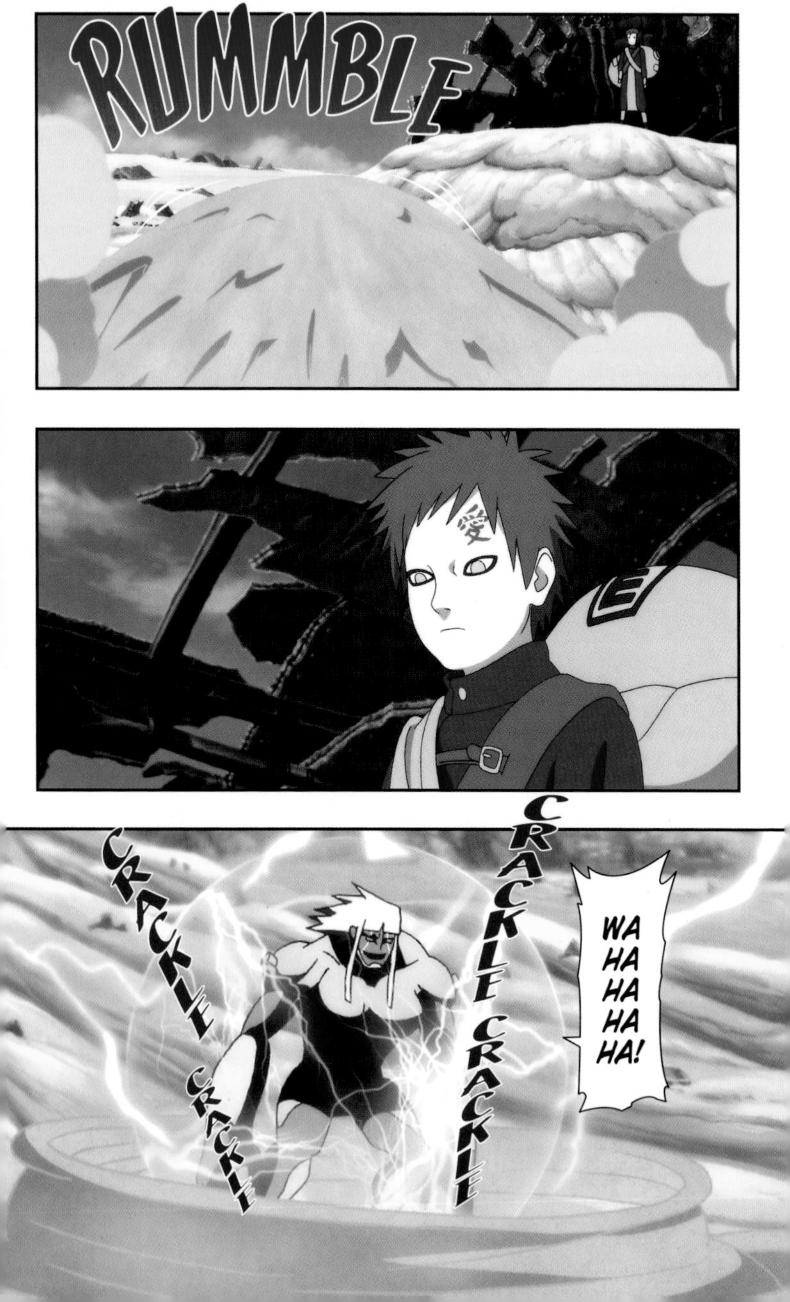
RUMMBLE
WA HA HA HA HA HA!
CRACKLE CRACKLE
CRACKLE CRACKLE

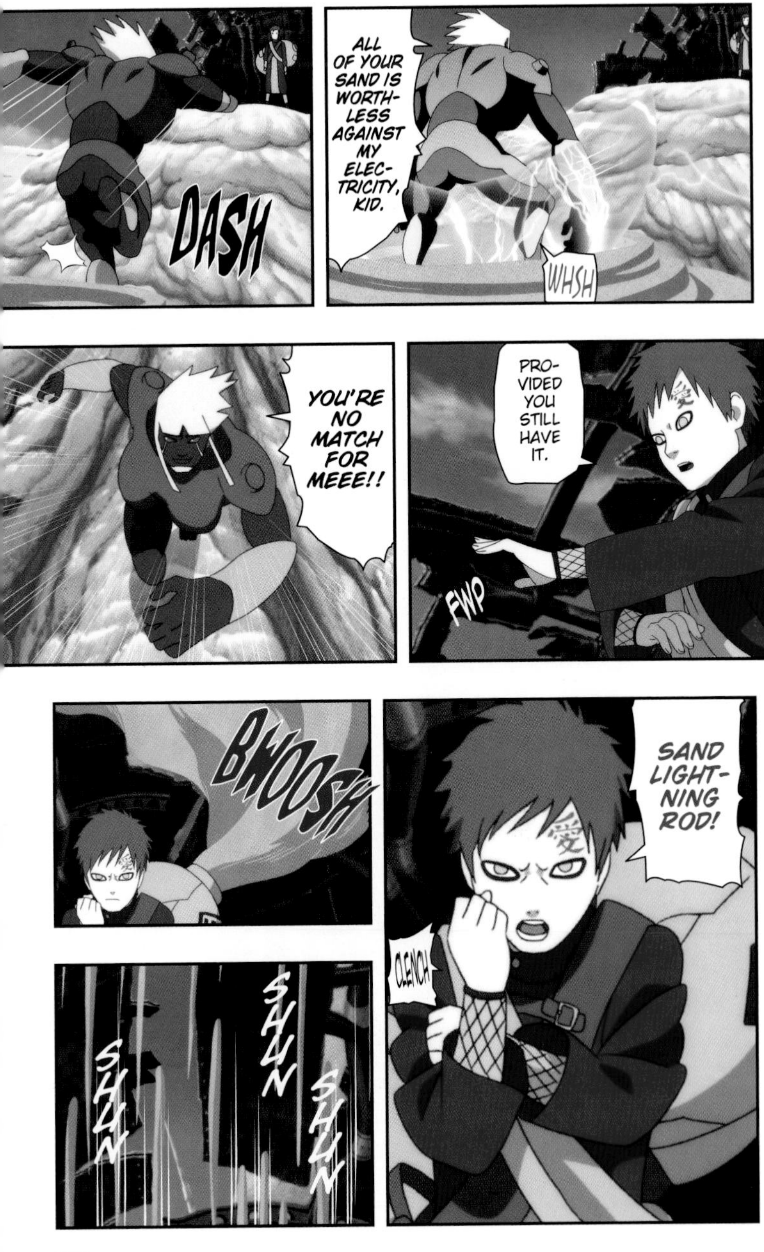
ALL OF YOUR SAND IS WORTHLESS AGAINST MY ELECTRICITY, KID.
WHSH
DASH
PROVIDED YOU STILL HAVE IT.
FWP
YOU'RE NO MATCH FOR MEEE!!
SAND LIGHTNING ROD!
CLENCH
BWOOSH
SHUN
SHUN
SHUN

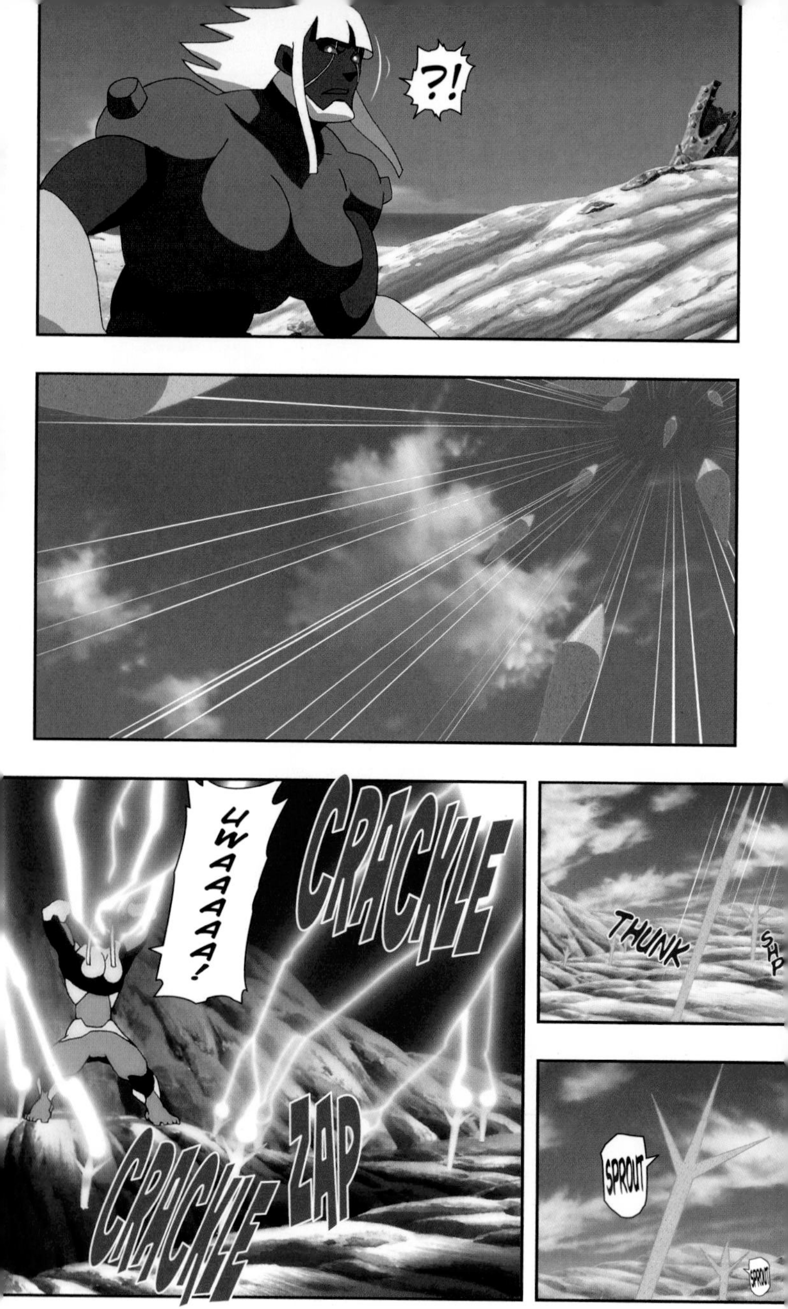
?!
THUNK
SHP
SPROUT
SPROUT
UWAAAAAAA!
CRACKLE
ZAP
CRACKLE

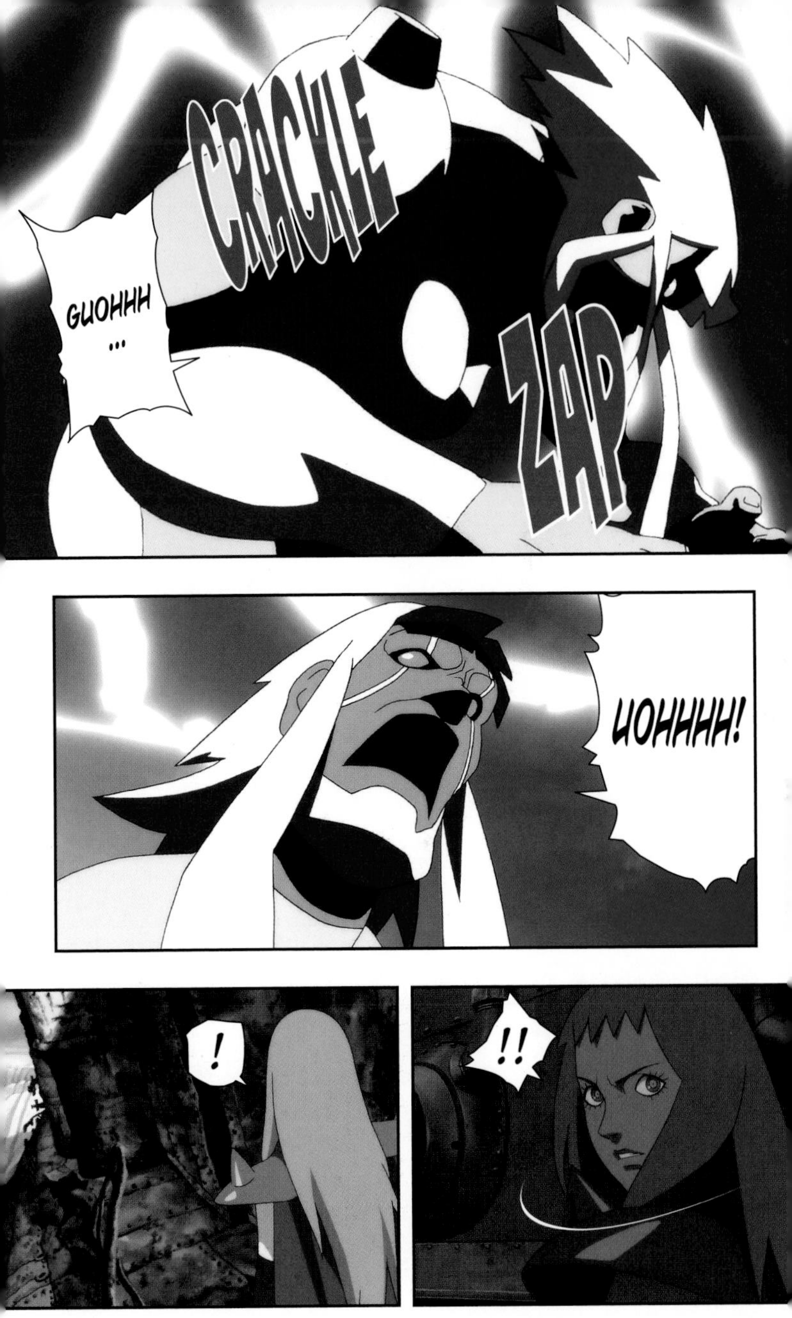
CRACKLE
ZAP
GUOHHH ...
UOHHHH!
!!
!

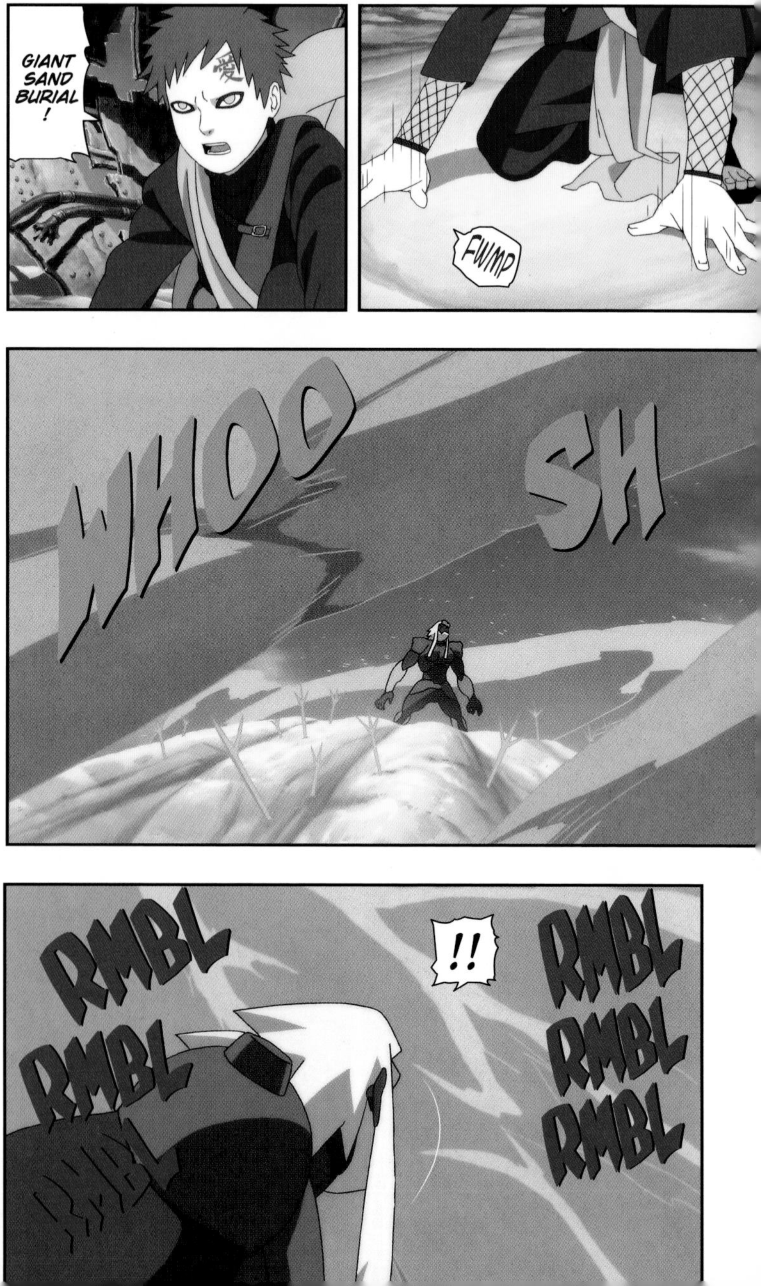
FWMP
GIANT SAND BURIAL!
WHOOSH
RMBL
RMBL
RMBL
!!
RMBL
RMBL

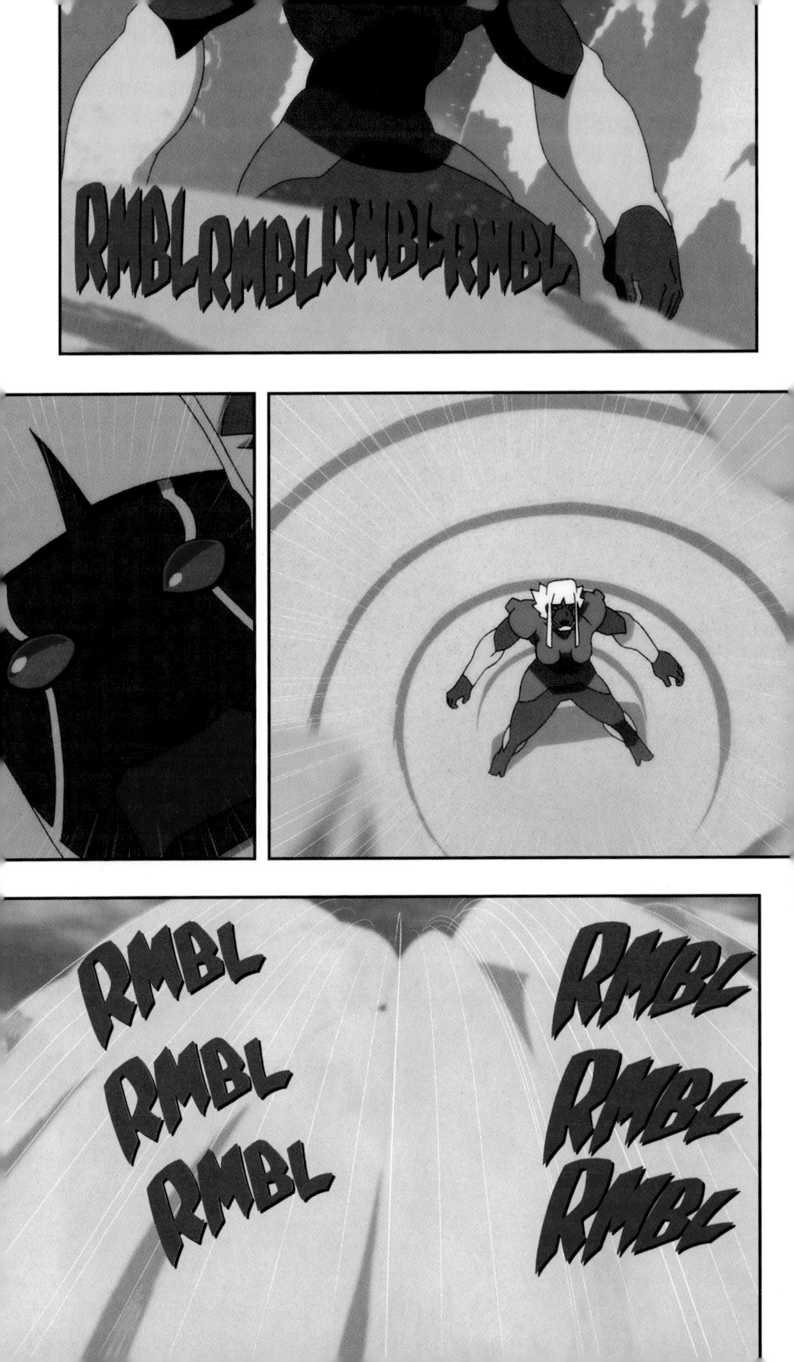
RMBLRMBLRMBLRMBL
RMBL
RMBL
RMBL
RMBL
RMBL
RMBL

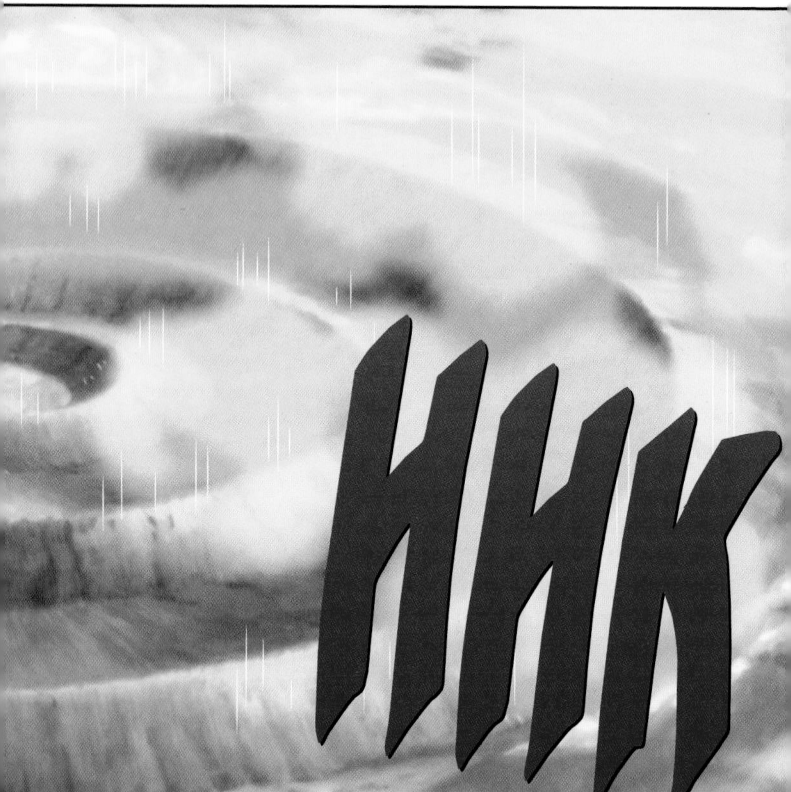
HHK
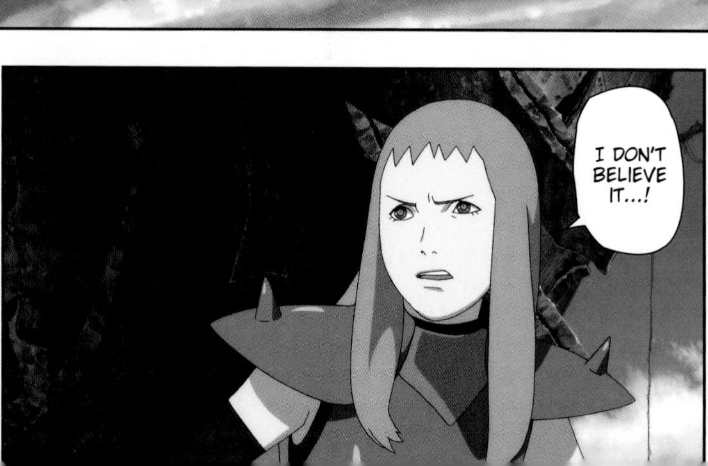
I DON'T BELIEVE IT...!

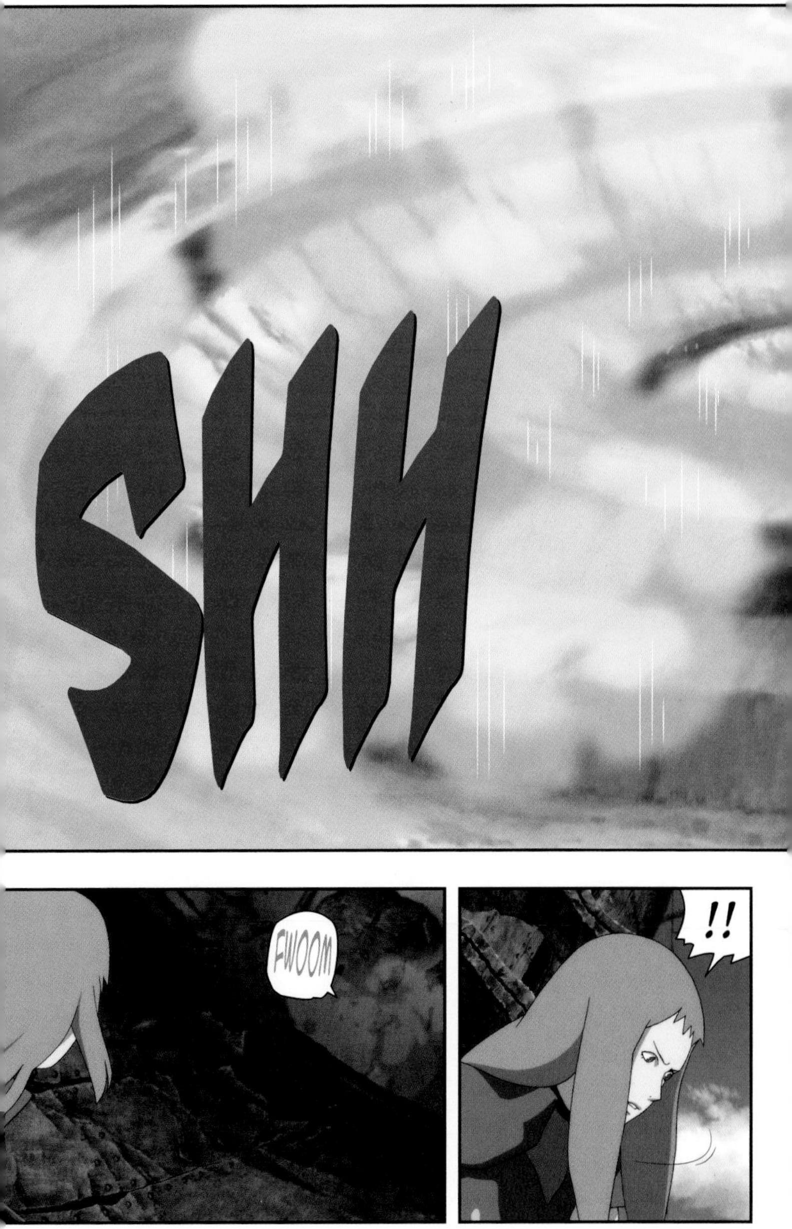
SHH
!!
FWOOM

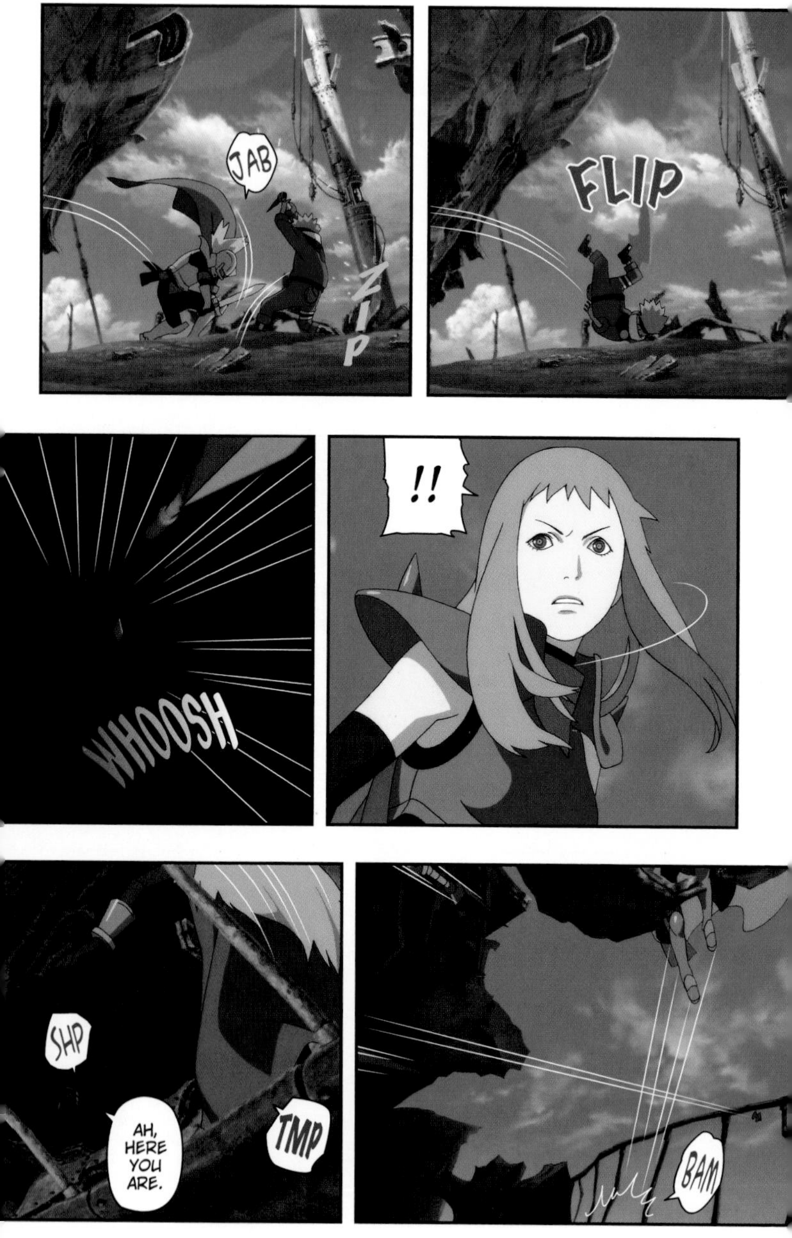
FLIP
JAB
ZIP
!!
WHOOSH
BAM
SHP
AH, HERE YOU ARE.
TMP

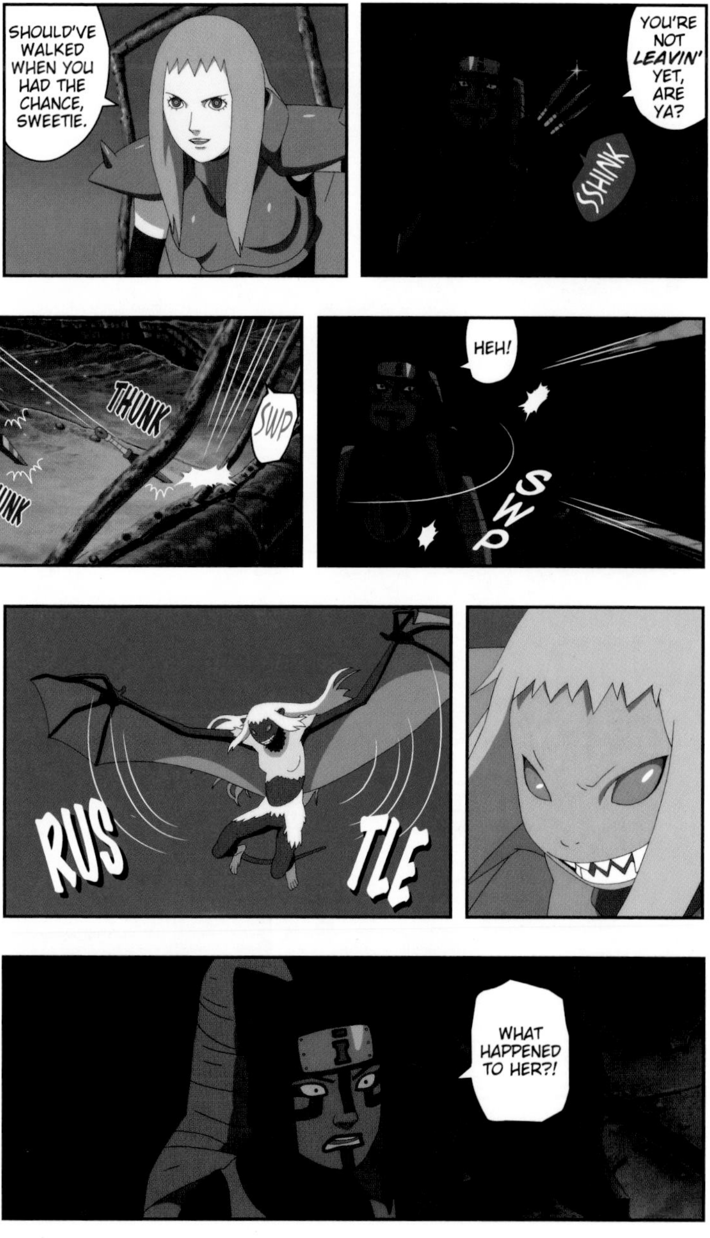
YOU'RE NOT LEAVIN' YET, ARE YA?
SSHINK
SHOULD'VE WALKED WHEN YOU HAD THE CHANCE, SWEETIE.
HEH!
SWP
SWP
THUNK
THUNK
RUS
TLE
WHAT HAPPENED TO HER?!

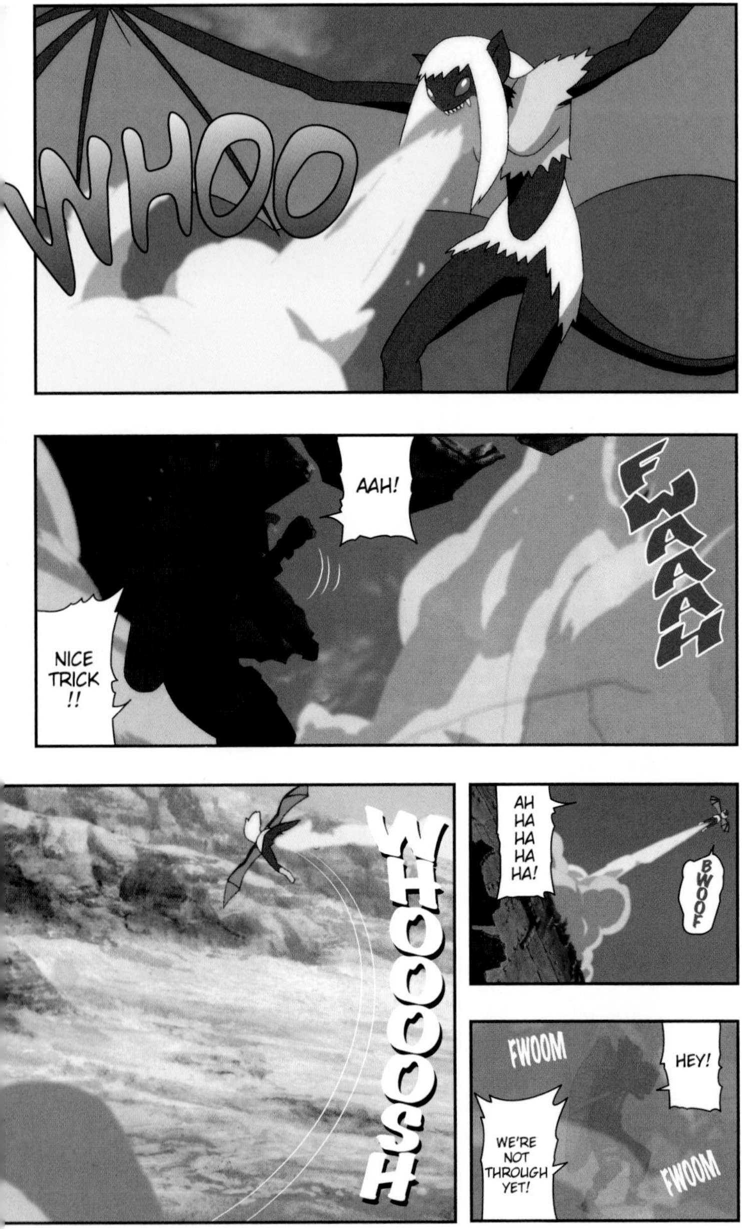
WHOO
FWAAAH
AAH!
NICE TRICK!!
AH HA HA HA HA!
BWOOF
HEY!
FWOOM
WE'RE NOT THROUGH YET!
FWOOM
WHOOOOSH

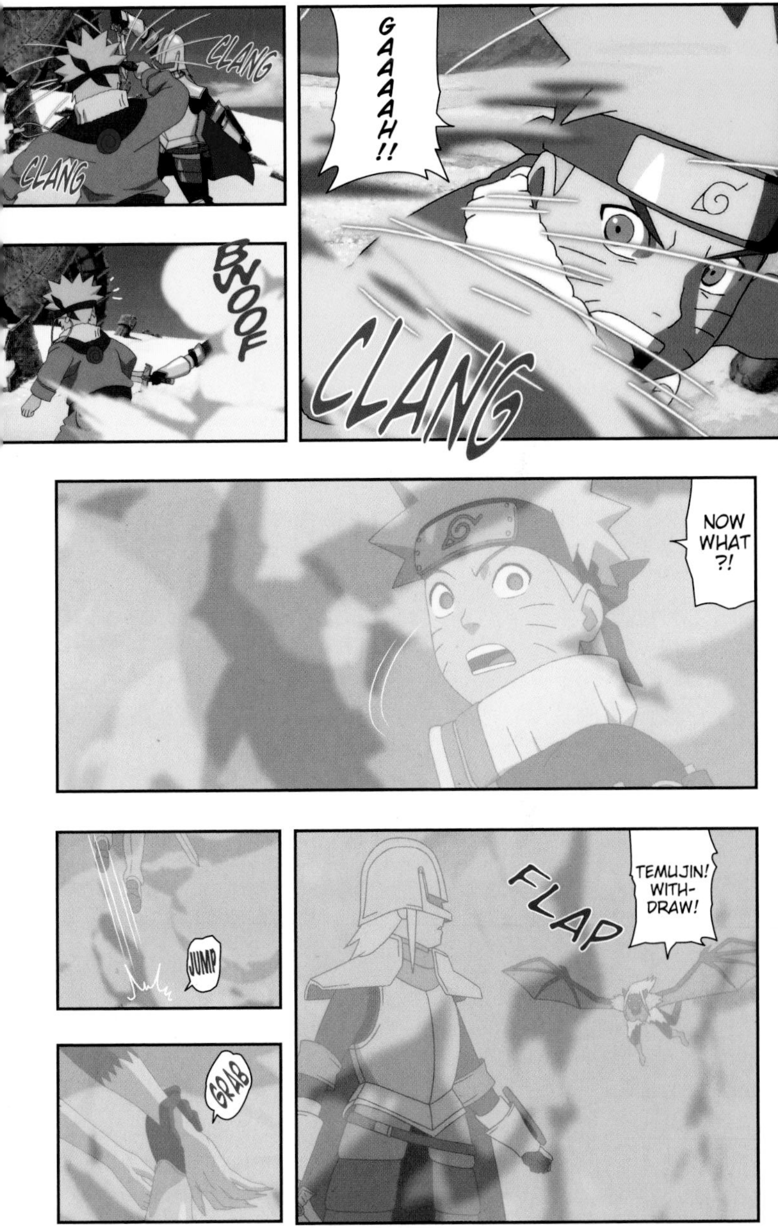
GAAAAAH!!
CLANG
CLANG
CLANG
BWOOF
NOW WHAT?!
TEMUJIN! WITH-DRAW!
FLAP
JUMP
GRAB

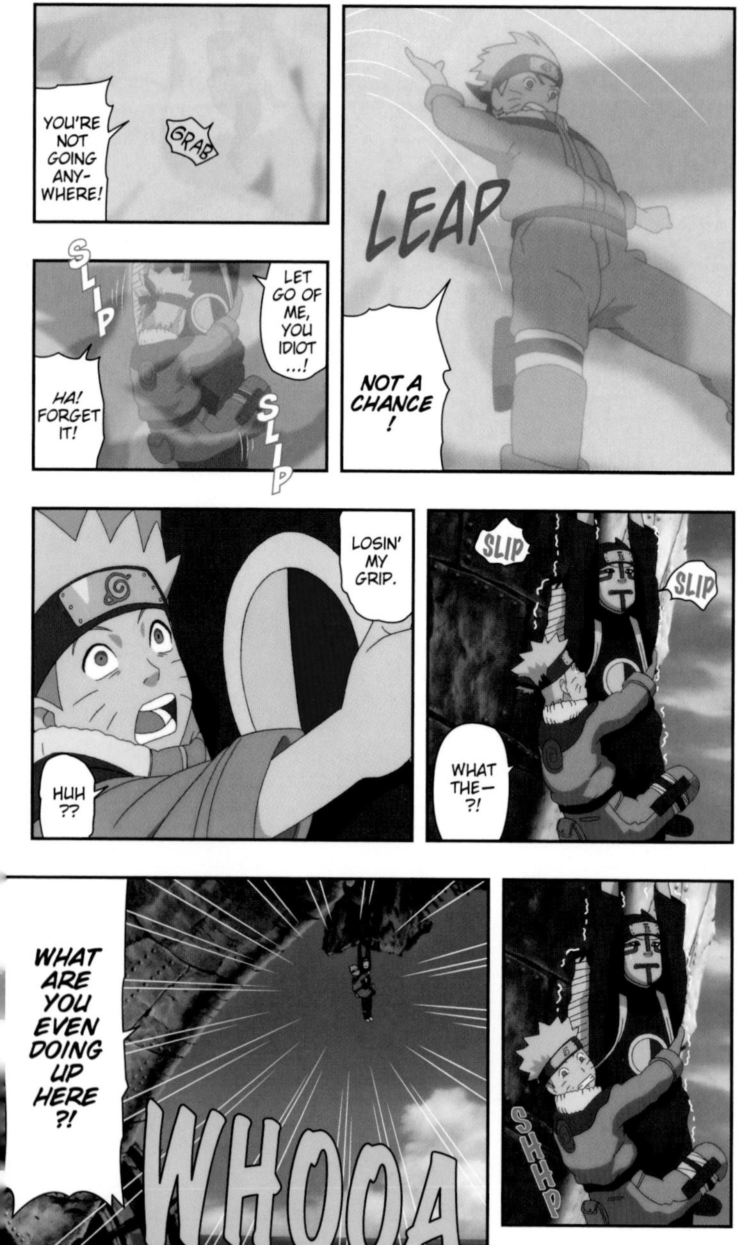
LEAP
NOT A CHANCE!
YOU'RE NOT GOING ANY-WHERE!
GRAB
LET GO OF ME, YOU IDIOT ...!
SLIP
SLIP
HA! FORGET IT!
SLIP
SLIP
WHAT THE— ?!
LOSIN' MY GRIP.
HUH ??
SHHP
WHAT ARE YOU EVEN DOING UP HERE ?!
WHOOA

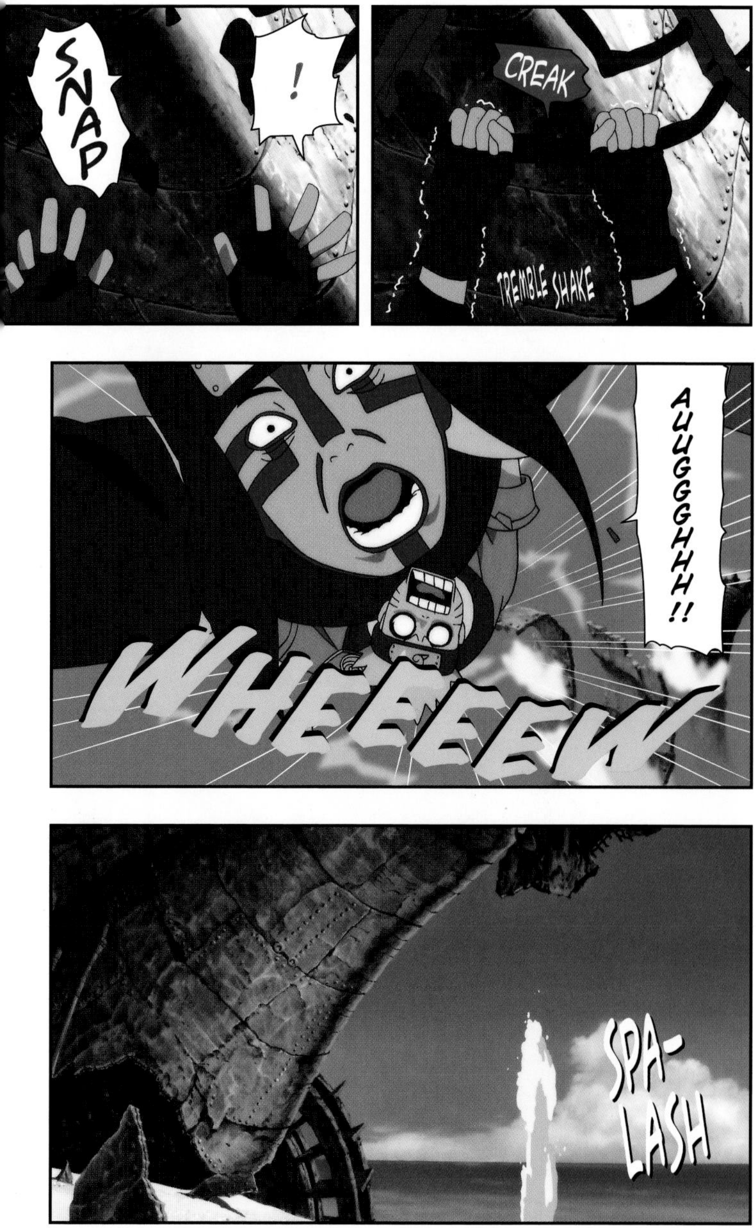
CREAK
TREMBLE SHAKE
SNAP
!
AUUGGGHHH!!
WHEEEEW
SPA-LASH

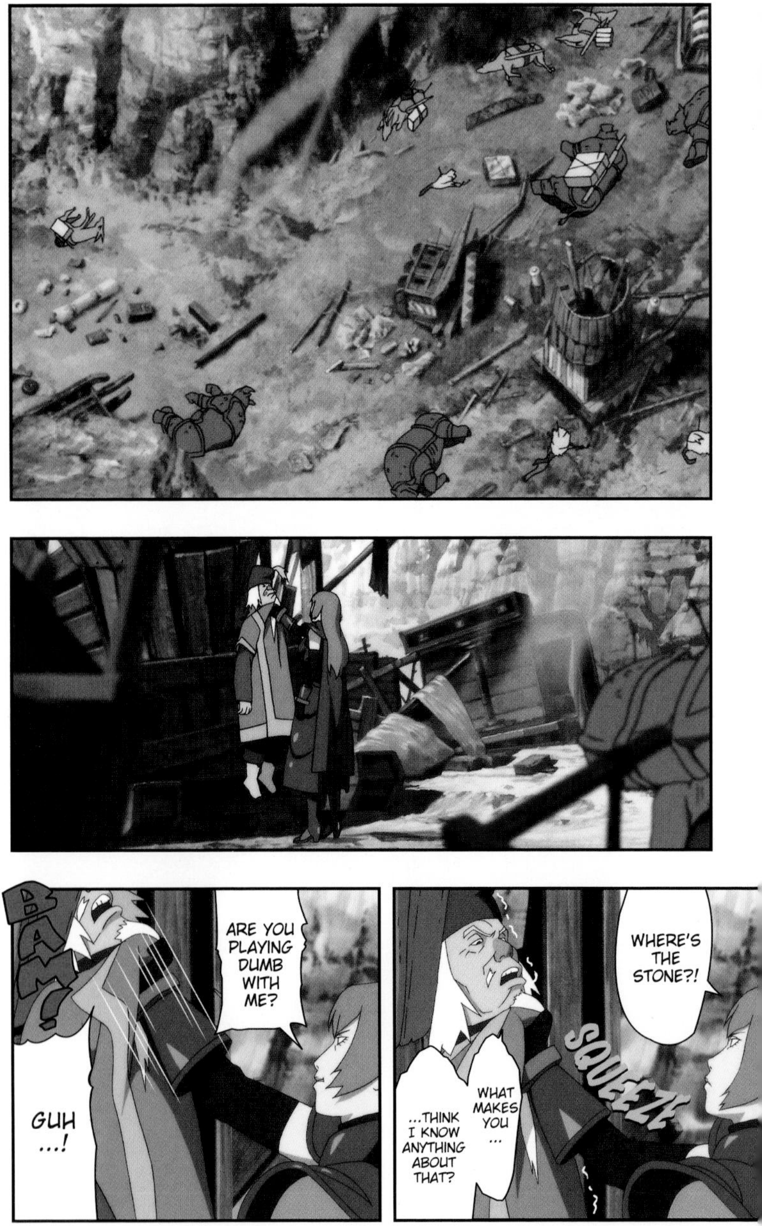
WHERE'S THE STONE?!
SQUEEZE
WHAT MAKES YOU ...
...THINK I KNOW ANYTHING ABOUT THAT?
ARE YOU PLAYING DUMB WITH ME?
BAM
GUH ...!

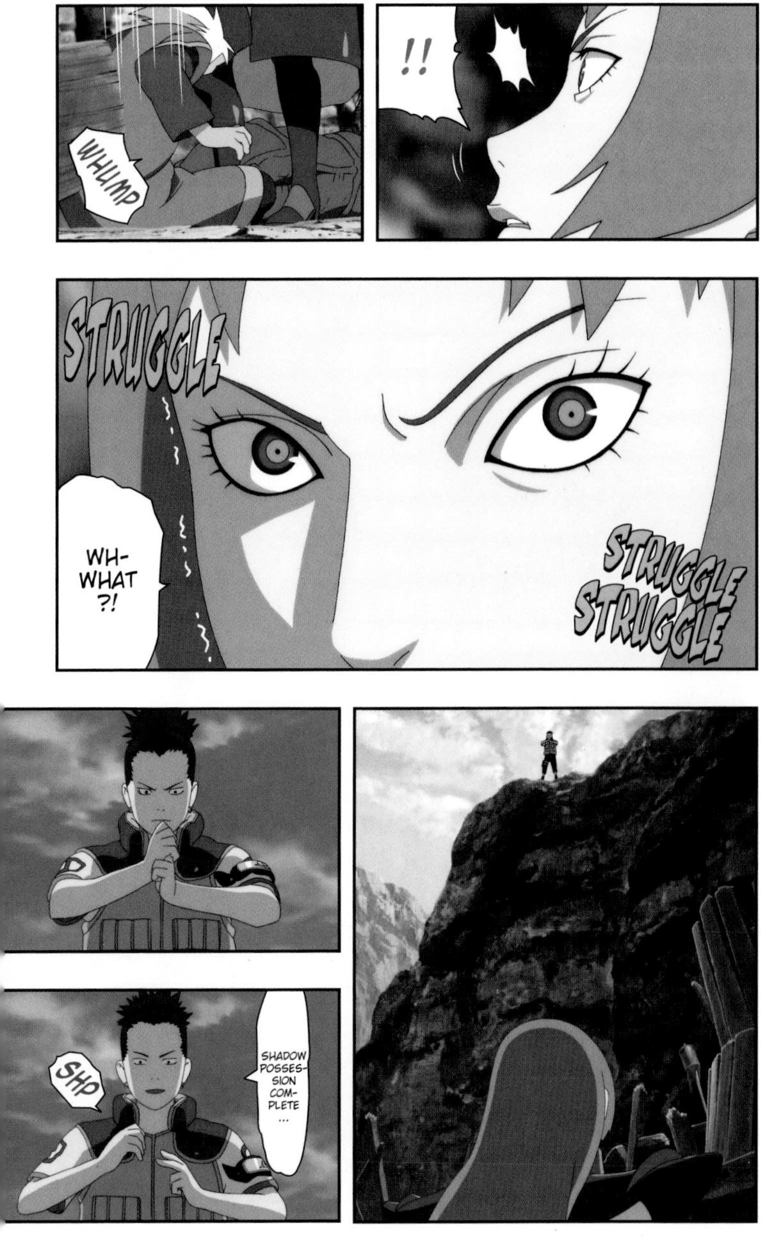
!!
WHUMP
STRUGGLE
STRUGGLE STRUGGLE
WH-WHAT?!
SHADOW POSSESSION COMPLETE...
SHP

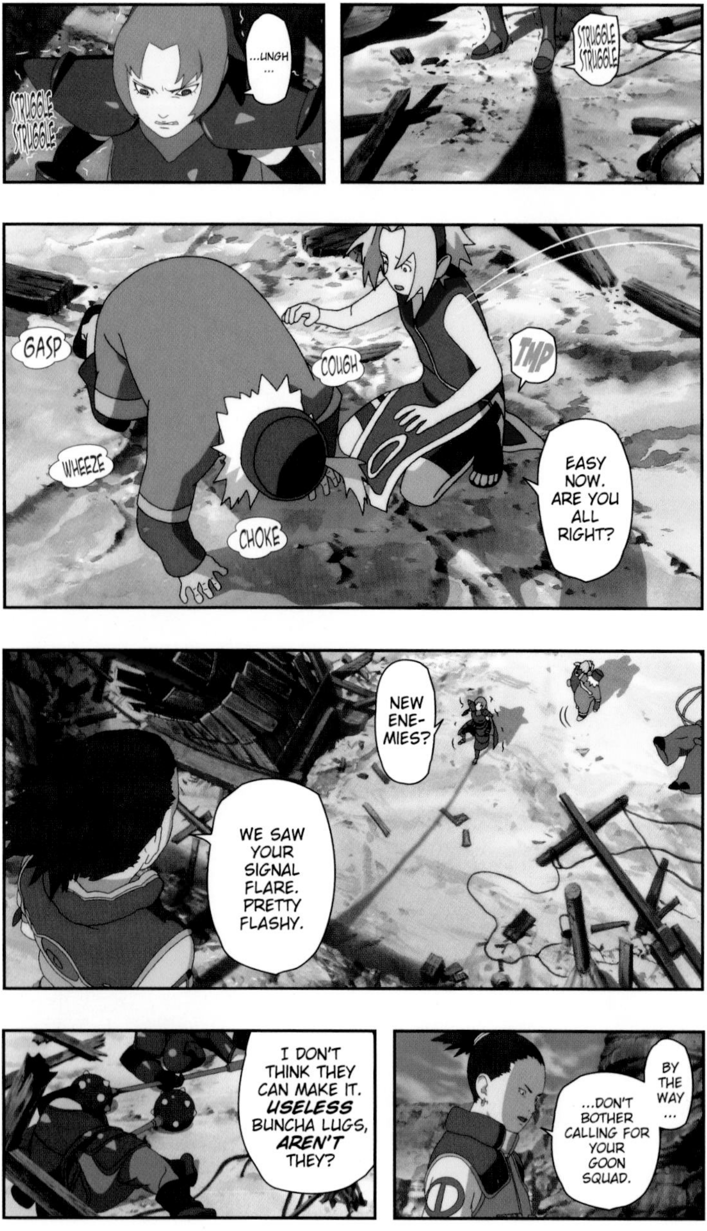
STRUGGLE STRUGGLE
...UNGH ...
STRUGGLE STRUGGLE
TMP
EASY NOW. ARE YOU ALL RIGHT?
COUGH
GASP
WHEEZE
CHOKE
NEW ENE-MIES?
WE SAW YOUR SIGNAL FLARE. PRETTY FLASHY.
BY THE WAY ...
...DON'T BOTHER CALLING FOR YOUR GOON SQUAD.
I DON'T THINK THEY CAN MAKE IT. ***USELESS*** BUNCHA LUGS, ***AREN'T*** THEY?

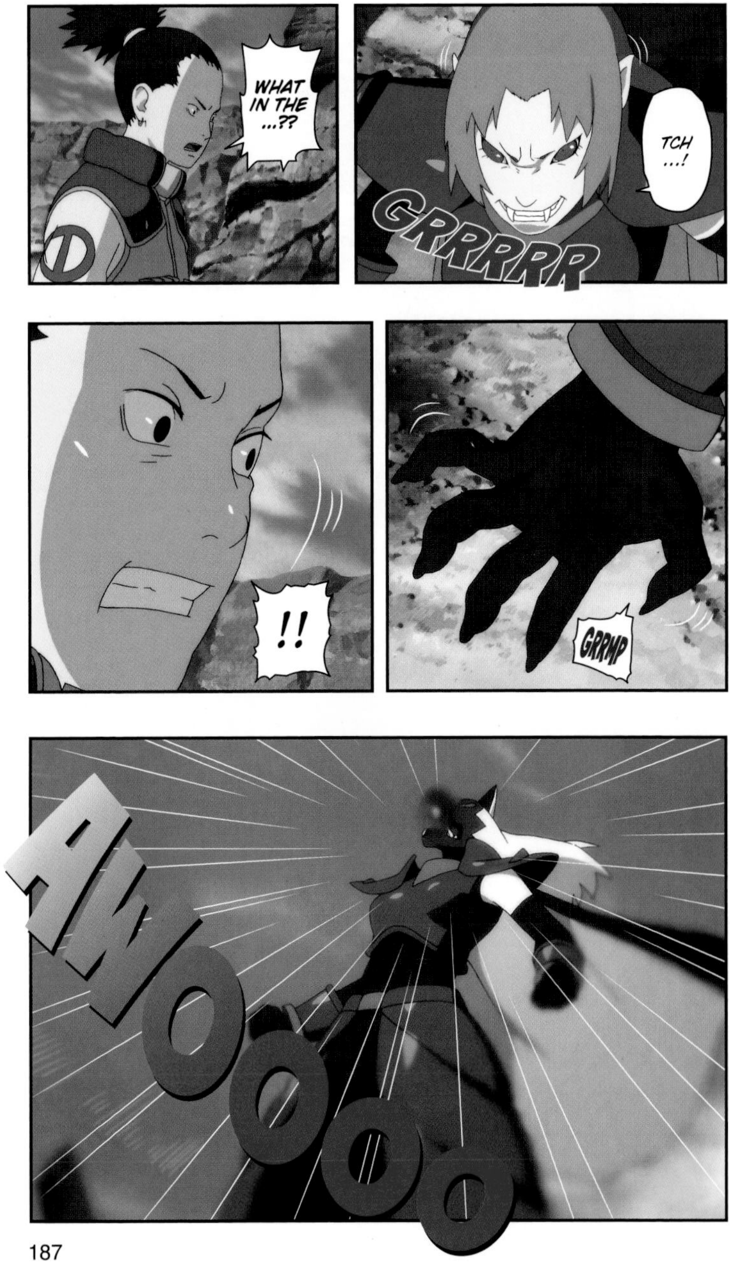
TCH ...!
GRRRRR
WHAT IN THE ...??
GRRMP
!!
AWOOOO

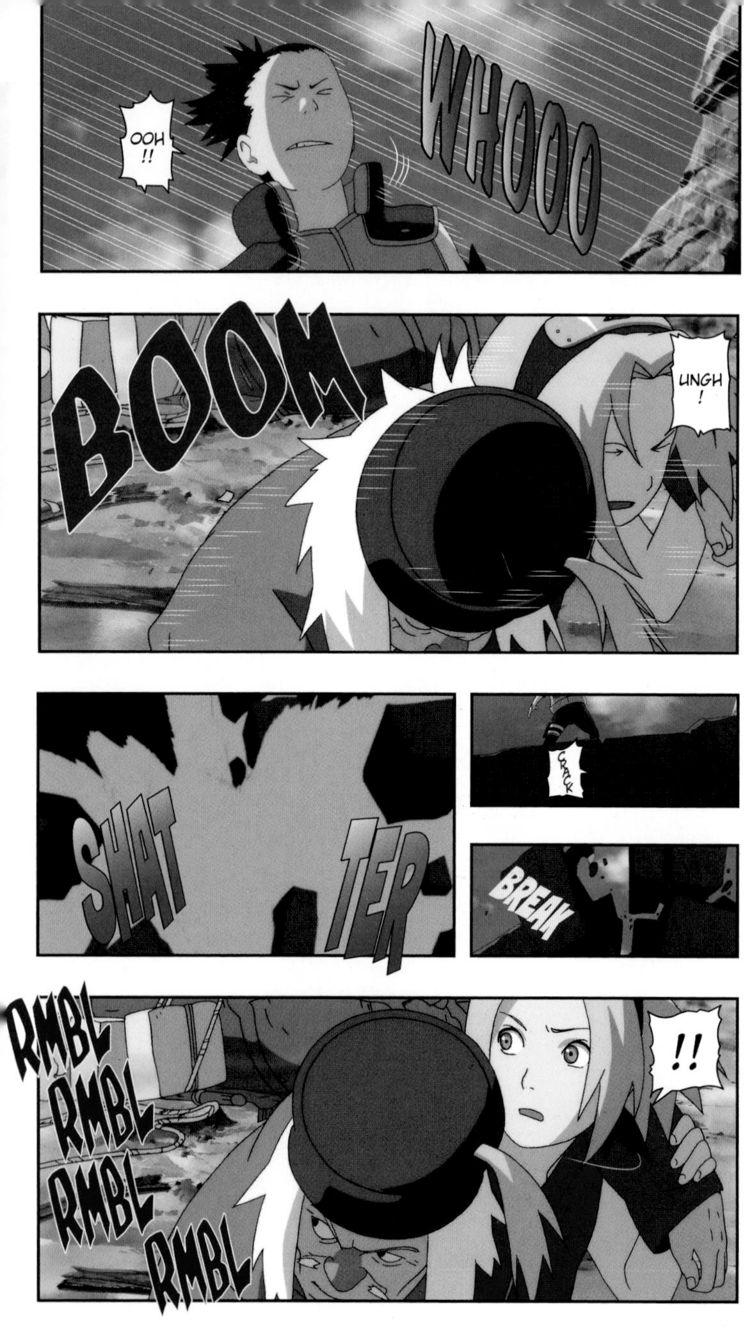
WHOOO
OOH!!
UNGH!
BOOM
CRACK
BREAK
SHATTER
!!
RMBL RMBL RMBL RMBL

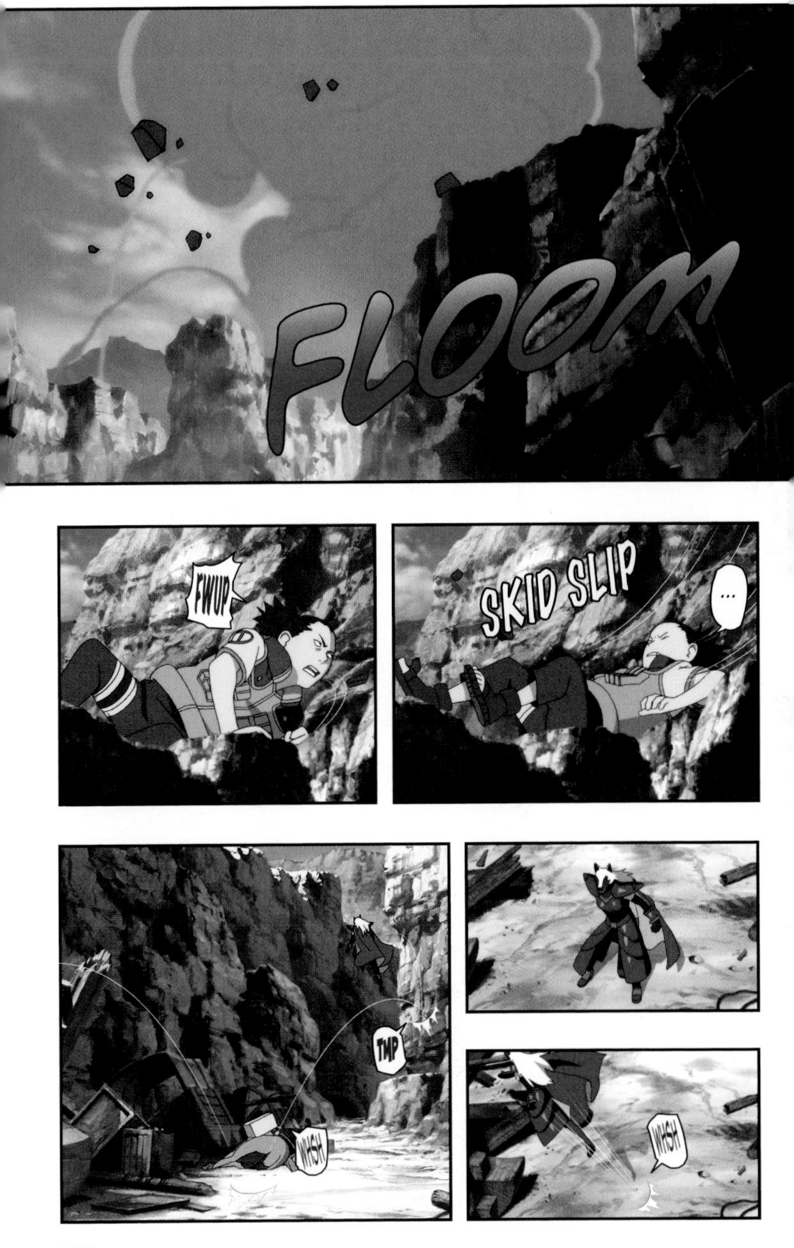
FLOOM
SKID SLIP
...
FWUP
WHSH
TMP
WHSH

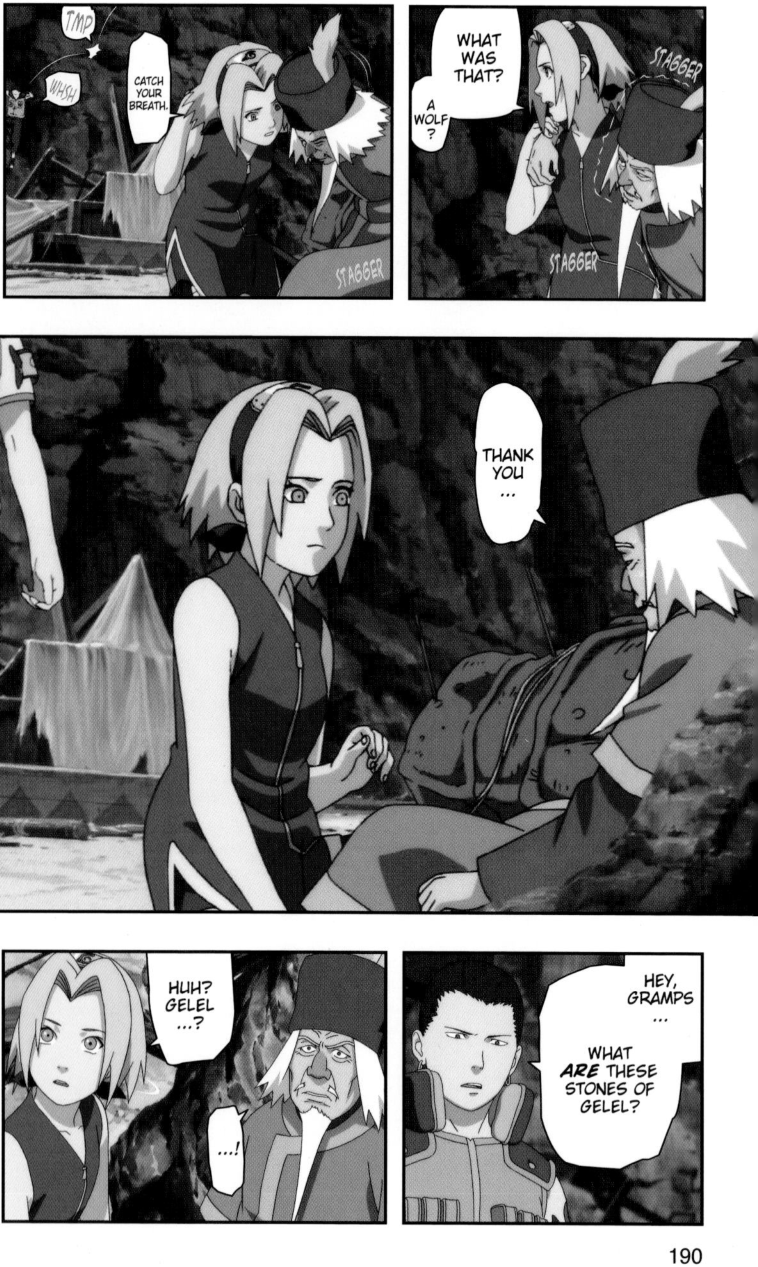

STAGGER
WHAT WAS THAT?
A WOLF?
STAGGER
TMP
WHSH
CATCH YOUR BREATH.
STAGGER
THANK YOU ...
HEY, GRAMPS ...
WHAT ARE THESE STONES OF GELEL?
HUH? GELEL ...?
...!

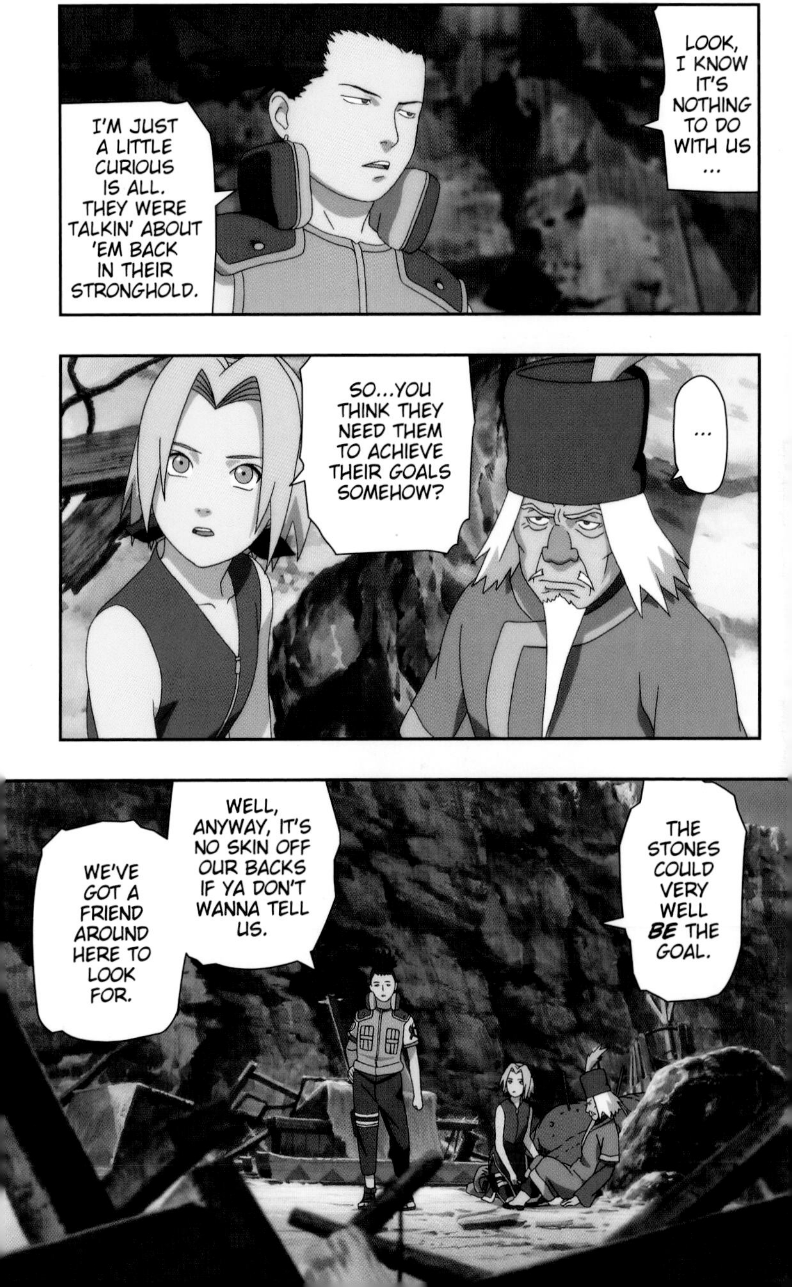
LOOK, I KNOW IT'S NOTHING TO DO WITH US ...
I'M JUST A LITTLE CURIOUS IS ALL. THEY WERE TALKIN' ABOUT 'EM BACK IN THEIR STRONGHOLD.
...
SO...YOU THINK THEY NEED THEM TO ACHIEVE THEIR GOALS SOMEHOW?
THE STONES COULD VERY WELL *BE* THE GOAL.
WELL, ANYWAY, IT'S NO SKIN OFF OUR BACKS IF YA DON'T WANNA TELL US.
WE'VE GOT A FRIEND AROUND HERE TO LOOK FOR.

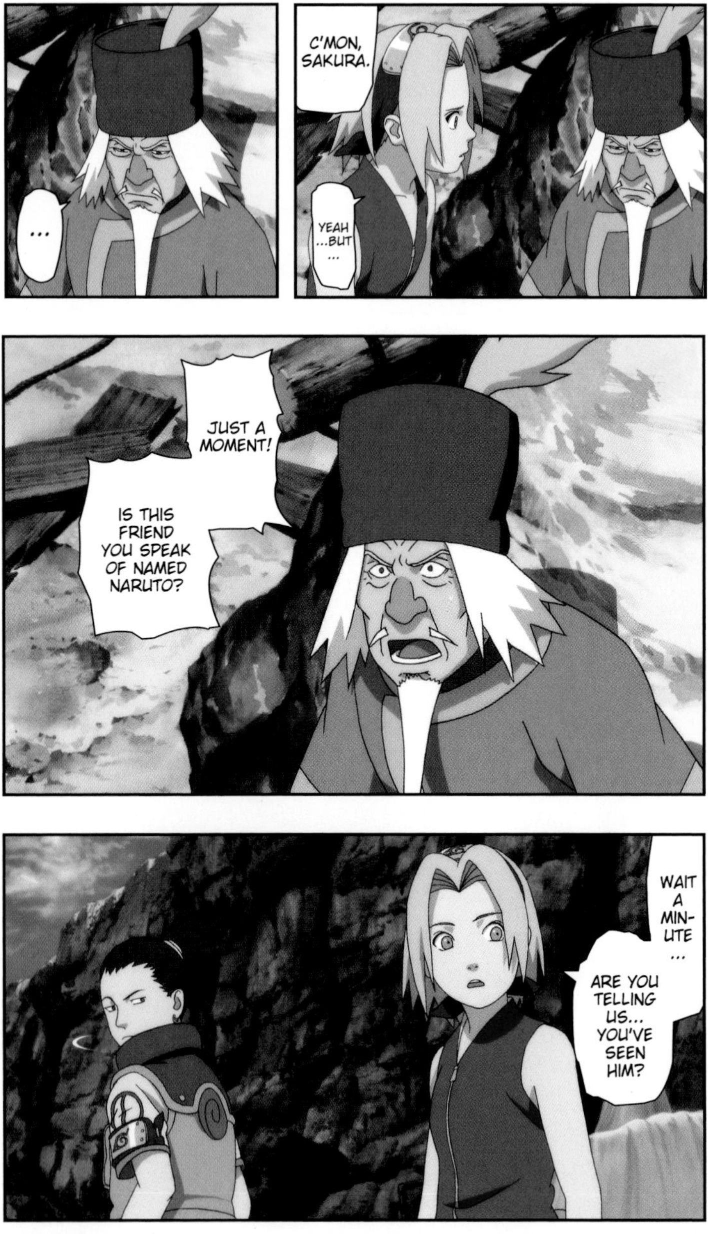
C'MON, SAKURA.
YEAH ...BUT ...
...
JUST A MOMENT!
IS THIS FRIEND YOU SPEAK OF NAMED NARUTO?
WAIT A MIN-UTE ...
ARE YOU TELLING US... YOU'VE SEEN HIM?

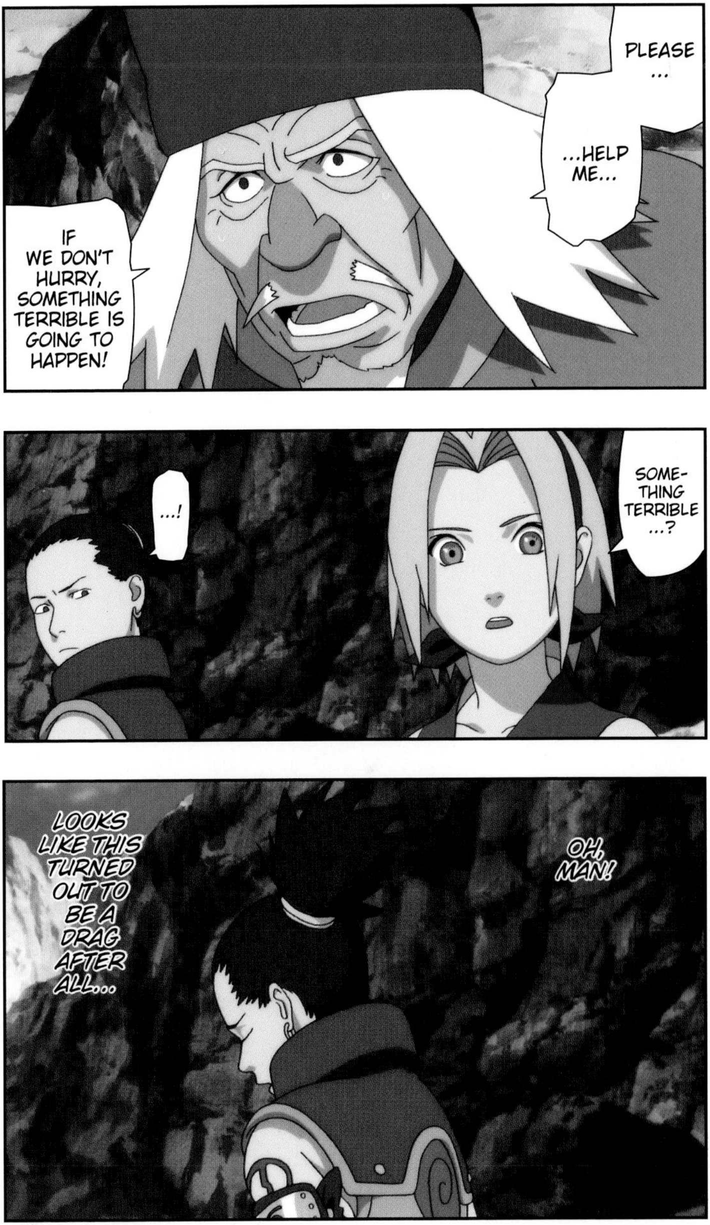
PLEASE ...
...HELP ME...
IF WE DON'T HURRY, SOMETHING TERRIBLE IS GOING TO HAPPEN!
SOME-THING TERRIBLE ...?
...!
OH, MAN!
LOOKS LIKE THIS TURNED OUT TO BE A DRAG AFTER ALL...

SHONEN JUMP

NARUTO

THE MOVIE

LEGEND of the STONE of GELEL

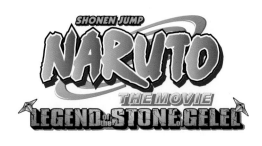

Chapter 5: A Thirst for Power!

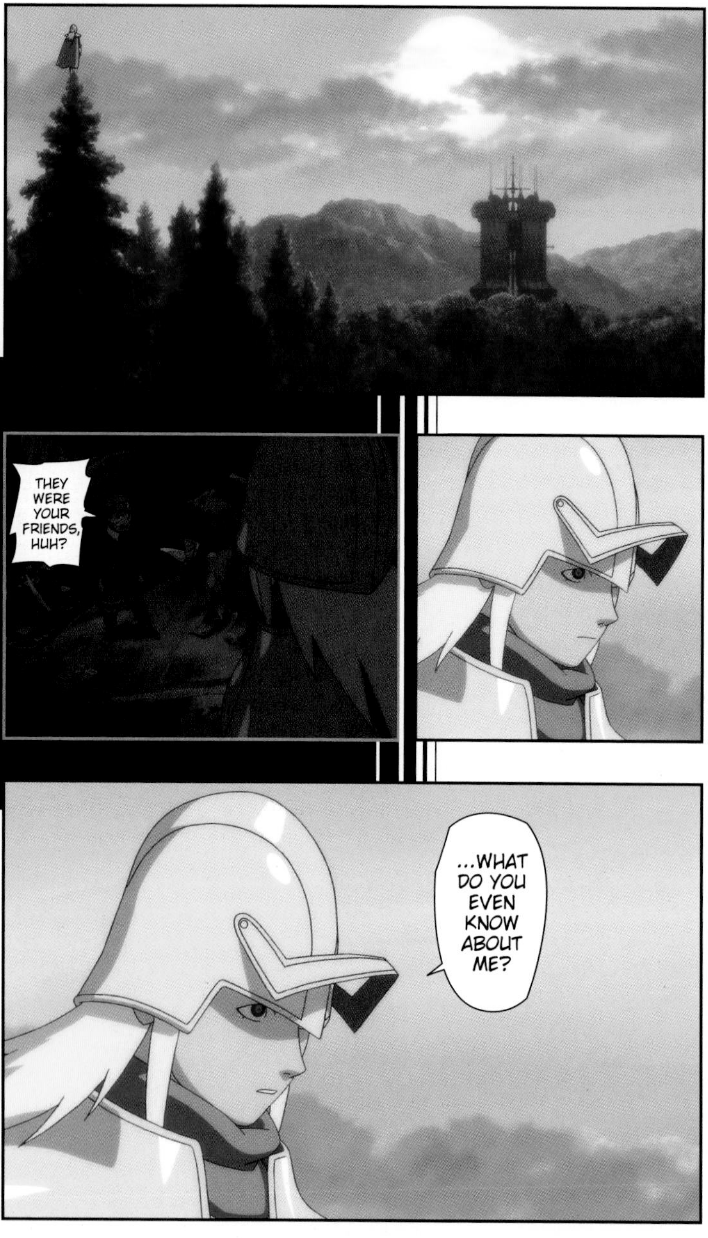
THEY WERE YOUR FRIENDS, HUH?
...WHAT DO YOU EVEN KNOW ABOUT ME?

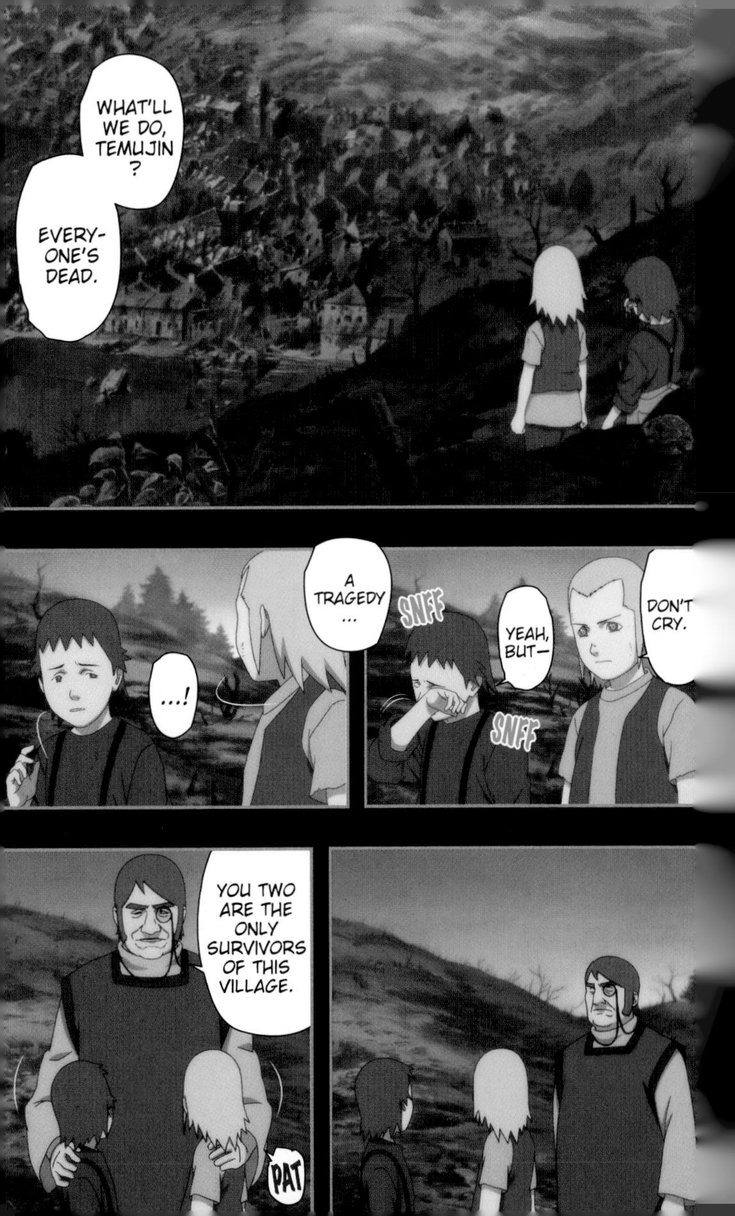

WHAT'LL WE DO, TEMUJIN?
EVERYONE'S DEAD.
DON'T CRY.
SNFF
YEAH, BUT—
SNFF
A TRAGEDY...
...!
YOU TWO ARE THE ONLY SURVIVORS OF THIS VILLAGE.
PAT

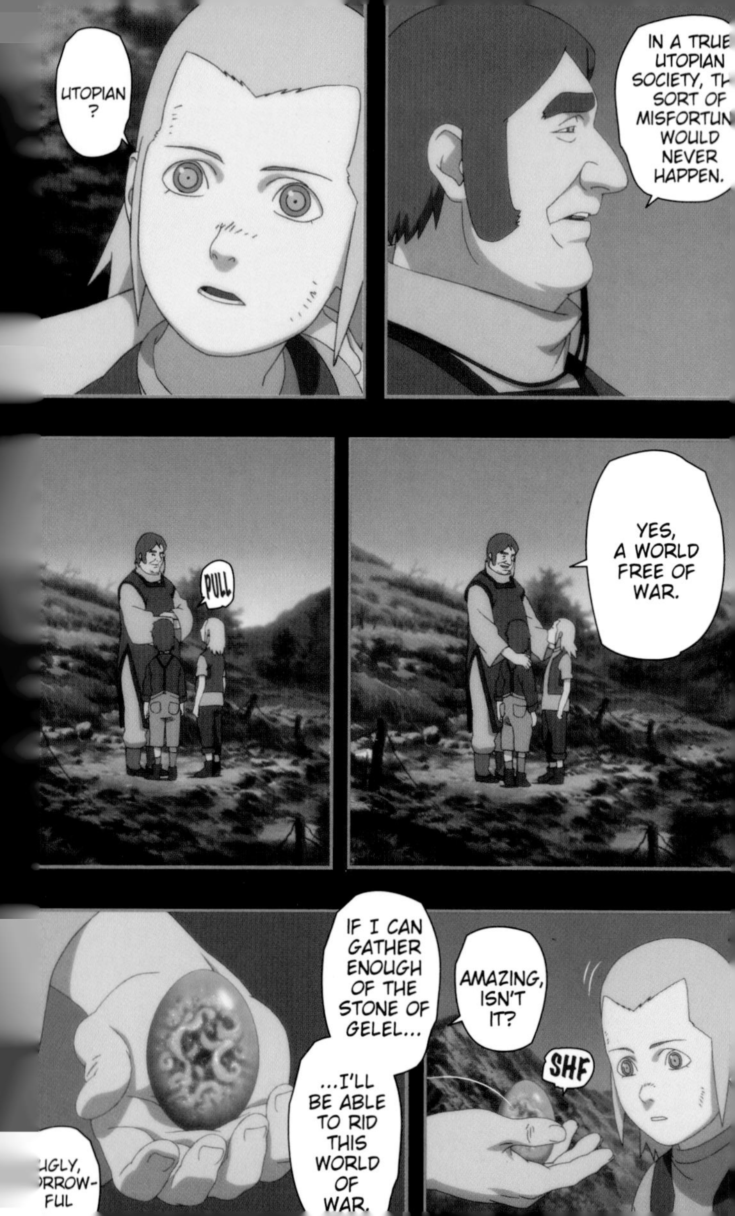
IN A TRUE UTOPIAN SOCIETY, TH SORT OF MISFORTUN WOULD NEVER HAPPEN.
UTOPIAN ?
YES, A WORLD FREE OF WAR.
PULL
AMAZING, ISN'T IT?
SHF
IF I CAN GATHER ENOUGH OF THE STONE OF GELEL...
...I'LL BE ABLE TO RID THIS WORLD OF WAR.
UGLY, RROW- FUL

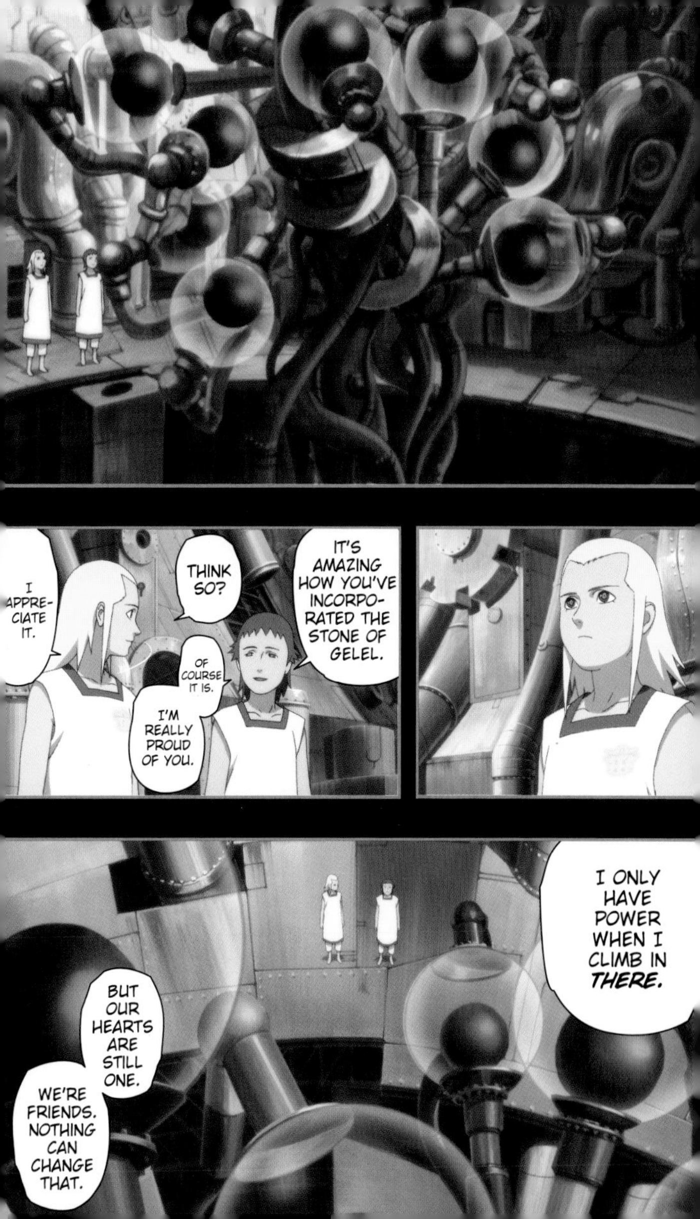
IT'S AMAZING HOW YOU'VE INCORPORATED THE STONE OF GELEL.
THINK SO?
OF COURSE IT IS.
I'M REALLY PROUD OF YOU.
I APPRECIATE IT.
I ONLY HAVE POWER WHEN I CLIMB IN *THERE.*
BUT OUR HEARTS ARE STILL ONE.
WE'RE FRIENDS. NOTHING CAN CHANGE THAT.

WE MUSTN'T LET OTHER VILLAGES SUFFER LIKE OURS DID.

WE GIVE OUR ALL...

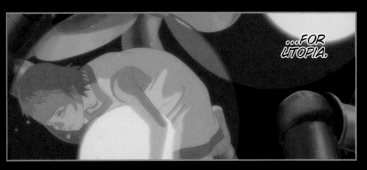

...FOR UTOPIA.

WHAT'S WRONG?

YOU BLIND LITTLE FOOL!

BEEP BEEP

THAT CARAVAN YOU WERE TRAIPSING AROUND WITH...

...HAD INFO ON THE STONE OF GELEL!

WHAT?!

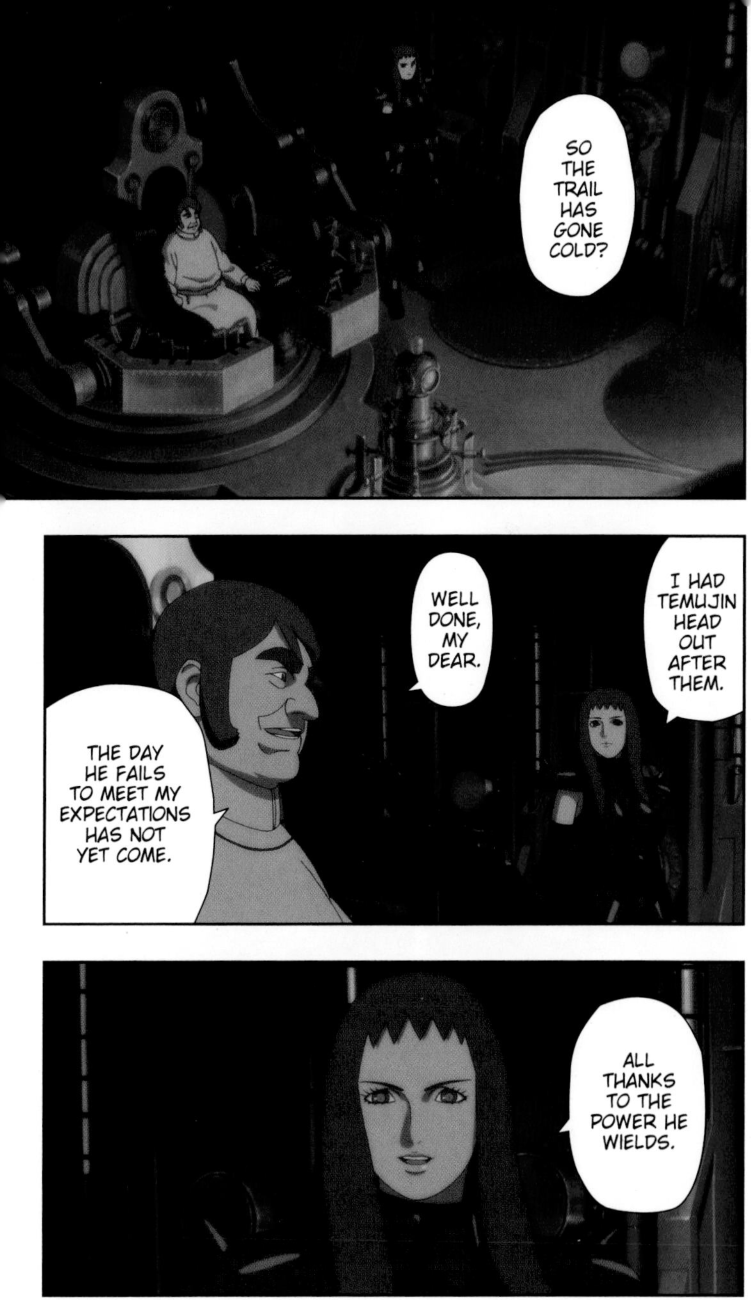
SO THE TRAIL HAS GONE COLD?
I HAD TEMUJIN HEAD OUT AFTER THEM.
WELL DONE, MY DEAR.
THE DAY HE FAILS TO MEET MY EXPECTATIONS HAS NOT YET COME.
ALL THANKS TO THE POWER HE WIELDS.

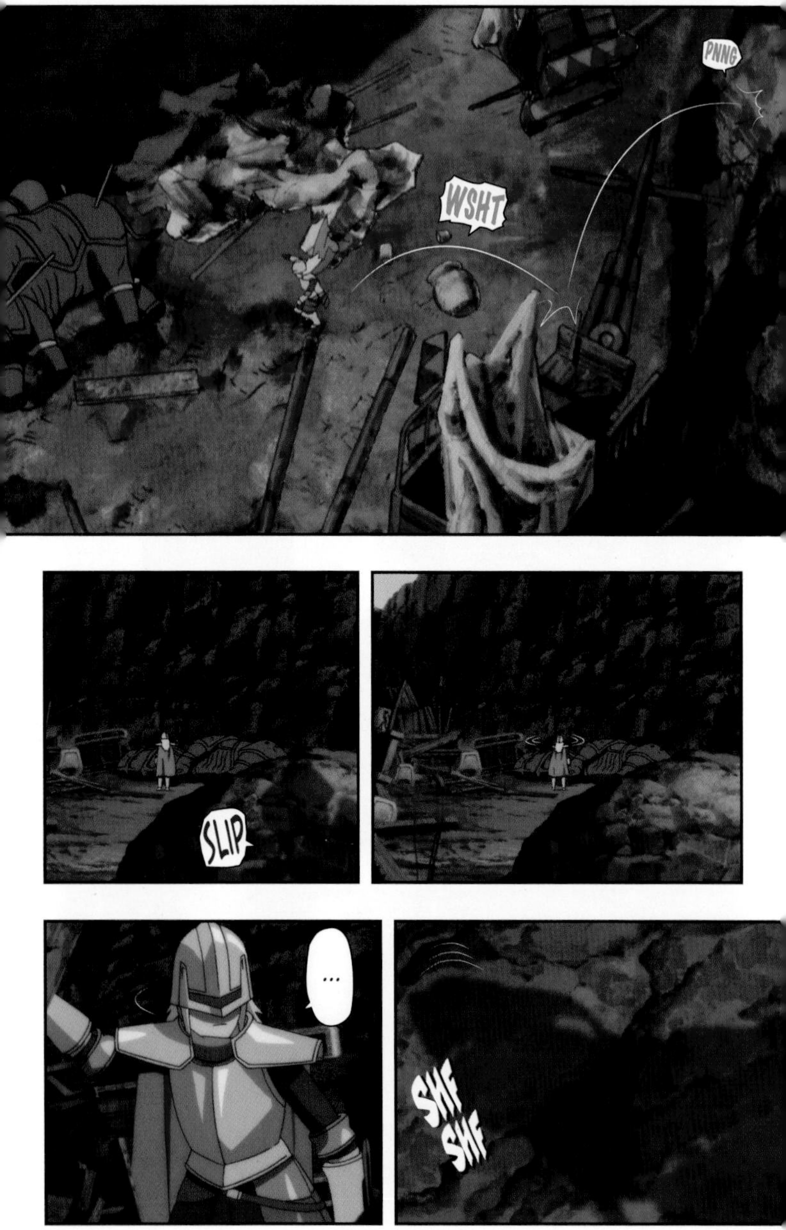
PNNG
WSHT
SLIP
SHF SHF
...

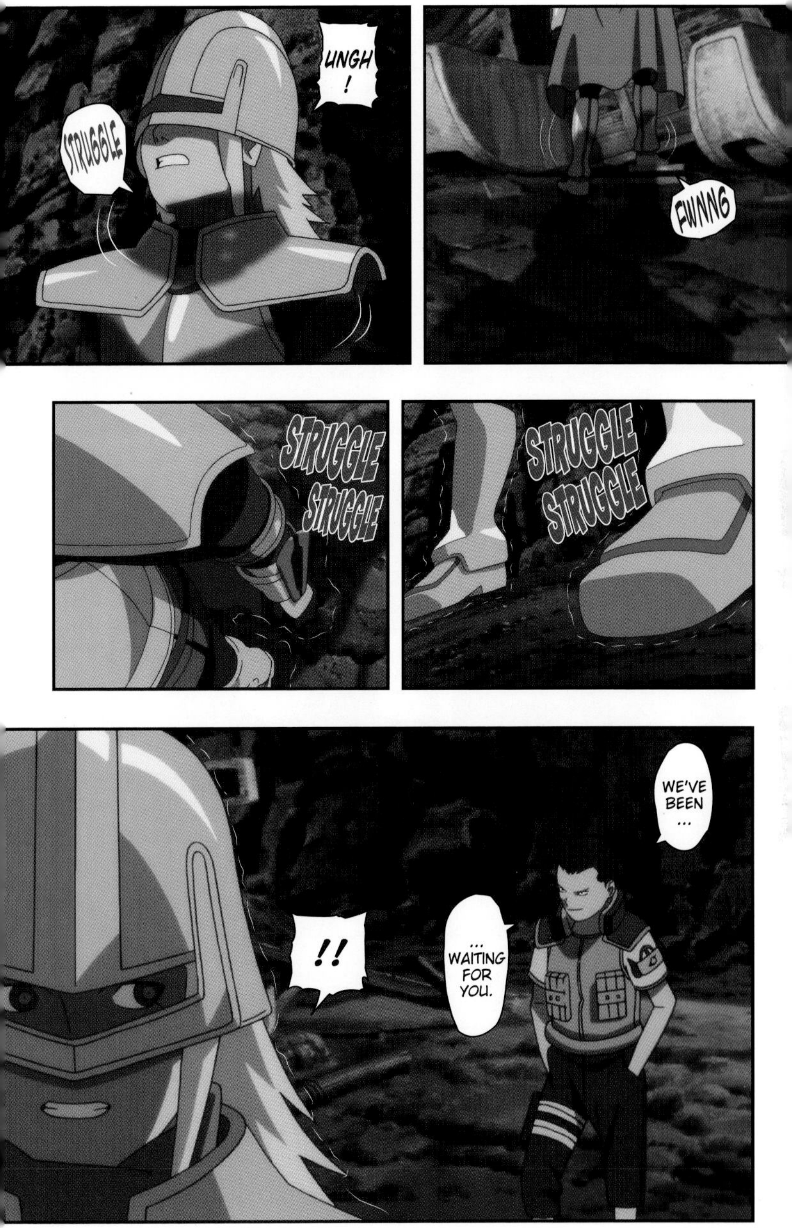
FWNNG
UNGH !
STRUGGLE
STRUGGLE STRUGGLE
STRUGGLE STRUGGLE
WE'VE BEEN ...
... WAITING FOR YOU.
!!

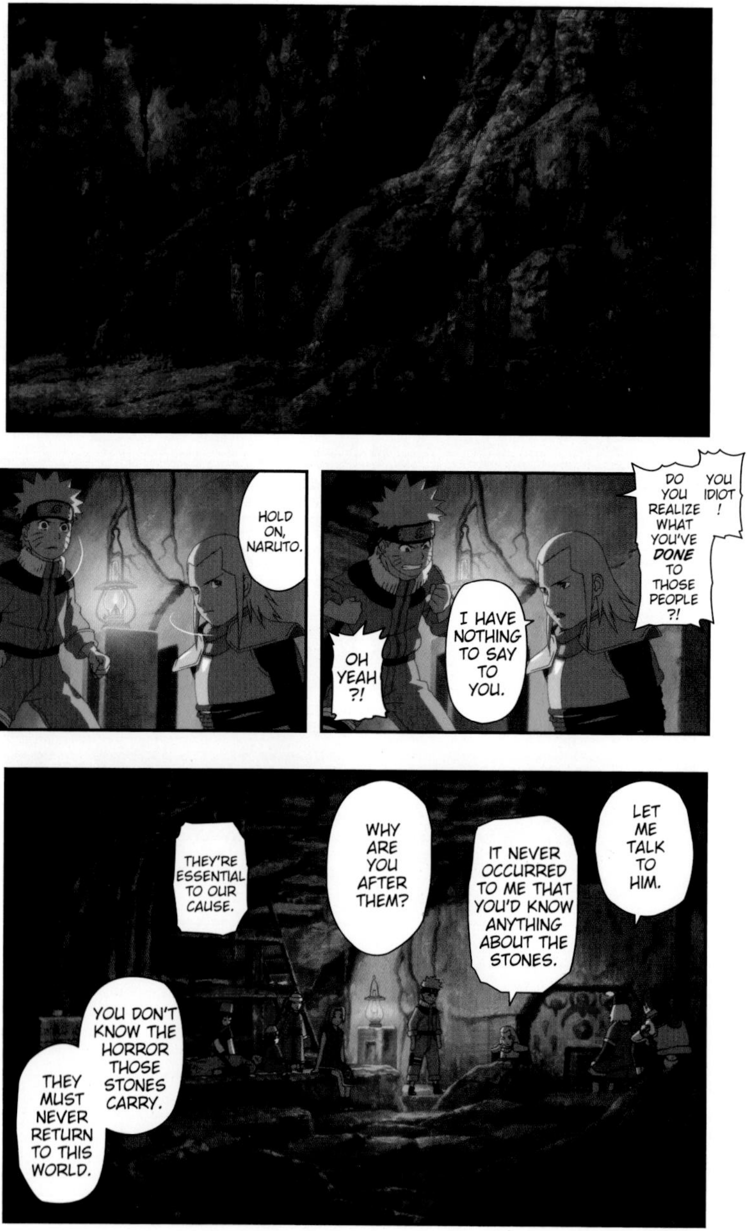
YOU IDIOT!
DO YOU REALIZE WHAT YOU'VE ***DONE*** TO THOSE PEOPLE?!
I HAVE NOTHING TO SAY TO YOU.
OH YEAH?!
HOLD ON, NARUTO.
LET ME TALK TO HIM.
IT NEVER OCCURRED TO ME THAT YOU'D KNOW ANYTHING ABOUT THE STONES.
WHY ARE YOU AFTER THEM?
THEY'RE ESSENTIAL TO OUR CAUSE.
YOU DON'T KNOW THE HORROR THOSE STONES CARRY.
THEY MUST NEVER RETURN TO THIS WORLD.

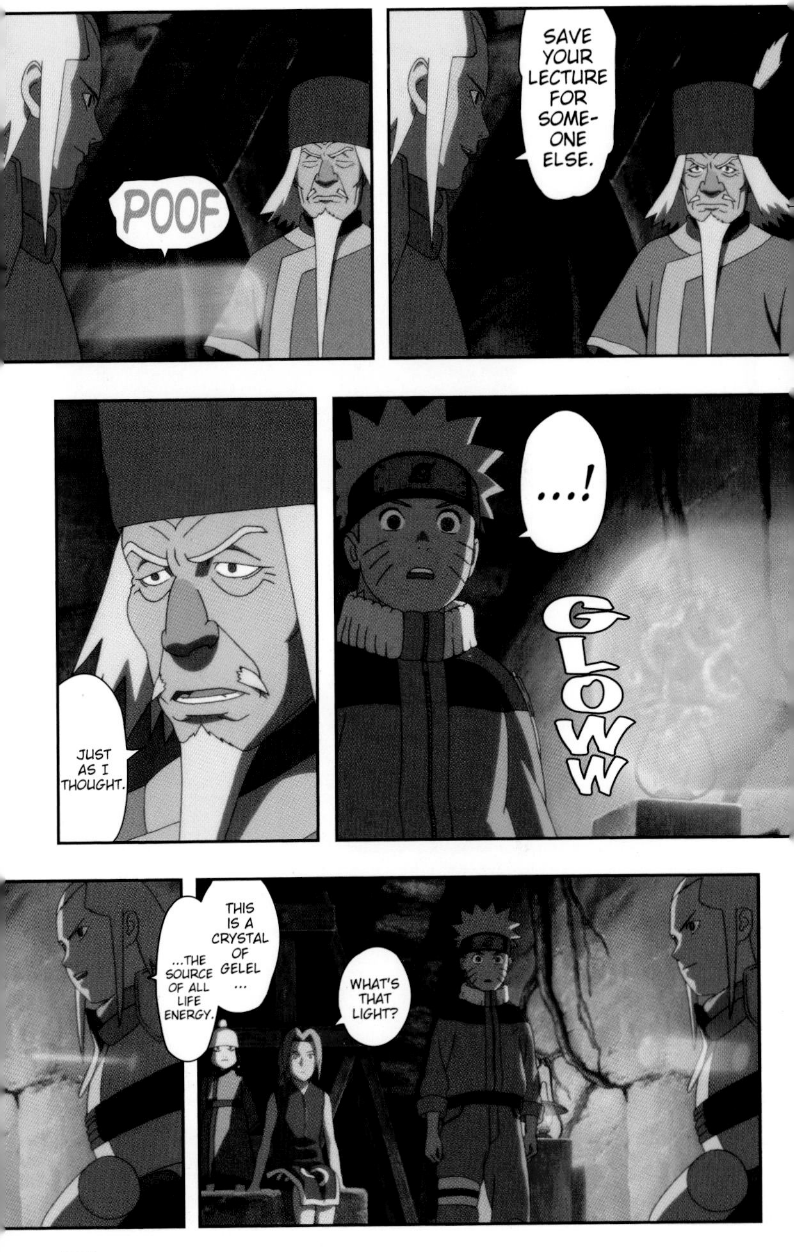
SAVE YOUR LECTURE FOR SOMEONE ELSE.
POOF
...!
GLOW
JUST AS I THOUGHT.
WHAT'S THAT LIGHT?
THIS IS A CRYSTAL OF GELEL...
...THE SOURCE OF ALL LIFE ENERGY.

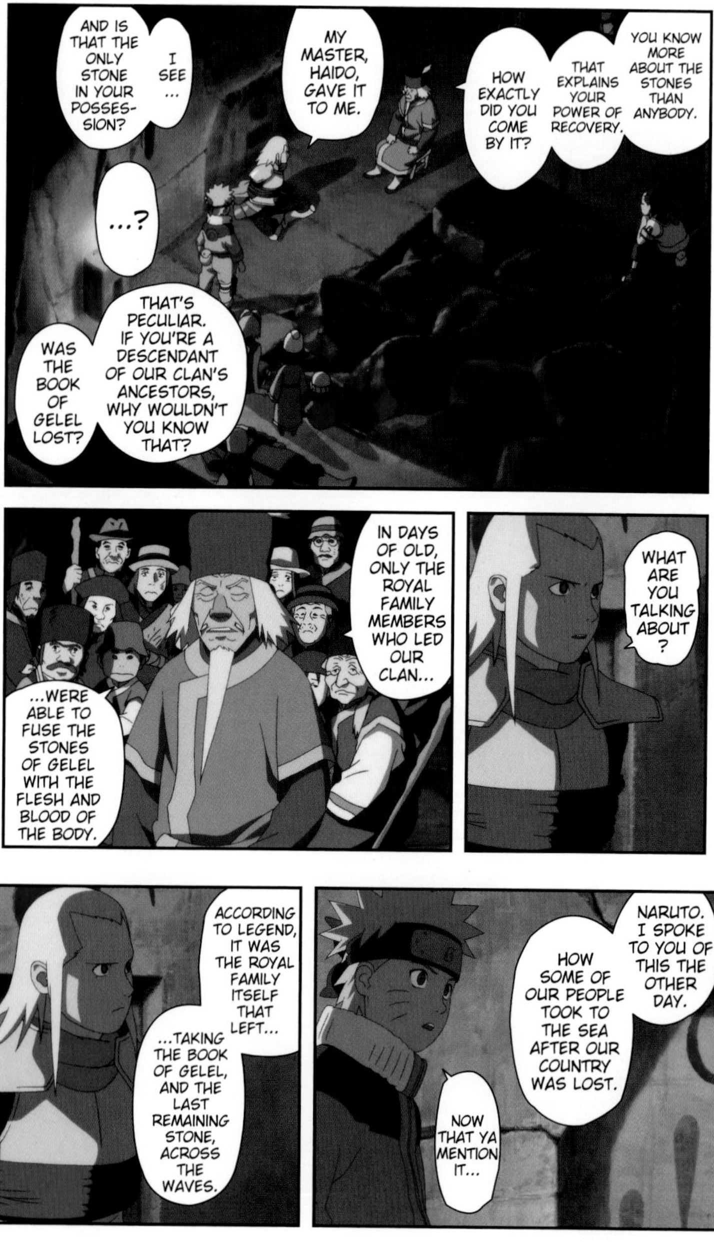
YOU KNOW MORE ABOUT THE STONES THAN ANYBODY.
THAT EXPLAINS YOUR POWER OF RECOVERY.
HOW EXACTLY DID YOU COME BY IT?
MY MASTER, HAIDO, GAVE IT TO ME.
I SEE...
AND IS THAT THE ONLY STONE IN YOUR POSSES-SION?
...?
THAT'S PECULIAR. IF YOU'RE A DESCENDANT OF OUR CLAN'S ANCESTORS, WHY WOULDN'T YOU KNOW THAT?
WAS THE BOOK OF GELEL LOST?
WHAT ARE YOU TALKING ABOUT?
IN DAYS OF OLD, ONLY THE ROYAL FAMILY MEMBERS WHO LED OUR CLAN...
...WERE ABLE TO FUSE THE STONES OF GELEL WITH THE FLESH AND BLOOD OF THE BODY.
NARUTO. I SPOKE TO YOU OF THIS THE OTHER DAY.
HOW SOME OF OUR PEOPLE TOOK TO THE SEA AFTER OUR COUNTRY WAS LOST.
NOW THAT YA MENTION IT...
ACCORDING TO LEGEND, IT WAS THE ROYAL FAMILY ITSELF THAT LEFT...
...TAKING THE BOOK OF GELEL, AND THE LAST REMAINING STONE, ACROSS THE WAVES.

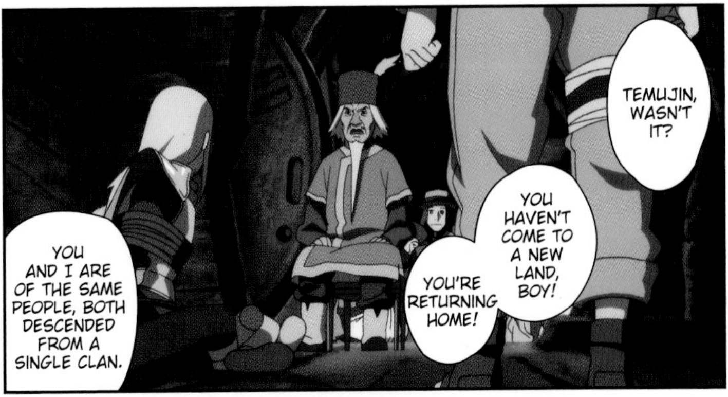
TEMUJIN, WASN'T IT?
YOU HAVEN'T COME TO A NEW LAND, BOY!
YOU'RE RETURNING HOME!
YOU AND I ARE OF THE SAME PEOPLE, BOTH DESCENDED FROM A SINGLE CLAN.

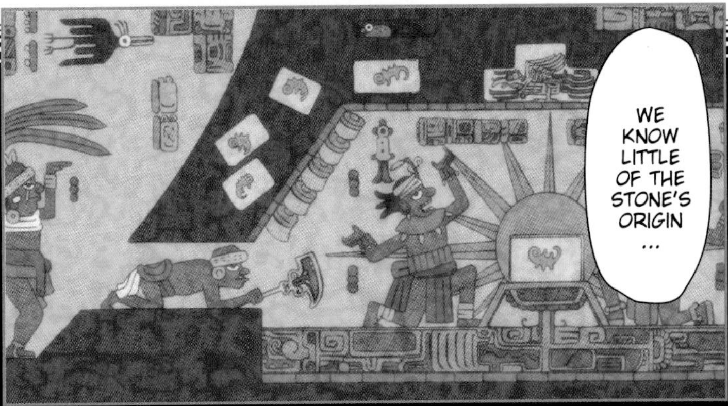
WE KNOW LITTLE OF THE STONE'S ORIGIN...

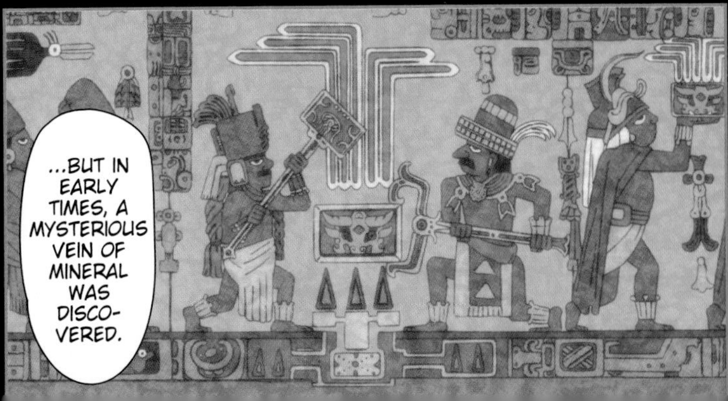
...BUT IN EARLY TIMES, A MYSTERIOUS VEIN OF MINERAL WAS DISCO-VERED.

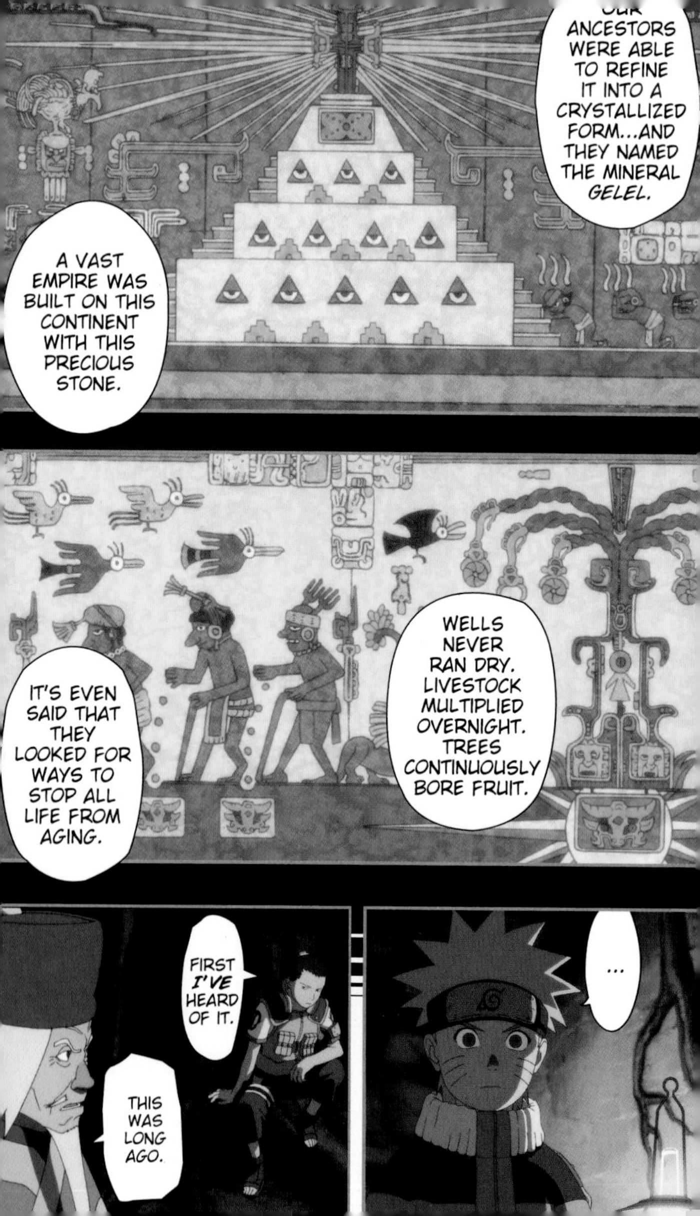
ANCESTORS WERE ABLE TO REFINE IT INTO A CRYSTALLIZED FORM...AND THEY NAMED THE MINERAL *GELEL.*
A VAST EMPIRE WAS BUILT ON THIS CONTINENT WITH THIS PRECIOUS STONE.
WELLS NEVER RAN DRY. LIVESTOCK MULTIPLIED OVERNIGHT. TREES CONTINUOUSLY BORE FRUIT.
IT'S EVEN SAID THAT THEY LOOKED FOR WAYS TO STOP ALL LIFE FROM AGING.
...
FIRST *I'VE* HEARD OF IT.
THIS WAS LONG AGO.

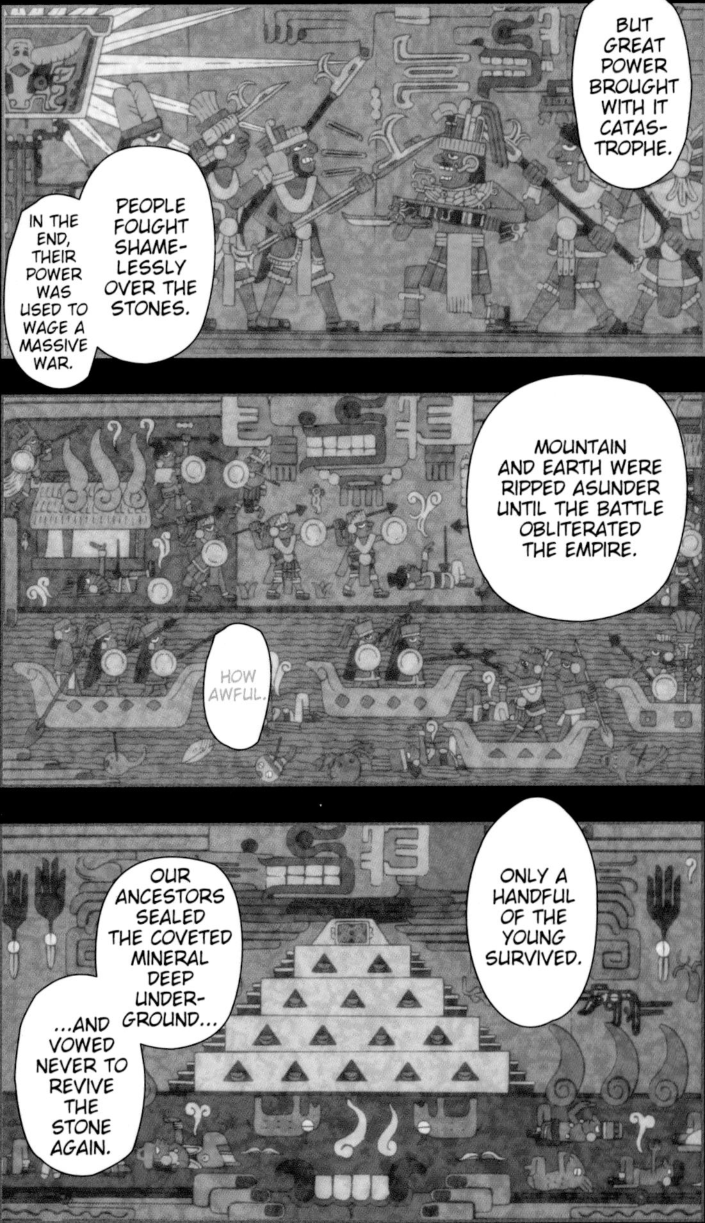
BUT GREAT POWER BROUGHT WITH IT CATASTROPHE.
PEOPLE FOUGHT SHAMELESSLY OVER THE STONES.
IN THE END, THEIR POWER WAS USED TO WAGE A MASSIVE WAR.
MOUNTAIN AND EARTH WERE RIPPED ASUNDER UNTIL THE BATTLE OBLITERATED THE EMPIRE.
HOW AWFUL.
ONLY A HANDFUL OF THE YOUNG SURVIVED.
OUR ANCESTORS SEALED THE COVETED MINERAL DEEP UNDERGROUND...
...AND VOWED NEVER TO REVIVE THE STONE AGAIN.

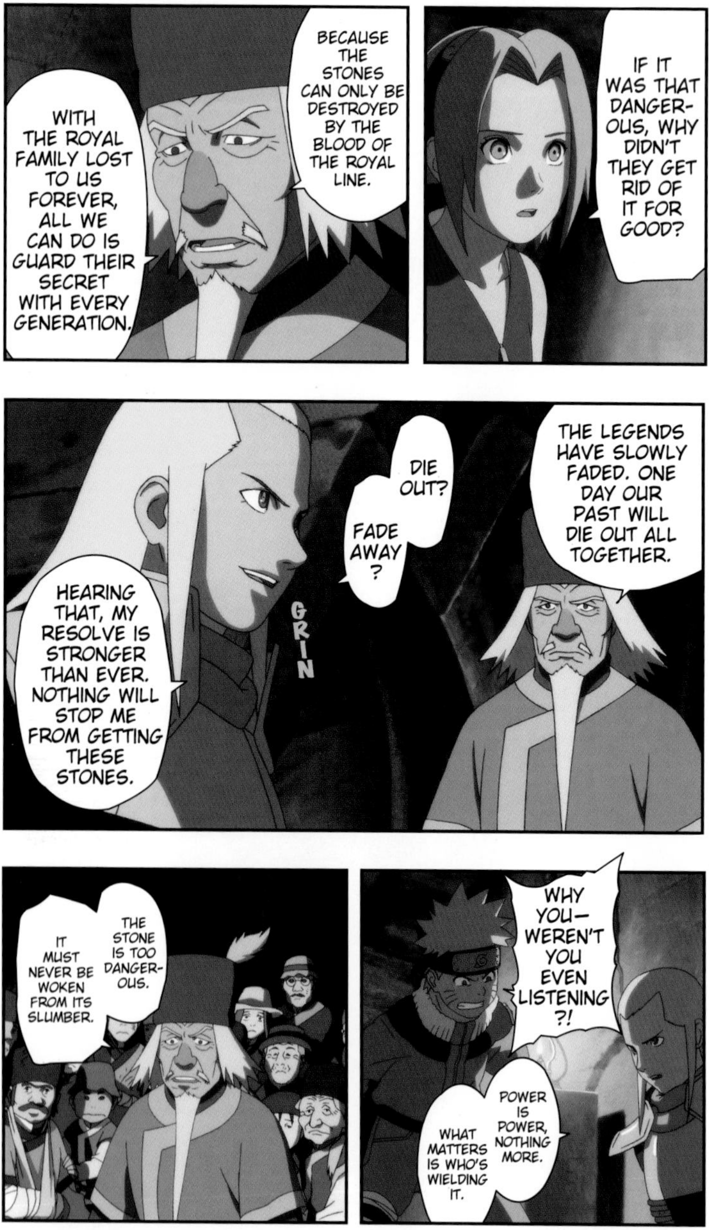
IF IT WAS THAT DANGER-OUS, WHY DIDN'T THEY GET RID OF IT FOR GOOD?
BECAUSE THE STONES CAN ONLY BE DESTROYED BY THE BLOOD OF THE ROYAL LINE.
WITH THE ROYAL FAMILY LOST TO US FOREVER, ALL WE CAN DO IS GUARD THEIR SECRET WITH EVERY GENERATION.
THE LEGENDS HAVE SLOWLY FADED. ONE DAY OUR PAST WILL DIE OUT ALL TOGETHER.
DIE OUT?
FADE AWAY?
GRIN
HEARING THAT, MY RESOLVE IS STRONGER THAN EVER. NOTHING WILL STOP ME FROM GETTING THESE STONES.
WHY YOU— WEREN'T YOU EVEN LISTENING?!
POWER IS POWER, NOTHING MORE.
WHAT MATTERS IS WHO'S WIELDING IT.
THE STONE IS TOO DANGER-OUS.
IT MUST NEVER BE WOKEN FROM ITS SLUMBER.

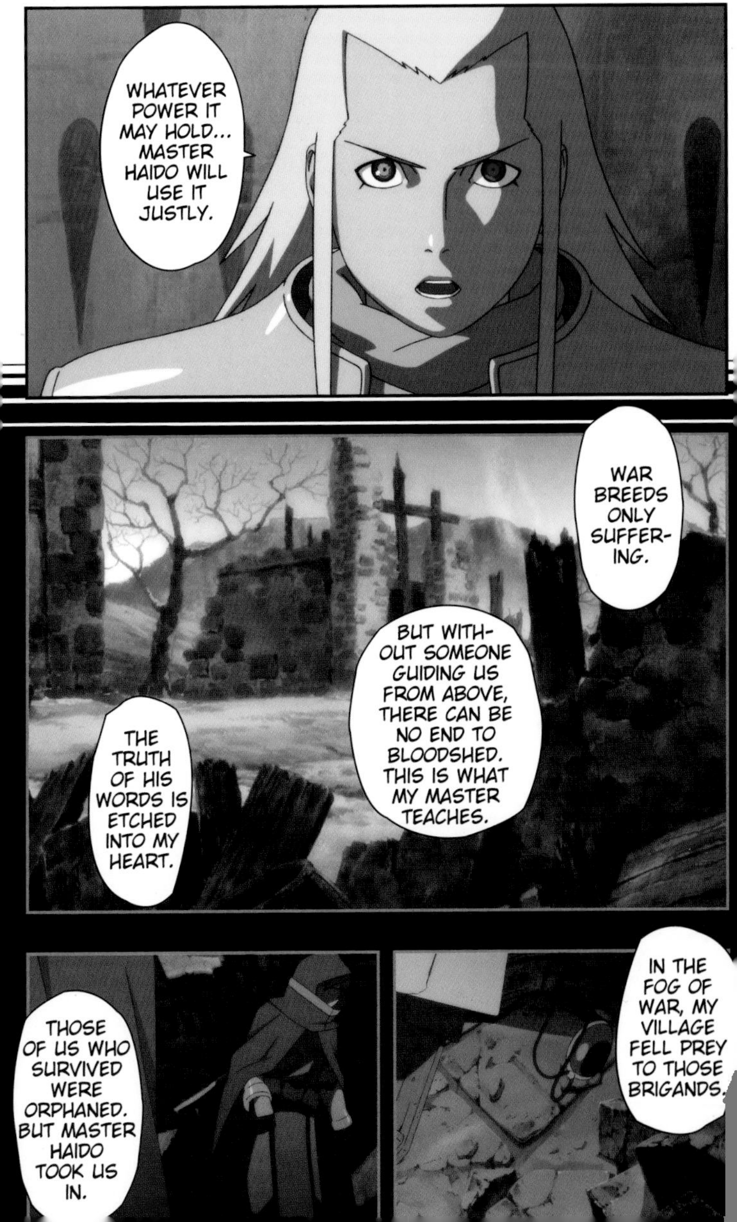
WHATEVER POWER IT MAY HOLD... MASTER HAIDO WILL USE IT JUSTLY.
WAR BREEDS ONLY SUFFER-ING.
BUT WITH-OUT SOMEONE GUIDING US FROM ABOVE, THERE CAN BE NO END TO BLOODSHED. THIS IS WHAT MY MASTER TEACHES.
THE TRUTH OF HIS WORDS IS ETCHED INTO MY HEART.
IN THE FOG OF WAR, MY VILLAGE FELL PREY TO THOSE BRIGANDS.
THOSE OF US WHO SURVIVED WERE ORPHANED. BUT MASTER HAIDO TOOK US IN.

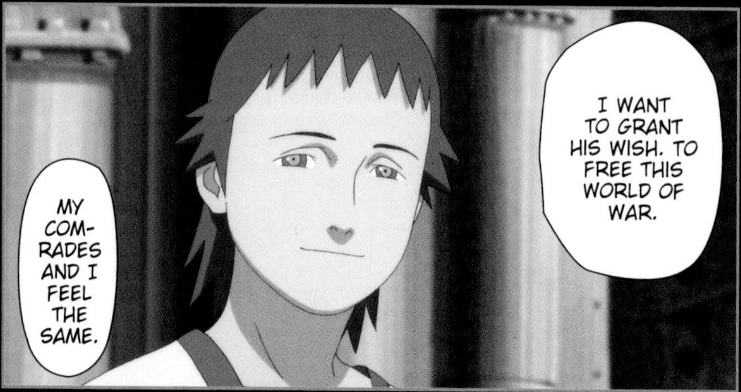
I WANT TO GRANT HIS WISH. TO FREE THIS WORLD OF WAR.
MY COM-RADES AND I FEEL THE SAME.

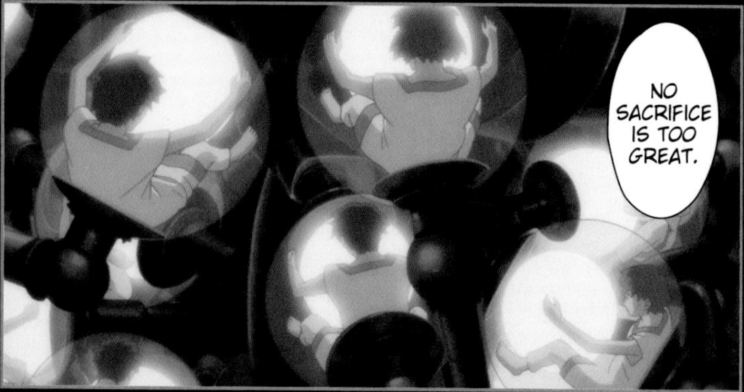
NO SACRIFICE IS TOO GREAT.

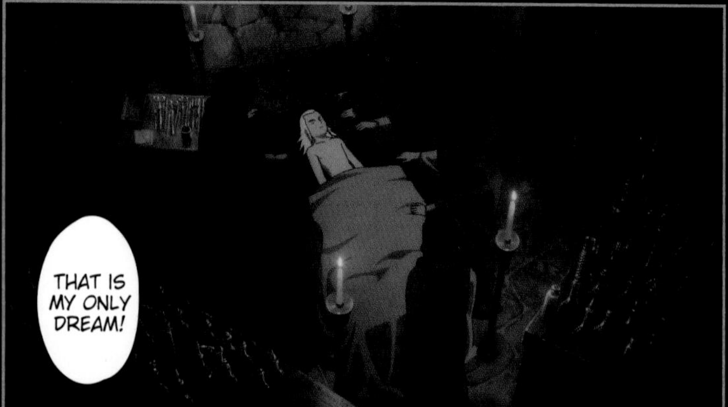
THAT IS MY ONLY DREAM!

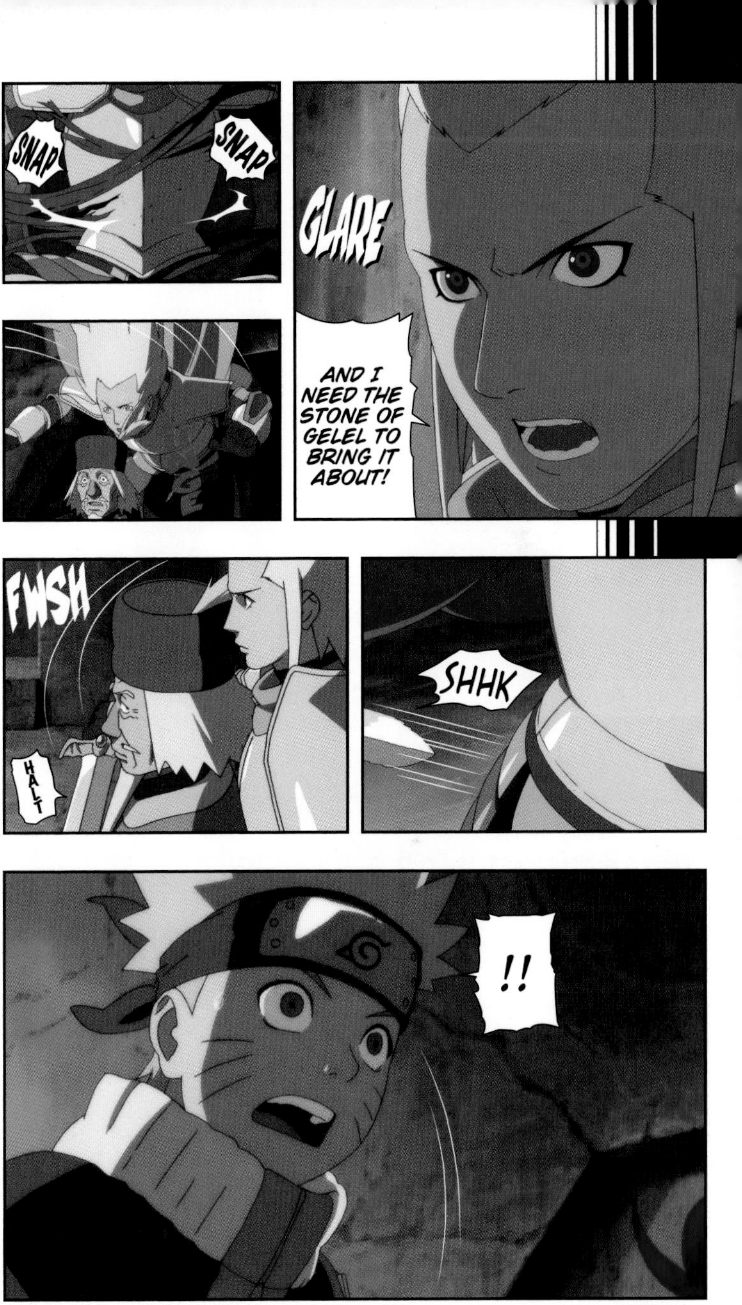
GLARE
AND I NEED THE STONE OF GELEL TO BRING IT ABOUT!
SNAP
SNAP
SHHK
FWSH
HALT
!!

HE WAS ...

... FAKING US OUT!

NO WAY!

WHACK

SWIP

CLANK

THAT'S TOO BAD.

I WILL NOT.

ALL RIGHT.

YOU'RE GOING TO TELL ME WHERE THE MINES OF GELEL ARE HIDDEN.

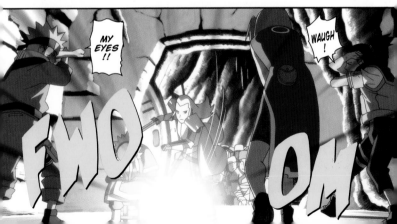

MY EYES !!

WAUGH !

FWO

OM

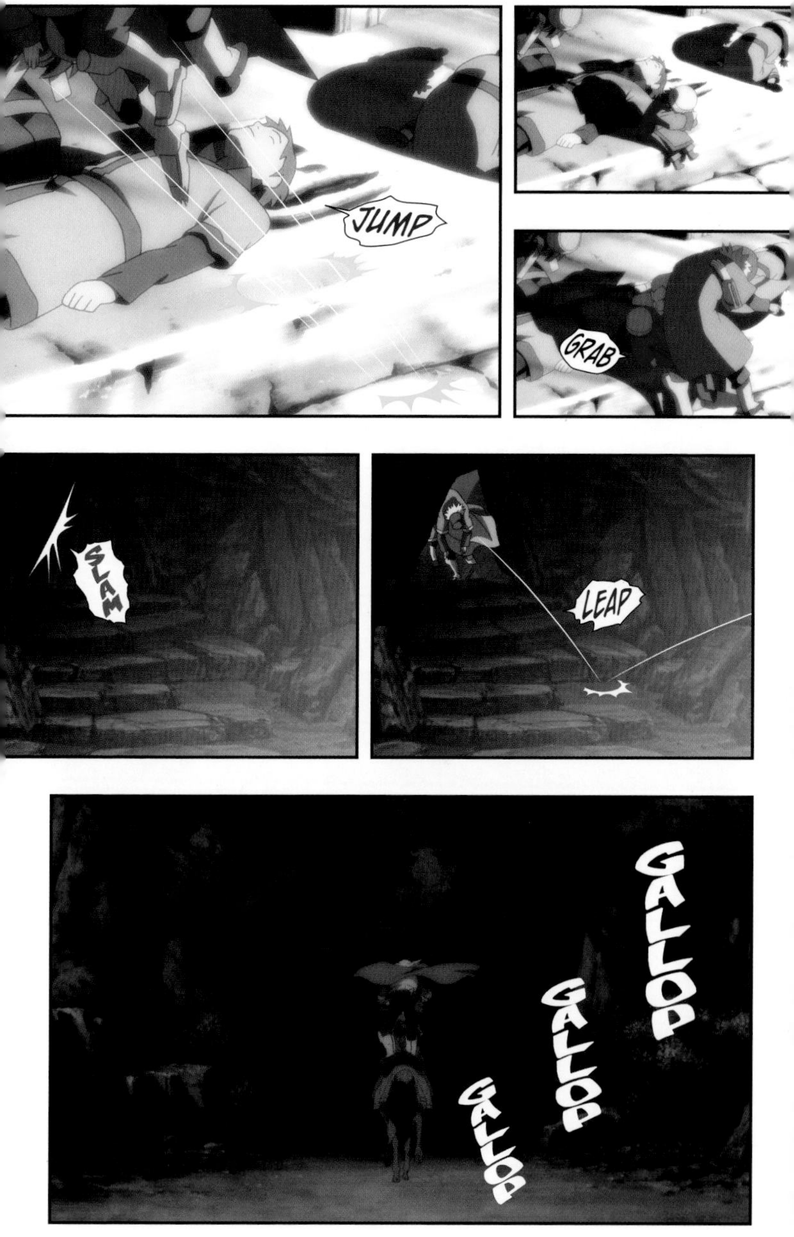
GRAB
JUMP
LEAP
SLAM
GALLOP
GALLOP
GALLOP

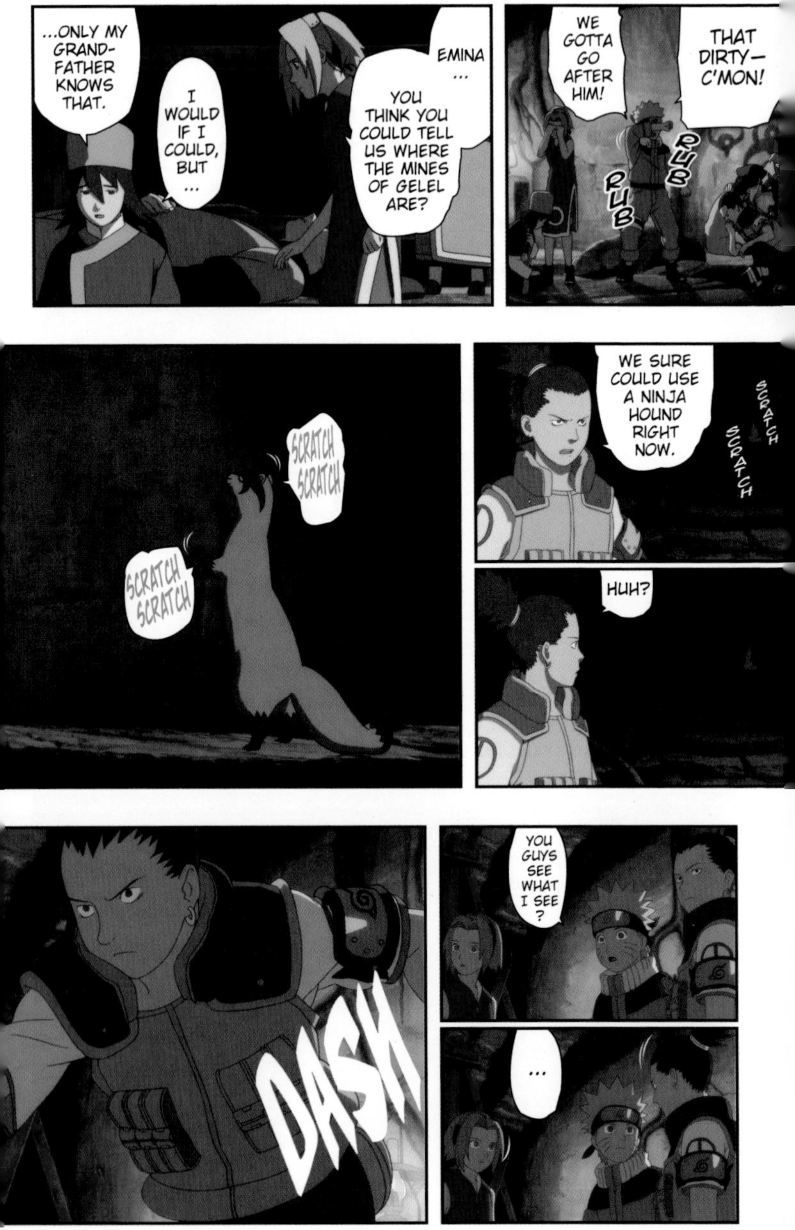

THAT DIRTY— C'MON!
WE GOTTA GO AFTER HIM!
RUB
RUB
EMINA ...
YOU THINK YOU COULD TELL US WHERE THE MINES OF GELEL ARE?
I WOULD IF I COULD, BUT ...
...ONLY MY GRANDFATHER KNOWS THAT.
WE SURE COULD USE A NINJA HOUND RIGHT NOW.
SCRATCH
SCRATCH
HUH?
SCRATCH SCRATCH
SCRATCH SCRATCH
YOU GUYS SEE WHAT I SEE?
...
DASH

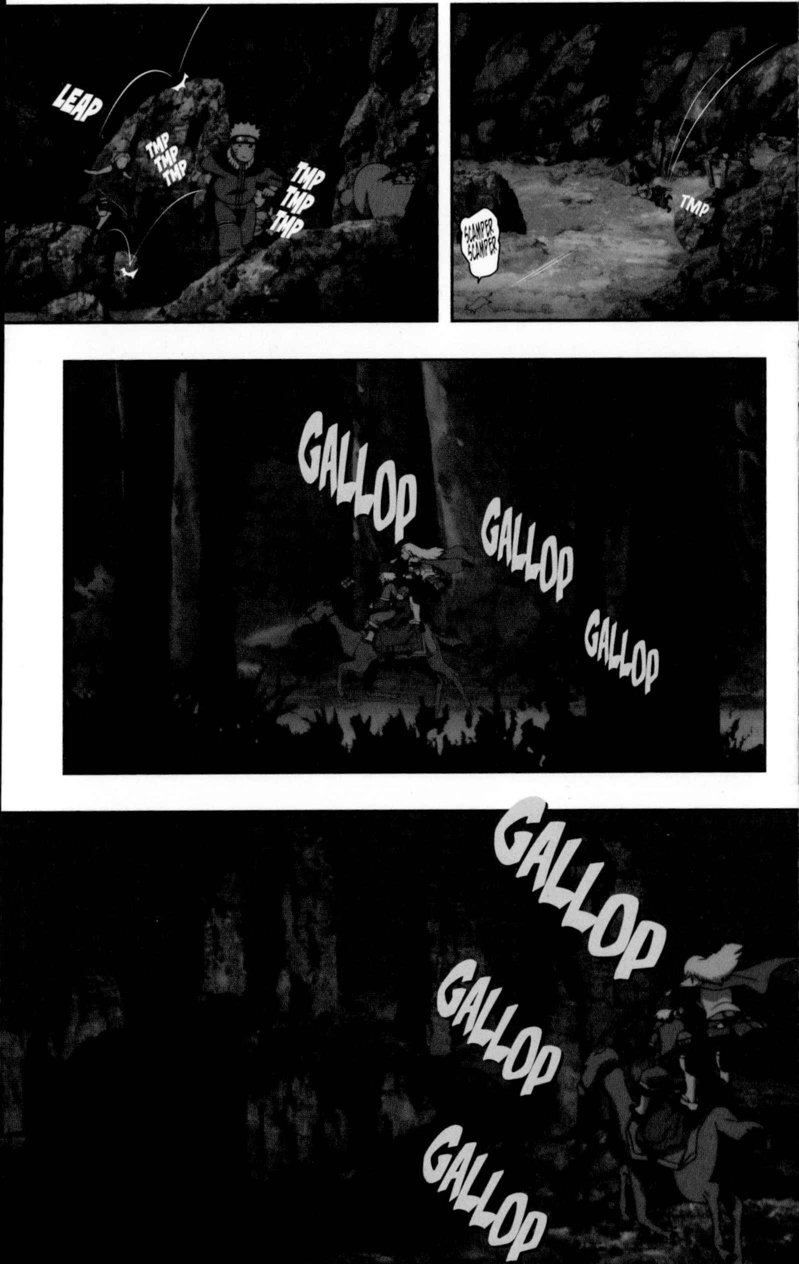
TMP
SCAMPER SCAMPER
LEAP
TMP TMP TMP
TMP TMP TMP
GALLOP
GALLOP
GALLOP
GALLOP
GALLOP
GALLOP

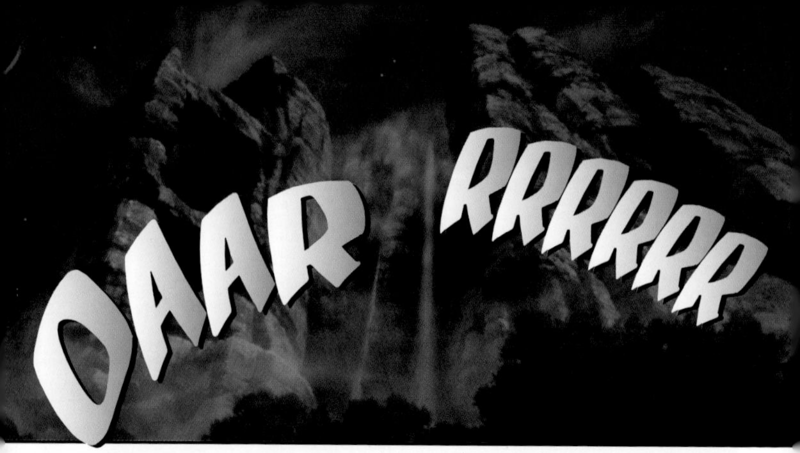
OAAR RRRRRRR
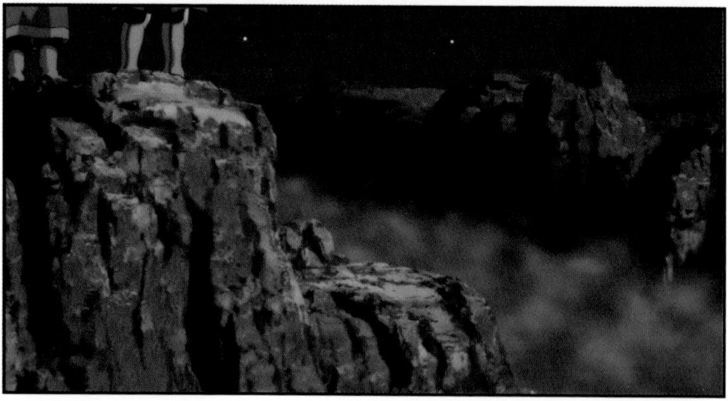
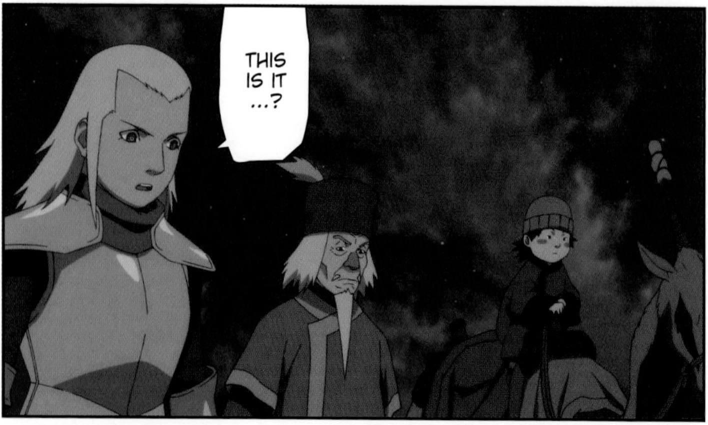
THIS IS IT ...?

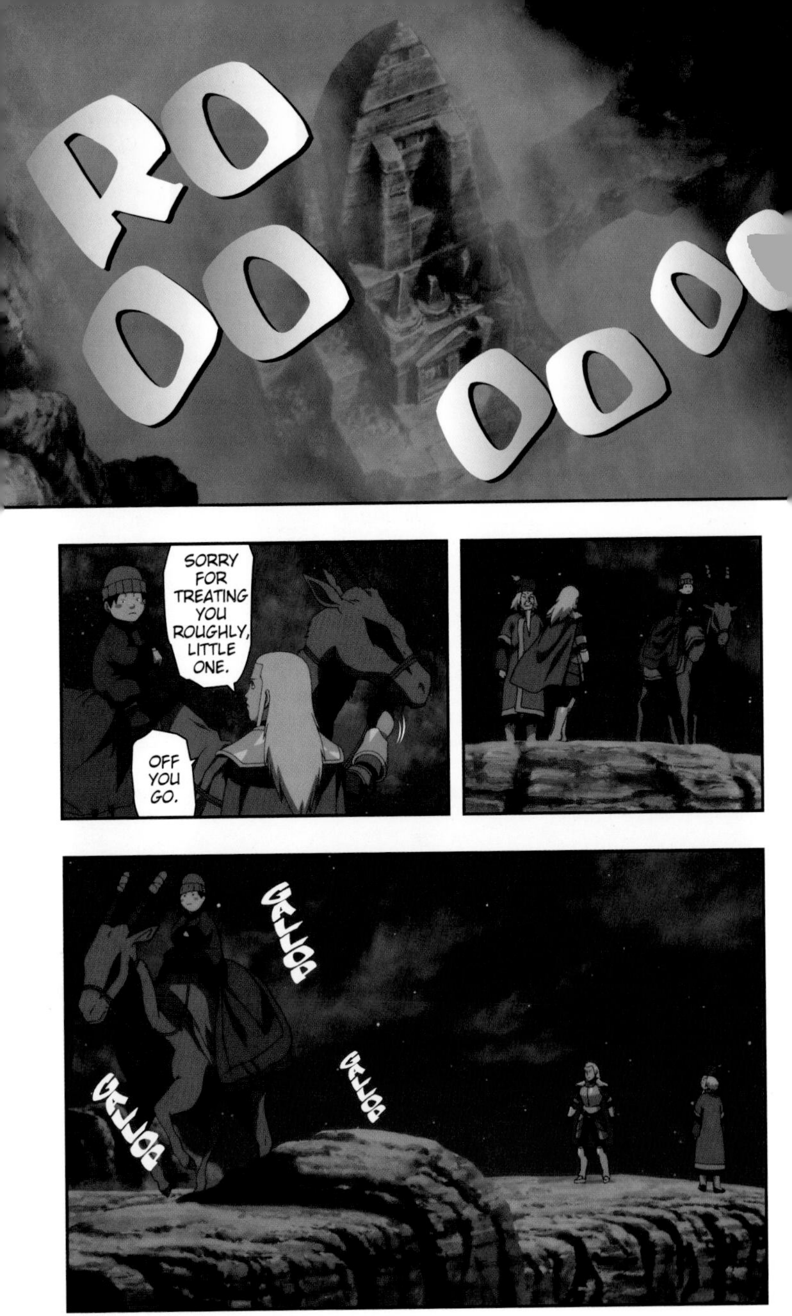
ROOOOOOOO
SORRY FOR TREATING YOU ROUGHLY, LITTLE ONE.
OFF YOU GO.
GALLOP
GALLOP
GALLOP

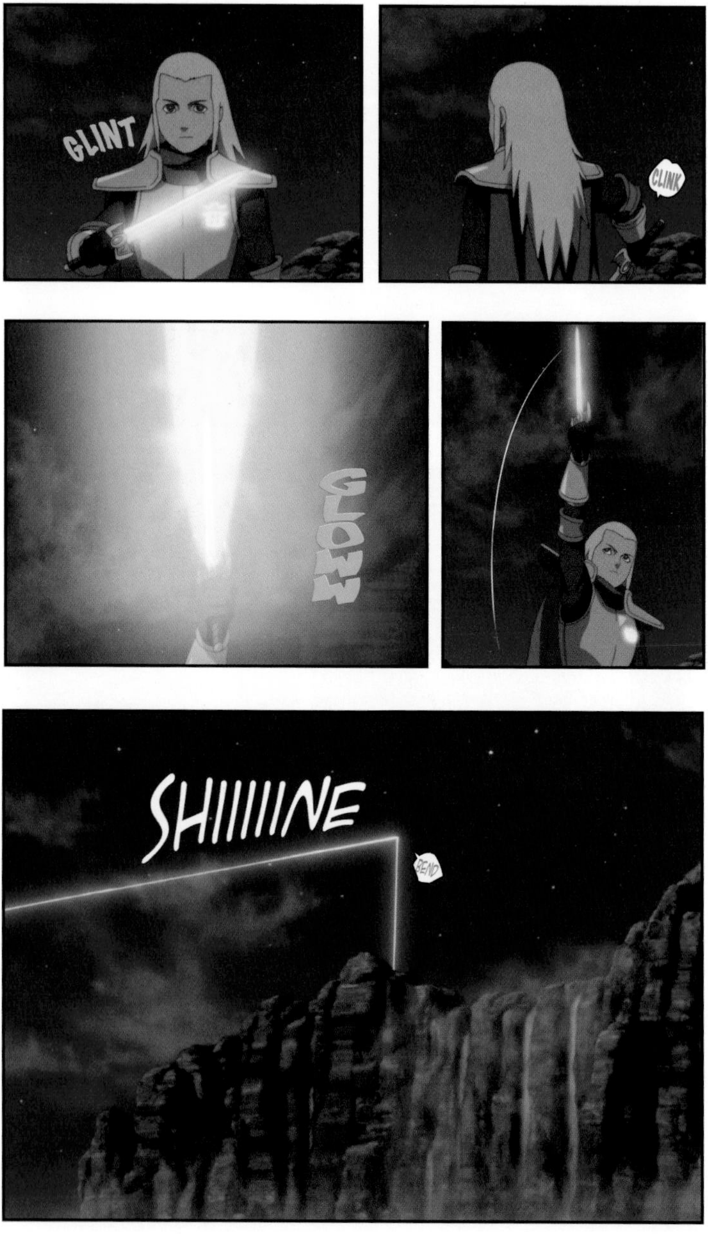

CLINK
GLINT
GLOWW
SHIIIINE
BEND

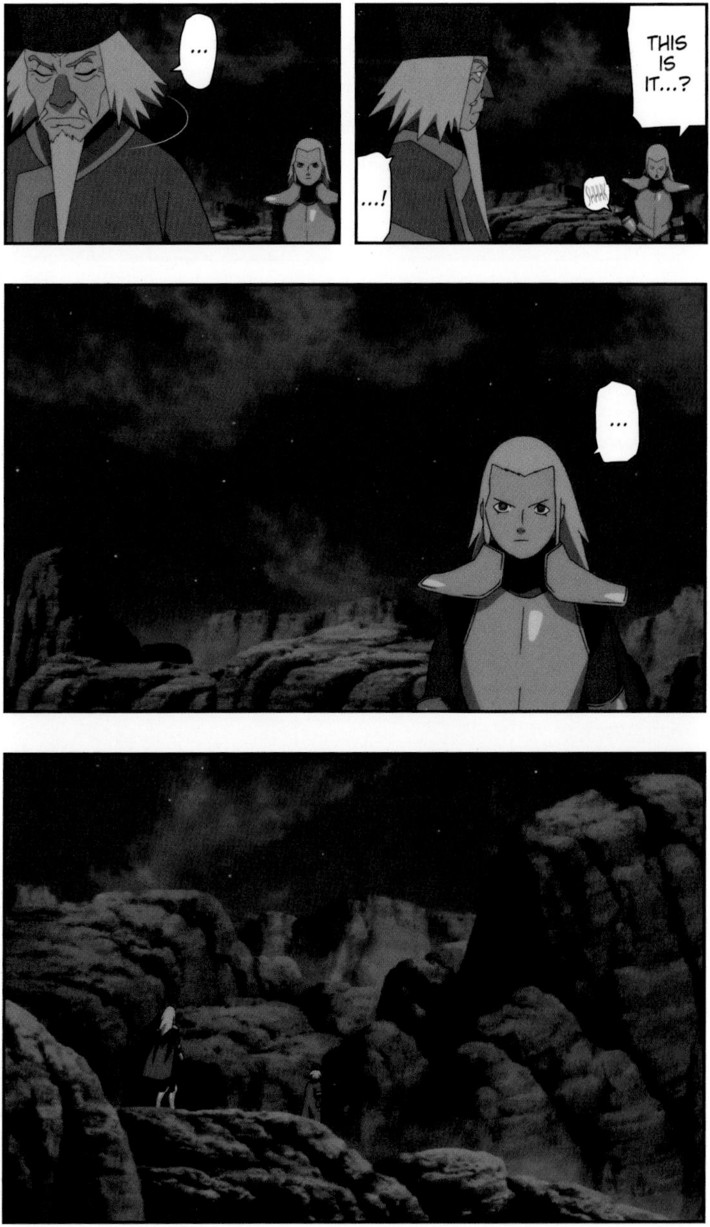

THIS IS IT...?
...!
...
...

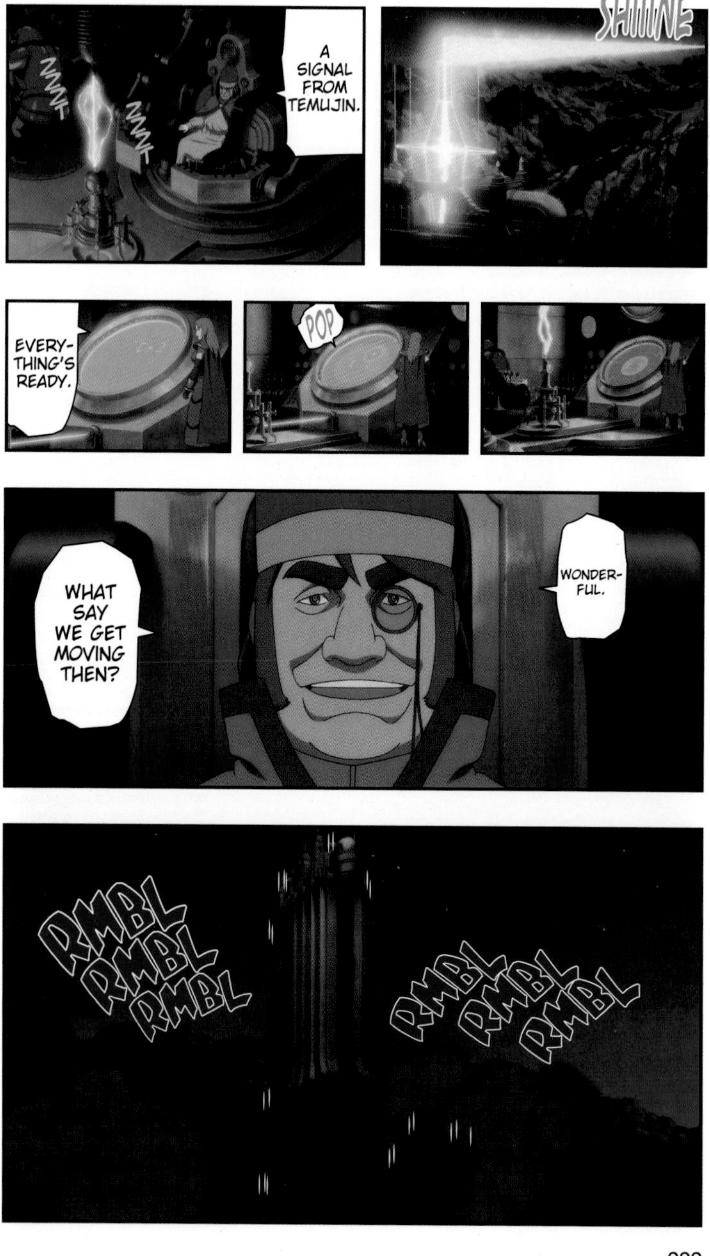
SHIIINE
A SIGNAL FROM TEMUJIN.
ZZZT
ZZZT
POP
EVERY-THING'S READY.
WONDER-FUL.
WHAT SAY WE GET MOVING THEN?
RMBL RMBL RMBL
RMBL RMBL RMBL

Chapter 6: Various Battles!

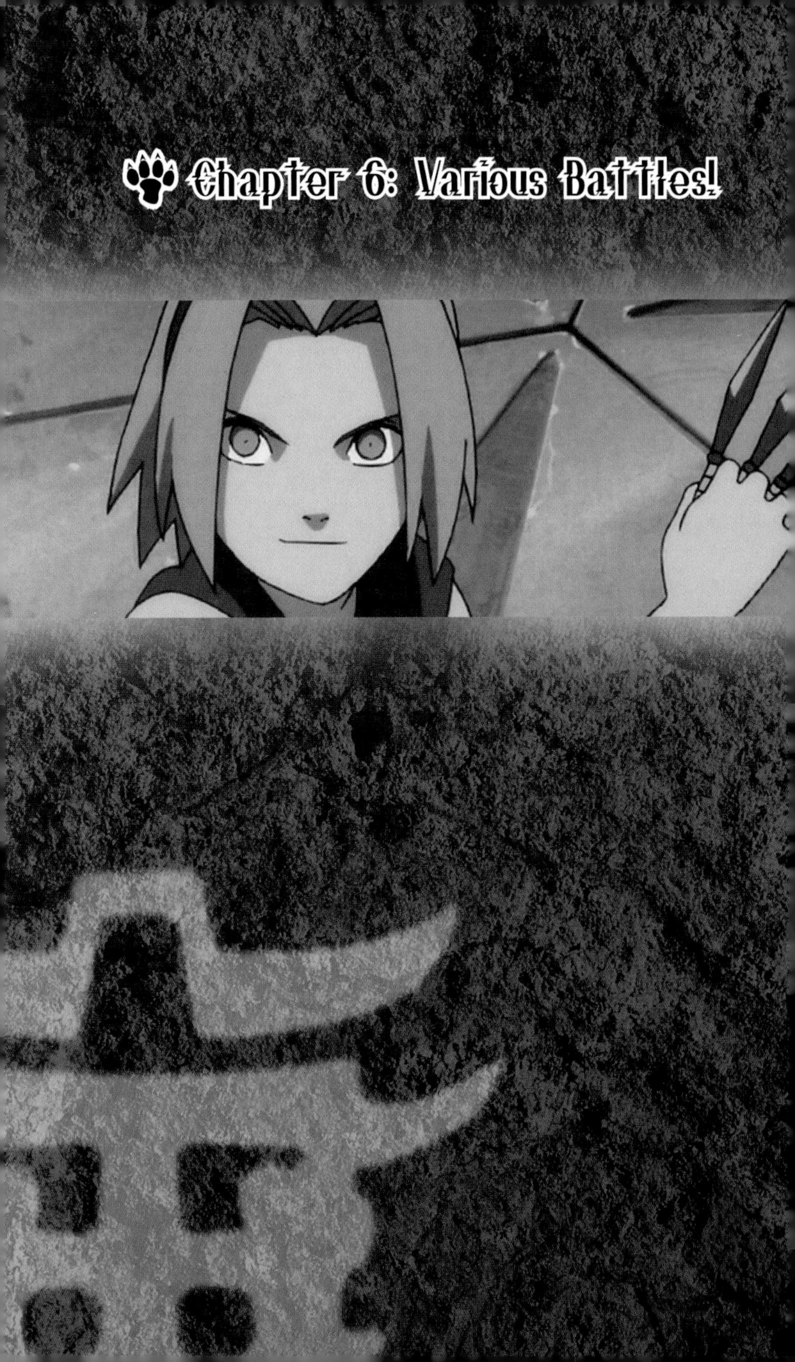

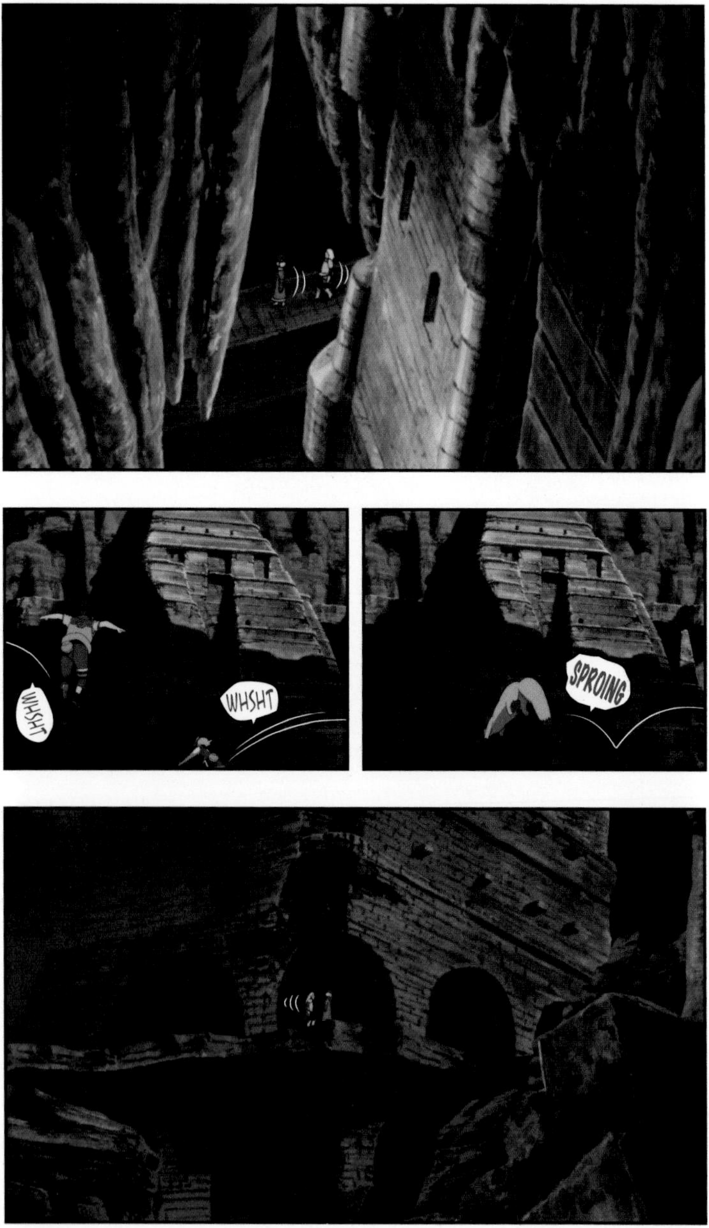
SPROING
WHSHT
WHSHT

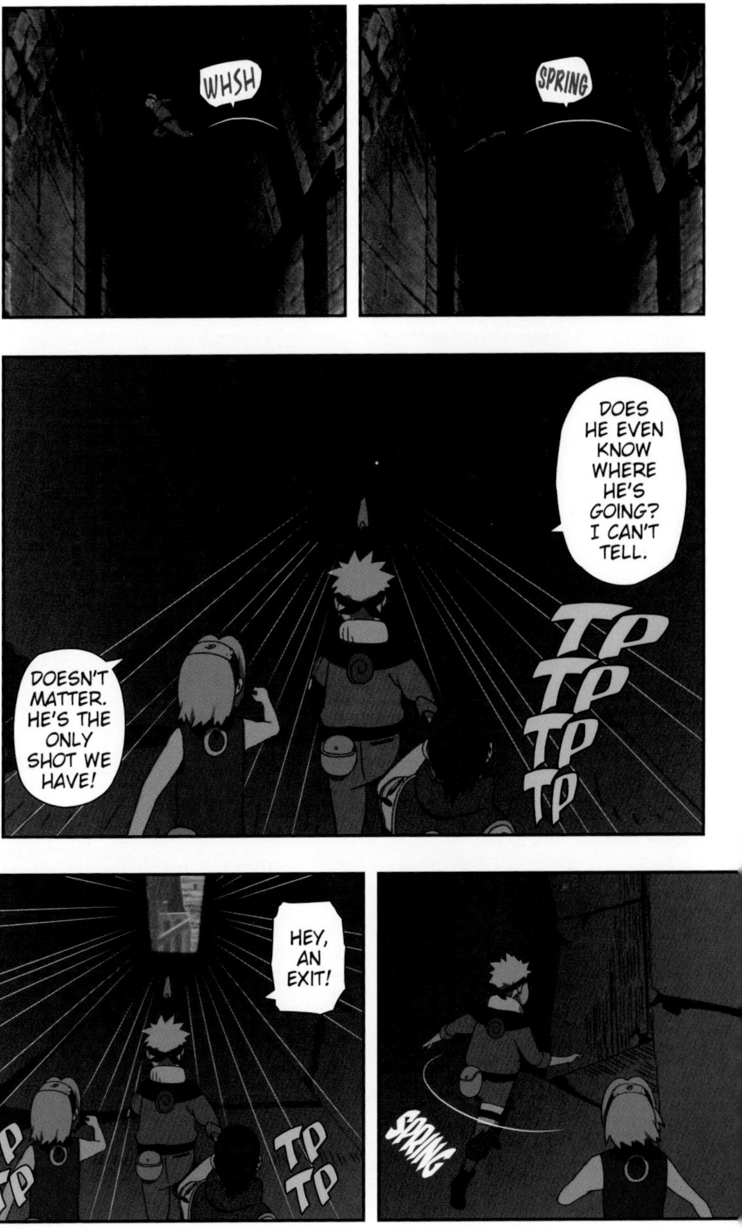
SPRING
WHSH
DOES HE EVEN KNOW WHERE HE'S GOING? I CAN'T TELL.
TP TP TP TP
DOESN'T MATTER. HE'S THE ONLY SHOT WE HAVE!
SPRING
HEY, AN EXIT!
TP TP
TP TP

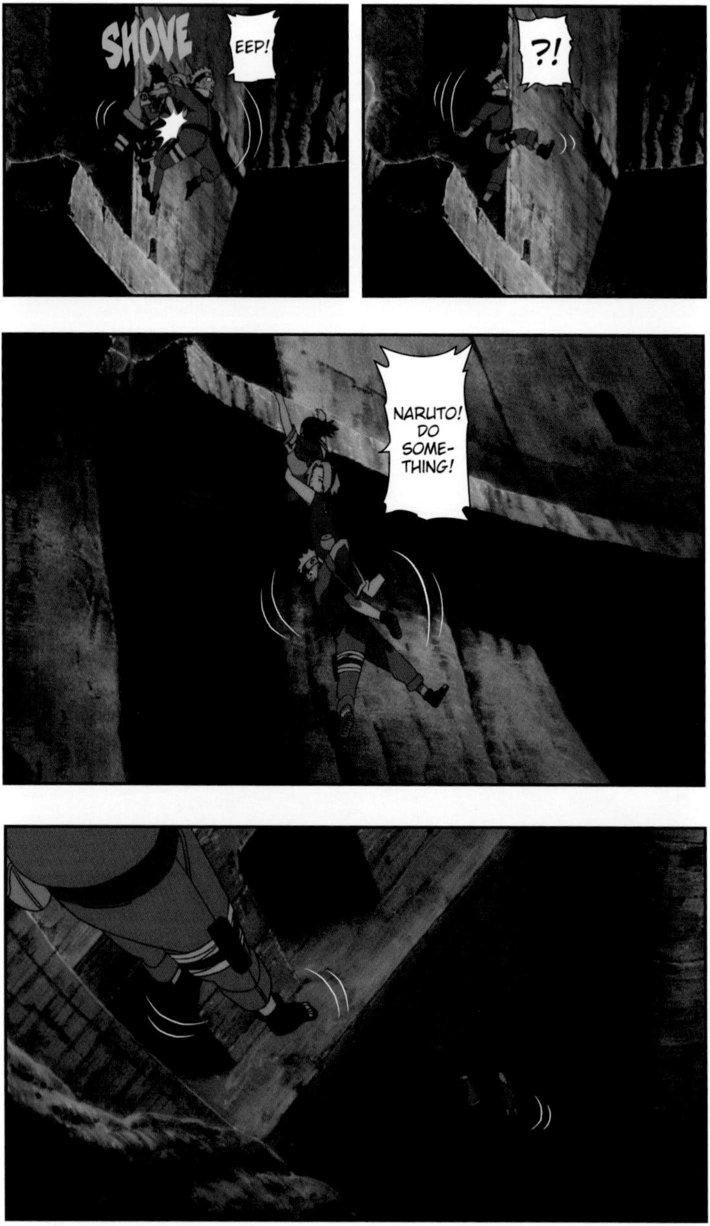
?!
SHOVE
EEP!
NARUTO! DO SOME-THING!

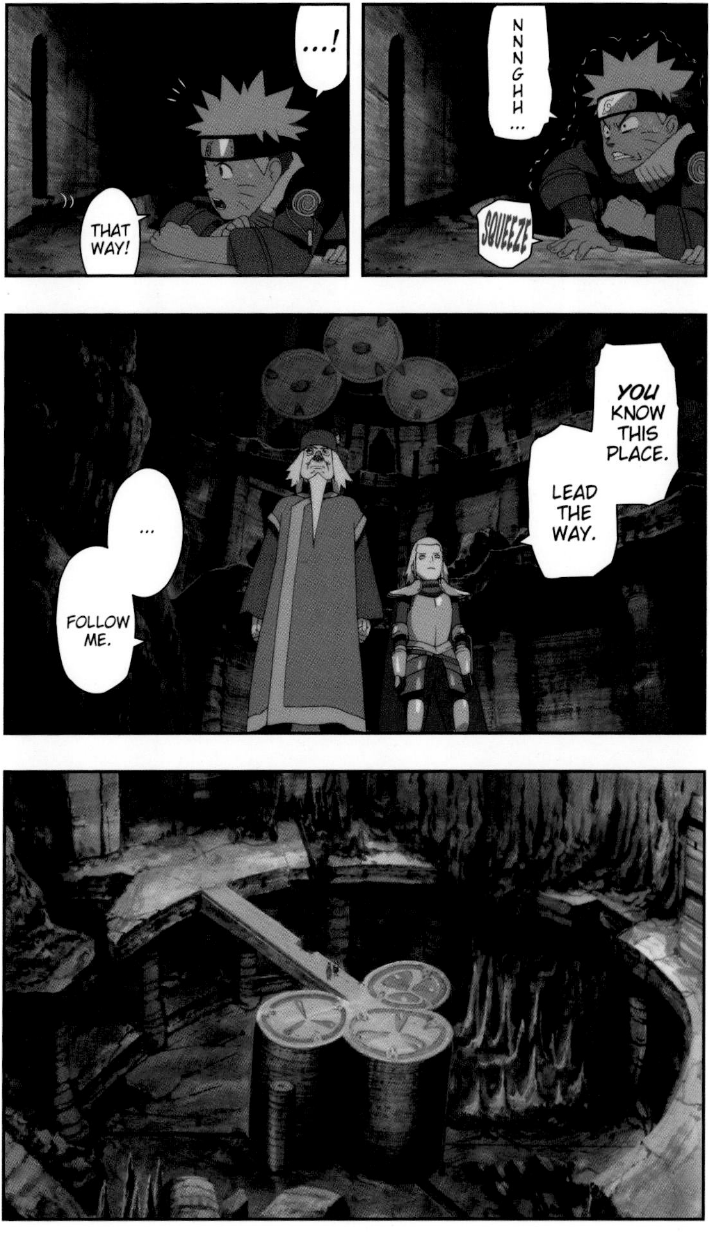
NNNGHH...
SQUEEZE
...!
THAT WAY!
YOU KNOW THIS PLACE.
LEAD THE WAY.
...
FOLLOW ME.

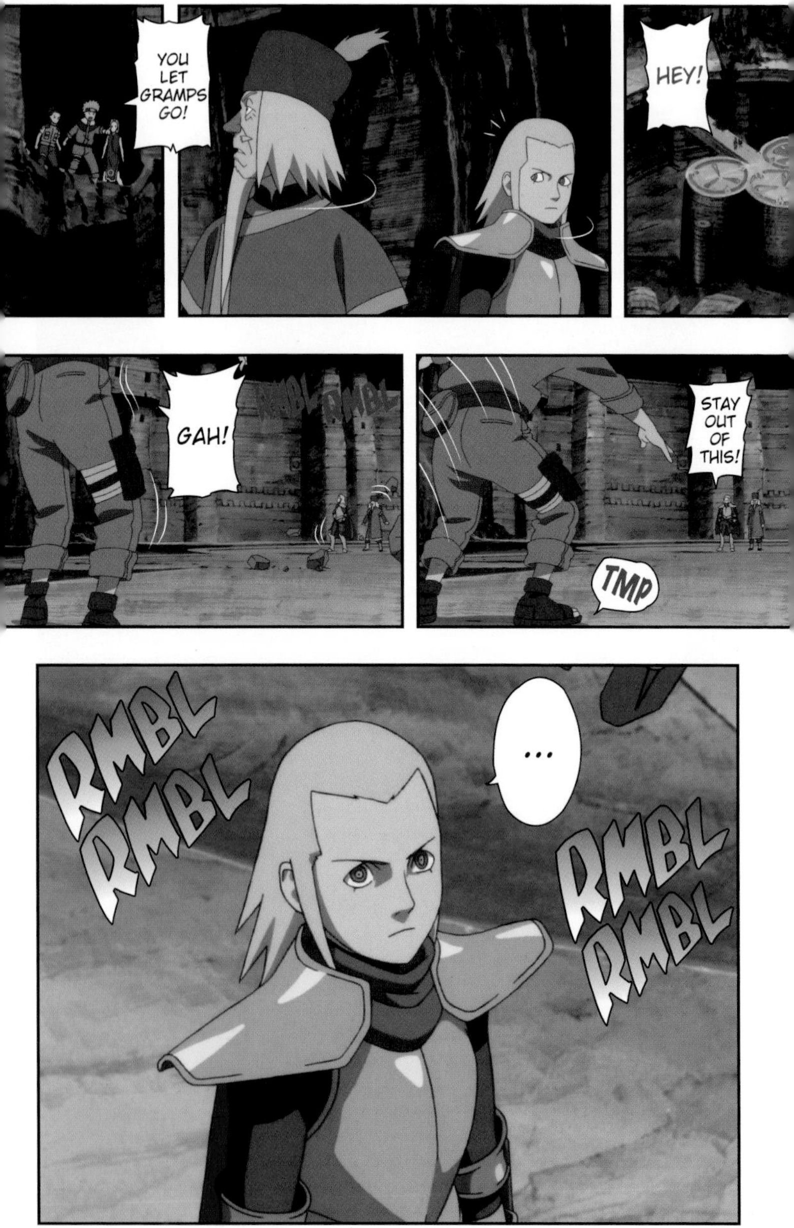
HEY!
YOU LET GRAMPS GO!
STAY OUT OF THIS!
TMP
GAH!
RMBL RMBL
...
RMBL RMBL
RMBL RMBL

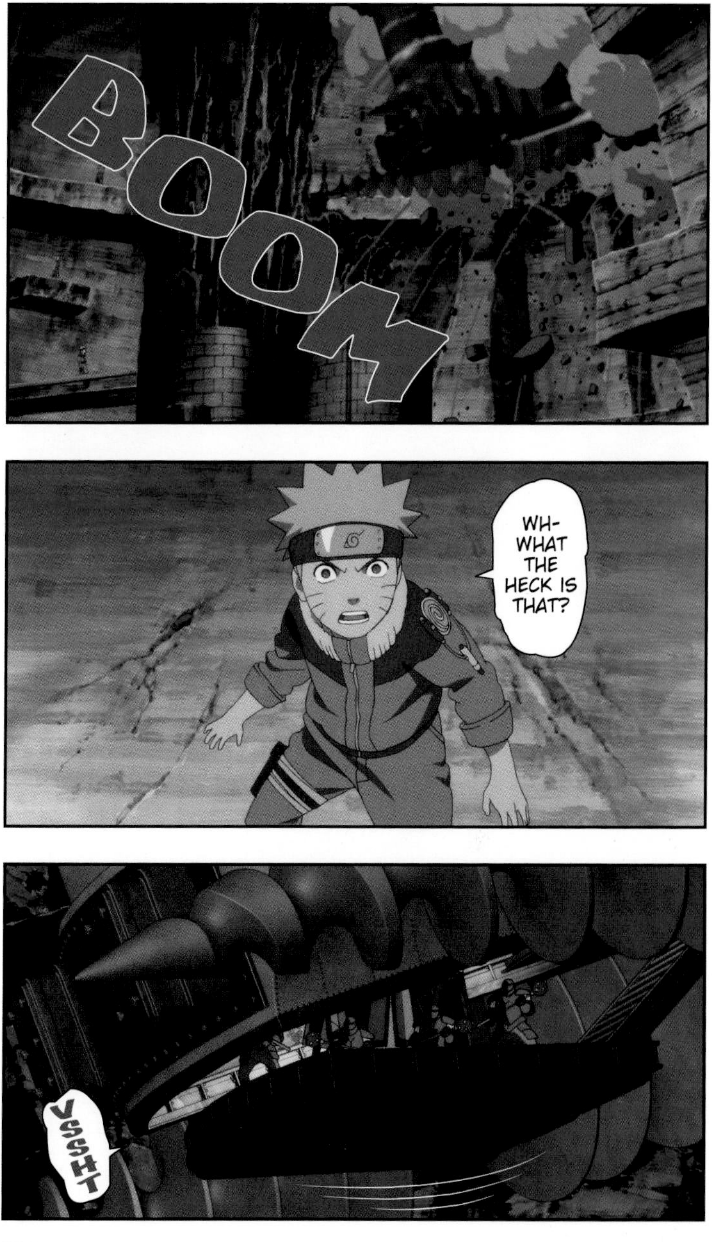
BOOM
WH- WHAT THE HECK IS THAT?
VSSHT

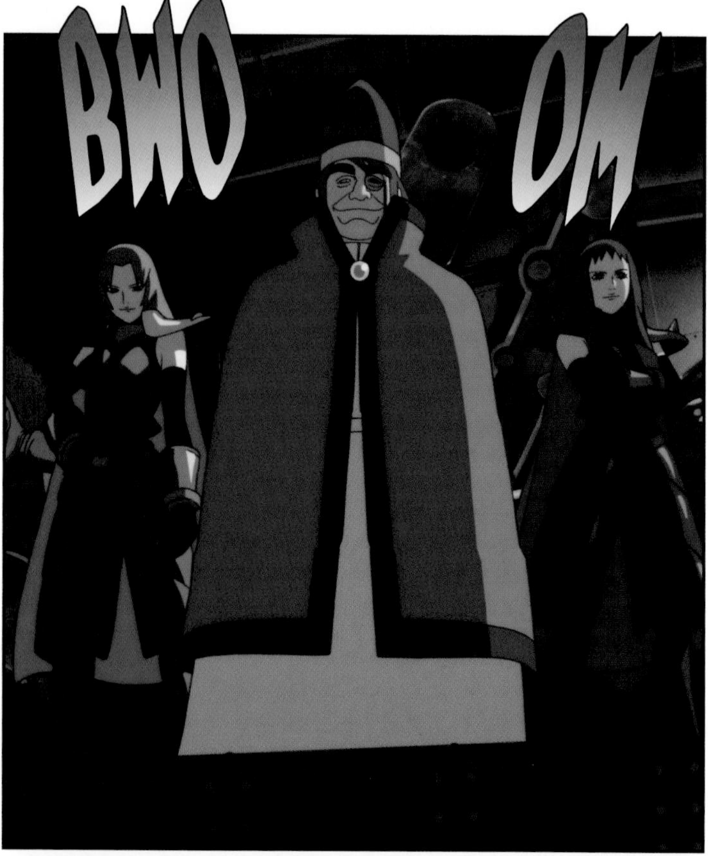
BWOOM

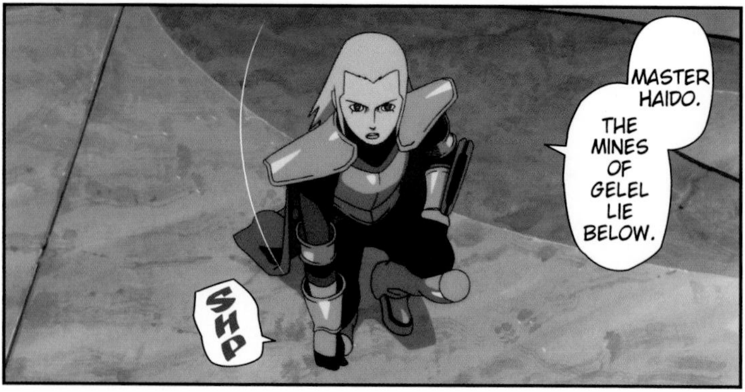
MASTER HAIDO.
THE MINES OF GELEL LIE BELOW.
SHP

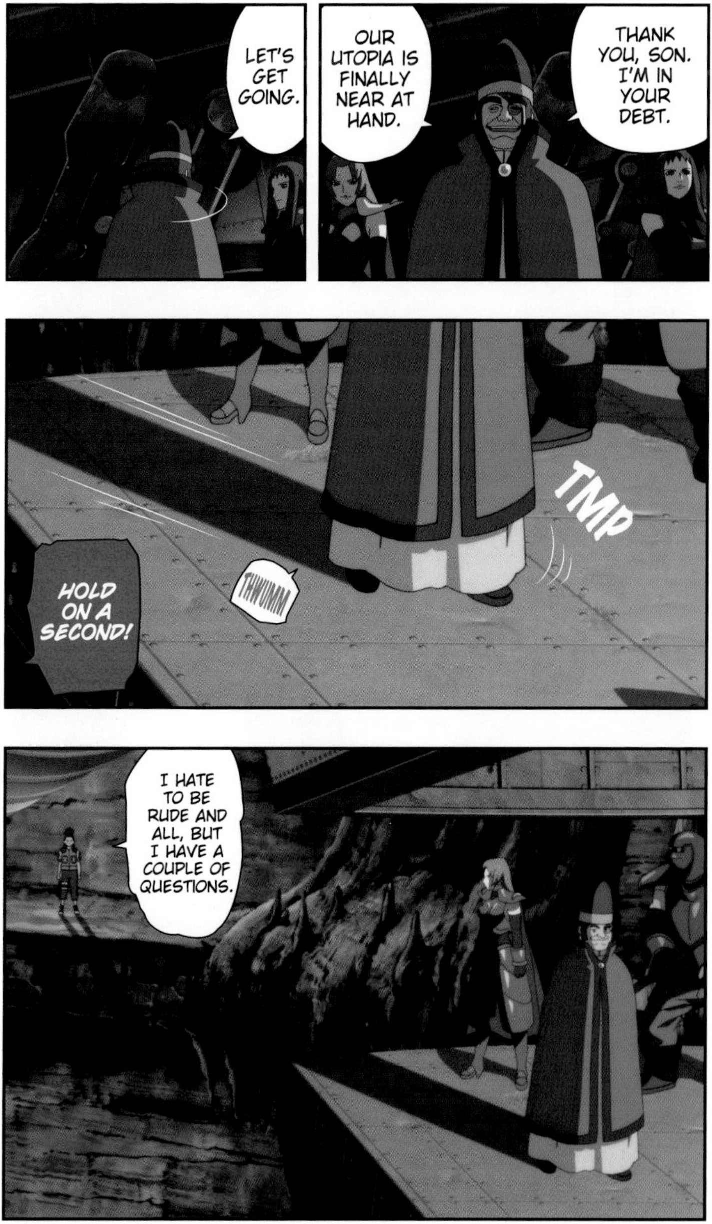
THANK YOU, SON. I'M IN YOUR DEBT.
OUR UTOPIA IS FINALLY NEAR AT HAND.
LET'S GET GOING.
TMP
THWUMM
HOLD ON A SECOND!
I HATE TO BE RUDE AND ALL, BUT I HAVE A COUPLE OF QUESTIONS.

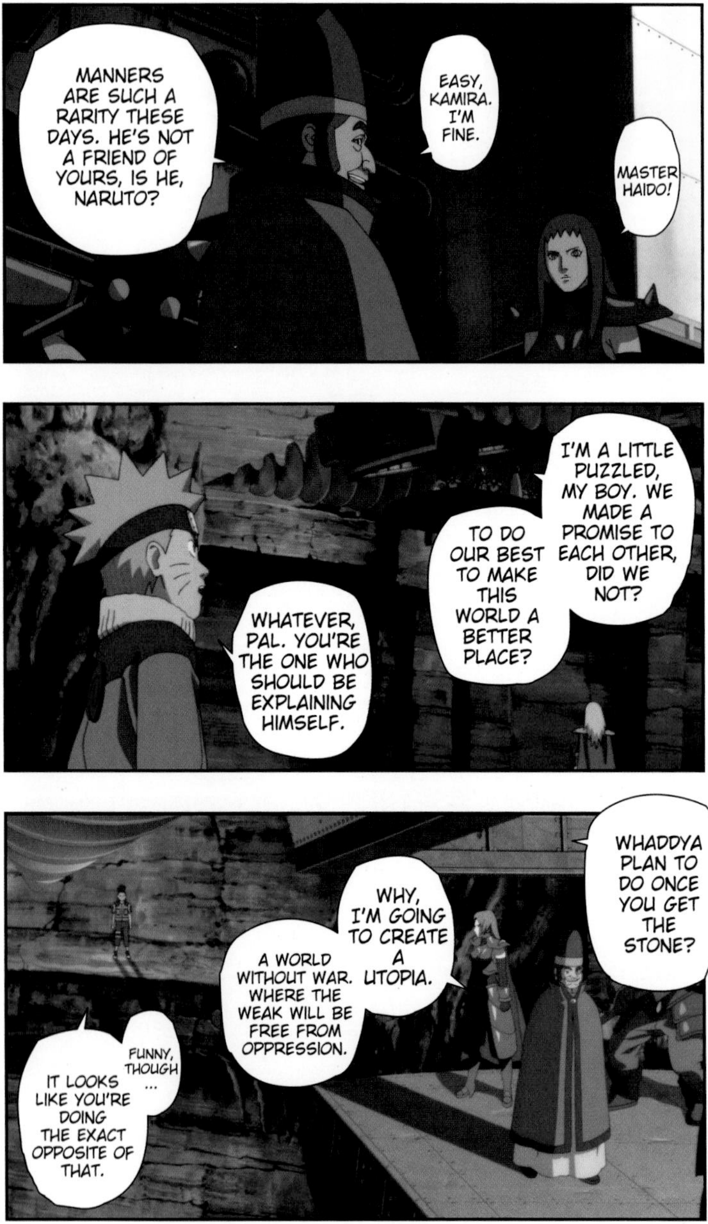
MASTER HAIDO!
EASY, KAMIRA. I'M FINE.
MANNERS ARE SUCH A RARITY THESE DAYS. HE'S NOT A FRIEND OF YOURS, IS HE, NARUTO?
I'M A LITTLE PUZZLED, MY BOY. WE MADE A PROMISE TO EACH OTHER, DID WE NOT?
TO DO OUR BEST TO MAKE THIS WORLD A BETTER PLACE?
WHATEVER, PAL. YOU'RE THE ONE WHO SHOULD BE EXPLAINING HIMSELF.
WHADDYA PLAN TO DO ONCE YOU GET THE STONE?
WHY, I'M GOING TO CREATE A UTOPIA.
A WORLD WITHOUT WAR. WHERE THE WEAK WILL BE FREE FROM OPPRESSION.
FUNNY, THOUGH...
IT LOOKS LIKE YOU'RE DOING THE EXACT OPPOSITE OF THAT.

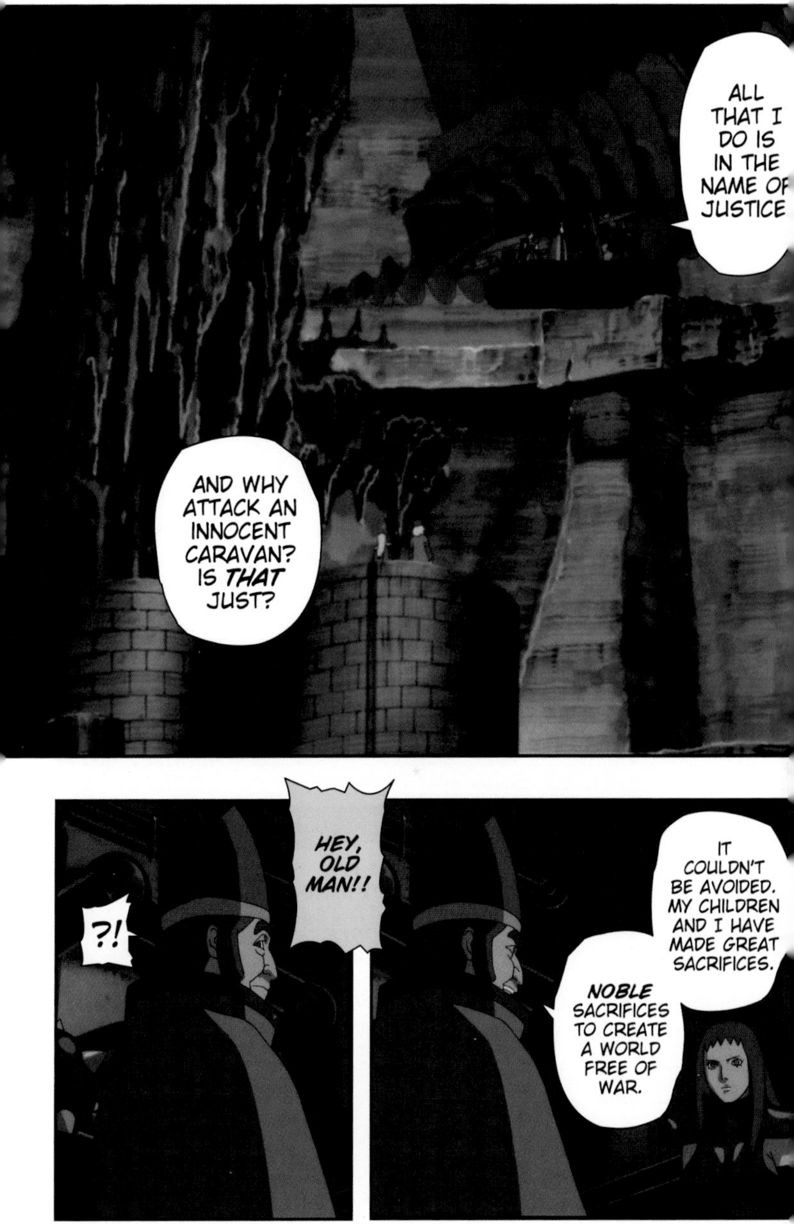
ALL THAT I DO IS IN THE NAME OF JUSTICE
AND WHY ATTACK AN INNOCENT CARAVAN? IS *THAT* JUST?
IT COULDN'T BE AVOIDED. MY CHILDREN AND I HAVE MADE GREAT SACRIFICES.
NOBLE SACRIFICES TO CREATE A WORLD FREE OF WAR.
HEY, OLD MAN!!
?!

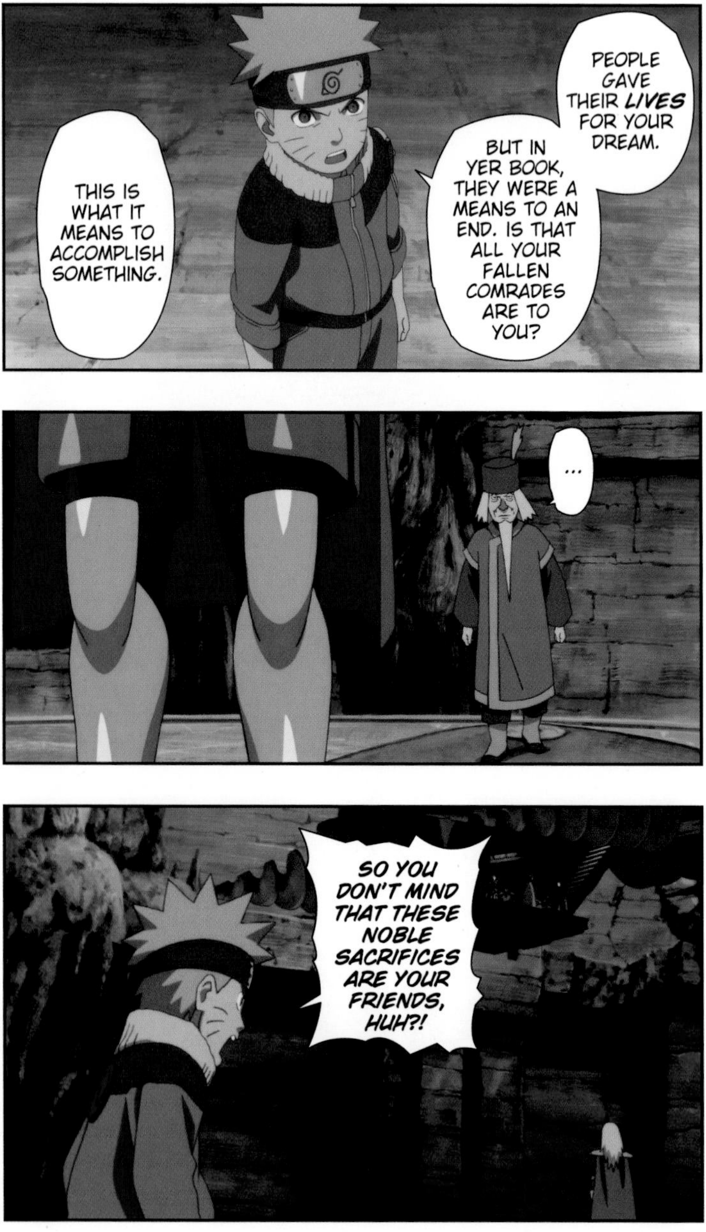
PEOPLE GAVE THEIR *LIVES* FOR YOUR DREAM.
BUT IN YER BOOK, THEY WERE A MEANS TO AN END. IS THAT ALL YOUR FALLEN COMRADES ARE TO YOU?
THIS IS WHAT IT MEANS TO ACCOMPLISH SOMETHING.
...
SO YOU DON'T MIND THAT THESE NOBLE SACRIFICES ARE YOUR FRIENDS, HUH?!

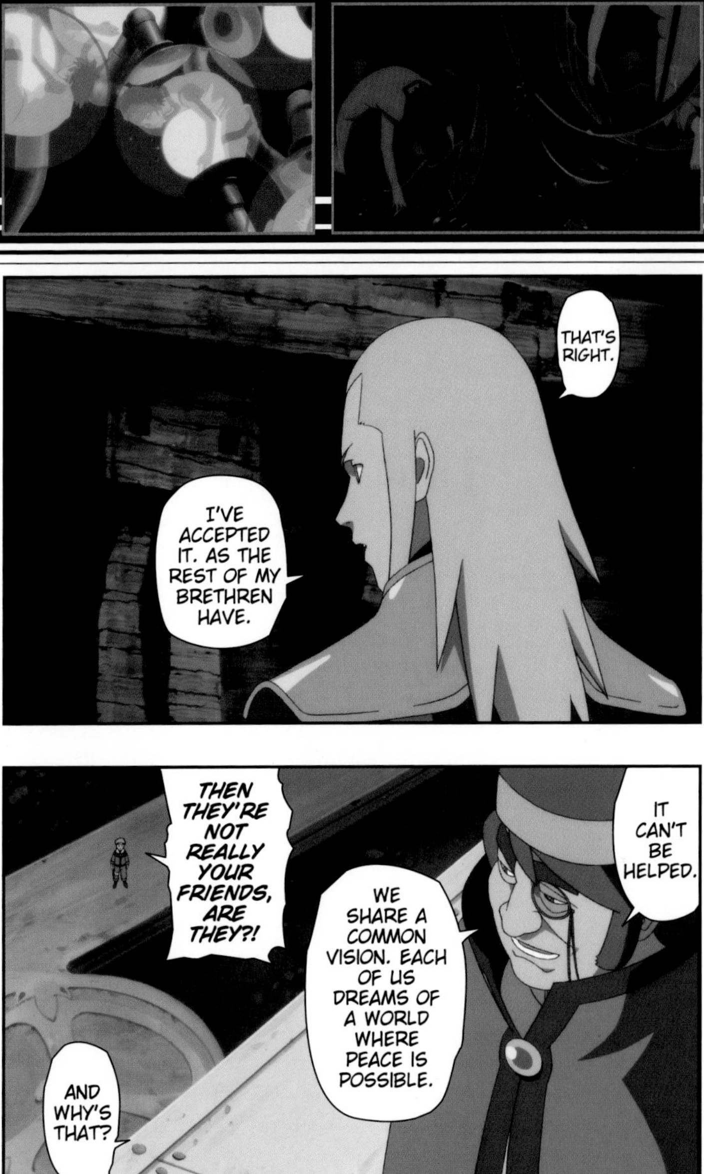
THAT'S RIGHT.
I'VE ACCEPTED IT. AS THE REST OF MY BRETHREN HAVE.
IT CAN'T BE HELPED.
WE SHARE A COMMON VISION. EACH OF US DREAMS OF A WORLD WHERE PEACE IS POSSIBLE.
THEN THEY'RE NOT REALLY YOUR FRIENDS, ARE THEY?!
AND WHY'S THAT?

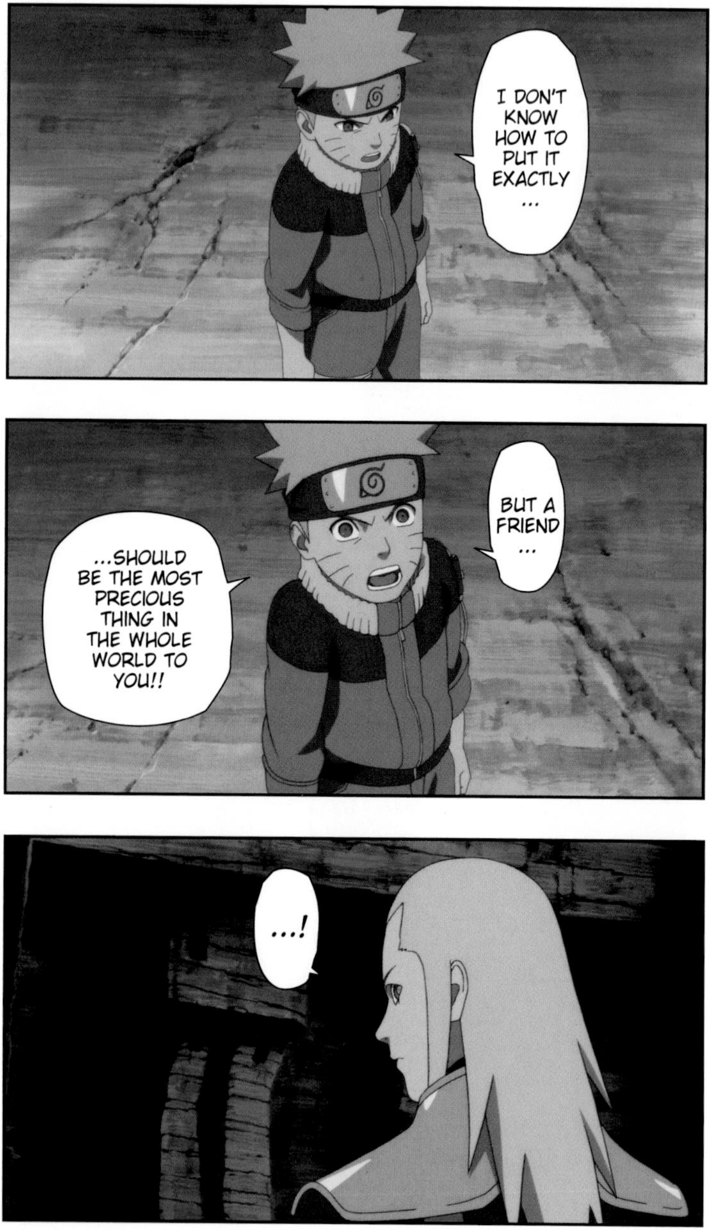
I DON'T KNOW HOW TO PUT IT EXACTLY ...
BUT A FRIEND ...
...SHOULD BE THE MOST PRECIOUS THING IN THE WHOLE WORLD TO YOU!!
...!

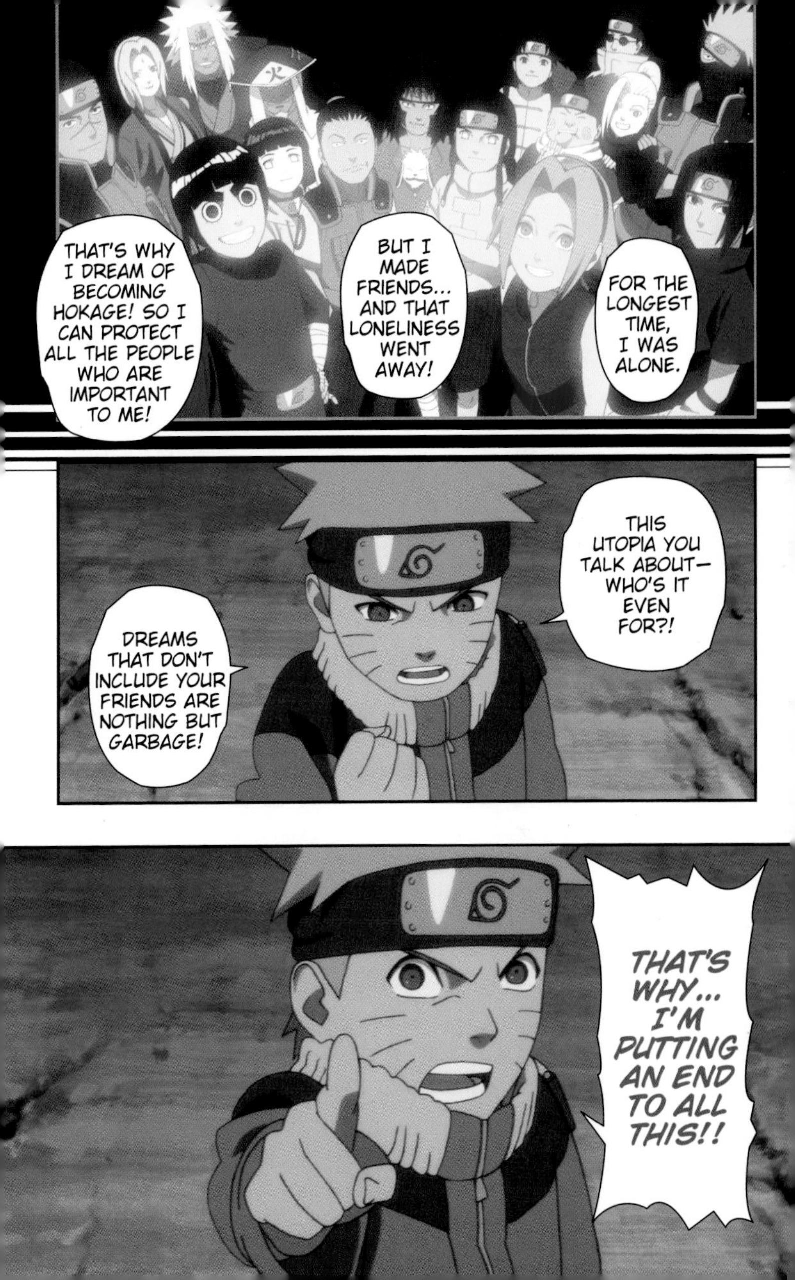
FOR THE LONGEST TIME, I WAS ALONE.
BUT I MADE FRIENDS... AND THAT LONELINESS WENT AWAY!
THAT'S WHY I DREAM OF BECOMING HOKAGE! SO I CAN PROTECT ALL THE PEOPLE WHO ARE IMPORTANT TO ME!
THIS UTOPIA YOU TALK ABOUT—WHO'S IT EVEN FOR?!
DREAMS THAT DON'T INCLUDE YOUR FRIENDS ARE NOTHING BUT GARBAGE!
THAT'S WHY... I'M PUTTING AN END TO ALL THIS!!

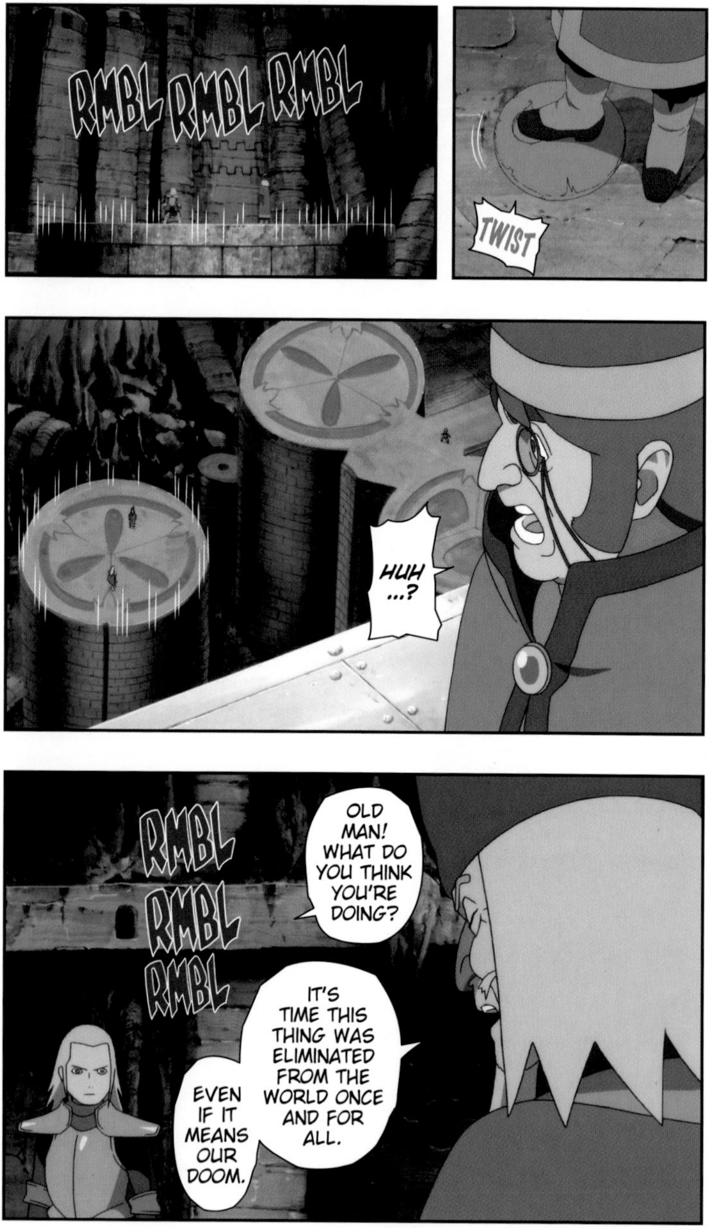
TWIST
RMBL RMBL RMBL
HUH ...?
OLD MAN! WHAT DO YOU THINK YOU'RE DOING?
RMBL RMBL RMBL
IT'S TIME THIS THING WAS ELIMINATED FROM THE WORLD ONCE AND FOR ALL.
EVEN IF IT MEANS OUR DOOM.

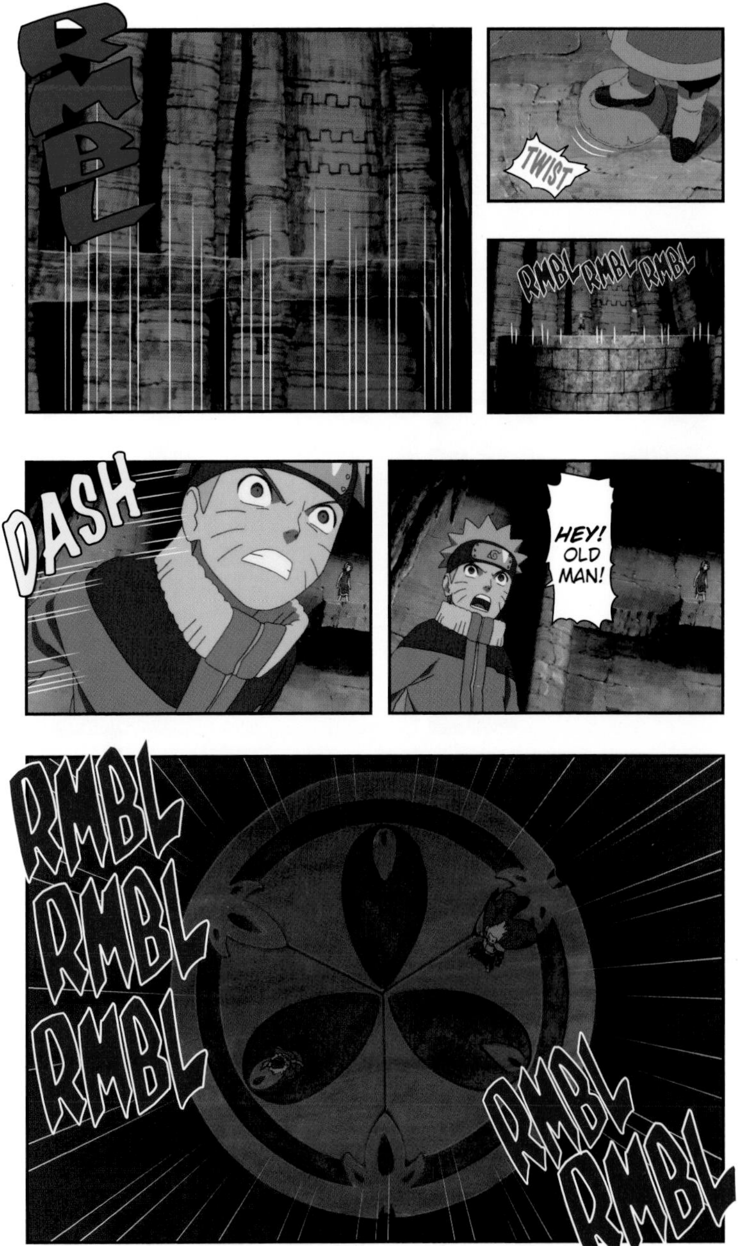
TWIST
RMBL RMBL RMBL
RMBL
HEY! OLD MAN!
DASH
RMBL RMBL RMBL
RMBL RMBL

RMBL RMBL RMBL RMBL

!

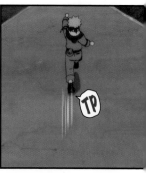

TP

TWIST

ELIMINATE THE STONES ...?!

AHH ....!

FLASH

!

RRGH
...!

THAT
CANNOT
BE
POS-
SIBLE
...!

FWIP
FWIP

WHUMP

HOP

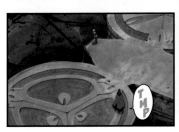

TMP

HE
MUST
KNOW
SOMETHING
...

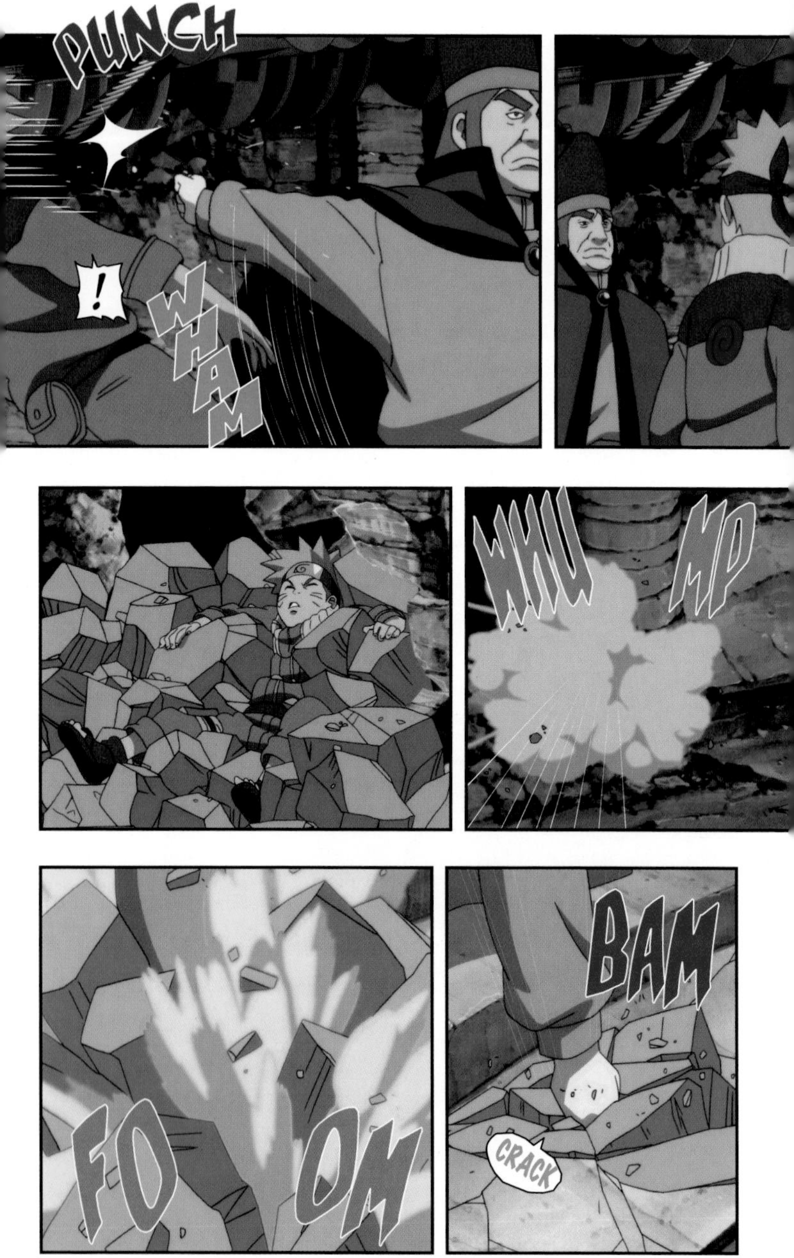
PUNCH
!
WHAM
WHUMP
BAM
CRACK
FOOM

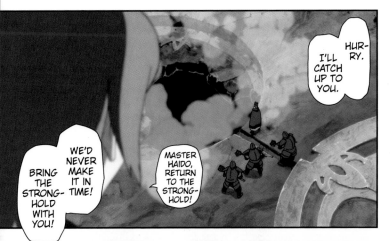

HUR-RY. I'LL CATCH UP TO YOU.

MASTER HAIDO, RETURN TO THE STRONG-HOLD!

WE'D NEVER MAKE IT IN TIME!

BRING THE STRONG-HOLD WITH YOU!

FWOOM

WHSH

ZIP

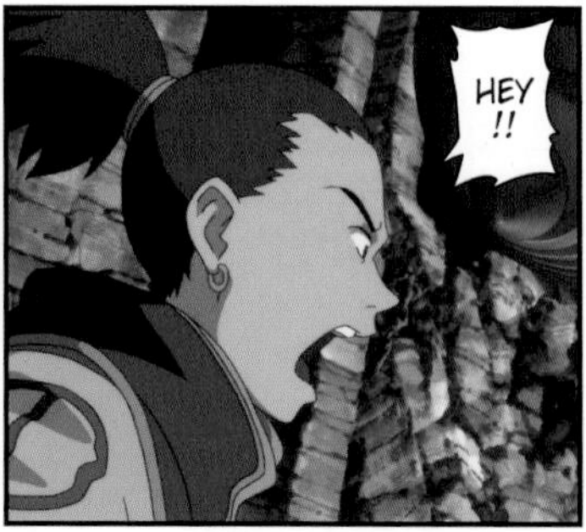
HEY !!

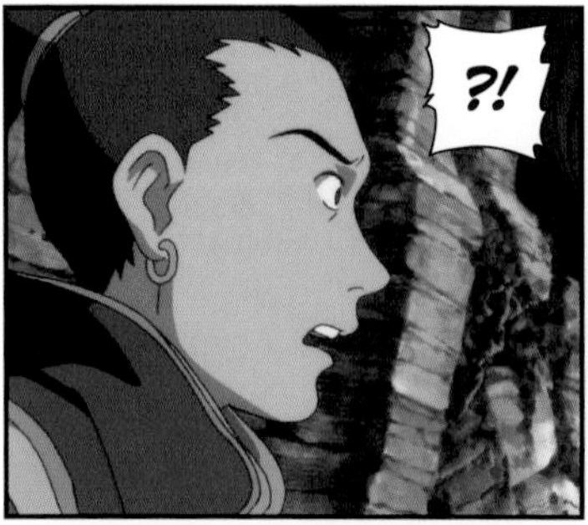
?!

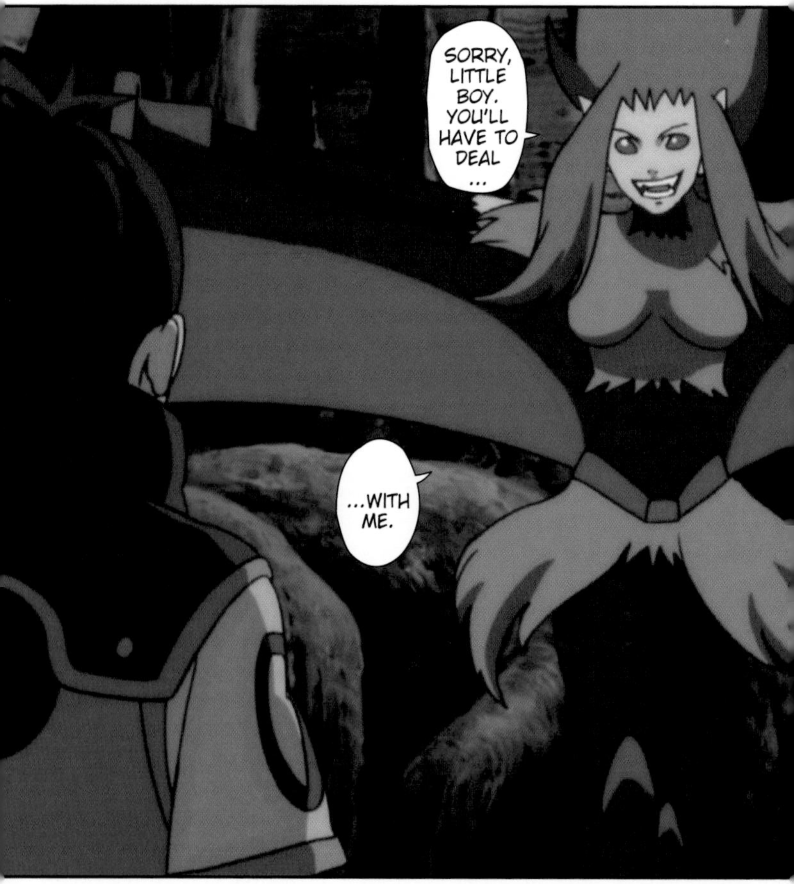
SORRY, LITTLE BOY. YOU'LL HAVE TO DEAL ...
...WITH ME.

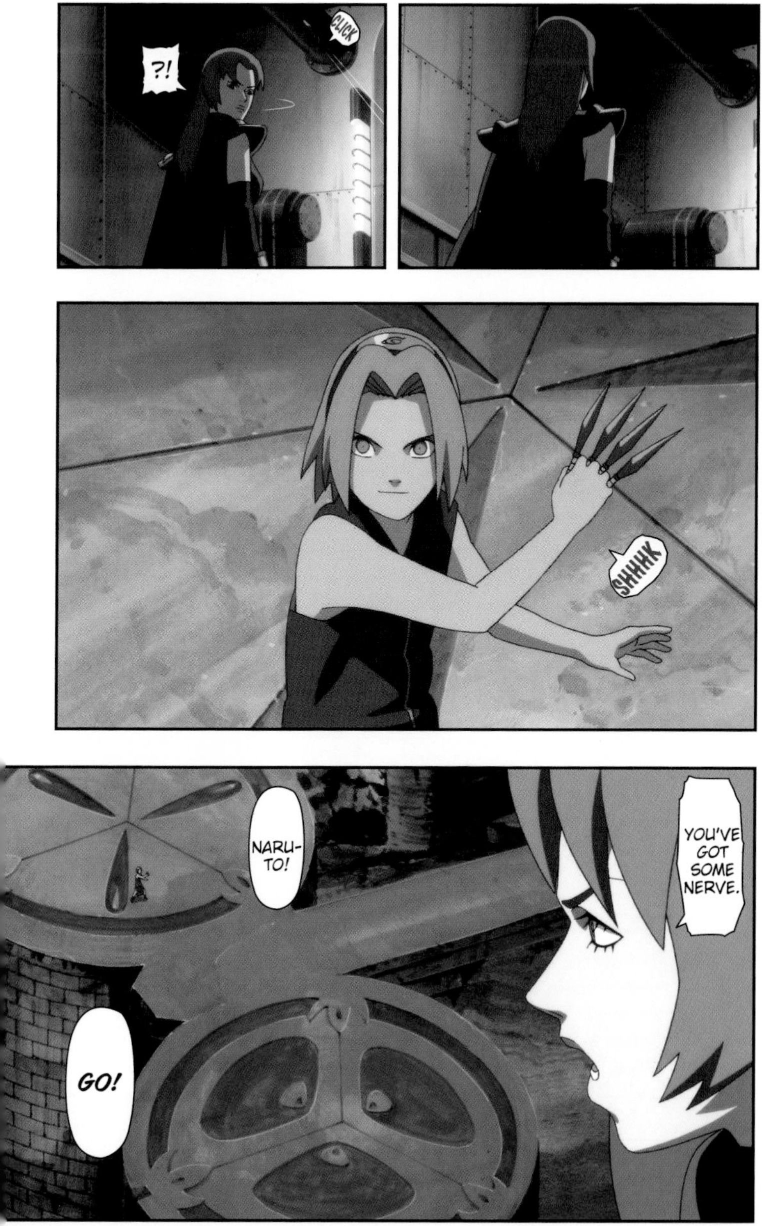
CLICK
?!
SHHHK
YOU'VE GOT SOME NERVE.
NARU- TO!
GO!

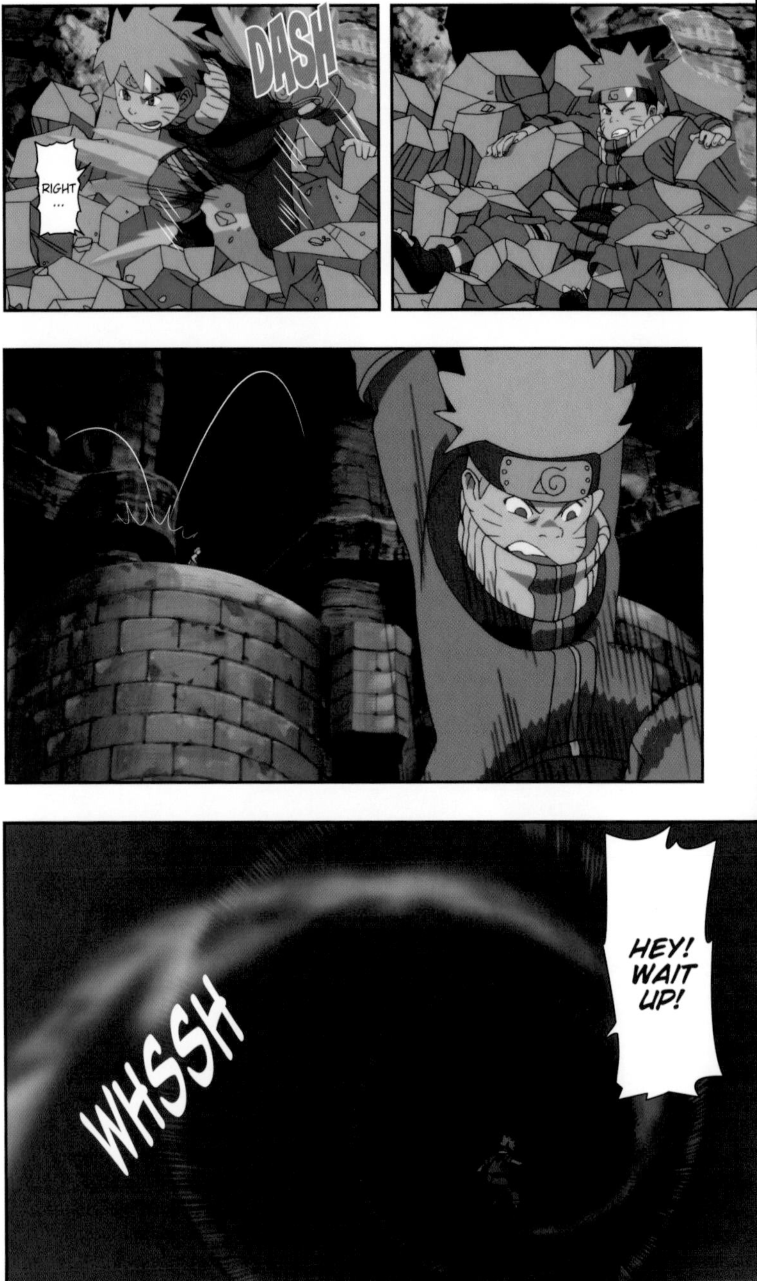
DASH
RIGHT ...
HEY! WAIT UP!
WHSSH

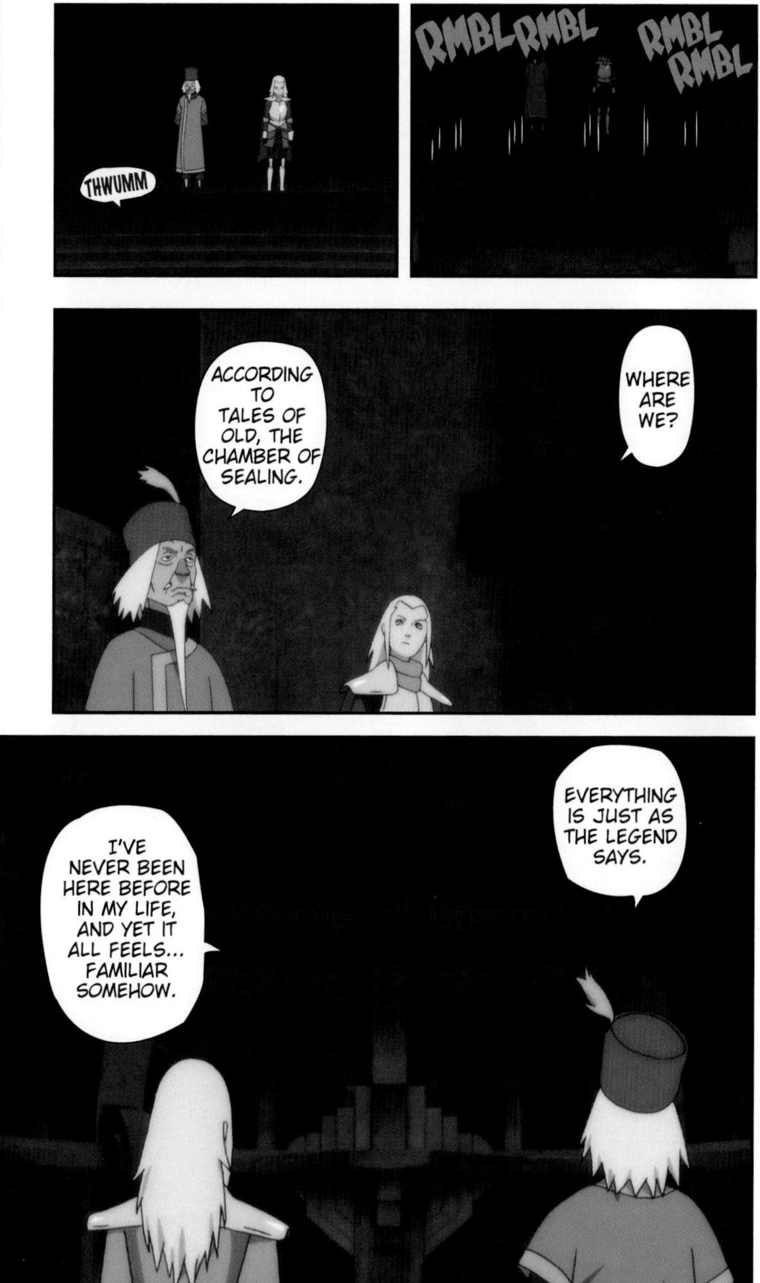
RMBL RMBL
RMBL RMBL
THWUMM
WHERE ARE WE?
ACCORDING TO TALES OF OLD, THE CHAMBER OF SEALING.
EVERYTHING IS JUST AS THE LEGEND SAYS.
I'VE NEVER BEEN HERE BEFORE IN MY LIFE, AND YET IT ALL FEELS... FAMILIAR SOMEHOW.

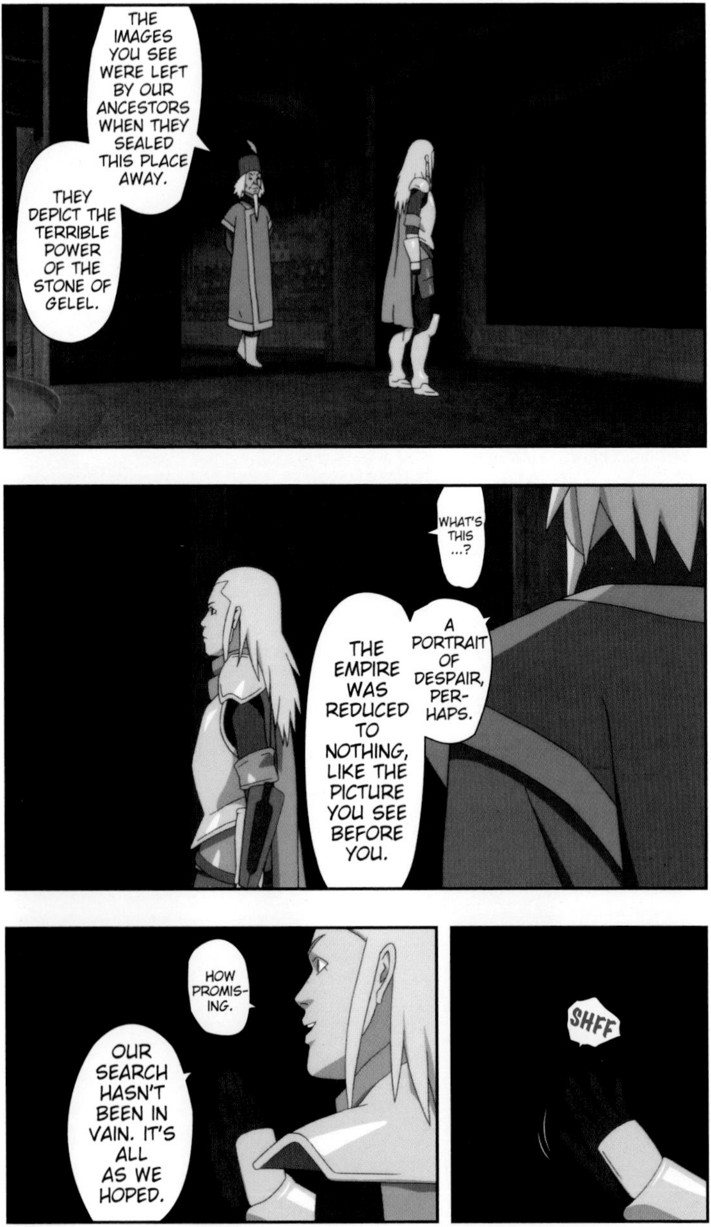
THE IMAGES YOU SEE WERE LEFT BY OUR ANCESTORS WHEN THEY SEALED THIS PLACE AWAY.
THEY DEPICT THE TERRIBLE POWER OF THE STONE OF GELEL.
WHAT'S THIS ...?
A PORTRAIT OF DESPAIR, PER-HAPS.
THE EMPIRE WAS REDUCED TO NOTHING, LIKE THE PICTURE YOU SEE BEFORE YOU.
SHFF
HOW PROMIS-ING.
OUR SEARCH HASN'T BEEN IN VAIN. IT'S ALL AS WE HOPED.

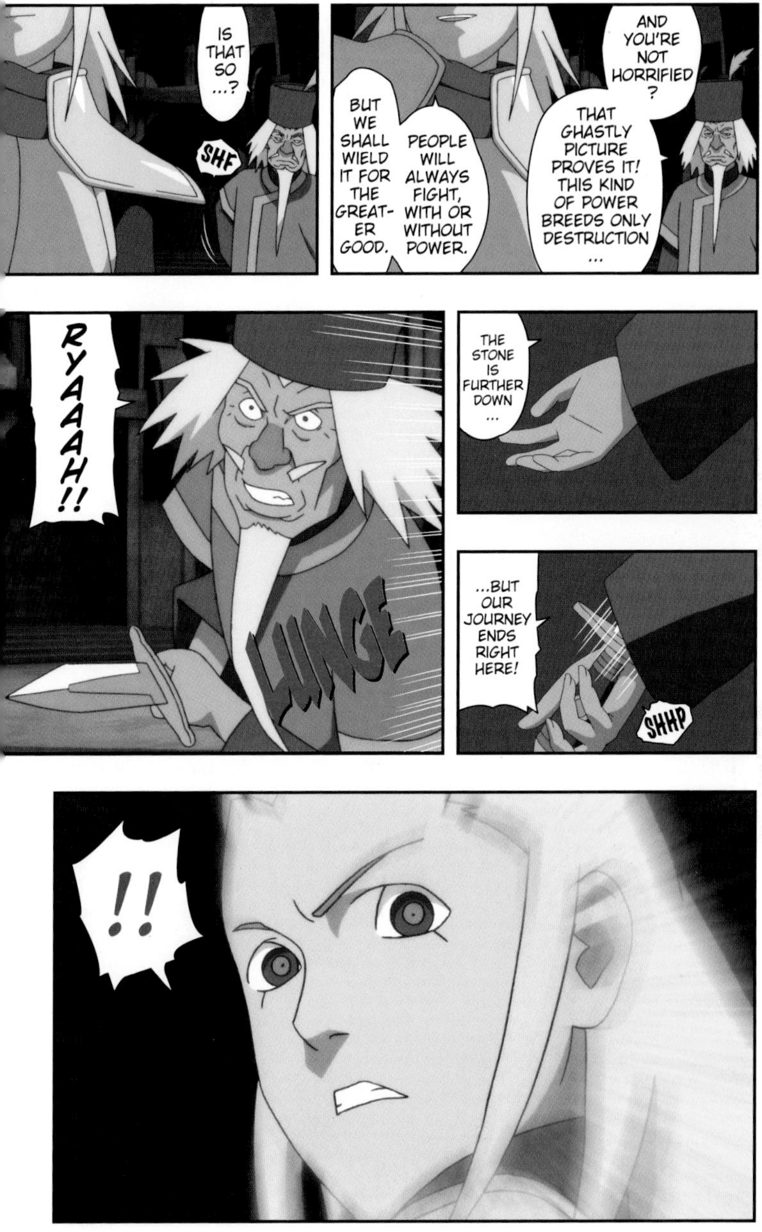
AND YOU'RE NOT HORRIFIED?
THAT GHASTLY PICTURE PROVES IT! THIS KIND OF POWER BREEDS ONLY DESTRUCTION...
PEOPLE WILL ALWAYS FIGHT, WITH OR WITHOUT POWER.
BUT WE SHALL WIELD IT FOR THE GREATER GOOD.
IS THAT SO...?
SHF
THE STONE IS FURTHER DOWN...
...BUT OUR JOURNEY ENDS RIGHT HERE!
SHHP
RYAAAH!!
LUNGE
!!

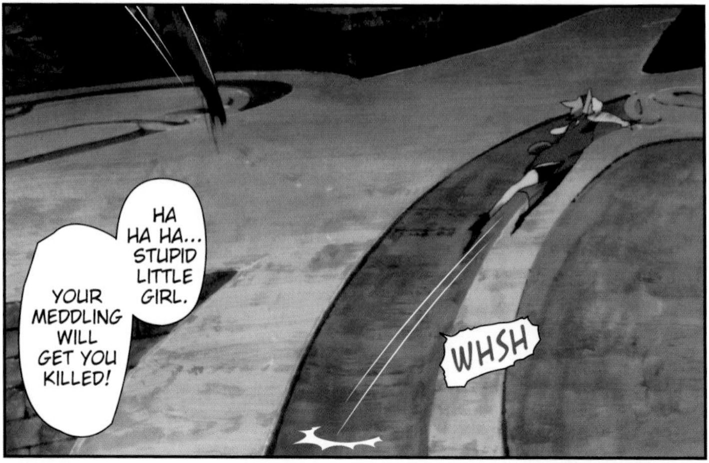
HA HA HA... STUPID LITTLE GIRL.
YOUR MEDDLING WILL GET YOU KILLED!
WHSH

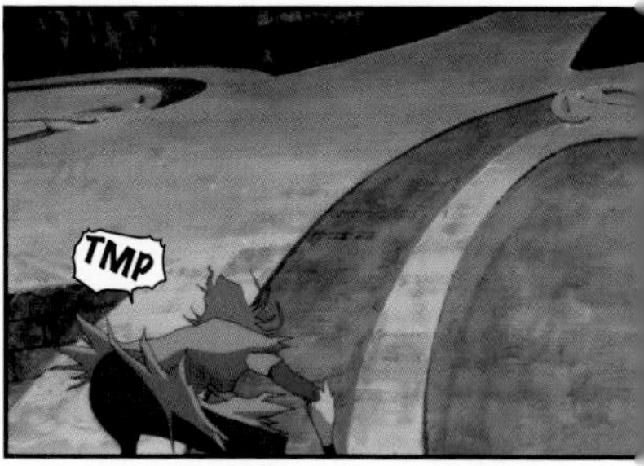
TMP

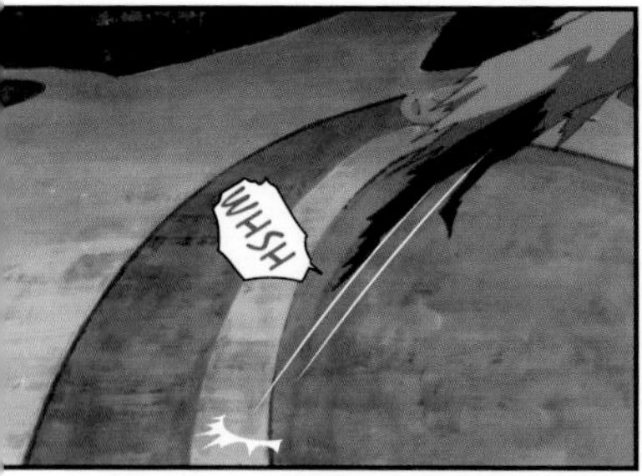
WHSH

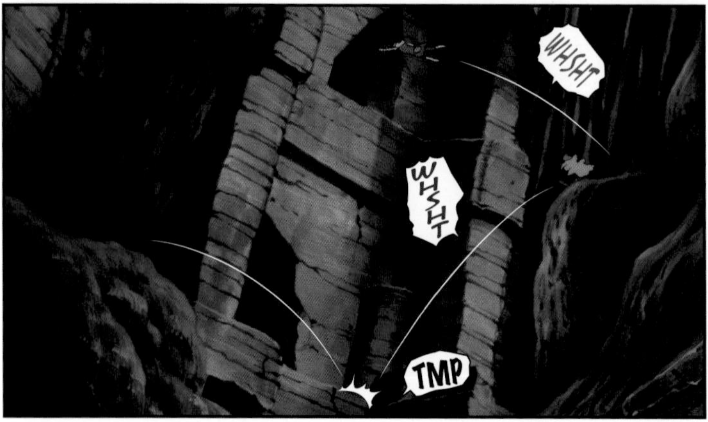
WHSHT
WHSHT
TMP

TOO SLOW!
SWISH
!!
LUNGE

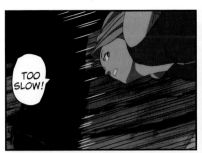

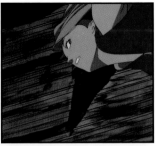

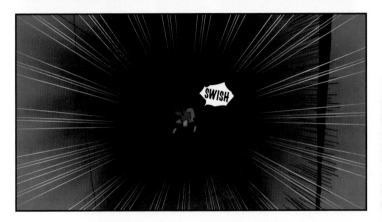

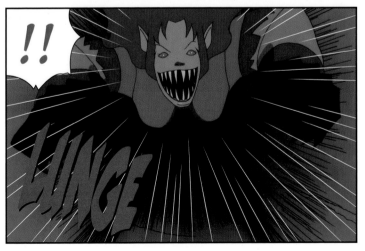

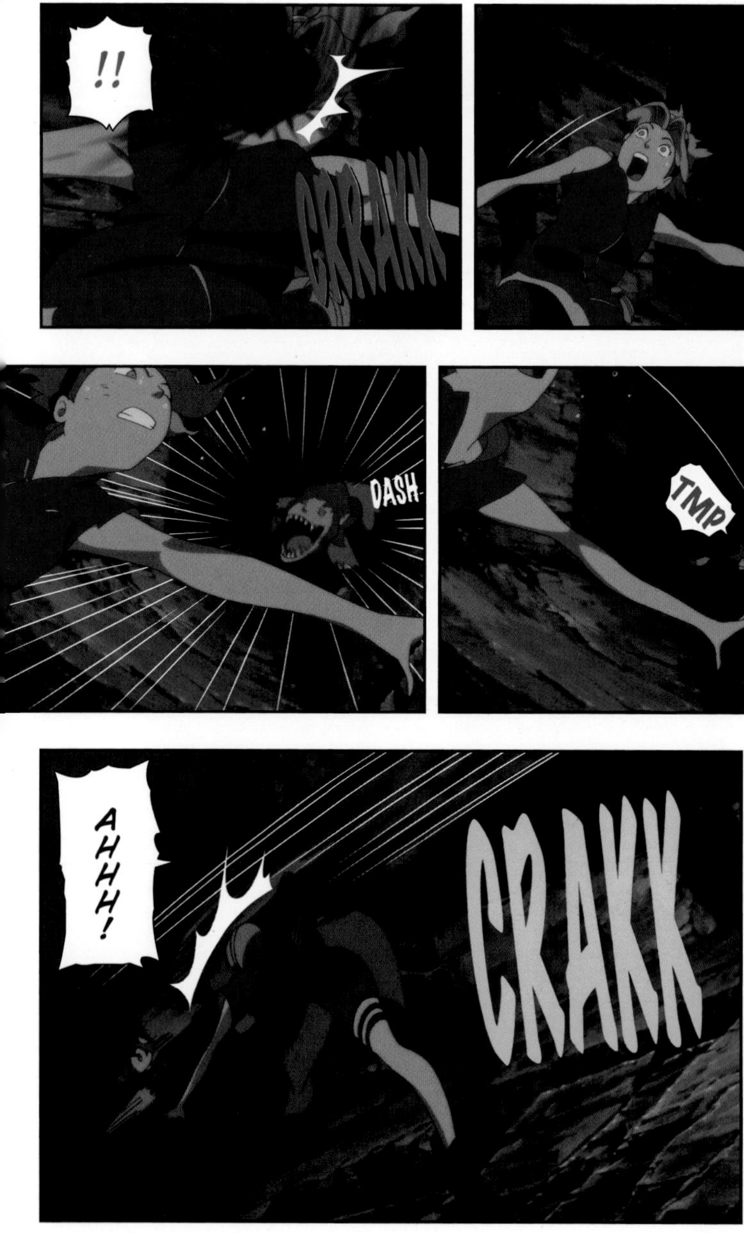
!!
CRRAKK
TMP
DASH
AHHH!
CRAKK

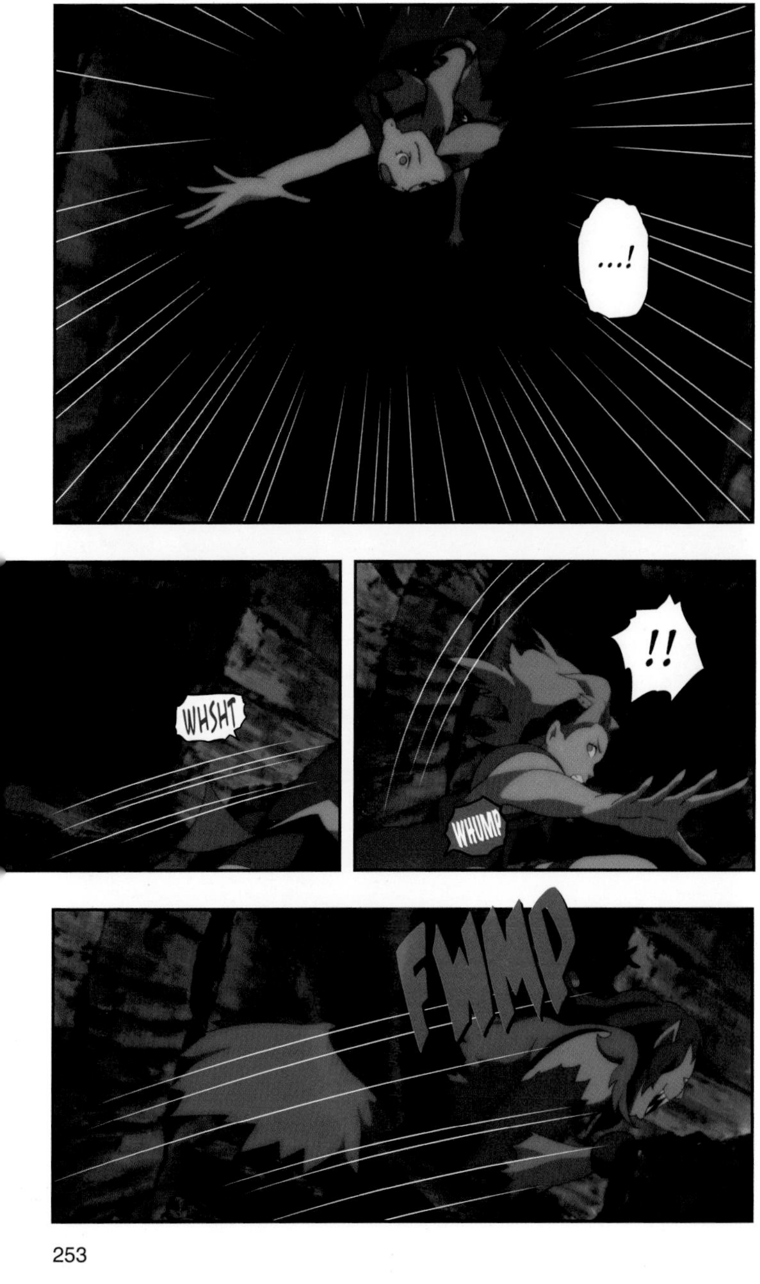
...!
!!
WHUMP
WHSHT
FWMP

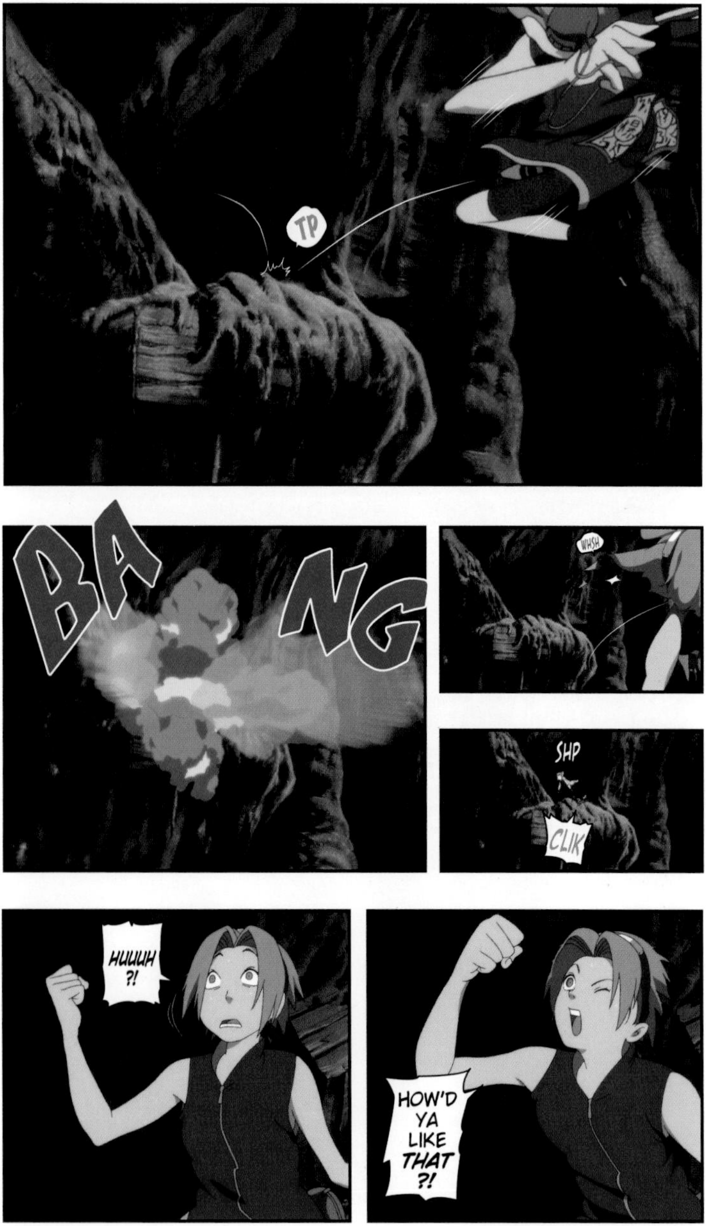
TP
WHSH
SHP
CLIK
BANG
HOW'D YA LIKE THAT?!
HUUUH?!

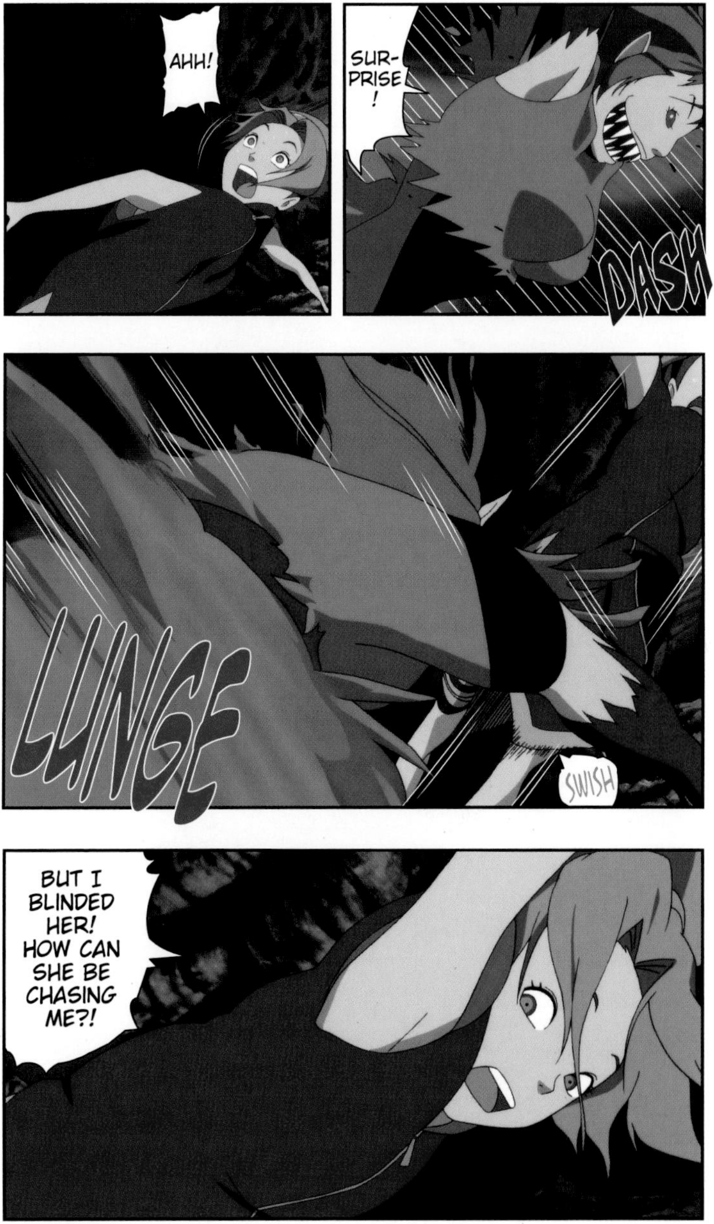
SUR-PRISE!
DASH
AHH!
SWISH
LUNGE
BUT I BLINDED HER! HOW CAN SHE BE CHASING ME?!

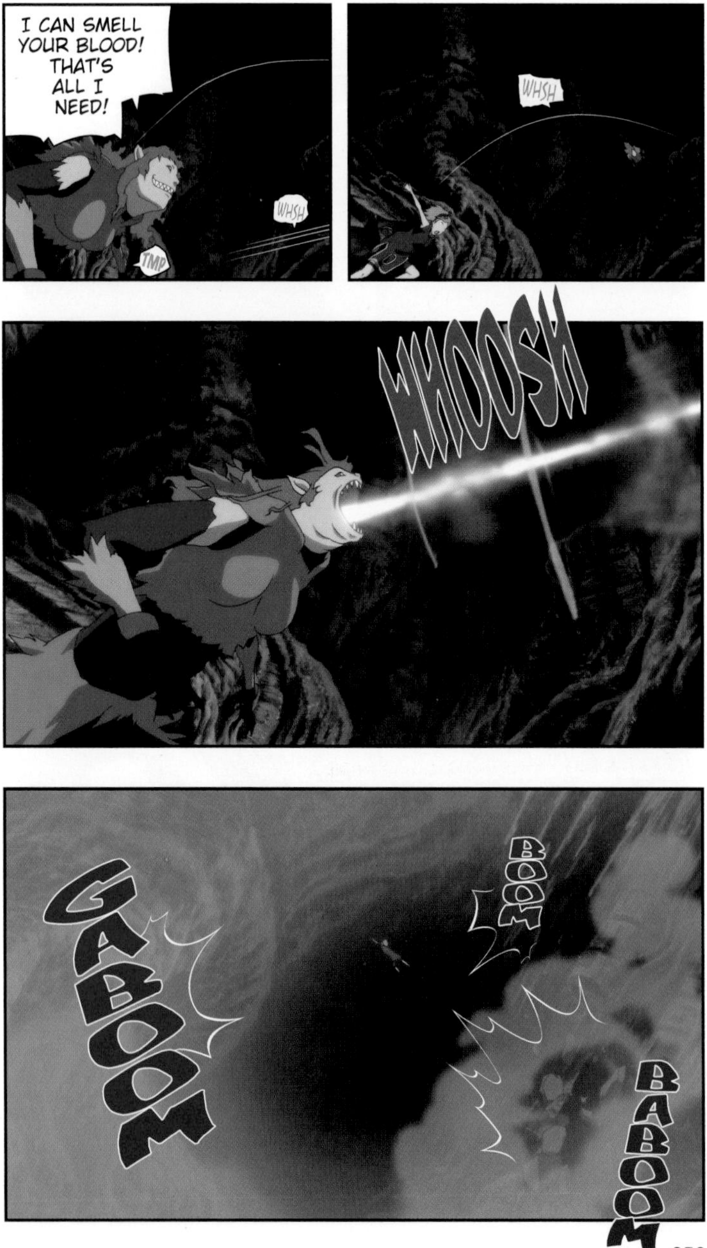
WHSH
I CAN SMELL YOUR BLOOD! THAT'S ALL I NEED!
WHSH
TMP
WHOOSH
BOOM
BABOOM
GABOOM

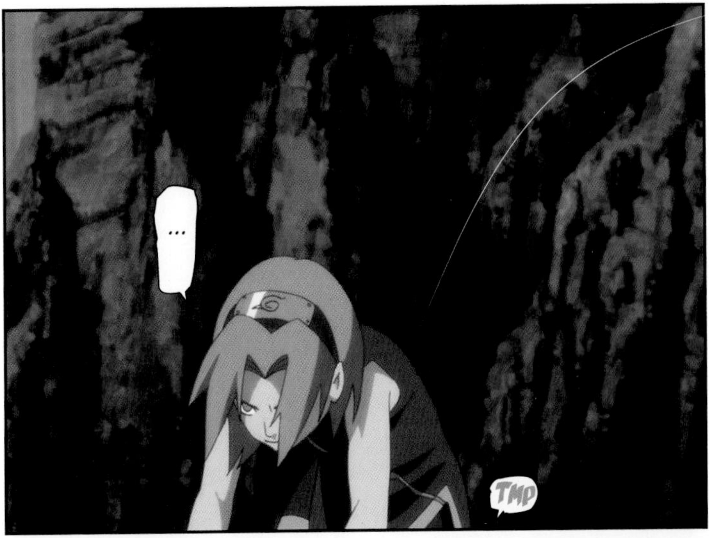
...
TMP
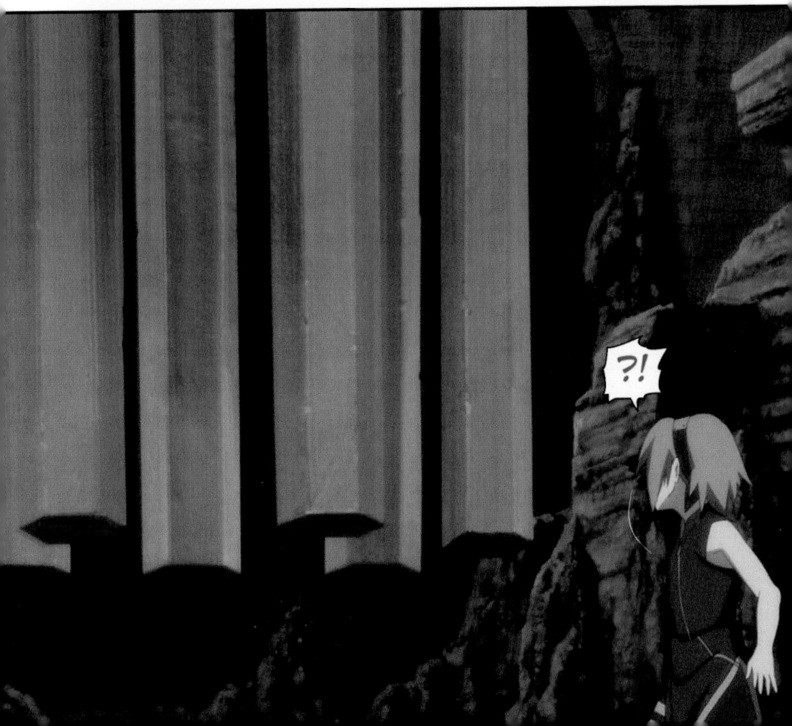
?!

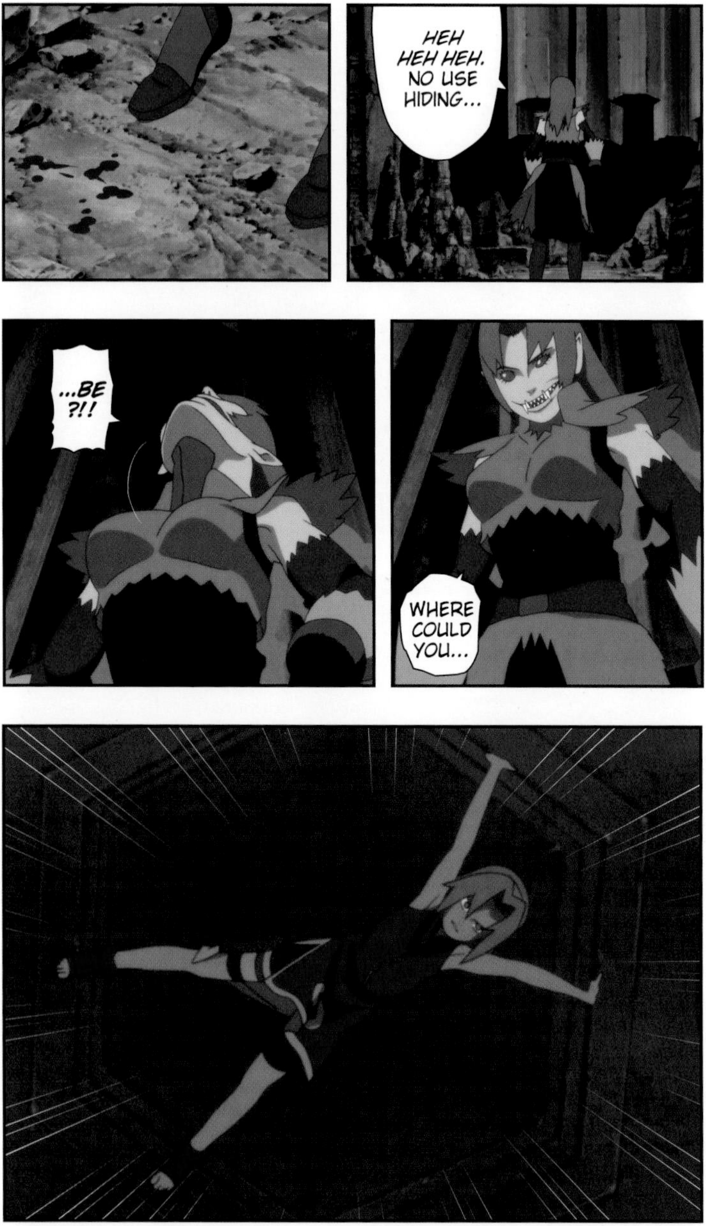
HEH HEH HEH. NO USE HIDING...
WHERE COULD YOU...
...BE ?!!

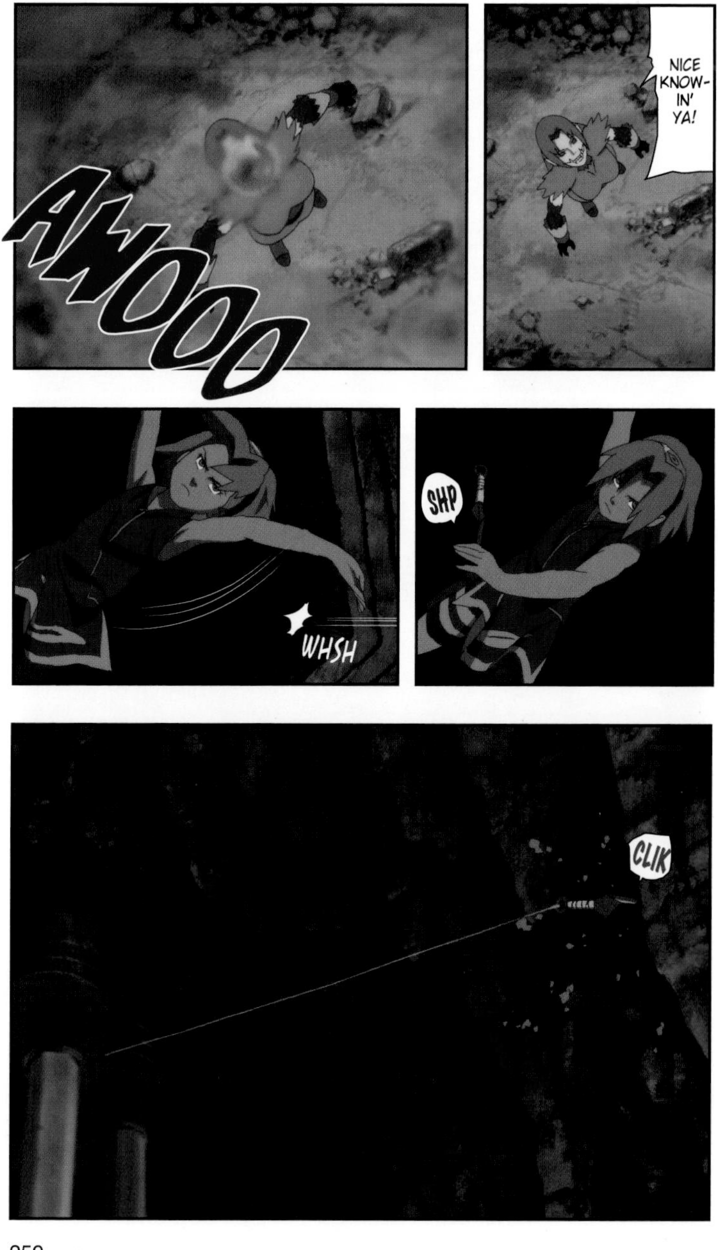
NICE KNOW-IN' YA!
AWOOO
SHP
WHSH
CLIK

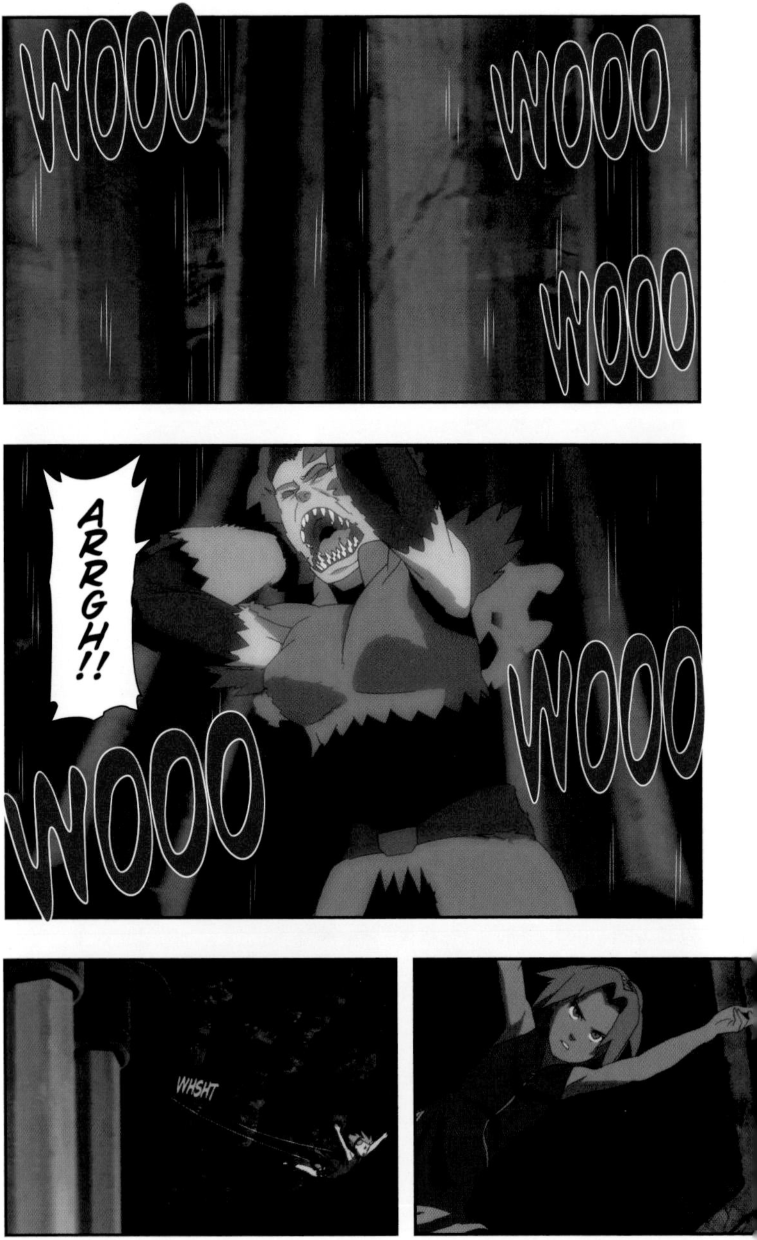
WOOO
WOOO
WOOO
ARRGH!!
WOOO
WOOO
WHSHT

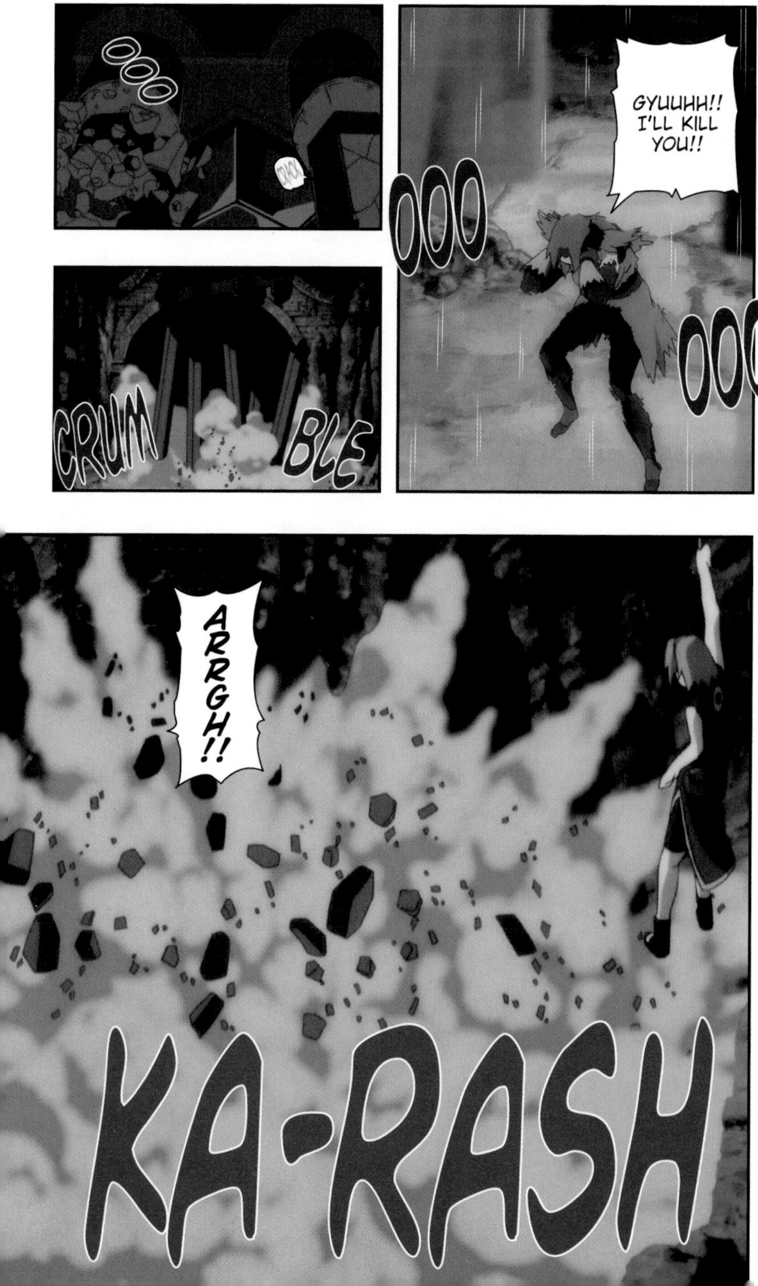
GYUUHH!! I'LL KILL YOU!!
OOO
OOO
OOO
CRACK
CRUM BLE
ARRGH!!
KA-RASH

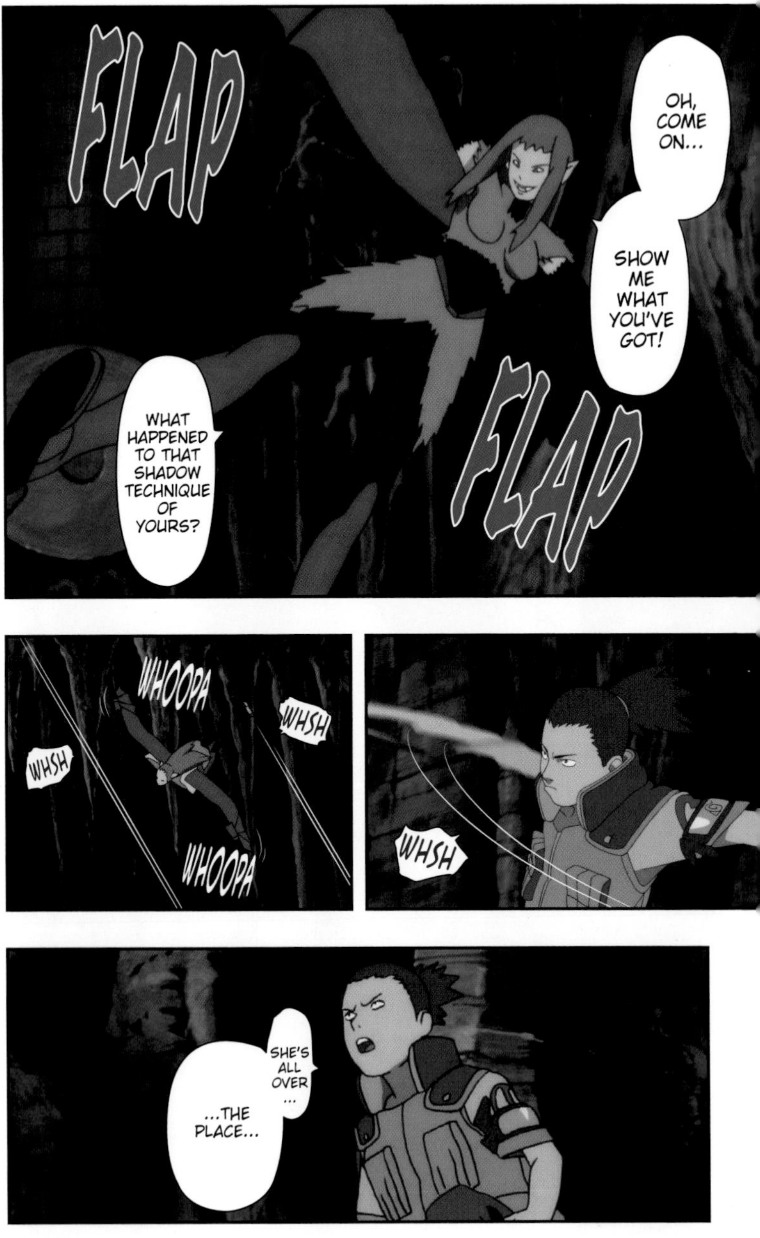
OH, COME ON...
SHOW ME WHAT YOU'VE GOT!
FLAP
FLAP
WHAT HAPPENED TO THAT SHADOW TECHNIQUE OF YOURS?
WHSH
WHOOPA
WHSH
WHSH
WHOOPA
SHE'S ALL OVER...
...THE PLACE...

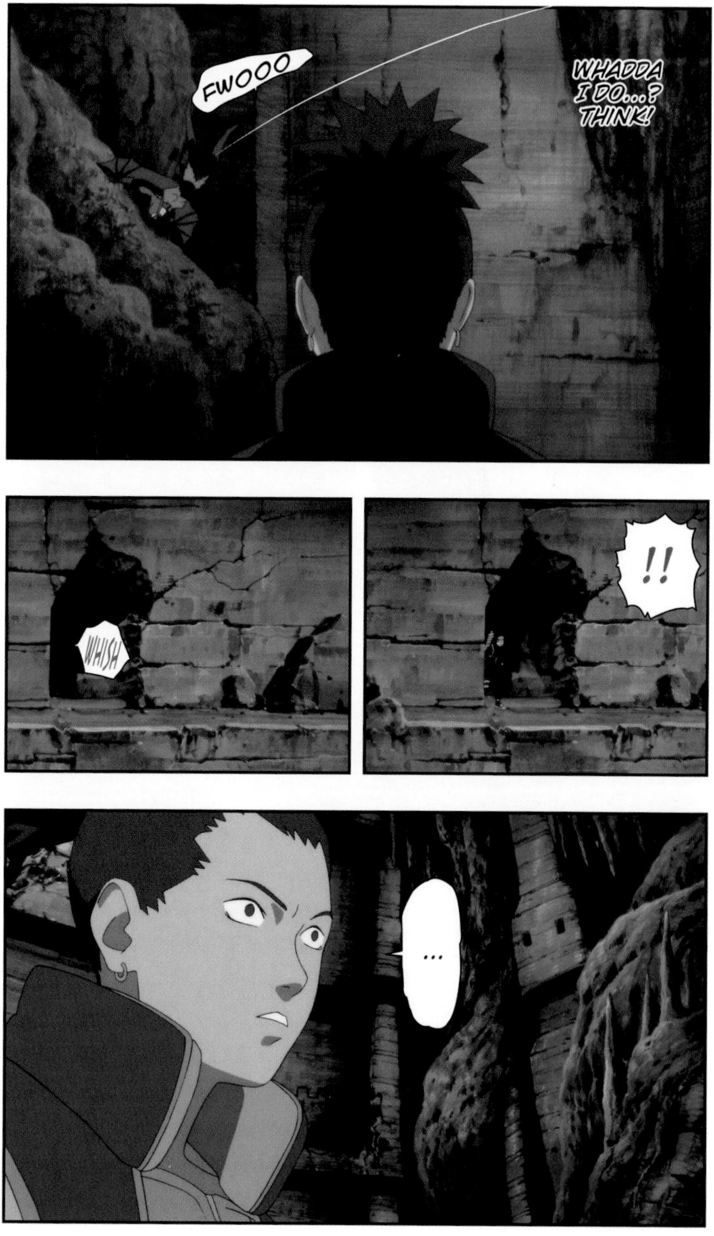
WHADDA I DO...? THINK!
FWOOO
!!
WHISH
...

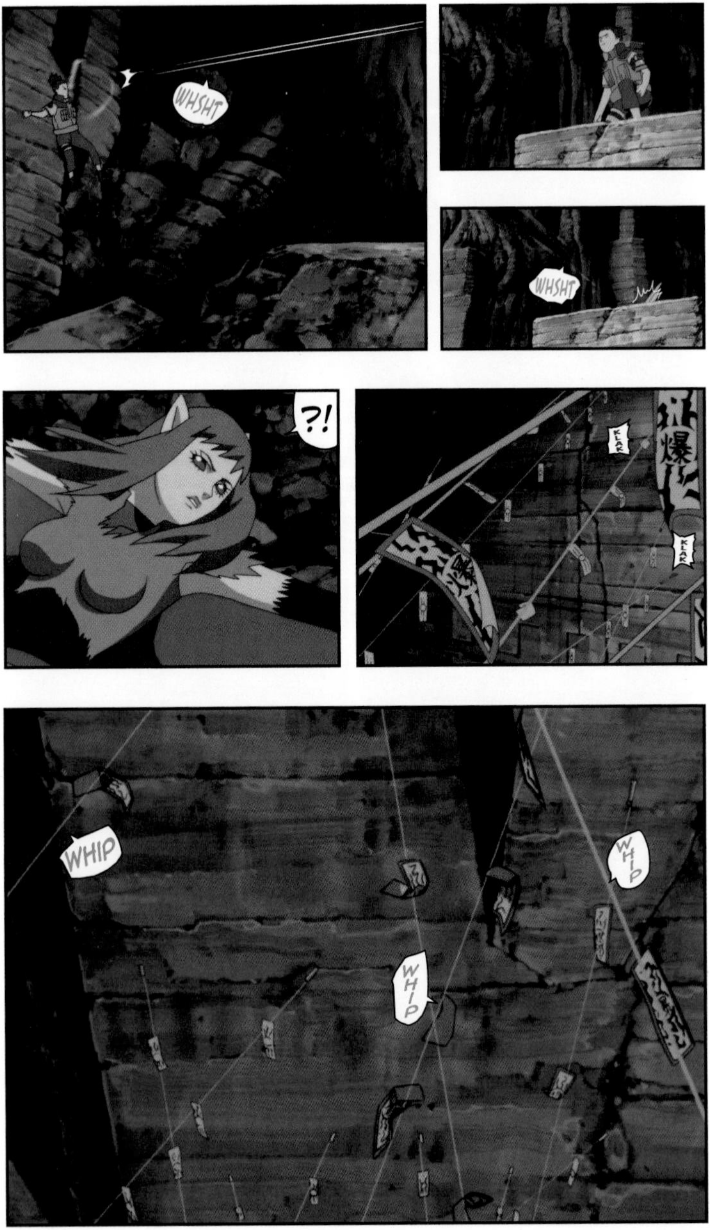
WHSHT
WHSHT
KLAK
KLAK
?!
WHIP
WHIP
WHIP

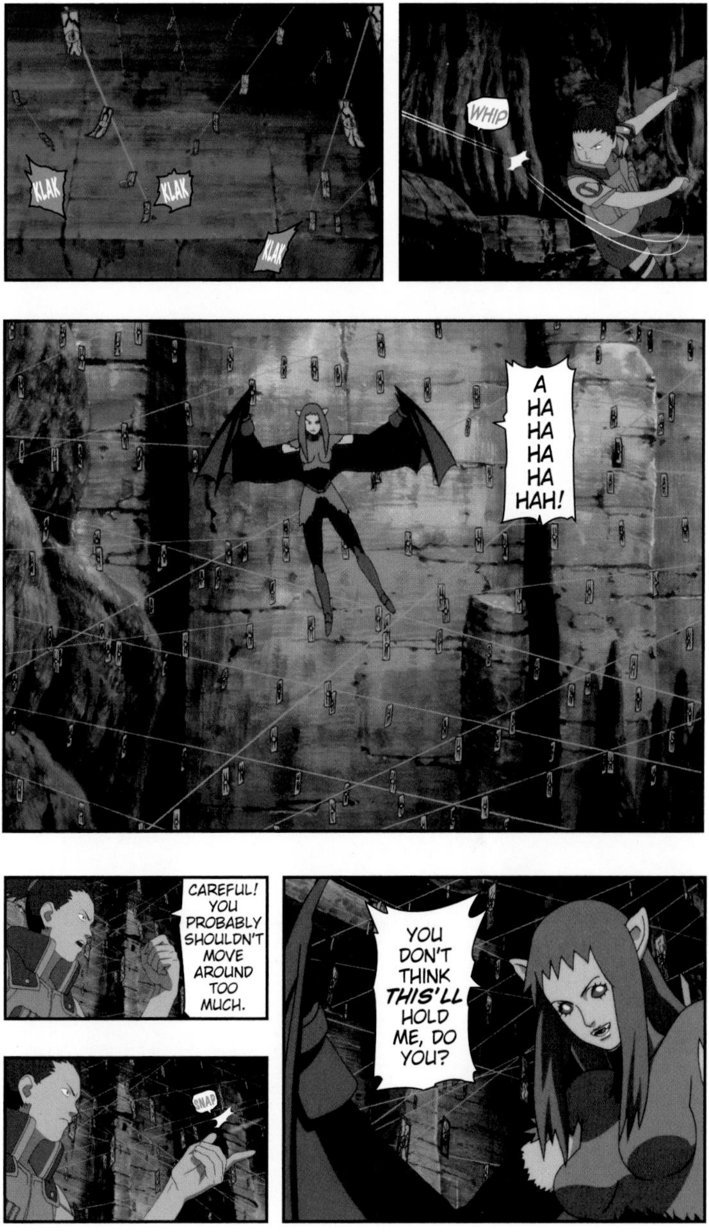
WHIP
KLAK
KLAK
KLAK
A HA HA HA HA HAH!
YOU DON'T THINK ***THIS'LL*** HOLD ME, DO YOU?
CAREFUL! YOU PROBABLY SHOULDN'T MOVE AROUND TOO MUCH.
SNAP

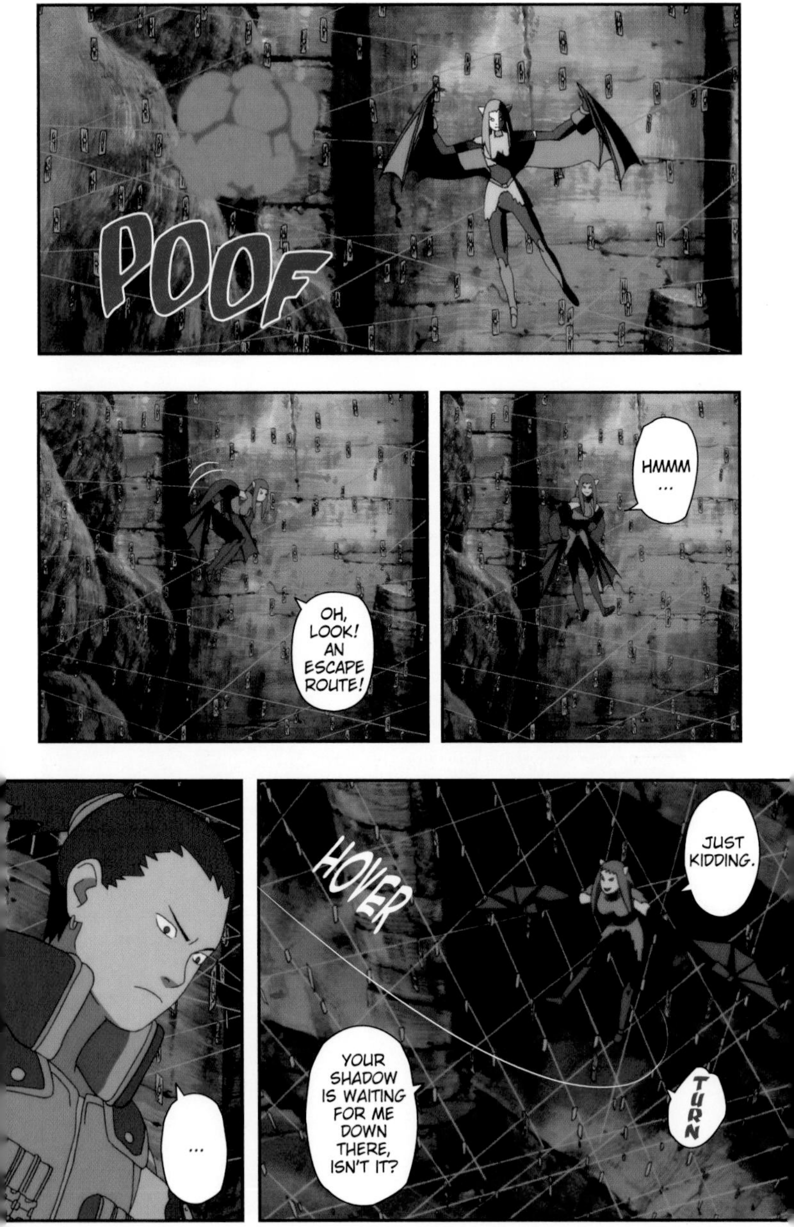
POOF
HMMM...
OH, LOOK! AN ESCAPE ROUTE!
JUST KIDDING.
HOVER
TURN
YOUR SHADOW IS WAITING FOR ME DOWN THERE, ISN'T IT?
...

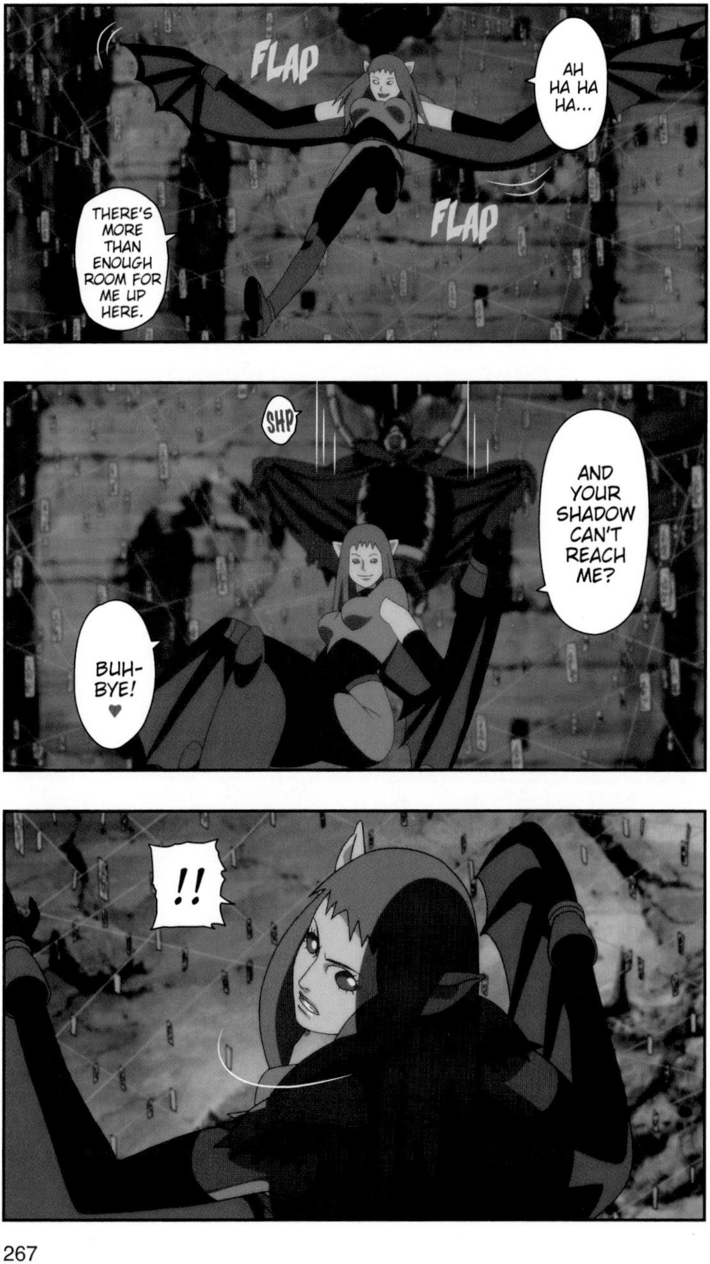
AH HA HA HA...
FLAP
FLAP
THERE'S MORE THAN ENOUGH ROOM FOR ME UP HERE.
SHP
AND YOUR SHADOW CAN'T REACH ME?
BUH-BYE! ♥
!!

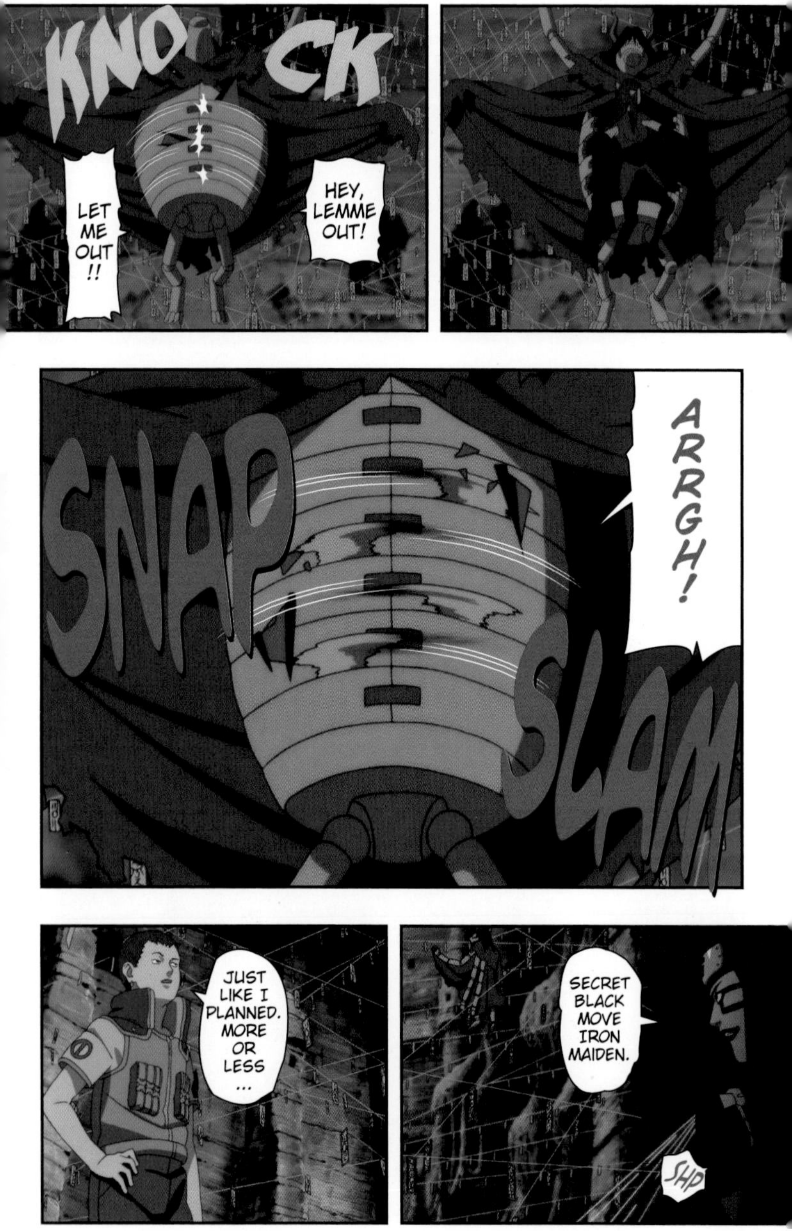
KNOCK
HEY, LEMME OUT!
LET ME OUT !!
ARRGH!
SNAP
SLAM
SECRET BLACK MOVE IRON MAIDEN.
SHP
JUST LIKE I PLANNED. MORE OR LESS ...

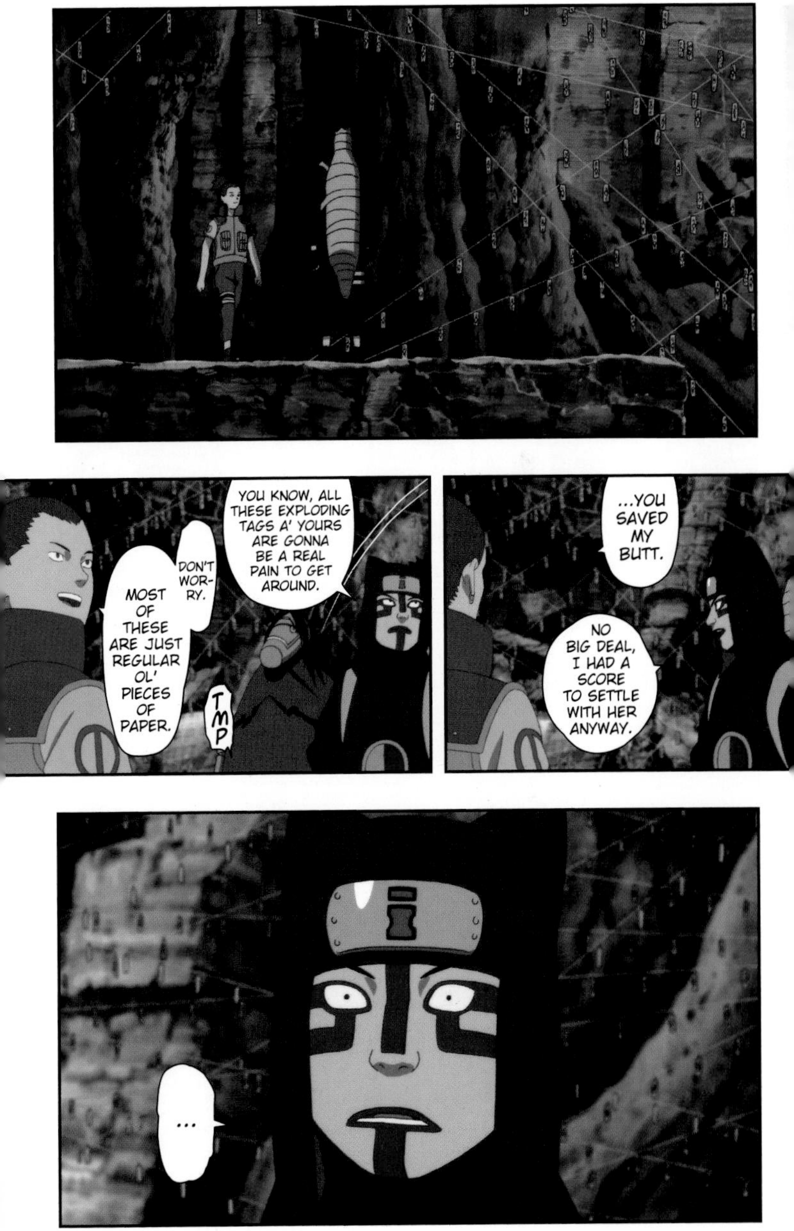
...YOU SAVED MY BUTT.
NO BIG DEAL, I HAD A SCORE TO SETTLE WITH HER ANYWAY.
YOU KNOW, ALL THESE EXPLODING TAGS A' YOURS ARE GONNA BE A REAL PAIN TO GET AROUND.
DON'T WOR-RY.
MOST OF THESE ARE JUST REGULAR OL' PIECES OF PAPER.
TMP
...

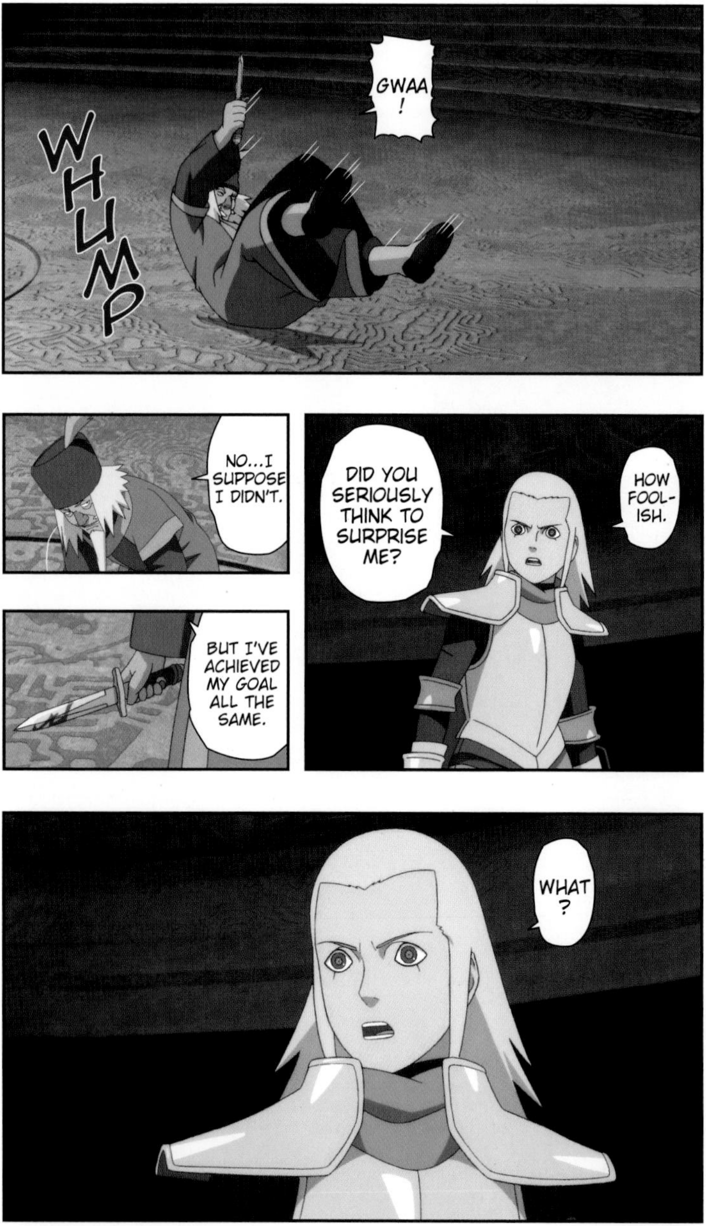
GWAA!
WHUMP
HOW FOOL-ISH.
DID YOU SERIOUSLY THINK TO SURPRISE ME?
NO...I SUPPOSE I DIDN'T.
BUT I'VE ACHIEVED MY GOAL ALL THE SAME.
WHAT?

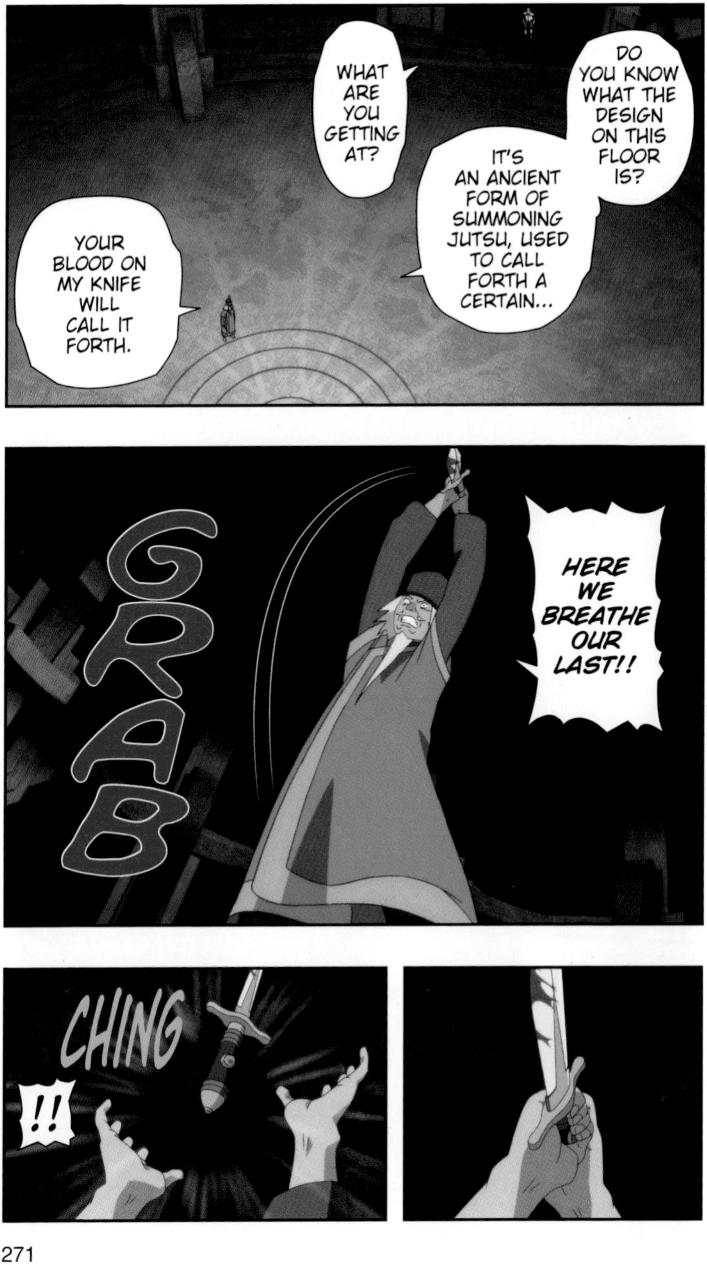
DO YOU KNOW WHAT THE DESIGN ON THIS FLOOR IS?
WHAT ARE YOU GETTING AT?
IT'S AN ANCIENT FORM OF SUMMONING JUTSU, USED TO CALL FORTH A CERTAIN...
YOUR BLOOD ON MY KNIFE WILL CALL IT FORTH.
HERE WE BREATHE OUR LAST!!
GRAB
CHING
!!

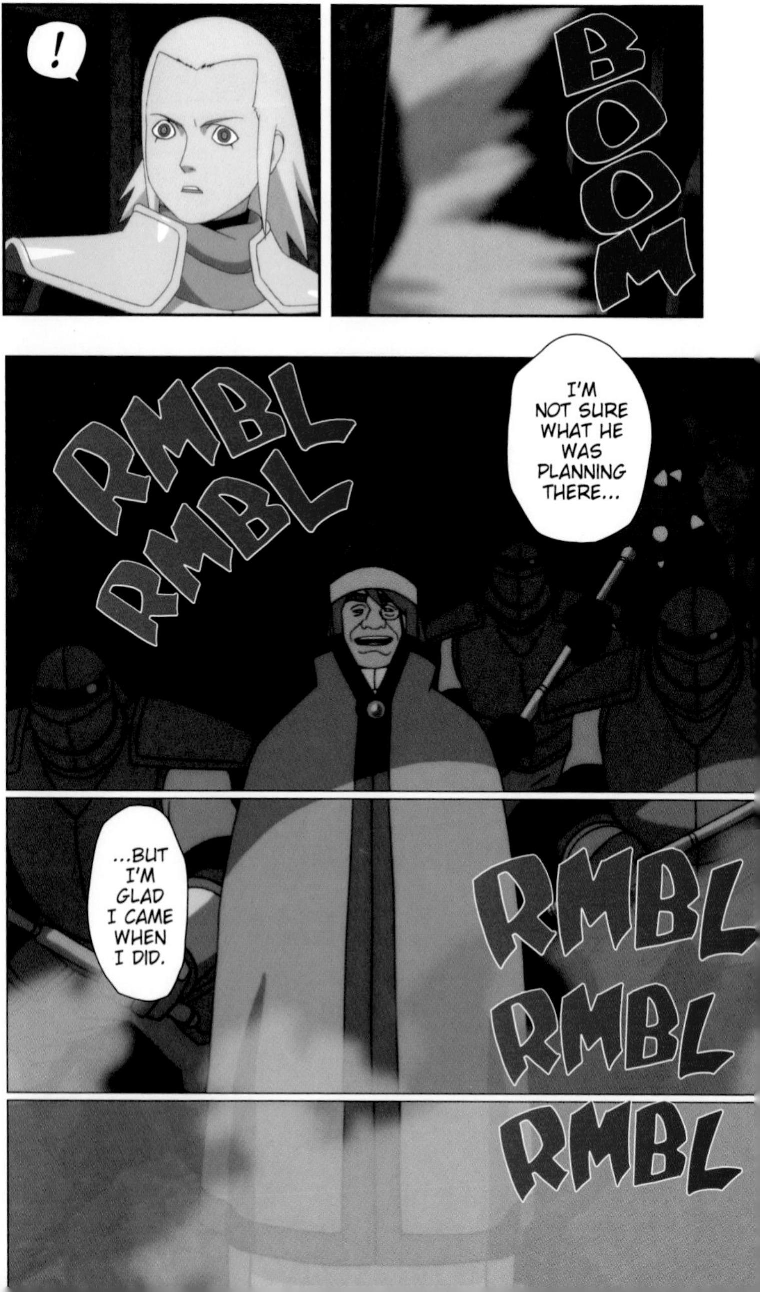
BOOM
!
I'M NOT SURE WHAT HE WAS PLANNING THERE...
RMBL RMBL
RMBL RMBL RMBL
...BUT I'M GLAD I CAME WHEN I DID.

Chapter 7: Never Give Up!

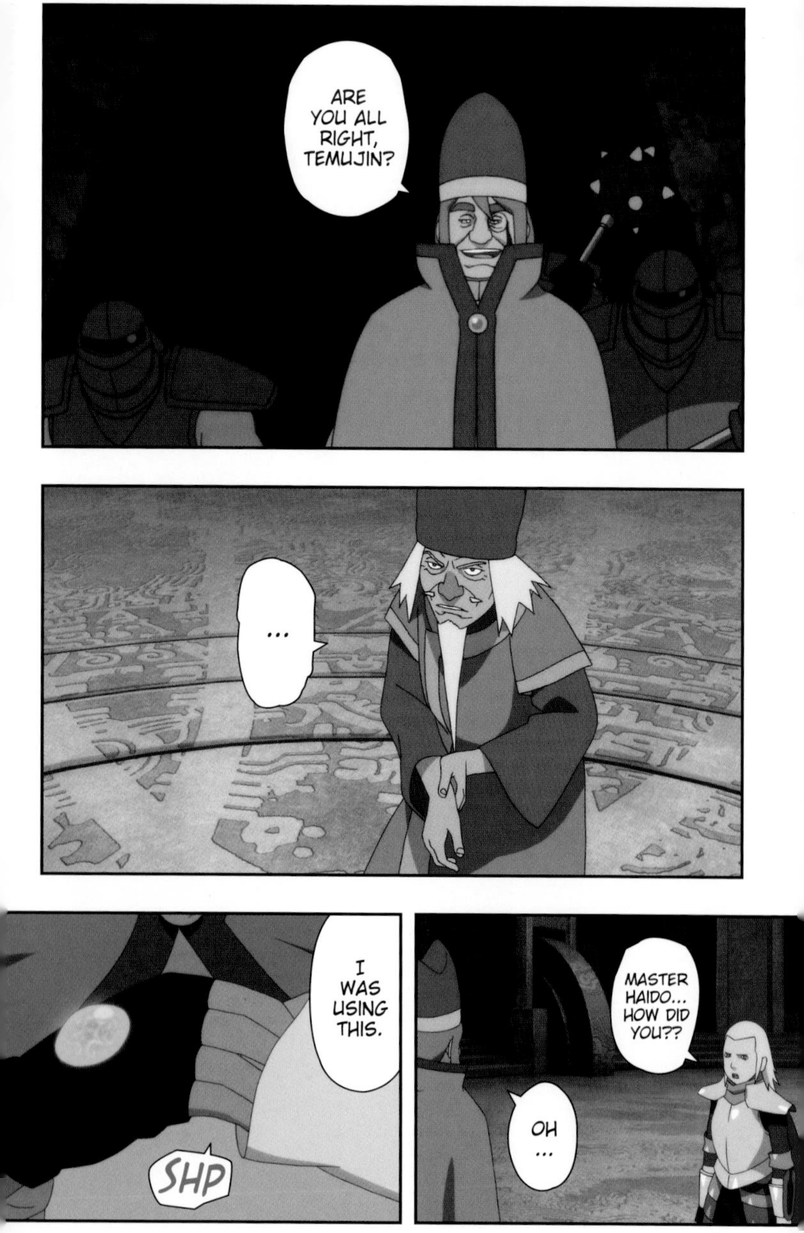
ARE YOU ALL RIGHT, TEMUJIN?
...
MASTER HAIDO... HOW DID YOU??
OH ...
I WAS USING THIS.
SHP

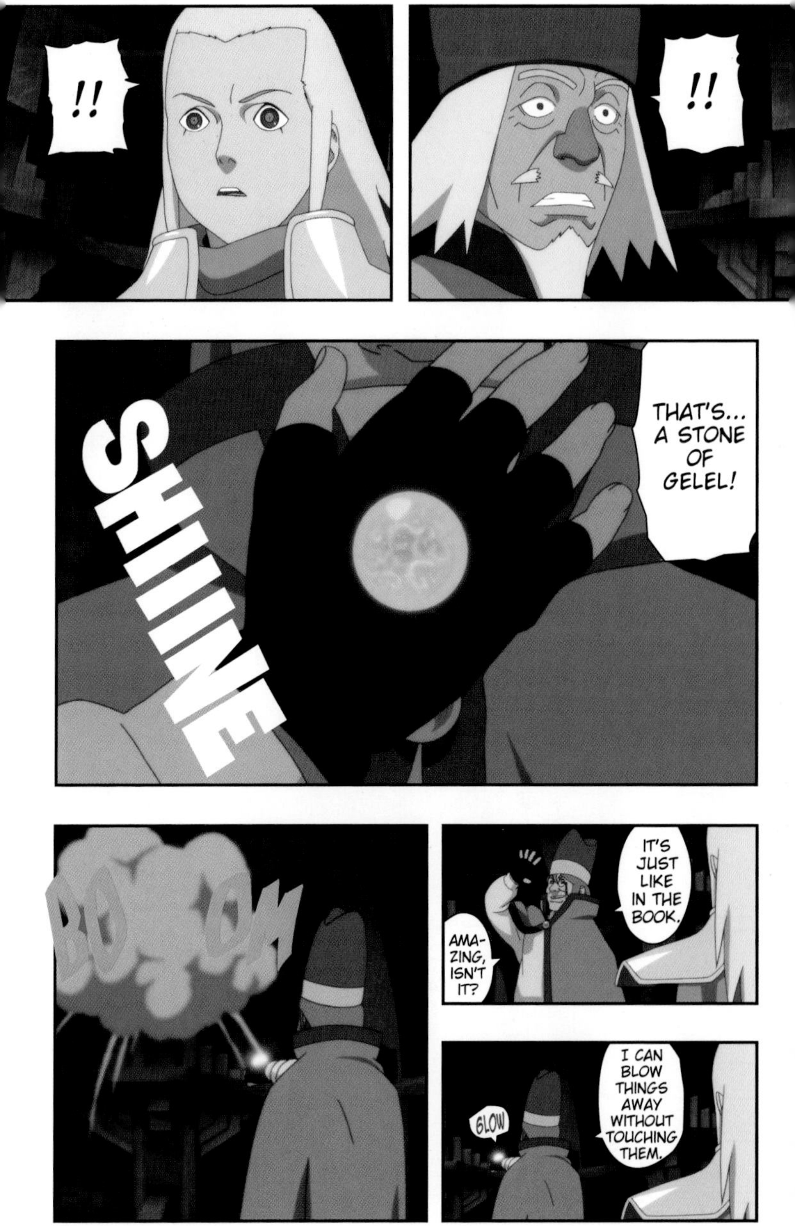
!!
!!
THAT'S... A STONE OF GELEL!
SHIINE
IT'S JUST LIKE IN THE BOOK.
AMAZING, ISN'T IT?
I CAN BLOW THINGS AWAY WITHOUT TOUCHING THEM.
GLOW
BOOM

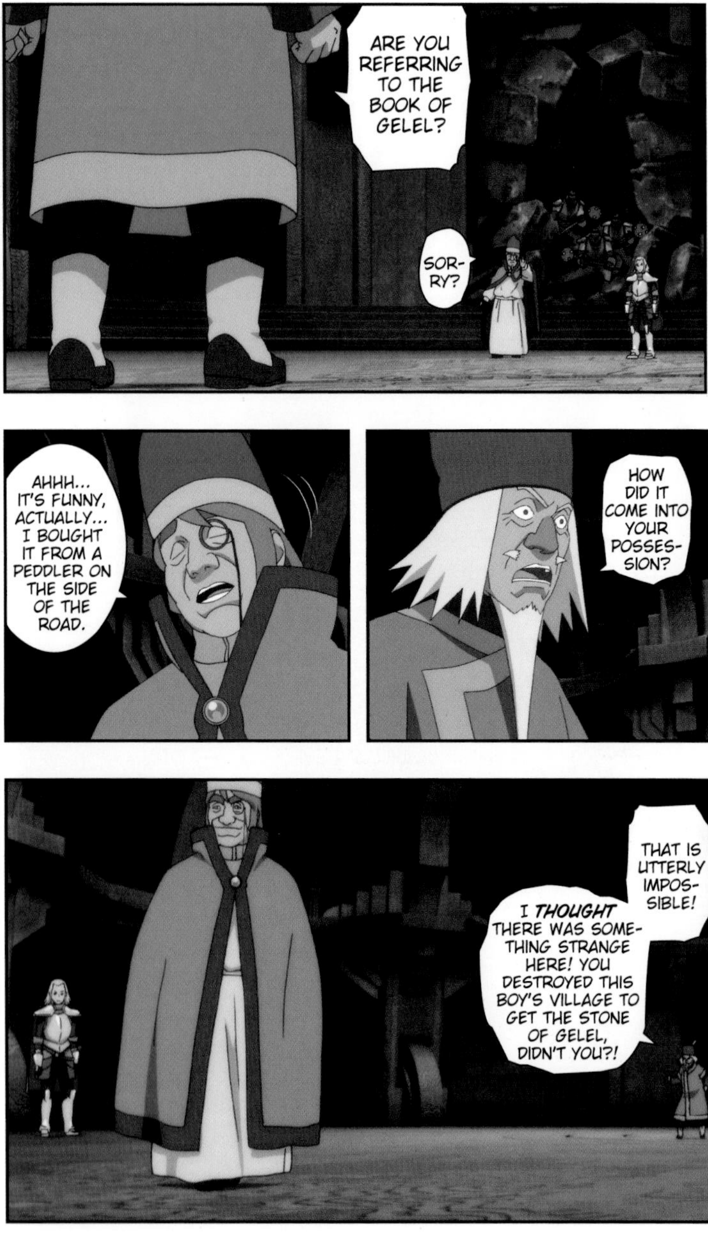
ARE YOU REFERRING TO THE BOOK OF GELEL?
SORRY?
HOW DID IT COME INTO YOUR POSSESSION?
AHHH... IT'S FUNNY, ACTUALLY... I BOUGHT IT FROM A PEDDLER ON THE SIDE OF THE ROAD.
THAT IS UTTERLY IMPOSSIBLE!
I *THOUGHT* THERE WAS SOMETHING STRANGE HERE! YOU DESTROYED THIS BOY'S VILLAGE TO GET THE STONE OF GELEL, DIDN'T YOU?!

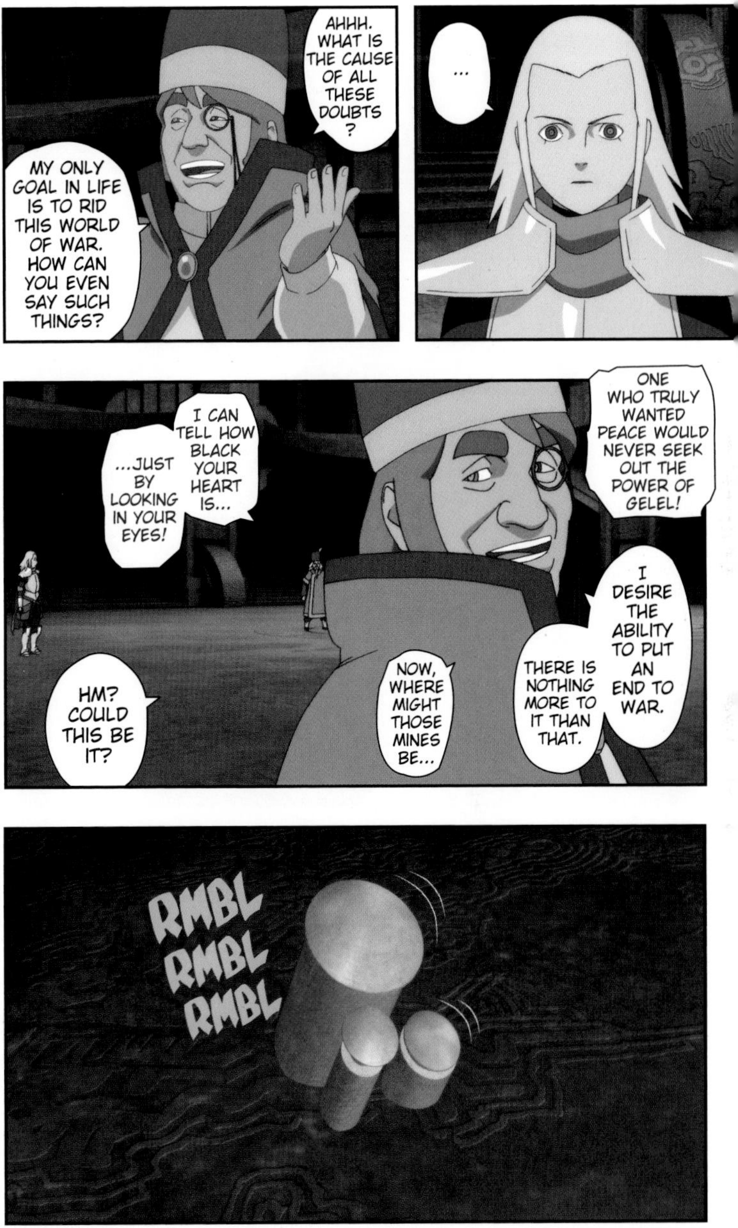
...
AHHH. WHAT IS THE CAUSE OF ALL THESE DOUBTS?
MY ONLY GOAL IN LIFE IS TO RID THIS WORLD OF WAR. HOW CAN YOU EVEN SAY SUCH THINGS?
ONE WHO TRULY WANTED PEACE WOULD NEVER SEEK OUT THE POWER OF GELEL!
I CAN TELL HOW BLACK YOUR HEART IS...
...JUST BY LOOKING IN YOUR EYES!
I DESIRE THE ABILITY TO PUT AN END TO WAR.
THERE IS NOTHING MORE TO IT THAN THAT.
NOW, WHERE MIGHT THOSE MINES BE...
HM? COULD THIS BE IT?
RMBL RMBL RMBL

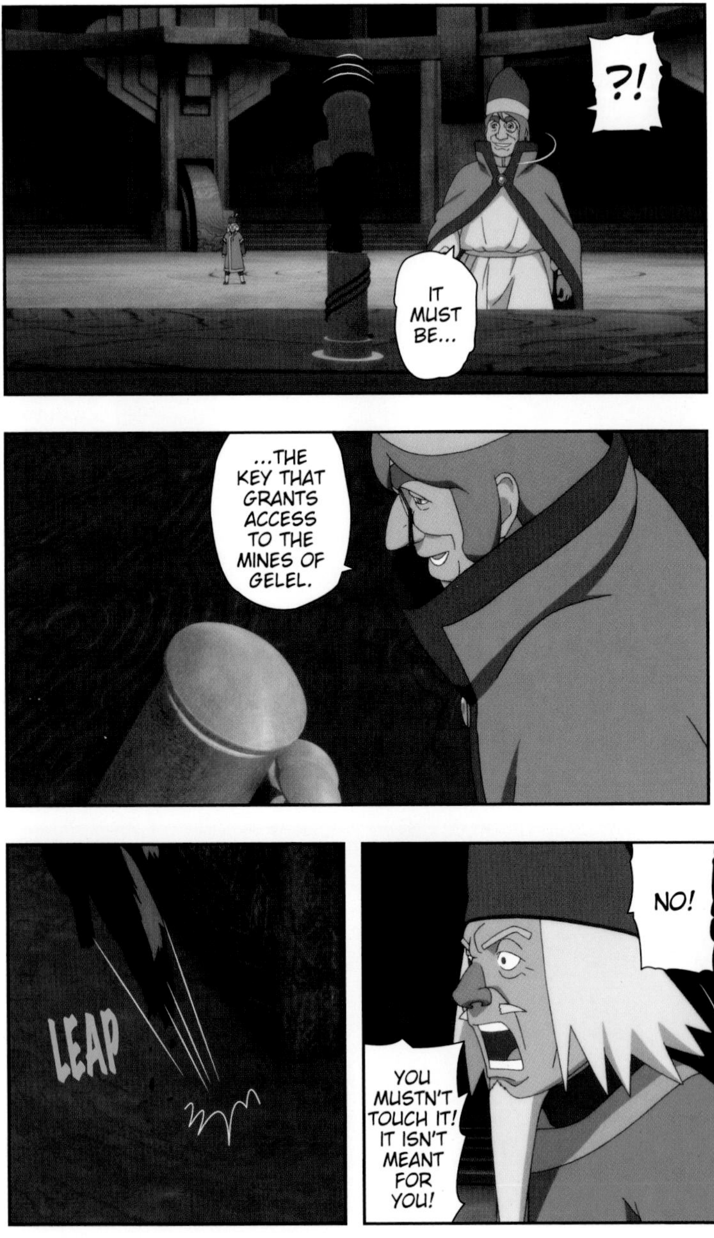
?!
IT MUST BE...
...THE KEY THAT GRANTS ACCESS TO THE MINES OF GELEL.
NO!
YOU MUSTN'T TOUCH IT! IT ISN'T MEANT FOR YOU!
LEAP

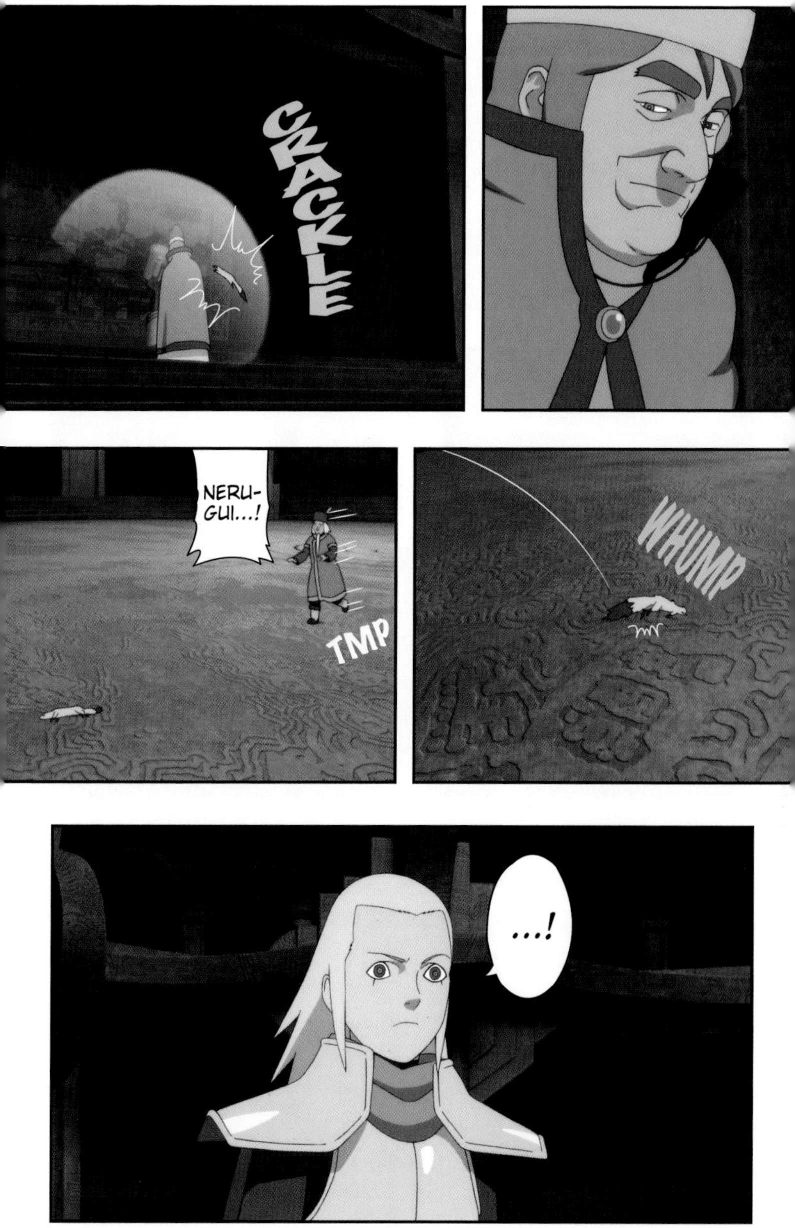
CRACKLE
WHUMP
NERU-GUI...!
TMP
...!

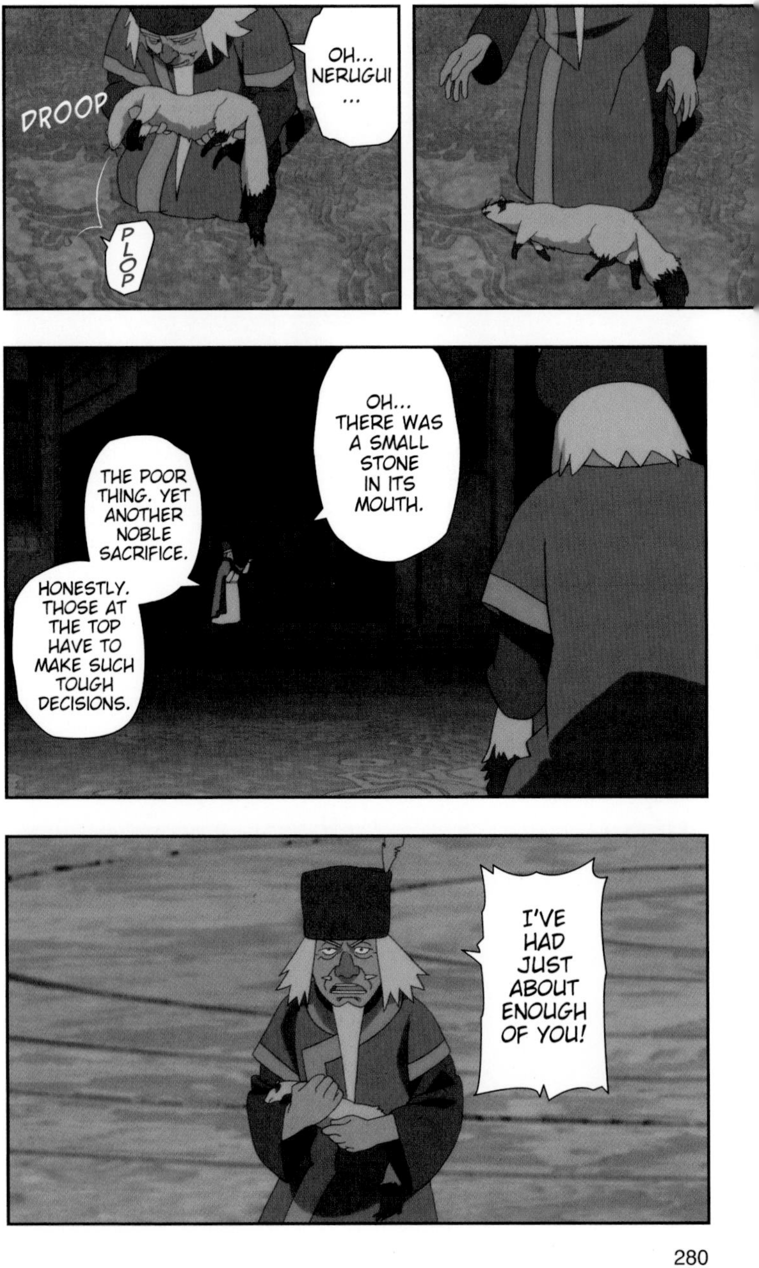
OH... NERUGUI ...
DROOP
PLOP
OH... THERE WAS A SMALL STONE IN ITS MOUTH.
THE POOR THING. YET ANOTHER NOBLE SACRIFICE.
HONESTLY. THOSE AT THE TOP HAVE TO MAKE SUCH TOUGH DECISIONS.
I'VE HAD JUST ABOUT ENOUGH OF YOU!

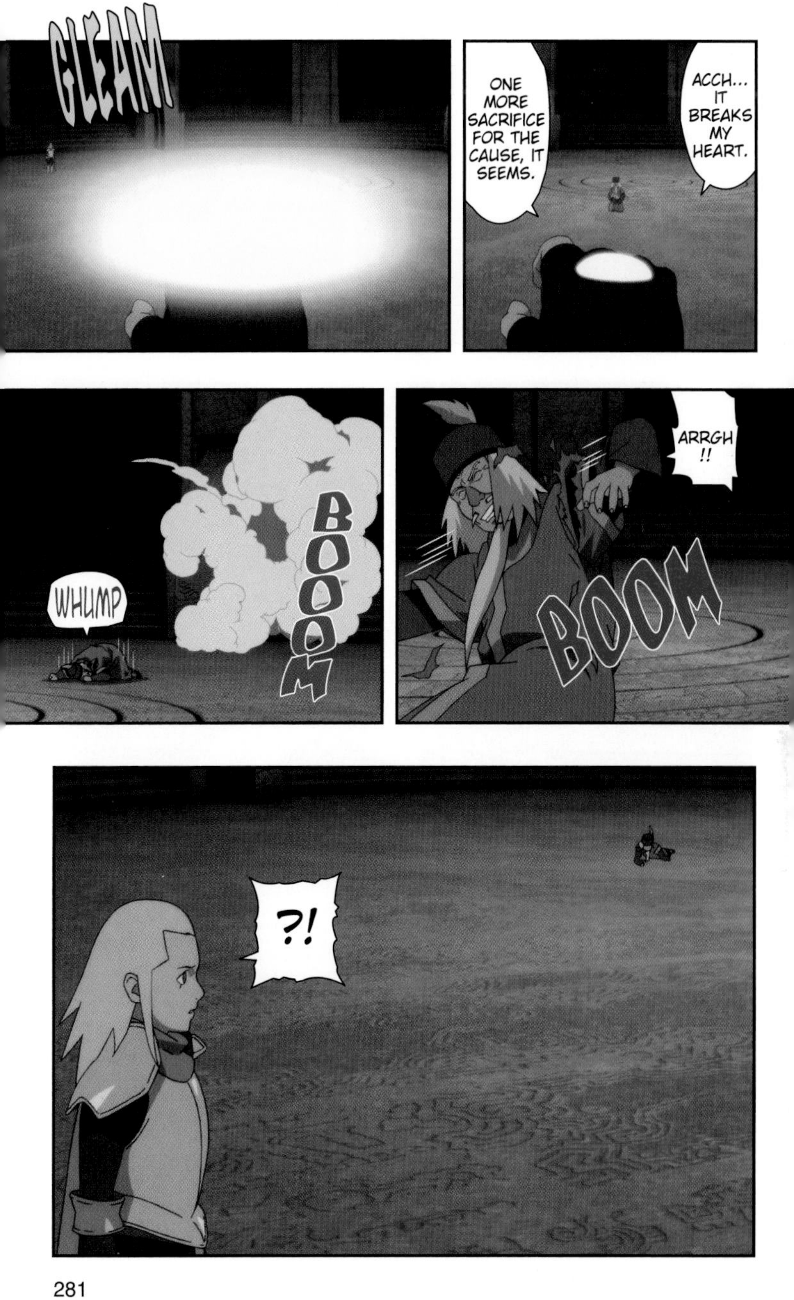
ACCH... IT BREAKS MY HEART.
ONE MORE SACRIFICE FOR THE CAUSE, IT SEEMS.
GLEAM
ARRGH!!
BOOM
BOOOOM
WHUMP
?!

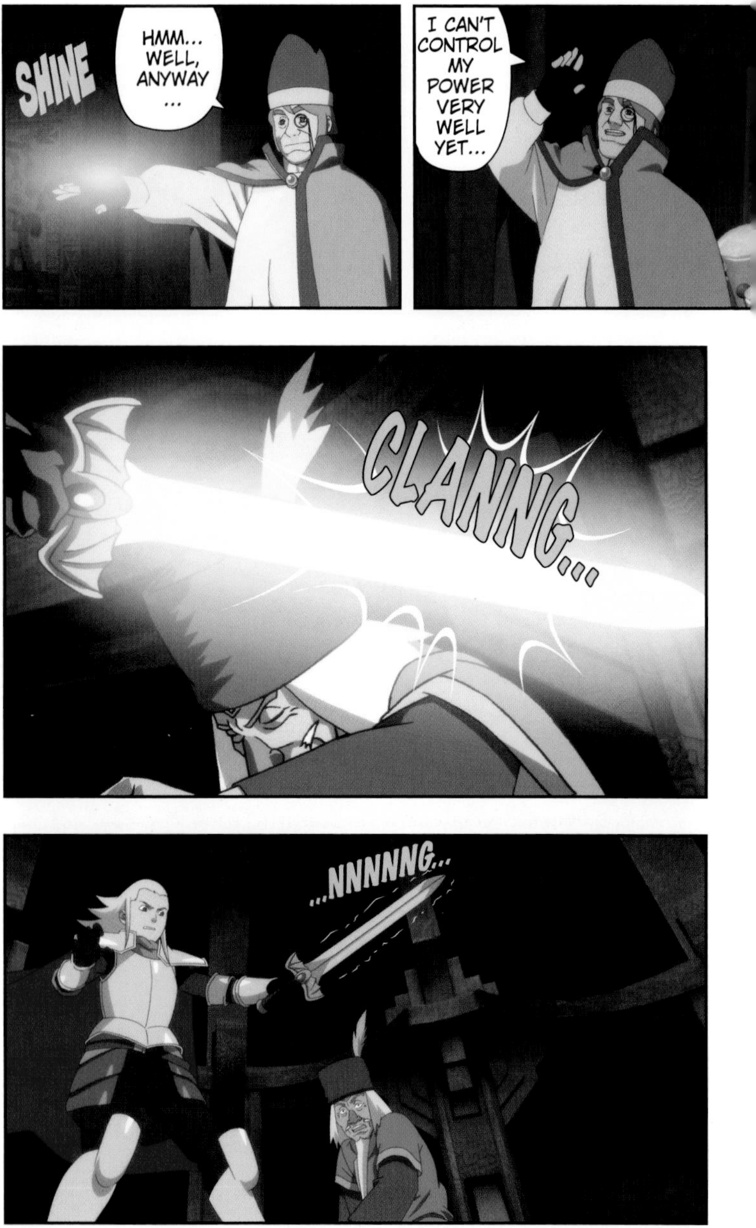
I CAN'T CONTROL MY POWER VERY WELL YET...
HMM... WELL, ANYWAY ...
SHINE
CLANNG...
...NNNNNG...

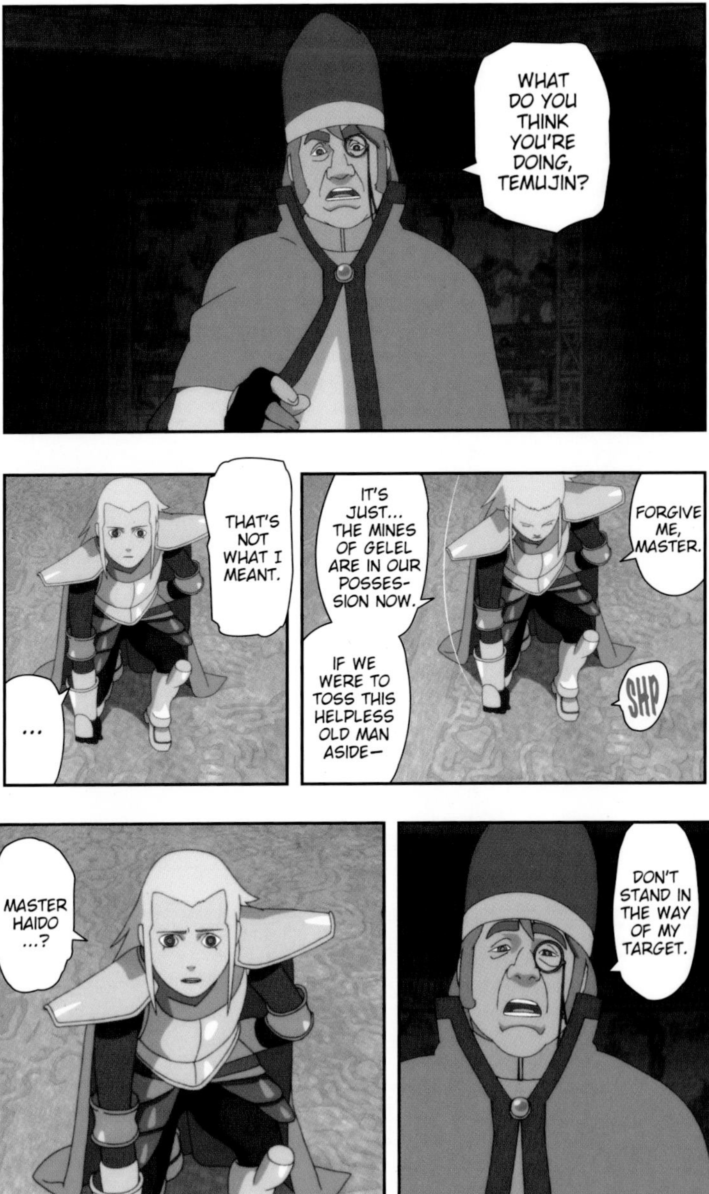
WHAT DO YOU THINK YOU'RE DOING, TEMUJIN?
FORGIVE ME, MASTER.
IT'S JUST... THE MINES OF GELEL ARE IN OUR POSSESSION NOW.
SHP
IF WE WERE TO TOSS THIS HELPLESS OLD MAN ASIDE—
THAT'S NOT WHAT I MEANT.
...
DON'T STAND IN THE WAY OF MY TARGET.
MASTER HAIDO ...?

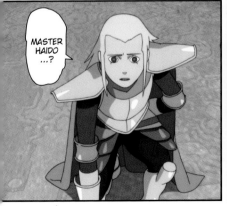

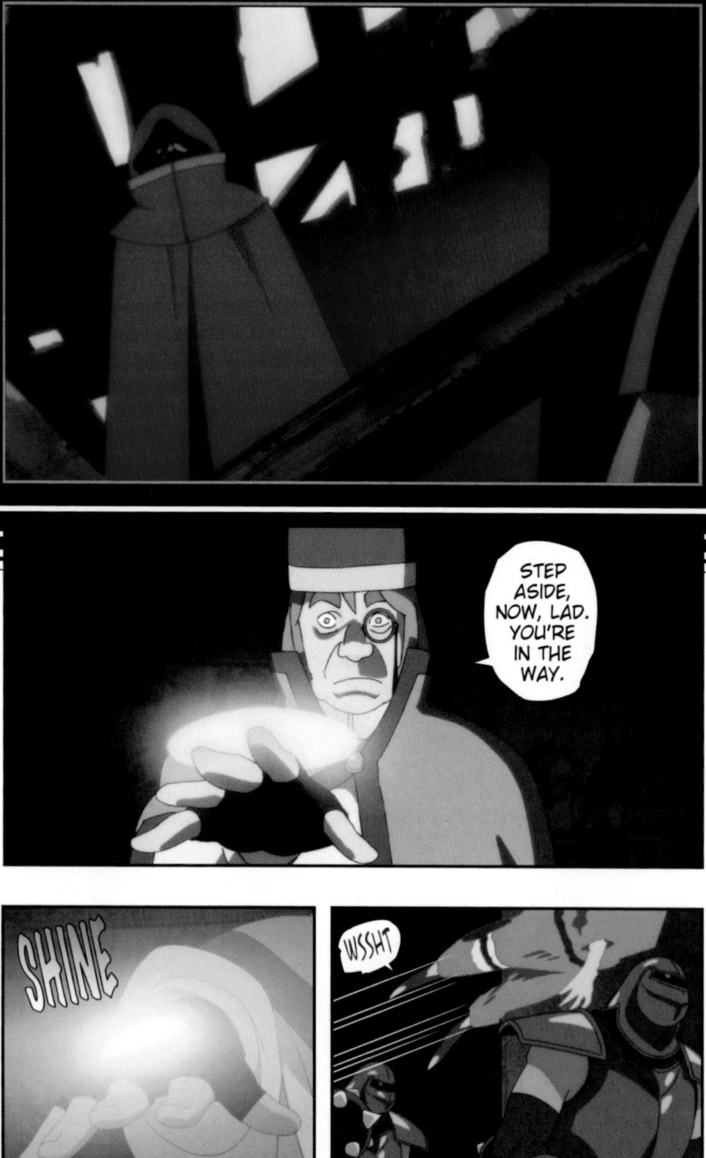
STEP ASIDE, NOW, LAD. YOU'RE IN THE WAY.
WSSHT
SHINE

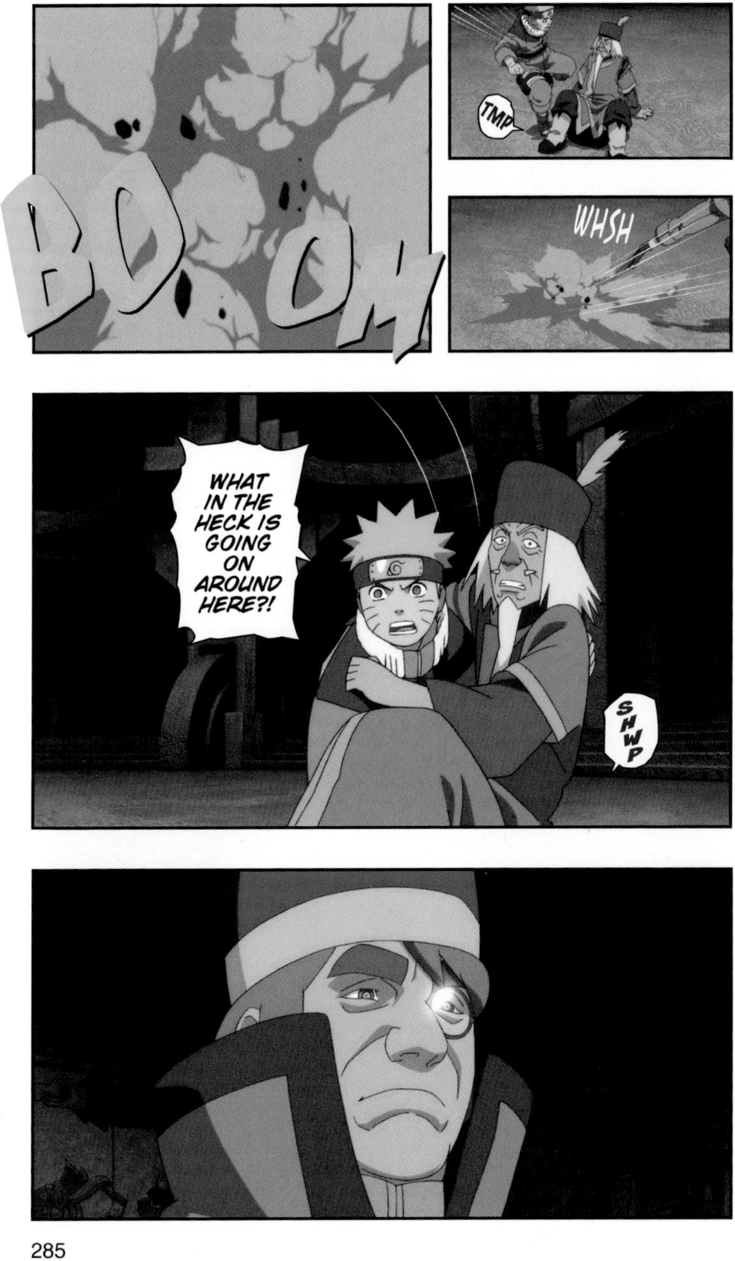
TMP
WHSH
BOOM
WHAT IN THE HECK IS GOING ON AROUND HERE?!
SHWP

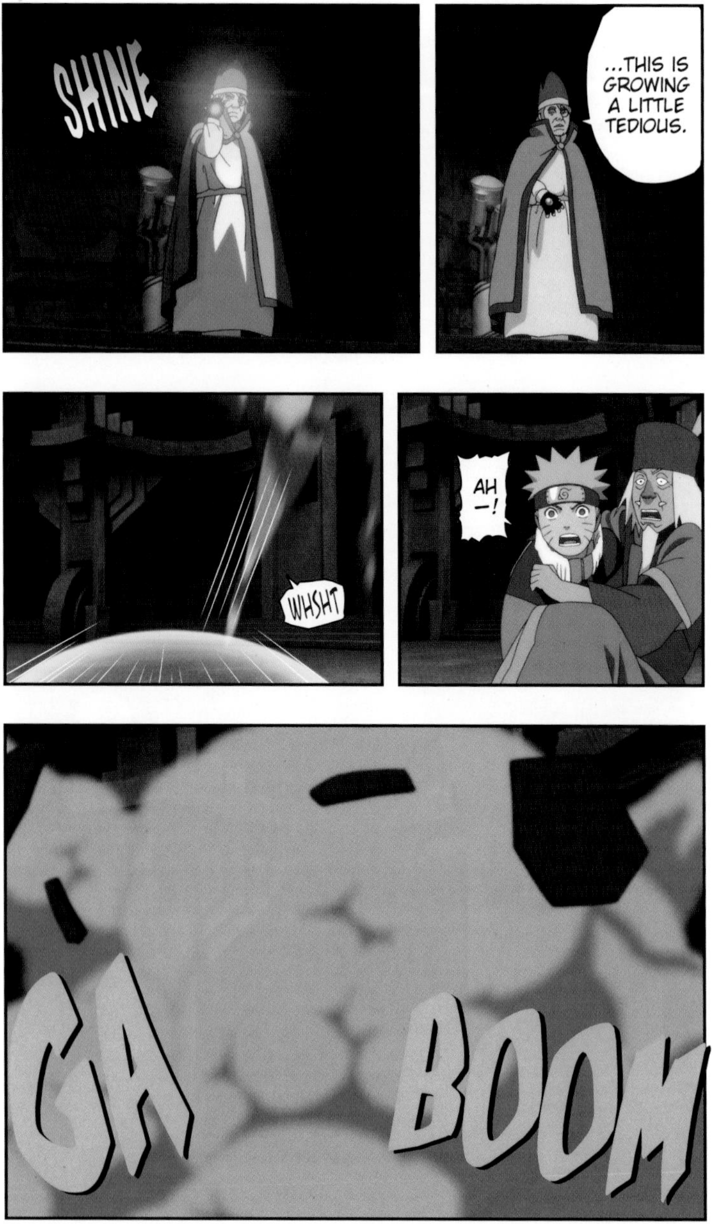
...THIS IS GROWING A LITTLE TEDIOUS.
SHINE
AH —!
WHSHT
GA BOOM

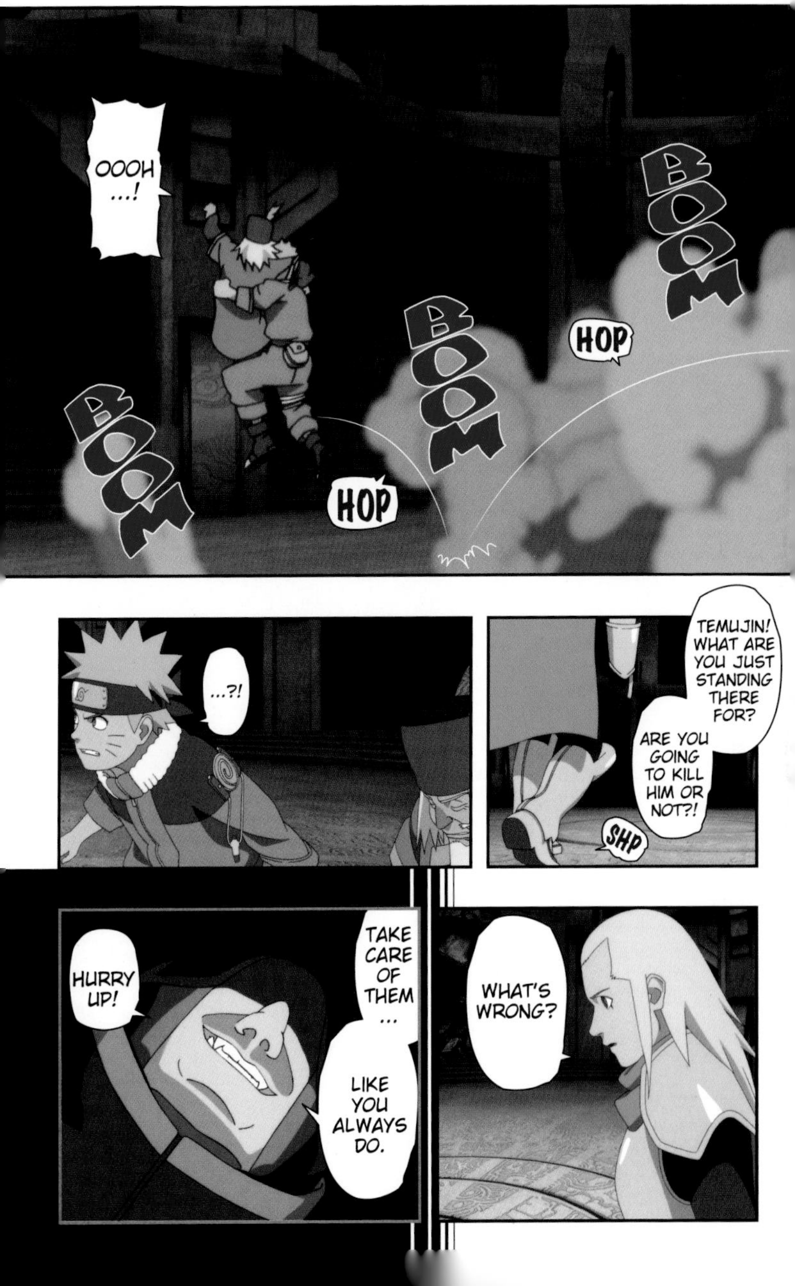
BOOM
HOP
BOOM
OOOH ...!
HOP
BOOM
TEMUJIN! WHAT ARE YOU JUST STANDING THERE FOR?
ARE YOU GOING TO KILL HIM OR NOT?!
SHP
...?!
WHAT'S WRONG?
TAKE CARE OF THEM ...
LIKE YOU ALWAYS DO.
HURRY UP!

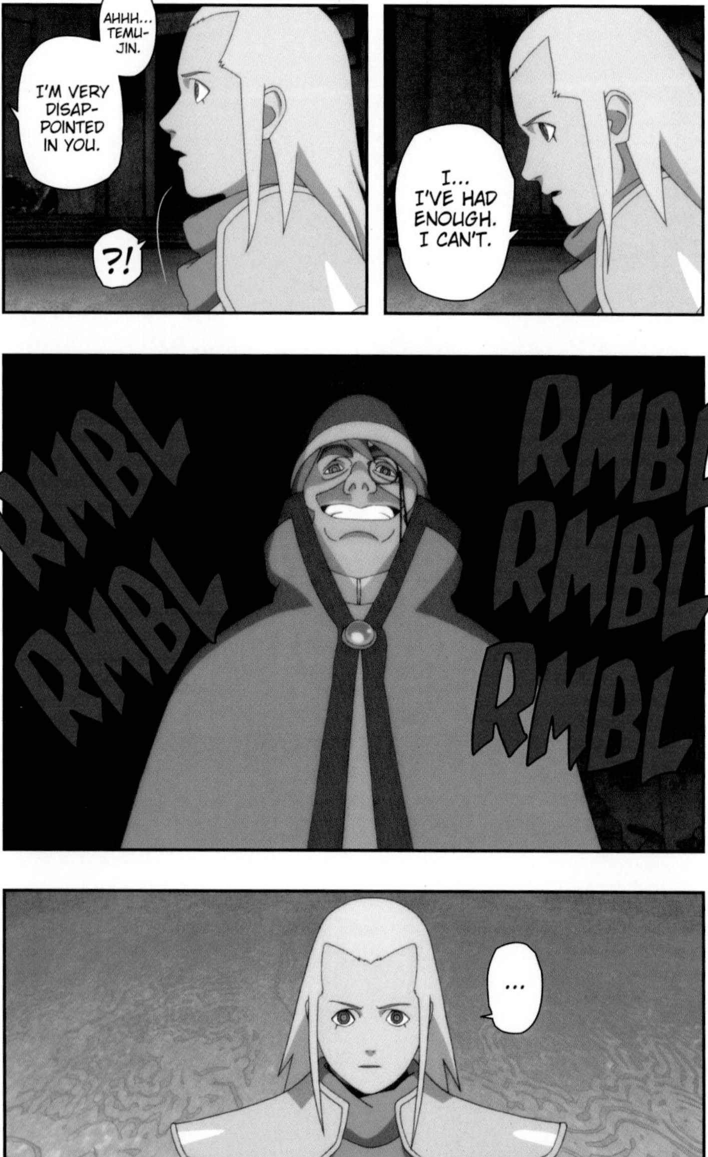
I... I'VE HAD ENOUGH. I CAN'T.
AHHH... TEMUJIN.
I'M VERY DISAPPOINTED IN YOU.
?!
RMBL RMBL RMBL RMBL
RMBL RMBL
...

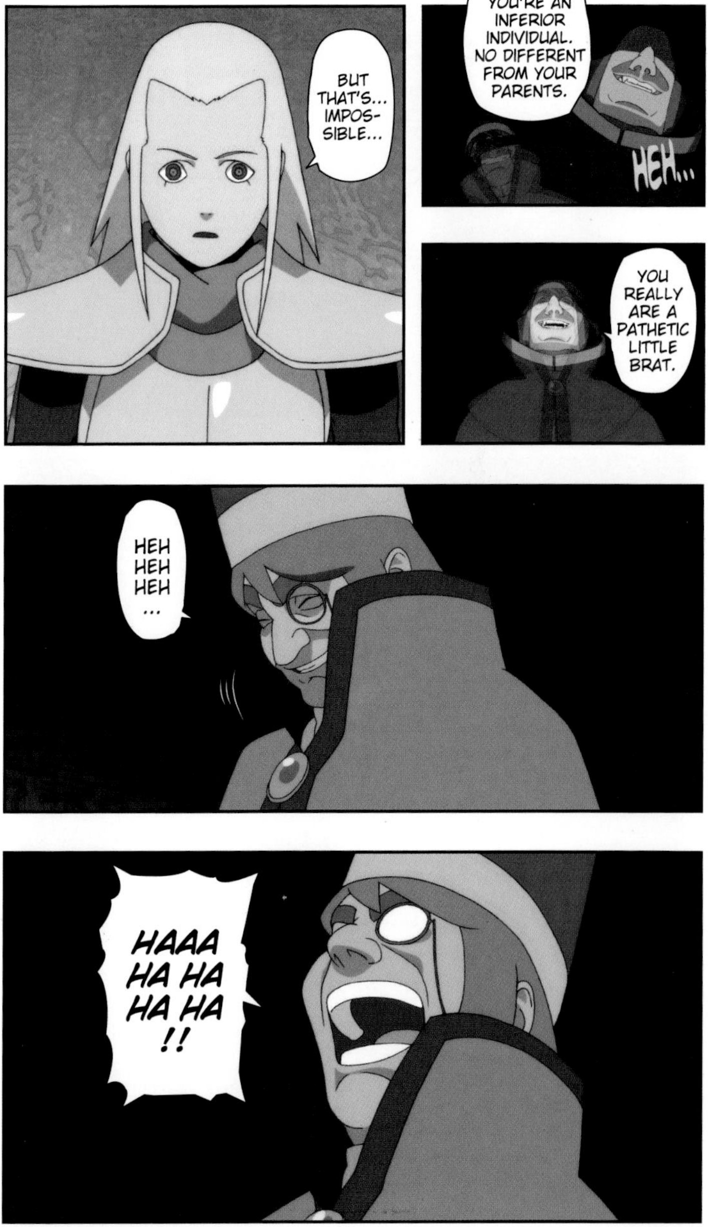
YOU'RE AN INFERIOR INDIVIDUAL. NO DIFFERENT FROM YOUR PARENTS.
HEH...
YOU REALLY ARE A PATHETIC LITTLE BRAT.
BUT THAT'S... IMPOSSIBLE...
HEH HEH HEH...
HAAA HA HA HA HA!!

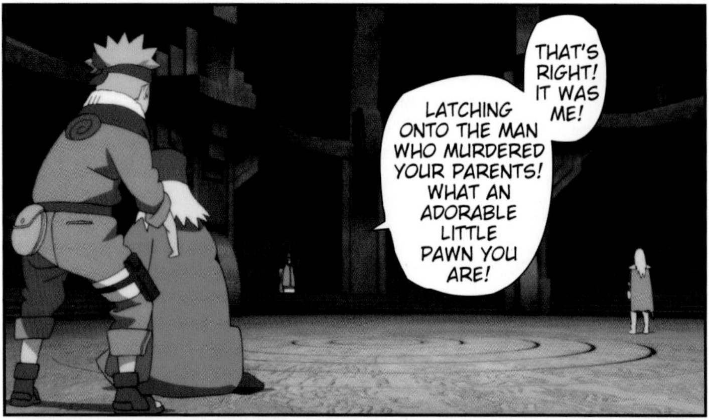
THAT'S RIGHT! IT WAS ME!
LATCHING ONTO THE MAN WHO MURDERED YOUR PARENTS! WHAT AN ADORABLE LITTLE PAWN YOU ARE!

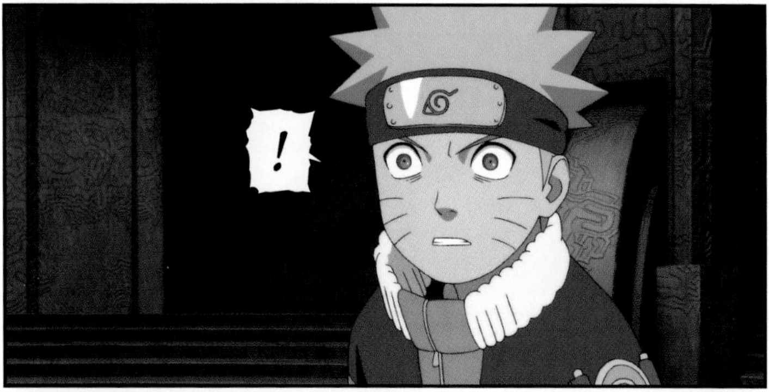
!

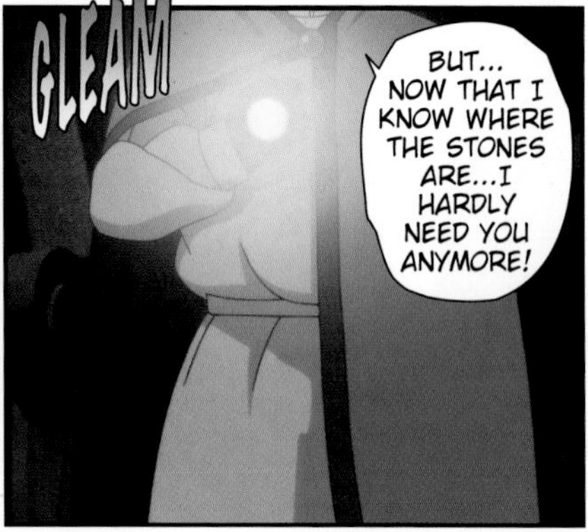
BUT... NOW THAT I KNOW WHERE THE STONES ARE...I HARDLY NEED YOU ANYMORE!
GLEAM

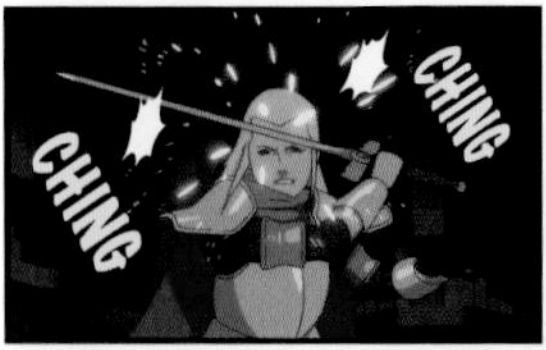
CHING
CHING

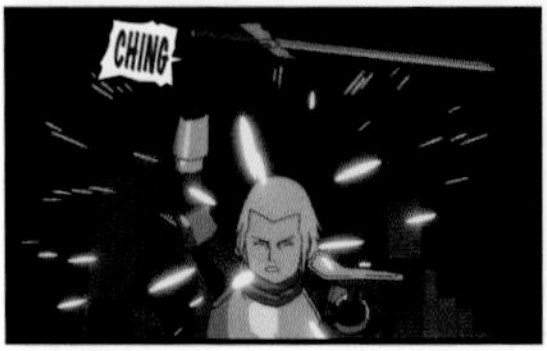
CHING

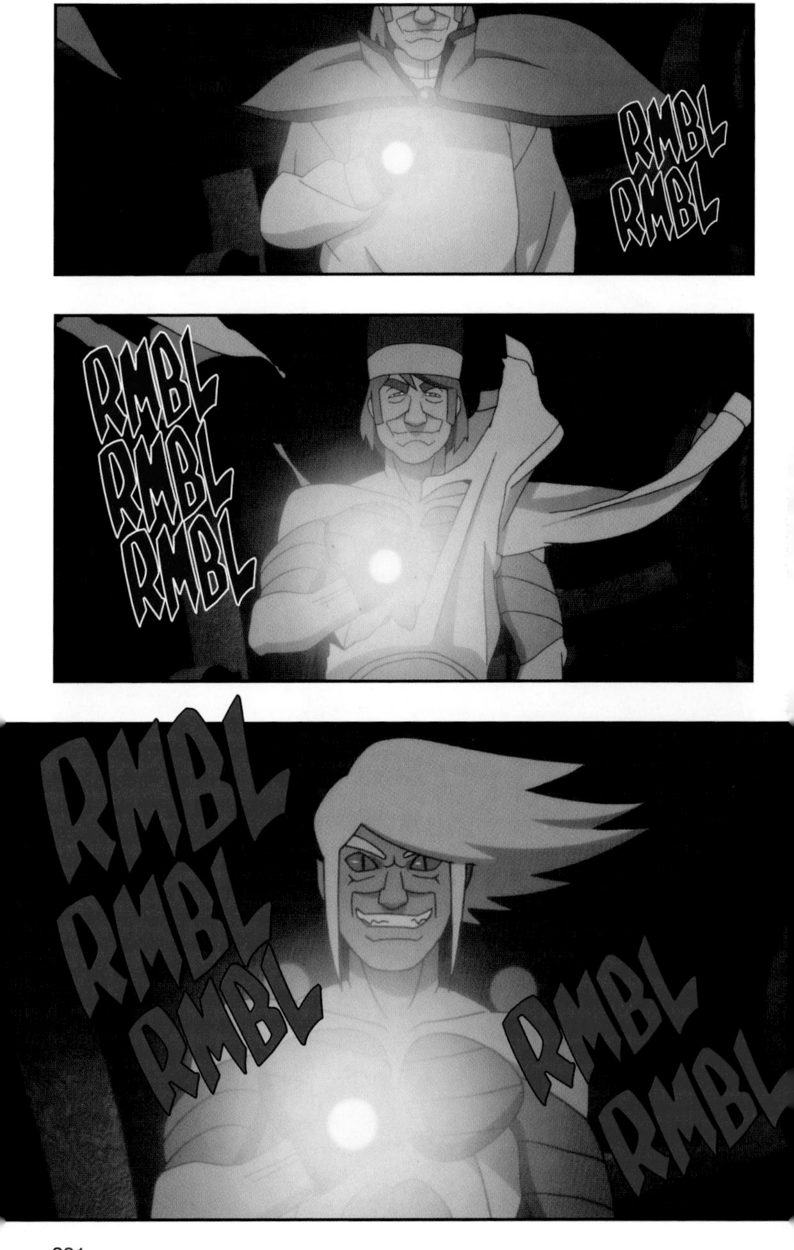
RMBL
RMBL
RMBL
RMBL
RMBL
RMBL
RMBL
RMBL
RMBL
RMBL

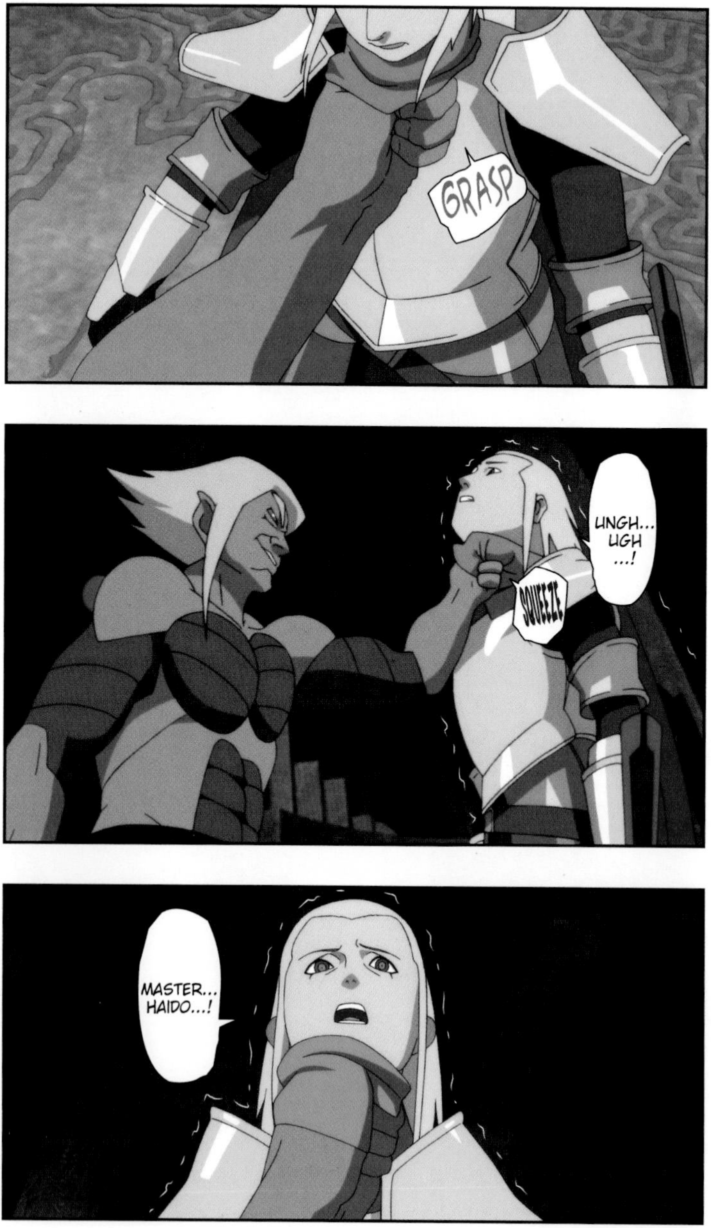
GRASP
UNGH... UGH ...!
SQUEEZE
MASTER... HAIDO...!

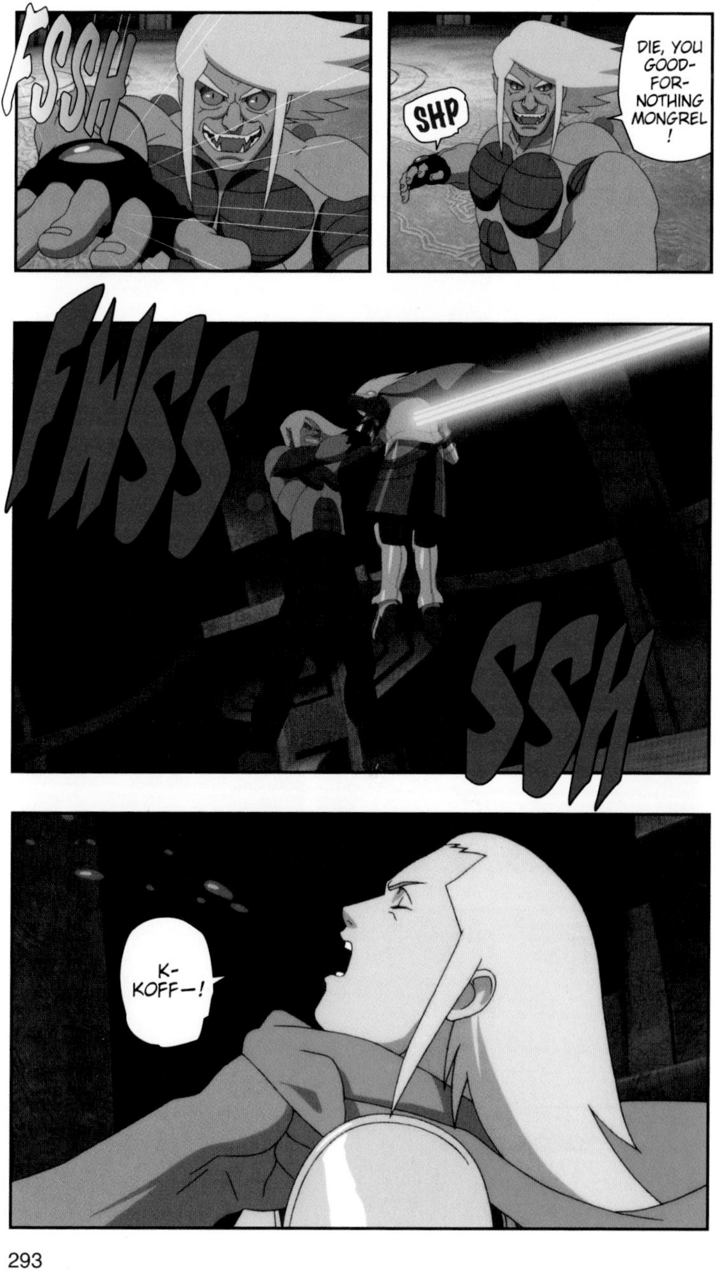
DIE, YOU GOOD-FOR-NOTHING MONGREL!
SHP
FSSH
FWSS
SSH
K-KOFF—!

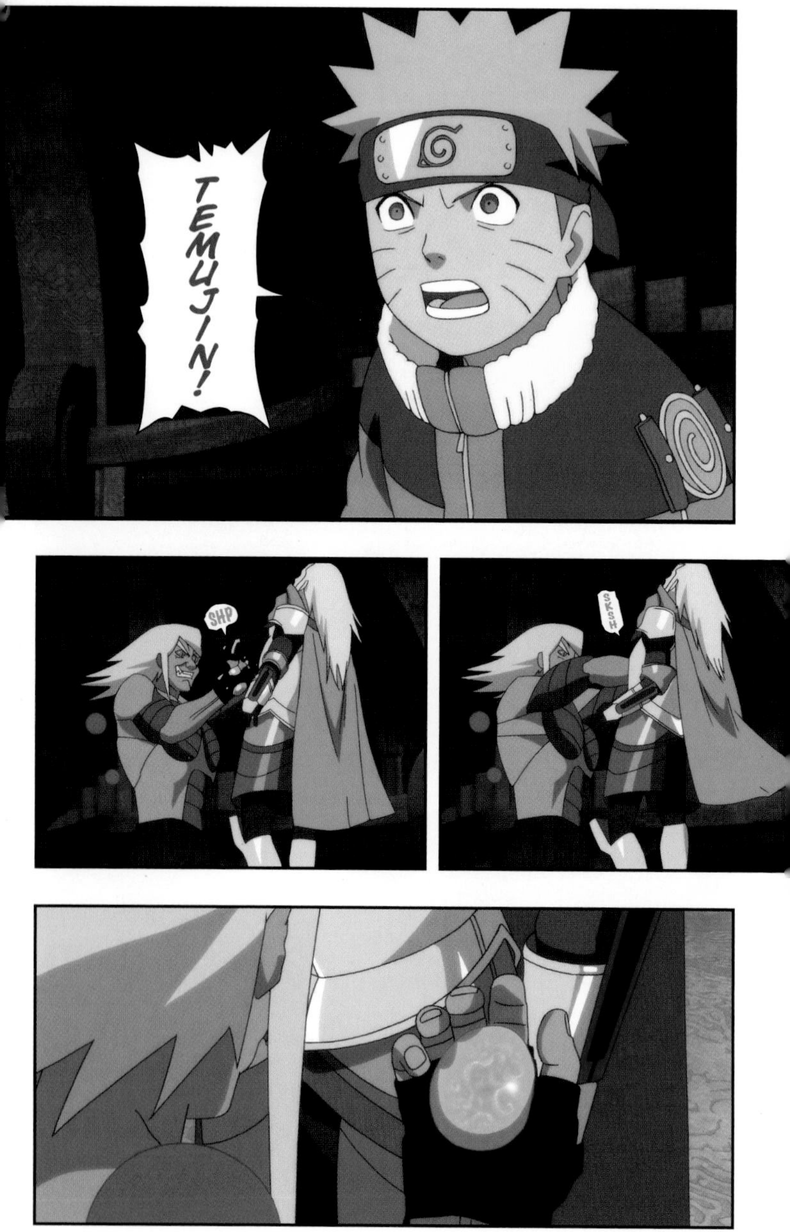
TEMUJIN!
SKSH
SHP

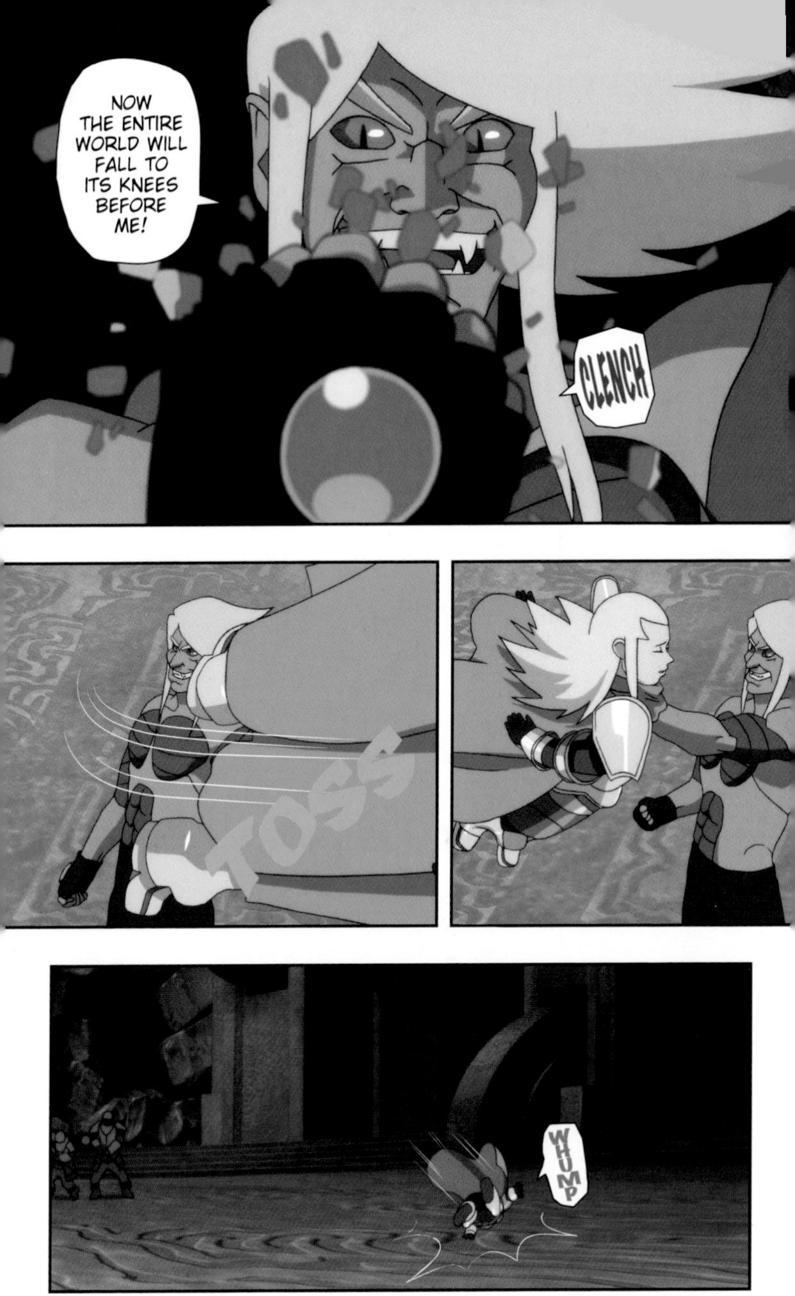
NOW THE ENTIRE WORLD WILL FALL TO ITS KNEES BEFORE ME!
CLENCH
TOSS
WHUMP

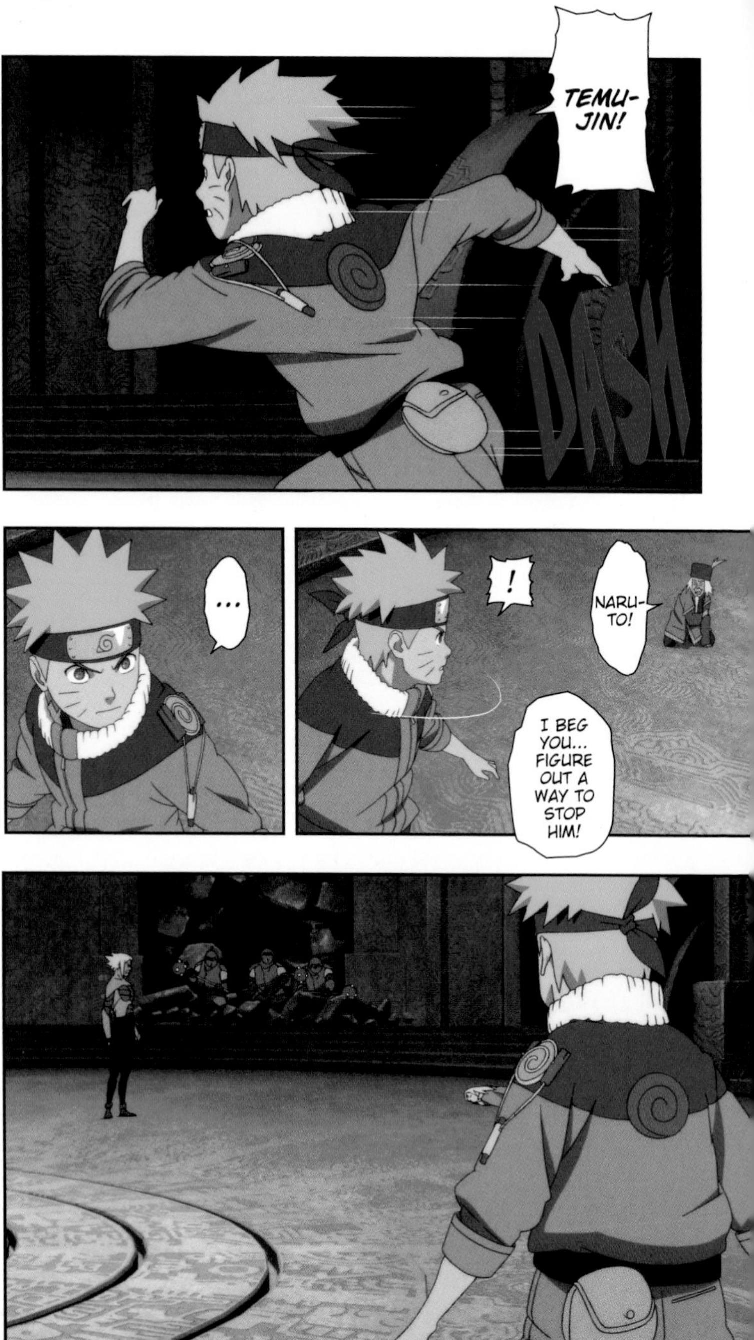
TEMU-JIN!
DASH
NARU-TO!
!
I BEG YOU... FIGURE OUT A WAY TO STOP HIM!
...

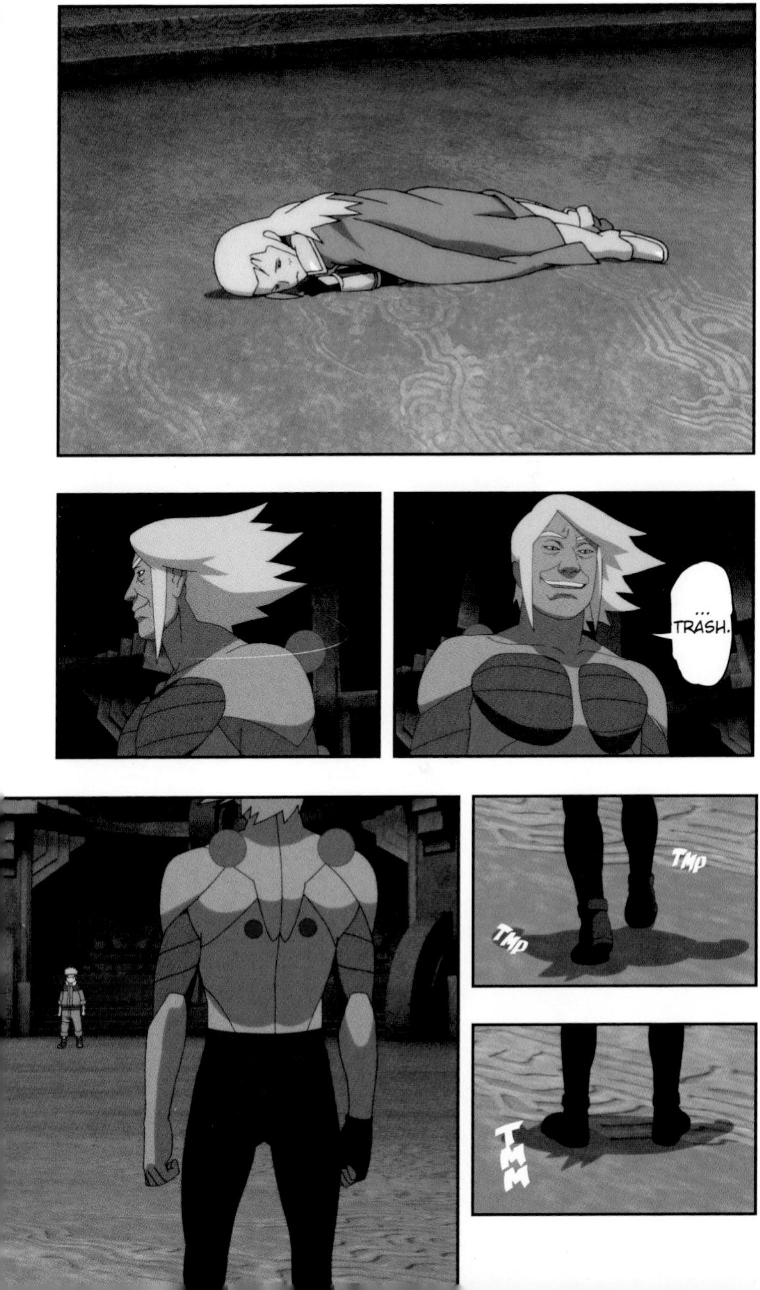
... TRASH.
TMP
TMP
TMM

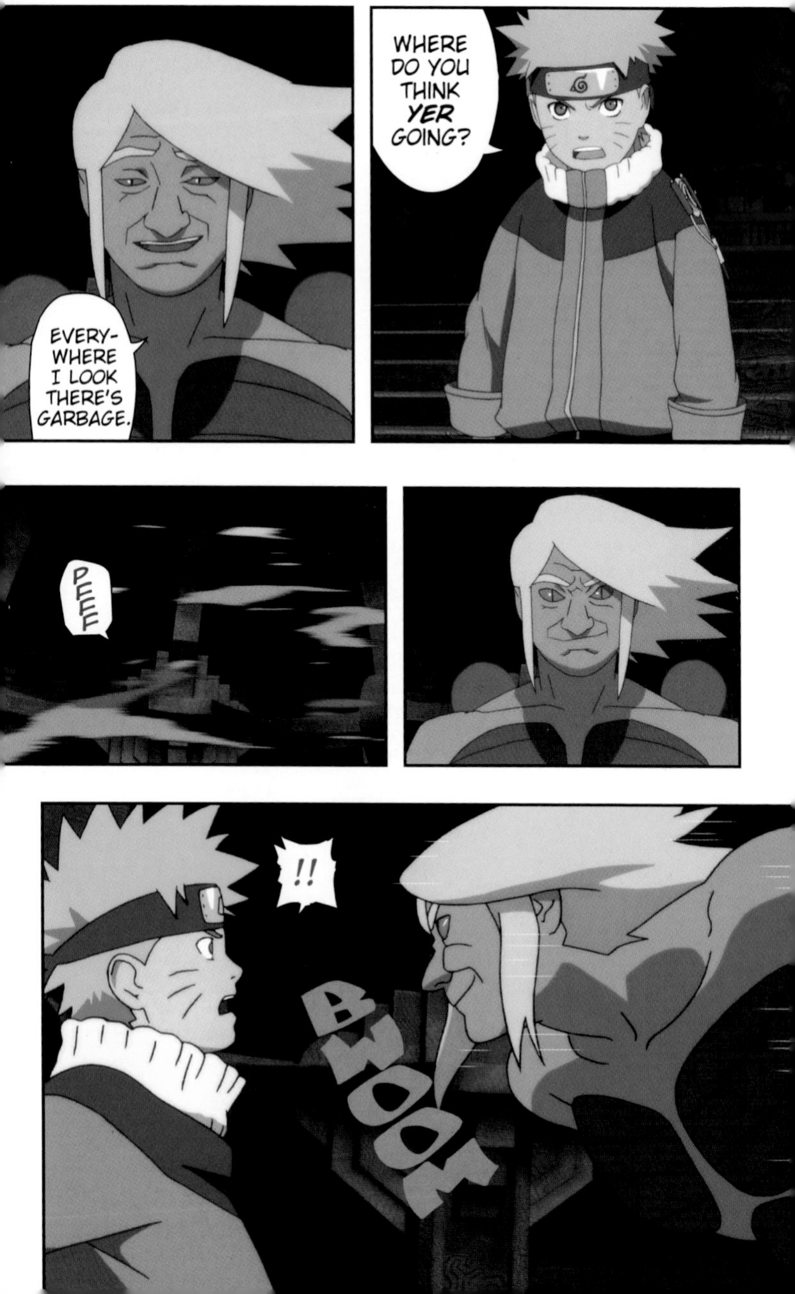
WHERE DO YOU THINK YER GOING?
EVERY-WHERE I LOOK THERE'S GARBAGE.
PFFF
!!
BWOOM

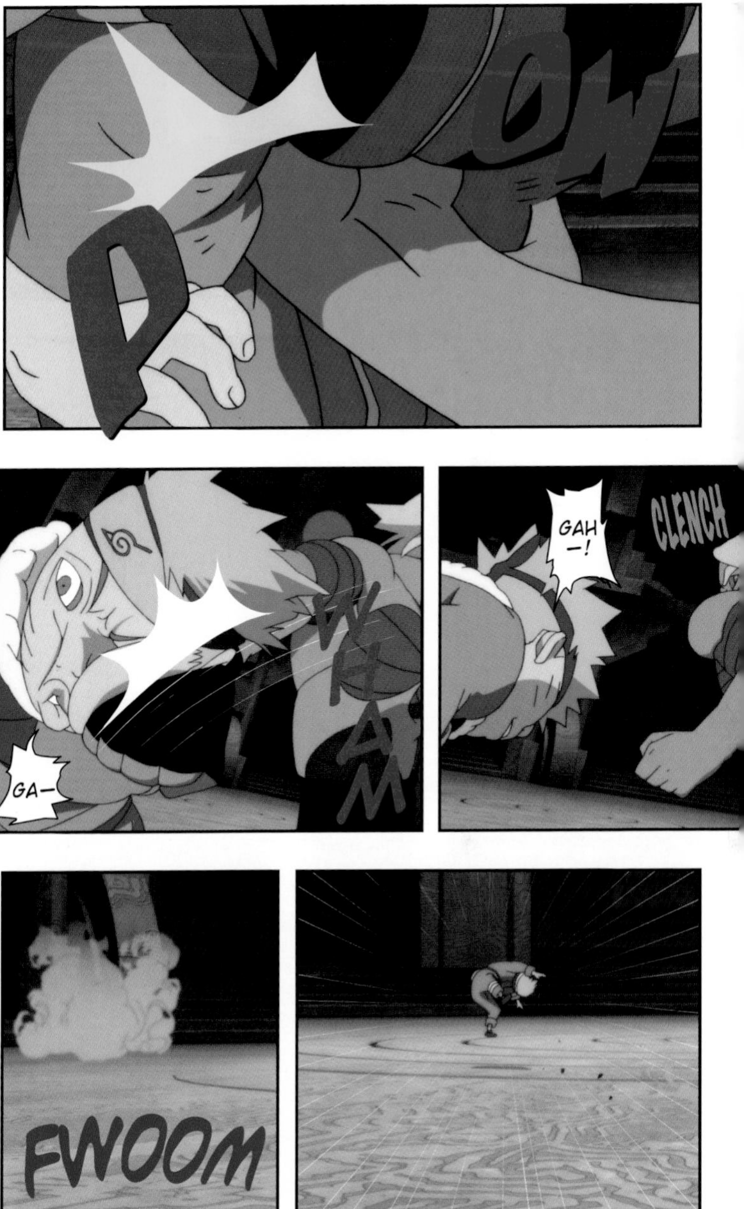
POW
CLENCH
GAH —!
WHAM
GA—
FWOOM

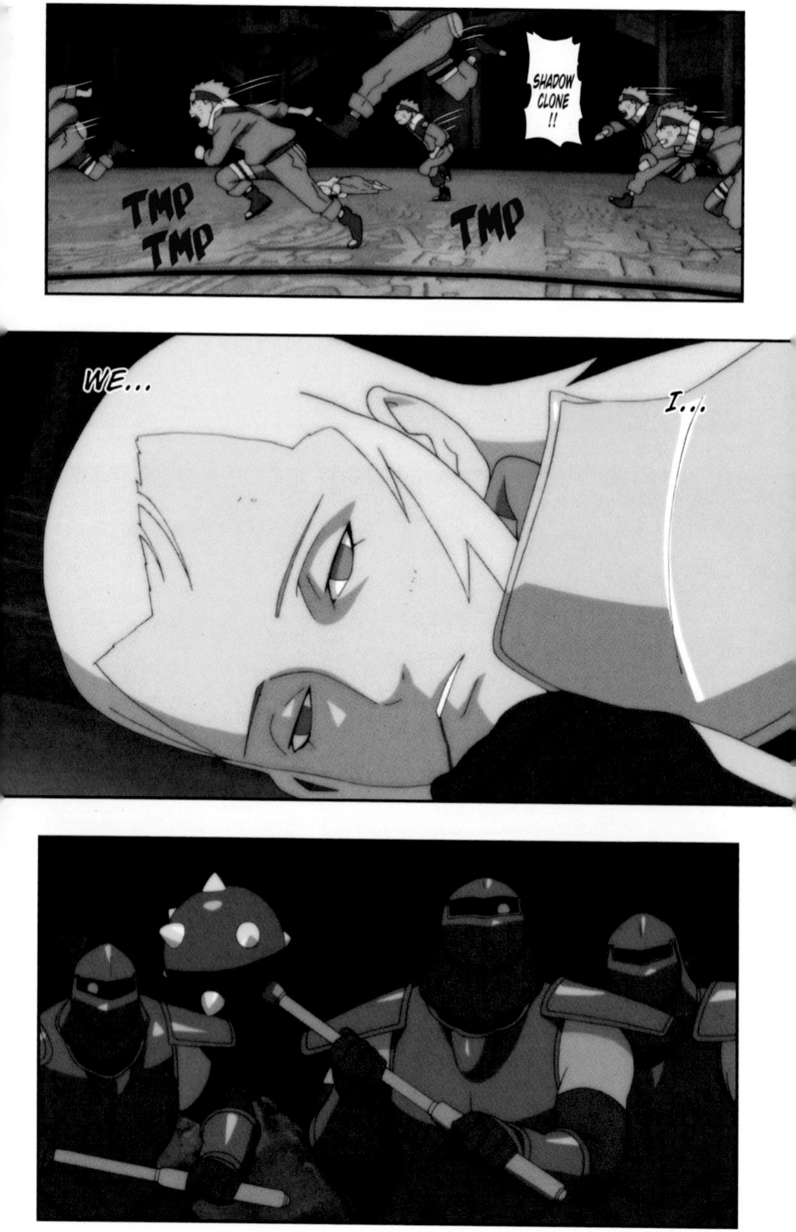
SHADOW CLONE !!
TMP
TMP TMP
I...
WE...

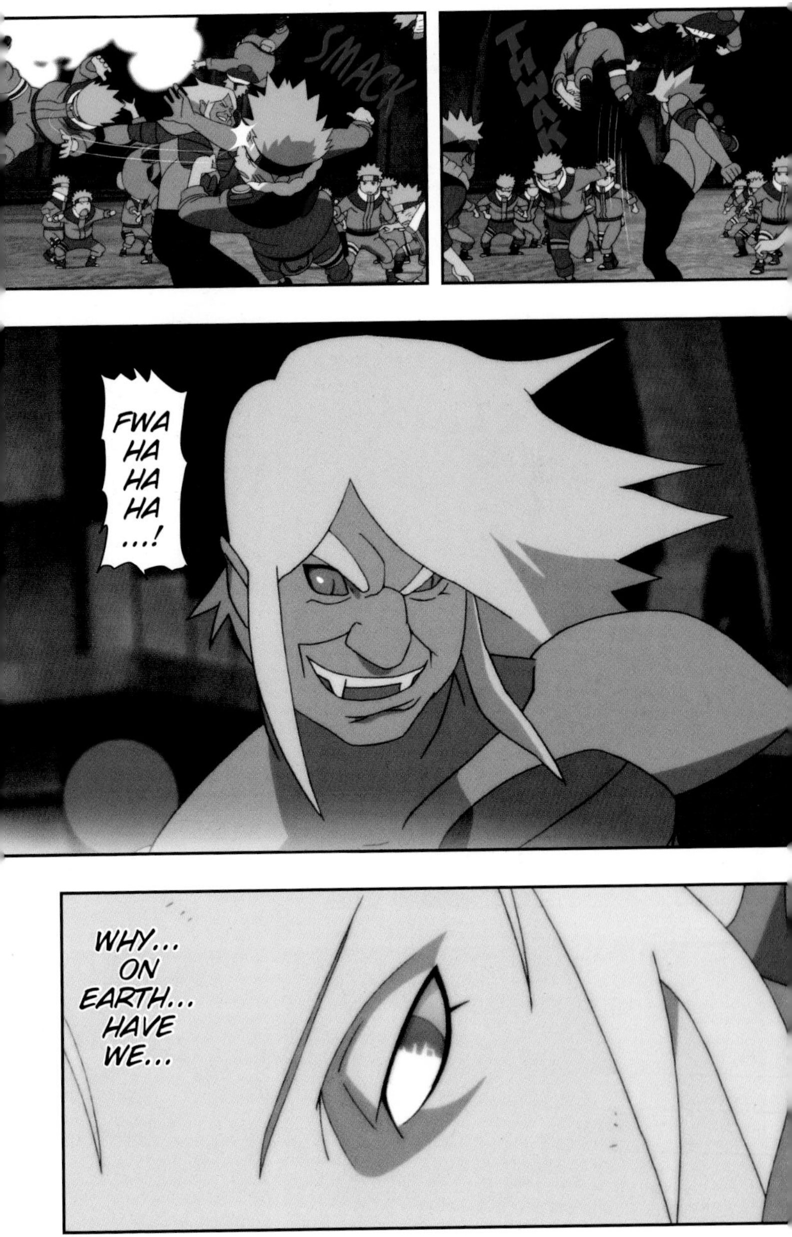
THWAK
SMACK
FWA HA HA HA ...!
WHY... ON EARTH... HAVE WE...

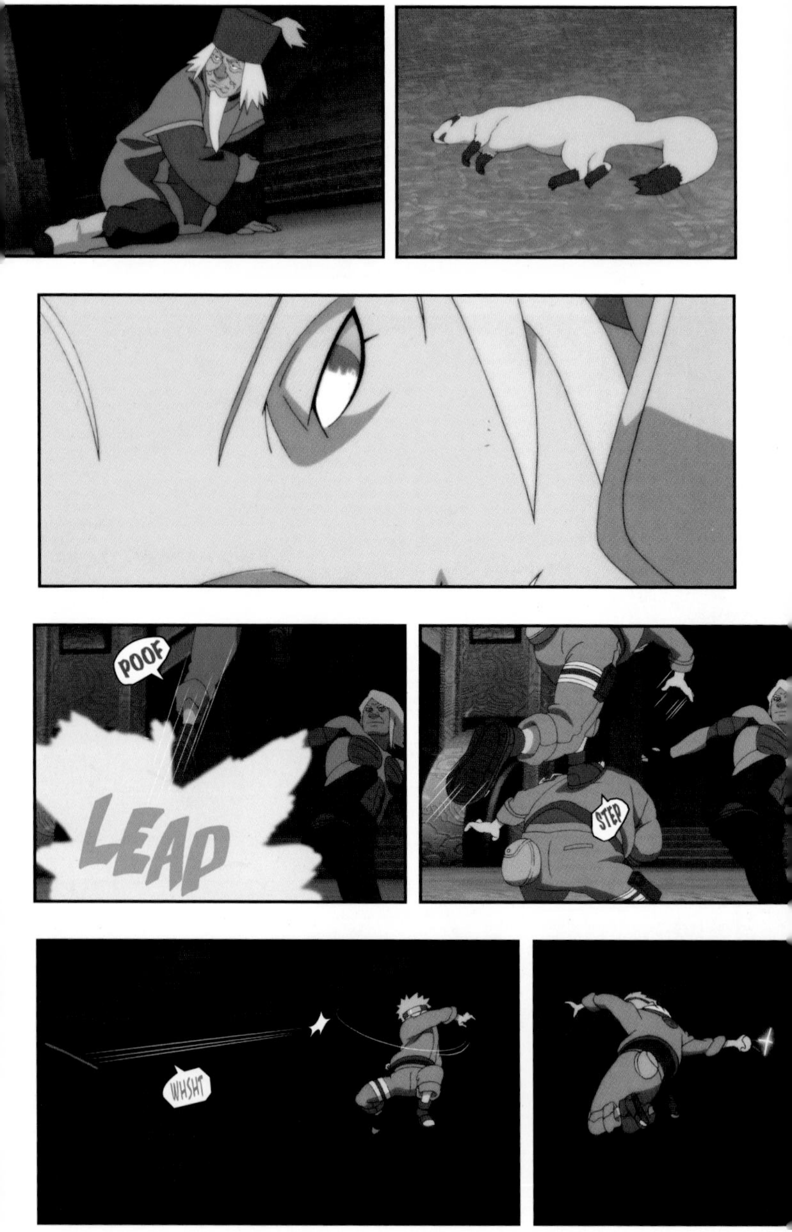
STEP
POOF
LEAP
WHSHT

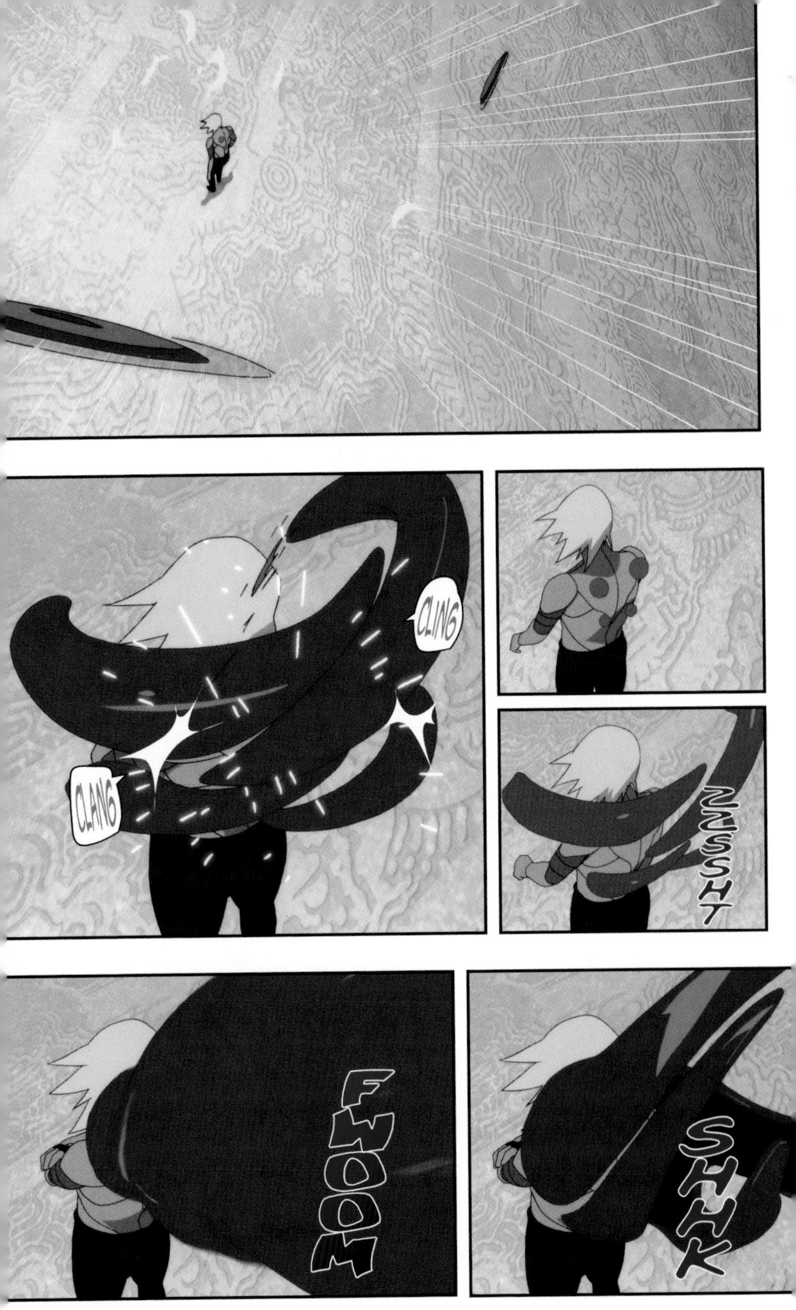
ZZSSHT
CLING
CLANG
SHHK
FWOOM

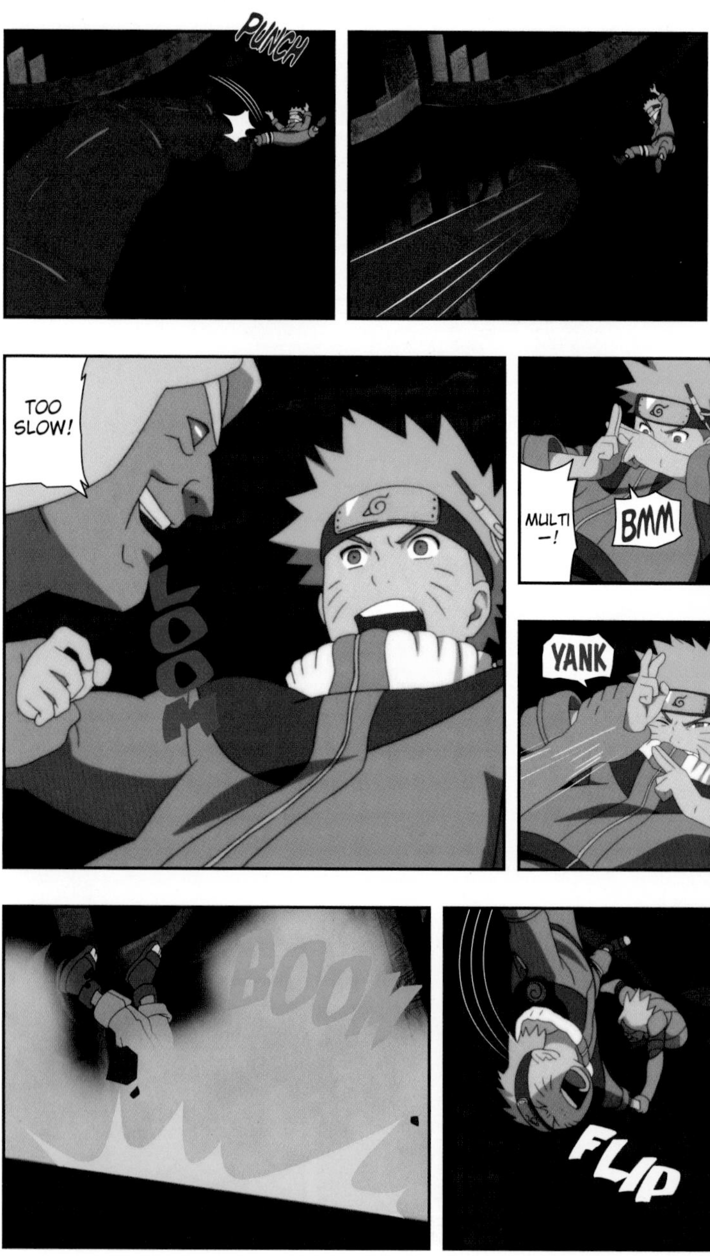
PUNCH
MULTI —!
BMM
YANK
TOO SLOW!
LOOM
FLIP
BOOM

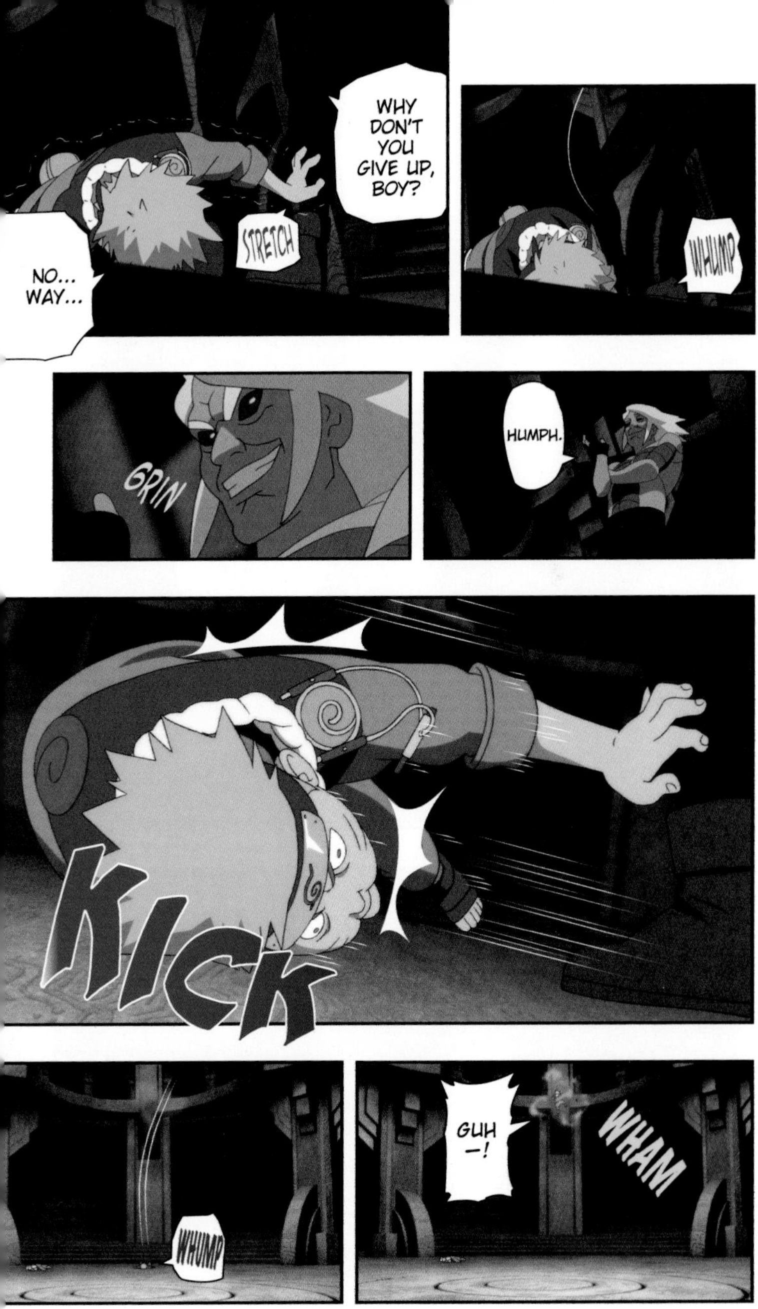
WHUMP
WHY DON'T YOU GIVE UP, BOY?
STRETCH
NO... WAY...
HUMPH.
GRIN
KICK
GUH—!
WHAM
WHUMP

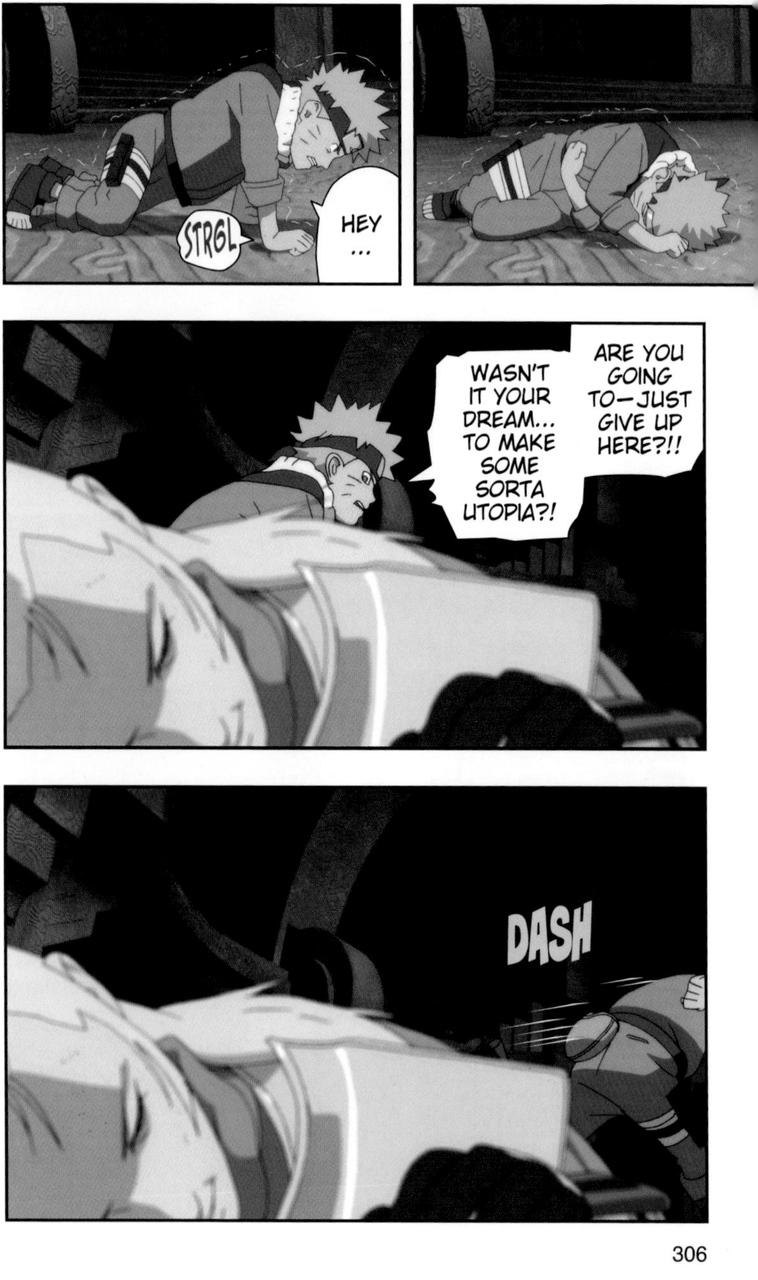
STRGL
HEY ...
ARE YOU GOING TO—JUST GIVE UP HERE?!!
WASN'T IT YOUR DREAM... TO MAKE SOME SORTA UTOPIA?!
DASH

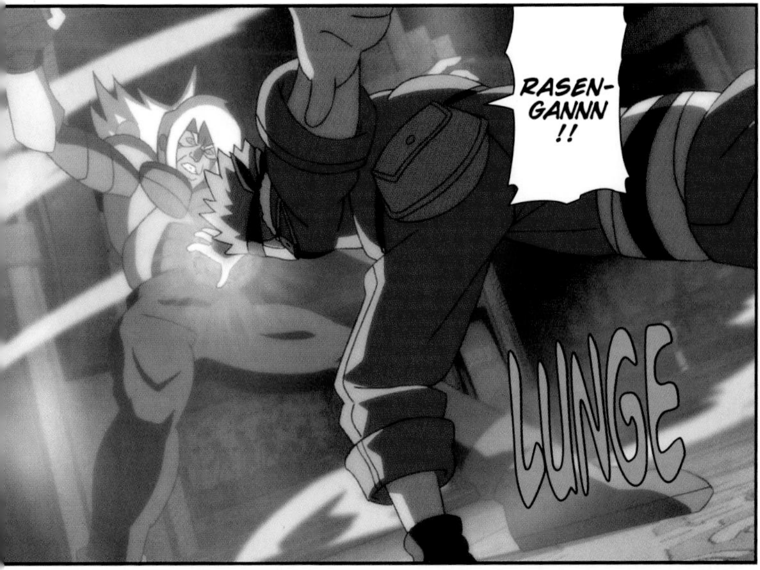
RASEN-
GANNN
!!
LUNGE
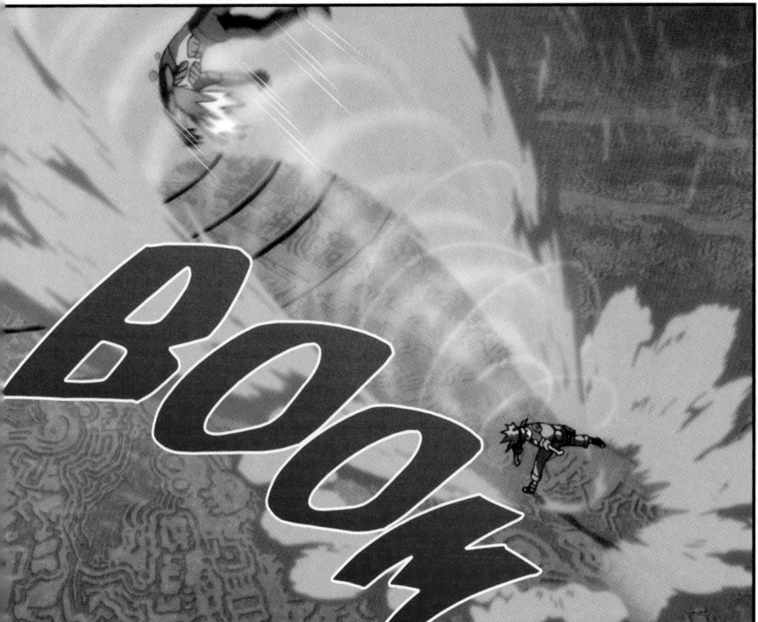
BOOM

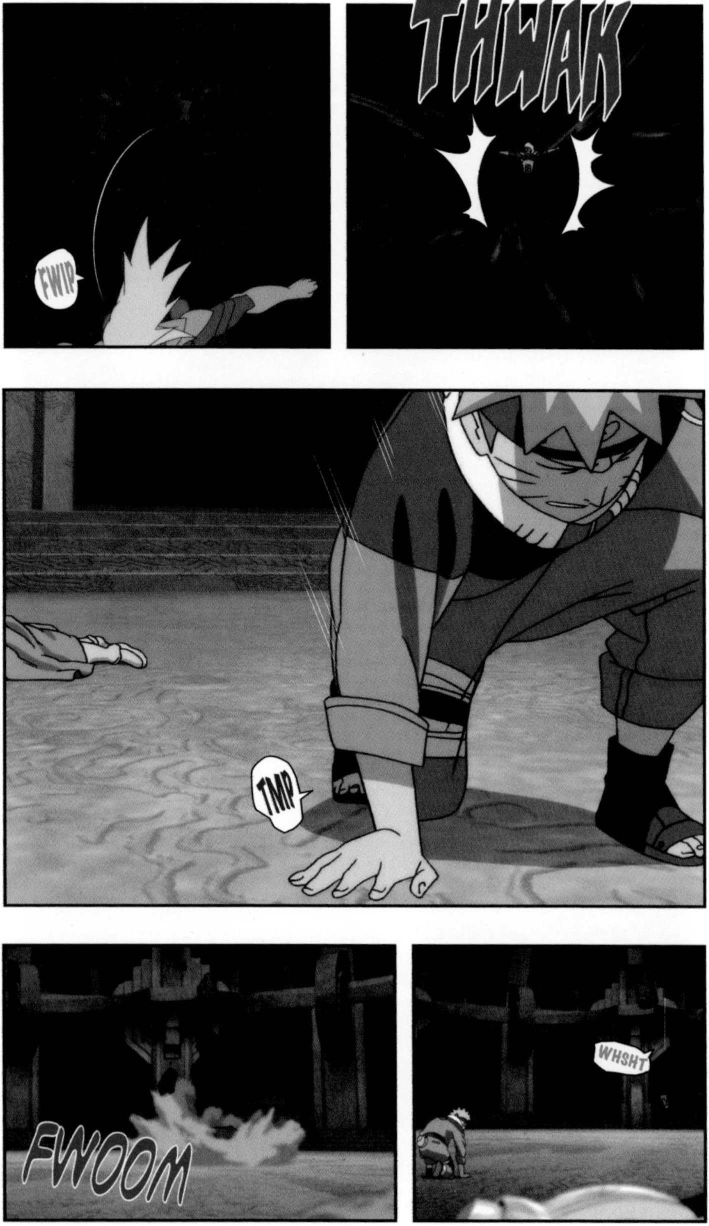
THWAK
FWIP
TMP
WHSHT
FWOOM

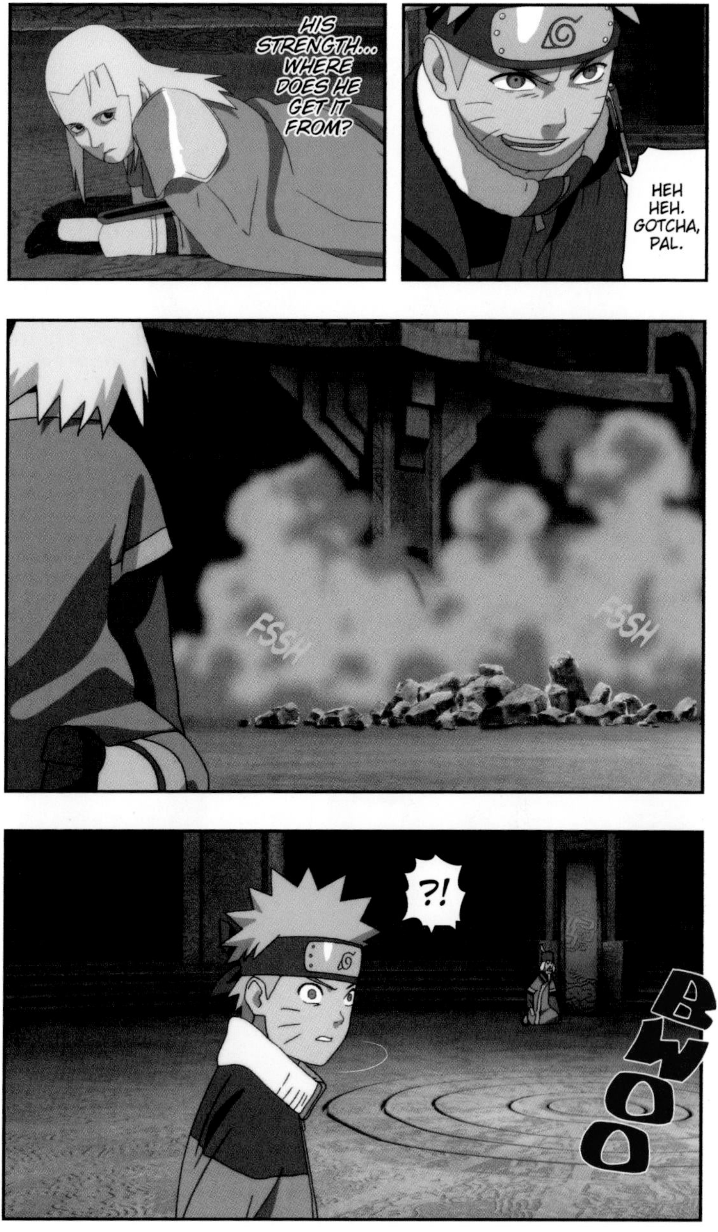
HEH HEH. GOTCHA, PAL.
HIS STRENGTH... WHERE DOES HE GET IT FROM?
FSSH
FSSH
?!
BWOO

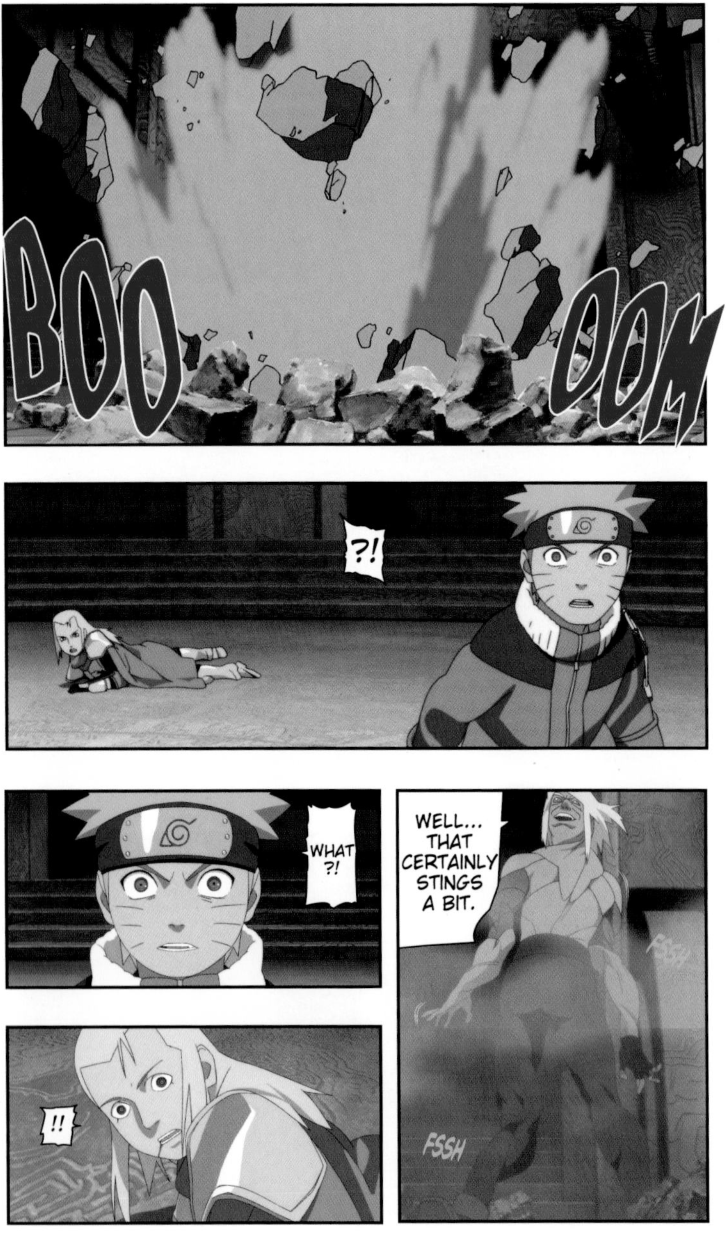
BOOOOM
?!
WELL... THAT CERTAINLY STINGS A BIT.
FSSH
FSSH
WHAT ?!
!!

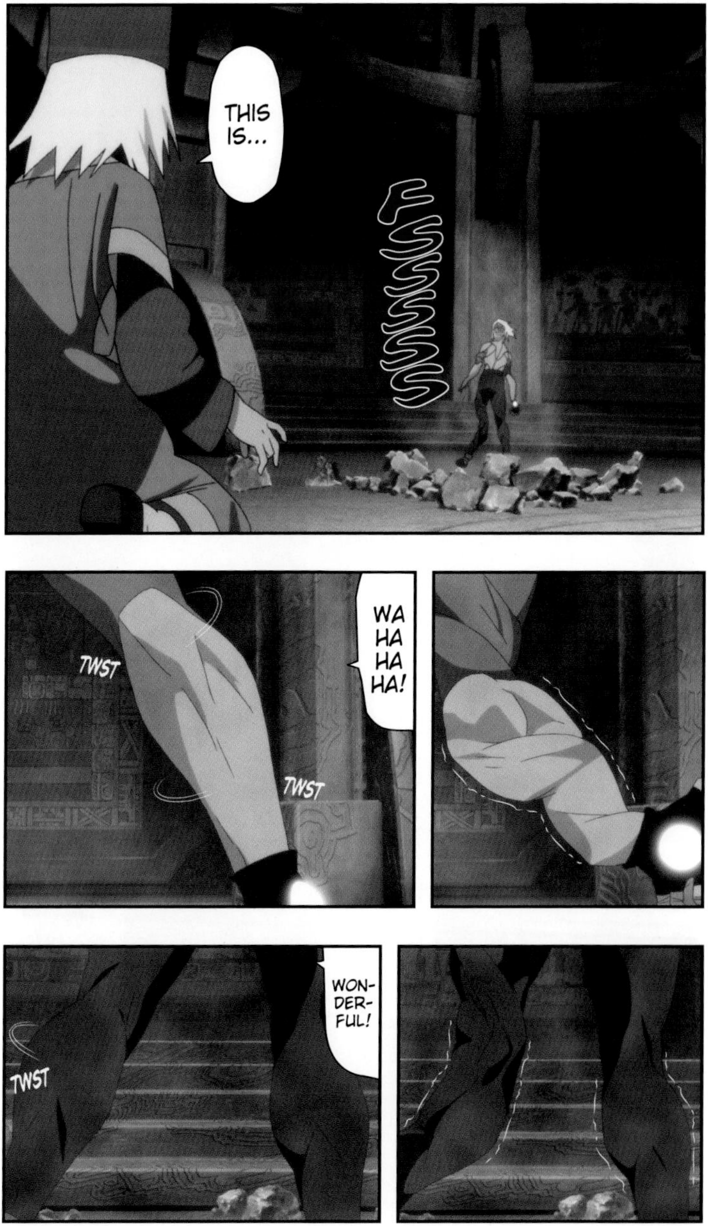
THIS IS...
FSSSSSS
WA HA HA HA!
TWST
TWST
WON-DER-FUL!
TWST

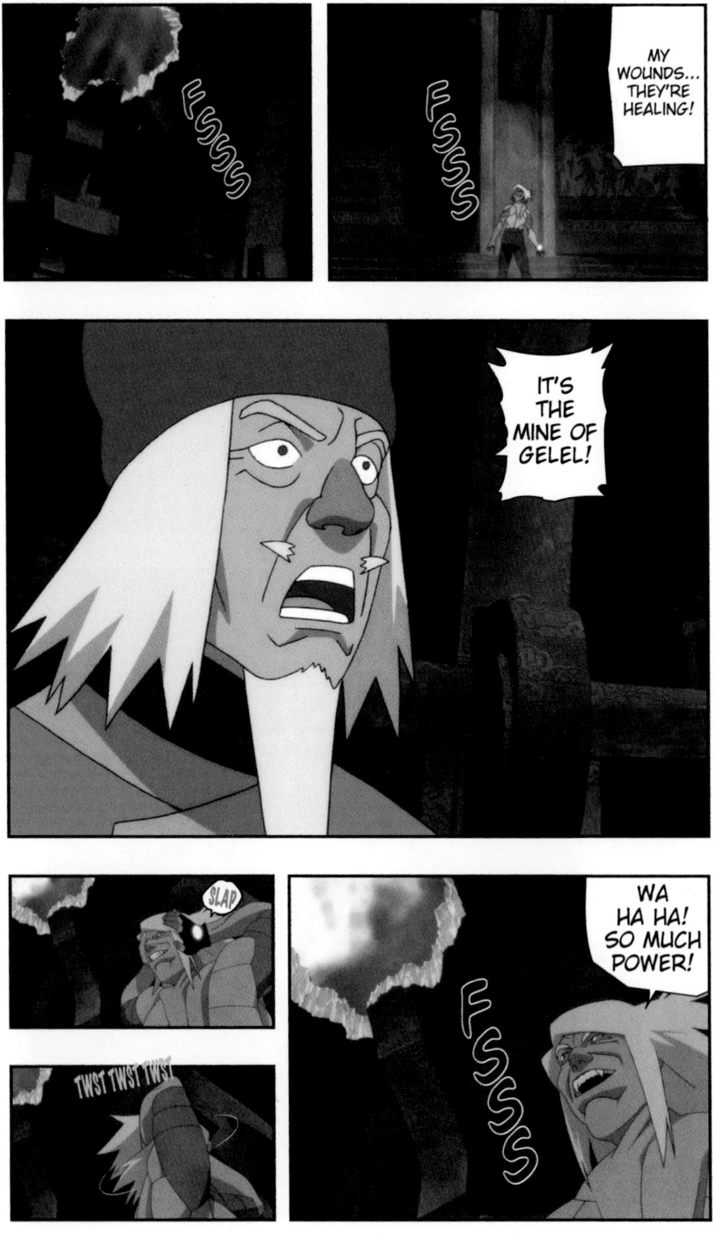
MY WOUNDS... THEY'RE HEALING!
FSSS
FSSS
IT'S THE MINE OF GELEL!
WA HA HA! SO MUCH POWER!
FSSS
SLAP
TWST TWST TWST

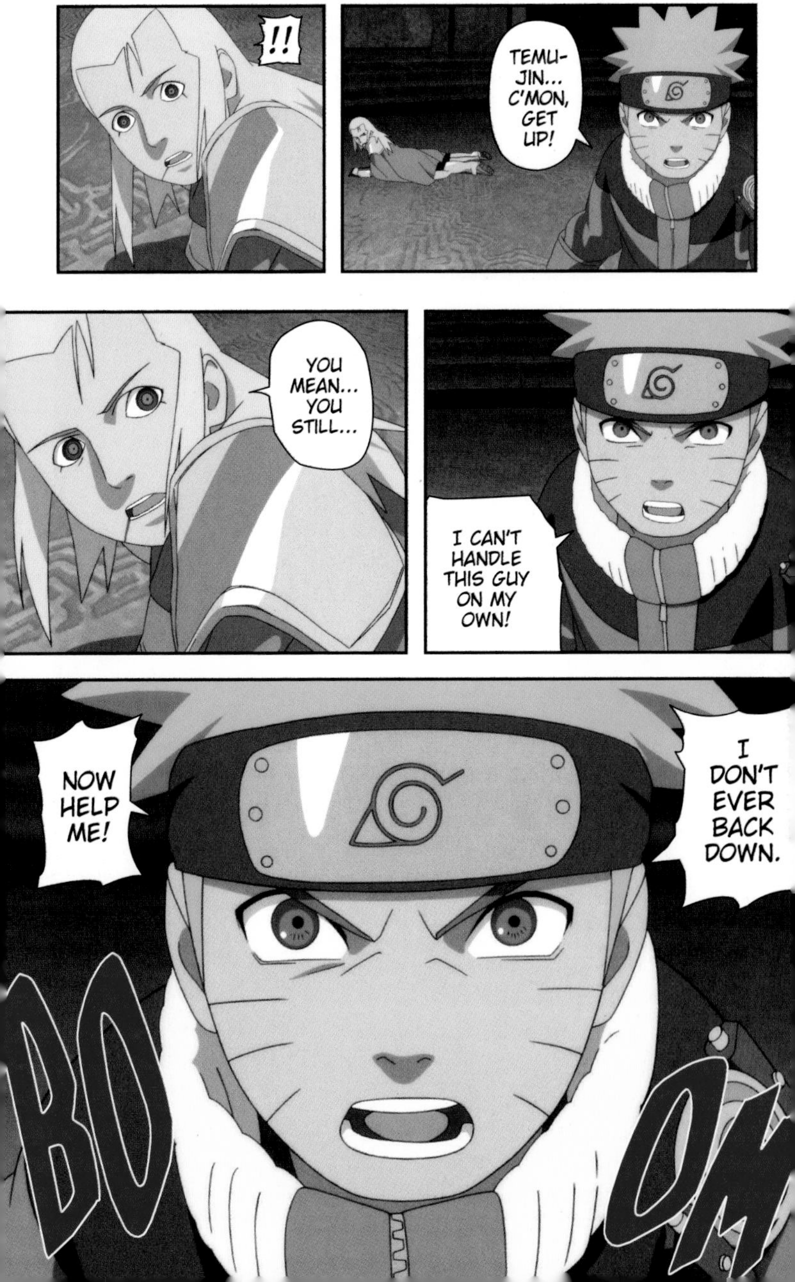
TEMU-JIN... C'MON, GET UP!
!!
I CAN'T HANDLE THIS GUY ON MY OWN!
YOU MEAN... YOU STILL...
I DON'T EVER BACK DOWN.
NOW HELP ME!
BOOM

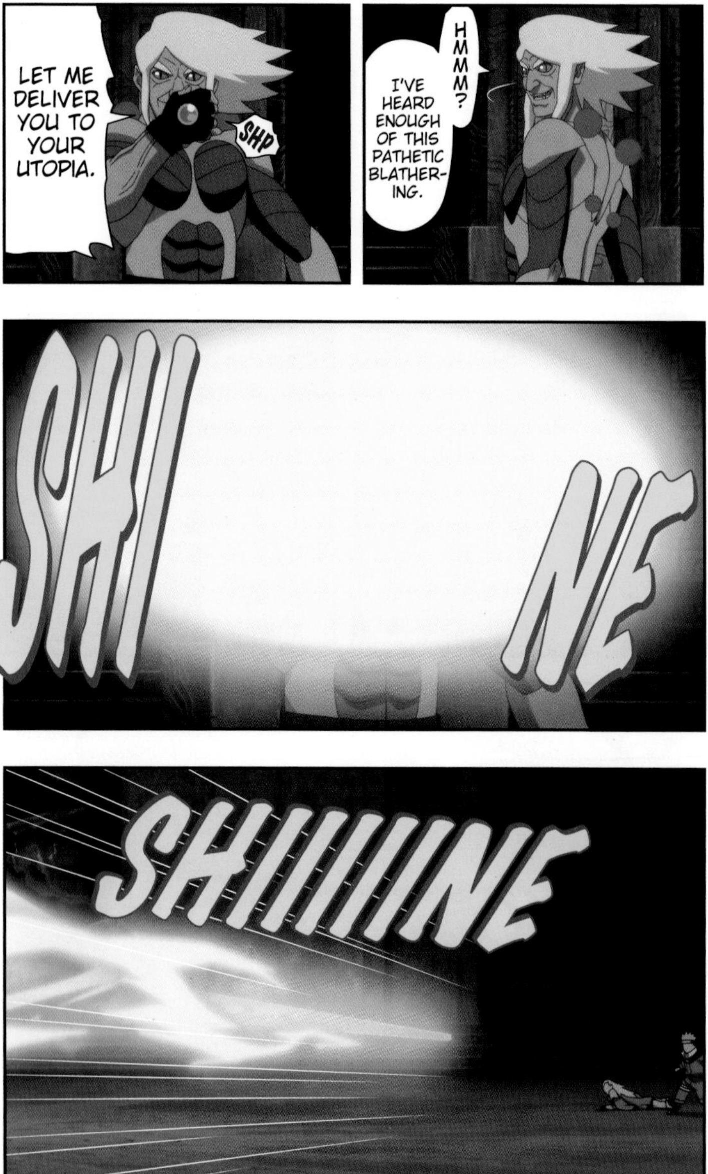
HMMMM?
I'VE HEARD ENOUGH OF THIS PATHETIC BLATHER-ING.
LET ME DELIVER YOU TO YOUR UTOPIA.
SHP
SHI NE
SHIIIIINE

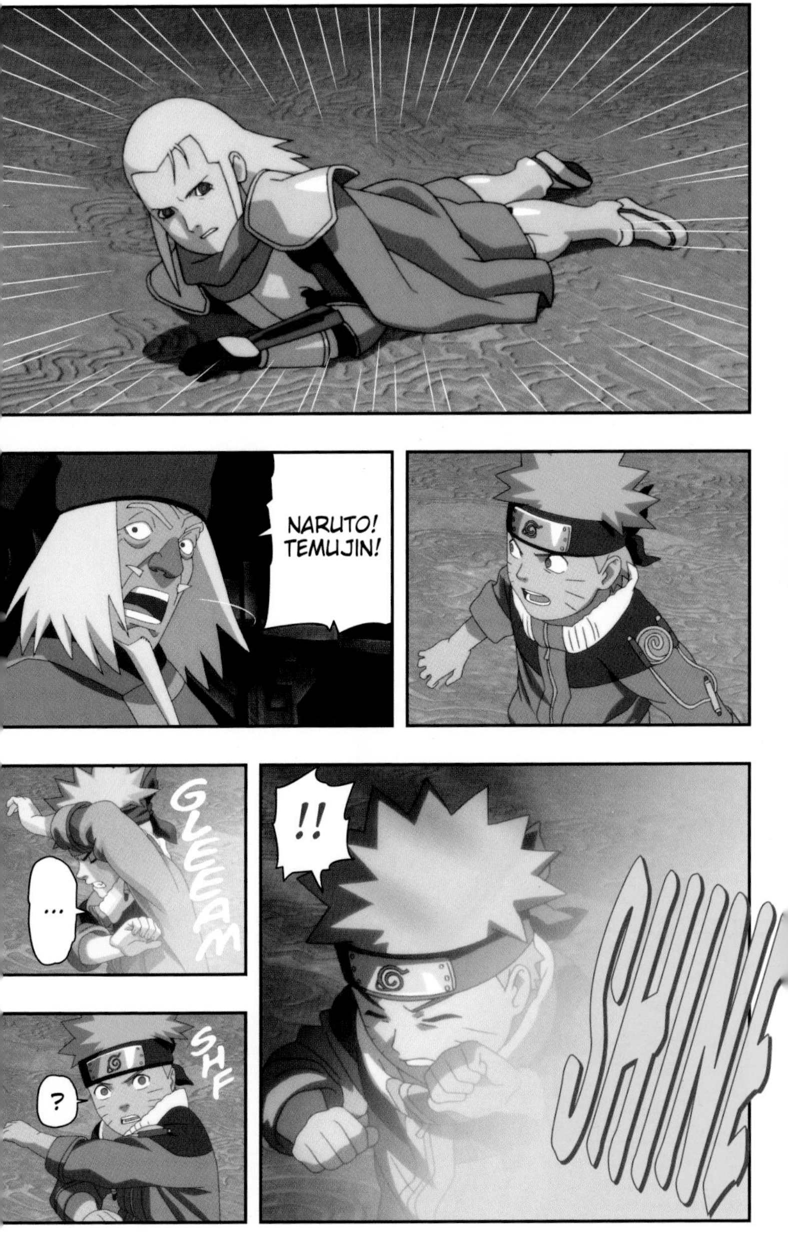
NARUTO! TEMUJIN!
!!
SHINE
GLEEAM
...
SHF
?

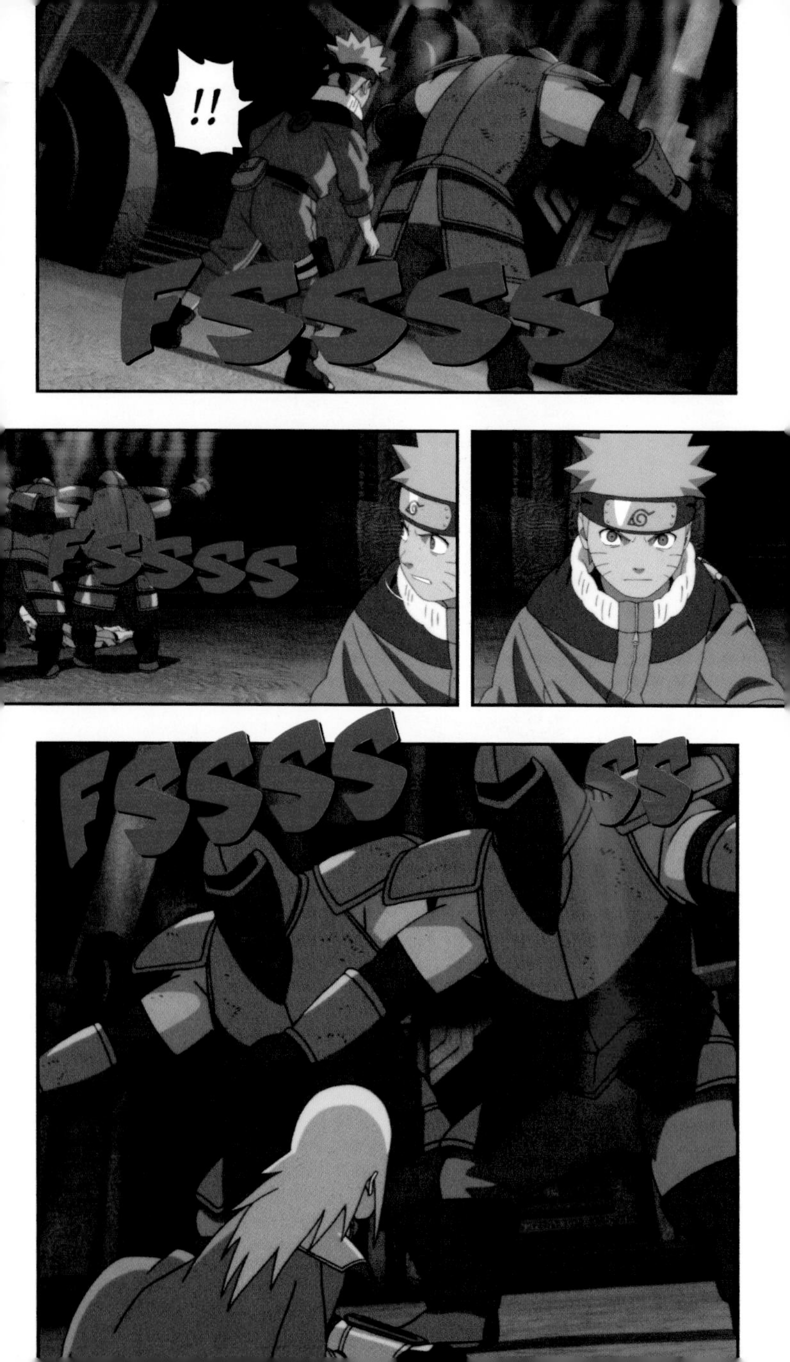
!!
FSSSSS
FSSSS
FSSSS
SS

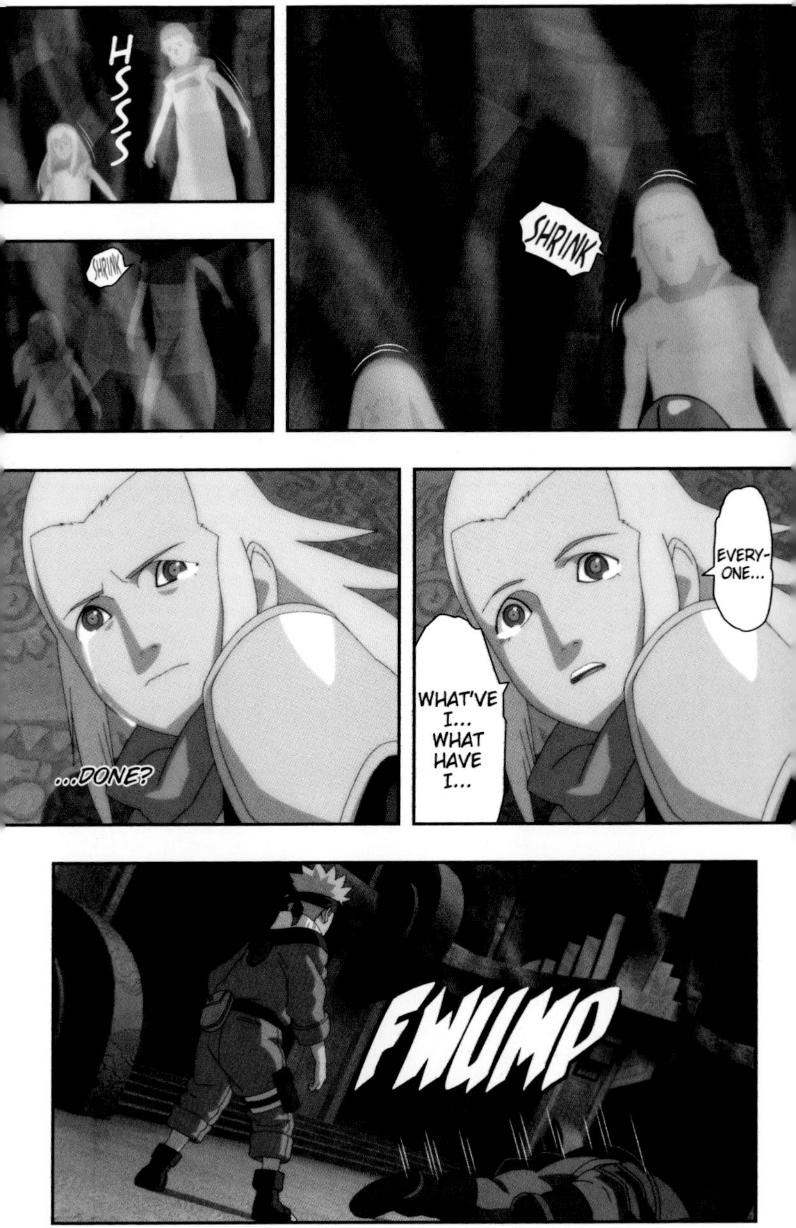
SHRINK
HSSS
SHRINK
EVERY-ONE...
WHAT'VE I... WHAT HAVE I...
...DONE?
FWUMP

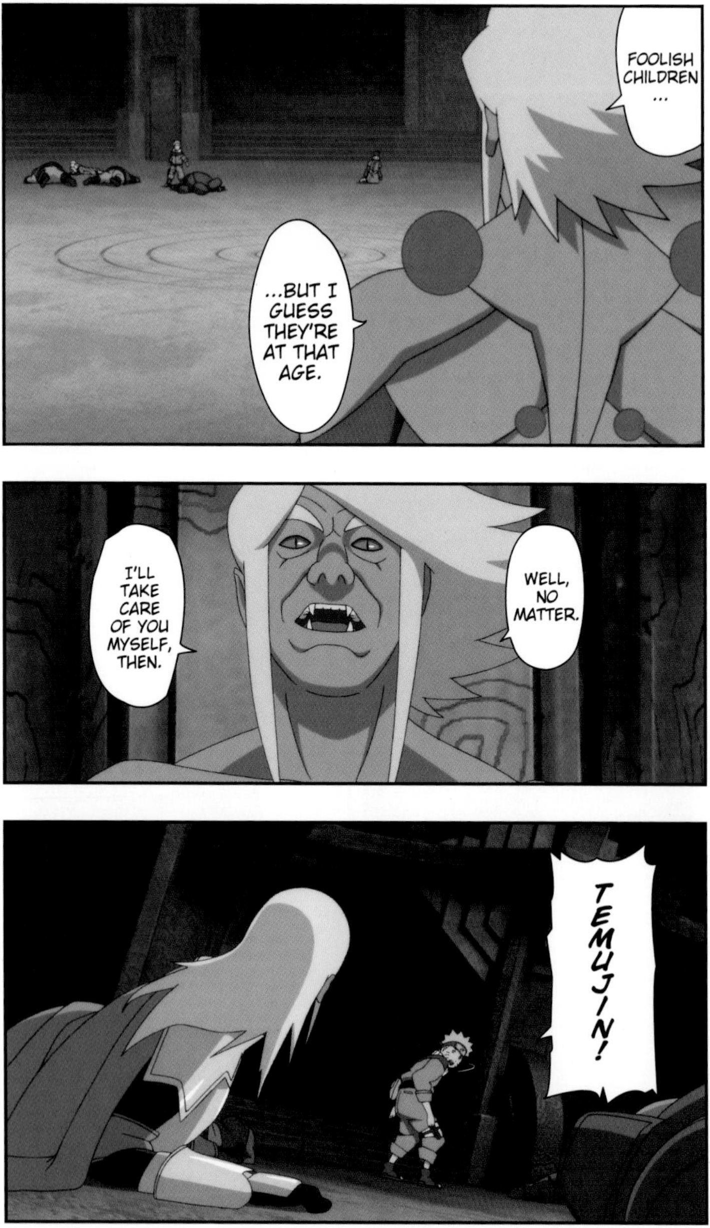
FOOLISH CHILDREN ...
...BUT I GUESS THEY'RE AT THAT AGE.
WELL, NO MATTER.
I'LL TAKE CARE OF YOU MYSELF, THEN.
TEMUJIN!

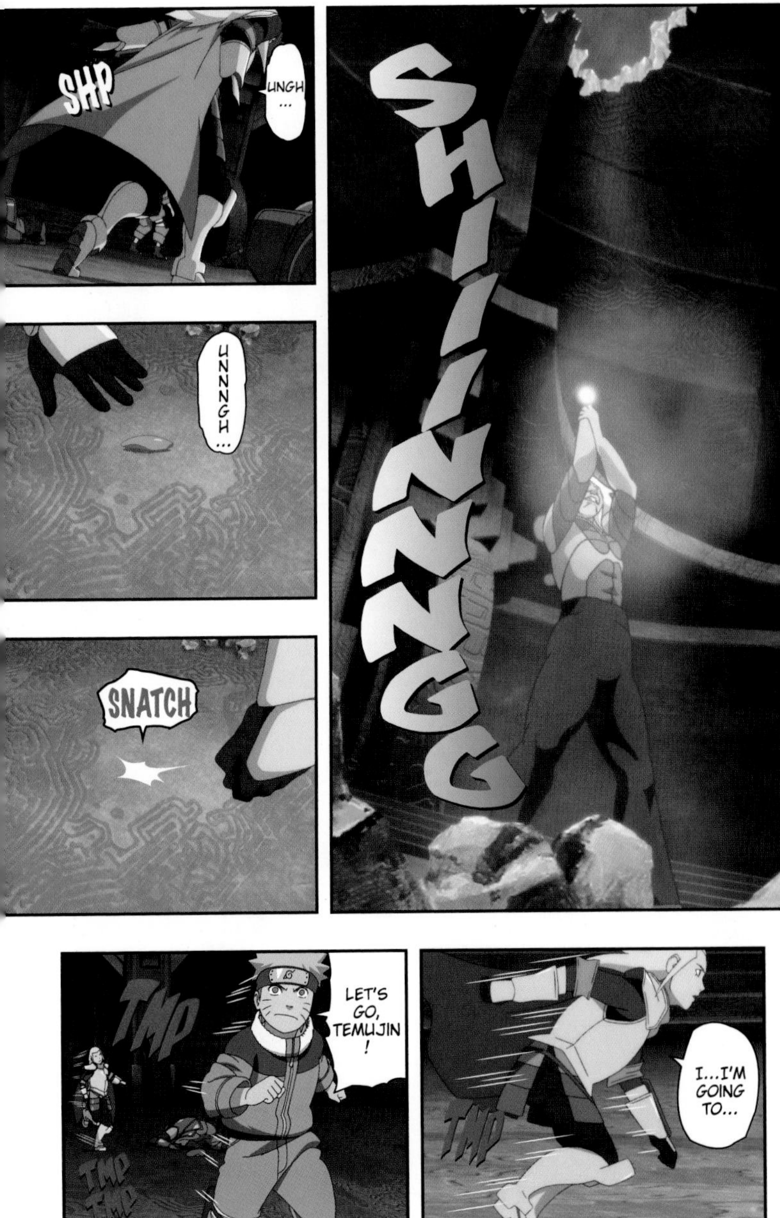
SHIIIINNNNGG
SHP
UNGH...
UNNNGH...
SNATCH
I...I'M GOING TO...
TMP
LET'S GO, TEMUJIN!
TMP
TMP TMP

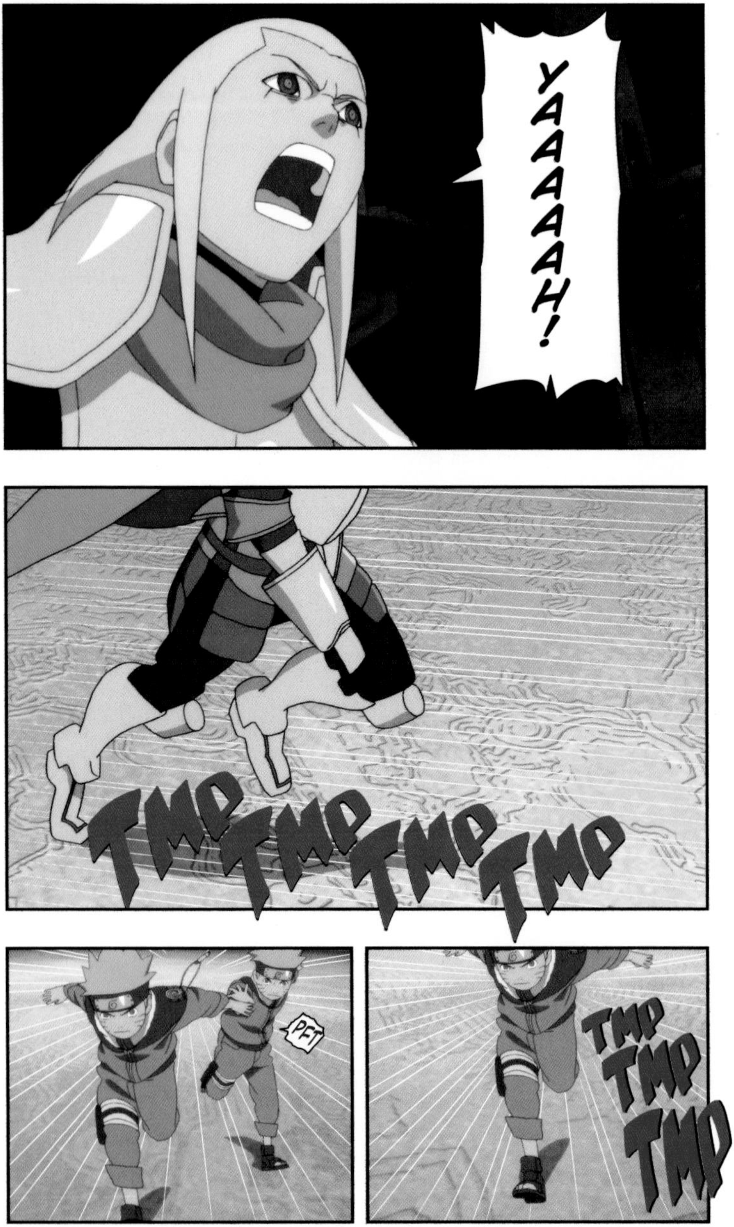
YAAAAAAH!
TMP TMP TMP TMP
TMP TMP TMP
PFT

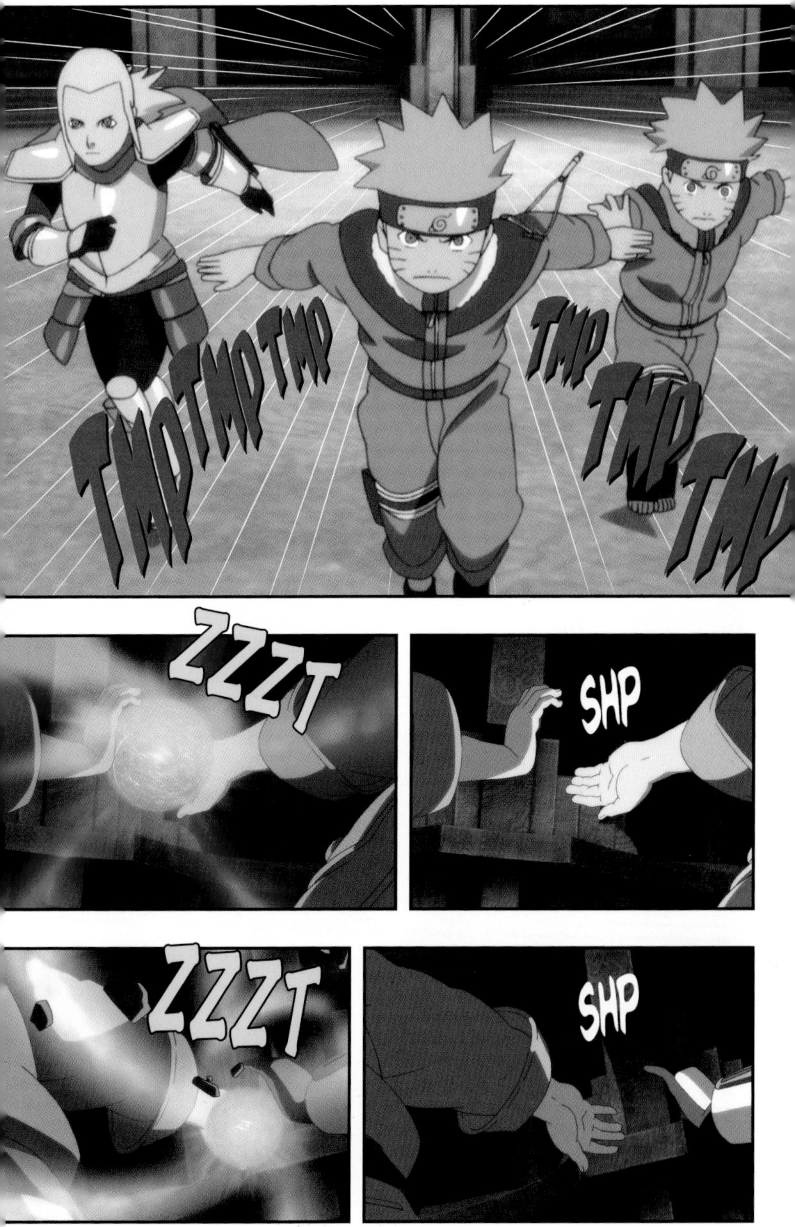
TMP
TMP
TMP
TMPTMPTMP
SHP
ZZZT
SHP
ZZZT

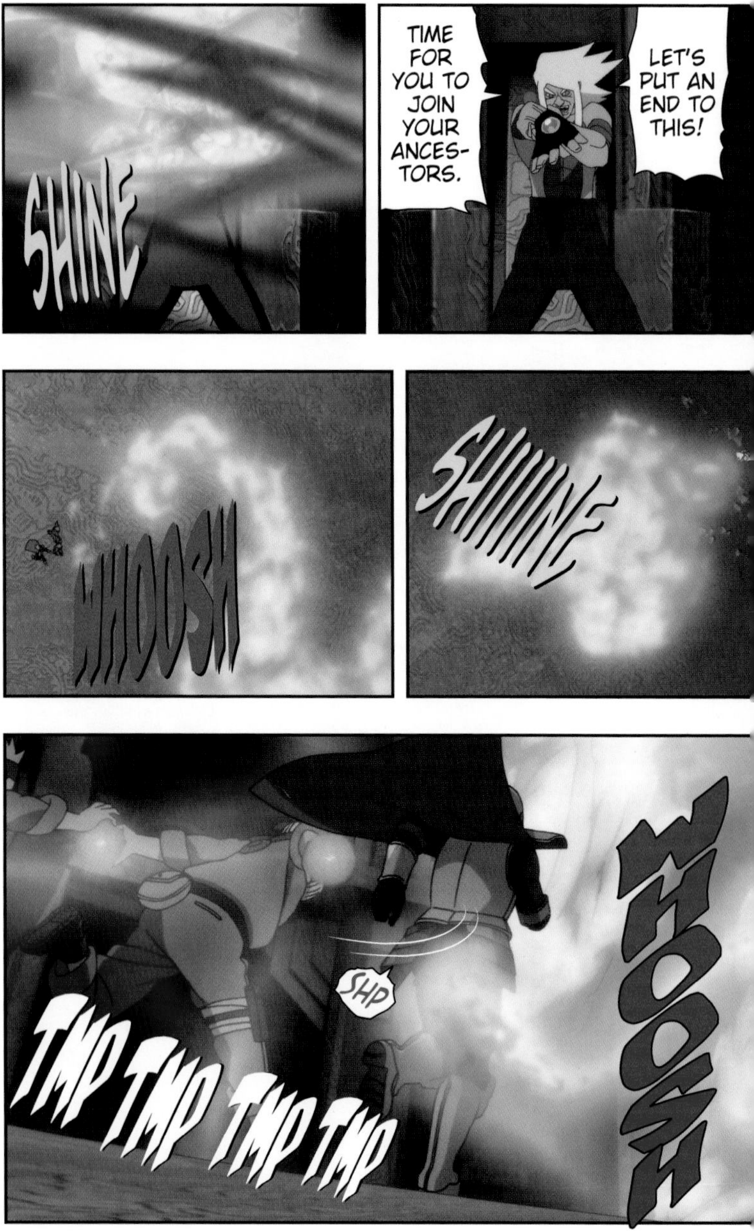
LET'S PUT AN END TO THIS!
TIME FOR YOU TO JOIN YOUR ANCES-TORS.
SHINE
SHIIINE
WHOOSH
WHOOSH
SHP
TMP TMP TMP TMP

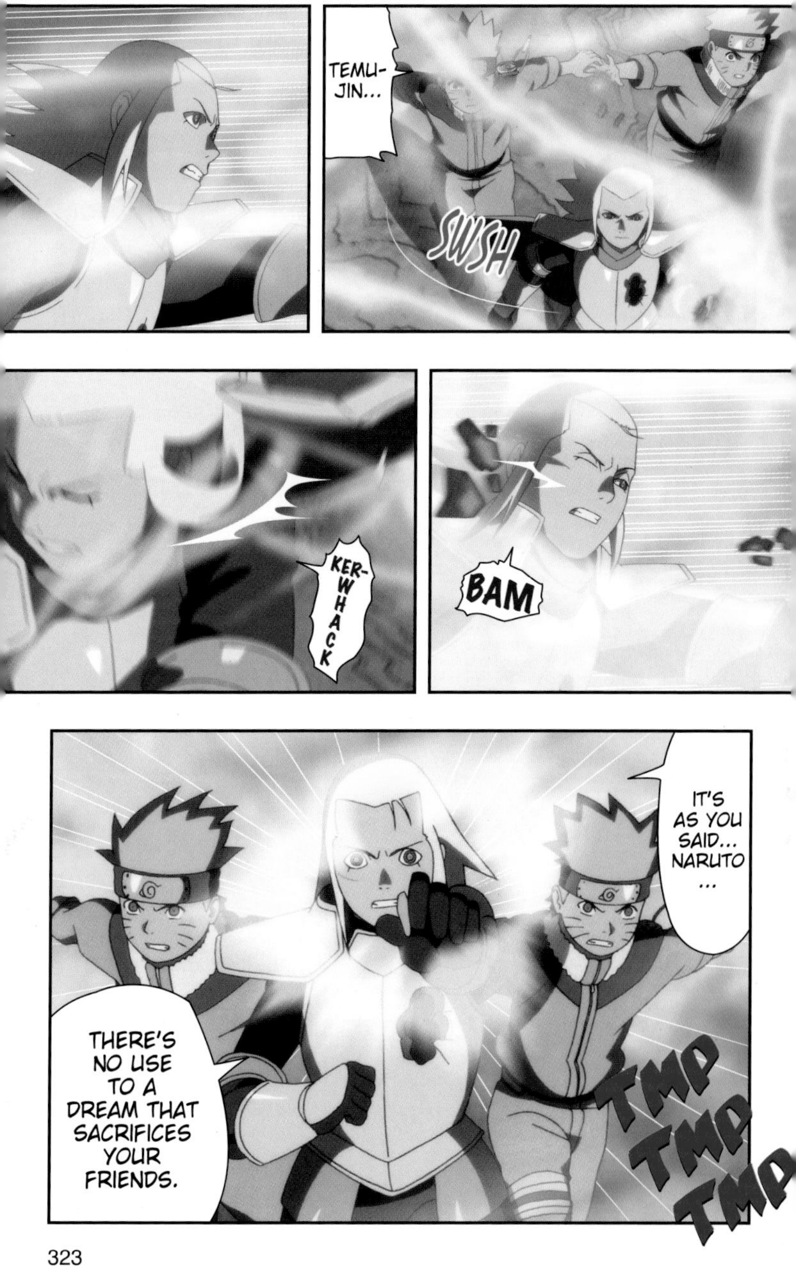
TEMUJIN...
SWSH
BAM
KER-WHACK
IT'S AS YOU SAID... NARUTO ...
THERE'S NO USE TO A DREAM THAT SACRIFICES YOUR FRIENDS.
TMP TMP TMP

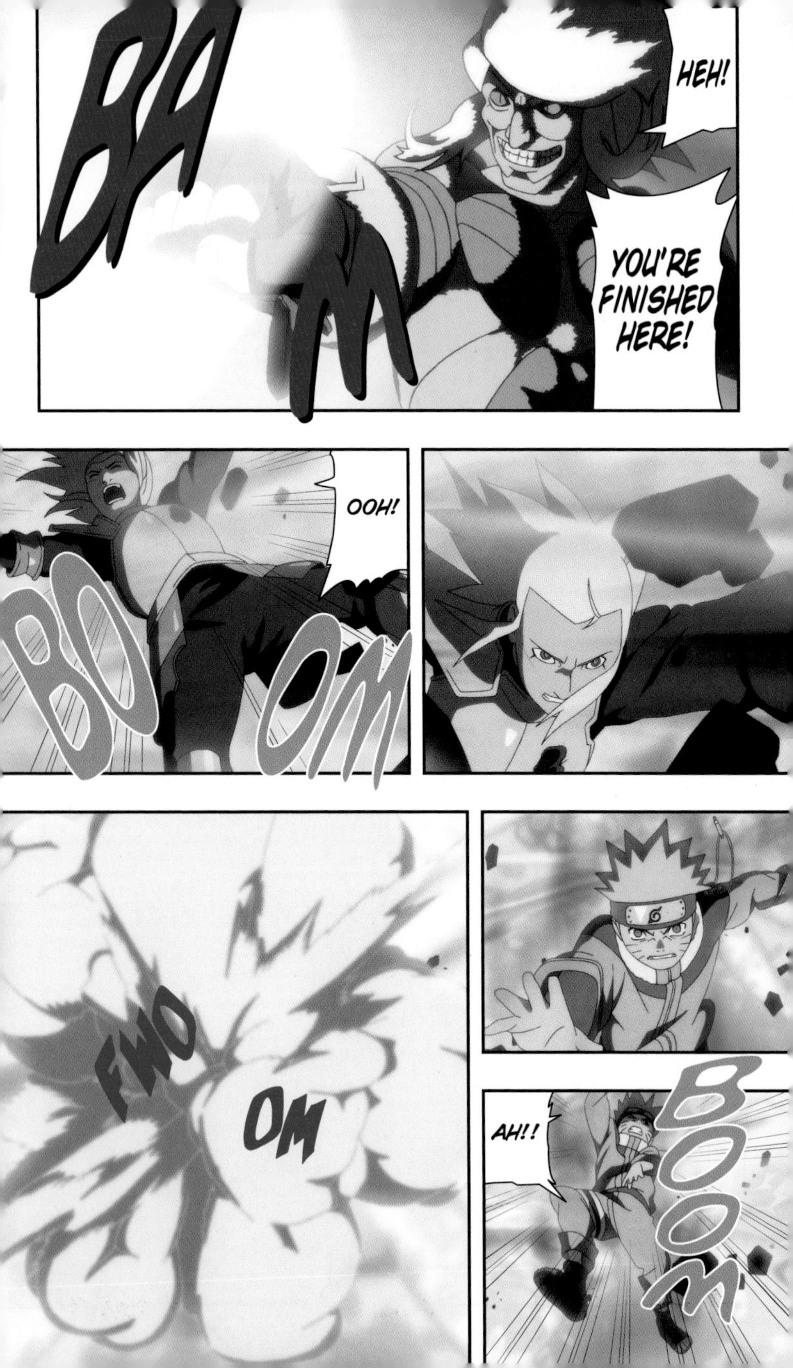
HEH!
YOU'RE FINISHED HERE!
BAM
OOH!
BOOM
BOOM
AH!!
FWOOM

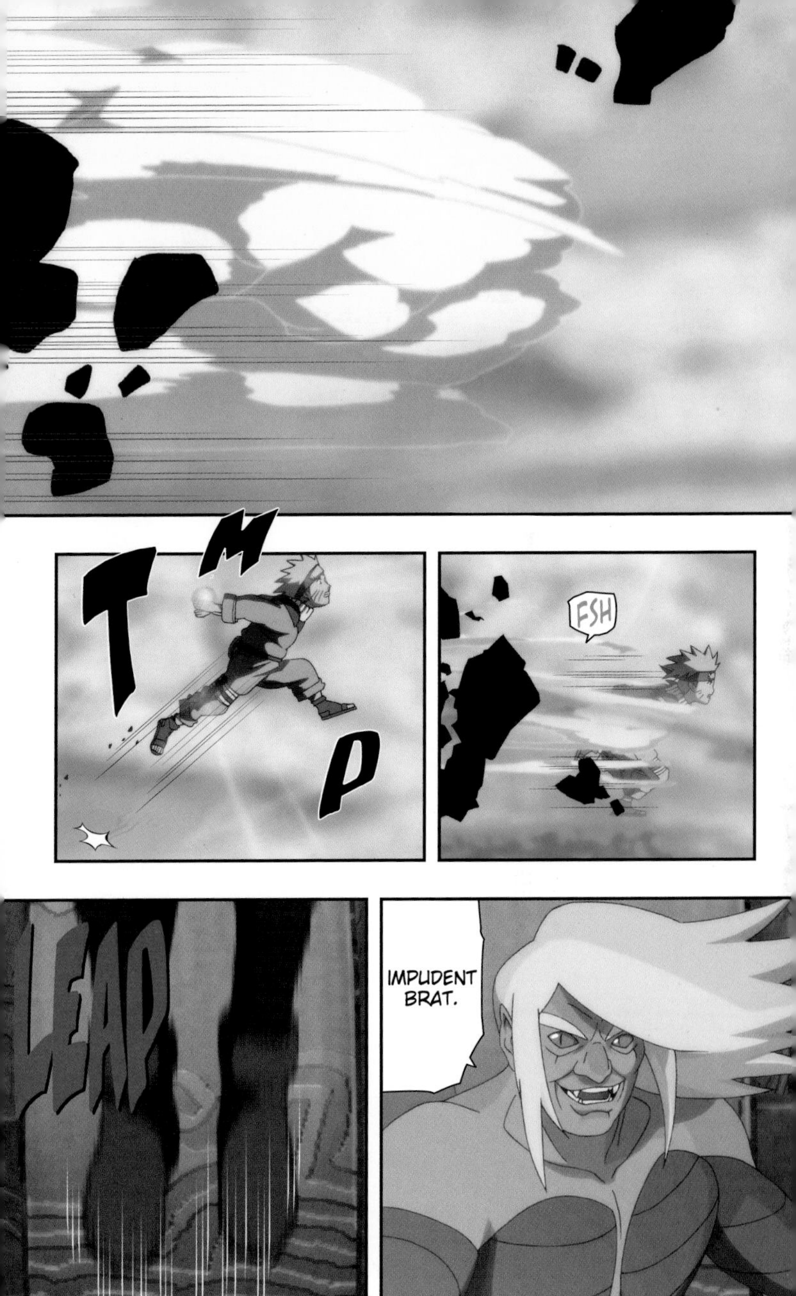
FSH
TMP
IMPUDENT BRAT.
LEAP

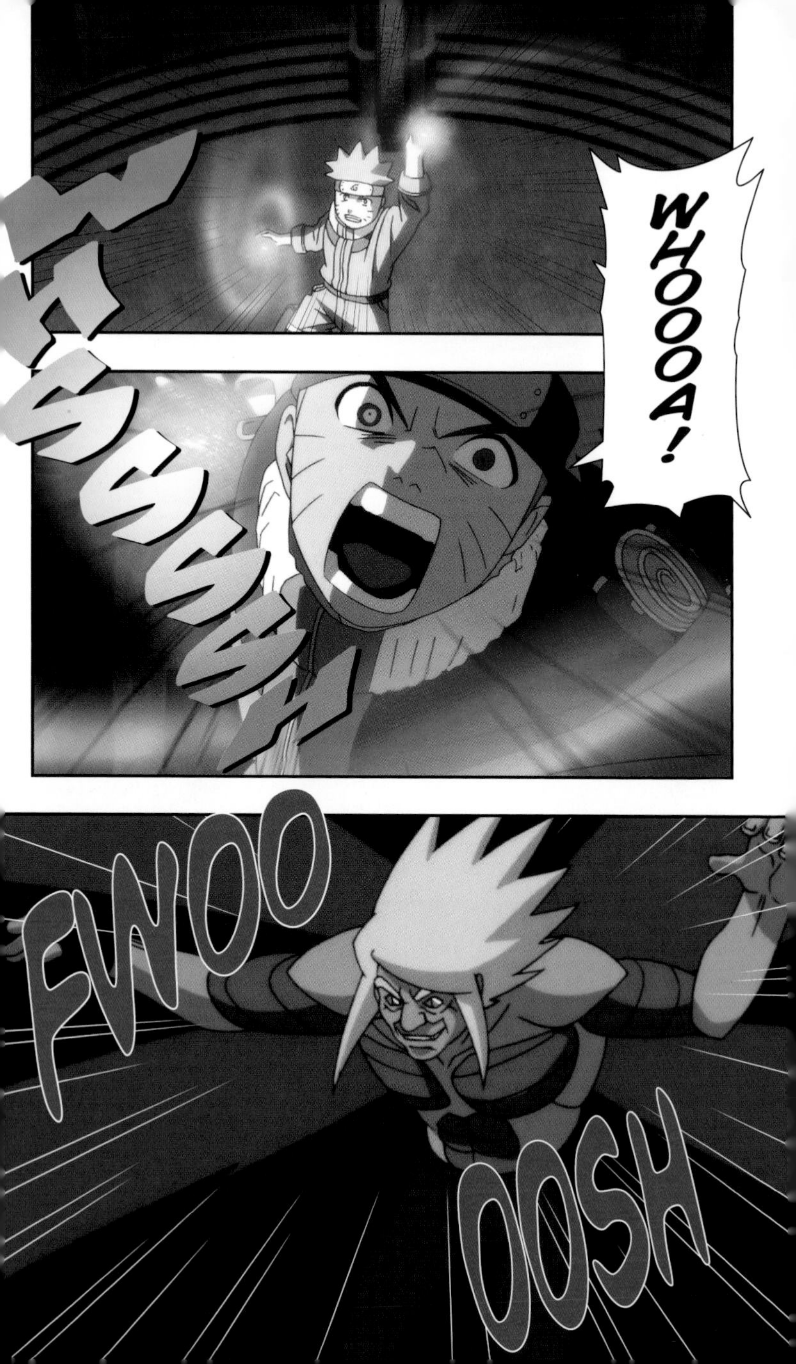
WHOOOOA!
WHSSSSH
FWOO
OOSH

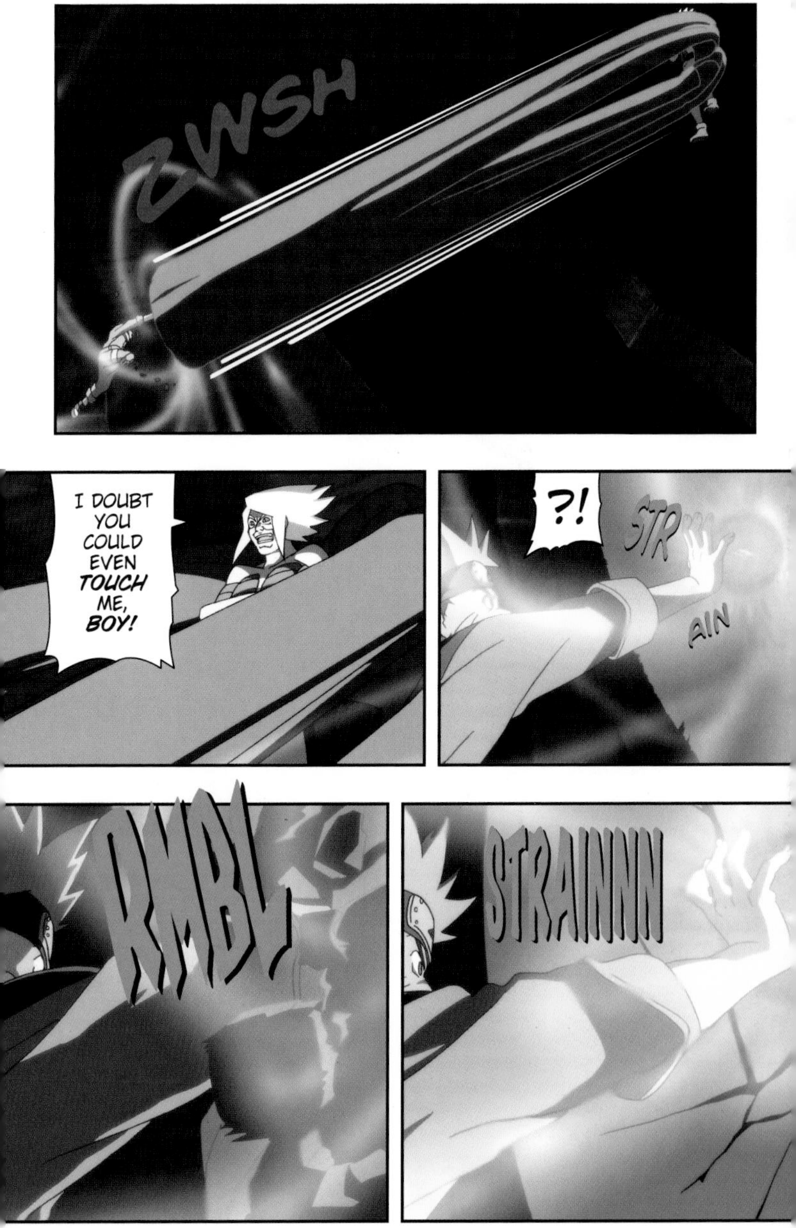
ZWSH
?!
STR
AIN
I DOUBT YOU COULD EVEN *TOUCH* ME, *BOY!*
STRAINNN
RMBL

SHP

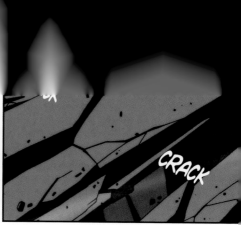

CRACK

WOULD YOU JUST DIE ALREADY?!!

AW, SHOVE IT!

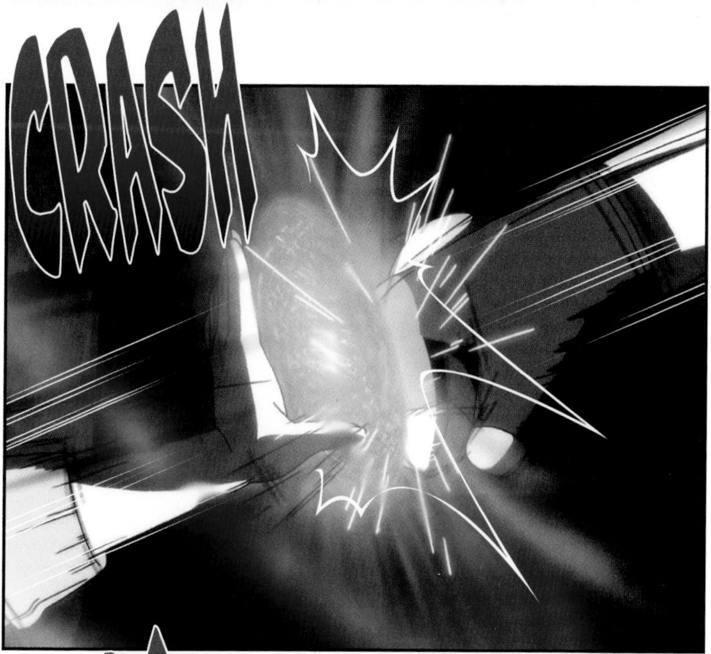
CRASH

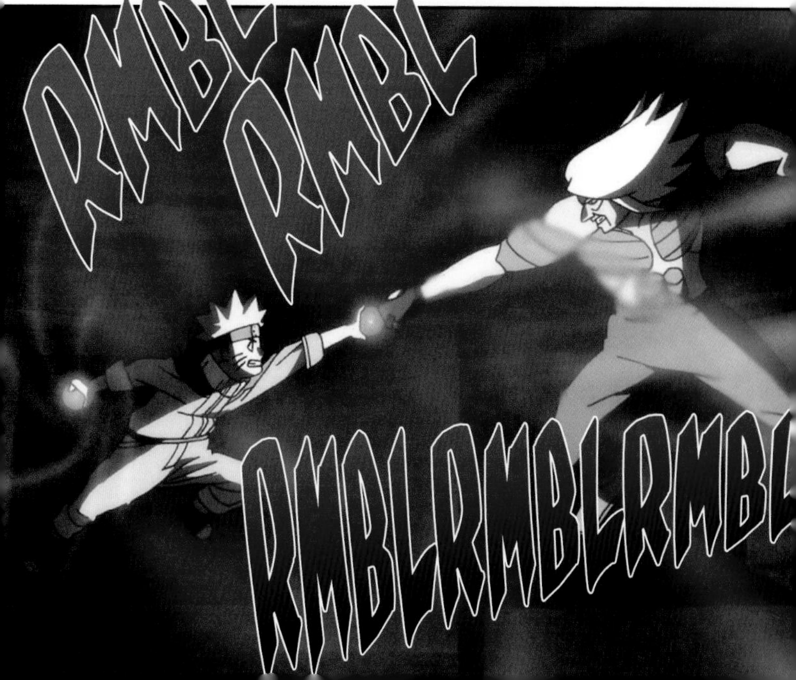
RMBL RMBL
RMBLRMBLRMBL

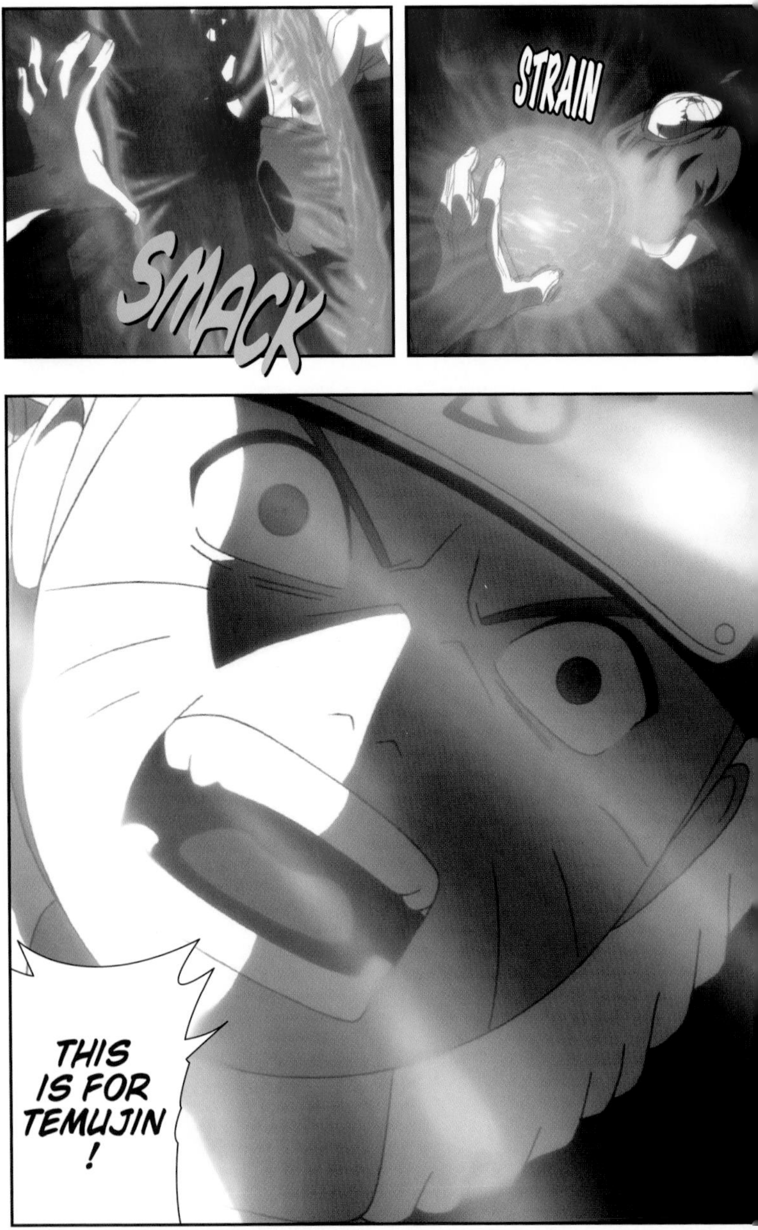
STRAIN
SMACK
THIS IS FOR TEMUJIN!

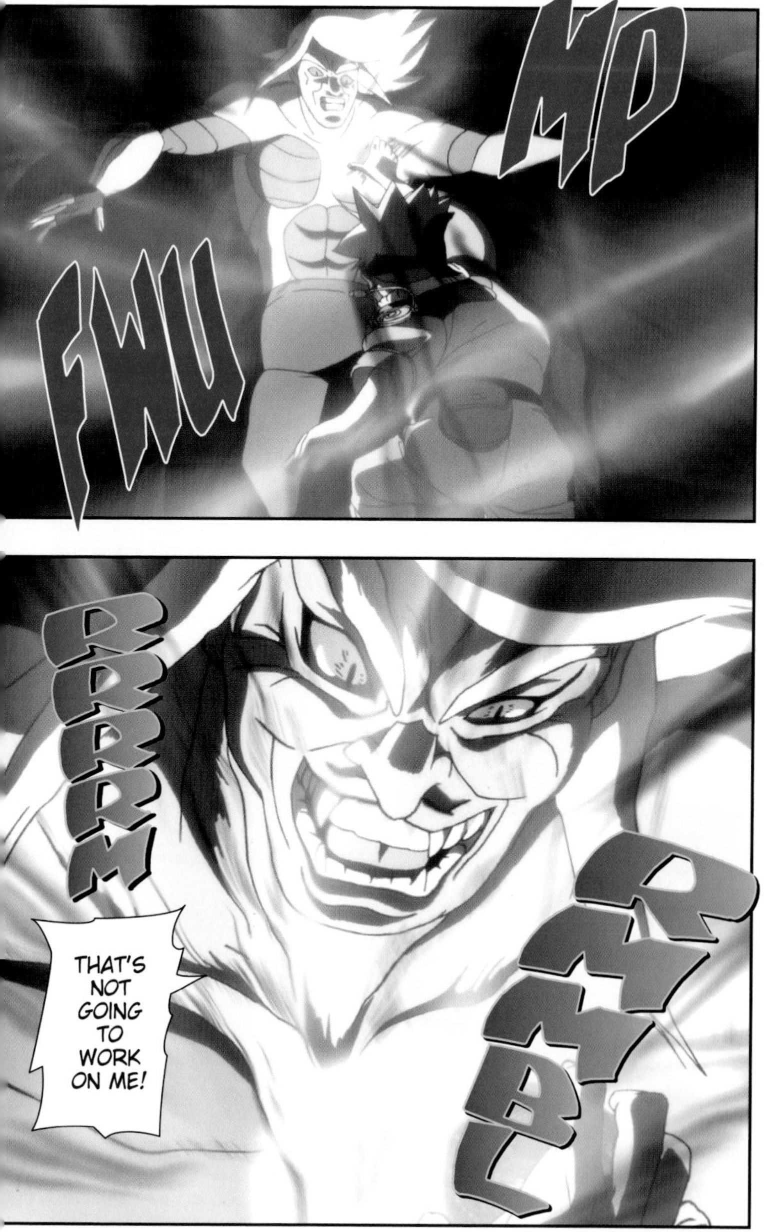
MP
FWU
RRRRRM
RMMBL
THAT'S NOT GOING TO WORK ON ME!

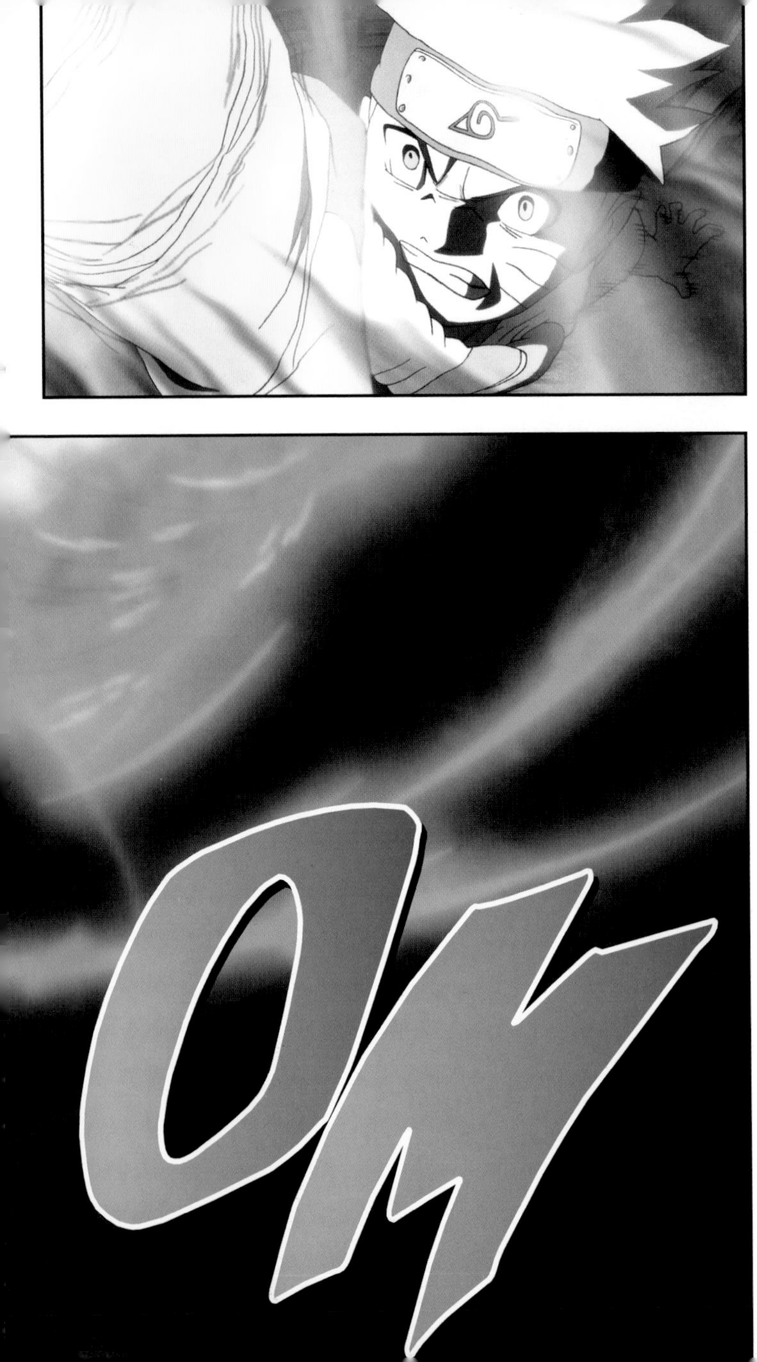
OM

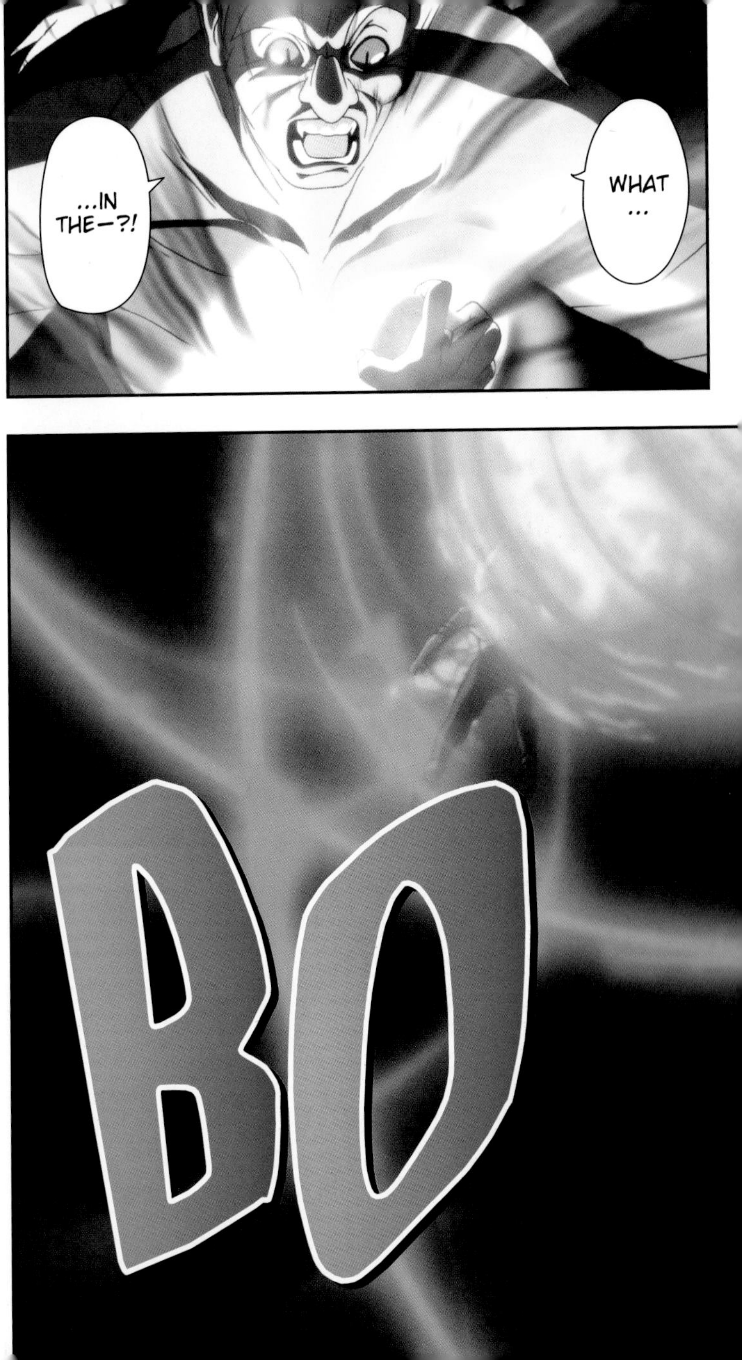
WHAT ...
...IN THE—?!
BO

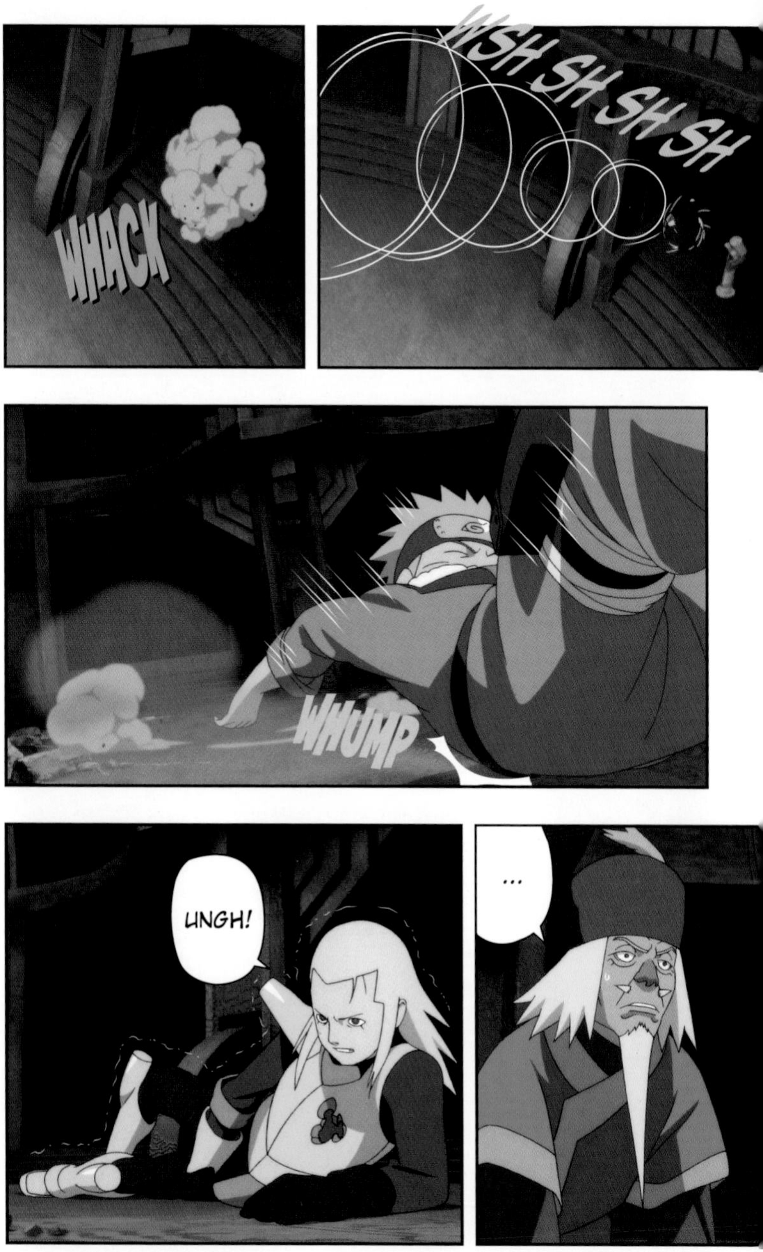
WSH SH SH SH
WHACK
WHUMP
...
UNGH!

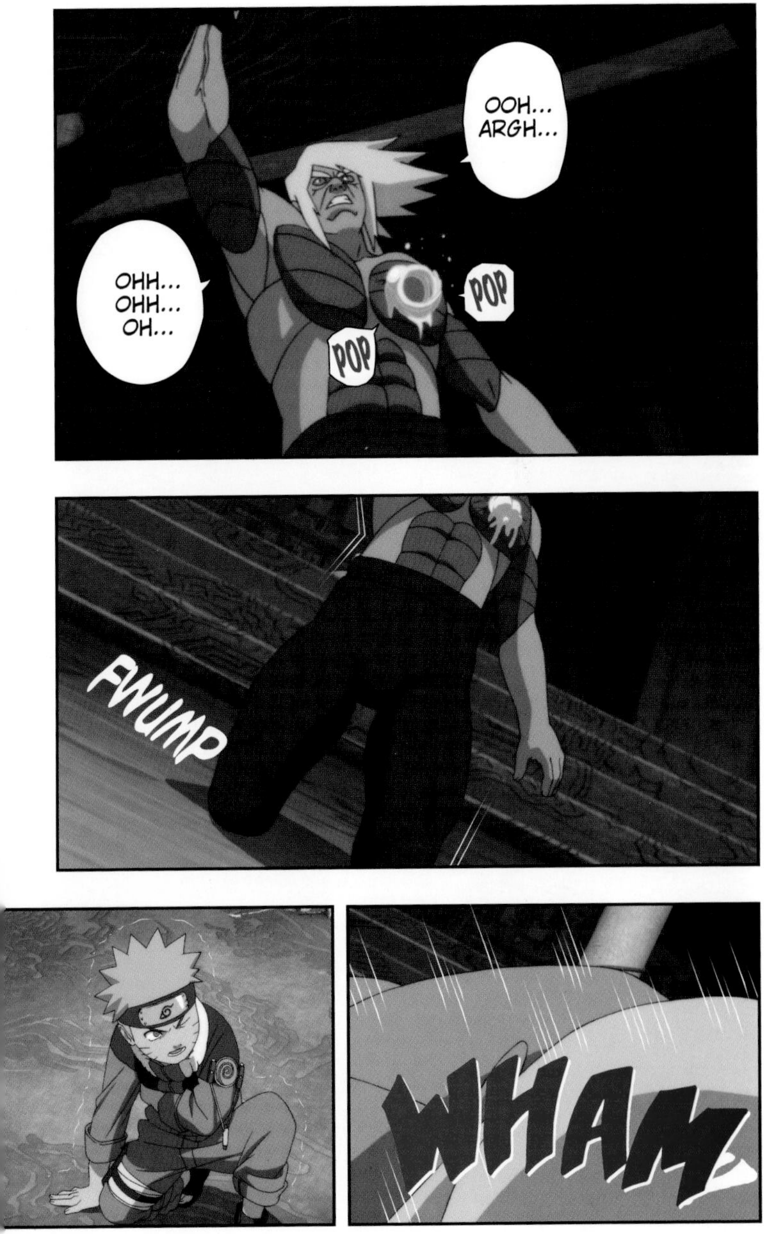
OOH... ARGH...
POP
OHH... OHH... OH...
POP
FWUMP
WHAM

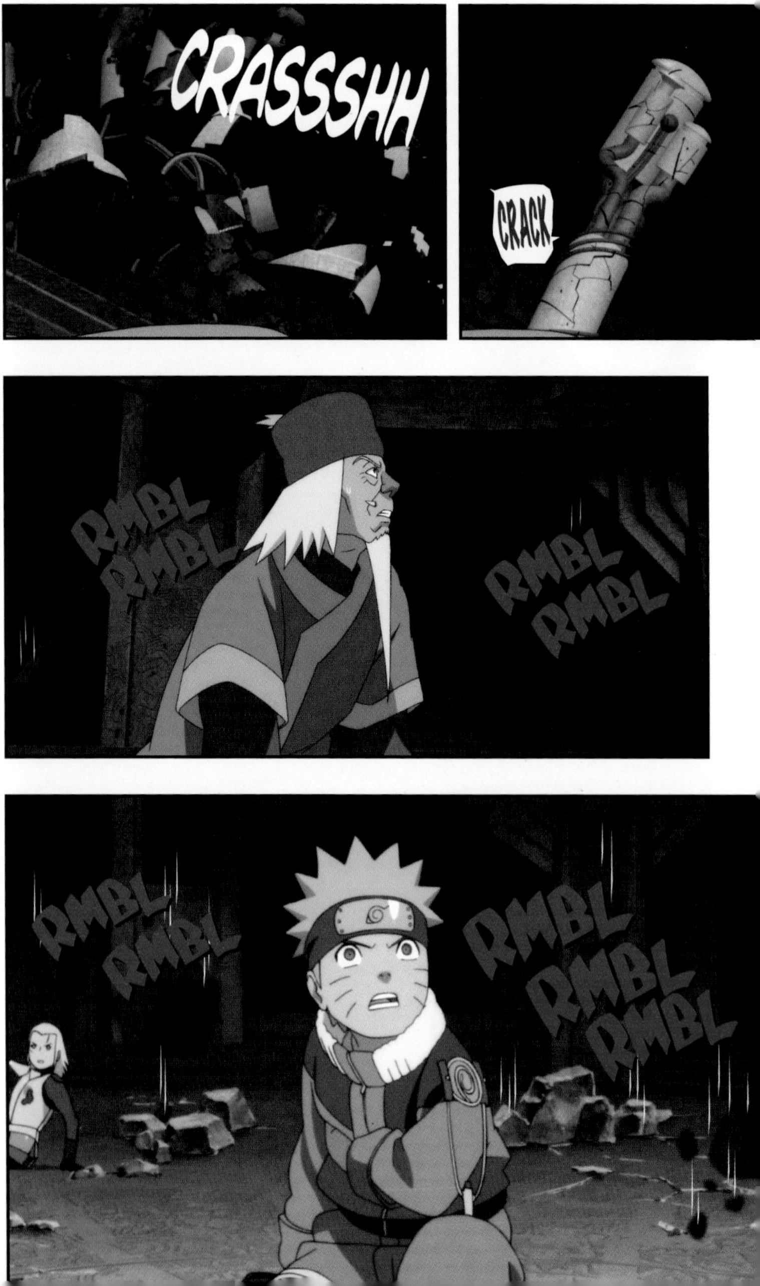
CRACK
CRASSSHH
RMBL RMBL
RMBL RMBL
RMBL RMBL RMBL
RMBL RMBL

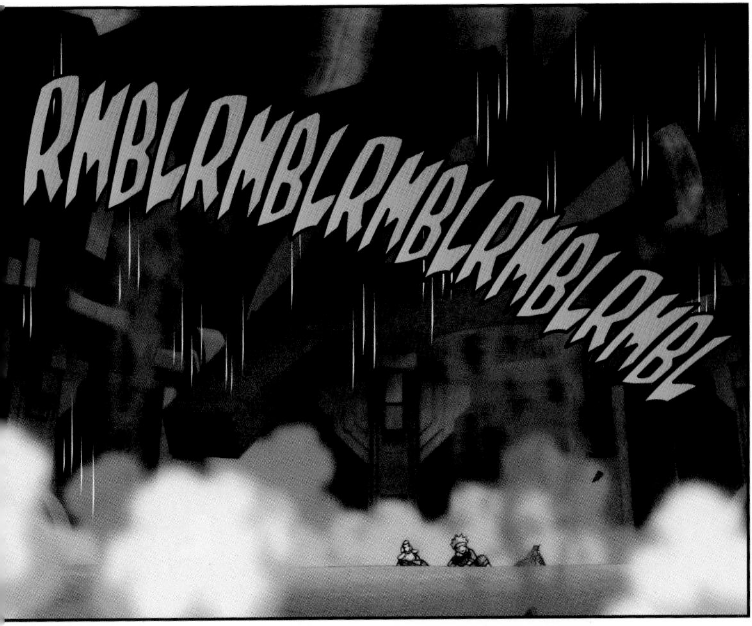
RMBLRMBLRMBLRMBLRMBLRMBL

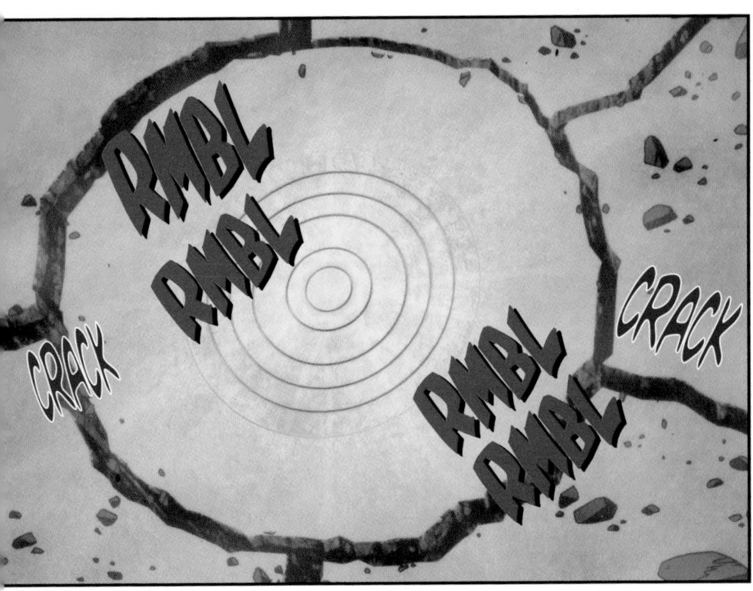
RMBL
RMBL
CRACK
RMBL
RMBL
CRACK

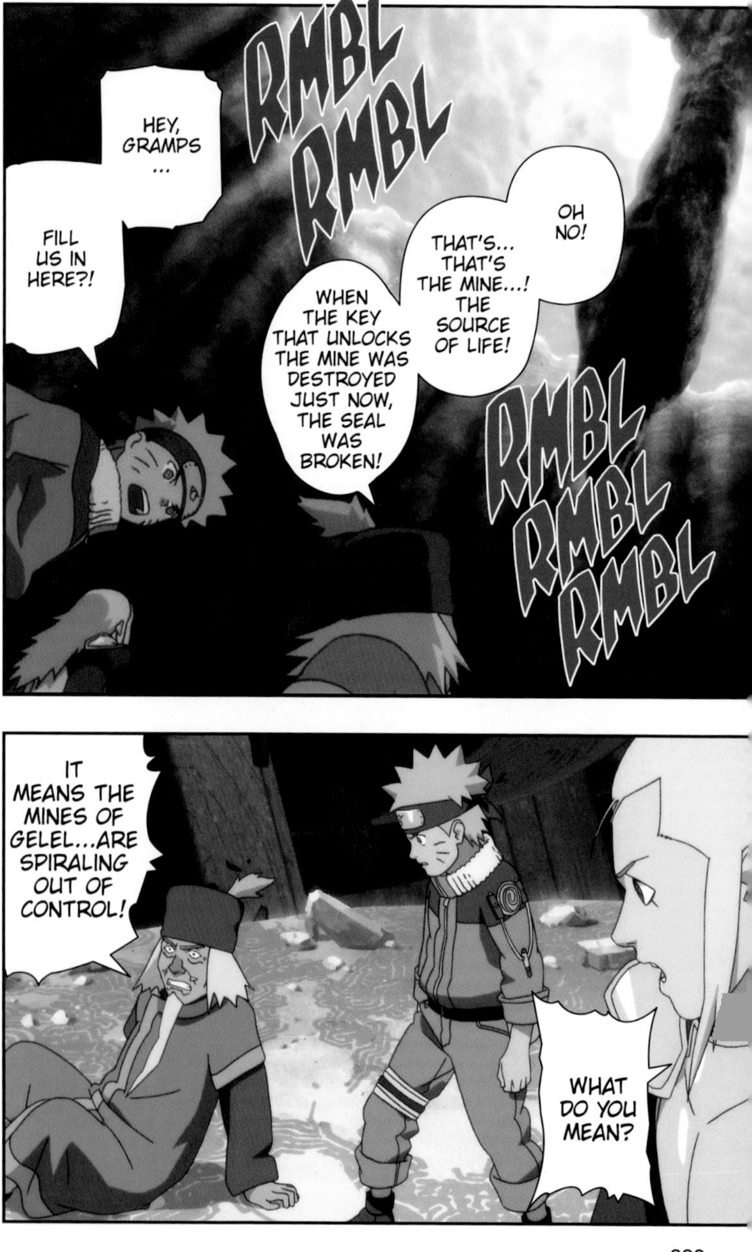
RMBL RMBL
OH NO!
THAT'S... THAT'S THE MINE...! THE SOURCE OF LIFE!
HEY, GRAMPS...
FILL US IN HERE?!
WHEN THE KEY THAT UNLOCKS THE MINE WAS DESTROYED JUST NOW, THE SEAL WAS BROKEN!
RMBL RMBL RMBL
WHAT DO YOU MEAN?
IT MEANS THE MINES OF GELEL...ARE SPIRALING OUT OF CONTROL!

Chapter 8: True Friends

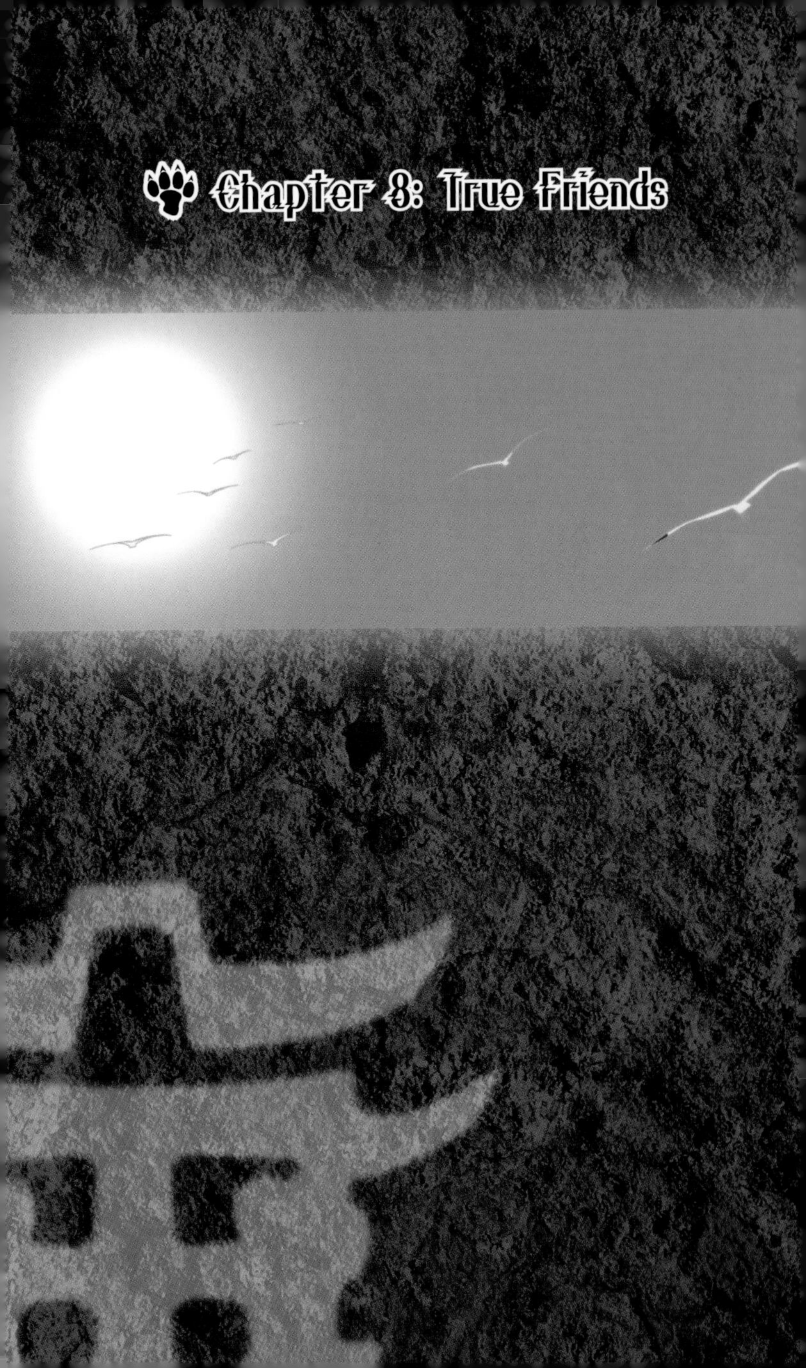

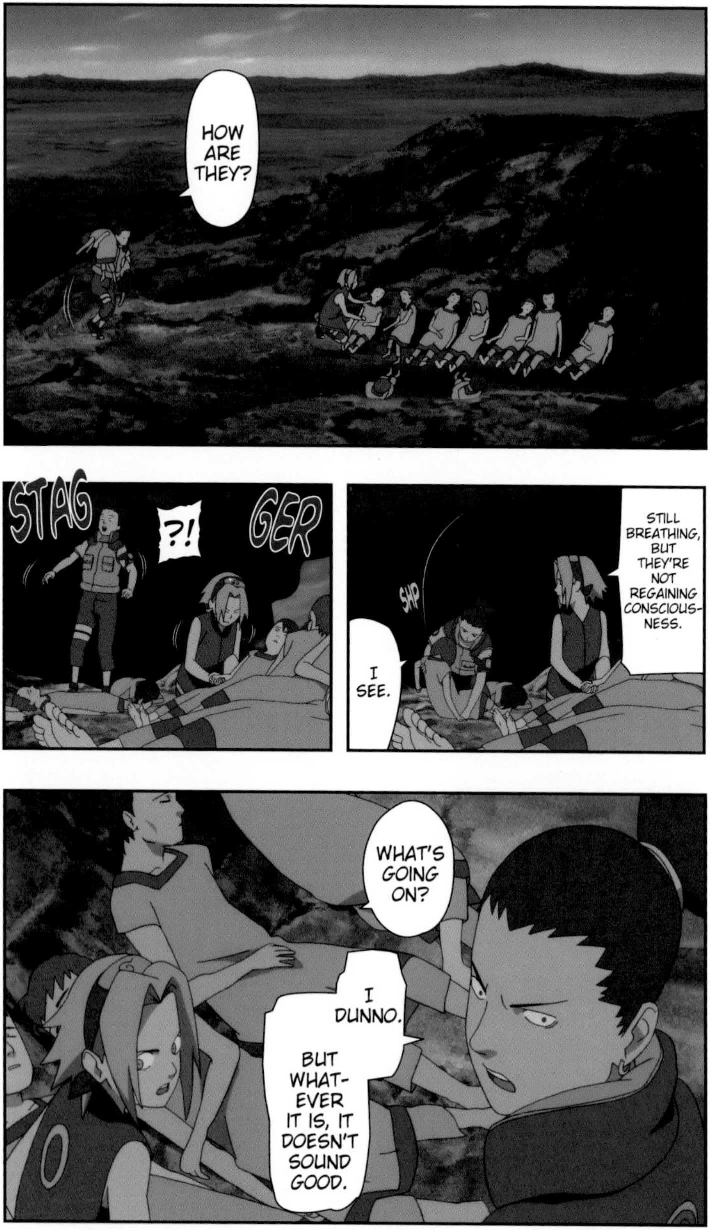

HOW ARE THEY?
STILL BREATHING, BUT THEY'RE NOT REGAINING CONSCIOUS-NESS.
SHP
I SEE.
GER
?!
STAG
WHAT'S GOING ON?
I DUNNO.
BUT WHAT-EVER IT IS, IT DOESN'T SOUND GOOD.

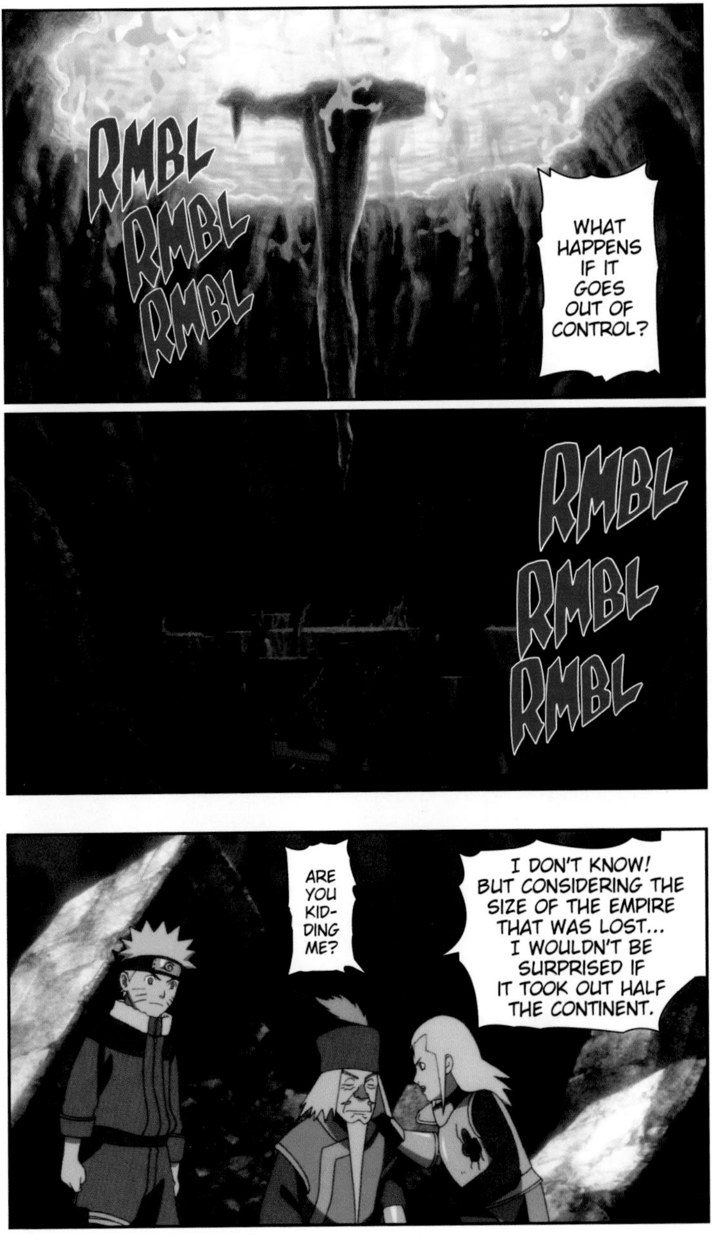
RMBL RMBL RMBL
WHAT HAPPENS IF IT GOES OUT OF CONTROL?
RMBL RMBL RMBL
I DON'T KNOW! BUT CONSIDERING THE SIZE OF THE EMPIRE THAT WAS LOST... I WOULDN'T BE SURPRISED IF IT TOOK OUT HALF THE CONTINENT.
ARE YOU KID-DING ME?

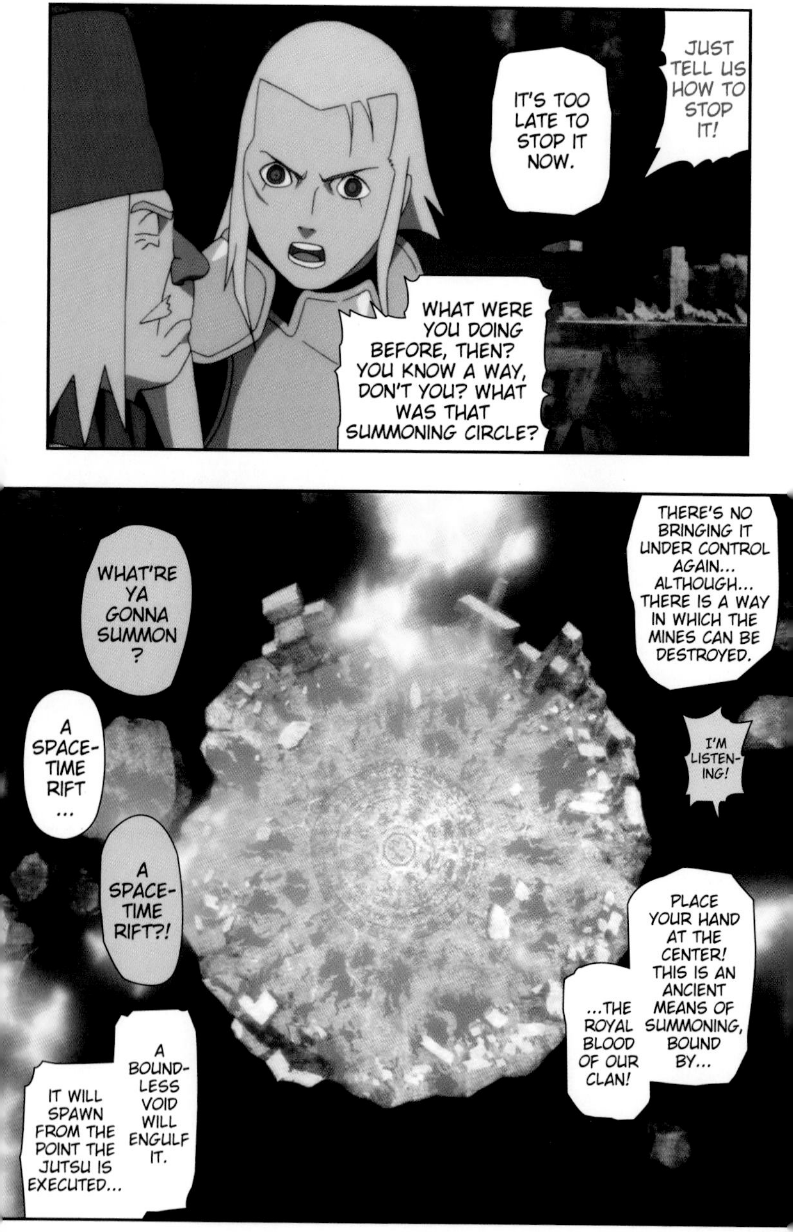
JUST TELL US HOW TO STOP IT!
IT'S TOO LATE TO STOP IT NOW.
WHAT WERE YOU DOING BEFORE, THEN? YOU KNOW A WAY, DON'T YOU? WHAT WAS THAT SUMMONING CIRCLE?
THERE'S NO BRINGING IT UNDER CONTROL AGAIN... ALTHOUGH... THERE IS A WAY IN WHICH THE MINES CAN BE DESTROYED.
I'M LISTENING!
PLACE YOUR HAND AT THE CENTER! THIS IS AN ANCIENT MEANS OF SUMMONING, BOUND BY...
...THE ROYAL BLOOD OF OUR CLAN!
WHAT'RE YA GONNA SUMMON?
A SPACE-TIME RIFT...
A SPACE-TIME RIFT?!
A BOUNDLESS VOID WILL ENGULF IT.
IT WILL SPAWN FROM THE POINT THE JUTSU IS EXECUTED...

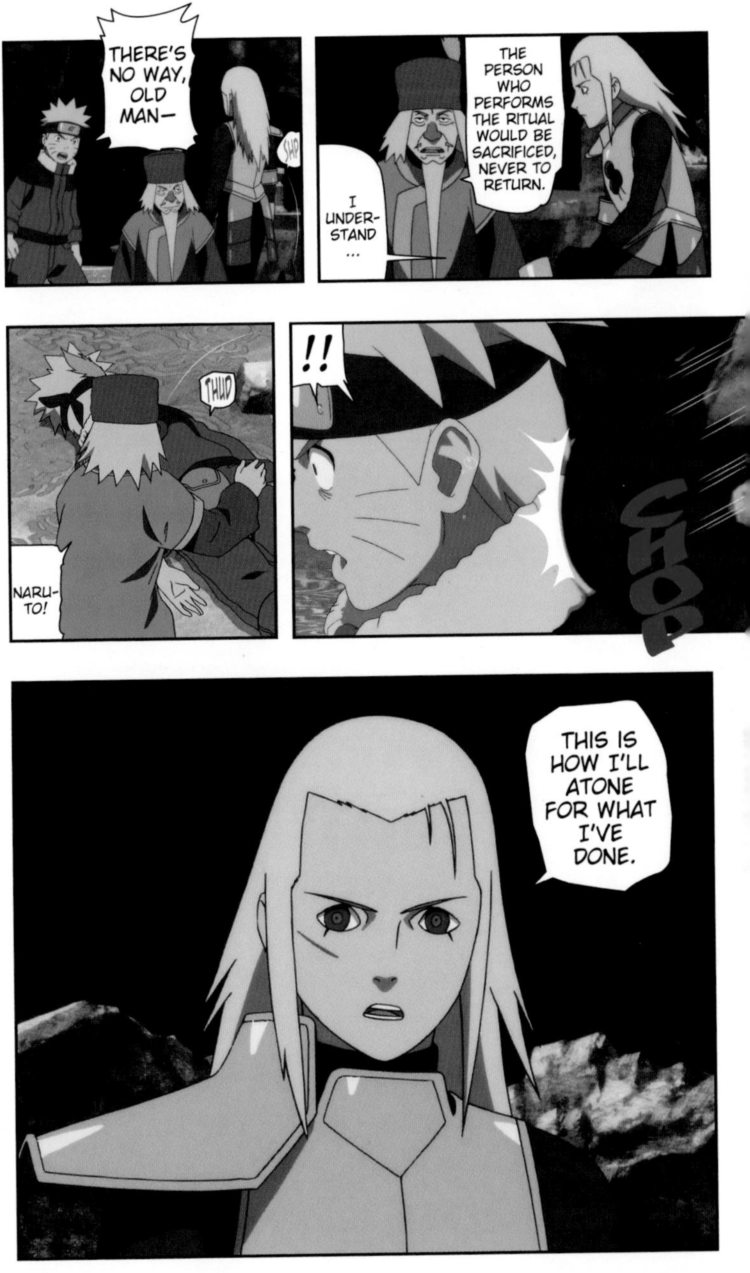
THE PERSON WHO PERFORMS THE RITUAL WOULD BE SACRIFICED, NEVER TO RETURN.
I UNDERSTAND...
SHP
THERE'S NO WAY, OLD MAN—
!!
CHOP
THUD
NARU-TO!
THIS IS HOW I'LL ATONE FOR WHAT I'VE DONE.

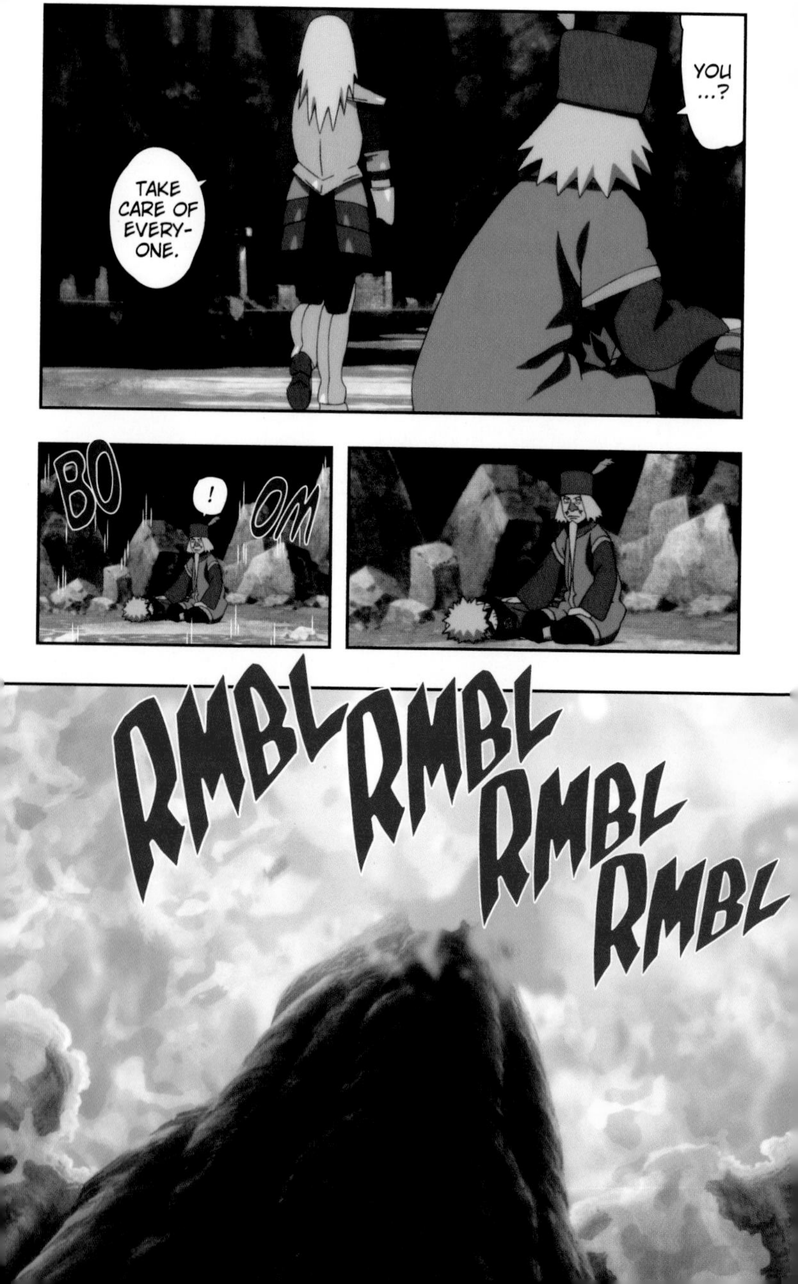
YOU ...?
TAKE CARE OF EVERY-ONE.
BOOM
!
RMBL RMBL RMBL RMBL

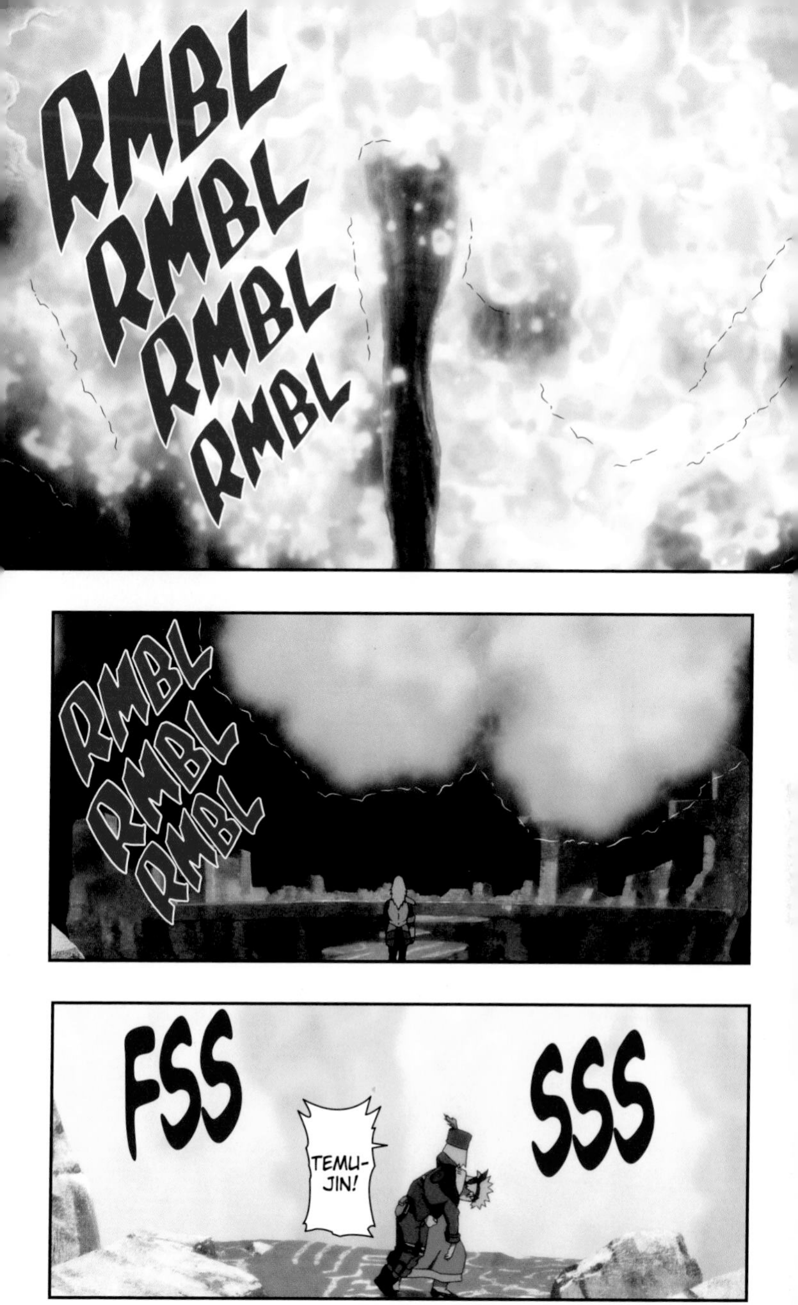
RMBL
RMBL
RMBL
RMBL
RMBL
RMBL
RMBL
FSS SSS
TEMU-JIN!

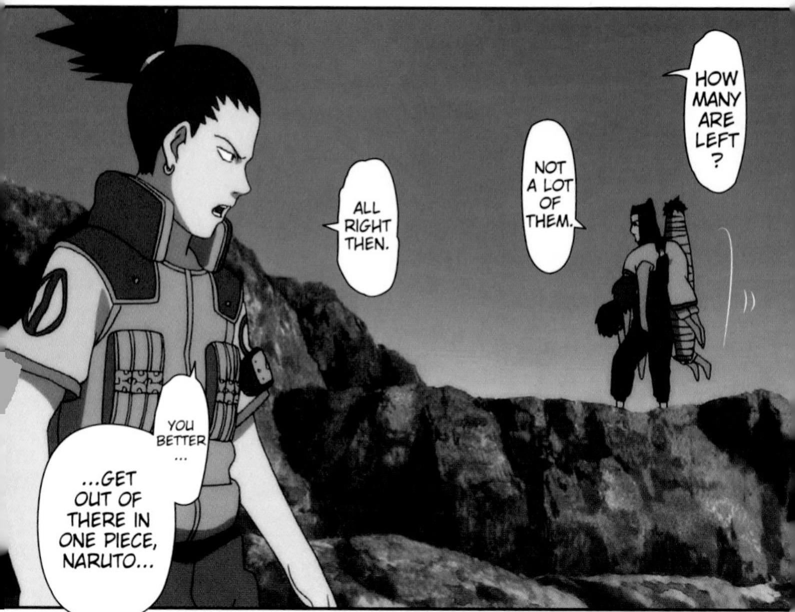
HOW MANY ARE LEFT?
NOT A LOT OF THEM.
ALL RIGHT THEN.
YOU BETTER...
...GET OUT OF THERE IN ONE PIECE, NARUTO...

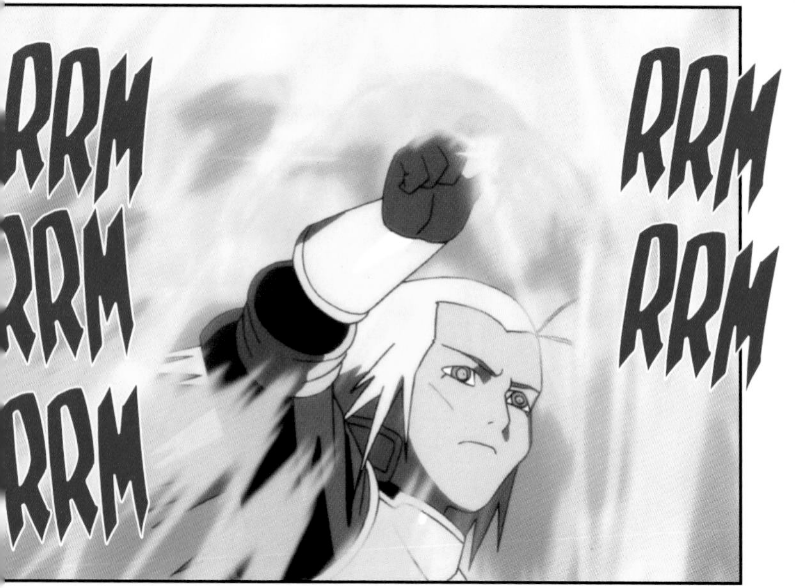
RRM RRM RRM
RRM RRM RRM

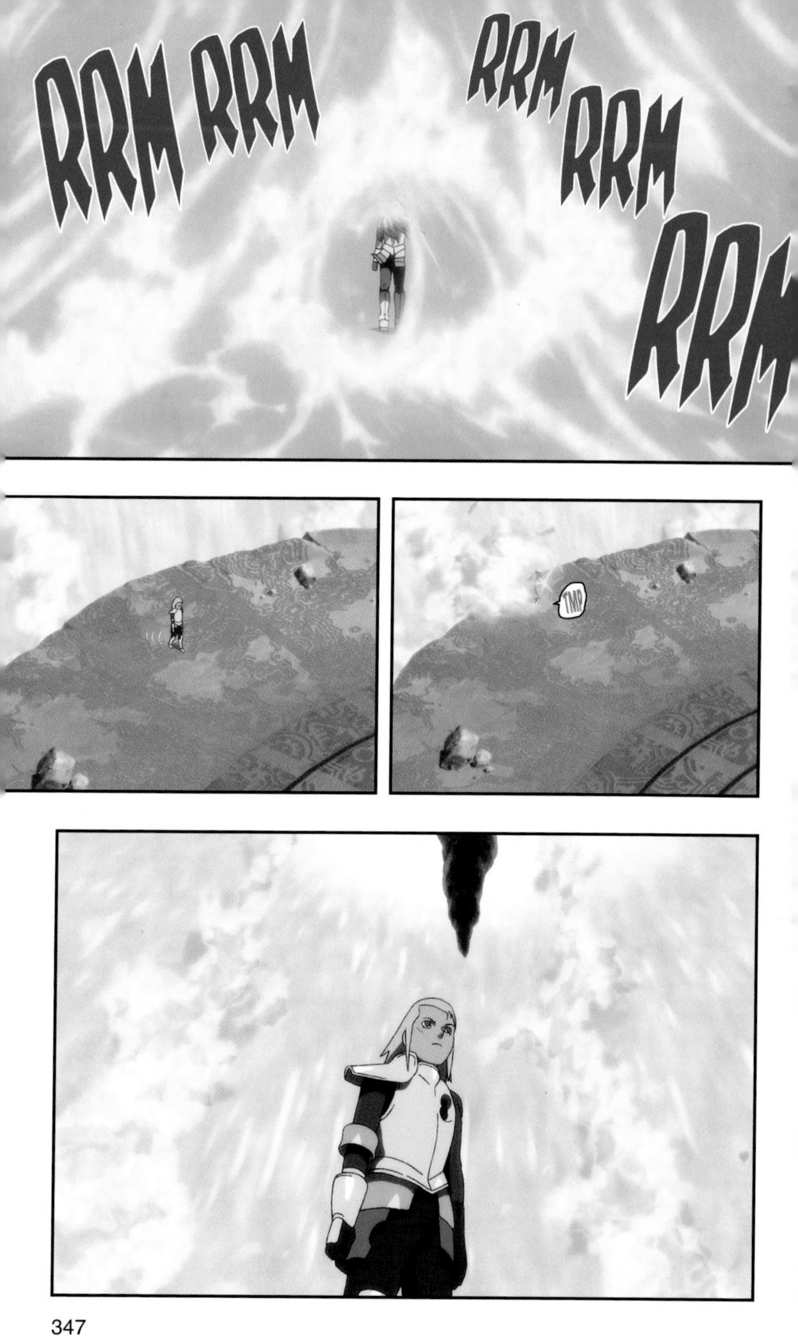
RRM RRM RRM
RRM RRM
TMP

...
TMP
BWSH

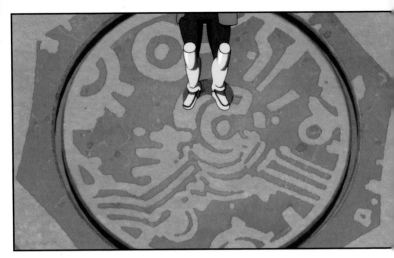

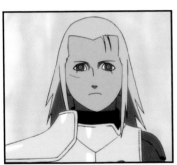

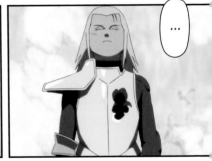

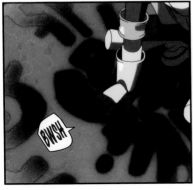

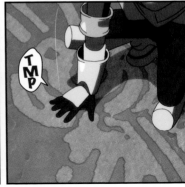

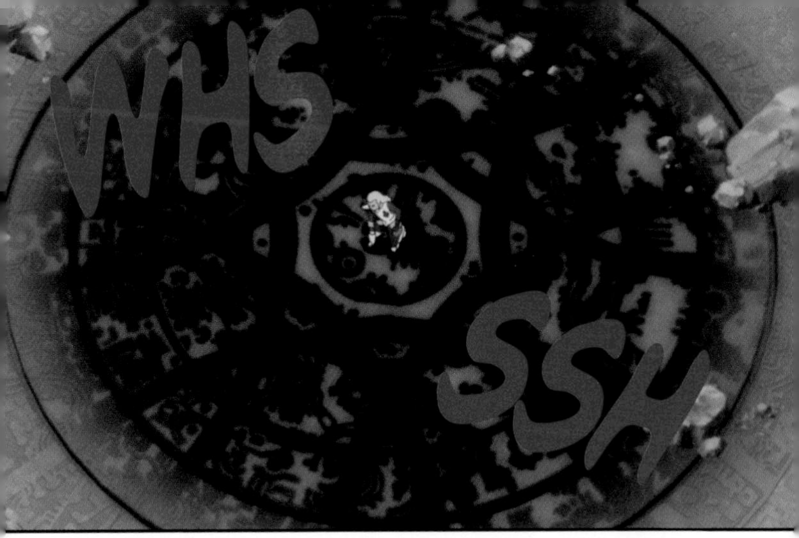
WHS
SSH
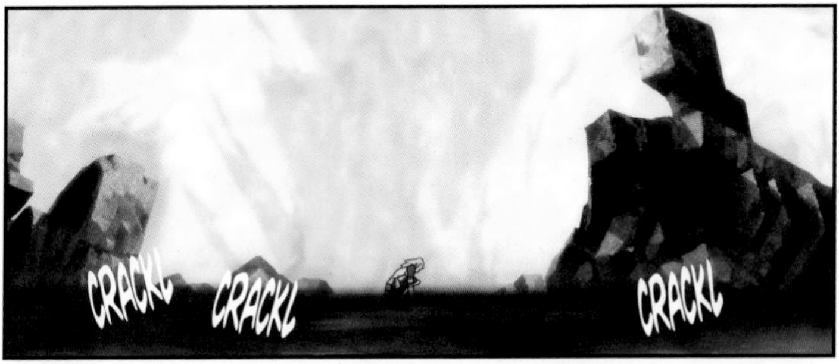
CRACKL
CRACKL
CRACKL
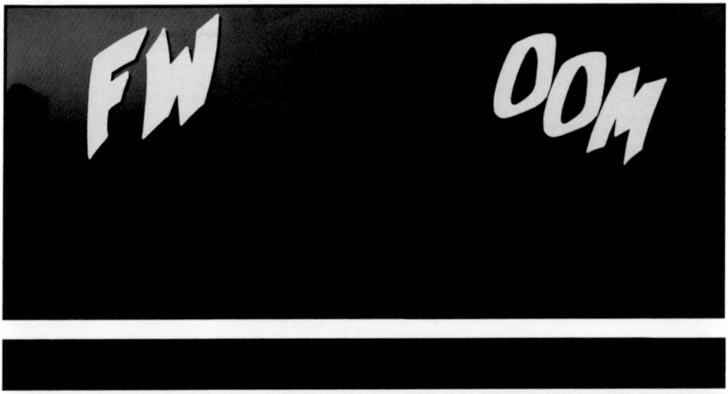
FW
OOM
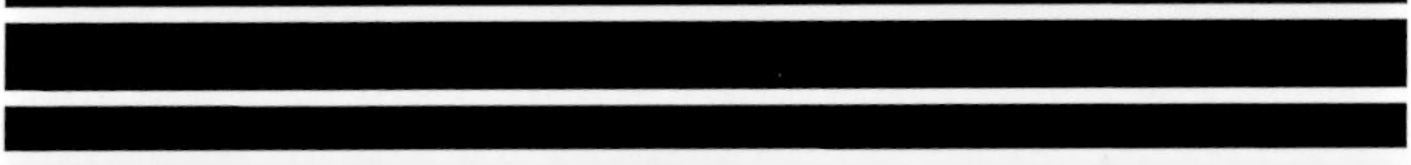

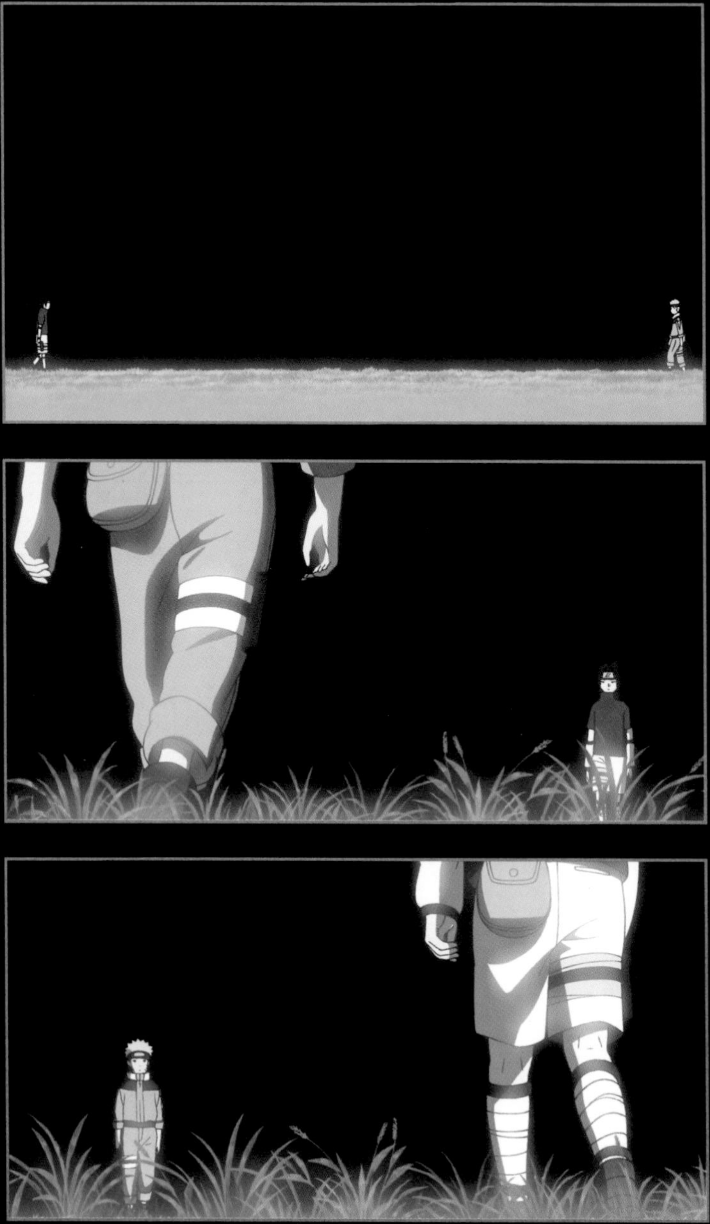

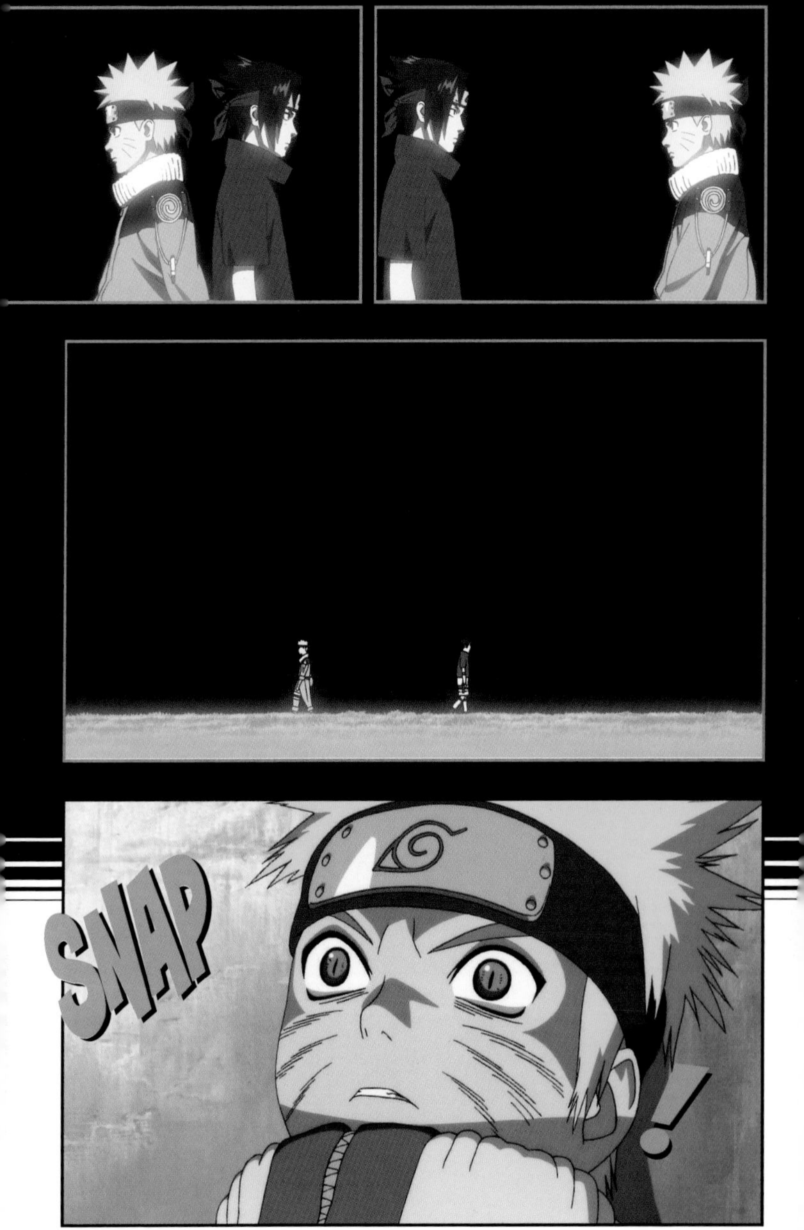
SNAP

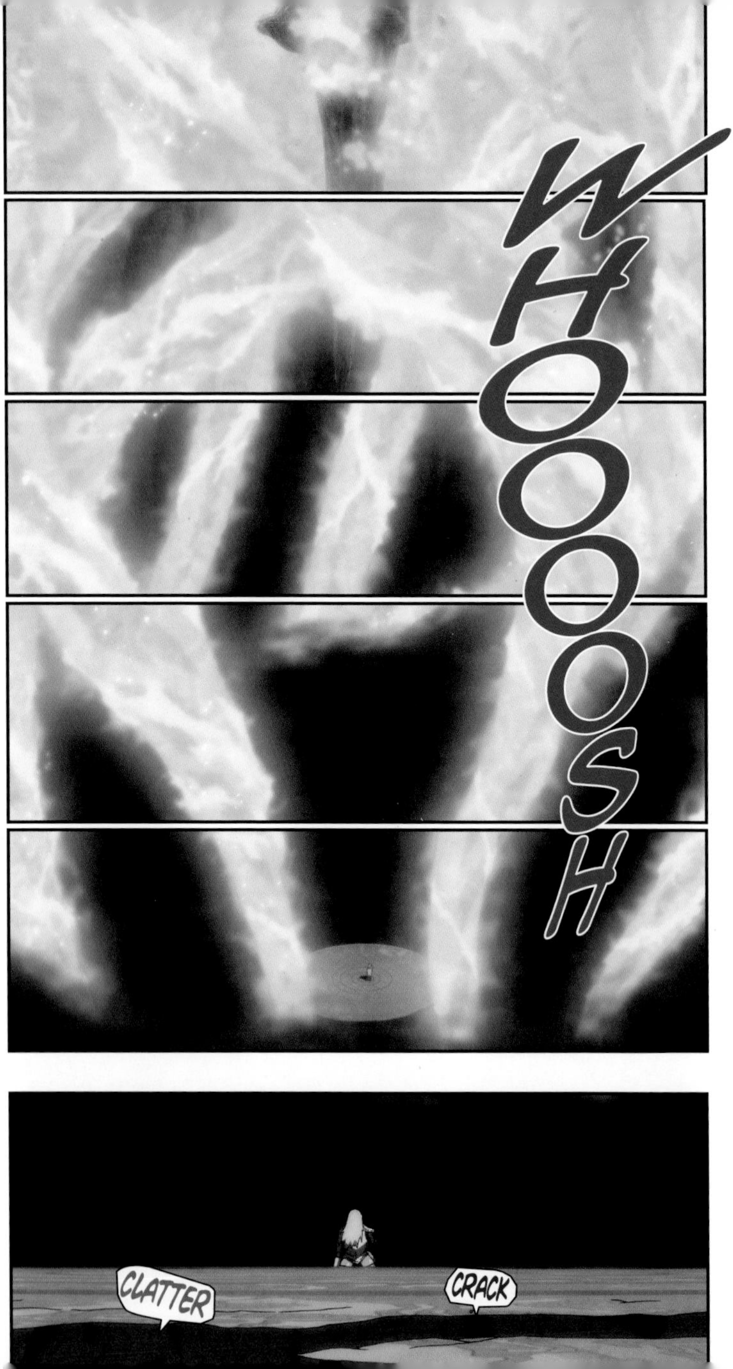
WHOOOOSH
CRACK
CLATTER

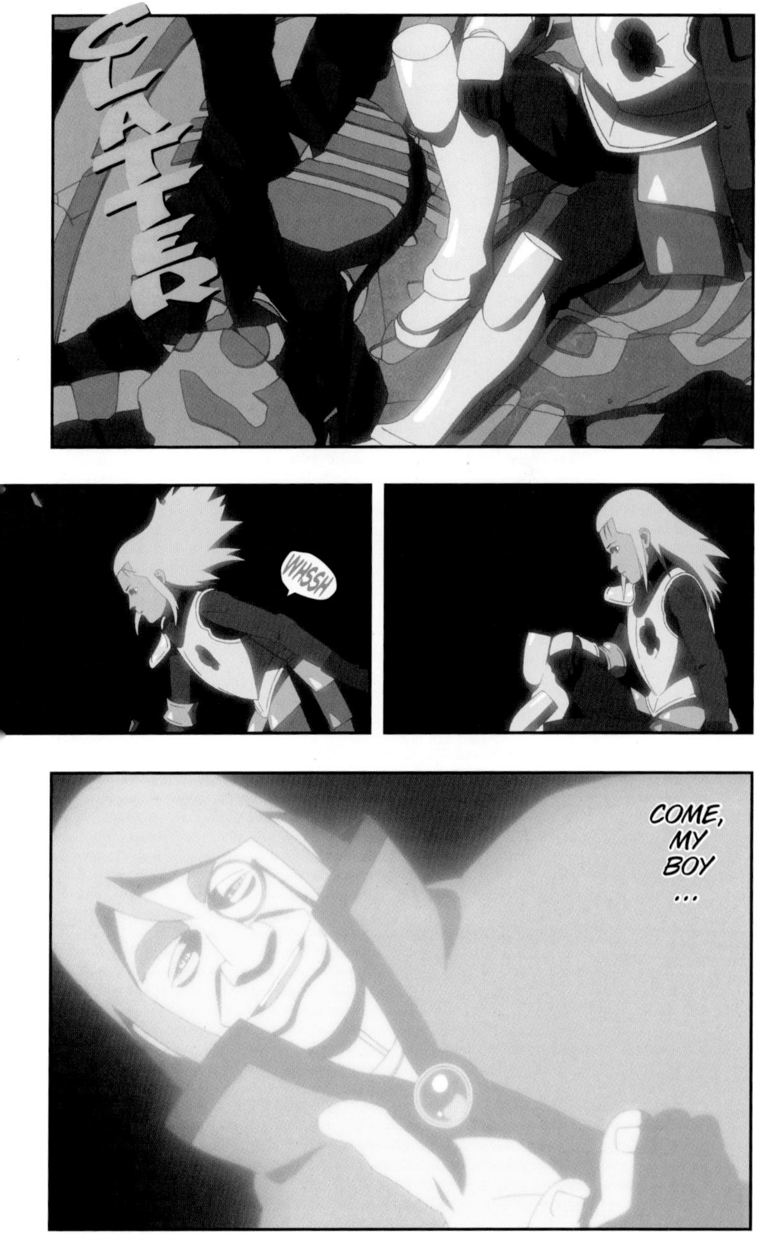
CLATTER
WHSSH
COME, MY BOY ...

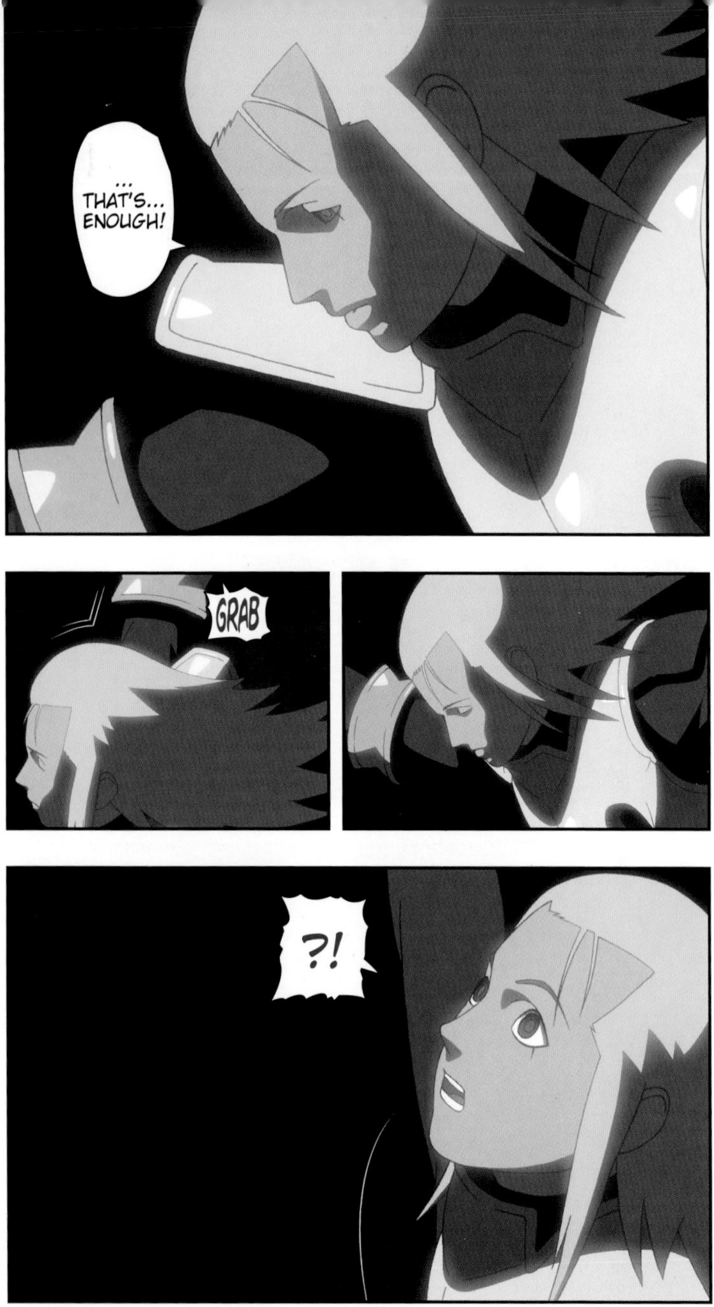
... THAT'S... ENOUGH!
GRAB
?!

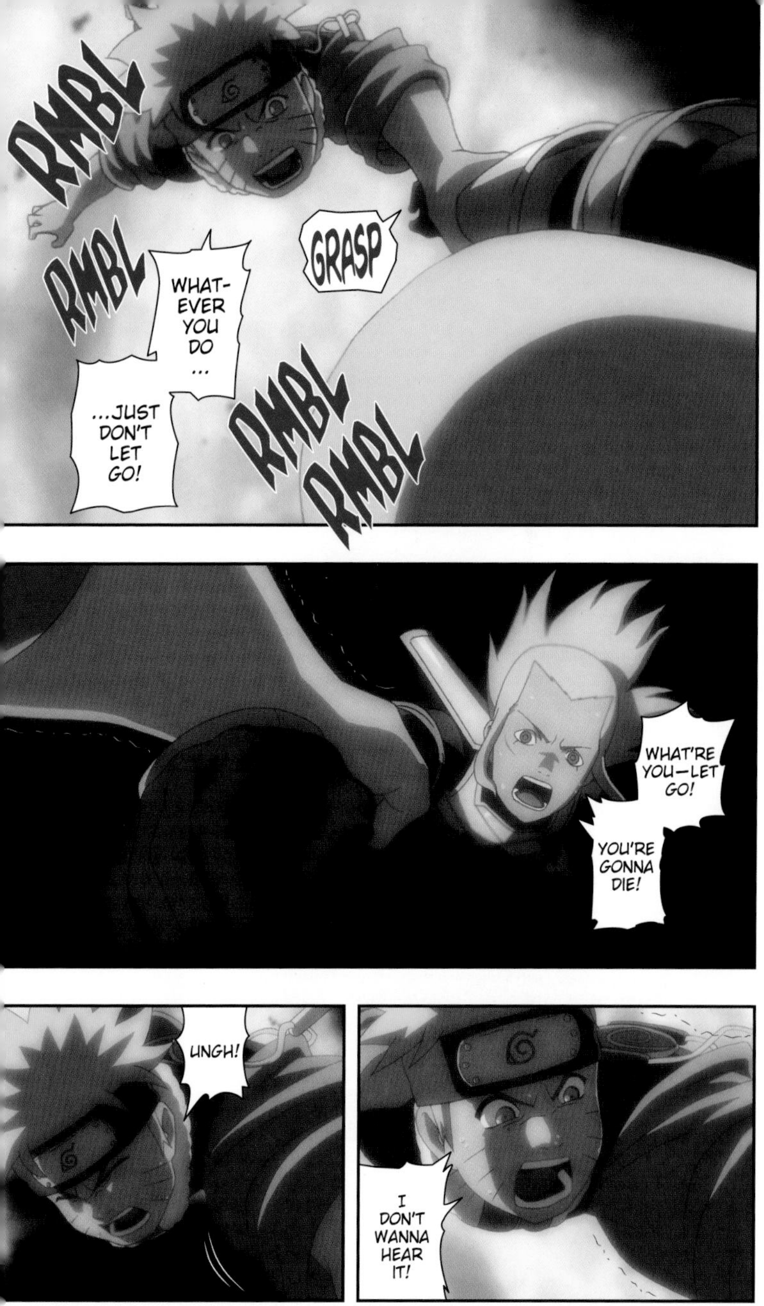
GRASP
WHATEVER YOU DO ...
...JUST DON'T LET GO!
RMBL
RMBL
RMBL RMBL
WHAT'RE YOU—LET GO!
YOU'RE GONNA DIE!
I DON'T WANNA HEAR IT!
UNGH!

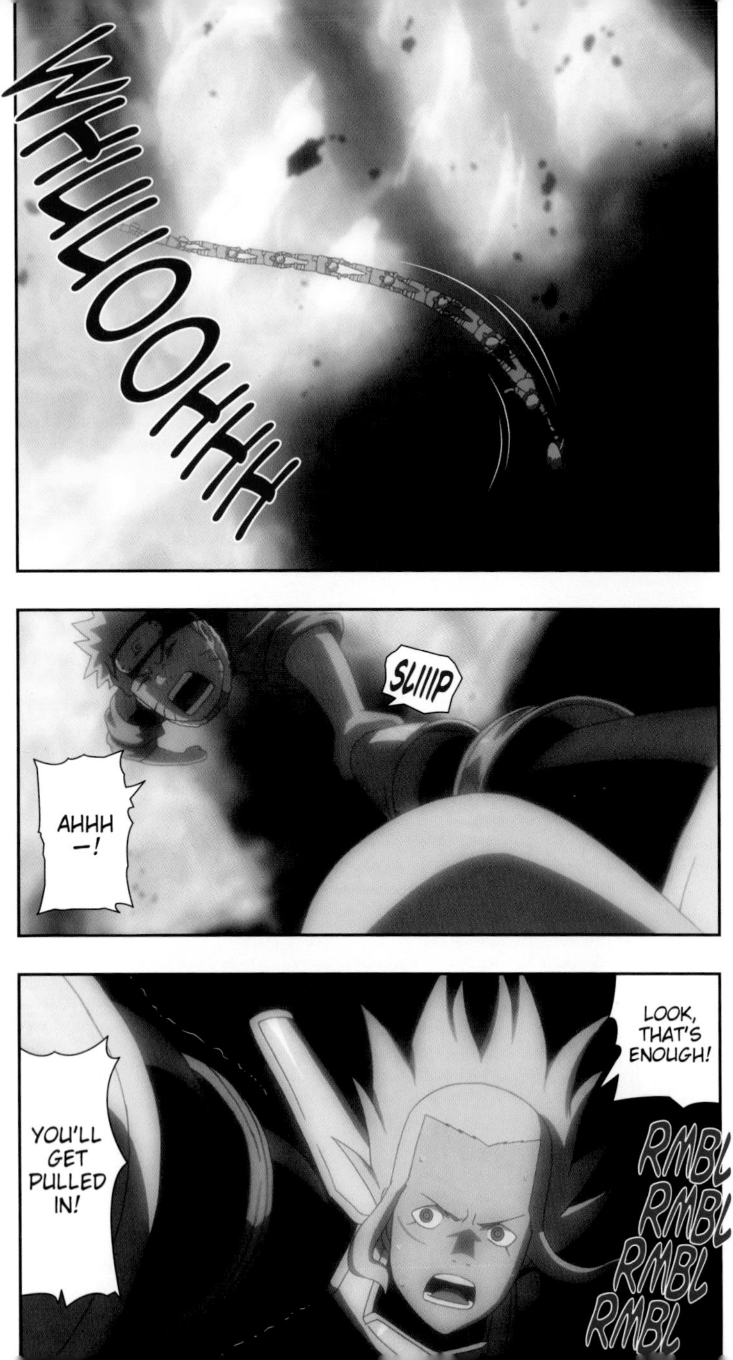
WHUOOHHH
SLIIIP
AHHH—!
LOOK, THAT'S ENOUGH!
RMBL RMBL RMBL RMBL
YOU'LL GET PULLED IN!

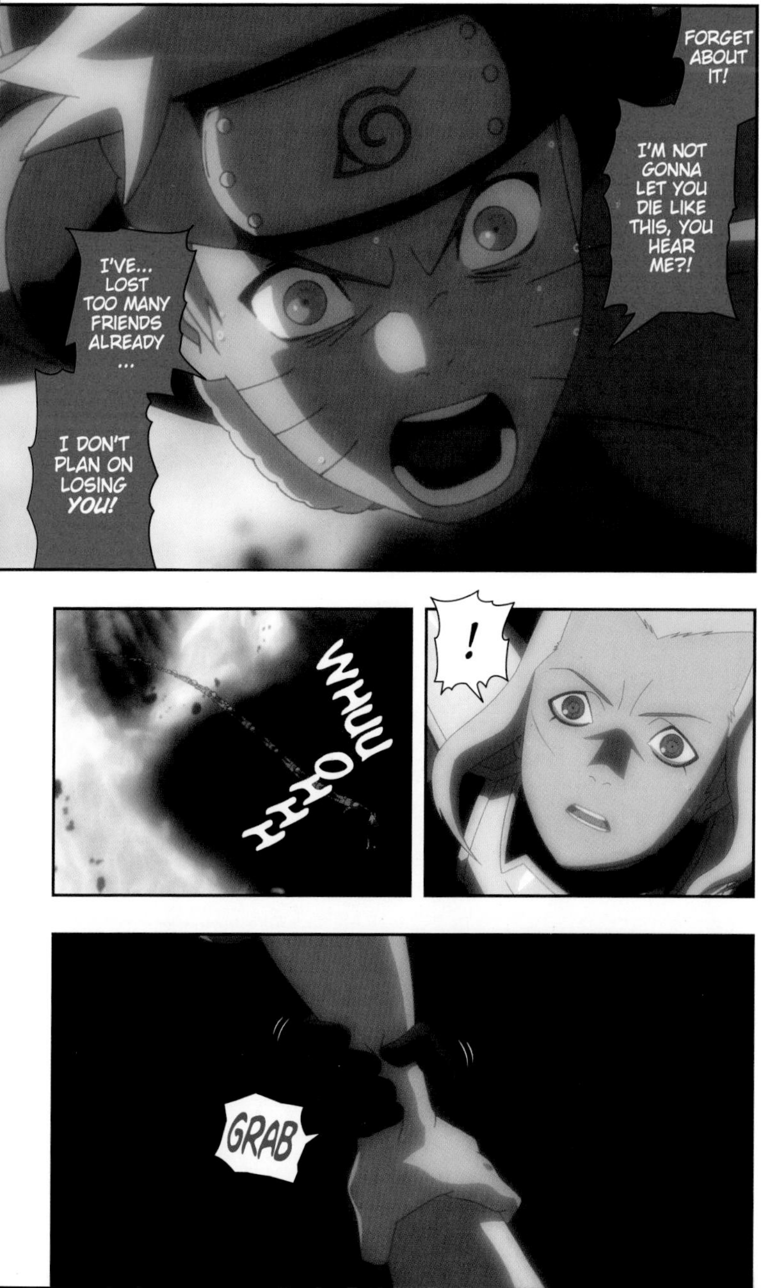
FORGET ABOUT IT!
I'M NOT GONNA LET YOU DIE LIKE THIS, YOU HEAR ME?!
I'VE... LOST TOO MANY FRIENDS ALREADY ...
I DON'T PLAN ON LOSING YOU!
!
GRAB

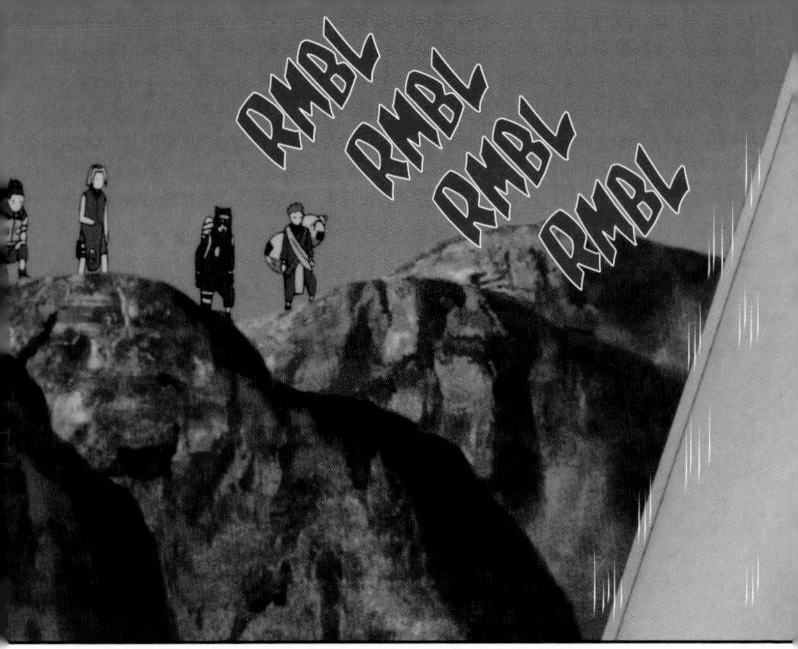
RMBL RMBL RMBL RMBL

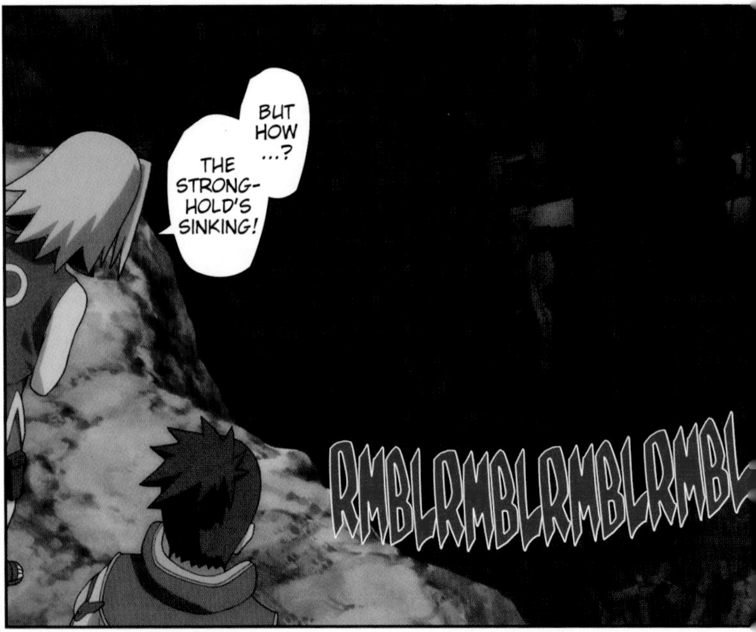
BUT HOW ...?
THE STRONG-HOLD'S SINKING!
RMBLRMBLRMBLRMBL

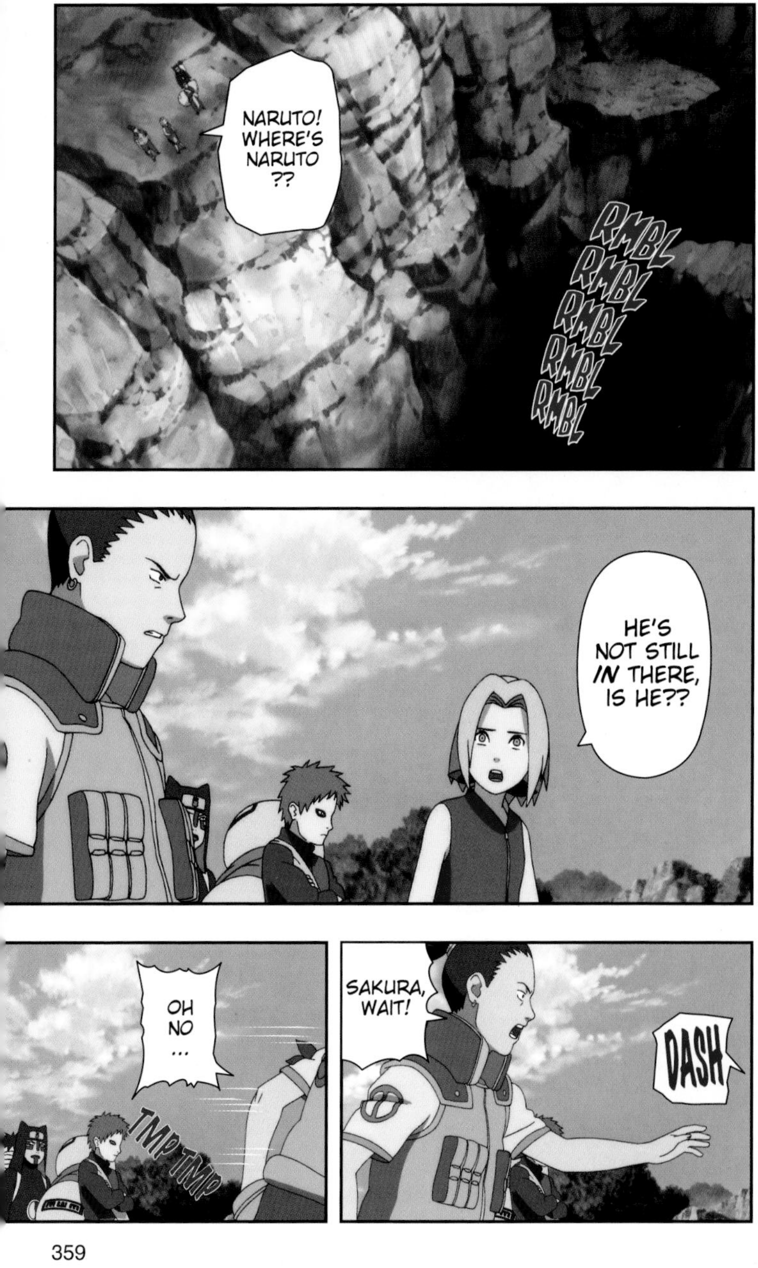
NARUTO! WHERE'S NARUTO ??
RMBL RMBL RMBL RMBL RMBL
HE'S NOT STILL *IN* THERE, IS HE??
SAKURA, WAIT!
DASH
OH NO ...
TMP TMP

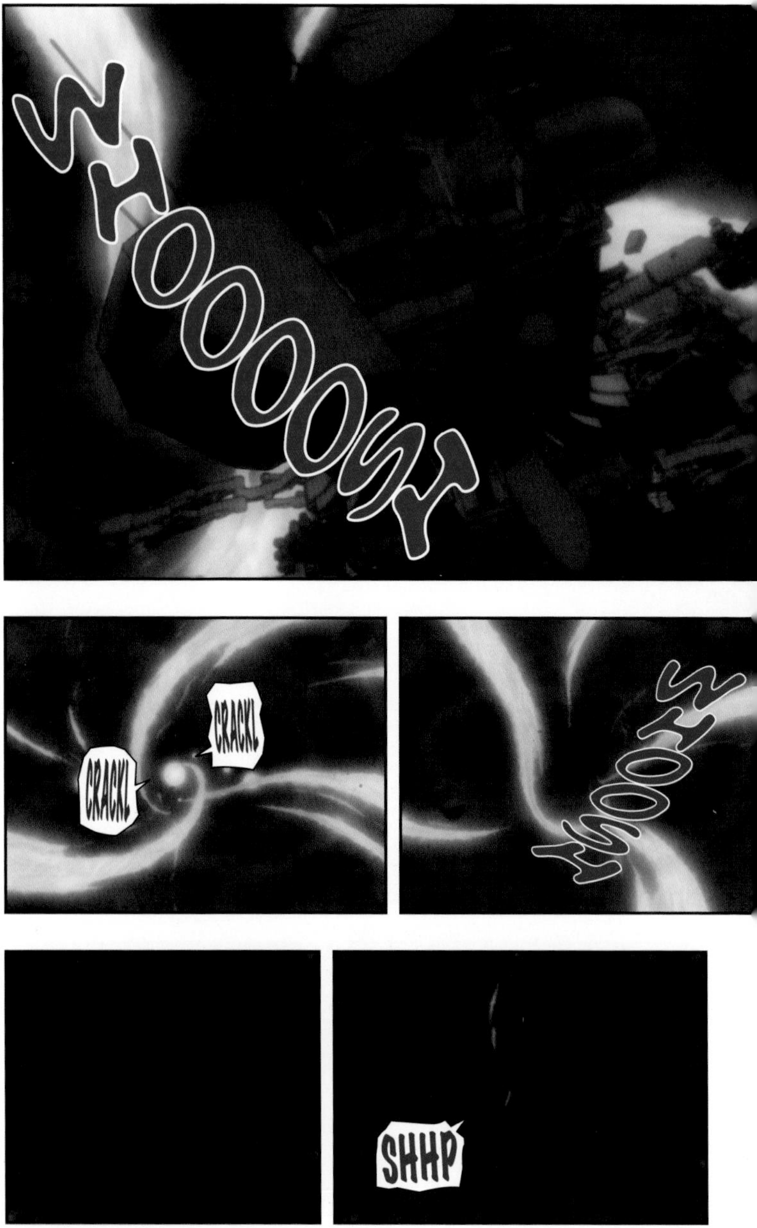
WHOOOOOSH
WHOOSH
CRACKL
CRACKL
SHHP

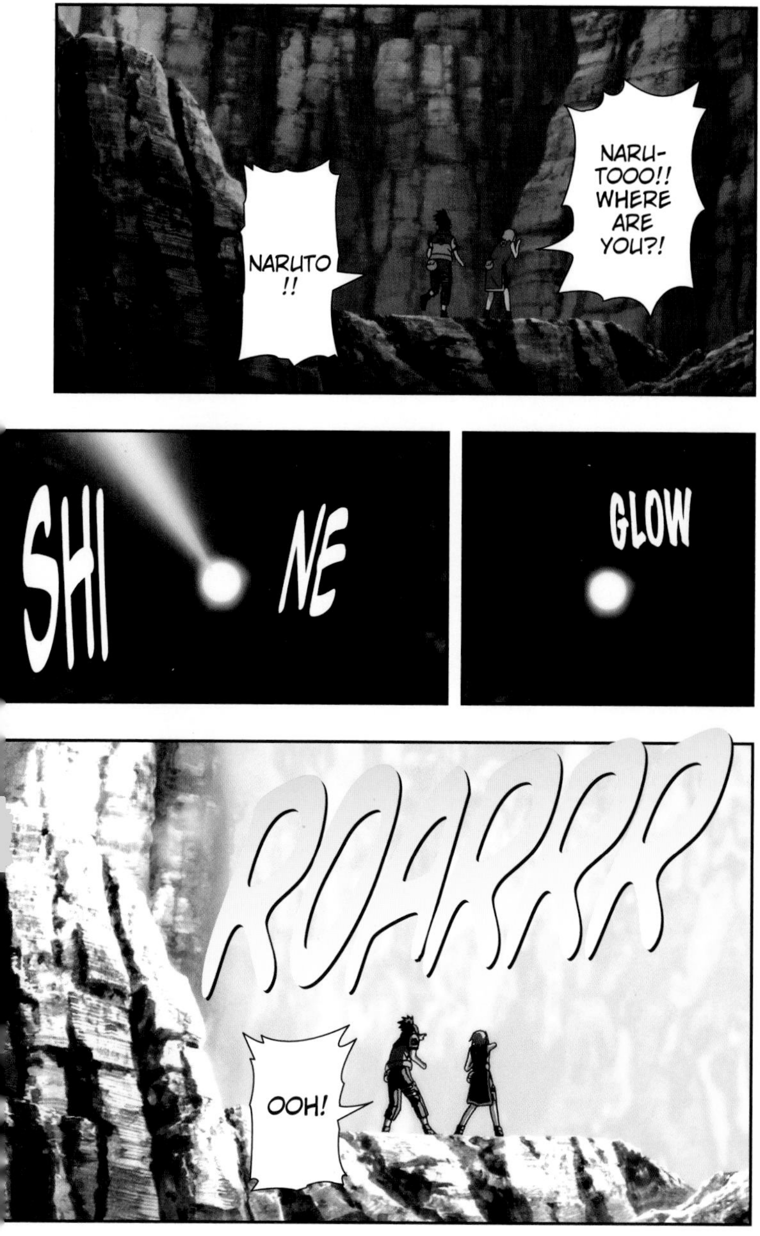
NARU-TOOO!! WHERE ARE YOU?!
NARUTO !!
GLOW
SHI NE
ROARRR
OOH!

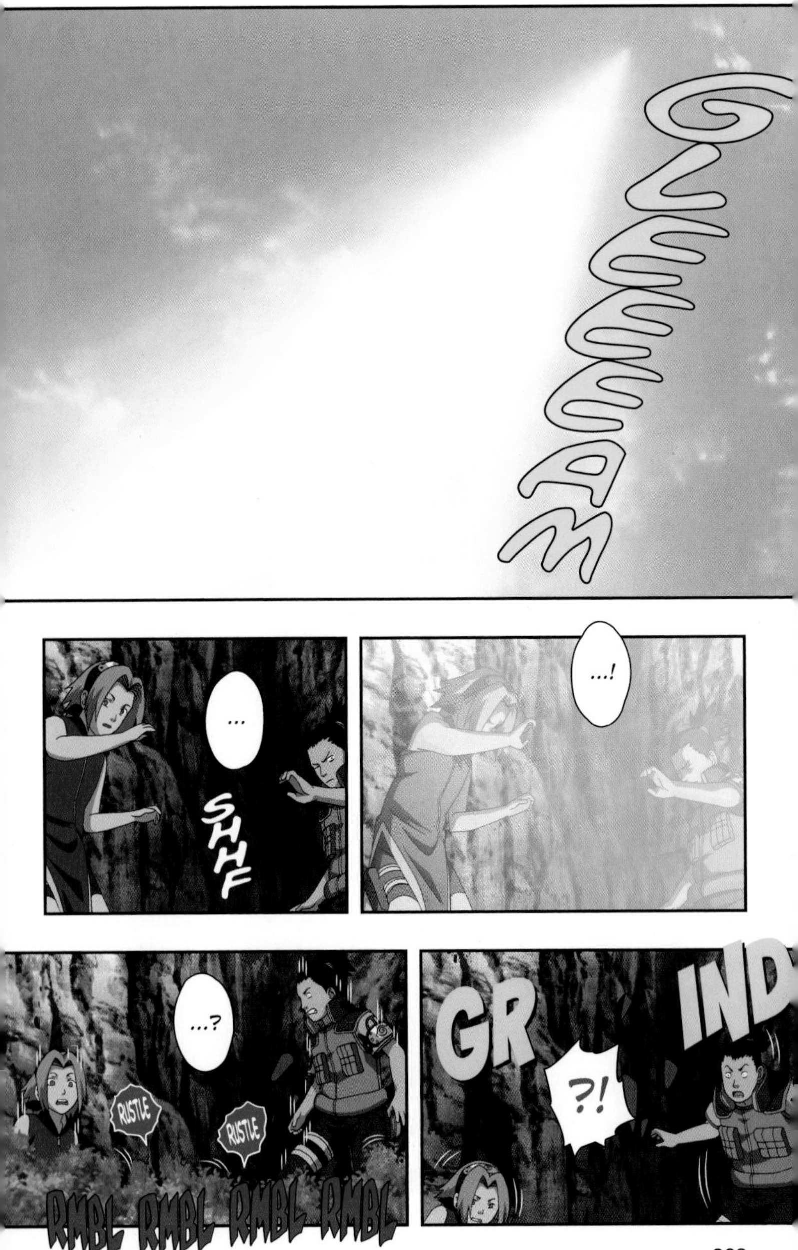
GLEEEEEAM
...!
...
SHHF
GR IND
?!
...?
RUSTLE
RUSTLE
RMBL RMBL RMBL RMBL

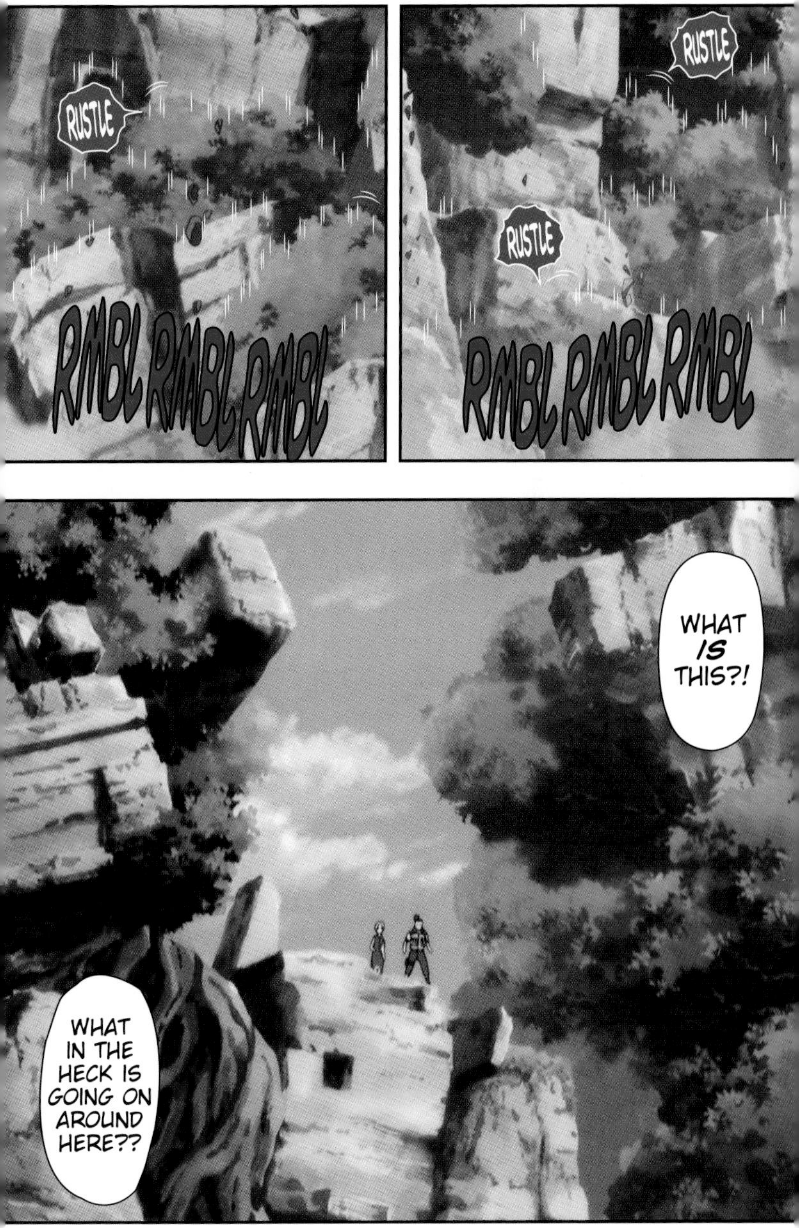
RUSTLE
RUSTLE
RMBL RMBL RMBL
RUSTLE
RMBL RMBL RMBL
WHAT *IS* THIS?!
WHAT IN THE HECK IS GOING ON AROUND HERE??

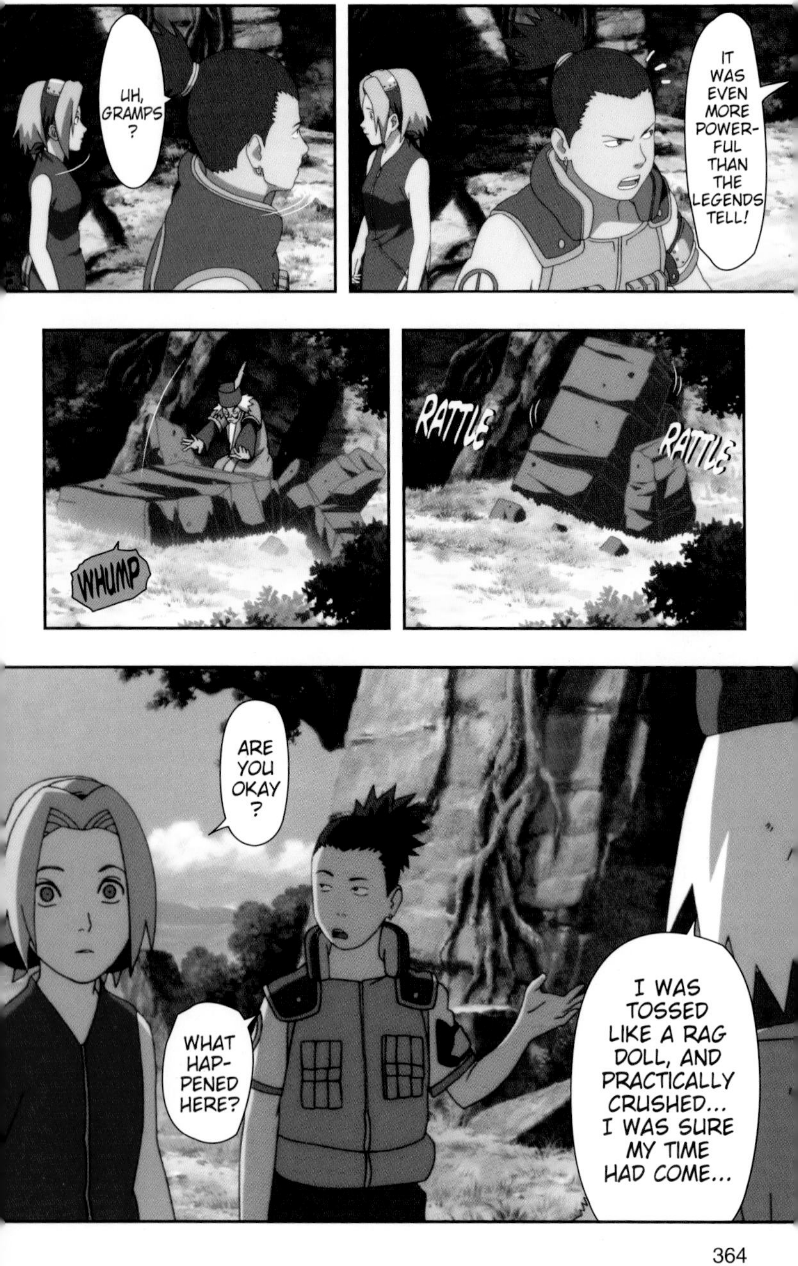
IT WAS EVEN MORE POWER-FUL THAN THE LEGENDS TELL!
UH, GRAMPS?
RATTLE
RATTLE
WHUMP
ARE YOU OKAY?
WHAT HAP-PENED HERE?
I WAS TOSSED LIKE A RAG DOLL, AND PRACTICALLY CRUSHED... I WAS SURE MY TIME HAD COME...

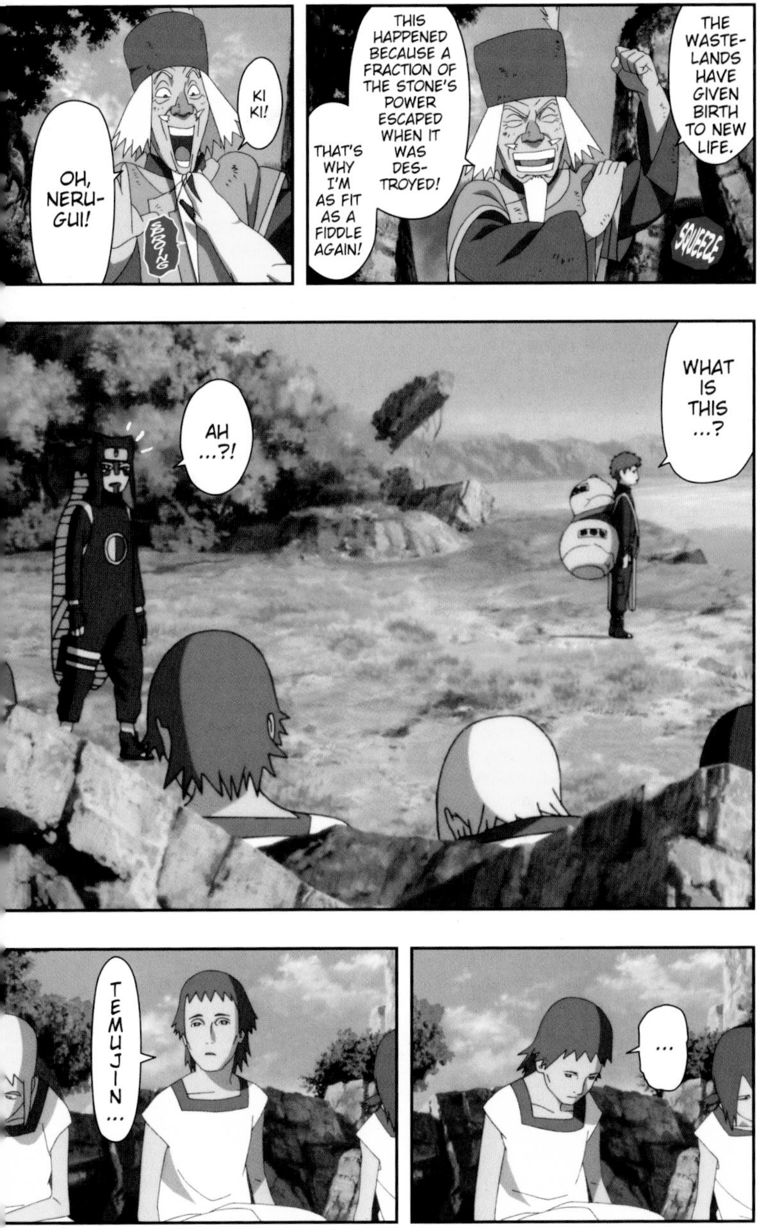

THE WASTE-LANDS HAVE GIVEN BIRTH TO NEW LIFE.
SQUEEZE
THIS HAPPENED BECAUSE A FRACTION OF THE STONE'S POWER ESCAPED WHEN IT WAS DES-TROYED!
THAT'S WHY I'M AS FIT AS A FIDDLE AGAIN!
KI KI!
OH, NERU-GUI!
SPROING
WHAT IS THIS ...?
AH ...?!
...
TEMUJIN ...

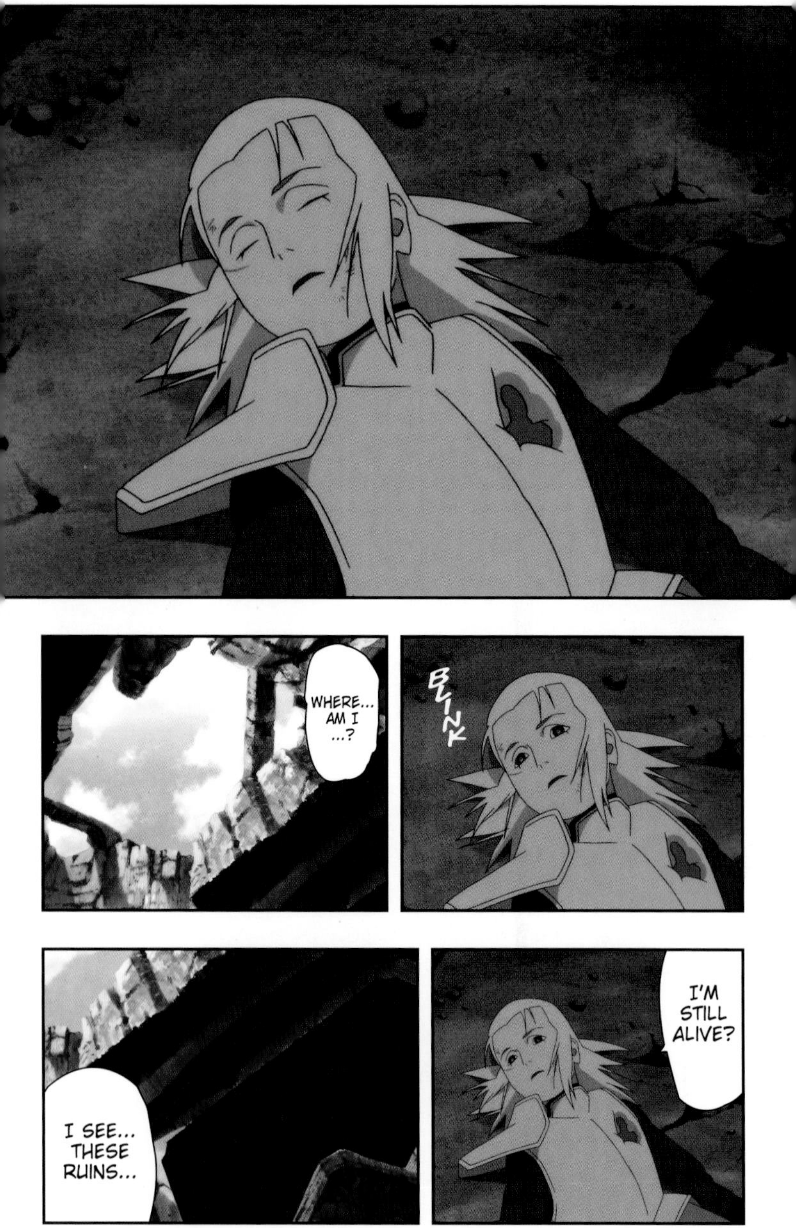
BLINK
WHERE... AM I ...?
I'M STILL ALIVE?
I SEE... THESE RUINS...

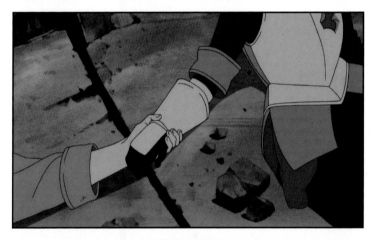

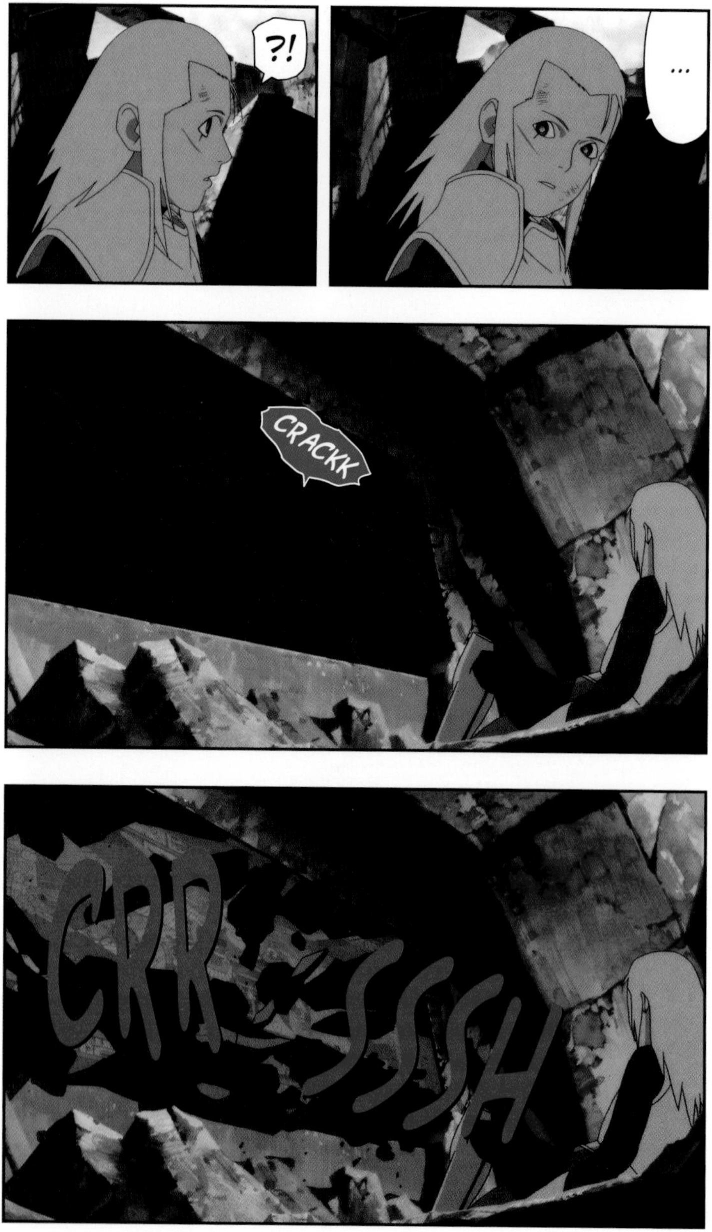
...
?!
CRACKK
CRRSSSH

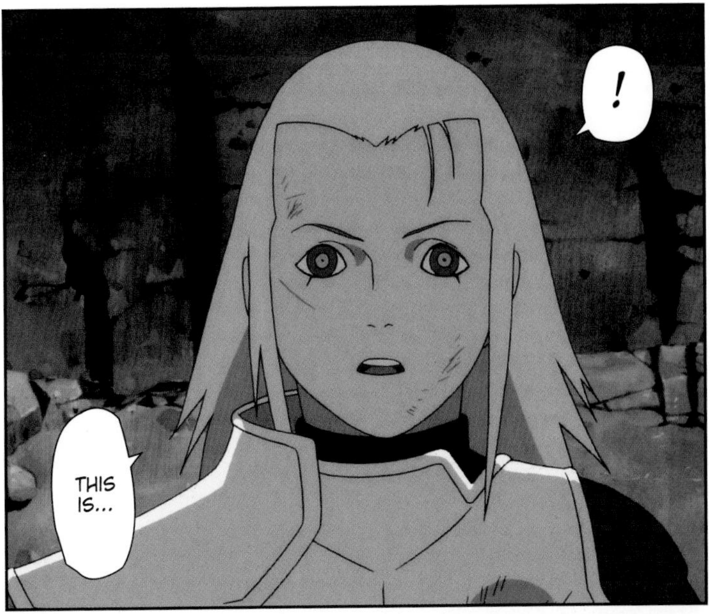
!
THIS IS...

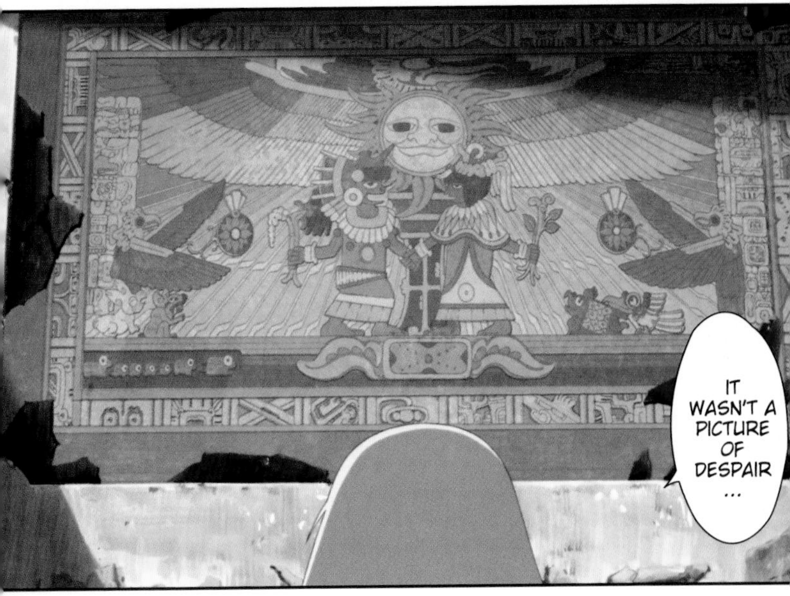
IT WASN'T A PICTURE OF DESPAIR ...

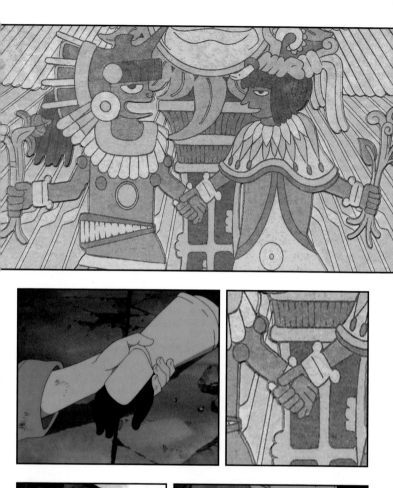

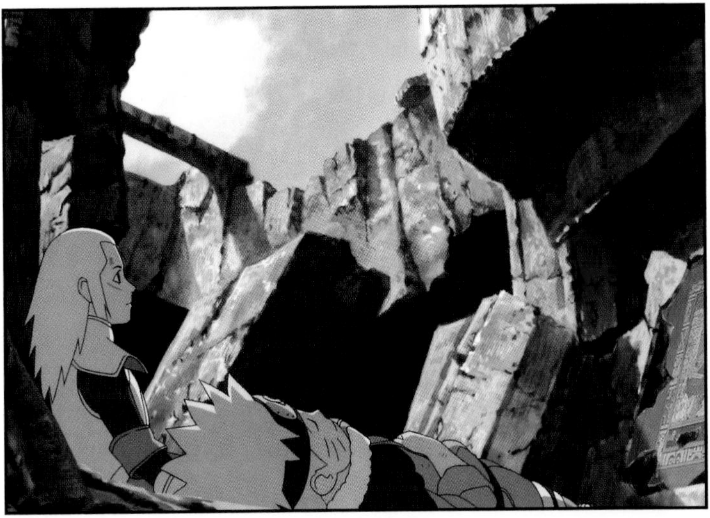

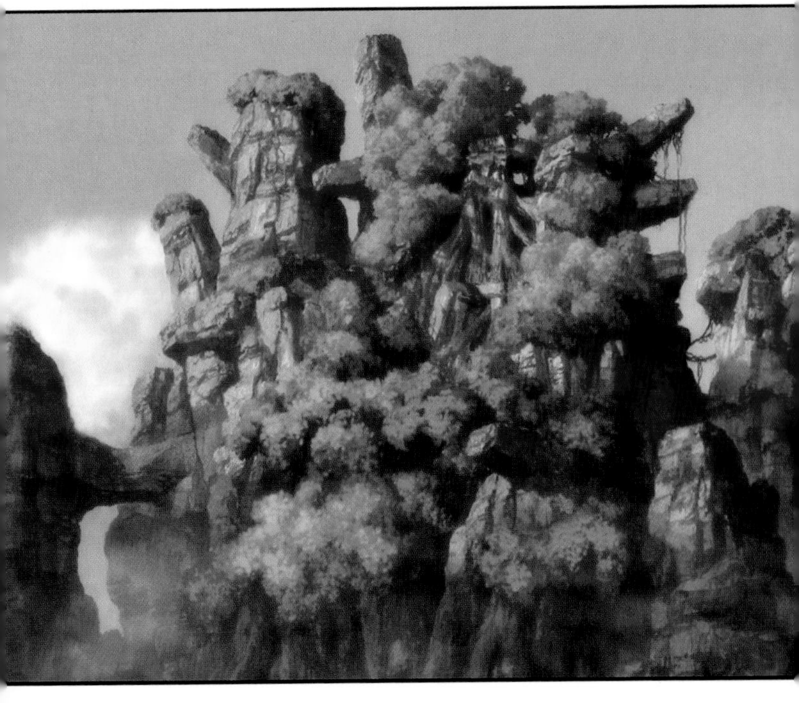

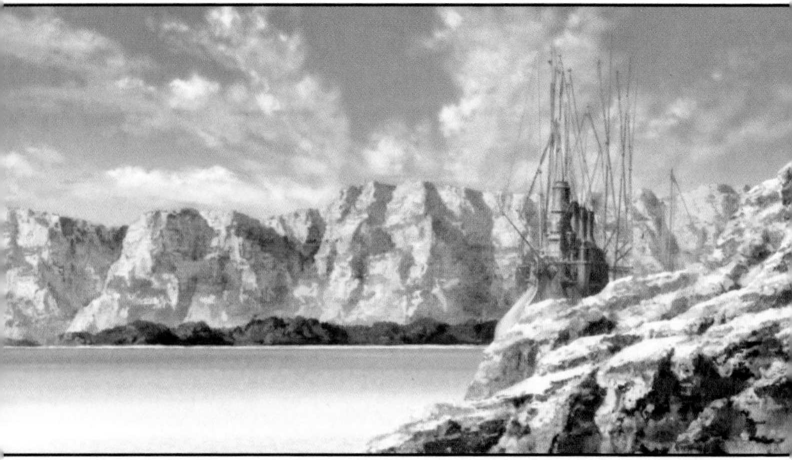

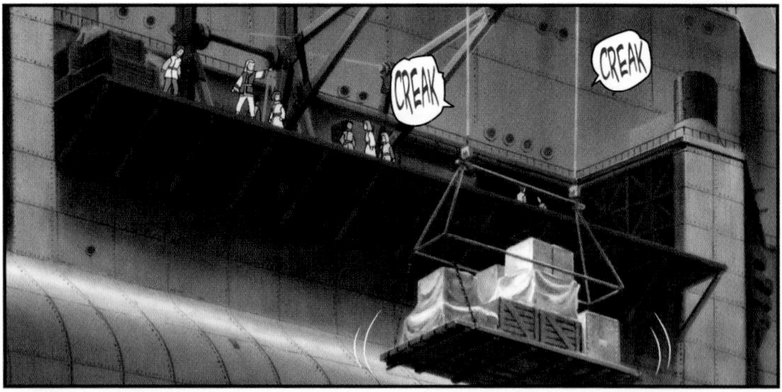
CREAK
CREAK

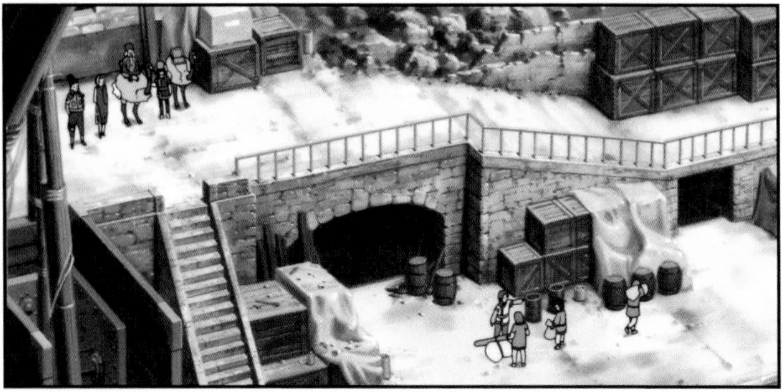

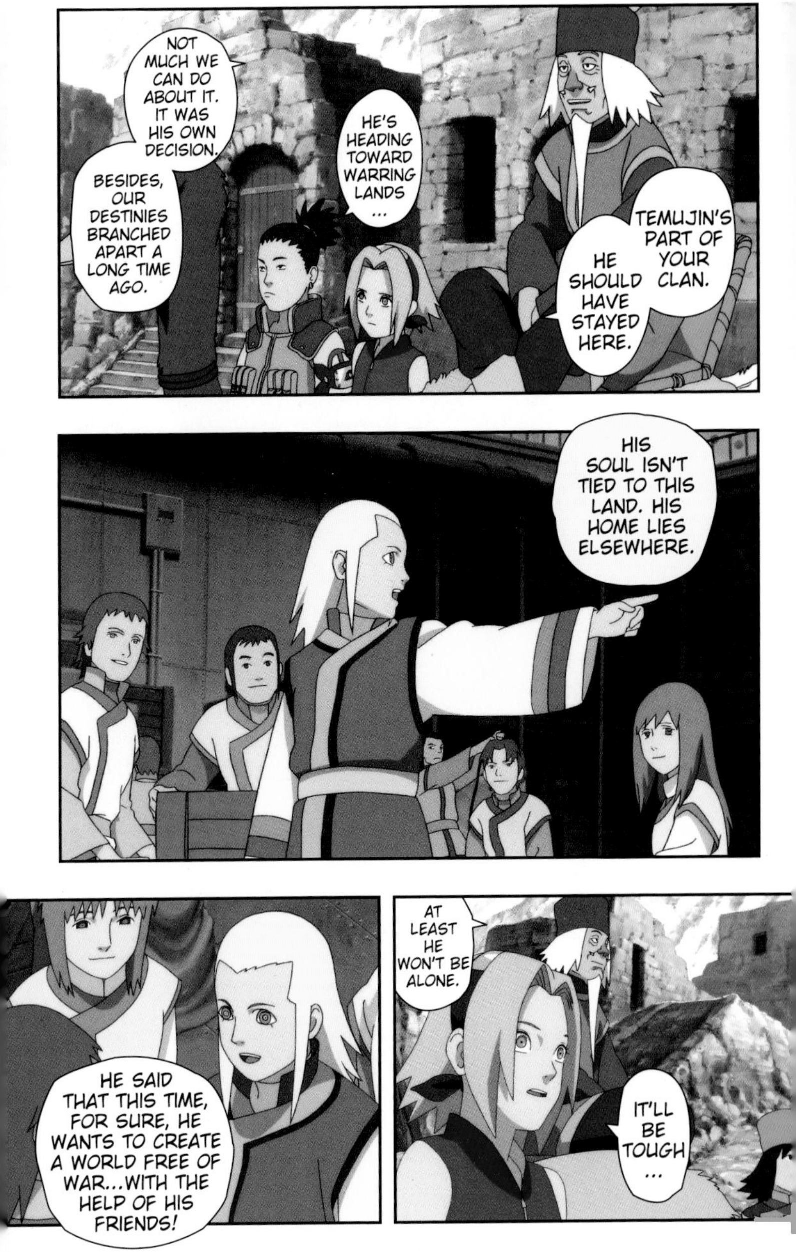
TEMUJIN'S PART OF YOUR CLAN. HE SHOULD HAVE STAYED HERE.
HE'S HEADING TOWARD WARRING LANDS ...
NOT MUCH WE CAN DO ABOUT IT. IT WAS HIS OWN DECISION.
BESIDES, OUR DESTINIES BRANCHED APART A LONG TIME AGO.
HIS SOUL ISN'T TIED TO THIS LAND. HIS HOME LIES ELSEWHERE.
AT LEAST HE WON'T BE ALONE.
IT'LL BE TOUGH ...
HE SAID THAT THIS TIME, FOR SURE, HE WANTS TO CREATE A WORLD FREE OF WAR...WITH THE HELP OF HIS FRIENDS!

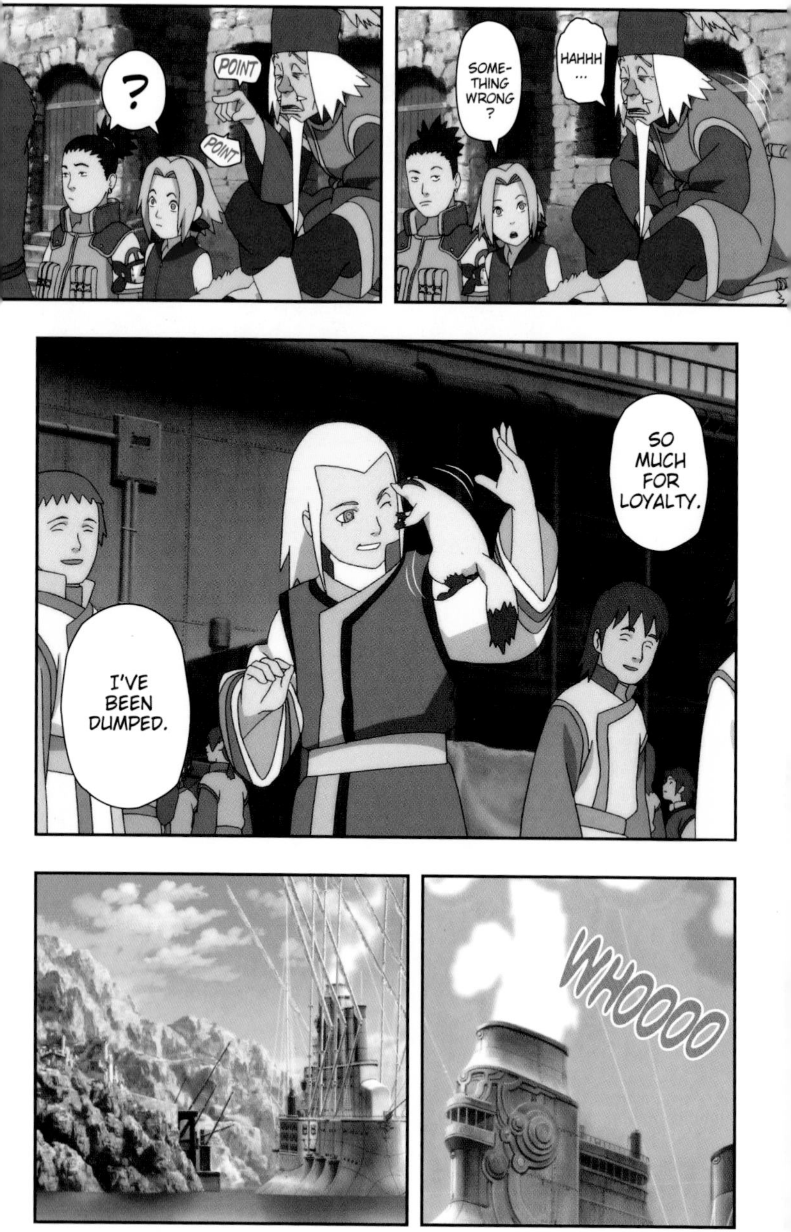
HAHHH ...
SOME-THING WRONG ?
POINT
?
POINT
SO MUCH FOR LOYALTY.
I'VE BEEN DUMPED.
WHOOOO

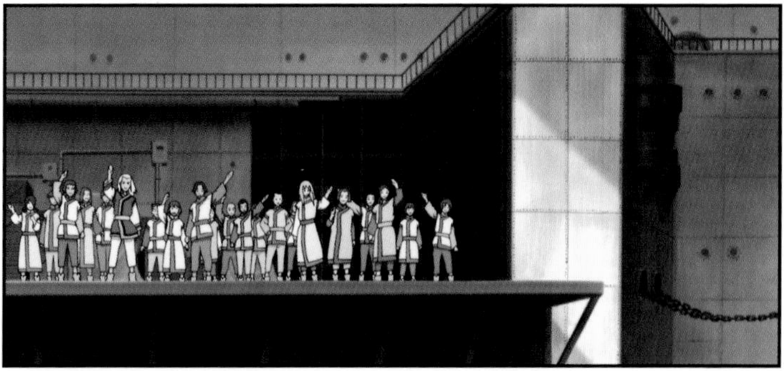

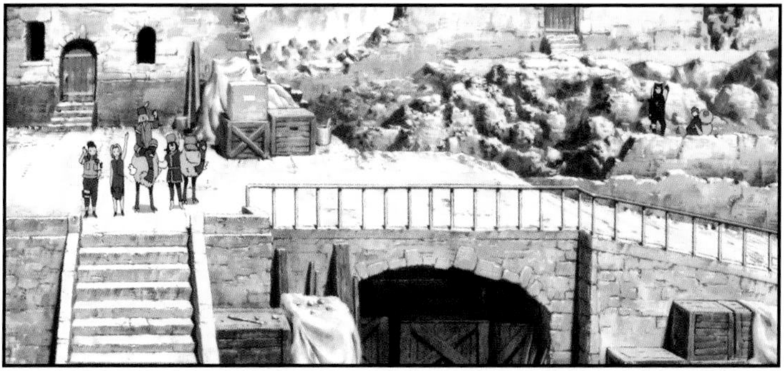

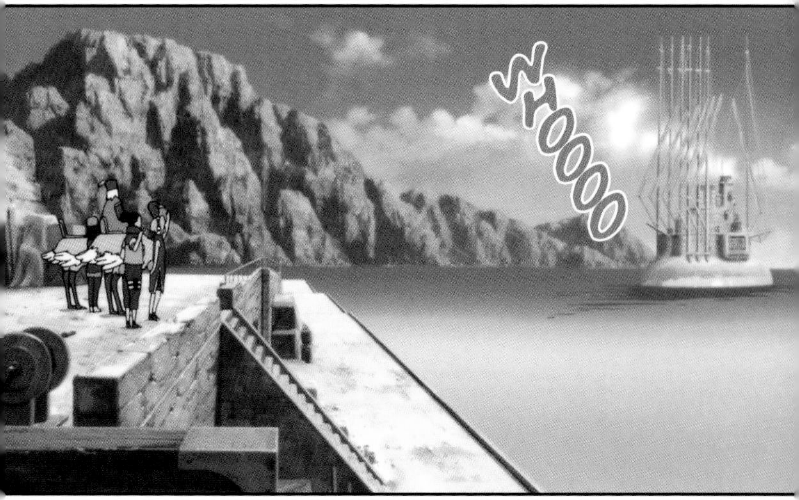
WHOOOO

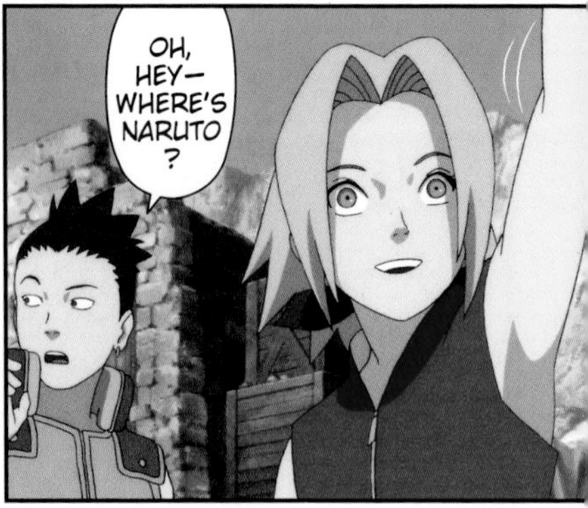
OH, HEY— WHERE'S NARUTO ?

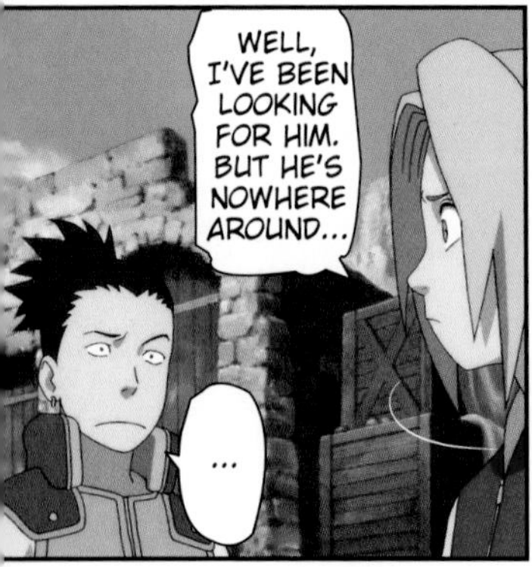
WELL, I'VE BEEN LOOKING FOR HIM. BUT HE'S NOWHERE AROUND...
...

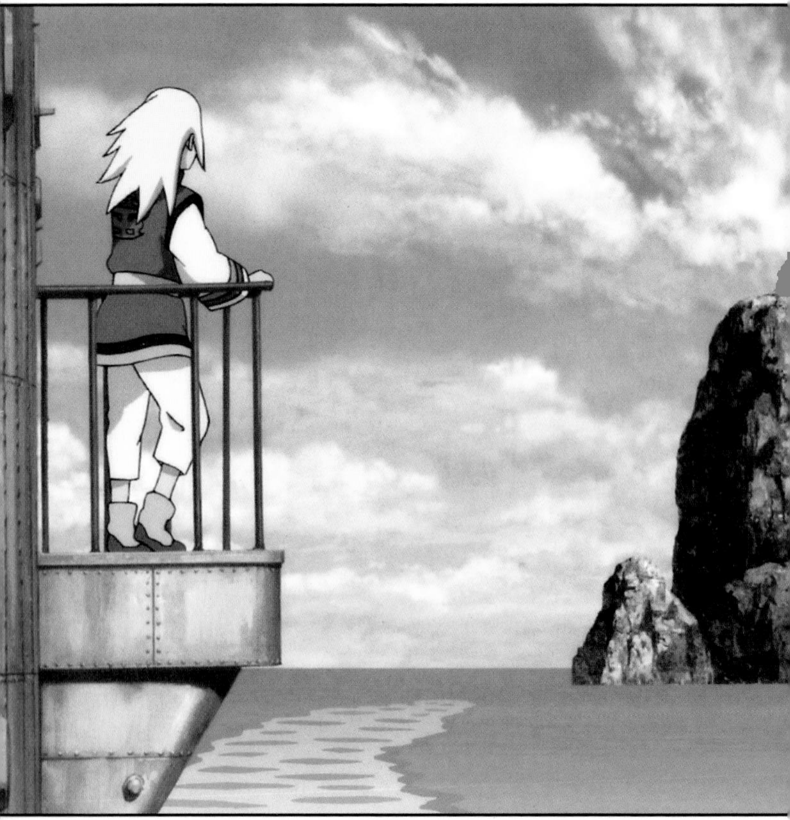

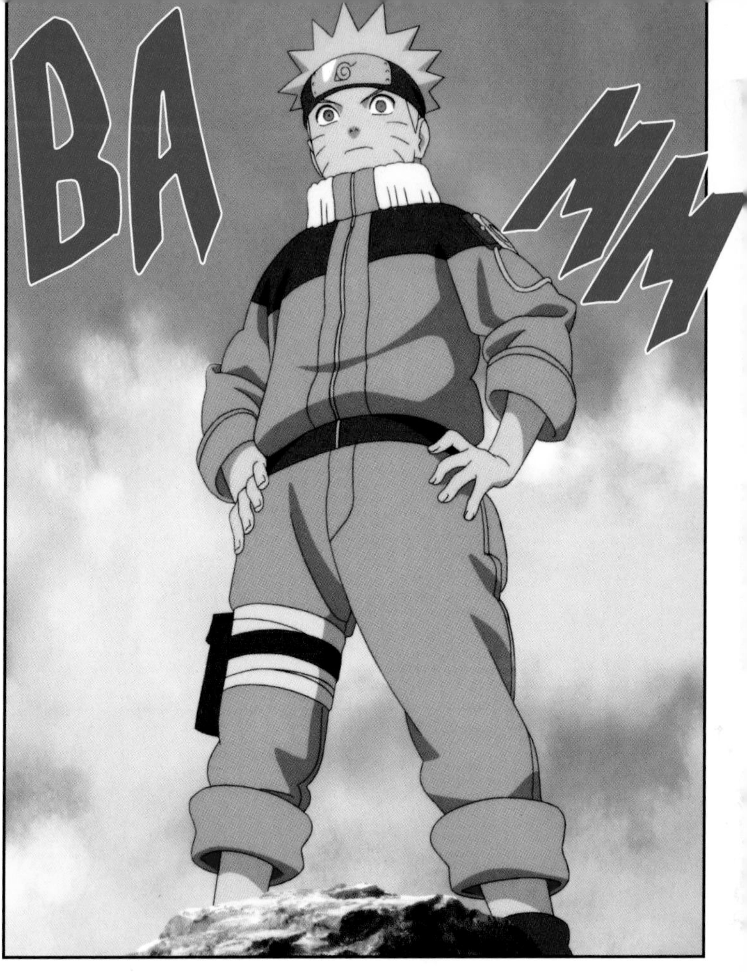
BA
MM

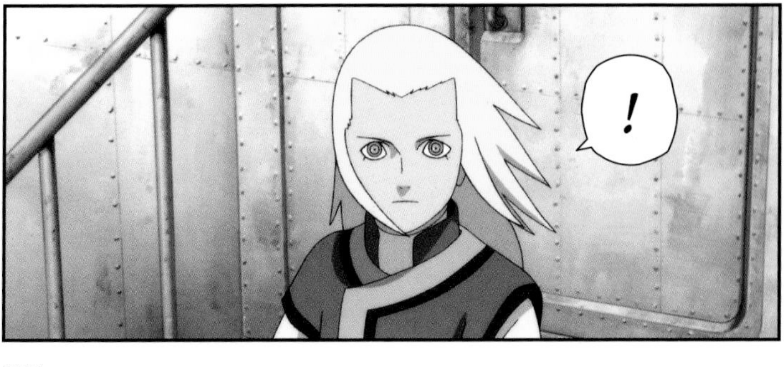
!

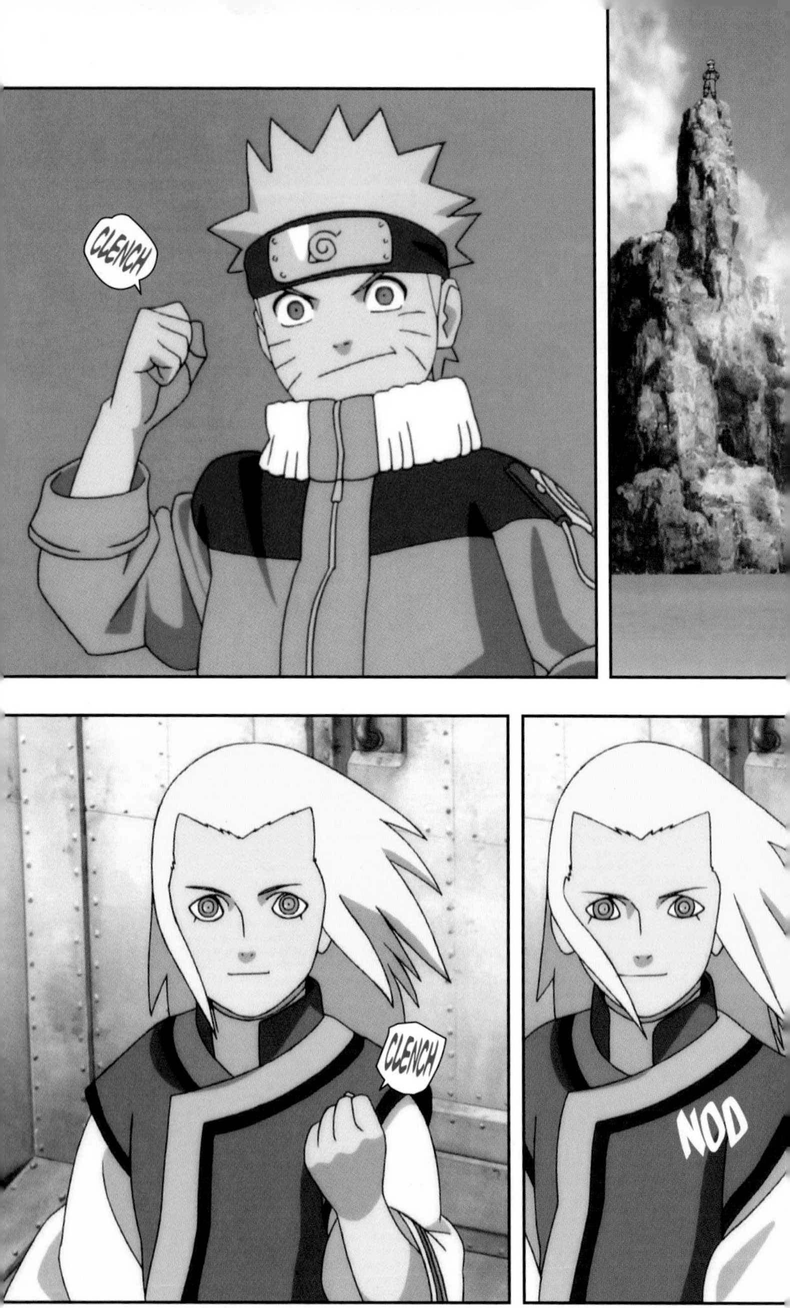
CLENCH
NOD
CLENCH

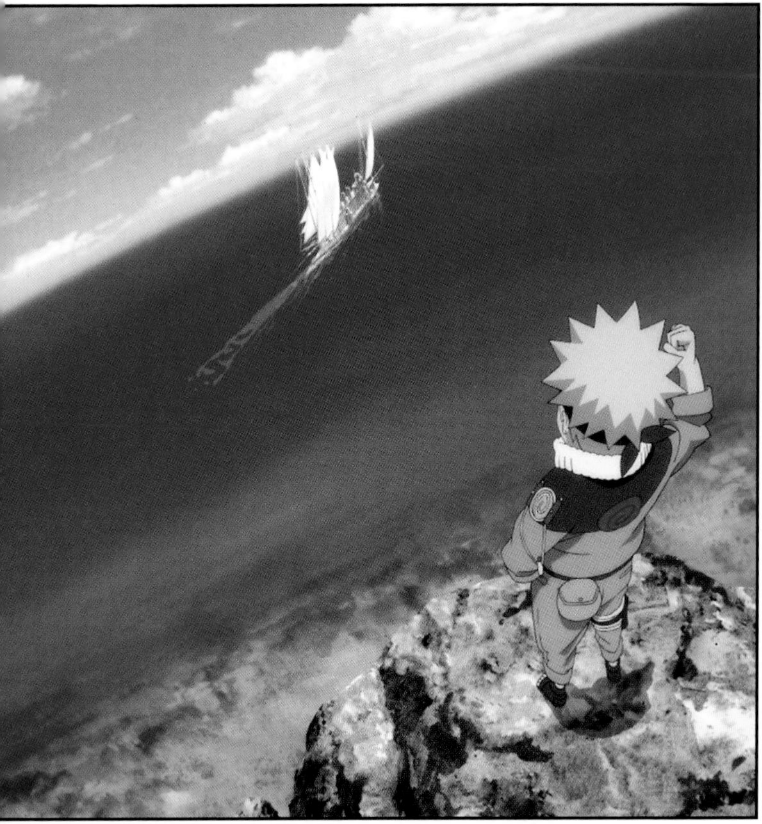

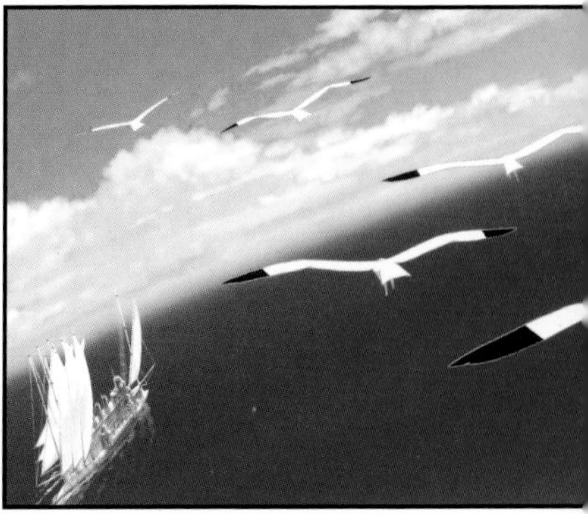

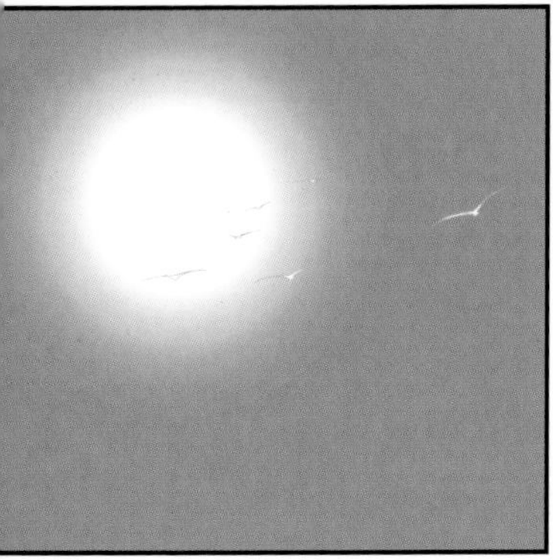

The End

ATSUSHI SATO
KAZUYA SUGIYAMA
TAISUKE YANAGISAWA
HIROKO MOMOTAKE
MAKOTO USAMI
REINA KANEKO
TOMONARI NAKAJIMA
YASUMITSU SUETAKE

HD24P Editing
Sony PCL
TOMOMI TAKEMURA
DAISUKE TSUKIOKA

HD Conversion
Sony PCL
TAKASHI KONO
HIKARU OOTSUKI

HD Coordination
Dinext
HIDEKI ITO

CMS Technical Supervisor
HIDEO MORITA

CMS Supervisor
TADASHI NAKAMURA
CMS Technician
ATSUHIKO TANAKA

Film Recording
TOKYO LABORATORY
LTD

Films
Kodak

Sound Effects
TAKUYA HASEGAWA
(SOUND BOX)

Sound Engineer
AKIRA NOGUCHI
(sound team •
DON JUAN)
The Tokyo Television
Center Co., Ltd.
EIJI HOTTA
MICHIHIKO IWANA
FUTOSHI UEDA

MA Studio
The Tokyo Television
Center Co., Ltd.

Sound Production
RAKUONSHA

Sound Producer
MASAHIRO TSUKADA

Digital Recording Engineer
NOBORU NISHIO

Theme Song
[Ding! Dong! Dang!]
Song by
TUBE
Lyrics by
NOBUTERU MAEDA
Composed by
MICHIYA HARUHATA
Arranged by
TUBE
(Sony Music Associated
Records Inc.)

Theme Song Promotion
JUNICHI SUGAWARA
SHINJI OZAWA
SYUICHIRO IMAIZUMI
TADAHITO KIMURA

Music Producers
MASAYUKI WATANABE
AI ABE

Recording Engineers
HITOSHI HASHIMOTO
JUNICHIRO OJIMA

Surround Mixing
Engineers
HITOSHI HASHIMOTO

Assistant Mixing Engineers
HIROMI SHINJOH
TETSUYA KANESHIGE
TOSHIHIKO KASAI
TAKASHI OHIZUMI

<MUSASHI Members>
Music Producers
KATSUNOSUKE
KOBARI
EMIKO OOIWA
HIROYUKI SAWANO
Japanese Drums
TAKARA OOTSUKA
Shamisen Guitar
HAJIME NISHI
Shakuhachi, Noukan, Flute
KINOHACHI
Guitar
MASAAKI IIZUKA
6 String Bass Guitar
ISAMU TAKITA
Drums
TAKEKI MIYAUCHI
Keyboard
YASUHARU TAKANASHI

Music Cooperation
TV TOKYO MUSIC

CONTINENTAL FAR
EAST INC.
TSUTOMU
KAWAHIGASHI

Assistant Voice Directors
AYAKO TERUI
KOJI ARITOMI

Assistant Animation
Producer
SYOJI MATSUI

Floor Coordinator
KUNIYUKI AOKI

Production Chief
SHIGEHIRO SUZUKI

Production Desk Manager
SHINYA KAWABATA
KAZUKI HIRAKAWA

Production Coordinators
MIKI KUROSAKA
KOICHI MACHIYAMA
TAKAHIRO NATORI
YUTA KIMURA
YUKIKO KUGIMIYA
NOZOMI KIKUCHI

Production Cooperation
MADHOUSE
MASAO MOROSAWA
YUTA HATTORI
TORU UMEOKA

DOGA KOBO
TATSUKO FUKUDO
MORITA EDITING
STUDIO
NANAE HAYASHI

JEONG HAENG GUEON
JOUNG SE KWON
JEONG GYUN JEONG

Acting Assistant
NAGI & RAKU (ferret)

Production
SYOHEI IZAWA
NORITAKA YAMAJI
YUJI NUNOKAWA
YOSHISHIGE
SHIMATANI
SHIGEKAZU TAKEUCHI
SOUICHI AKIYAMA
ATSUSHI TAKEUCHI

Project Cooperation
KEISUKE IWATA
KAZUHIKO TORISHIMA
MICHIYUKI HONMA
KEN HAGINO

Producers
NORIKO KOBAYASHI
KAZUTERU OSHIKIRI

Project Cooperation
SHUEISHA/SHONEN
JUMP
MASAHIKO IBARAKI
MASANA TAKAHASHI
KOSUKE YAHAGI

Associate Producers
YUKAKO MATSUSAKO
TAKASHI HARADA
TAKUYUKI HIROBE
MASATO TAKAMI
KAZUMICHI UEDA
YUKIO YOSHIMURA
TAIHEI YAMANISHI

Marketing Producer
MASAKI NAKAYAMA

Marketing Coordinators
AKITO TAKAHASHI
NOBUHIRO FUKUDA
SAYAKA ONO

Movie Trailer Producer
MASAYUKI OHHIRA

Movie Trailer Director
DAISUKE FUKUNAGA

Naruto Movie Project
TV TOKYO
TETSUO NAKAO
HARUYUKI IGUCHI

SHUEISHA
TSUNEO OYAMA
KENICHIRO USHIKI

PIERROT
HIROMICHI UCHIDA
MIKIO IGARASHI
KOTA KITAMURA
EMIKO YAKAME

TOHO
KAZUHIKO SETA
GENKI KAWAMURA

Aniplex
HIDEO KATSUMATA
YUUKI HOSHIJIMA
OSAMU TAKESUE
KAZUKO YAMAMOTO

Dentsu
RIICHITO NAKAMURA
ATSUSHI HIGASHIYAMA

BANDAI
KEISUKE FURUSAWA
CHUYA ISHIDA

Sponsored by
TOMY
SHIRYO OKUAKI
MASAYA SAWADA
HITOSHI NOMURA

ENSKY
KOICHI SOMEYA
HIRONOBU KAMADA

SHOWA NOTE
SHIGERU KATAGISHI
TOMIO HIGANO
MAMIKO ABE

MOVIC
MASAKI YASUDA
TOSHIHIKO SUZUKI

Cooperation
FAMILYMART
famima.com

SHINYOKOHAMA
RAUMEN MUSEUM
ANRAKUTEI

Animation Production
studio
PIERROT

Distributed by
TOHO

Produced by
Naruto Movie Project
TV TOKYO
SHUEISHA
PIERROT
TOHO
Aniplex
dentsu
BANDAI

CARD 14
Director
HIROTSUGU
KAWASAKI

CARD 15
© 2002 MASASHI
KISHIMOTO © NMP
2005
English Production By
VIZ Media, LLC

Executive Producers
HIDEMI FUKUHARA
AKIRA FUJITA

Producer
JAMIE SIMONE

Production Supervisors
ALVIN LU
WILLIAM GERMAIN

Co-Producers
JASON BERGENFELD
MIKI MACALUSO

Associate Producer
MITSUKO KITAJIMA

Music Coordinator
WILLIAM GERMAIN

Creative Consultant
JOEL ENOS

Distributed By
VIZ Media, LLC

Casting By
JAMIE SIMONE

Voice Director
MARY ELIZABETH
MCGLYNN

Cast:
MAILE FLANAGAN
KATE HIGGINS
TOM GIBIS
ROGER CRAIG SMITH
DOUGLAS RYE
MICHELLE RUFF
MONA MARSHALL
JENNIER HALE
LIAM O'BRIEN
CRISPIN FREEMAN
STEVE BLUM
KEITH SILVERSTEIN
KYLE HEBERT
KARI WALGREN
MICHAEL LINDSAY
MEGAN
HOLLINGSHEAD
SAM RIEGEL

Post Production
Supervisor
DENNY DENSMORE

Video Editor
TERRY MARLIN
LINDSEY MYERS

Additional Video
Compositing
DAVID BUTTERWORTH

Recording Engineer
DAVID W. BARR
ERIC LEWIS

English Adaptation By
LIAM O'BRIEN

Re-Recording Mixer
MARK ETTEL C.S.A.

Production Manager
LAURA LOPEZ

Production Coordinators
SEAN KELLEY
JESSICA RENSLOW

Produced at
STUDIOPOLIS, INC.
STUDIO CITY, CA USA

© 2002 MASASHI
KISHIMOTO © NMP
2005

Original Author
MASASHI KISHIMOTO
SHUEISHA/SHONEN JUMP

Screenpay
HIROTSUGU KAWASAKI
YUKA MIYATA

Continuity
HIROTSUGU KAWASAKI
MAMORU SASAKI
SHINICHI FUKUYAMA
KOICHI ARAI

Character Design
TETSUYA NISHIO

Mechanic Design
YASUMITSU SUETAKE

Concept Design
MASAAKI ENDO
HIDETSUGU ITO

Animation Directors
TETSUYA NISHIO
TATSUYA TOMARU

Art Director
SATOSHI MATSUOKA
MUTSUO KOZEKI

Color Design
KAYOKO NISHI

Music
TOSHIO MASUDA &
MUSASHI PROJECT

Recording Director
CHIHARU KAMIO

Sound Director
YASUNORI EBINA

Director of Cinematography
ATSUHO MATSUMOTO

Editor
YUKIE OIKAWA
SEIJI MORITA

CAST
Naruto Uzumaki
JUNKO TAKEUCHI
Temujin
GAMON KAAI
Sakura Haruno
CHIE NAKAMURA
Shikamaru Nara
SHOTARO MORIKUBO
Gaara
AKIRA ISHIDA
Kankuro
YASUYUKI KASE
Fugai
URARA TAKANO
Kamira
SACHIKO KOJIMA
Ranke
HOKO KUWASHIMA
Temujin's Childhood Friend
TAKAKO HONDA
Young Temujin
YUKO KATO
Sand Ninja
TOMOYUKI SHIMURA
FUMITOSHI MIYAJIMA
TAKAHIRO YOSHINO
MASAYUKI KATO
KEKO SAKUE

Voice Cooperation for
[Caravan no Tami]
GENKI PROJECT

Emina
TOMOKA KUROKAWA
(Special Appearance)
Haido
AKIO NOJIMA
Kahiko
NACHI NOZAWA

Assistant Animation Directors
YASUYUKI SHIMIZU
MASAHIRO SATO
SYUICHI KANEKO
MAMORU SASAKI

Key Animation
MASAAKI END
HIDETSUGU ITO
NORIO MATSUMOTO
MASAHIRO SATO
MAMORU SASAKI
NOBUTOSHI OGURA
YASUYUKI SHIMIZU
HIROFUMI MASUDA
TAKAO MAKI
AKIKO YAMAGUCHI
MIWA SASAKI
KAZUYOSHI YAGINUMA
YUKO HIRASAWA
HIROYUKI OGURA
SHIGERU KIMIJIMA
HIROTAKA KINOSHITA
KAZUNOBU HOSHI
ICHIRO UNO

HISASHI EGUCHI
KEISHI HASHIMOTO
TETSUYA KUMAGAI
KOICHI ARAI
HIROYUKI HORIUCHI
OKIO YAMADA
MAMIKO NAKANISHI
TAKASHI MUKODA
TOSHIHARU SUGIE
KENJI YAZAKI
TOSHIHIKO MASUDA
MITSUNORI MURATA
YUZO SATO
TSUTOMU SUZUKI
ERIKO KUBOKAWA

KEIKO SHIMIZU
TADASHI MATSUZAKI
HIROOMI YAMAKAWA
YUICHI ENDO
MASAHIRO NERIKI
TADAKATSU YOSHIDA
TADASHI FUKUDA
HIROKO OGURI
FUMIYO KIMURA
MASAHARU TADA
HARUO MIYAGAWA
KAN SAITO
HARUO SOTOZAKI
AKIHIRO TSUDA

SHINJI HASHIMOTO
HIROYUKI OKIURA
KATSUHIRO NAKAJIMA
HIROTO TANAKA
TSUTOMU AWADA
MICHIO MIHARA
SYUICHI KANEKO
HIROSHI SHIMIZU
YOSHIHARU SHIMIZU
TETSUYA NISHIO
TENSAI OKAMURA
TSUGUYUKI KUBO
YASUMITSU SUETAKE

Second Key Animation
MAMORU OHTAKE
HIDEHITO TANAKA
AKIRA YAMAUCHI
JUNICHI TAKADATE
MASAYUKI KATO
RYUTA YANAGI
MASAYUKI KOUDA

DR MOVIE
KYOUNG KANG ANIA
MADHOUSE

Art
JUNICHI TANIGUCHI
AKEMI KONNO

Backgrounds
MASANORI KIKUCHI
HIROSHI TAKIGUCHI

MADHOUSE
HISASHI IKEDA
SHIGEYO UEHARA
MASAKO OKADA
JUNKO INA
MASATOSHI KAI
SEIKI TANAKA
SYUICHI HIRATA
DR MOVIE
PARK YONG IL
KO HYO SOON
KIM MI KYUENG
NA KUM YOUNG
PARK KYEONG SOOK
PARK JONG IM
LEE JUN HO
JEON KEUK SUN
CHA JU SUN
LEE BONG SU
LEE YOON HO

Background Cooperation
STUDIO WYETH
MINORU NAKAMURA

Art Digital Support
TOSHIKI TAKEYA

In-between Animation
PIERROT
KUMIKO KAWASHIMA
RINAKO NISHIHARA
MEGUMI HATTA
ERIKO MURAKAMI
MIKA NAIKI
AIKA KAWASAKI
KIM BRUGES
PIERROT FUKUOKA
MIFUMI TOMITA
MIKA OOKUBO
ETSUKO KIMURA
MIHO INOUE
KIM BOMIN
EMI KIRIKIHIRA

OH PRODUCTION
MIHOKO UDA
SHINICHI KUNIYASU
TOSHIMITSU KUROYANAGI
JINKO TSUJI
MINAKO SEKIHARA
MISUZU ICHINOSE
YOSHIE FUJIWARA

NARA ANIMATION STUDIO
HWANG JI NA
CHOI HEE EUN
PARK EUN JOO
KIM JI EUN
LEE SUN ME
OCK MI YOUNG
CHOI DO YOUNG
AN MI GYEONG
KIM MI SUK
CHO HYE JUNG
YOUN EUN JU
YUN JOUNG HYE
BARK SU GYONG
SUNG JI YOUNG
BYEON HYE SOON
YI BO RUEM
LEE KYOUNG AE
JOUNG HYEUN SOO
HAN SUENG JIN

SEONG BO YANG HAENG
CHO HYUN MI
PARK EUN A
SONG HYUN JOO
KO KUN AE
LIM KAB SOOK
MIN HO JEONG
JEON EUN KYUNG
BAE YONG O
DR MOVIE
GU IN HOI
KIM OK JU
SONG JI YOUNG
LEE MI OK
LEE JAE DEUCK
LEE JEONG EUN
LIM HEY JIN
JANG CHEL HO
PYUN EUN ME
HAN EUN JIN
YOUN MYUNG HEE
JEONG YOUN HEE
MITSUE AKIYAMA
KAZUE TSUNODA
MAYUMI SUZUKI
MADHOUSE
STUDIO_MAT
RADIX 02
HAYASHI Co., Ltd.
Triple A

Color Correction
KAYOKO NISHI
MAYUMI NAGASHIMA
NAOKO KODAMA
YUKI KASE

Animation Inspection
MITSUKO TOSHIMA
HIROKO TEZUKA

Digital Painting
PIERROT FUKUOKA
YUKIE MATSUZAKI
YUKIKO TANISHIMA
SHINNOSUKE NAGARE
HITOMI SHIMOGANNA
MAMI YARIWAKE
STUDIO KILLY
TOSHIKO IWAKIRI
NAOMI TAKAHASHI
SAYURI TAKAGI
MIYOKO YOSHIDA
MICHIKO IKUSHIMA
HIROMI TSUCHIYA
KAORI ISHIKAWA
YOSHISHIGE IWAKIRI
KAORU NAKAGAMA
SEONG BO YANG HAENG
GUEON O SOOK
YOU HYE JEONG
SEO KYUNG HWA
KOOK KUI SEON
HWANG JEONG SIL
KIM JEONG HWAN
LIM MAE IL

BAE IN HWA

NARA ANIMATION STUDIO
CHO SEOUNG SUK
JEONG JI HYUN
PARK KUYUNG SUK
LIM HO YOUNG
OH YOUNG SUK
SON EUN SUK
SON EUN SUK
KIM MI JOUNG
HAN MYUNG SUN
CHUN HYUN JOO
LEE MI JOUNG

DR MOVIE
KIM KANG IN
LEE KUN HAE
CHOI HEE KYOUNG
CHOI SOON LEE
KIM MIN JU

JUN JUNG SUK
KEUM JEONG MIN
SEO SUNG HEE
JUNG HEE JUNG
LEE YOUNG SHIM
SHIN HYE MI
CHOI KI JEONG
PARK YUN HEE

MADHOUSE
HAYASHI Co., Ltd.
Triple A
STUDIO TARGE
KONOHANA
STUDIO LAGOON
YOSHIKO TAKIGUCHI

Filming
KAORI KAWASHIMA
YUKA NAKAYA
HISAKO TAMADA
TOSHIO KAIDO
MAI UEMATSU
KUMIKO KIMURA
KAORI SAKAMOTO
ANNA TORII

STUDIO COSMOS DIGITAL
FACTORY
TORU SUGAWARA
NORIKAZU YAMAGUCHI
HIROSHI YOSHIDA
KATSUYOSHI KISHI
YUKO ORIKASA
YUMIKO MORIMOTO
KOICHI GONDA
SHINJI IKEGAMI
TOMOHIRO NISHIYAMA
HISAYUKI SADAMATSU
TOSHINO YASUNO
TARO OKUZAWA
FUJIKO TABATA
KAZUHIRO UDAGAWA
NAOHISA HAIJIMA
YUJI SHIRAI

STUDIO YOU
MIYOSHI TAZAWA
KENTARO ARAGAKI
TAKASHI UENO
WELZ ANIMATION STUDIO
MUNEHIRO KASUYA
SYUHEI YABUTA
MASAHIKO YAGI
TAKAKO BABA
RIE AWAJI

Paint Inspection
IZUMI MURASAKI
TOMOE IMAMURA
YOSHIKO SHIMIZU
MAKIKO YAGIHASHI
YUKIE MATSUZAKI
HITOMI SHIMOGANNA
MAMI YARIWAKE

Background Retouching
YURI SHIMIZU
KAORU NAGASAWA
TOMOE MURAMATSU
MAKIKO YAGIHASHI
KIMIKO KOJIMA

CG Effects
SHINJI YAGINUMA
NAOMI WADA
NOBUO KIMURA
KAZUKO OYANAGI
KENJI IKEDA

3DCGI Director
XINHON WU
3 DCGI IKIF+
YUTAKA HAMANAKA
YUTA SEO
YUKO OKUMURA

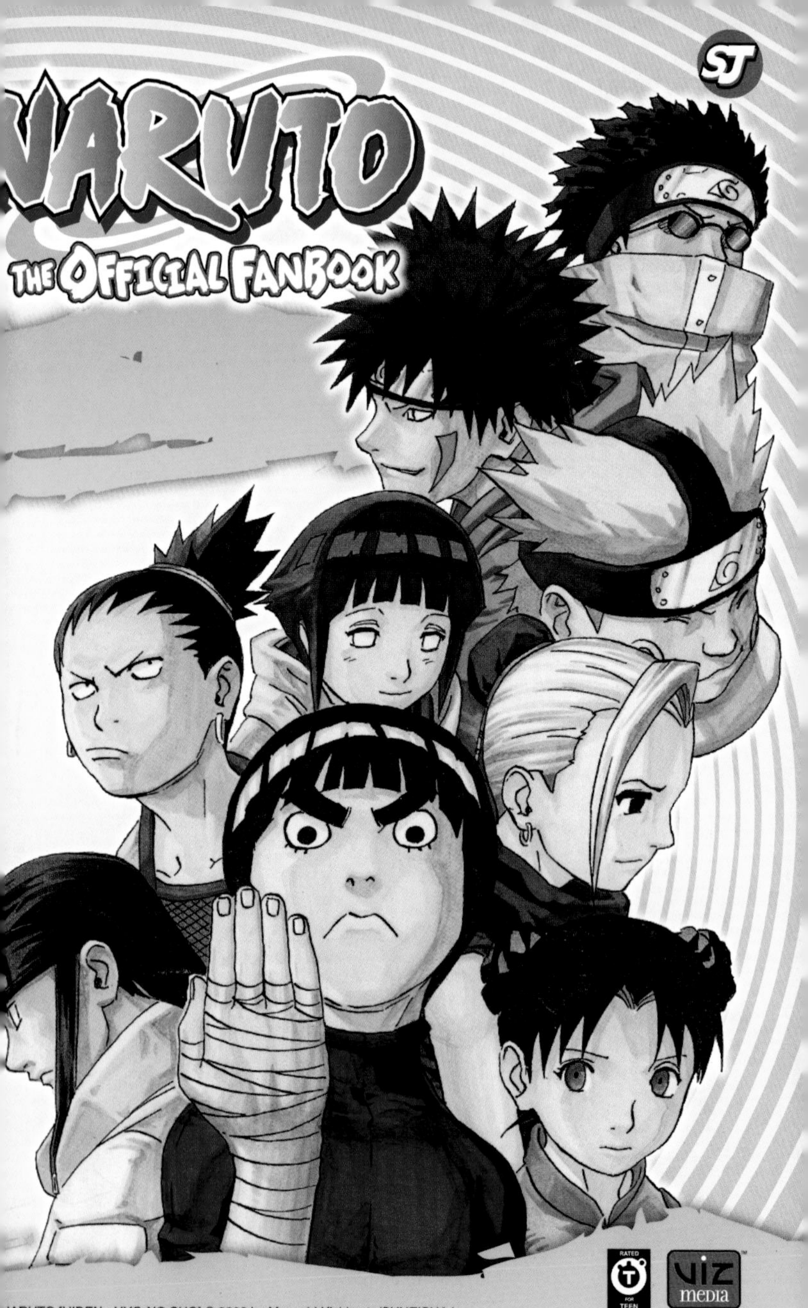
SJ
NARUTO
THE OFFICIAL FANBOOK
RATED T FOR TEEN
ratings.viz.com
VIZ media
www.viz.com

BY FANS FOR FANS!

THE ULTIMATE SOURCE THAT YOU HELPED CREATE.

Get all the inside secrets with:
- Official maps
- Character profiles
- Fold-out poster
- Previously hidden revelations

Plus, the original 45-page NARUTO manga!

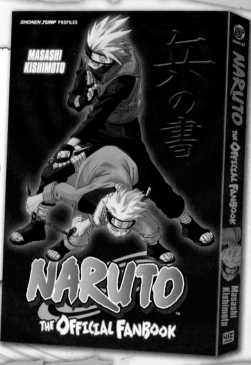

WWW.NARUTO.COM

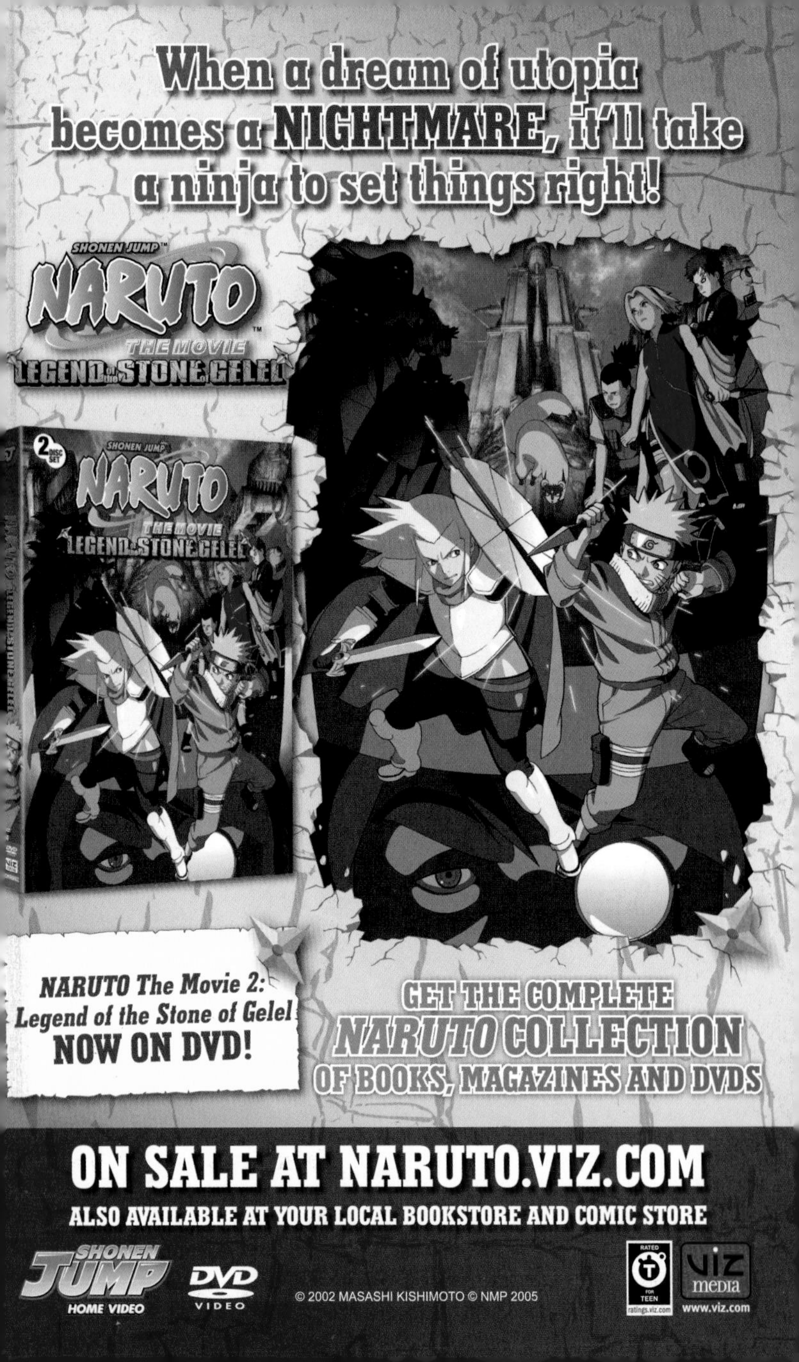
When a dream of utopia becomes a NIGHTMARE, it'll take a ninja to set things right!
SHONEN JUMP
NARUTO
THE MOVIE
LEGEND OF THE STONE OF GELEL
2 DISC SET
NARUTO The Movie 2: Legend of the Stone of Gelel NOW ON DVD!
GET THE COMPLETE NARUTO COLLECTION OF BOOKS, MAGAZINES AND DVDS
ON SALE AT NARUTO.VIZ.COM
ALSO AVAILABLE AT YOUR LOCAL BOOKSTORE AND COMIC STORE
SHONEN JUMP HOME VIDEO
DVD VIDEO
© 2002 MASASHI KISHIMOTO © NMP 2005
RATED T FOR TEEN
ratings.viz.com
viz media
www.viz.com